Lecture Notes in Computer Science 15617

Founding Editors

Gerhard Goos
Juris Hartmanis

AF167718

The series Lecture Notes in Computer Science (LNCS), including its subseries Lecture Notes in Artificial Intelligence (LNAI) and Lecture Notes in Bioinformatics (LNBI), has established itself as a medium for the publication of new developments in computer science and information technology research, teaching, and education.

LNCS enjoys close cooperation with the computer science R & D community, the series counts many renowned academics among its volume editors and paper authors, and collaborates with prestigious societies. Its mission is to serve this international community by providing an invaluable service, mainly focused on the publication of conference and workshop proceedings and postproceedings. LNCS commenced publication in 1973.

Shivakumara Palaiahnakote ·
Stephanie Schuckers · Jean-Marc Ogier ·
Prabir Bhattacharya · Umapada Pal ·
Saumik Bhattacharya

Editors

Pattern Recognition

ICPR 2024 International Workshops and Challenges

Kolkata, India, December 1, 2024
Proceedings, Part IV

 Springer

Editors
Shivakumara Palaiahnakote
University of Salford
Salford, UK

Jean-Marc Ogier
Université de La Rochelle
La Rochelle, France

Umapada Pal ⓘ
Indian Statistical Institute
Kolkata, West Bengal, India

Stephanie Schuckers
University of North Carolina at Charlotte
Charlotte, NC, USA

Prabir Bhattacharya
Concordia University
Montreal, QC, Canada

Saumik Bhattacharya
IIT Kharagpur
Kharagpur, West Bengal, India

ISSN 0302-9743   ISSN 1611-3349 (electronic)
Lecture Notes in Computer Science
ISBN 978-3-031-88216-6   ISBN 978-3-031-88217-3 (eBook)
https://doi.org/10.1007/978-3-031-88217-3

President's Address

On behalf of the Executive Committee of the International Association for Pattern Recognition (IAPR), I am pleased to welcome you to the 27th International Conference on Pattern Recognition (ICPR 2024), the main scientific event of the IAPR.

After a completely digital ICPR in the middle of the COVID pandemic and the first hybrid version in 2022, we can now enjoy a fully back-to-normal ICPR this year. I look forward to hearing inspirational talks and keynotes, catching up with colleagues during the breaks and making new contacts in an informal way. At the same time, the conference landscape has changed. Hybrid meetings have made their entrance and will continue. It is exciting to experience how this will influence the conference. Planning for a major event like ICPR must take place over a period of several years. This means many decisions had to be made under a cloud of uncertainty, adding to the already large effort needed to produce a successful conference. It is with enormous gratitude, then, that we must thank the team of organizers for their hard work, flexibility, and creativity in organizing this ICPR. ICPR always provides a wonderful opportunity for the community to gather together. I can think of no better location than Kolkata to renew the bonds of our international research community.

Each ICPR is a bit different owing to the vision of its organizing committee. For 2024, the conference has six different tracks reflecting major themes in pattern recognition: Artificial Intelligence, Pattern Recognition and Machine Learning; Computer and Robot Vision; Image, Speech, Signal and Video Processing; Biometrics and Human Computer Interaction; Document Analysis and Recognition; and Biomedical Imaging and Bioinformatics. This reflects the richness of our field. ICPR 2024 also features two dozen workshops, seven tutorials, and 15 competitions; there is something for everyone. Many thanks to those who are leading these activities, which together add significant value to attending ICPR, whether in person or virtually. Because it is important for ICPR to be as accessible as possible to colleagues from all around the world, we are pleased that the IAPR, working with the ICPR organizers, is continuing our practice of awarding travel stipends to a number of early-career authors who demonstrate financial need. Last but not least, we are thankful to the Springer LNCS team for their effort to publish these proceedings.

Among the presentations from distinguished keynote speakers, we are looking forward to the three IAPR Prize Lectures at ICPR 2024. This year we honor the achievements of Tin Kam Ho (IBM Research) with the IAPR's most prestigious King-Sun Fu Prize "for pioneering contributions to multi-classifier systems, random decision forests, and data complexity analysis". The King-Sun Fu Prize is given in recognition of an outstanding technical contribution to the field of pattern recognition. It honors the memory of Professor King-Sun Fu who was instrumental in the founding of IAPR, served as its first president, and is widely recognized for his extensive contributions to the field of pattern recognition.

The Maria Petrou Prize is given to a living female scientist/engineer who has made substantial contributions to the field of Pattern Recognition and whose past contributions, current research activity and future potential may be regarded as a model to both aspiring and established researchers. It honours the memory of Professor Maria Petrou as a scientist of the first rank, and particularly her role as a pioneer for women researchers. This year, the Maria Petrou Prize is given to Guoying Zhao (University of Oulu), "for contributions to video analysis for facial micro-behavior recognition and remote biosignal reading (RPPG) for heart rate analysis and face anti-spoofing".

The J.K. Aggarwal Prize is given to a young scientist who has brought a substantial contribution to a field that is relevant to the IAPR community and whose research work has had a major impact on the field. Professor Aggarwal is widely recognized for his extensive contributions to the field of pattern recognition and for his participation in IAPR's activities. This year, the J.K. Aggarwal Prize goes to Xiaolong Wang (UC San Diego) "for groundbreaking contributions to advancing visual representation learning, utilizing self-supervised and attention-based models to establish fundamental frameworks for creating versatile, general-purpose pattern recognition systems".

During the conference we will also recognize 21 new IAPR Fellows selected from a field of very strong candidates. In addition, a number of Best Scientific Paper and Best Student Paper awards will be presented, along with the Best Industry Related Paper Award and the Piero Zamperoni Best Student Paper Award. Congratulations to the recipients of these very well-deserved awards!

I would like to close by again thanking everyone involved in making ICPR 2024 a tremendous success; your hard work is deeply appreciated. These thanks extend to all who chaired the various aspects of the conference and the associated workshops, my ExCo colleagues, and the IAPR Standing and Technical Committees. Linda O'Gorman, the IAPR Secretariat, deserves special recognition for her experience, historical perspective, and attention to detail when it comes to supporting many of the IAPR's most important activities. Her tasks became so numerous that she recently got support from Carolyn Buckley (layout, newsletter), Ugur Halici (ICPR matters), and Rosemary Stramka (secretariat). The IAPR website got a completely new design. Ed Sobczak has taken care of our web presence for so many years already. A big thank you to all of you!

This is, of course, the 27th ICPR conference. Knowing that ICPR is organized every two years, and that the first conference in the series (1973!) pre-dated the formal founding of the IAPR by a few years, it is also exciting to consider that we are celebrating over 50 years of ICPR and at the same time approaching the official IAPR 50th anniversary in 2028: you'll get all information you need at ICPR 2024. In the meantime, I offer my thanks and my best wishes to all who are involved in supporting the IAPR throughout the world.

September 2024   Arjan Kuijper
                                                              President of the IAPR

Preface

The 27th International Conference on Pattern Recognition Workshops (ICPRW 2024), were held at Kolkata, West Bengal, India on Sunday, December 1, 2024, one day earlier than the main ICPR conference. A total of 31 workshop submissions were received and were carefully reviewed by the IAPR Conferences and Meetings committee and the workshop chairs. Of these, 24 workshops were approved, and finally 21 took place.

Of the 21 accepted workshops, 10 were full-day events (physical or hybrid), 8 were half-day events (physical or hybrid), and 3 were half-day virtual events. Many of the workshops received sponsorship, endorsement or approval from the International Association for Pattern Recognition (IAPR).

ICPR 2024 marked the return of the main conference to a fully in-person format, workshops still had the option of being held in person or remotely. This meant we could meet many colleagues face to face again and make new connections to support scientific collaborations and (perhaps) even some new friendships.

Publishing the proceedings of a scientific conference such as ICPR serves a number of purposes: establish a permanent record of the research presented; report on current research concerns and accomplishments of the participants; make new research visible to the scientific community and other audiences, to promote collaboration, innovation, and discovery; disseminate the latest research findings to researchers, academics, industry professionals, and other practitioners; and support the shared goal of staying up to date with developments in the fast-moving field of artificial intelligence and pattern recognition.

These volumes constitute the refereed proceedings of 19 of the 21 ICPR 2024 workshops. The wide range of topics covered is a testament to the ever-widening concerns of AI researchers as they creatively find ways to apply artificial intelligence to domains far from its historical concerns. The ICPR 2024 workshops addressed problems in pattern recognition, artificial intelligence, computer vision, and image and sound analysis, and the contributions reflect the most recent applications related to healthcare, biometrics, ethics, multimodality, cultural heritage, imagery, affective computing, and de-escalation. The following workshops took place at ICPR 2024:

[W1] A2I – Affective Artificial Intelligence
[W2] ABC with ML – Advancing Brain–Computer Interfaces with Machine Learning
[W4] AIHA – Artificial Intelligence for Healthcare Application
[W7] FAIRBIO – Fairness in Biometric Systems
[W8] FBE – Facial and Body Expressions
[W9] G2SP-CV – Graph Learning and Graph Signal Processing Algorithms in Computer Vision
[W10] IMTA – Image Mining: Theory and Applications
[W11] MADiMA – Multimedia Assisted Dietary Management
[W12] MCMI – Multi- and Cross-modal Information for Enhanced Pattern Recognition
[W13] MMVPR – Multi-modal Visual Pattern Recognition

[W14] MPRSS – Multimodal Pattern Recognition of Social Signals in Human–Computer Interaction
[W15] PRHA – Pattern Recognition in Healthcare Analytics
[W16] PRRS – Pattern Recognition in Remote Sensing
[W17] RRPR – Reproducible Research in Pattern Recognition
[W18] SPRCV – Sustainable Pattern Recognition and Computer Vision Developments: Balancing Innovation and Environmental Responsibility
[W19] VAIB – Visual Observation and Analysis of Vertebrate and Insect Behavior
[W20] WCWCE – Challenges in Wireless Capsule Endoscopy
[W21] WICV – Infrared Computer Vision
[W22] WILD – Multimedia Forensics in the Wild
[W23] WIMUE – Intelligent Mobility in Unstructured Environments
[W24] XAIE – Explainable and Ethical AI

With the exception of [W17] and [W19], these proceedings contain the 183 papers accepted at the above workshops, distributed as follows:

LNCS 15614, Part I includes papers from [W1], [W2], [W7]
LNCS 15615, Part II includes papers from [W4], [W8]
LNCS 15616, Part III includes papers from [W9], [W10]
LNCS 15617, Part IV includes papers from [W11], [W12], [W13], [W16]
LNCS 15618, Part V includes papers from [W14], [W15], [W18], [W20]
LNCS 15619, Part VI includes papers from [W21], [W22], [W23], [W24]

January 2025

Shivakumara Palaiahnakote
Stephanie Schuckers
Jean-Marc Ogier
Prabir Bhattacharya
Umapada Pal
Saumik Bhattacharya

ICPR 2024 Conference and Workshops Organization

General Chairs

Umapada Pal	Indian Statistical Institute, Kolkata, India
Josef Kittler	University of Surrey, UK
Anil Jain	Michigan State University, USA

Conference Program Chairs

Apostolos Antonacopoulos	University of Salford, UK
Subhasis Chaudhuri	Indian Institute of Technology, Bombay, India
Rama Chellappa	Johns Hopkins University, USA
Cheng-Lin Liu	Institute of Automation, Chinese Academy of Sciences, China

Conference Publication Chairs

Ananda S. Chowdhury	Jadavpur University, India
Wataru Ohyama	Tokyo Denki University, Japan

Competition Chairs

Richard Zanibbi	Rochester Institute of Technology, USA
Lianwen Jin	South China University of Technology, China
Laurence Likforman-Sulem	Télécom Paris, France

Workshop Chairs

P. Shivakumara	University of Salford, UK
Stephanie Schuckers	Clarkson University, USA
Jean-Marc Ogier	Université de la Rochelle, France
Prabir Bhattacharya	Concordia University, Canada

Tutorial Chairs

B. B. Chaudhuri	Indian Statistical Institute, Kolkata, India
Michael R. Jenkin	York University, Canada
Guoying Zhao	University of Oulu, Finland

Doctoral Consortium Chairs

Véronique Eglin	CNRS, France
Daniel P. Lopresti	Lehigh University, USA
Mayank Vatsa	Indian Institute of Technology, Jodhpur, India

Organizing Chairs

Saumik Bhattacharya	Indian Institute of Technology, Kharagpur, India
Palash Ghosal	Sikkim Manipal University, India

Organizing Committee

Santanu Phadikar	West Bengal University of Technology, India
SK Md Obaidullah	Aliah University, India
Sayantari Ghosh	National Institute of Technology Durgapur, India
Himadri Mukherjee	West Bengal State University, India
Nilamadhaba Tripathy	Clarivate Analytics, USA
Chayan Halder	West Bengal State University, India
Shibaprasad Sen	Techno Main Salt Lake, India

Finance Chairs

Kaushik Roy	West Bengal State University, India
Michael Blumenstein	University of Technology Sydney, Australia

Awards Committee Chair

Arpan Pal	Tata Consultancy Services, India

Sponsorship Chairs

P. J. Narayanan   Indian Institute of Technology, Hyderabad, India
Yasushi Yagi   Osaka University, Japan
Venu Govindaraju   University at Buffalo, USA
Alberto Bel Bimbo   Università di Firenze, Italy

Exhibition and Demonstration Chairs

Arjun Jain   FastCode AI, India
Agnimitra Biswas   National Institute of Technology, Silchar, India

International Liaison, Visa Chair

Balasubramanian Raman   Indian Institute of Technology, Roorkee, India

Publicity Chairs

Dipti Prasad Mukherjee   Indian Statistical Institute, Kolkata, India
Bob Fisher   University of Edinburgh, UK
Xiaojun Wu   Jiangnan University, China

Women in ICPR Chairs

Ingela Nystrom   Uppsala University, Sweden
Alexandra B. Albu   University of Victoria, Canada
Jing Dong   Institute of Automation, Chinese Academy of
                               Sciences, China
Sarbani Palit   Indian Statistical Institute, Kolkata, India

Event Manager

Alpcord Network

Workshop Committees

[W1] A2I – Affective Artificial Intelligence

Organizers

Sanjay Ghosh	Indian Institute of Technology, Kharagpur, India
Shreya Ghosh	Curtin University, Australia
Abhinav Dhall	Flinders University, Australia
Tom Gedeon	Curtin University, Australia

Program Committee

Lownish Sookha	Indian Institute of Technology, Ropar, India
Prashant Patil	Indian Institute of Technology, Guwahati, India
Shruti Shantiling Phutke	Griffith University, Australia
Yue Yao	Curtin University, Australia
Rakibul Hasan	Curtin University, Australia
Surbhi Madan	Indian Institute of Technology, Ropar, India
Gulshan Sharma	Indian Institute of Technology, Ropar, India
Hrishav Bakul Barua	Monash University, Australia
Deepak Kumar	Indian Institute of Technology, Roorkee, India
Ruining Yang	Northeastern University, USA
Akanksha Chuchra	Indian Institute of Technology, Ropar, India
Baibei Ji	Soochow University, China
Phyo Yee	Indian Institute of Technology, Ropar, India

[W2] ABC with ML – Advancing Brain–Computer Interfaces with Machine Learning

Organizers

Amit Konar	Jadavpur University, India
Sriparna Saha	Indian Institute of Technology, Patna, India
Rajdeep Chatterjee	Kalinga Institute of Industrial Technology (KIIT), India
Sricheta Parui	Kalinga Institute of Industrial Technology (KIIT), India

Deborsi Basu	Indian Institute of Technology, Kharagpur, India
Ashok Kumar Das	Indian Institute of Technology, Hyderabad, India

Program Committee

Anup Kumar Haldar	Warsaw University of Technology, Poland
Arpan Pal	TCS Innovation Lab, Kolkata, India
Atanu Kundu	Heritage Institute of Technology, India
Avirup Banerjee	University of Oxford, UK
Badri N Subudhi	Indian Institute of Technology, Jammu, India
Chandreyee Chowdhury	Jadavpur University, India
Chengappa M. R.	Hewlett Packard Enterprise, India
Chintan Kumar Mandal	Jadavpur University, India
Chittaranjan Hens	Indian Institute of Technology, Hyderabad, India
Chittaranjan Pradhan	Kalinga Institute of Industrial Technology (KIIT), India
Constantinos Patsakis	University of Piraeus, Greece
Debabrata Samanta	Christ University, India
Debarshi Kumar Sanyal	Indian Association of Cultivation Science, Kolkata, India
Debasis Giri	Maulana Abul Kalam Azad University of Technology, India
Debbrota Paul Chowdhury	SNU Kolkata, India
Dharavath Ramesh	Indian Institute of Technology (ISM), Dhanbad, India
Deepak Gangadharan	Indian Institute of Technology, Hyderabad, India
Dibakar Ghosh	Indian Statistical Institute (ISI), Kolkata, India
Dwarikanath Mahapatra	Inception Institute of AI, Abu Dhabi, UAE
Gadadhar Sahoo	Indian Institute of Technology (ISM) Dhanbad, India
Himansu Das	Kalinga Institute of Industrial Technology (KIIT), India
Hrudaya Kumar Tripathy	Kalinga Institute of Industrial Technology (KIIT), India
Imon Mukherjee	Indian Institute of Technology, Kalyani, India
Ishan Roy Chowdhury	Mercedes Benz R&D, India
Jayita Saha	Dayananda Sagar University, Bengaluru, India
Joy Dutta	Khalifa University, Abu Dhabi, UAE
Kamalesh Karmakar	Techno International, Kolkata, India
Kuntal Ghosh	Indian Statistical Institute Kolkata, India
Madhabananda Das	Kalinga Institute of Industrial Technology (KIIT), India

Madhurima Ray	Dell EMC, Oregon, USA
Manas Lenka	Kalinga Institute of Industrial Technology (KIIT), India
Manoj Kumar Mishra	Kalinga Institute of Industrial Technology (KIIT), India
Matangini Chattopadhyay	Jadavpur University, India
Monideepa Roy	Kalinga Institute of Industrial Technology (KIIT), India
Moumita Roy	IEM Kolkata, Kolkata, India
Mohammad Shahidehpour	Illinois Institute of Technology, USA
Muhammet Uzuntarla	Bülent Ecevit University, Turkey
Nabanita Ganguly	Maulana Abul Kalam Azad University of Technology, India
Nazma B. J. Naskar	Kalinga Institute of Industrial Technology (KIIT), India

[W4] AIHA – Artificial Intelligence for Healthcare Application

Organizers

Nicole Dalia Cilia	University of Enna, Kore, Italy
Francesco Fontanella	University of Cassino and Southern Lazio, Italy
Claudio Marrocco	University of Cassino and Southern Lazio, Italy

Program Committee

Berdakh Abibullaev	University of Houston, USA
George Azzopardi	University of Groningen, Netherlands
Anselmo Cardoso De Paiva	Federal University of Maranhao, Brazil
Jesus G. Cruz-Garza	University of Houston, USA
Vittorio Cuculo	University of Milan, Italy
Antonio Cunha	University of Trás-os-Montes and Alto Douro, Portugal
Tiziana D'Alessandro	University of Cassino and Southern Lazio, Italy
Alessandro De Nunzio	Lunex, Luxembourg
Claudio De Stefano	University of Cassino and Southern Lazio, Italy
Moises Diaz	University of Las Palmas de Gran Canaria, Spain
Maria Fazio	University of Messina, Italy
David Fofi	Université de Bourgogne, France
Adrian Galdran	University Pompeu Fabra, Spain
Donato Impedovo	University of Bari, Italy

Xavier Lladó	University of Girona, Spain
Elena Marchiori	Radboud University, Netherlands
Robert Martì	University of Girona, Spain
Murad Megjhani	University of Columbia, USA
Mario Molinara	University of Cassino and Southern Lazio, Italy
Emanuele Nardone	University of Cassino and Southern Lazio, Italy
Arnau Oliver	University of Girona, Spain
Antonio Parziale	University of Salerno, Italy
Ciro Russo	University of Cassino and Southern Lazio, Italy
Carlo Sansone	University of Naples Federico II, Italy
Alessandra Scotto di Freca	University of Cassino and Southern Lazio, Italy
Desirè Sidibè	Université d'Évry Val d'Essonne, France
Omar Tahri	University of Burgundy, France
Francesco Tortorella	University of Salerno, Italy
Gennaro Vessio	University of Bari, Italy

[W7] FAIRBIO – Fairness in Biometric Systems

Organizers

Philipp Terhörst	University of Paderborn, Germany
Kiran Raja	Norwegian University of Science and Technology (NTNU), Norway
Christian Rathgeb	University of Applied Sciences (Hochschule Darmstadt), Germany
Abhijit Das	BITS Pilani Hyderabad University, India
Ana Filipa Sequeira	INESC TEC, Portugal
Antitza Dantcheva	Inria, France
Sambit Bakshi	National Institute of Technology Rourkela (NITR), India
Raghavendra Ramachandra	Norwegian University of Science and Technology (NTNU), Norway
Naser Damer	Fraunhofer Institute for Computer Graphics Research (IGD), Germany

Program Committee

Abu Sufian	CNR-ISASI, Italy
Ana F. Sequeira	INESC, Portugal
André Dörsch	Hochschule Darmstadt, Germany
Anubhooti Jain	Indian Institute of Technology, Jodhpur, India

Anudeep Vurity	George Mason University, USA
Christian Rathgeb	Hochschule Darmstadt, Germany
Colton R. Crum	University of Notre Dame, USA
Eli J. Laird	Southern Methodist University, USA
Ivan DeAndres-Tame	Universidad Autónoma de Madrid, Spain
Marco Leo	National Research Council of Italy, Italy
Rishabh Ranjan	Indian Institute of Technology, Jodhpur, India
Ruben Vera-Rodriguez	Universidad Autónoma de Madrid, Spain
Subhankar Ghosh	University of Technology Sydney, Australia
Zitong Yu	Great Bay University, China

[W8] FBE – Facial and Body Expressions

Organizers

Vittorio Murino	Istituto Italiano di Tecnologia, Italy
Moi Hoon Yap	Manchester Metropolitan University, UK
Federico Pernici	University of Florence, Italy
Federico Becattini	University of Siena, Italy
Luca Cultrera	University of Florence, Italy
Lorenzo Berlincioni	University of Florence, Italy

Program Committee

Alex Ergasti	University of Parma, Italy
Emre Girgin	Boğaziçi University, Turkey
Gonzalo Garrido-López	Universidad Politécnica de Madrid, Spain
Guido Borghi	University of Modena and Reggio Emilia, Italy
Nélida Mirabet-Herranz	Eurecom, France
Pavlos Tosidis	Aristotle University of Thessaloniki, Greece
Tomaso Fontanini	University of Parma, Italy
Gabriele Magrini	University of Florence, Italy

[W9] G2SP-CV – Graph Learning and Graph Signal Processing Algorithms in Computer Vision

Organizers

Thierry Bouwmans	La Rochelle Université, France
Jhony H. Giraldo	LTCI, Télécom Paris, Institut Polytechnique de Paris, France
Ananda S. Chowdhury	Jadavpur University, India
Badri N. Subudhi	Indian Institute of Technology, Jammu, India

Program Committee

Thierry Bouwmans	La Rochelle Université, France
Jhony H. Giraldo	LTCI, Télécom Paris, Institut Polytechnique de Paris, France
Ananda S. Chowdhury	Jadavpur University, India
Badri N. Subudhi	Indian Institute of Technology, Jammu, India
Mehgna Kapoor	Indian Institute of Technology, Jammu, India
Anindya Mondal	University of Surrey, UK
Manoj Panda	GIET University, India
Ujjwal Karn	Meta, USA
Anastasia Zakharova	La Rochelle Université, France

[W10] IMTA – Image Mining: Theory and Applications

Organizers

Vera Yashina	Russian Academy of Sciences, Moscow, Russia
Davide Moroni	National Research Council of Italy (CNR), Pisa, Italy
Heinrich Niemann	Friedrich-Alexander-University of Erlangen-Nuremberg, Germany
Maria Antonietta Pascali	National Research Council of Italy (CNR), Pisa, Italy
Bernd Radig	Technical University Munich, Germany
Gerhard Ritter	University of Florida, Gainesville, USA
Igor Gurevich	Russian Academy of Sciences, Moscow, Russia
Maria Antonietta Pascali	National Research Council of Italy (CNR), Pisa, Italy

Program Committee

Sergey Ablameyko	Belarusian State University and Belarusian Academy of Sciences, Belarus
Sara Colantonio	National Research Council of Italy (CNR), Pisa, Italy
Daniela Giorgi	National Research Council of Italy (CNR), Pisa, Italy
Manuel Grana	Universidad del País Vasco, San Sebastian, Spain
Vassilis Kaburlasos	Eastern Macedonia and Thrace Institute of Kavala, Greece
Claudia Landi	University of Modena and Reggio Emilia, Italy
Anatoly Nemirko	Saint Petersburg Electrotechnical University (LETI), Russia
Heinrich Niemann	Friedrich-Alexander University of Erlangen-Nuremberg, Germany
Maria Antonietta Pascali	National Research Council of Italy (CNR), Pisa, Italy
Gerhard Ritter	University of Florida, Gainesville, USA
Ovidio Salvetti	National Research Council of Italy (CNR), Pisa, Italy
Humberto Sossa	Instituto Politécnico Nacional (IPN), Mexico City, Mexico

[W11] MADiMA – Multimedia Assisted Dietary Management

Organizers

Stavroula Mougiakakou	University of Bern, Switzerland
Keiji Yanai	University of Electro-Communications, Tokyo, Japan
Dario Allegra	University of Catania, Italy
Yoko Yamakata	University of Tokyo, Japan
Lorenzo Brigato	University of Bern, Switzerland

Program Committee

Lorenzo Catania	University of Catania, Italy
Jingjing Chen	Fudan University, China
Anastasios Delopoulos	Aristotle University of Thessaloniki, Greece
Christos Diou	Harokopio University of Athens, Greece

Ichiro Ide	Nagoya University, Japan
Aulo Gelli	International Food Policy Research Institute, USA
Ioannis Papathanail	University of Bern, Switzerland
Raimondo Schettini	Università degli Studi di Milano-Bicocca, Italy

[W12] MCMI – Multi- and Cross-modal Information for Enhanced Pattern Recognition

Organizers

Moreno La Quatra	Kore University of Enna, Italy
Nicole Dalia Cilia	Kore University of Enna, Italy
Vincenzo Conti	Kore University of Enna, Italy
Salvatore Sorce	Kore University of Enna, Italy
Giovanni Garraffa	Kore University of Enna, Italy
Valerio Mario Salerno	Kore University of Enna, Italy

Program Committee

Mauro Castelli	University of Lisbon, Portugal
Tiziana D'Alessandro	University of Cassino and Southern Lazio, Italy
Wellington Santos	Universidade Federal de Pernambuco, Brazil
Alessandro Bruno	IULM University, Italy
Md Fahim Faysal	Nvidia, USA
Alkis Koudounas	Politecnico di Torino, Italy
Eliana Pastor	Politecnico di Torino, Italy
Carmelo Militello	Italian National Research Council (CNR), Italy
Emanuele Nardone	University of Cassino and Southern Lazio, Italy
Lala Shakti Swarup Ray	DFKI Kaiserslautern, Germany
Flavio Giobergia	Politecnico di Torino, Italy
Lorenzo Vaiani	Politecnico di Torino, Italy
Antonio Parziale	University of Salerno, Italy
Giovanni Pilato	ICAR-CNR, Italy
Leonardo Rundo	University of Salerno, Italy

[W13] MMVPR – Multi-modal Visual Pattern Recognition

Organizers, Program Committee

Tianyang Xu	Jiangnan University, China
Xiao-Jun Wu	Jiangnan University, China
Josef Kittler	University of Surrey, UK
Umapada Pal	Indian Statistical Institute, India
Jiwen Lu	Tsinghua University, China
Xi Li	Zhejiang University, China
Vasile Palade	Coventry University, UK
Xuefeng Zhu	Jiangnan University, China
Linze Li	Jiangnan University, China
Xiao Yang	Jiangnan University, China
Yifan Pan	Jiangnan University, China
Minzhi Li	Jiangnan University, China
Han Zang	Jiangnan University, China
Youchen Xie	Jiangnan University, China

[W14] MPRSS – Multimodal Pattern Recognition of Social Signals in Human–Computer Interaction

Organizers

Mariofanna Milanova	University of Arkansas at Little Rock, USA
Friedhelm Schwenker	Ulm University, Germany

[W15] PRHA – Pattern Recognition in Healthcare Analytics

Organizers

Arzucan Özgür	Boğaziçi University, Turkey
İnci M. Baytaş	Boğaziçi University, Turkey
Bert Arnrich	Hasso Plattner Institute (HPI) and University of Potsdam, Germany
Ujjwal Maulik	Jadavpur University, India

Program Committee

Gökçe Uludoğan	Boğaziçi University, Turkey
Hakime Öztürk	German Cancer Research Center, Germany
Sudipta Banerjee	New York University, USA
Özlem Özcan	Boğaziçi University, Turkey
Junguk Hur	University of North Dakota, USA
Burak Suyunu	Boğaziçi University, Turkey
Guanjie Huang	Penn State University and Facebook, USA
İlknur Karadeniz	Özyeğin University, Turkey

[W16] PRRS – Pattern Recognition in Remote Sensing

Organizers

Ribana Roscher	Forschungszentrum Jülich and University of Bonn, Germany
Ujjwal Verma	Manipal Institute of Technology, India
Johannes Leonhardt	University of Bonn, Germany
Sylvain Lobry	Université de Paris, France
Charlotte Pelletier	Université Bretagne Sud, IRISA, France
Marc Rußwurm	Wageningen University, Netherlands

Program Committee

Marc Chaumont	LIRMM (Montpellier), University of Nîmes, France
John Kerekes	Rochester Institute of Technology, USA
Jan Dirk Wegner	University of Zurich, Switzerland
Paolo Gamba	University of Pavia, Italy
Nicolas Audebert	LASTIG Lab, France
Martin Weinmann	Karlsruhe Institute of Technology, Germany
Franz Rottensteiner	Leibniz Universitat Hannover, Germany
Eckart Michaelsen	Fraunhofer-IOSB, Germany
Loic Landrieu	École nationale des ponts et chaussées (ENPC), France
Selim Aksoy	Bilkent University, Turkey
Michele Volpi	Swiss Data Science Center, ETH Zürich, Switzerland
Diego Marcos	Inria, France
Jocelyn Chanussot	Grenoble Institute of Technology, France

Fabio Dell'Acqua   University of Pavia, Italy
Camille Kurtz   Université Paris Cité, France
Dino Ienco   INRAE, France
Florence Tupin   Télécom Paris, France
Ananya Gupta   Google

[W17] RRPR – Reproducible Research in Pattern Recognition

Organizers

Bertrand Kerautret   LIRIS, Université de Lyon 2, France
Miguel Colom   ENS Paris-Saclay, France
Daniel Lopresti   Lehigh University, USA
Pascal Monasse   LIGM, École des Ponts, France
Benjamin Perret   LIGM, ESIEE Paris, Université Gustave Eiffel,
                                 France
Hugues Talbot   CentraleSupélec, Paris, France
Burak Yildiz   Delft University of Technology, The Netherlands
Jean-Michel Morel   ENS Paris-Saclay, France
Federico Bolelli   University of Modeno and Reggio Emilia, Italy

Program Committee

Fabien Baldacci   LaBRI, Université de Bordeaux, France
Jenny Benois-Pineau   LaBRI, Université de Bordeaux, France
Partha Bhowmick   Indian Institute of Technology, Kharagpur, India
Arindam Biswas   IIEST, Shibpur, India
Alexandre Boulch   Valeo.ai, France
Luc Brun   GREYC, Ensicaen, Caen, France
Leszek Chmielewski   Warsaw University of Life Sciences, Poland
David Coeurjolly   LIRIS, CNRS, Lyon, France
Miguel Colom   Centre Borelli, ENS Paris-Saclay, France
Carlos Crispim-Junior   LIRIS, Université de Lyon 2, France
Isabelle Debled-Rennesson   LORIA, Université de Lorraine, France
Maxime Devanne   IRIMAS, Université de Haute-Alsace, France
Pascal Desbarats   LaBRI, Université de Bordeaux, France
Éléonore Dufresne   ICube, University of Strasbourg, France
Philippe Even   LORIA, Université de Lorraine, France
Véronique Eglin   LIRIS, INSA Lyon, France
Yukiko Kenmochi   GREYC, France

Bertrand Kerautret	LIRIS, Université de Lyon 2, France
Adrien Krähënbühl	ICube, University of Strasbourg, France
Pierre Kraemer	ICube, University of Strasbourg, France
Jacques-Olivier Lachaud	LAMA, Université Savoie Mont Blanc, France
Daniel Lopresti	Lehigh University, USA
Vincent Mazet	ICube, University of Strasbourg, France
Enric Meinhardt	CMLA, ENS Paris Saclay, France
Nicolas Mellado	CNRS, IRIT, Université de Toulouse, France
Cyril Meyer	ICube, University of Strasbourg, France
Pascal Monasse	LIGM, École des Ponts ParisTech, France
Nelson Monzón	Universidad de las Palmas de Gran Canaria, Spain
Jean-Michel Morel	ENS Paris-Saclay, France
Serge Miguet	LIRIS, Université de Lyon 2, France
Pierre Moulon	Zillow Group, USA
Khadija Musayeva	Université Côte d'Azur, France
Phuc Ngo	LORIA, Université de Lorraine, France
Thanh Phuong Nguyen	University of Toulon, France
Nicolas Passat	CReSTIC, Reims, France
Benjamin Perret	ESIEE, Université Gustave Eiffel, France
Fabien Pierre	LORIA, Université de Lorraine, Nancy, France
François Rousseau	LaTIM Telecom Bretagne, France
Tristan Roussillon	LIRIS, INSA Lyon, France
Loïc Simon	GREYC, Ensicaen, France
Isabelle Sivignon	GIPSA Lab, Grenoble, France
Robin Strand	Uppsala University, Sweden
Hugues Talbot	CentraleSupélec, Paris, France
Iulia Tkachenko	LIRIS, Université de Lyon 2, France
Laure Tougne	LIRIS, Université de Lyon 2, France
Antoine Vacavant	Institut Pascal, Clermont-Ferrand, France
Jonathan Weber	IRIMAS, Université de Haute-Alsace, France
Laurent Wendling	LIPADE, Université Paris Cité, France
Burak Yildiz	Delft University of Technology, Delft, The Netherlands

[W18] SPRCV – Sustainable Pattern Recognition and Computer Vision Developments: Balancing Innovation and Environmental Responsibility

Organizers

Dilip K. Prasad	UiT, Arctic University of Norway, Norway
Balasubramanian Raman	Indian Institute of Technology, Roorkee, India
Krishan Berwal	National Institute of Technology, Kurukshetra, India
Debi Prosad Dogra	Indian Institute of Technology, Bhubaneswar, India
Ajit Bopardikar	University of Houston, USA
Balvinder Singh	Samsung Electronics, India
Ayan Kumar Bhunia	University of Surrey and Sony, UK
Samir Malakar	UiT, Arctic University of Norway, Norway
Arif Ahmed	XIM University, India
Iti Chaturvedi	James Cook University, Australia
Ayush Somani	UiT, Arctic University of Norway, Norway

Program Committee

Alexander Horsch	UiT, Arctic University of Norway, Norway
Sweta Thakur	King's Own Institute, Australia
M. Tanveer	Indian Institute of Technology, Indore, India
Samarjit Kar	NIT Durgapur, India
Debashis De	West Bengal University of Technology, India
Sasaram Ranvir Singh	IIT Guhahati, India
Rakesh Chandra Balabantaray	Indian Institute of Technology, Bhubaneswar, India
Anoworul Habib	UiT, Arctic University of Norway, Norway
Pinaki Nath Chowdhury	Sony, UK
Rohit Agarwal	UiT, Arctic University of Norway, Norway
Saher Tariq	UiT, Arctic University of Norway, Norway
Aaron Celeste	UiT, Arctic University of Norway, Norway
Krishna Agarwal	UiT, Arctic University of Norway, Norway
Debaleena Roy	Aston University, UK
Ranvir Soni	UTNT, India
Tapas Nayak	TCS Research, India
Malay Bhattacharyya	ISI Kolkata, India
Sriparna Saha	Indian Institute of Technology, Patna, India

Ashwin Ittoo	University of Liège, Belgium
Mitchell Fulton	University of Colorado, USA
Aneeshan Sain	Sony UK
Abhinanda R. Punnakal	UiT, Arctic University of Norway, Norway
Agneet Chatterjee	Arizona State University, USA
Mahesh Kumar H Kolekar	Indian Institute of Technology, Patna, India
Himanshu Buckchash	UiT, Arctic University of Norway, Norway
Alok Ranjan	Bosch, India
Samarendra Das	ICAR, National Institute on Foot and Mouth Disease, India
Akanksha Priyadarshini	Aurassure, India
Sudip Kumar Naskar	Jadavpur University, India
Björn Schuller	Imperial College London, UK and TU München, Germany
Petia Radeva	University of Barcelona, Spain
Manu Rastogi	AMD, USA
Nirwan Banerjee	UiT, Arctic University of Norway, Norway
Iqra Qasim	UiT, Arctic University of Norway, Norway
N. S. Chaudhari	Indian Institute of Technology, Indore, India
Alok Negi	UPES, Dehradun, India

[W19] VAIB – Visual Observation and Analysis of Vertebrate and Insect Behavior

Organizers

Robert Fisher	University of Edinburgh, UK
Simone Palazzo	Università di Catania, Italy
Sai Ravela	MIT, USA

Program Committee

John K. Atanbori	University of Lincoln, UK
Tsevi Beatus	Hebrew University of Jerusalem, Israel
Margrit Betke	Boston University, USA
Bas Boom	Imec OnePlanet, Netherlands
Alexandra Branzan Albu	University of Victoria, Canada
Tilo Burghardt	University of Bristol, UK
Joachim Denzler	Universität Jena, Germany
Andrew French	Nottingham University, UK

Lakshmi N. Govindarajan	Brown University, USA
Anthony Hoogs	Kitware, USA
Xiaoyi Jiang	Universität Münster, Germany
Martin Kampel	TU Wien, Austria
Walter Kropatsch	TU Wien, Austria
Michael Mangan	University of Sheffield, UK
Rémi Megret	University of Puerto Rico, USA
Majid Mirmehdi	University of Bristol, UK
Seyed Mojtaba Marvasti Zadeh	University of Alberta, Canada
Nils Napp	State University of New York at Buffalo, USA
Ronald Poppe	Universiteit Utrecht, Netherlands
Eric Psota	University of Nebraska-Lincoln, USA
Benjamin Risse	Universität Münster, Germany
Sylvie Treuillet	University of Orleans, France
Y. Xiao	University of West England, UK

[W20] WCWCE – Challenges in Wireless Capsule Endoscopy

Organizers, Program Committee

Suchendra M. Bhandarkar	University of Georgia, USA
Kiran Raja	Norwegian University of Science and Technology (NTNU), Norway
Kishor Upla	Sardar Vallabhbhai National Institute of Technology (SVNIT), India
Sudhish N. George	National Institute of Technology, Calicut, India
Marius Pedersen	Norwegian University of Science and Technology (NTNU), Norway
Anuja Vats	Norwegian University of Science and Technology (NTNU), Norway

[W21] WICV – Infrared Computer Vision

Organizers

Ajith Abraham	Bennett University, India
Manoj Sharma	Bennett University, India
Avinash Upadhyay	Visual Cognition Laboratory, India
Ankit Shukla	Visual Cognition Laboratory, India

Swati Bhugra	Visual Cognition Laboratory, India
Brejesh Lall	Indian Institute of Technology, Delhi, India
Prerna Mukherjee	Jawaharlal Nehru University, India
Amit Singhal	Netaji Subhas University of Technology, Delhi

[W22] WILD – Multimedia Forensics in the Wild

Organizers

Sebastiano Battiato	University of Catania, Italy
Giulia Boato	University of Trento, Italy
Alessandro Ortis	University of Catania, Italy
Nasir Memon	New York University, USA

Program Committee

Roberto Caldelli	CNIT, Italy
Luisa Verdoliva	University of Napoli Federico II, Italy
Oliver Giudice	iCTLAb, Catania, Italy
Alessandro Ortis	University of Catania, Italy
Luca Guarnera	University of Catania, Italy
Rainer Boehme	University of Innsbruck, Austria
Giovanni Puglisi	University of Cagliari, Italy
Pedro Comensana	University of Vigo, Spain
Anderson Rocha	University of Campinas, Brazil
Edward J. Delp	Purdue University, USA
Fernando Perez-Gonzalez	University of Vigo, Spain
Christian Riess	Friedrich-Alexander-Universität Erlangen-Nürnberg, Germany
Bin Li	Shenzen University, China
Alessandro Piva	University of Florence, Italy
Marco Fontani	Amped Software, Italy
Mattias Kirchner	Kitware, USA
Remi Cogranne	Université de technologie de Troyes, France
Rongrong Ni	Institute of Information Science (IIS), China
Benedetta Tondi	University of Siena, Italy
Davide Cozzolino	University of Napoli Federico II, Italy
Irene Amerini	Roma La Sapienza, Italy

Paolo Bestagini	Politecnico di Milano, Italy
Siwei Lyu	Buffalo University, USA
Pawel Korus	New York University, USA

[W23] WIMUE – Intelligent Mobility in Unstructured Environments

Organizers

Ayesha Choudhary	Jawaharlal Nehru University, India
Indu Sreedevi	Technological University, Delhi, India

Program Committee

S. Indu	Delhi Technological University, India
Ayesha Choudhary	Jawaharlal Nehru University, India
Ajay Kaushik	University of Derby, UK
Any Gupta	National Informatics Centre, India
J. Panda	Delhi Technological University, India
Pramod Soni	Galgotias University, India
Shraddha Chaudhary	NorthCap University, India
Gurjeet Walia	Defence Research and Development Organisation, India
Nidhi Goel	Indira Gandhi Delhi Technical University for Women, India
N. Jayanthi	Delhi Technological University, India
Bhavnesh Jaiant	Delhi Technological University, India
Ehtesham Hassan	Kuwait College of Science and Technology, Kuwait
Uma Mudenagudi	KLE Technological University, India
Aditi Kapoor	iKites Technologies, India
Aditi Saran	Jawaharlal Nehru University, India

[W24] XAIE – Explainable and Ethical AI

Organizers

Jenny Benois-Pineau	LaBRI and Université de Bordeaux, France
Romain Bourqui	LaBRI and Université de Bordeaux, France
Romain Giot	LaBRI and Université de Bordeaux, France
Dragutin Petkovic	San Francisco State University, USA

Program Committee

Carlos Toxtli	Clemson University, USA
Celine Hudelot	CentraleSupélec, France
Damien Garreau	Université Côte d'Azur, France
David Auber	Université de Bordeaux, France
Dragutin Petkovic	San Francisco State University, USA
Georges Quénot	Laboratoire d'Informatique de Grenoble, CNRS, France
Hervé Le Borgne	CEA LIST, France
Jenny Benois-Pineau	LaBRI, France
Luis Gustavo Nonato	University of São Paulo, Brazil
Mark Keane	University College Dublin and Insight SFI Centre for Data Analytics, Ireland
Romain Xu Darme	CEA LIST, France
Stefanos Kollias	National Technical University of Athens, Greece
Thomas Baltzer Moeslund	Aalborg University, Denmark
Vicent Botti	Universitat Politècnica de València, Spain
Victoria Bourgeais	Université de Bordeaux, France
Wassila Ouerdane	CentraleSupélec, France
Weiru Liu	University of Bristol, UK

Contents – Part IV

W13

W16

W11

Benchmarking Post-Hoc Unknown-Category Detection in Food Recognition

Lubnaa Abdur Rahman[1] ID, Ioannis Papathanail[2] ID, Lorenzo Brigato[2] ID, and Stavroula Mougiakakou[2](✉) ID

[1] Graduate School for Cellular and Biomedical Sciences, ARTORG Center, University of Bern, Bern, Switzerland
[2] ARTORG Center, University of Bern, Bern, Switzerland
stavroula.mougiakakou@unibe.ch

Abstract. Food recognition models often struggle to distinguish between seen and unseen samples, frequently misclassifying samples from unseen categories by assigning them an in-distribution (ID) label. This misclassification presents significant challenges when deploying these models in real-world applications, particularly within automatic dietary assessment systems, where incorrect labels can lead to cascading errors throughout the system. Ideally, such models should prompt the user when an unknown sample is encountered, allowing for corrective action. Given no prior research exploring food recognition in real-world settings, in this work we conduct an empirical analysis of various post-hoc out-of-distribution (OOD) detection methods for fine-grained food recognition. Our findings indicate that virtual logit matching (ViM) performed the best overall, likely due to its combination of logits and feature-space representations. Additionally, our work reinforces prior notions in the OOD domain, noting that models with higher ID accuracy performed better across the evaluated OOD detection methods. Furthermore, transformer-based architectures consistently outperformed convolution-based models in detecting OOD samples across various methods.

Keywords: Open Set Food Recognition · Out of Distribution · Image-based Automatic Dietary Assessment

1 Introduction

The rise in non-communicable diseases (NCDs), contributing to 74% of global annual deaths, presents a significant burden on global health [40]. It is well-known that maintaining a healthy diet is key to preventing and managing conditions like malnutrition, cardiovascular diseases, and diabetes while promoting

Supplementary Information The online version contains supplementary material available at https://doi.org/10.1007/978-3-031-88217-3_1.

overall well-being [39]. To effectively adhere to dietary interventions, continuous and accurate dietary monitoring and assessment are primordial. For long, this has been addressed through traditional dietary assessment methods led by dietitians, such as food frequency questionnaires and 24-hour recalls. However, not only are they time-consuming but also error-prone due to their reliance on people's memory, introducing subjective biases and inaccuracies [33].

To overcome these challenges and streamline the process, image-based automatic dietary assessment systems have been proposed by leveraging advancements in artificial intelligence (AI) and computer vision (CV) [22,37]. Such systems have proven effective in multiple settings, such as monitoring malnutrition in hospitalized patients [31], ensuring adherence to specific diets [32], and for everyday use under real-life conditions [30]. These have further demonstrated accuracy comparable to that of dietitians [22]. Typically, in an image-based automatic dietary assessment system, a meal image is captured and goes through the different modules of food segmentation, recognition, and volume estimation, all aggregated into the nutritional content of the meal [1,2]. One key component of this pipeline is food recognition, whereby the fine-grained label assigned to the food plays a crucial role in the retrieval of nutritional contents from the food composition databases.

Despite the vast number of potential food classes reflecting the global diversity of foods and eating habits, most food recognition models are practically limited to a predefined set of categories. In real-world applications like automatic dietary assessment systems, test samples from user-captured meal images [30] can be out-of-distribution (OOD), meaning that they belong to categories not seen during training. These OOD samples may present novel food categories or come from entirely different domains, originating from the initial stage of the automatic dietary assessment pipeline, whereby food segmentation models may mistakenly segment non-food items as food [7].

Consequently, when an unknown sample is provided as input, the recognition model is prone to misclassifying this OOD data as an in-distribution (ID) instance. This misclassification occurs because recognition models are typically trained under the closed-world assumption [5], where the test data is assumed to be drawn independently and identically distributed (IID) from the same distribution as the training data [42]. This problem eventually leads to inaccuracies in the automatic dietary assessment pipeline, which could potentially be dangerous.

For example, in [28], carbohydrate intake coming from an automatic dietary assessment serves as input for the personalized recommendation of insulin dosing for people with diabetes. Ideally, the food recognition model should distinguish between what it has not been exposed to and, therefore, prompt an OOD warning to enable the user to assign a proper food label.

Significant advancements have been achieved in the field of open-world multiclass image recognition, particularly in OOD detection [18,38] and enhancing the applicability of recognition models for open-world scenarios [5]. However, up to date, there remains a conspicuous gap in modeling these findings to the problem of fine-grained food recognition. As such, in this work, our primary contribution is delving into OOD detection for fine-grained food recognition by applying and assessing the performance of several state-of-the-art methods for differentiating between OOD and ID data. We focus on post-hoc methods, given their advantage of not requiring adjustment to training strategies and simple plug-and-play deployment.

2   Related Works

The core challenge of OOD detection is to create a scoring mechanism that accurately differentiates between ID and OOD samples. This is inherently complex due to the unpredictable and vast nature of OOD distributions, which are difficult to model or estimate beforehand. There has been increasing interest in developing efficient OOD detection methods that do not require training adjustments, unlike approaches in [17,44], which can be time- and computationally-consuming. Several works focused on establishing post-hoc scoring mechanisms applicable to pre-trained models, which usually assess model confidence using softmax probabilities from the classification layer [13,19]. [5] proposed adjusting class probabilities to improve OOD handling as an attempt to make recognition models more "open" to real-world scenarios.

Other methods leverage feature space metrics by modeling class-conditional distributions within the feature space [18]. Logit-based methods have also gained traction as a viable alternative with approaches like [12,20]. Other methods proposed combining logit-based while leveraging [38] representations within the feature space. Some additionally propose modifications to the network's activations during inference, such as clipping or pruning, before applying scoring methods [34,35]. While these methods have been extensively evaluated on standard open-set benchmarks using ID datasets such as CIFAR-10 [16] and ImageNet1K [8], their applicability to the fine-grained food recognition, remains unexplored.

3   Materials and Methods

Our task here is to first train different models for multi-class fine-grained food recognition and apply the existing different post-hoc OOD methods to further assess their performance. All the experiments described in this section, including Sects. 3.1 to 3.3, were run with acceleration on NVIDIA RTX A6000 with the exception of the training of the Shifted Window - T variant (Swin-T) [21] which was on RTX 4090[1].

3.1   Datasets
In Distribution. For the ID dataset to train the model on, we utilize the Food-101 dataset [6], a well-known fine-grained food recognition dataset comprising 101,000 images categorized into 101 distinct food classes covering diverse cuisines. We use the standard train/test splits of 75,750/25,250 images.

---

[1] Computations were performed on UBELIX (https://www.id.unibe.ch/hpc), the HPC cluster at the University of Bern.

Out of Distribution

Food Datasets. As no prior work exists on OOD detection within the food domain and no benchmark OOD datasets are available for this task, we, therefore, utilize the open-source food recognition datasets presented in Table 1. Overlapping and similar categories are removed (as described in Sect. 3.1). We also provide the list of categories used for each dataset in the Supplementary Materials: Supplementary A - OOD. Specifically for Indian20 [29] and UECFoodPixComplete [27], since there were multiple foods per image, we further used annotations provided by the dataset creators to produce single food item images. We show some examples of the images from each dataset in Fig. 1.

Table 1. Food Dataset Overview and Image Counts

Dataset	Cuisine	#Images
African Foods Dataset [4]	African (Cameroon, Ghana)	1,751
FoodX-251 [15]	Mixed Cuisines	6,561
Indian20 [29]	Indian	37,067
UECFoodPixComplete [27]	Japanese	8,758
Food2K [24]	Mixed Cuisines	262,777
THFOOD-50 [36]	Thai	1,534
ISIA FOOD-500 [23]	Mixed Cuisines	98,482

Non-food Datasets. To compare with common benchmarks and address scenarios specifically in dietary assessment pipelines where segmentation models may inaccurately segment non-food items as well, we use the OOD datasets presented in Table 2. For all datasets, we utilized the testing splits, except for the ImageNet1K dataset [8], where we used the validation set after filtering it to include only non-food items. We use the ImageNet1K to also evaluate whether pretraining affects OOD detection in the ResNet-18, ResNet-50 [11], and Swin-T [21] models. Examples of images from each dataset are shown in Fig. 1.

Table 2. Non-Food Dataset Overview and Image Counts

Dataset	Type	#Images
CIFAR10 [16]	Animals & Vehicles	10,000
iSUN [41]	Scenes	8,925
ImageNet1K (non-food items) [8]	Diverse	47,150
Places365 [43]	Scenes	328,500
SVHN [25]	Street View House Numbers	26,032

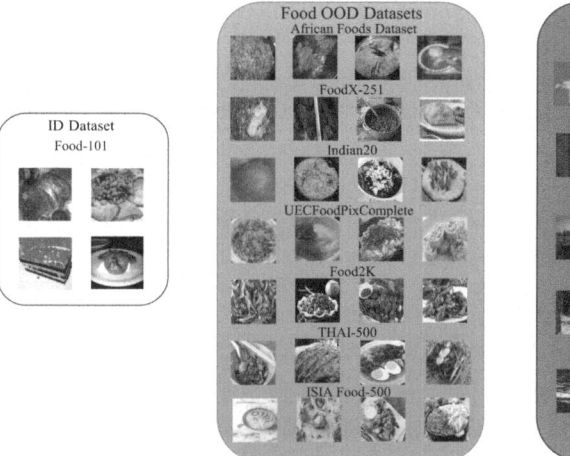

Fig. 1. Example of images present in ID and OOD datasets

Removal of Overlapping and Similar Categories. To remove overlapping categories, we compared word-for-word patterns between the OOD datasets and the ID dataset, eliminating any matching entries from the OOD datasets. Additionally, given the complexity of lexicons, including synonyms and words with different meanings across languages, we further processed the categories of the OOD datasets. For this task, we used Llama-3-8B-Instruct [3]. We instructed Llama-3 to act as a global cuisine expert to identify whether any OOD categories were synonymous or represented similar categories to those in the in-distribution dataset. For example, "Beef tenderloin" from Food2k was removed because it encompasses the ID category "Filet mignon" from Food-101.

3.2 Training

We evaluated four models, chosen based on recent works [26,38], two CNN-based, ResNet18 and ResNet50 [11], and two transformer-based architectures, the Vision Transformer with B variant patch 16 (ViT-B/16) [9], and the Swin-T [21]. All models were trained with a batch size of 64, and the images were resized to 224×224. The training specifics and ID accuracy achieved by the different models are presented in Table 3. To compare OOD detection performance between fine-tuned models and models trained from scratch (-S), we focused on ResNet-18 and ResNet-50.

3.3 Post-Hoc OOD Detection

Preliminaries. We begin by outlining the general framework whereby the input space can be denoted by $\mathcal{X} = \mathbb{R}^d$ and the output space by $\mathcal{Y} = \{1, 2, \ldots, C\}$. The model is provided with a training set $\mathcal{D} = \{(\mathbf{x}_i, y_i)\}_{i=1}^{N}$, sampled from an

Table 3. Training Specifics and ID Performance

Model	Pre-training	Scheduler	Optimizer	LR	WD	Epochs	Accuracy
ResNet-18	ImageNet-1K	Linear	SGD	0.001	0	50	77.71%
ResNet-18-S	None	Cosine	SGD	0.1	0.0001	100	65.04%
ResNet-50	ImageNet-1K	Cosine	SGD	0.001	0.0001	50	82.91%
ResNet-50-S	None	Cosine	SGD	0.1	0.0001	100	67.62%
ViT-B	ImageNet-21K	Cosine	SGD	0.001	0	15	**89.34%**
Swin-T	ImageNet-1K	Linear	Adam	0.00001	0	15	87.73%

unknown joint distribution $P(\mathcal{X}, \mathcal{Y})$. Let P_{in} represent the marginal probability distribution on $\mathcal{X}$. We recall that the principle of OOD detection is traditionally modeled as a binary classification problem whereby the ID is considered as the positive class and the OOD the negative class. At a specific evaluation time, the goal is to determine whether an input sample $\mathbf{x} \in \mathcal{X}$ belongs to the ID P_{in} or the OOD P_{out}. The distribution of P_{out} represents unknowns that may be encountered during deployment, whereby the label set has no overlap with ID labels $\mathcal{Y}$ and should not be predicted by the model. As such, post-hoc OOD detection follows the pipeline as expressed in Algorithm 1. λ represents the cutoff threshold to distinguish between ID and OOD samples. Following common practice, we choose λ such that 95% of the ID data is correctly classified.

Algorithm 1. Recognition Model with Post-hoc OOD Detection

---

function POSTHOCOODDETECTION(trained_model, deployment_data)
    for each sample $\mathbf{x}$ in deployment_data **do**
        Extract features $\mathbf{f}(\mathbf{x})$ from the input using the model's feature extractor
        Compute the score $S(\mathbf{f}(\mathbf{x}))$ using a scoring function
        if $S(\mathbf{f}(\mathbf{x})) \geq \lambda$ **then**
            label ← "in"   ▷ ID sample
            predicted_label ← trained_model.classifier($\mathbf{f}(\mathbf{x})$)
        else
            label ← "out"   ▷ OOD sample
            predicted_label ← "unknown"
        end if
        output predicted_label
    end for
end function

Benchmarked OOD Methods. In this section, we describe the post-hoc OOD baselines evaluated in this work. For the entailing section, let $z = [z_1, z_2, \ldots, z_C] \in \mathbb{R}^C$ be the logits for a sample, where C is the number of ID classes and z_i represents the logit for class i.

Maximum Softmax Probability. [13]: The maximum softmax probability score (MSP) is based on the observation that correctly classified ID examples tend to have higher softmax probabilities than OOD examples. The softmax probability for class i is given by: $p(y = i|x) = \frac{\exp(z_i)}{\sum_{j=1}^{C} \exp(z_j)}$. The MSP score $MSP(x)$ is then computed as:

$$MSP(x) = \max_i p(y = i|x) \qquad (1)$$

ODIN [19]: The Out-of-DIstribution detector for Neural networks (ODIN) method applies temperature scaling to adjust the softmax scores, enhancing the separation between ID and OOD data. The softmax score $S_i(x; T)$ for class i at temperature T is given by:

$$S_i(x; T) = \frac{\exp(z_i/T)}{\sum_{j=1}^{C} \exp(z_j/T)} \qquad (2)$$

In our experiments, we set T to 1000 as in previous work [14,19].

OpenMax [5]: OpenMax replaces the standard softmax layer with a layer that recalibrates the output probabilities by modeling the uncertainty for each class by fitting a Weibull distribution, $W(\lambda_i, k_i)$ for each class i. Here, λ_i and k_i are the scale and shape parameters of the Weibull distribution, respectively for each class. The original logits z_i are adjusted by reducing the score for the top classes based on the tail probability that they belong to an unknown class computed by $z_i' = z_i \cdot (1 - W(\lambda_i, k_i, z_i))$, where $W(\lambda_i, k_i, z_i)$ represents the Weibull cumulative distribution function for class i, evaluated at logit z_i. After adjusting the logits, a recalibrated softmax probability distribution is computed using the adjusted logits z'. The probability that the input belongs to a known class is then given by:

$$p(y = i|x) = \frac{\exp(z_i')}{\sum_{j=1}^{C} \exp(z_j') + \exp(z_\alpha')} \qquad (3)$$

where z_α' is the score for the unknown class, which is derived from the tail probabilities of the Weibull distributions.

KL Matching [12]: Kullback-Leibler (KL) Matching captures the typical shape of each class's posterior distribution by creating class-wise posterior distribution templates. It compares the network's softmax posterior distribution $p(y|x)$ to the class-wise template distributions $q(y|c)$, where c is the class template. The anomaly score $KL(x)$ is computed as:

$$KL(x) = \min_c D_{\mathrm{KL}}\left(p(y|x) \parallel q(y|c)\right) \qquad (4)$$

where D_{KL} is the Kullback-Leibler divergence. A higher $KL(x)$ score indicates a greater likelihood that the input is OOD, as the posterior distribution of the input deviates significantly from the class-wise templates.

Mahalanobis [18]: This method leverages Gaussian distributions to model the class-conditional distributions resulting in a Mahalanobis distance-based scores. By estimating the generative classifier parameters from a pre-trained softmax neural classifier, the empirical class means and covariances are calculated using the activations on training data. Let μ_i represent the empirical mean vector for class i, and let Σ represent the shared covariance matrix, both of which were estimated using the training set. Given a new input test sample x, the Mahalanobis distance between the feature representation $f(x)$ and the class mean μ_i is given as: $d_M(f(x), \mu_i) = (f(x) - \mu_i)^T \Sigma^{-1}(f(x) - \mu_i)$. This quantity measures how far the feature representation of the input $f(x)$ is from the mean of the distribution for class i. To detect OOD data, the confidence score, $M(x)$, is:

$$M(x) = \max_i \left\{ -d_M(f(x), \mu_i) \right\} \tag{5}$$

Inputs exhibiting larger $M(x)$ scores (i.e., lower confidence scores) are more likely to be classified as OOD.

Maximum Logit [12]: The MaxLog score uses the negative of the maximum of the unnormalized logits as an anomaly score which is given by:

$$MaxLog(x) = -\max_i z_i \tag{6}$$

Energy [20]: The Energy score maps each input to a single non-probabilistic scalar that is lower for ID data and higher for OOD ones. It is computed as the negative log-sum-exp of the logits, effectively distinguishing OOD samples based on their lower energy values compared to ID data. The Energy score $E(x)$ for a given input x is:

$$E(x) = -\log \left(\sum_{i=1}^{C} \exp(z_i) \right) \tag{7}$$

ViM [38]: Virtual-logit Matching (ViM) combines a class-agnostic score from the feature space with the ID class-specific logits. First, the feature space offset using vector $o = -\left(W^T\right)^+ b$, where W and b are the weights and biases from the fully connected layer. The principal subspace P is obtained via eigen decomposition on the training data (in our experiments, we use the whole training set). The residual $x_{P\perp}$ is then computed as the projection of feature x onto the orthogonal complement of P. Next, the norm of the residual $x_{P\perp}$ is scaled to create a virtual logit, $l_0 := \alpha \|x_{P\perp}\| = \alpha \sqrt{x^\top R R^\top x}$, where α is a scaling factor derived from the training data and R represents the matrix whose columns span the orthogonal complement of the principal subspace P. The virtual logit l_0 is then appended to the original logits z, forming a new logit vector $[z_1, z_2, \ldots, z_C, l_0]$. The ViM score is then given as the softmax probability corresponding to the virtual logit:

$$ViM(x) = \frac{e^{l_0}}{\sum_{i=1}^{C} e^{z_i} + e^{l_0}} \tag{8}$$

ReAct [34]: Rectified Activation (ReAct), designed to reduce the model's over-confidence, works by applying rectifications to the activations applied to the penultimate layer of the network and truncates activations to a certain limit, τ. After truncation, the outputs can be combined with the Eq. 7 scoring function for OOD detection. In our experiments, we run ReAct with different values of τ and show the best results in Tables 4 and 5.

DICE [35]: Directed Sparsification (DICE) introduces sparsity into the activations of the penultimate layer using a contribution matrix derived from the whole training set to retain the most significant weights. Sparsity is applied by zeroing out a certain percentage of the lowest activations based on a sparsity parameter ρ where higher values of ρ correspond to a larger proportion of weights being dropped. Once the "unimportant" weights are removed, scoring functions such as Eq. 7 or 1 can be utilized. In our experiments, consistent with [35], Eq. 7 provided the best results. Various values of ρ were tested, and the optimal value for each model is reported in Tables 4 and 5.

Evaluation Metrics. We used two key metrics for evaluating OOD detection methods:

- FPR95: The false positive rate (FPR) at 95% true positive rate (TPR), which is computed as: FPR95 = P(False Positive | TPR = 95%).
- Area Under the Receiver Operating Characteristic Curve (AUROC): It is defined as: AUROC = $\int_0^1$ TPR dFPR.

4 Results and Discussion

The average performance results across the food-related and non-food-related datasets are presented in Fig. 2. We additionally provide the detailed results for each architecture and method for food OOD datasets in Table 4 and non-food OOD datasets in Table 5. Due to the poorer performance of models trained from scratch, we instead report the detailed results of ResNet-18-S and ResNet-50-S in the Supplementary Materials: Experiments.

Overall, we observed that all methods evaluated gave the best performance with the ViT-B model, which was also the model with the highest ID accuracy (Table 3), for both food and non-food OOD datasets, as seen in Fig. 2e. Particularly, OpenMax [5] and ViM [38] achieve the lowest FPR at TPR 95% with values of 31.4, and 37.4 in food OOD datasets (Table 4). On the other hand, for non-food OOD datasets, most methods excelled with FPR95 between 0.2-1.3, with the exception of the Mahalanobis [18], which had a relatively higher average FPR95 of 26.5 (Table 5). The Swin-T model also showed high performance, with the lowest FPR95 of 51.1 in food OOD detection using OpenMax, and 0.7 in non-food OOD detection using ViM as seen in Fig. 2f, and Tables 4 and 5.

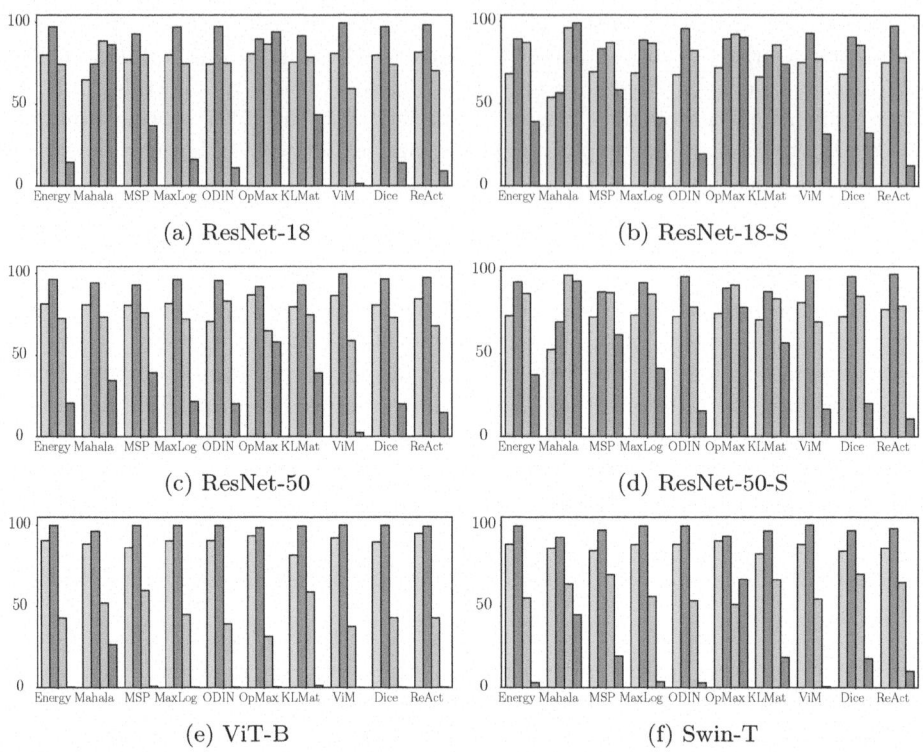

Fig. 2. Average results for different methods for different models for food and non-foods. The color-coded metrics are as follows: AUROC for foods , AUROC for non-foods , FPR95 Foods , and FPR95 for non-foods . (Color figure online)

However, these patterns did not extend consistently to the CNN-based architectures. With ResNet-18 and ResNet-50, ViM outperformed other methods by delivering the lowest FPR95 scores for both food and non-food OOD datasets. In contrast, OpenMax underperformed with these CNN models.

The pre-trained models consistently outperformed those trained from scratch, likely due to the lower ID accuracy of the latter. In our runs, we also noted that even models pre-trained on ImageNet-1K, such as ResNet-18 and ResNet-50 with ViM, and Swin-T with ViM, MaxLog, and Energy, produced relatively low FPR95 scores for the OOD ImageNet-1K (non-food items) dataset. This potentially suggests that the dataset on which the model was pre-trained does not heavily impact OOD performance, as models trained from scratch, such as ResNet-18-S and ResNet-50-S, exhibited significantly less favorable FPR95 and AUROC scores for the same datasets.

The overall metrics indicate that OOD detection methods performed better on non-food datasets than on food datasets (Fig. 2). Simpler scoring functions,

Table 4. Detailed performance for Food OOD dataset expressed by FPR95 / AUROC. Best results are represented by **FPR95**.

Model	Method	African	FX251	Indian	UECFPC	Food2K	THF50	ISIA F500	Average
RN18	MSP	77.1 / 79.3	79.7 / 78.2	79.9 / 77.7	79.7 / 76.8	79.9 / 77.7	81.5 / 76.9	83.3 / 73.9	80.2 / 77.2
	ODIN	76.6 / 73.7	76.1 / 76.2	63.7 / 77.9	75.8 / 71.2	71.5 / 78.3	82.7 / 71.4	78.7 / 72.6	75.0 / 74.5
	OpenMax	81.7 / 83.4	91.7 / 78.5	83.7 / 82.9	85.0 / 81.6	87.9 / 81.2	87.2 / 80.2	88.5 / 77.0	86.5 / 80.7
	KL Matching	74.2 / 78.2	79.9 / 76.5	77.7 / 76.9	77.6 / 75.1	77.4 / 75.5	80.4 / 74.4	82.1 / 72.1	78.5 / 75.5
	Mahalanobis	82.5 / 68.8	92.3 / 61.9	79.6 / 73.3	89.1 / 67.0	91.9 / 62.2	93.8 / 59.2	91.1 / 62.1	88.6 / 64.9
	MaxLog	69.3 / 84.0	75.3 / 80.6	73.8 / 80.8	73.4 / 79.2	73.3 / 81.4	77.7 / 78.4	79.9 / 75.7	74.7 / 80.0
	Energy	69.1 / 84.1	75.0 / 80.5	73.1 / 80.8	72.9 / 79.1	72.5 / 81.4	78.0 / 78.2	79.7 / 75.5	74.3 / 80.0
	ViM	55.6 / 81.4	64.2 / 82.5	53.6 / 84.6	61.3 / 78.9	54.7 / 82.5	58.5 / 79.8	67.7 / 76.3	**59.4** / 80.8
	ReAct τ=1.75	59.0 / 87.1	74.3 / 80.7	64.3 / 84.0	68.3 / 81.5	69.9 / 82.5	78.2 / 78.8	78.2 / 76.4	70.3 / 81.6
	DICE ρ=0.01	68.4 / 83.9	75.2 / 80.2	73.2 / 80.4	72.8 / 79.0	72.4 / 81.3	77.2 / 78.4	80.0 / 75.3	74.2 / 79.8
RN50	MSP	73.5 / 82.5	98.5 / 77.0	80.9 / 94.2	73.2 / 81.9	79.1 / 75.1	79.7 / 91.6	75.4 / 81.2	75.7 / 80.4
	ODIN	86.0 / 68.9	96.7 / 86.1	70.2 / 89.6	74.8 / 73.3	64.6 / 84.1	66.1 / 84.1	78.8 / 76.0	83.1 / 70.4
	OpenMax	50.3 / 90.5	99.2 / 74.3	84.3 / 95.5	66.2 / 87.8	87.1 / 62.8	87.3 / 95.1	64.1 / 87.1	64.7 / 86.7
	KL Matching	72.1 / 81.8	98.3 / 75.8	80.2 / 93.4	72.1 / 81.1	74.2 / 74.4	79.1 / 90.8	74.1 / 80.1	74.7 / 79.4
	Mahalanobis	56.7 / 87.8	99.0 / 78.5	79.3 / 93.8	67.2 / 83.8	80.7 / 73.2	81.2 / 92.3	75.7 / 79.9	73.2 / 80.7
	MaxLog	69.1 / 84.1	98.6 / 73.2	81.6 / 94.1	66.8 / 83.6	79.1 / 70.8	80.9 / 91.7	70.7 / 83.0	71.9 / 81.4
	Energy	69.7 / 84.1	98.6 / 73.4	81.4 / 94.1	66.6 / 83.5	79.1 / 70.8	80.8 / 91.6	70.9 / 83.0	77.4 / 81.3
	ViM	36.5 / 92.7	99.4 / 66.4	85.3 / 95.6	37.8 / 91.8	89.2 / 57.1	86.5 / 94.2	64.2 / 85.9	**58.7** / 86.3
	ReAct τ=1	57.7 / 88.1	99.1 / 72.4	84.1 / 94.4	61.5 / 85.1	84.2 / 63.4	85.5 / 94.7	67.8 / 87.9	70.0 / 85.1
	DICE ρ=0.05	68.3 / 84.0	98.6 / 73.3	81.8 / 94.1	66.7 / 83.6	79.3 / 70.8	80.9 / 91.6	70.7 / 83.0	72.3 / 81.5
ViT-B	MSP	56.8 / 86.6	62.5 / 86.1	55.5 / 88.0	62.8 / 84.4	55.8 / 88.0	61.1 / 85.2	63.8 / 84.9	59.8 / 86.2
	ODIN	33.6 / 92.3	45.1 / 89.8	30.0 / 93.4	41.7 / 89.1	34.3 / 92.3	44.0 / 88.7	46.7 / 88.7	39.3 / 90.6
	OpenMax	26.1 / 94.3	42.8 / 91.9	28.3 / 94.5	33.8 / 92.2	24.7 / 94.6	29.0 / 93.9	35.4 / 92.5	**31.4** / 93.4
	KL Matching	55.6 / 81.4	64.2 / 82.5	53.6 / 84.6	61.3 / 78.9	54.0 / 83.1	58.5 / 79.8	63.8 / 79.9	58.7 / 81.4
	Mahalanobis	41.1 / 91.2	59.4 / 87.2	43.6 / 91.1	56.8 / 86.1	48.8 / 89.9	56.8 / 87.3	58.2 / 86.5	52.1 / 88.5
	MaxLog	40.1 / 92.0	50.7 / 89.7	35.4 / 93.2	48.6 / 88.5	38.9 / 92.3	50.5 / 88.6	51.3 / 88.7	45.1 / 90.4
	Energy	37.1 / 92.4	49.0 / 89.8	32.5 / 93.6	46.3 / 88.7	36.4 / 92.5	48.7 / 88.7	49.6 / 88.9	42.8 / 90.7
	ViM	28.5 / 94.1	48.2 / 90.0	25.1 / 95.3	36.8 / 91.7	24.5 / 95.2	53.4 / 88.9	45.7 / 90.0	37.4 / 92.2
	ReAct τ=1	36.9 / 99.4	49.2 / 97.0	32.1 / 92.0	46.6 / 95.2	36.2 / 92.6	49.6 / 99.1	49.1 / 89.1	42.8 / 94.9
	DICE ρ=0.08	37.2 / 91.3	47.9 / 89.4	32.0 / 93.2	44.6 / 88.4	35.3 / 92.2	50.3 / 87.9	53.2 / 85.1	42.9 / 89.6
SWIN-T	MSP	64.7 / 85.8	69.4 / 84.7	66.9 / 85.4	68.2 / 84.0	68.3 / 85.0	72.4 / 83.2	74.4 / 80.1	69.2 / 84.0
	ODIN	43.1 / 91.6	56.4 / 88.4	46.7 / 90.6	51.6 / 88.0	50.9 / 89.1	61.2 / 86.0	63.1 / 83.3	53.3 / 88.2
	OpenMax	51.7 / 90.2	55.4 / 90.0	53.1 / 91.1	50.9 / 90.1	42.9 / 91.9	49.9 / 90.9	53.7 / 87.8	**51.1** / 90.3
	KL Matching	62.7 / 84.2	67.6 / 83.2	62.5 / 84.1	65.6 / 81.9	63.9 / 82.9	69.6 / 80.3	71.8 / 78.0	66.3 / 82.1
	Mahalanobis	63.0 / 86.2	65.8 / 85.8	55.8 / 89.1	67.6 / 84.4	54.8 / 88.2	70.6 / 83.1	67.1 / 82.2	63.5 / 85.6
	MaxLog	45.5 / 91.9	58.3 / 88.4	49.4 / 90.5	54.2 / 87.7	54.2 / 88.8	64.2 / 85.5	65.5 / 83.1	55.9 / 88.0
	Energy	43.6 / 92.2	58.0 / 88.4	48.0 / 90.7	53.1 / 87.8	53.3 / 88.9	63.8 / 85.5	65.2 / 83.1	55.0 / 88.1
	ViM	43.4 / 92.4	59.7 / 88.3	35.5 / 93.0	52.7 / 87.7	51.3 / 89.2	74.3 / 82.5	64.3 / 83.4	54.5 / 88.1
	ReAct τ=0.75	56.0 / 88.8	64.4 / 86.3	69.2 / 85.1	67.1 / 84.2	62.0 / 86.9	64.9 / 85.1	68.1 / 84.0	64.5 / 85.8
	DICE ρ=0.1	58.6 / 88.8	69.6 / 84.6	79.2 / 81.1	74.0 / 81.5	66.9 / 85.2	67.0 / 84.0	72.9 / 82.1	69.7 / 83.9

such as Energy, MaxLog, and ODIN, proved particularly effective on non-food datasets (Table 5) where the feature space is well-separated. The better performance on non-food datasets is likely due to the clearer feature distinction between ID and OOD data, clearly visible in Fig. 1. However, certain methods, such as OpenMax and Mahalanobis, performed unexpectedly poorly on non-food items, with FPR95 values exceeding 70 in some cases (Figs. 2a,2b,2d and 2f and

Table 5. Detailed performance for Non-Food dataset expressed by FPR95 / AUROC. Best results are represented by **FPR95**.

Model	Method	CIFAR10	SVHN	iSUN	places365	ImageNet1k	Average
RN18	MSP	31.2 / 94.5	17.0 / 97.1	30.4 / 94.6	44.8 / 91.2	60.5 / 86.3	36.8 / 92.7
	ODIN	0.7 / 99.8	0 / 100	3.6 / 99.2	18.2 / 95.7	31.8 / 92.0	10.9 / 97.3
	OpenMax	97.4 / 90.0	97.3 / 91.6	97.5 / 89.5	95.1 / 88.5	82.6 / 88.8	94.0 / 89.7
	KL Matching	42.5 / 93.4	27.7 / 95.9	38.1 / 93.6	49.7 / 90.2	58.9 / 85.7	43.4 / 91.7
	Mahalanobis	88.1 / 75.4	87.4 / 83.3	91.5 / 71.4	89.5 / 65.4	74.8 / 76.4	86.2 / 74.4
	MaxLog	7.3 / 98.6	2.2 / 99.4	7.5 / 98.7	19.9 / 96.3	43.1 / 91.3	16.0 / 96.8
	Energy	5.5 / 98.9	1.4 / 99.6	5.6 / 99.0	17.3 / 96.7	41.2 / 91.5	14.2 / 97.1
	ViM	0.3 / 99.7	0.4 / 99.7	0.3 / 99.6	1.8 / 99.3	3.6 / 98.8	**1.3** / 99.4
	ReAct τ=1.75	3.5 / 99.2	0.2 / 99.9	3.4 / 99.3	10.5 / 97.9	27.1 / 94.8	8.9 / 98.2
	DICE ρ=0.01	4.6 / 99.1	1.3 / 99.7	4.5 / 99.2	17.6 / 96.6	41.3 / 91.4	13.8 / 97.2
RN50	MSP	38.6 / 93.0	20.3 / 96.7	35.9 / 93.8	45.0 / 91.6	56.1 / 88.7	39.2 / 92.8
	ODIN	6.9 / 98.6	0.0 / 99.9	14.0 / 97.4	39.0 / 91.4	40.8 / 90.6	20.1 / 95.6
	OpenMax	63.7 / 90.8	59.1 / 92.3	54.4 / 92.8	56.0 / 92.1	56.4 / 91.4	57.9 / 91.9
	KL Matching	39.8 / 92.8	21.1 / 96.7	36.0 / 93.9	43.8 / 91.9	54.2 / 88.8	39.0 / 92.8
	Mahalanobis	42.6 / 92.9	28.1 / 95.4	38.2 / 94.0	27.2 / 95.3	36.6 / 92.7	34.5 / 94.1
	MaxLog	19.6 / 96.7	5.9 / 98.8	17.2 / 97.1	25.7 / 95.3	39.7 / 92.5	21.6 / 96.1
	Energy	18.3 / 96.9	5.6 / 98.8	15.8 / 97.2	24.5 / 95.5	38.6 / 92.6	20.6 / 96.2
	ViM	0.1 / 99.9	0.0 / 100.0	0.1 / 99.9	2.9 / 99.2	8.7 / 98.3	**2.4** / 99.5
	ReAct τ=1	13.2 / 97.7	6.0 / 98.9	10.3 / 98.2	14.0 / 97.4	29.1 / 94.7	14.5 / 97.4
	DICE ρ=0.05	16.5 / 97.1	2.4 / 99.5	13.7 / 97.5	28.2 / 94.7	39.1 / 92.3	20.0 / 96.2
ViT-B	MSP	0.2 / 100.0	0.2 / 100.0	0.2 / 99.9	1.5 / 99.6	3.2 / 99.3	1.1 / 99.8
	ODIN	0.0 / 100.0	0.0 / 100.0	0.0 / 100.0	0.8 / 99.8	1.1 / 99.7	0.4 / 99.9
	OpenMax	0.1 / 98.3	0.1 / 99.0	0.1 / 98.5	0.7 / 98.4	1.6 / 98.2	0.5 / 98.5
	KL Matching	0.3 / 99.7	0.4 / 99.7	0.3 / 99.6	1.8 / 99.3	3.6 / 98.8	1.3 / 99.4
	Mahalanobis	28.8 / 96.2	43.5 / 94.6	23.7 / 96.6	16.7 / 97.3	19.8 / 96.8	26.5 / 96.3
	MaxLog	0.0 / 100.0	0.0 / 100.0	0.0 / 100.0	0.7 / 99.8	1.1 / 99.7	0.4 / 99.9
	Energy	0.0 / 100.0	0.0 / 100.0	0.0 / 100.0	0.6 / 99.8	1.0 / 99.7	0.3 / 99.9
	ViM	0.0 / 100.0	0.0 / 100.0	0.0 / 100.0	0.5 / 99.9	0.7 / 99.8	**0.2** / 99.9
	ReAct τ=1	0.0 / 100.0	0.0 / 100.0	0.0 / 100.0	0.6 / 97.0	1.0 / 99.3	0.3 / 99.3
	DICE ρ=0.08	0.0 / 100.0	0.0 / 100.0	0.0 / 100.0	0.5 / 99.8	0.8 / 99.7	0.3 / 99.9
SWIN-T	MSP	16.2 / 97.5	3.8 / 99.2	10.7 / 98.3	26.9 / 95.7	39.6 / 92.9	19.4 / 96.7
	ODIN	0.6 / 99.8	0.1 / 100.0	0.2 / 99.9	3.4 / 99.2	11.5 / 97.7	3.2 / 99.3
	OpenMax	72.8 / 92.4	92.8 / 91.8	83.4 / 91.1	39.2 / 95.1	43.9 / 94.4	66.4 / 93.0
	KL Matching	16.9 / 97.2	4.5 / 98.6	13.4 / 97.5	23.2 / 95.9	34.7 / 92.9	18.6 / 96.4
	Mahalanobis	42.9 / 93.4	75.4 / 86.4	46.8 / 93.3	24.0 / 95.7	34.2 / 92.9	44.7 / 92.4
	MaxLog	0.7 / 99.8	0.1 / 100.0	0.3 / 99.9	4.0 / 99.2	13.3 / 97.6	3.7 / 99.3
	Energy	0.4 / 99.9	0.1 / 100.0	0.2 / 99.9	3.3 / 99.3	11.7 / 97.8	3.2 / 99.4
	ViM	0.0 / 100.0	0.0 / 100.0	0.0 / 100.0	0.8 / 99.8	2.7 / 99.4	**0.7** / 99.8
	ReAct τ=0.75	5.4 / 98.7	0.9 / 99.7	3.4 / 99.0	12.8 / 97.6	28.8 / 94.8	10.2 / 97.9
	DICE ρ=0.1	18.6 / 96.9	5.0 / 98.2	11.2 / 97.6	15.8 / 97.1	38.5 / 92.9	17.8 / 96.5

Table 5). While these methods may work well in some scenarios, they are not universally reliable across all model architectures and dataset types. On the other hand, ViM showed consistent performance across different OOD datasets and model architectures, proving its adaptability. This suggests that ViM effectively uses both class-agnostic and class-specific information, even in highly variable food-related datasets.

Mahalanobis, in particular, struggled across the board, especially with food-related datasets, which are inherently more challenging due to their fine-grained nature. On the other hand, techniques that involve activation rectification and pruning, such as ReAct and DICE, generally outperformed simpler scoring functions like Energy, with ReAct consistently outperforming DICE in all runs. This further emphasizes the importance of reducing redundant activations. Differently from the original work [35], DICE performed better using a smaller values of ρ for activation pruning.

Additionally, transformer models clearly outperformed CNN-based ones, as reported by recent works [10]. This could be possibly attributed not only to their higher ID accuracy but also to their ability to better handle complex variations in data, owing to their more abstract and high-dimensional feature representations.

5   Conclusion

In this work, we assessed various post-hoc OOD detection methods within the domain of fine-grained food recognition. Our results showed that ViM [38], performed better generally - not only did it stand out in recognizing non-foods but it was always among the top-3 methods when it came to detecting food as OOD. Additionally, we note that model architecture and ID accuracy have a great impact on OOD detection performances. This work underscores the need for continued research into specialized OOD detection strategies tailored to fine-grained food recognition, particularly as these models find increasing application in real-world systems such as automatic dietary assessments.

Acknowledgements. This work was partly supported by the European Commission and the Swiss Confederation - State Secretariat for Education, Research and Innovation (SERI) within the projects 101057730 Mobile Artificial Intelligence Solution for Diabetes Adaptive Care (MELISSA) and 101080117 BETTER4U.

References

1. Abdur Rahman, L., Papathanail, I., Brigato, L., Mougiakakou, S.: A comparative analysis of sensor-, geometry-, and neural-based methods for food volume estimation. In: Proceedings of the 8th International Workshop on Multimedia Assisted Dietary Management, pp. 21–29 (2023)
2. Abdur Rahman, L., Papathanail, I., Brigato, L., Spanakis, E.K., Mougiakakou, S.: Chapter 6 - food recognition and nutritional apps. In: Klonoff, D.C., Kerr, D., Espinoza, J.C. (eds.) Diabetes Digital Health, Telehealth, and Artificial Intelligence, pp. 73–83. Academic Press (2024)

3. AI@Meta: Llama 3 model card (2024). https://github.com/meta-llama/llama3/blob/main/MODEL_CARD.md
4. Ataguba, G., Ezekiel, R., Daniel, J., Ogbuju, E., Orji, R.: African foods for deep learning-based food recognition systems dataset. Data Brief **53**, 110092 (2024)
5. Bendale, A., Boult, T.E.: Towards open set deep networks. In: Proceedings of the IEEE Conference on Computer Vision and Pattern Recognition, pp. 1563–1572 (2016)
6. Bossard, L., Guillaumin, M., Van Gool, L.: Food-101 – mining discriminative components with random forests. In: Fleet, D., Pajdla, T., Schiele, B., Tuytelaars, T. (eds.) ECCV 2014. LNCS, vol. 8694, pp. 446–461. Springer, Cham (2014). https://doi.org/10.1007/978-3-319-10599-4_29
7. Dehais, J., Anthimopoulos, M., Mougiakakou, S.: Food image segmentation for dietary assessment. In: Proceedings of the 2nd International Workshop on Multimedia Assisted Dietary Management, pp. 23–28 (2016)
8. Deng, J., Dong, W., Socher, R., Li, L.J., Li, K., Fei-Fei, L.: ImageNet: A Large-Scale Hierarchical Image Database. In: CVPR09 (2009)
9. Dosovitskiy, A., et al.: An image is worth 16x16 words: Transformers for image recognition at scale. arXiv preprint arXiv:2010.11929 (2020)
10. Fort, S., Ren, J., Lakshminarayanan, B.: Exploring the limits of out-of-distribution detection. Adv. Neural. Inf. Process. Syst. **34**, 7068–7081 (2021)
11. He, K., Zhang, X., Ren, S., Sun, J.: Deep residual learning for image recognition. In: Proceedings of the IEEE Conference on Computer Vision and Pattern Recognition, pp. 770–778 (2016)
12. Hendrycks, D., et al.: Scaling out-of-distribution detection for real-world settings. arXiv preprint arXiv:1911.11132 (2019)
13. Hendrycks, D., Gimpel, K.: A baseline for detecting misclassified and out-of-distribution examples in neural networks. arXiv preprint arXiv:1610.02136 (2016)
14. Hsu, Y.C., Shen, Y., Jin, H., Kira, Z.: Generalized odin: detecting out-of-distribution image without learning from out-of-distribution data. In: Proceedings of the IEEE/CVF Conference on Computer Vision and Pattern Recognition, pp. 10951–10960 (2020)
15. Kaur, P., Sikka, K., Wang, W., Belongie, S., Divakaran, A.: Foodx-251: a dataset for fine-grained food classification. arXiv preprint arXiv:1907.06167 (2019)
16. Krizhevsky, A., Hinton, G., et al.: Learning multiple layers of features from tiny images (2009)
17. Lee, K., Lee, H., Lee, K., Shin, J.: Training confidence-calibrated classifiers for detecting out-of-distribution samples. arXiv preprint arXiv:1711.09325 (2017)
18. Lee, K., Lee, K., Lee, H., Shin, J.: A simple unified framework for detecting out-of-distribution samples and adversarial attacks. In: Advances in Neural Information Processing Systems vol. 31 (2018)
19. Liang, S., Li, Y., Srikant, R.: Enhancing the reliability of out-of-distribution image detection in neural networks. arXiv preprint arXiv:1706.02690 (2017)
20. Liu, W., Wang, X., Owens, J., Li, Y.: Energy-based out-of-distribution detection. Adv. Neural. Inf. Process. Syst. **33**, 21464–21475 (2020)
21. Liu, Z., et al.: Swin transformer: Hierarchical vision transformer using shifted windows. In: Proceedings of the IEEE/CVF International Conference on Computer Vision (ICCV) (2021)
22. Lu, Y., et al.: gofoodtm: an artificial intelligence system for dietary assessment. Sensors **20**(15), 4283 (2020)

23. Min, W., et al.: Isia food-500: a dataset for large-scale food recognition via stacked global-local attention network. In: Proceedings of the 28th ACM International Conference on Multimedia, pp. 393–401 (2020)
24. Min, W., et al.: Large scale visual food recognition. IEEE Trans. Pattern Anal. Mach. Intell. **45**(8), 9932–9949 (2023)
25. Netzer, Y., Wang, T., Coates, A., Bissacco, A., Wu, B., Ng, A.Y., et al.: Reading digits in natural images with unsupervised feature learning. In: NIPS Workshop on Deep Learning and Unsupervised Feature Learnin, vol. 2011, p. 4. Granada (2011)
26. Oh, J.H., Falahkheirkhah, K., Bhargava, R.: Are we ready for out-of-distribution detection in digital pathology? In: International Conference on Medical Image Computing and Computer-Assisted Intervention, pp. 78–89. Springer (2024). https://doi.org/10.1007/978-3-031-72117-5_8
27. Okamoto, K., Yanai, K.: UEC-FoodPIX complete: a large-scale food image segmentation dataset. In: Proceedings of ICPR Workshop on Multimedia Assisted Dietary Management(MADiMa) (2021)
28. Panagiotou, M., et al.: A complete AI-based system for dietary assessment and personalized insulin adjustment in type 1 diabetes self-management. In: International Conference on Computer Analysis of Images and Patterns, pp. 77–86. Springer (2023)
29. Pandey, D., et al.: Object detection in indian food platters using transfer learning with yolov4. In: 2022 IEEE 38th International conference on data engineering workshops (ICDEW), pp. 101–106. IEEE (2022)
30. Papathanail, I., et al.: The nutritional content of meal images in free-living conditions-automatic assessment with gofoodtm. Nutrients **15**(17), 3835 (2023)
31. Papathanail, I., et al.: Evaluation of a novel artificial intelligence system to monitor and assess energy and macronutrient intake in hospitalised older patients. Nutrients **13**(12), 4539 (2021)
32. Papathanail, I., et al.: A feasibility study to assess Mediterranean diet adherence using an AI-powered system. Sci. Rep. **12**(1), 17008 (2022)
33. Ravelli, M.N., Schoeller, D.A.: Traditional self-reported dietary instruments are prone to inaccuracies and new approaches are needed. Front. Nutr. **7**, 90 (2020)
34. Sun, Y., Guo, C., Li, Y.: React: out-of-distribution detection with rectified activations. Adv. Neural. Inf. Process. Syst. **34**, 144–157 (2021)
35. Sun, Y., Li, Y.: Dice: Leveraging sparsification for out-of-distribution detection. In: European Conference on Computer Vision, pp. 691–708. Springer (2022). https://doi.org/10.1007/978-3-031-20053-3_40
36. Termritthikun, C., Kanprachar, S.: Nu-ResNet: deep residual networks for Thai food image recognition. J. Telecommun., Electron. Comput. Eng. (JTEC) **10**(1-4), 29–33 (2018)
37. Vasiloglou, M.F., et al.: A comparative study on carbohydrate estimation: Gocarb vs. dietitians. Nutrients **10**(6), 741 (2018)
38. Wang, H., Li, Z., Feng, L., Zhang, W.: Vim: out-of-distribution with virtual-logit matching. In: Proceedings of the IEEE/CVF Conference on Computer Vision and Pattern Recognition, pp. 4921–4930 (2022)
39. World Health Organization: Unhealthy diets. https://www.emro.who.int/noncommunicable-diseases/causes/unhealthy-diets.html
40. World Health Organization: Noncommunicable diseases. https://www.who.int/news-room/fact-sheets/detail/noncommunicable-diseases (September 2023)
41. Xu, P., Ehinger, K.A., Zhang, Y., Finkelstein, A., Kulkarni, S.R., Xiao, J.: Turkergaze: crowdsourcing saliency with webcam based eye tracking. arXiv preprint arXiv:1504.06755 (2015)

42. Yang, J., Zhou, K., Li, Y., Liu, Z.: Generalized out-of-distribution detection: a survey. Int. J. Comput. Vision, pp. 1–28 (2024)
43. Zhou, B., Lapedriza, A., Khosla, A., Oliva, A., Torralba, A.: Places: A 10 million image database for scene recognition. IEEE Trans. Pattern Anal. Mach. Intell. (2017)
44. Zhou, W., Liu, F., Chen, M.: Contrastive out-of-distribution detection for pre-trained transformers. arXiv preprint arXiv:2104.08812 (2021)

Calorie-Aware Food Image Editing with Image Generation Models

Kohei Yamamoto⬤, Honghui Yuan⬤, and Keiji Yanai⁽⊠⁾⬤

The University of Electro-Communications, Tokyo, Japan
{yamamoto-k,yuan-h,yanai}@mm.inf.uec.ac.jp

Abstract. With the development of AI models such as ChatGPT, artificial intelligence has become deeply integrated into our daily lives. Additionally, the growing focus on health and wellness has accelerated the development of AI applications in healthcare. In the realm of dietary management, some smartphone applications offer automated calorie calculation and nutrient tracking features. However, these systems often rely on nutrition facts labels, making it challenging for users to visually comprehend the portion sizes corresponding to their desired caloric intake. To address this limitation, this paper proposes a novel food image editing model that incorporates image generation AI to adjust the caloric content of food images. Our model begins by extracting features, such as estimated current calories, food regions, and visual attributes, from input food images. Subsequently, a conditional edge image is generated based on the desired caloric value and food regions. By providing these features into an image generation model, our model produces a new food image that aligns with the specified caloric target. This approach enables accurate and visually intuitive dietary management.

Keywords: Generative AI · Food Image Editing · Food Image Generation · Food Calorie Estimation

1 Introduction

In the field of artificial intelligence research, language models and vision-language models trained on massive amounts of data using Transformers [16] have been rapidly evolving. Furthermore, generative AI, represented by ChatGPT[1], is becoming increasingly prevalent in society. In the field of image generative AI such as Stable Diffusion [13], midjourney[2], and DeepFloyd IF[3] are well-known. However, it is not possible to accurately generate images that match one's imagination, and it takes time and trial and error to generate images that are manipulated in size or that conform to physical laws. In particular, human hands, eating behavior, quantities, and characters are difficult for generative AI to accurately

---

[1] https://openai.com/chatgpt.
[2] https://www.midjourney.com/.
[3] https://www.deepfloyd.ai/deepfloyd-if.

© The Author(s), under exclusive license to Springer Nature Switzerland AG 2025
S. Palaiahnakote et al. (Eds.): ICPR 2024 Workshops, LNCS 15617, pp. 19–33, 2025.
https://doi.org/10.1007/978-3-031-88217-3_2

represent, and they are useful for distinguishing generated images from real ones. Food images remain a challenging domain for generative AI. Even with text prompts combining a food category and quantity, it is highly unlikely that the generated image will strictly adhere to the textual description. In fact, when an image is generated using Stable Diffusion v1.4 with the prompt "a photo of spaghetti for one person," the result is as shown in Fig. 1. Although it is instructed in English to be for one person, the output image is more than one serving.

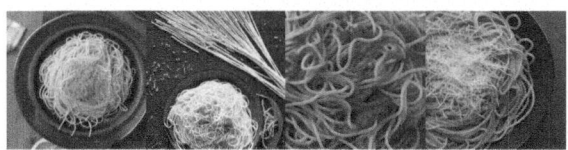

Fig. 1. Output images generated by Stable Diffusion v1.4 with the input "a photo of spaghetti for one person"

Moreover, as sports facilities improve, new health equipment is developed, and health promotion activities increase, health consciousness is rising across society. Today, it's easy to track exercise and manage diets using smartwatches and apps, making health management more accessible.

Diet-tracking apps, for instance, can automatically calculate calories and record nutrients, offering increasingly sophisticated features. However, these calculations often rely on standardized values from food labels, which can lead to inaccuracies when portion sizes vary. Additionally, it is not always easy to visually estimate the amounts specified on food labels.

In this study, we propose a food image editing model that considers calorie amounts by combining an image generation model and a food calorie estimation model.

To generate images that consider calorie amounts, we need an original image and the desired calorie amount value as inputs.

The main contributions of this paper are as follows:

- We propose a method by combining an image synthesis model and a food calorie estimation model to modify a given food image into a food image with the specified calorie amount, which enables us to visually grasp the change in calorie amount and to manage diet appropriately.
- By the comprehensive experiments, we confirmed the effectiveness of the proposed method.

2   Related Work

2.1   Calorie Estimation from Images

There are primarily two methods for estimating calorie content from images. The first method involves using a reference object while the second method directly estimates calorie content using deep learning.

In the method using a reference object, Kim *et al.* [6] conducted a study. Their study first places a reference paper in front of the food and detects the corners of the paper to recognize the three-dimensional space. Next, they manually construct a 2D mesh of the food and project it into 3D to calculate the volume. Finally, the calorie content is calculated based on the volume.

On the other hand, in the method using deep learning directly, studies by Ege *et al.* [2] and Maeta [9] exist.

Ege *et al.* proposed three methods for estimating calorie content from images. Among the three methods, it was found that accuracy improved by simultaneously learning calorie content, category classification, ingredient estimation, and cooking procedures.

Based on the study by Ege *et al.* , Maeta used the Swin Transformer V2, a state-of-the-art deep learning model, and an original output function, Auto-Binning Softmax-Regression, to improve accuracy. Similar to Ege *et al.* 's study, this work performs simultaneous learning to estimate both calorie amounts and food category.

In this work, we like to estimate calorie content even in images without reference objects, and therefore adopt Maeta's method, which is the latest method for directly predicting calorie content using deep learning.

2.2   Food Image Generation

Many studies on food image synthesis used the Recipe1M [17] dataset. Cook-GAN [20] by Zhu *et al.* is a text image generation model that considers ingredients and procedures using a cooking simulator sub-network. CookGAN [3] by Han *et al.* generates meal images conditioning the generation network with an attention-based ingredients-image association model for associating food items with images. ChefGAN [12] by Pan *et al.* used an image-recipe embedding model to generate a similar representation of a recipe and an image and generate the image considering the recipe.

2.3   Deep Learning Applications for Food

Deep learning applications for food transformation mainly include food transformation and food recognition.

For food transformation research, there are mobile food transformation apps by Tanno *et al.* [14], food image transformation by Horita *et al.* [4], and Enchanting Your Noodles by Nakano *et al.* [10]. For food recognition research, there are CaloriesCaptorGlass by Naritomi *et al.* [11] and CalorieCam360 by Terauchi *et al.* [15].

The research by Tanno *et al.* and Horita *et al.* on food transformation uses cCycleGAN, which adds a conditioning vectors to the generator and discriminator of CycleGAN [21] to enable conditioning. The mobile app of Tanno *et al.* is a product that allows you to convert meals on your smartphone and experience meal transformation closely.

Nakano *et al.* 's research, transforms simple ingredients such as somen noodles and rice into "attractive" dishes such as ramen, curry, and fried rice through a VR headset. This research is the first food editing research using VR in the food domain, and by changing the type of food in the video in real time, it was possible to obtain effects other than visual effects, such as changing the taste of the food being eaten.

Naritomi *et al.* 's research on food recognition calculates the volume of food using AR glasses, and displays the volume and calorie content in 3D. Previous studies often measure calorie content from two-dimensional images. However, by using AR glasses, it is possible to estimate calorie content using the depth of food, which is difficult to predict in 2D.

Terauchi *et al.* proposed a system that can recognize food, estimate calorie content, and measure food intake using commercially available 360-degree cameras, which have become widespread in recent years. By using 360-degree cameras, it has become possible for multiple people to simultaneously record food log.

This study differs from these applied studies in that it focuses on food image editing rather than food transformation, and it utilizes recent diffusion models for transforming food amounts.

3   Method

3.1   Overview of the Method

In this study, it is necessary to adjust the overall shape of food, which requires powerful image control.

ControlNet [19] is representative of the method using additional networks. ControlNet fixes the diffusion model to be used and learns a new encoder part of the diffusion network. This allows us to take advantage of the generative capabilities of the diffusion model while avoiding overfitting even with small datasets and promoting early convergence of learning. It can generate images with various conditions such as Canny images, OpenPose images, and depth images. Due to its high controllability, it is very often used in the creation of human images and manga generation.

Therefore, we decided to use ControlNet [19] for this study. In order to get SoftEdge images, we required the detection of the food region. Therefore, we used Grounded-Segment-Anything (Grounded-SAM)[4] for food region detection. Furthermore, a calorie estimation model is required to determine how much to expand or contract the food region based on the calorie amount. Finally, a

---

[4] https://github.com/IDEA-Research/Grounded-Segment-Anything.

mechanism is needed to adjust the appearance, and in this case, we decided to use LoRA [5] and Reference-only[5].

Considered these points, the proposed method has the structure shown in Fig. 2.

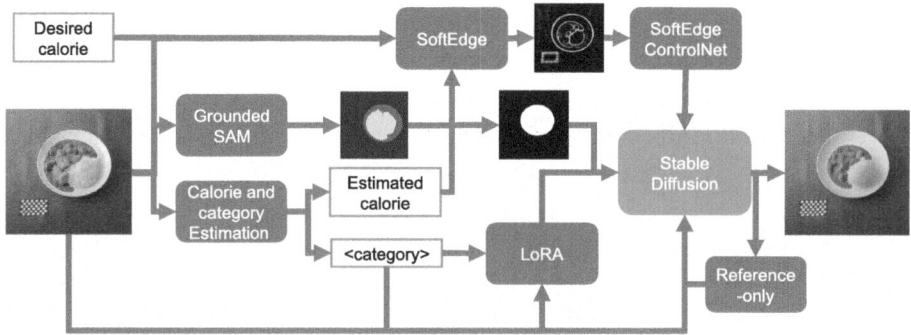

Fig. 2. Structure of the proposed method

As inputs, the model takes an input image and the desired calorie amount after transformation. First, the input image is provided to the calorie estimation model to obtain the calorie amount and category. At the same time, by inputting the input image and prompt "a photo of food" to Grounded-SAM, the bounding box and the segmentation mask are obtained. Next, the segmentation mask obtained from Grounded-SAM is fine-tuned for SoftEdge image editing. Based on the fine-tuned segmentation mask and the ratio of the desired calorie amount to the measured calorie amount, the SoftEdge image of the input image is adjusted. Furthermore, LoRA is learned from a single image, and Reference-only is used to obtain appearance features. Finally, using the input image, segmentation mask, SoftEdge image, LoRA, and Reference-only obtained so far, a food image with the adjusted calorie amount is generated.

3.2   Calorie Estimation

In order to generate an image considering the calorie amount, it is necessary to estimate the current calorie amount of the input image. Therefore, in this study, we used Maeda's model [9] as the calorie estimation model. Maeda's model is trained on a food image dataset with calorie information created by Ege *et al.* [1]. Ege's dataset contains 15 food category and 4,877 images, from 6 recipe sites.

However, in this study, in order to obtain higher calorie detection accuracy, we collected a dataset for additional learning. Similar to Ege *et al.* , we collected images of 14 food categories for which there were in excess of 100 images from recipe sites with calorie information. By retraining Maeda's model using these images, we aimed to improve the accuracy of the calorie recognition model.

---

[5] https://github.com/Mikubill/sd-webui-controlnet/discussions/1236.

3.3 Grounded-SAM

In this study, we primarily adjust the quantity using ControlNet [19] with Soft-Edge images. To edit the SoftEdge image, it is necessary to recognize which area contains food or a plate. Therefore, we used Grounded-SAM, which obtains a bounding box and segmentation mask of an object by inputting arbitrary text and an image. Figure 3 is shown the structure of Grounded-SAM.

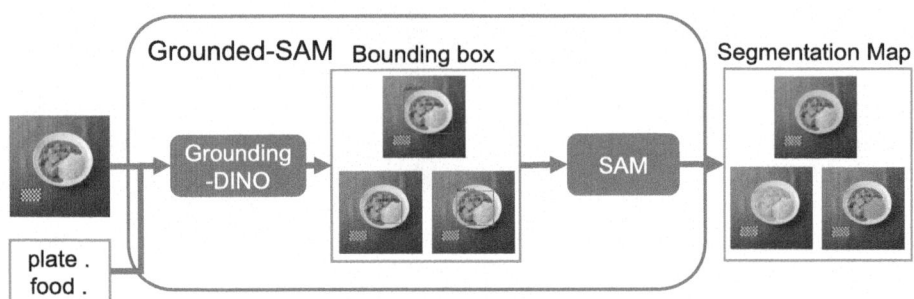

Fig. 3. Structure of Grounded-SAM.

Grounded-SAM is an open segmentation model that uses Grounding-DINO [8] and Segment Anything (SAM) [7]. Grounded-SAM performs object detection with the zero-shot object detection model Grounding-DINO and performs segmentation with SAM based on the bounding boxes. In this study, to detect the plate and food areas, we input an image and "plate. food." into Grounded-SAM to segment the plate and food areas. Note that Grounded-SAM text entry is to be separated by a period, and "plate. food." means that plates and foods are recognized separately.

3.4 Fine-Tuning the Segmentation Mask and Editing the SoftEdge

In this section, we obtain the SoftEdge image to transform the food quantity. In general, the segmentation mask obtained by Grounded-SAM is too narrow to edit the SoftEdge image. We expand the mask by 10% so that the line drawing can be edited easily.

By adjusting the segmentation mask, one food area is obtained for one plate area. Based on this, the food area in SoftEdge image is edited to the desired calorie amount as shown in Fig. 4.

First, the input image is converted to a SoftEdge image. The SoftEdge image is generated by Holistically-nested Edge Detection (HED) [18], an image-to-image prediction deep learning model composed of a convolutional network. Second, the food area and background are separated using the adjusted segmentation mask. Third, the food area of the SoftEdge image is adjusted. The editing is performed by considering the ratio of the desired calorie amount to

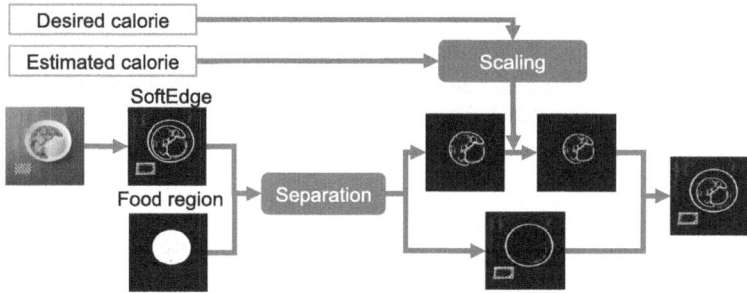

Fig. 4. Editing the SoftEdge image. The figure shows the case where the SoftEdge image is resized to $\frac{2}{3}^{\frac{1}{3}} \fallingdotseq 0.874$ times in the vertical and horizontal directions, assuming the desired calorie amount is 400 kcal and the measured calorie amount is 600 kcal.

the measured calorie amount as the volume ratio, and using the area ratio to perform a resizing process. Since the calorie amount is obtained by volume, if the vertical and horizontal (and depth) sizes are simply multiplied by n times, the volume ratio (calorie amount) becomes n^3 times larger. If we want to increase the calorie amount by n times, we need to multiply the vertical and horizontal sizes of the area by $n^{\frac{1}{3}}$. For example, if the desired calorie intake is 400 kcal and the measured calorie intake is 600 kcal, the volume ratio of the food area's SoftEdge image is $4 : 6 = \frac{2}{3} : 1$. Therefore, by resizing both the length and width by a factor of $\frac{2}{3}^{\frac{1}{3}} \fallingdotseq 0.874$, the desired volume (calorie amount) can be obtained. Finally, by combining the edited SoftEdge image with the plate area SoftEdge image, a SoftEdge image for generating images with the adjusted calorie amount is obtained. Note that the fine-tuning of the segmentation mask and the editing of the SoftEdge image work similarly even when there are multiple plates or foods. Furthermore, since the segmentation map is used as an inpainting mask for the diffusion model, only when increasing the calorie amount, the plate mask is also enlarged in proportion here.

3.5   Preserving Appearance

As described in the previous subsection, ControlNet [19] can adjust the shape of the food. However, ControlNet does not preserve the food appearance. Therefore, in this work, we use two mechanisms, LoRA [5] and Reference-only[6], to preserve the appearance.

LoRA is an additional network that learns only the differences in weights for new concepts while fixing the weights of the learned network.

In Stable Diffusion, training of LoRA is performed by inserting it into the linear layer of the attention layer. Since it is a very lightweight network, training is easy, and it is also used to easily express features such as style, characters, background, and pose.

---

[6] https://github.com/Mikubill/sd-webui-controlnet/discussions/1236.

In addition to LoRA, Reference-only is also used to preserve the appearance. Reference-only is a structure as shown in Fig. 5, that can reflect the appearance features of the original image by saving the intermediate features of self-attention without conditioning at each layer and combining them with the calculation of attention keys and values with condition.

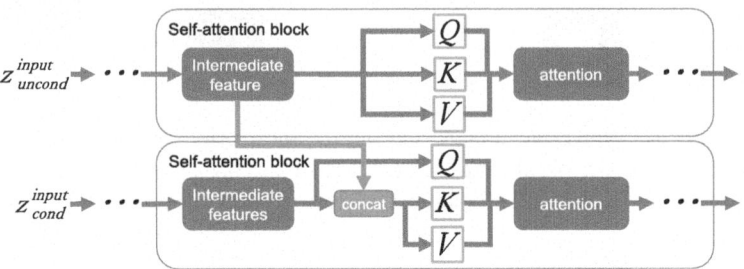

Fig. 5. Structure of Reference-only.

Although Reference-only does not require training of networks unlike LoRA, it is necessary to have intermediate features without conditioning. Therefore, the image generation time increases. In this study, we use both LoRA and Reference-only to preserve the appearance of the original image.

Finally, as shown in Fig. 6, an image with an adjusted calorie amount is generated using the input image, segmentation mask, edited SoftEdge image, and LoRA obtained so far.

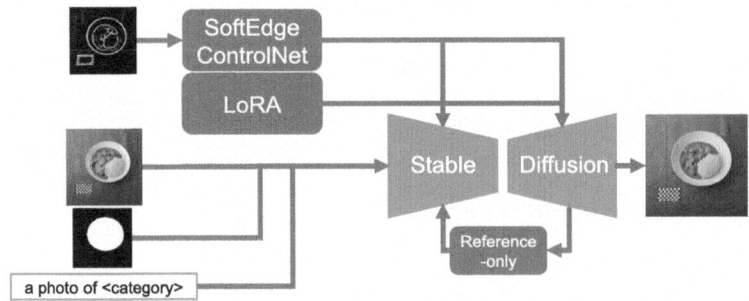

Fig. 6. The final output part of the proposed method.

To generate a calorie-edited image, we use Stable Diffusion's inpainting mechanism. For the prompt, we use "a photo of <category>" where <category> is the category name estimated by the calorie estimation model. As the inpainting mask, we use the combination of all the plate and food areas obtained so far. Furthermore, the pre-trained LoRA and Reference-only for preserving the appearance are also used to generate the final calorie-edited image.

4   Experiments

Since both the images in Ege's dataset [1] and the dataset collected in this experiment were collected from the internet, there may be inconsistencies between images and calorie amount information. Therefore, a part of the dataset, UEC-FoodCal (tentative), which was collected independently in collaboration with a company with chefs and registered dietitians, is used for generating calorie-edited images and comparing them with actual calorie amounts.

4.1   Calorie Estimation

Referencing Ege's model [1], we collected recipes and images from online recipe sites for 14 dishes. Using only the collected images this time, we retrained Maeta's model [9] and evaluated these model. Table 1 shows the results of calorie recognition for Maeta's model and the retrained model. The images used for evaluation are 1/5 of each dataset, approximately 1,000 images for Ege's dataset and approximately 7400 images for collected dataset.

Table 1. Calorie Recognition Results. Bold indicates the best accuracy among all data. Red indicates the best performance for each dataset.

		Original		Re-trained	
		Ege *et al.* [1]	new dataset	Ege *et al.* [1]	new dataset
Calorie	Absolute error [kcal]↓	87.5	161.0	166.4	**80.0**
	Relative error [%] ↓	27.8	68.1	61.7	**25.5**
	Ratio within 20% error ↑	0.536	0.301	0.240	**0.623**
Category	Top-1 accuracy [%] ↑	**89.2**	27.9	46.8	73.0

The results showed that the models achieved the higher calorie estimation accuracy for the datasets they were trained on. However, considering the larger number of training images, higher image resolution, and more evaluation images, the retrained model in this study is considered to be more effective. For category estimation, the original model seems to be more effective. However, this may be because the data used in Ege's dataset was well-curated from 7 recipe sites, resulting in similar recipes and photography styles. In this study, we decided to generate images with adjusted calorie amounts using the retrained model, which was trained on the larger dataset.

4.2   Calorie-Aware Edited Food Images

We present the results of the edited images when generating various sizes in Fig. 7.

For all the images, the categories are estimated correctly, and the calorie values are also reasonably estimated. Moreover, the segmentation map is obtained,

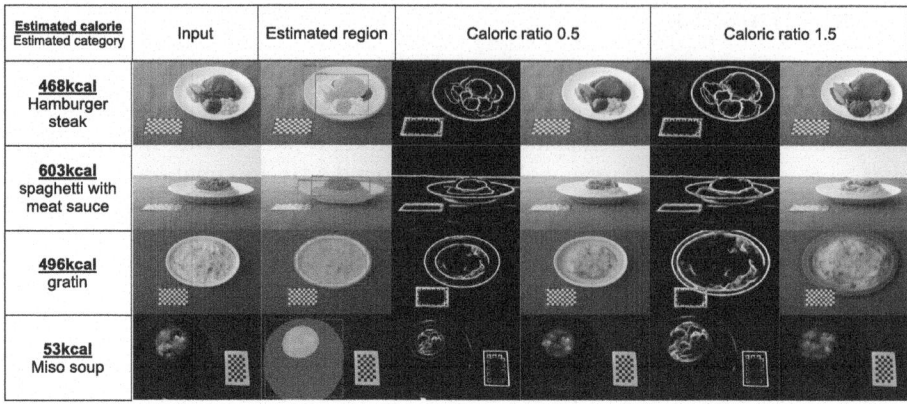

Fig. 7. Results of edited images. The calorie amount estimated by the calorie estimation model and the category are described to the left of the input image.

the SoftEdge image is edited, and it can be seen that the food area of the generated image is changed. In the top row, like the hamburger steak, it can be seen that if there is a word for another food, such as "steak", it may deviate from the original image. However, the side dishes relatively maintain their shape and color, and the amount of food itself is also changing. Additionally, miso soup images in the bottom row, a significant area is dyed with a deep black, and it can be seen that in some cases, the contour of the plate cannot be captured in the SoftEdge image. Even in such cases, changes in the amount of food can be seen.

Furthermore, Fig. 8 shows the modified images when the size of the meal is changed to various sizes with the seed value of the Stable Diffusion set to 0.

Comparing the original image with the generated image, although it is successful in enlarging the food area of the generated image, it sometimes fails to reduce it. When increasing the size of the meal, the larger food area than we expect is generated. However, we can obtain some reduced amount of food images by generating multiple candidates with different seed values. Furthermore, the ratio of the food area to the overall resolution is similar to the ideal ratio of the food area to the input image, except when the calorie amount is reduced to 0.3 times. Therefore, we can say that the food amount change is also successful.

4.3 Comparison with Real Image

Here, we show how much difference there is from the actual amount of food by comparing generated images with real amount-changed images. Figure 9 shows the real and generated images. Note that when the original images are compared with each other, the size of the plate and the angle of view are different depending on the size of the meal. In addition, when the ratio of the meal area detected by Grounded-SAM between the input image and the converted image is regarded as

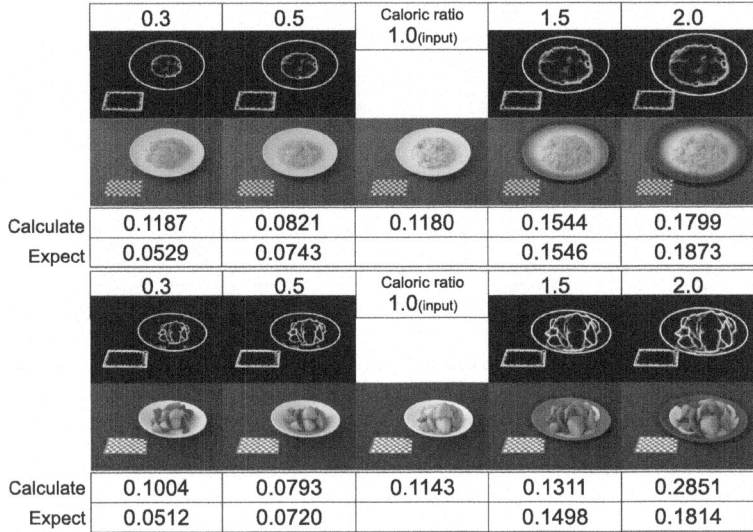

0.3	0.5	Caloric ratio 1.0(input)	1.5	2.0
Calculate				
0.1187	0.0821	0.1180	0.1544	0.1799
Expect				
0.0529	0.0743		0.1546	0.1873

0.3	0.5	Caloric ratio 1.0(input)	1.5	2.0
Calculate				
0.1004	0.0793	0.1143	0.1311	0.2851
Expect				
0.0512	0.0720		0.1498	0.1814

Fig. 8. Calorie-modified images when changing to various sizes. "Calculate" represents the ratio of the food area estimated by Grounded-SAM to the entire edited image. "Expect" indicates the ratio of the ideal food area to the entire input image.

the area ratio, the volume ratio is regarded as the calorie ratio, and the calculated value of "(the food area ratio to the entire screen of the edited image/the food area ratio to the entire screen of the input image) $\left(\frac{3}{2}\right)$" is regarded as the calorie ratio by the food area.

Comparing the real image and the generated image, we can say that although the shapes are different, the visual amount of food is similar. It is not possible to simply compare the real images with the generated images because plates are different. However, by comparing the generated image with the input image, the size can be recognized, which can be said to be a strength of this method. Looking at the calorie ratio by food area, when it was edited with the calorie ratio of 0.5, the value was far from the designated calorie amount ratio, but when it was edited with the calorie ratio of 1.5, the value was close to the designated calorie amount ratio.

4.4 Quantitative Evaluation

In the food image modification considering calorie amounts, it is important to estimate the calorie amount and to actually reduce or enlarge the meal. Consequently, no fixed quantitative evaluation exists for this task.

In the image generation in consideration of the calorie amount, it is important how much the meal area is actually increased or decreased according to the desired calorie amount. Therefore, in this subsection the evaluation is made by measuring the ratio of calories by meal area of the input image.

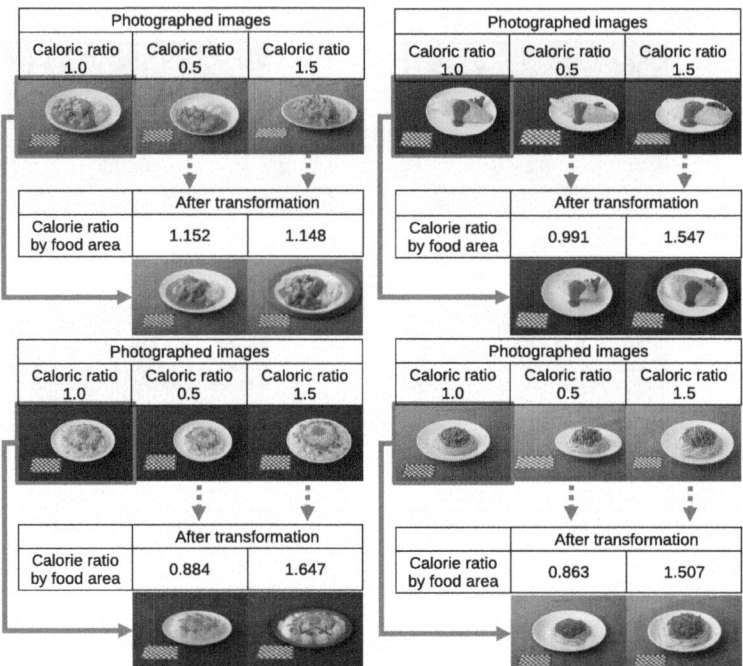

Fig. 9. Comparison of the real amount-changed image with the generated image. The lower part shows the output image when the calorie amount (0.5 times or 1.5 times the reference calorie amount) in the same column is input with the image in the upper left of each category as the input. Note that the size of the plate and the angle of view of the photographed image differ depending on the size of the meal. In addition taken Images at ×0.5 and ×1.5 are reference images for comparison and are not used for processing.

In case of x0.5, the calorie ratio should be 0.5 in the ideal case, while it should be 1.5 in case of x1.5. However, there are differences depending on the category, such as curry, stir-fried noodles, and pilaf, which showed appropriate values, and hamburger steak, miso soup, and omurice, which had excessively high calorie ratios. Regarding the average value over all the categories, we can see that it often takes a slightly larger calorie ratio than groundtruth value, 0.5 or 1.5. In addition, regarding the deviation, it can be seen that the values of hamburger steak and miso soup are scattered.

Table 2. Calorie ratio of food regions for 100 generated images for each category and calorie ratio. Values represent mean ± standard deviation.

Food Category	Estimated Calorie Ratio at x0.5	Estimated Calorie Ratio at x1.5
Nikujaga	0.522 ± 0.0417	2.485 ± 1.3268
Fried rice	0.507 ± 0.0378	1.905 ± 1.0061
Chirashi-sushi	0.428 ± 0.1687	1.257 ± 0.5095
Curry	0.559 ± 0.0714	1.558 ± 0.6483
Stir-fried noodles	0.511 ± 0.0112	1.530 ± 0.2707
Gratin	0.498 ± 0.0544	1.397 ± 0.2116
Hamburg steak	1.184 ± 0.1941	2.683 ± 1.4070
Miso soup	1.321 ± 1.6865	3.576 ± 1.5958
Mixed rice	1.505 ± 0.9103	1.716 ± 0.2736
Omelet rice	0.818 ± 0.1661	1.932 ± 0.9982
Pilaf	0.511 ± 0.0104	1.561 ± 0.5165
Potato salad	0.730 ± 0.2682	1.523 ± 0.3880
Spaghetti with meat sauce	0.374 ± 0.1403	1.260 ± 0.6171
Cream stew	0.572 ± 0.1448	1.381 ± 0.4155
All categories average	0.717 ± 0.2790	1.840 ± 0.7275

5   Conclusion

In this paper, we proposed a method for food image editing considering calorie amounts. By using Maeta's model for calorie recognition and collecting a new dataset of images with calorie information, we were able to make the estimated calorie amount more accurate. Additionally, we used Grounded-SAM to detect the food area and adjusted the detected segmentation map. By editing the SoftEdge image, we generated food images considering arbitrary desired calorie amounts. Furthermore, by performing inpainting using these data, we were able to generate food images with changed calorie amounts. In quantitative evaluation, it was confirmed that the size change was appropriately performed based on the region.

Future challenges include discovering a powerful size changing mechanism, and developing a calorie estimator that considers the actual size or increases the number of food types. Although in this study we used ControlNet with a SoftEdge image as a size changing mechanism, we believe that intermediate features like Reference-only and ControlNet using a segmentation map of the food area may be effective. Furthermore, since each model in the mechanism of this research can be replaced, if a better model is available, it is possible to increase the number of estimated categories and improve the accuracy of calorie estimation. Therefore, a more versatile model can be created by constructing an upgraded calorie estimator applicable to a wider variety of foods.

We believe that calorie estimation and the generation of food images based on calorie amounts are effective for health management and adjusting food intake.

We hope that our work stimulates new food computing researches on calorie-aware food image synthesis and modification.

Acknowledgments. This work was supported by JSPS KAKENHI Grant Numbers, 22H00540 and 22H00548.

References

1. Ege, T., Yanai, K.: Image-based food calorie estimation using knowledge on food categories, ingredients and cooking directions. In: Proceedings of ACM International Conference on Multimedia, pp. 367–375 (2017)
2. Ege, T., Yanai, K.: Simultaneous estimation of food categories and calories with multi-task CNN. In: Proceedings of IAPR International Conference on Machine Vision Applications (MVA), pp. 198–201 (2017). https://doi.org/10.23919/MVA.2017.7986835
3. Han, F., Guerrero, R., Pavlovic, V.: CookGAN: meal Image Synthesis from Ingredients. In: Proceedings of IEEE/CFV Winter Conference on Applications of Computer Vision (2020)
4. Horita, D., Tanno, R., Shimoda, W., Yanai, K.: Food category transfer with conditional cyclegan and a large-scale food image dataset. In: Proceedings of the Joint Workshop on Multimedia for Cooking and Eating Activities and Multimedia Assisted Dietary Management, pp. 67–70 (2018)
5. Hu, E.J., et al.: Lora: Low-rank adaptation of large language models. In: arXiv preprint arXiv:2106.09685 (2021)
6. Kim, J.h., Lee, D.s., Kwon, S.k.: Food classification and meal intake amount estimation through deep learning. Appl. Sci. **13**, 5742 (05 2023). https://doi.org/10.3390/app13095742
7. Kirillov, A., et al.: Segment anything. In: Proceedings of IEEE International Conference on Computer Vision. pp. 3992–4003 (2023). https://api.semanticscholar.org/CorpusID:257952310
8. Liu, S., et al.: Grounding DINO: Marrying dino with grounded pre-training for open-set object detection. In: arXiv preprint arXiv:2303.05499 (2023)
9. Maeta, K.: Estimating calorie content from meal images using vision transformer. In: Master's Thesis, The University of Electro-Communications (2023)
10. Nakano, K., Horita, D., Sakata, N., Kiyokawa, K., Yanai, K., Narumi, T.: Enchanting your noodles: Gan-based real-time food-to-food translation and its impact on vision-induced gustatory manipulation. In: Proceedings of IEEE Conference on Virtual Reality and 3D User Interfaces, pp. 1096–1097 (2019)
11. Naritomi, S., Yanai, K.: CalorieCaptorGlass: food calorie estimation based on actual size using hololens and deep learning. In: Proc.of IEEE Conference on Virtual Reality and 3D User Interfaces Abstracts and Workshops, pp. 818–819 (2020)
12. Pan, S., Dai, L., Hou, X., Li, H., Sheng, B.: ChefGAN: food image generation from recipes. In: Proceedings of ACM International Conference on Multimedia, pp. 4244–4252 (2020)
13. Rombach, R., Blattmann, A., Lorenz, D., Esser, P., Ommer, B.: High-resolution image synthesis with latent diffusion models. In: Proceedings of IEEE Computer Vision and Pattern Recognition, pp. 10684–10695 (2022)

14. Tanno, R., Horita, D., Shimoda, W., Yanai, K.: Magical rice bowl: a real-time food category changer. In: Proceedings of ACM International Conference on Multimedia, pp. 1244–1246 (2018)
15. Terauchi, K., Yanai, K.: CalorieCam360: simultaneous eating action recognition of multiple people using an omnidirectional camera. In: Proceedings of ACM International Conference on Multimedia Retrieval, pp. 644–648 (2023)
16. Vaswani, A., et al.: Attention is all you need. In: Proceedings of Neural Information Processing Systems, vol. 30 (2017)
17. Wang, H., Sahoo, D., Liu, C., Lim, E.p., Hoi, S.C.: Learning cross-modal embeddings with adversarial networks for cooking recipes and food images. In: Proceedings of IEEE Computer Vision and Pattern Recognition, pp. 11572–11581 (2019)
18. Xie, S., Tu, Z.: Holistically-nested edge detection. In: Proceedings of IEEE International Conference on Computer Vision, pp. 1395–1403 (2015)
19. Zhang, L., Rao, A., Agrawala, M.: Adding conditional control to text-to-image diffusion models. In: Proceedings of IEEE International Conference on Computer Vision (2023)
20. Zhu, B., Ngo, C.W.: CookGAN: causality based text-to-image synthesis. In: Proceedings of IEEE Computer Vision and Pattern Recognition (2020)
21. Zhu, J.Y., Park, T., Isola, P., Efros, A.A.: Unpaired image-to-image translation using cycle-consistent adversarial networks. In: Proceedings of IEEE Computer Vision and Pattern Recognition, pp. 2223–2232 (2017)

Improving Food Segmentation Through Selecting Suitable Feature Representations of Image Pixels

Ziyi Zhu and Ying Dai[✉]

Faculty of Software and Information Science, Iwate Prefectural University, Takizawa 020-0693, Iwate, Japan
g236t002@s.iwate-pu.ac.jp, dai@iwate-pu.ac.jp

Abstract. Food segmentation is essential for dietary monitoring, yet it faces significant challenges due to the scarcity of pixel-level labels and the need to accurately segment foods from new images. We propose a novel method that addresses these challenges by leveraging selectively pre-trained convolutional neural network (CNN) deep features for pixel-wise clustering, requiring minimal pixel-level labels. We begin by generating pixel-wise feature representations from a convolutional layer and concatenated multiple layers. We then select the most suitable representations, perform pixel-wise clustering by k-means, and choose the clusters with the best clustering quality. Our method performed well on three public food segmentation datasets, achieving an aAcc of 0.8967 and mIoU 0.8094 on UECFOODPIX COMPLETE, 0.8750 and 0.7768 on FoodSeg103, and 0.9304 and 0.8373 on UNIMIB2016. These results show that our method achieves segmentation performance close to supervised models while reducing reliance on extensive pixel-level labels. It also adapts well to diverse food images, making it suitable for various applications.

Keywords: food segmentation · pixel-wise feature representation · k-means clustering · clustering quality assessment

1 Introduction

Food computing has become a critical research area due to the growing demand for automated diet management and health monitoring systems. The increasing prevalence of diet-related conditions like obesity and diabetes highlights the need for accurate food analysis. Food image segmentation is essential in this context, enabling precise identification and separation of food items for applications such as calorie estimation and nutritional assessment.

However, food segmentation is challenging due to the diverse visual features of food items and the complexities of real-world scenarios. Variations in shape, color, and texture across food categories, along with complex backgrounds and inconsistent lighting, make accurate segmentation difficult. These challenges necessitate advanced algorithms to effectively handle the complexities of real-world food images.

S. Palaiahnakote et al. (Eds.): ICPR 2024 Workshops, LNCS 15617, pp. 34–48, 2025.
https://doi.org/10.1007/978-3-031-88217-3_3

Current food segmentation methods [1–5] primarily rely on deep learning models, which are trained on pixel-level annotated food image datasets to generate pixel-level masks. While effective in some cases, these methods are limited by the scarcity of large-scale annotated datasets, as pixel-level annotation is time-consuming and labor-intensive. This constraint hampers accurate segmentation across diverse food types and limits the models' ability to generalize to complex real-world scenarios.

To address these challenges, some researchers have utilized class-level labels and techniques like Class Activation Mapping [6–8] or saliency detection [10] for food segmentation. However, these methods often activate only partial regions of food items, struggles with multi-dish images, and is affected by class imbalance, leading to underrepresentation of less common categories. Additionally, its reliance on limited food category labels hinders its effectiveness in segmenting a broader range of food categories.

Zhu, Z. et al. [11] introduced a new framework for food ingredient segmentation that avoids the reliance on CAM. Their method extracts feature maps directly from an ingredient classification model and uses pixel-wise clustering to generate masks, enhancing flexibility across various ingredients. However, it still faces challenges in complex scenarios, particularly with multiple food categories or intricate backgrounds.

Building upon the segmentation framework proposed by [11], we introduce a novel approach that enhances segmentation accuracy by generating multiple pixel-level feature representations and selectively filtering them for clustering-based segmentation. The primary goal is to achieve class-agnostic food segmentation in complex scenarios. The key modules of our method include:

Generate multiple Pixel-Level Feature Representations: Our approach extracts feature maps from different CNN layers and selectively concatenates those with low cosine similarity, as these features contain diverse and complementary information.

Select Suitable Pixel-wise Representations: we use two metrics to select the most suitable set of features for food segmentation. The first metric evaluates the clustering quality of each pixel, while the second measures the alignment between the clusters and the true categories.

Segmentation of Food Images Using Selected Features: We use k-means to cluster the pixels in food images, select the clustering results with the highest quality, and generate the final segmentation masks. The main contributions of this research are as follows:

1. We propose a novel approach for food segmentation that does not require extensive pixel-level image datasets for training. The approach consists of the following steps: generating multiple pixel-wise feature representations, selecting the most suitable representations, and using these selected features to segment food images.
2. We validated the effectiveness of our method on three public food segmentation datasets: UECFOODPIX COMPLETE [2], FoodSeg103 [14], and UNIMIB2016 [15]. Our results demonstrate that the method performs well across various food images and achieves segmentation performance close to that of fully supervised models on all three datasets.

2   Related Work

2.1   Food Segmentation

Food segmentation is a critical step in food Recognition [12] for dietary monitoring [13], enabling precise identification and analysis of food items within images. Sharma et al. [3] introduced a network called GourmetNet, which adopts the Waterfall Atrous Spatial Pooling (WASPv2) module, and employs dual attention (channel and spatial) mechanisms for multi-scale waterfall features to improve the food segmentation performance. Okamoto et al. [4] introduced a region-based segmentation model for multiple-dish segmentation. Furthermore, Aguilar et al. [16] proposed a method using Bayesian deep learning, which includes uncertainty estimation to enhance segmentation. While these methods have demonstrated effectiveness, they rely heavily on datasets with pixel-level annotations for training.

As the high cost and labor of pixel-level annotations became apparent, the focus shifted to weakly supervised methods [6, 7, 9, 10]. Wang et al. [6] introduced pseudo-label generation based on Class Activation Maps (CAMs) to create pixel-wise annotations for training segmentation network. Cai et al. [7] refined CAM using the SEAM mechanism [17], which incorporates multi-scale information for improved accuracy. Furthermore, Shimoda et al. [9] enhanced food segmentation accuracy by comparing outputs from a food category classifier and a food/non-food classifier, using their differences to estimate plate regions. Futagami et al. [10] combined saliency detection with GrabCut to improve food region extraction. However, both CAM and saliency map methods face challenges such as activating only partial regions of food items and difficulties in handling multi-dish images.

Recently, Lan et al. [18] introduced the FoodSAM. This framework utilizes the Segment Anything Model (SAM) [19] to perform multi-level segmentation on food images, including semantic segmentation, instance segmentation, and panoptic segmentation. Additionally, [20] introduced the OVFoodSeg framework for open-vocabulary food image segmentation. However, these methods still rely on large-scale pre-training datasets and requires substantial computational resources, limiting its use in resource-constrained environments.

In comparison, our approach provides a simpler and more efficient solution. We achieve food segmentation by selecting the highest-quality clustering from multiple pixel-wise feature representations generated from different CNN layers. This method not only achieves high-quality segmentation but also operates effectively in resource-limited settings, making it a more practical and accessible solution than existing methods.

2.2   Clustering Quality Assessment

Accurate segmentation, especially in complex tasks like food segmentation, relies on effective clustering quality assessment. The Silhouette Coefficient (SC) evaluates the compactness of points within clusters and their separation from others, with values ranging from -1 to 1, where higher values indicate better local clustering. However, SC's focus on local performance can overlook global clustering consistency with true labels, leading to suboptimal feature selection.

To address this, we introduce the Center Similarity (CS) metric, which measures global alignment by comparing the cosine similarity between cluster centers and true label centers. High CS values indicate strong global alignment. By combining SC and CS, we offer a comprehensive clustering evaluation approach that ensures both local accuracy and global consistency, leading to more accurate segmentation results.

3   Methodology

In this section, we introduce a novel approach for food image segmentation. The overall pipeline is illustrated in Fig. 1.

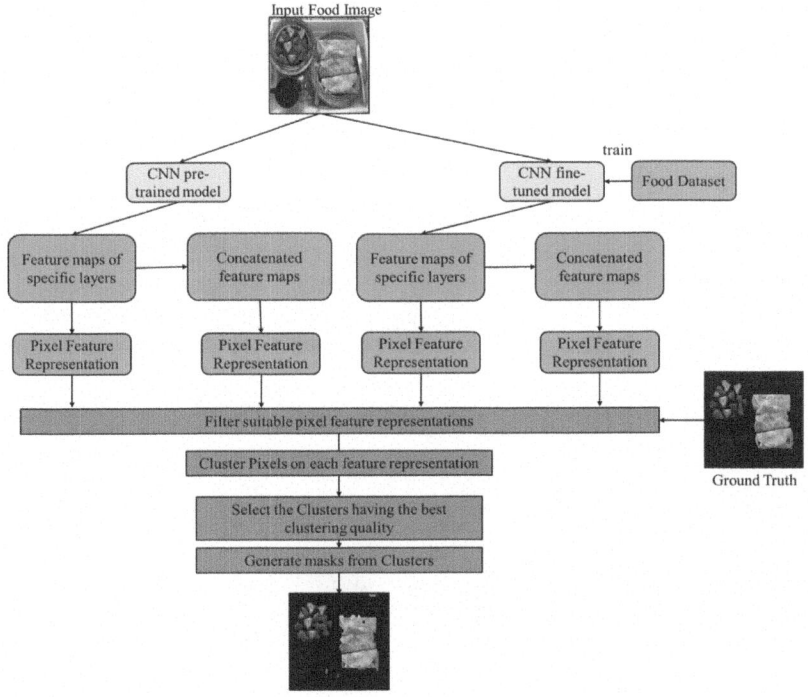

Fig. 1. Diagram of selecting suitable Pixel Feature Representations for Food Segmentation

3.1   Backbone

For the backbone of our image segmentation framework, we utilized the EfficientNet-B0 model [21], pre-trained on a large-scale ImageNet dataset. We selected EfficientNet-B0 due to its optimal balance between computational efficiency and accuracy [22]. To improve its performance for food image segmentation, we fine-tuned the EfficientNet-B0 model on a custom dataset comprising both food and non-food images. The detailed process of fine-tuning this model will be elaborated in the subsequent Implementation Details section.

3.2 Generation of Multiple Pixel-Wise Feature Representations

To obtain diverse pixel-wise feature representations, we extract feature maps from the final stages of the EfficientNet-B0 model (Blocks 16, 17, and 18). We select these deeper blocks for their high-level features, which are essential for capturing complex object representations. Although these layers capture semantically rich features, they often fail to retain important details such as colors, textures, and edges, which are essential for accurate segmentation. A possible solution to this issue is to concatenate feature maps from other layers.

To enhance feature diversity and reduce redundancy, we calculate cosine similarity between each pair of feature maps to guide the concatenation process. Based on the similarity results, we then select and concatenate low-similarity features. As shown in Fig. 2, we observed that Blocks 9, 8, 5, 4, 2, and 1 exhibit the most dissimilar features compared to Blocks 18, 17, and 16. Leveraging this, we implemented a concatenation strategy to fuse these diverse features. The effectiveness of this approach will be analyzed in subsequent experiments.

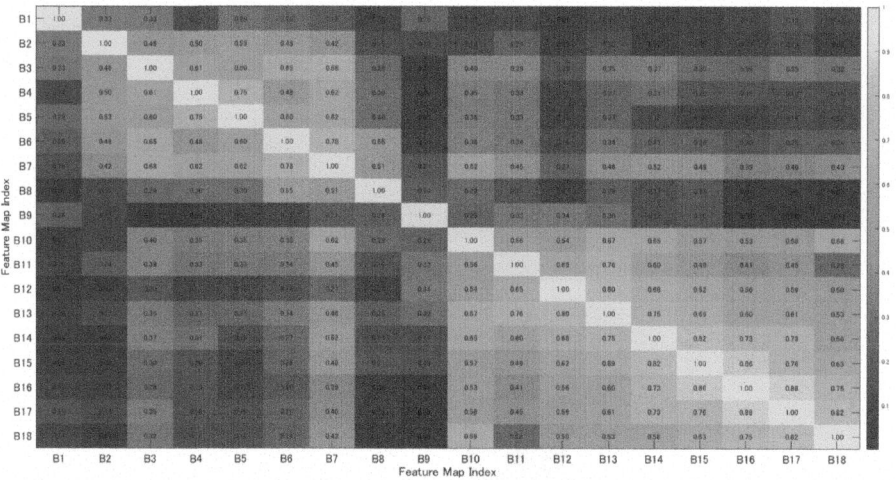

Fig. 2. Similarity matrix of CNN feature maps across different layers for a food image.

Finally, these feature representations, whether extracted from specific layers or created by concatenating multiple layers of a Convolutional Neural Network (CNN) model, are encoded as high-dimensional feature vectors at the pixel level, referred to as pixel-wise feature representations.

3.3 Selection of Suitable Pixel-Wise Feature Representations

Given that there are currently 21 (3 single-layer features and 18 multi-layer concatenated features) feature representations, we have identified that computing each of them during the subsequent clustering and quality analysis process is highly time-intensive.

Consequently, we need to find a way to select a smaller, more essential set of feature representations.

We propose a method for selecting the most suitable pixel-wise feature representations for food image segmentation. As illustrated in Fig. 3, multiple pixel-wise features are first extracted from each image. To evaluate the effectiveness of these features in distinguishing food pixels from non-food pixels, we employ two metrics for clustering quality assessment.

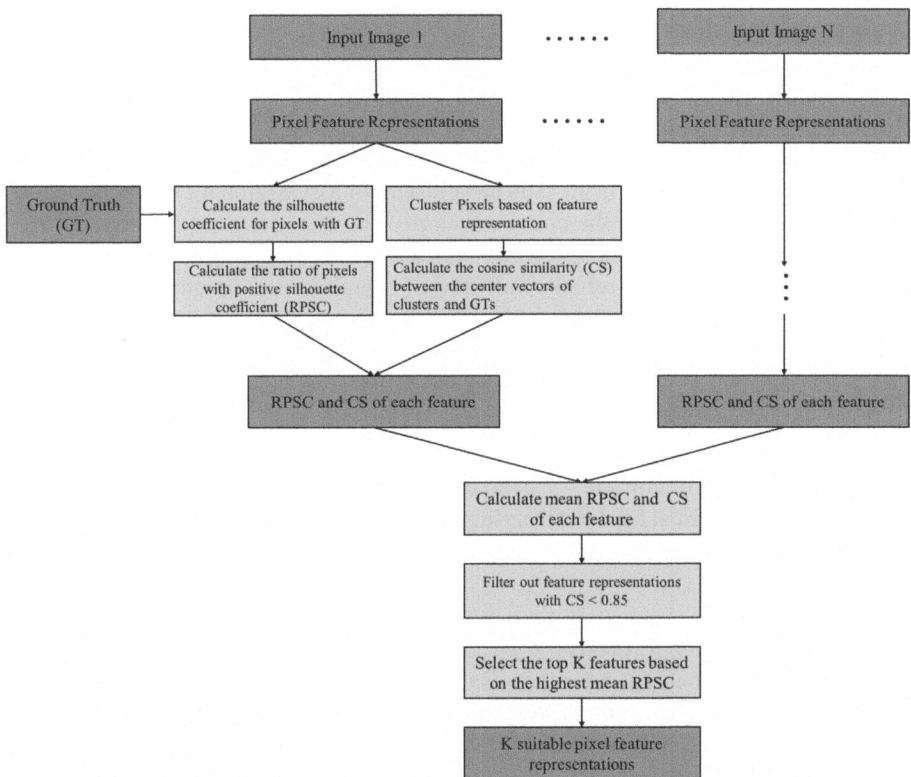

Fig. 3. Diagram of Selection of Suitable Pixel-wise Feature Representations

The first metric, RPSC (Ratio of Pixels with a positive Silhouette Coefficient), evaluates the local clustering quality by measuring how well pixels are grouped together within clusters. To calculate the RPSC, we set a threshold for the Silhouette Coefficient (e.g., 0) and determine the proportion of GT pixels that exceed this threshold. A higher RPSC value indicates better local clustering quality, making it a reliable measure for evaluating different pixel feature representations. The RPSC is calculated as follows:

$$\text{RPSC} = \frac{1}{N}\sum\nolimits_{i=1}^{N} I(S_i > 0) \tag{1}$$

where N is the total number of pixels, I is an indicator function.

$$S_i = \frac{b_i - a_i}{\max(a_i, b_i)} \tag{2}$$

$$a_i = \frac{1}{|C_i| - 1} \sum_{j \in C_i, j \neq i} d(i, j) \tag{3}$$

$$b_i = \min_{C_k \neq C_i} \frac{1}{|C_k|} \sum_{j \in C_k} d(i, j) \tag{4}$$

where, $|C_i|$ is the number of points in the cluster C_i to which i belongs, $|C_k|$ is the number of points in the nearest neighboring cluster C_k to which i does not belong, and $d(i, j)$ is the distance between points i and j.

The second metric, cosine similarity (CS), compares the center vectors of Ground Truth labels (GT) with those from k-means clusters to assess global clustering quality. To calculate CS, we measure the cosine similarity between the cluster centers and the ground truth centers. A higher CS value indicates better alignment between clusters and ground truth, making it a reliable indicator of overall clustering quality. The Center Similarity is calculated as follows:

$$CS = \frac{1}{n} \sum_{i=1}^{n} \frac{C_i^A \bullet C_i^B}{\|C_i^A\| \|C_i^B\|} \tag{5}$$

where n is the number of clusters, C_i^A denotes the center vector of the $i-$th cluster in the clustering results obtained by the clustering methods. C_i^B represents the center vector of the $i-$th cluster in the ground truth clustering. $\|C_i^A\|$ and $\|C_i^B\|$ are the Euclidean norms of the vectors.

The RPSC and CS values are first calculated for each image to assess local and global clustering quality, respectively. These values are then averaged across the dataset to provide a comprehensive and robust evaluation of the pixel feature representations. To select the top K pixel feature representations, we begin by filtering out those with a mean CS value below 0.85, ensuring only those with strong global clustering alignment are considered. The remaining representations are then ranked by their average RPSC values in descending order, as higher RPSC indicates better local clustering quality. Finally, the top K representations with the highest RPSC values are selected.

3.4 Food Segmentation

After selecting the top K pixel feature representations, we process new food images for segmentation. Using these selected features, we apply the K-means clustering algorithm to segment image pixels into two clusters. For each clustering result, we calculate the Positive Silhouette Coefficient Ratio (RPSC) to assess clustering quality. The result with the highest RPSC is chosen as the optimal clustering. The corresponding cluster labels are then used to create the segmentation mask, where the two labels are assigned values of 1 and 0 to represent different regions. These labels are directly converted into a binary segmentation mask, but it's important to note that the labels do not inherently indicate "food" or "non-food".

We use the fine-tuned CNN model from Sect. 3.1 to classify each segmented region as either food or non-food. For performance evaluation, we adopt the following procedure to assign labels to each segmented result: leveraging the pixel-level ground truth, we compute the proportion of food pixels within each region. If this proportion exceeds 50%, the region is assigned a "food" label; otherwise, it is assigned a "non-food" label.

4 Experiments

4.1 Implementation Details

Datasets. To evaluate the performance of food segmentation, we utilize three public datasets: UECFoodPix Complete [2], FoodSeg103 [14], and UNIMIB2016 [15]. Each of these datasets originally contains multiple classes of food items. The UEC-FoodPix Complete dataset includes 102 dishes, comprising 9,000 training images and 1,000 test images. The FoodSeg103 dataset consists of 7,118 images, covering 103 food ingredients. This dataset includes 4,983 training images and 2,135 test images. The UNIMIB2016 dataset consists of 1,027 images, covering 73 food categories, with 667 training images and 360 test images. To align with our objective of segmenting food regions from non-food regions within images, we preprocessed all these datasets by merging all food-related classes into a single unified food class, while categorizing all other pixels as non-food.

Backbone Model. For feature extraction, we utilized two versions of the EfficientNet-B0 model as the backbone. The first is a pre-trained EfficientNet-B0 model (PM), while the second is a re-trained version of the same model (RM) on the custom food vs. non-food dataset. This dataset is built on the Food5K dataset [23], which includes 2,500 food images and 2,500 non-food images. To increase the diversity of the dataset samples, 9,982 single-ingredient food images from the SI110 dataset [11] were added, providing cleaner visuals without distracting backgrounds. Additionally, 2,066 background-removed, multi-ingredient dish images from the MIF110 dataset [11] were incorporated to increase the variety of food presentations. Finally, we collected 1,000 food images from the internet and extracted non-food regions from these images, such as tableware, tablecloths, and plates. Ultimately, we selected 2,600 non-food images to include in the dataset. During the training phase, we unfroze all layers of the pre-trained model, allowing fine-tuning of the original parameters. The model was trained with a mini-batch size of 32 over 20 epochs. We used an initial learning rate of 1e-4, which was adjusted using a piecewise learning rate schedule that reduced the learning rate by a factor of 0.1 every 5 epochs.

Selecting Suitable Pixel-wise Feature Representations. We randomly selected images and their corresponding masks from the training sets of the three datasets mentioned earlier. To ensure consistent feature selection, we compared results from sample sizes of 150 and 300. In the first round, 50 images were sampled per dataset, totaling 150 samples, and in the second round, 100 images per dataset, totaling 300 samples. To maintain computational efficiency in food segmentation, we limited the selection to a maximum of three feature representations.

Evaluation Metrics. We evaluate our proposed segmentation framework by three metrics: average accuracy (aAcc), mean accuracy (mAcc) and mean Intersection over Union (mIoU). Average Accuracy (aAcc) is defined as the mean of the pixel-wise accuracy across all classes, calculated as the ratio of correctly identified pixels to the total number of pixels in each class is defined as

$$aAcc = \frac{\sum_{i=1}^{N} TP_i}{\sum_{i=1}^{N} TP_i + FN_i} \tag{6}$$

Mean Accuracy (mAcc) is defined as the average of the accuracy values computed for each class individually. It can be formulated as

$$mAcc = \frac{1}{N} \sum_{i=1}^{N} \frac{TP_i}{TP_i + FN_i} \tag{7}$$

Mean Intersection over Union (mIoU) measures the overlap between the predicted segmentation and the ground truth, averaged across all classes, and is defined as

$$mIoU = \frac{1}{N} \sum_{i=1}^{N} \frac{TP_i}{TP_i + FP_i + FN_i} \tag{8}$$

where TP_i (true positives) is the number of correctly identified pixels belonging to class i, TN_i (true negatives) is the number of correctly identified pixels not belonging to class i, FP_i (false positives) is the number of pixels incorrectly identified as class i, and FN_i (false negatives) is the number of pixels belonging to class i but incorrectly identified as another class. N represents the total number of classes in the dataset.

Additionally, we evaluate the performance of food classification on the segmented results using three metrics: Precision, Recall, and F1 score. Precision is the ratio of correctly predicted positive instances to all predicted positives, while recall is the ratio of correctly predicted positive instances to all actual positives. The F1 score, which is the harmonic mean of precision and recall, provides a single metric that balances both precision and recall. These metrics are defined as:

$$Precision = \frac{TP}{TP + FP} \tag{9}$$

$$Recall = \frac{TP}{TP + FN} \tag{10}$$

$$F1 \ score = 2 \times \frac{precison * recall}{precison + recall} \tag{11}$$

where TP (True Positives) represents the correctly predicted positive instances, FP (False Positives) represents the incorrectly predicted positive instances, and FN (False Negatives) represents the actual positive instances that were incorrectly predicted as negative.

4.2   Selecting Suitable Pixel-Wise Feature Representations for Food Segmentation

We extracted features from both the pre-trained model (PM) and the retrained model (RM), focusing on three specific layers for single-layer features and combining these with features from other layers for multi-layer concatenated features. This approach resulted in a total of 42 feature representations. We calculated the mean RPSC and CS values for each feature representation in both sampling rounds (Sample 50 and Sample 100). Feature representations with a mean CS lower than 0.85 were filtered out. The remaining feature representations are listed in Table 1.

From Table 1, we observed that most of the feature representations remaining after CS value filtering were from the pre-trained model, suggesting that its features are more robust and generalizable. In contrast, the retrained model likely overfitted to its dataset, leading to less effective features. We also found that concatenated features generally had higher PSCR values than single-layer features, suggesting that feature fusion improves pixel clustering quality. However, not all concatenated features had higher CS values, implying that while fusion enhances local clustering, it may disrupt global clustering. We identified the top three features by ranking them based on mean RPSC values: Block17 + 9 (F1), Block16 + 9 (F2), and Block17 + 4 (F3) from the pre-trained model.

Table 1. Feature Representations Remaining After Filtering with mCS > 0.85.

Model	Features	Sample 50		Sample 100	
		mRPSC	mCS	mRPSC	mCS
PM	Block 17 + 9	**0.9524**	0.8879	**0.9471**	0.8805
PM	Block 16 + 9	**0.9500**	0.8595	**0.9430**	0.8578
PM	Block 17 + 4	**0.9444**	0.8876	**0.9399**	0.8938
RM	Block 17 + 9	0.9385	0.8686	0.9397	0.8547
PM	Block 16 + 4	0.9443	0.9084	0.9370	0.9075
RM	Block 15 + 4	0.9449	0.8574	0.9365	0.8569
PM	Block 15 + 2	0.9348	0.8609	0.9247	0.8605
PM	Block 17 + 2	0.9309	0.9080	0.9235	0.8930
PM	Block 16 + 2	0.9312	0.9018	0.9217	0.9064
PM	Block 17	0.9207	0.9066	0.9147	0.8982
PM	Block 16	0.9216	0.9039	0.9125	0.9070
RM	Block 17	0.9145	0.8842	0.9121	0.8734

4.3   Segmentation Results

Our segmentation model grouped image pixels into two categories, producing two segmentation masks with initially unknown categories. To evaluate performance, we matched these masks to Ground Truth (GT) masks using the Jaccard index. The mask with the higher Jaccard value was assigned to the corresponding GT category.

As shown in Fig. 4, our method performs well across diverse food images and datasets. Furthermore, as shown in Table 2, we compared our results with SOTA. Since the model performs binary class-agnostic segmentation, the mAcc and mIoU metrics are computed by matching the predicted segment masks to the food/non-food ground truth masks across two categories.

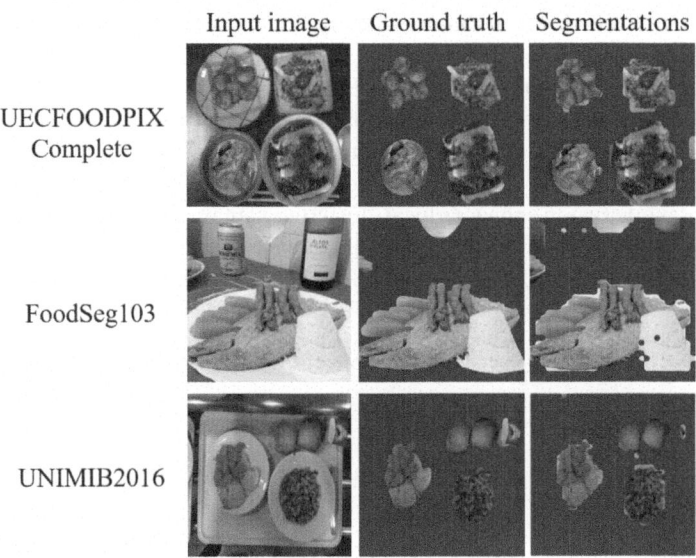

Fig. 4. Visualization of segmentation results from three food segmentation image datasets.

From Table 2, the model achieved an aAcc of 0.8967(+0.012) and mIoU of 0.8094(+0.148) on the UECFOODPIX COMPLETE dataset compared to FoodSAM, and a 0.9304(-0.0539) aAcc and 0.8375(+0.0664) on the UNIMIB2016 dataset compared to BayesianDeepLabv3 + [16]. On the FoodSeg103 dataset, we achieved an aAcc of 0.875 (-0.0664) and a mIoU of 0.7768 (-0.1112) compared to the SAM fine-tuned with LoRA [24]. This study shares our objective of segmenting food and background, but it utilizes pixel-level annotations from both the FoodSeg103 and UECFOODPIX COMPLETE datasets to train their model. These results indicate that with limited pixel label data, our model delivers near-SOTA segmentation performance.

Further analysis showed that the method performed best on the UECFOODPIX COMPLETE and UNIMIB2016 datasets with three feature candidates (K = 3), yielding the highest aAcc values. On the FoodSeg103 dataset, the highest aAcc was achieved with two features (K = 2). The third feature on UECFOODPIX COMPLETE and UNIMIB2016 had the highest mean center similarity, likely contributing to superior aAcc values. On FoodSeg103, the second feature had the highest mean similarity. These results suggest that prioritizing feature representations with higher mean center similarity enhances segmentation performance and improves efficiency, as better results are achieved with fewer features.

Table 2. Comparison of segmentation performance (K represents the number of feature representation candidates for selecting).

Datasets	Model	aAcc	mAcc	mIoU
UECFOODPIX COMPLETE	BayesianGourmetNet [16]	0.8805	0.7817	0.6616
	FoodSAM [18]	0.8847	0.7801	0.6614
	Ours(K = 1)	0.8812	0.8956	0.7879
	Ours(K = 2)	0.8880	0.9003	0.7977
	Ours(K = 3)	**0.8967**	0.9054	**0.8094**
FoodSeg103	CCNet-Finetune[14]	0.8770	0.5380	0.4130
	FoodSAM [18]	0.8410	0.5827	0.4642
	SAM fine-tuned + LoRA[24]	**0.9414**	–	**0.8880**
	Ours(K = 1)	0.8621	0.8688	0.7582
	Ours(K = 2)	0.8750	0.8818	0.7768
	Ours(K = 3)	0.8720	0.8736	0.7717
UNIMIB2016	BayesianDeepLabv3 + [16]	**0.9843**	0.8271	0.7717
	BayesianGourmetNet [16]	0.9816	0.8646	0.8076
	Ours(K = 1)	0.9015	0.9254	0.7925
	Ours(K = 2)	0.9022	0.9242	0.7935
	Ours(K = 3)	0.9304	0.9386	**0.8373**

We further employed the fine-tuned food/non-food classification model, described in the Backbone section, to assign each segment to food or non-food categories, due to the class-agnostic segmentation. As shown in Table 3, the model's overall recognition capability is highly reliable, with an F1 score of approximately 0.9012 on the UEC-FOODPIX COMPLETE dataset and 0.8834 on the FoodSeg103 dataset. The average F1 score on the UNIMIB2016 dataset is slightly lower, at 0.8876. These results indicate that our segmentation approach effectively supports high-quality food recognition.

4.4 Discussion

In this section, we demonstrate cases where RPSC limitations led to incorrect clustering selections from candidate feature representations, as highlighted in Fig. 5.

Firstly, in Fig. 5(a) and 5(b), one class is nested within another, forming a non-convex structure. K-means clustering, which assumes clusters are convex and similarly sized, struggles to correctly handle such nested or overlapping classes. This assumption leads to a shift in the cluster centroids, resulting in inaccurate clustering outcomes. Even though

Table 3. Classification performance of segmentation results across three datasets.

Datasets	Category	Precision	Recall	F1
UECFOODPIX COMPLETE	Food	0.8878	0.9148	0.9009
	Non-Food	0.9146	0.8876	0.9011
	Average	0.9012	0.9012	0.9012
FoodSeg103	Food	0.8895	0.8859	0.8792
	Non-Food	0.8773	0.8811	0.8877
	Average	0.8834	0.8835	0.8834
UNIMIB2016	Food	0.8215	0.9945	0.8997
	Non-Food	0.9929	0.7827	0.8754
	Average	0.9072	0.8886	0.8876

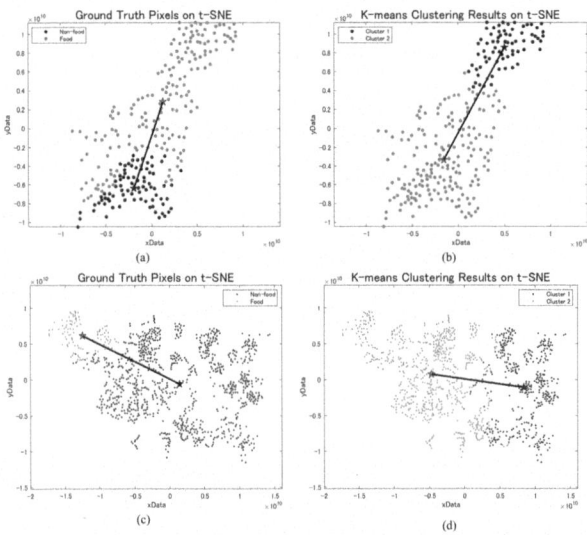

Fig. 5. t-SNE visualizations comparing true pixel class distributions and k-means clustering results, highlighting issues with nested structures, class imbalance, and RPSC limitations.

we filtered out feature representations with low mean CS values during the selection process, this issue can still arise in some representations during testing. To address this, a potential improvement could involve dynamically detecting these nested structures or using clustering algorithms that do not rely on convexity assumptions, which would be better suited for handling such complex data. Secondly, Fig. 5(c) and 4(d) illustrate the impact of class imbalance, where certain classes contain significantly more pixels than others. This imbalance causes K-means to pull cluster centers toward the larger classes, creating a bias that results in suboptimal clustering.

These clustering failures received higher RPSC values because RPSC primarily measures local clustering quality, which may not fully capture the overall data structure. As a result, RPSC can overlook issues like nested structures and class imbalances, leading to the selection of suboptimal clustering results.

4.5 Conclusion

This study proposed a simple yet effective method for food image segmentation, designed to distinguish between food and non-food regions within an image. The core of our approach involved extracting various pixel-wise feature representations using convolutional neural networks (CNNs), selectively fusing low-similarity features with single-layer features, and implementing a novel feature selection algorithm that required minimal supervision with only 50 to 100 pixel-wise labeled samples. This algorithm was based on the clustering quality analysis of pixel-wise feature representations. Additionally, we employed a clustering-based segmentation method to achieve accurate food image segmentation. We validated the effectiveness of our method on three public food segmentation datasets: UECFOODPIX COMPLETE [2], FoodSeg103 [14], and UNIMIB2016 [15]. Our results demonstrate that the method performs well across various food images and achieves segmentation performance close to that of fully supervised models on all three datasets. This method represents a meaningful contribution to food image segmentation, especially in contexts where pixel-level labeled data is scarce. By minimizing the need for extensive labeling, our approach enhances efficiency while maintaining high accuracy, addressing a key challenge in the field.

Given the limitations identified in this study, future work will focus on developing more robust clustering algorithms capable of better handling non-convex structures and class imbalances. Additionally, enhancing the RPSC metric to more effectively account for both local and global clustering quality will be essential. By addressing these challenges, we aim to improve the accuracy and broaden the applicability of our method in more complex food segmentation scenarios.

Acknowledgments. This work was partly supported by JSPS KAKENHI Grant Number JP22K12095 and JKA Subsidy Program for Keirin and Auto Racing.

References

1. Aslan, S., Ciocca, G., Mazzini, D., Schettini, R.: Benchmarking algorithms for food localization and semantic segmentation. Int. J. Mach. Learn. Cybern. **11**, 2827–2847 (2020)
2. Okamoto, K., Yanai, K.: UEC-FoodPix Complete: A Large-Scale Food Image Segmentation Dataset. ICPR Workshops (2020)
3. Sharma, U., Artacho, B., Savakis, A.E.: GourmetNet: food segmentation using multi-scale waterfall features with spatial and channel attention. Sensors (Basel, Switzerland) **21** (2021)
4. Okamoto, K., Adachi, K., Yanai, K.: Region-based food calorie estimation for multiple-dish meals. In: Proceedings of the 13th International Workshop on Multimedia for Cooking and Eating Activities (2021)

5. Siemon, M.S., Shihavuddin, A.S., Ravn-Haren, G.: Sequential transfer learning based on hierarchical clustering for improved performance in deep learning based food segmentation. Sci. Rep. **11** (2021)

6. Wang, Y., Zhu, F.M., Boushey, C.J., Delp, E.J.: Weakly supervised food image segmentation using class activation maps. IEEE Int. Conf. Image Process. (ICIP) **2017**, 1277–1281 (2017)

7. Cai, Q., Abhayaratne, C.: SSDB-Net: a single-step dual branch network for weakly supervised semantic segmentation of food images. In: 2023 IEEE 25th International Workshop on Multimedia Signal Processing (MMSP), pp. 1–6 (2023)

8. Shimoda, W., Yanai, K.: CNN-Based Food Image Segmentation Without Pixel-Wise Annotation. ICIAP Workshops (2015)

9. Shimoda, W., Yanai, K.: Weakly-supervised plate and food region segmentation. IEEE Int. Conf. Multimedia Expo (ICME) **2020**, 1–6 (2020)

10. Futagami, T., Hayasaka, N.: Improvement in automatic food region extraction based on saliency detection. Int. J. Food Prop. **25**, 634–647 (2022)

11. Zhu, Z., Dai, Y.: A new CNN-based single-ingredient classification model and its application in food image segmentation. J. Imaging **9** (2023)

12. Aguilar, E., Remeseiro, B., Bolaños, M., Radeva, P.: Grab, Pay, and Eat: semantic food detection for smart restaurants. IEEE Trans. Multimedia **20**, 3266–3275 (2017)

13. Aslan, S., Ciocca, G., Schettini, R.: Semantic food segmentation for automatic dietary monitoring. In: 2018 IEEE 8th International Conference on Consumer Electronics - Berlin (ICCE-Berlin), pp. 1–6 (2018)

14. Wu, X., Fu, X., Liu, Y., Lim, E., Hoi, S.C., Sun, Q.: A large-scale benchmark for food image segmentation. In: Proceedings of the 29th ACM International Conference on Multimedia (2021)

15. Ciocca, G., Napoletano, P., Schettini, R.: Food recognition: a new dataset, experiments, and results. IEEE J. Biomed. Health Inform. **21**, 588–598 (2017)

16. Aguilar, E., Nagarajan, B., Remeseiro, B., Radeva, P.: Bayesian deep learning for semantic segmentation of food images. Comput. Electr. Eng. **103**, 108380 (2022)

17. Wang, Y., Zhang, J., Kan, M., Shan, S., Chen, X.: Self-supervised equivariant attention mechanism for weakly supervised semantic segmentation. IEEE/CVF Conf. Comput. Vision Pattern Recogn. (CVPR) **2020**, 12272–12281 (2020)

18. Lan, X., et al.: FoodSAM: Any Food Segmentation. ArXiv, abs/2308.05938 (2023)

19. Kirillov, A., et al.: Segment anything. IEEE/CVF Int. Conf. Comput. Vision (ICCV) **2023**, 3992–4003 (2023)

20. Wu, X., Yu, S., Lim, E., Ngo, C.: OVFoodSeg: Elevating Open-Vocabulary Food Image Segmentation via Image-Informed Textual Representation. ArXiv, abs/2404.01409 (2024)

21. Tan, M., Le, Q.V.: EfficientNet: Rethinking Model Scaling for Convolutional Neural Networks. ArXiv, abs/1905.11946 (2019)

22. Ahdi, M.W., et al.: Convolutional neural network (CNN) EfficientNet-B0 model architecture for paddy diseases classification. In: 2023 14th International Conference on Information & Communication Technology and System (ICTS). IEEE (2023)

23. Singla, A., Yuan, L., Ebrahimi, T.: Food/Non-food Image classification and food categorization using pre-trained GoogLeNet model. In: Proceedings of the 2nd International Workshop on Multimedia Assisted Dietary Management (2016)

24. Alahmari, S.S., Gardner, M.R., Salem, T.: Segment anything in food images. IEEE/CVF Conf. Comput. Vision Pattern Recogn. Workshops (CVPRW) **2024**, 3715–3720 (2024)

MFP3D: Monocular Food Portion Estimation Leveraging 3D Point Clouds

Jinge Ma[1]($\boxtimes$), Xiaoyan Zhang[2], Gautham Vinod[1], Siddeshwar Raghavan[1], Jiangpeng He[1], and Fengqing Zhu[1]

[1] Elmore Family School of Electrical and Computer Engineering, Purdue University, West Lafayette, USA
ma859@purdue.edu
[2] College of Artificial Intelligence, Anhui University, Hefei, China

Abstract. Food portion estimation is crucial for monitoring health and tracking dietary intake. Image-based dietary assessment, which involves analyzing eating occasion images using computer vision techniques, is increasingly replacing traditional methods such as 24-hour recalls. However, accurately estimating the nutritional content from images remains challenging due to the loss of 3D information when projecting to the 2D image plane. Existing portion estimation methods are challenging to deploy in real-world scenarios due to their reliance on specific requirements, such as physical reference objects, high-quality depth information, or multi-view images and videos. In this paper, we introduce MFP3D, a new framework for accurate food portion estimation using only a single monocular image. Specifically, MFP3D consists of three key modules: (1) a 3D Reconstruction Module that generates a 3D point cloud representation of the food from the 2D image, (2) a Feature Extraction Module that extracts and concatenates features from both the 3D point cloud and the 2D RGB image, and (3) a Portion Regression Module that employs a deep regression model to estimate the food's volume and energy content based on the extracted features. Our MFP3D is evaluated on MetaFood3D dataset, demonstrating its significant improvement in accurate portion estimation over existing methods.

Keywords: Food Portion Estimation · 3D Point Cloud · Monocular Image · Multimodality Model

1 Introduction

The significance of a person's diet on their overall health and well-being is paramount. Chronic diseases such as diabetes are linked to poor dietary habits, therefore understanding one's nutritional intake is of utmost significance [1]. There has been a shift from traditional dietary methods towards image-based dietary assessment due to the ease of usage, fewer measurement or self-reporting

Supplementary Information The online version contains supplementary material available at https://doi.org/10.1007/978-3-031-88217-3_4.

errors, and improved accuracy in the estimation of nutritional content from eating occasion images [2,3].

However, accurate portion estimation is very challenging domain-specific problem compared to food recognition [11,19,24,30,31,33]. Even domain experts, such as trained dietitians, cannot accurately estimate the nutritional content of the food from eating occasion images alone [4,23,25]. Directly using monocular image for portion or nutrition estimation is an ill-posed problem due to the loss of 3D information when projecting from the 3D world coordinate to the 2D image plane.

To combat this issue, many existing methods rely on various assumptions such as the availability of a physical reference in the image, such as a checkerboard pattern [5], or the presence of a high-quality depth map with real-world physical units of depth [6]. Methods such as [7–9] rely on multiple views, videos, or depth maps, which may be difficult to obtain in real-world applications. Most existing methods that handle the 3D shape of food typically rely on input images with physical references [28], and few are able to solely depend on monocular images as input.

In this paper, we propose MFP3D, a new monocular food portion estimation pipeline, that reconstructs a point cloud representation of the food, and uses a multimodal approach for 3D and 2D feature adaptation for accurate portion estimation. Our MFP3D consists of three modules: 1) a *3D Reconstruction Module* where the monocular image serves as the input to a depth-estimation network. The estimated depth map is then used to reconstruct a 3D point cloud representation of the food, 2) a *Feature Extraction Module* which comprises a 3D feature extractor network and a 2D feature extractor network, and 3) a *Portion Regression Module* where the extracted features are combined and passed through a deep regression model to estimate the food's volume and energy. Our MFP3D demonstrates significant improvements compared to existing methods on the MetaFood3D dataset [32], which includes 637 food objects across 108 categories, with diverse modalities and detailed nutritional data.

The main contributions of our paper can be summarized as follows:

- We introduce an end-to-end food portion estimation framework, which uses only a monocular RGB image as input and significantly outperforms existing methods without requiring additional information such as the depth map or physical references.
- We have innovatively utilized 3D point cloud features for food portion estimation.
- We propose to combine the 2D image and corresponding 3D point cloud features in a multimodal approach for accurate portion estimation.

2   Related Works

Food Portion Estimation. Different classes of portion estimation methods use different representations or inputs to recreate the lost 3D information during image capture. These include multi-view methods [7,8], depth-based methods [9, 10], model-based methods [5], and deep-learning based methods [6,12]. The use of 3D food models in [5] shows the efficacy of utilizing such representations of food. The method relies on using predefined 3D models of food and recreating the eating occasion image using the 3D model through object and camera pose estimation. However, the input to this method is constrained by the requirement of a physical reference (checkerboard pattern) in the eating occasion image. Further, food objects that don't fit the geometrical shape of its corresponding 3D model (e.g. whole avocado as compared to sliced avocado) will not achieve reasonable estimates for the food volume. Alternatively, the voxel reconstruction methods require some predefined knowledge of the scene such as in [6] where the distance between the camera and image plane is a known constant. Further, the depth map captured in [6] using a high-quality Intel RealSense RGBD camera makes it easy to capture the distance between the camera and the object in real-world units. However, without this information, there would need to be some scaling between the ground-truth volume and the voxel volume which would require knowledge of ground-truth volume for accurate results [5]. Our method alleviates these concerns by reconstructing the 3D point cloud representation through an estimated depth map while also using its representation for portion estimation.

3D Point Cloud. 3D point clouds can be sampled from real meshes obtained via 3D scanners or reconstructed from 2D images using existing methods such as depth estimation and 3D mesh reconstruction. Zoedepth [13] estimates depth maps for each pixel from monocular images, with depth values representing the coordinates of points in the third dimension. TripoSR [14] is one of the best-performing models for 3D mesh reconstruction from a single image. It directly reconstructs meshes, which can then be sampled to obtain 3D point clouds.

3D point cloud perception models extract features from a set of three-dimensional coordinates, performing downstream tasks such as classification and segmentation. PointNet [15] was the first model introduced to handle unordered point cloud data. Improving upon its performance, CurveNet [16] introduces continuous sequences of point segments, termed curves, into a ResNet-style network to enhance point cloud geometry learning by effectively aggregating features. Subsequent models introduced many improvements such as using advanced convolution, transformer structures, neighbor clustering, or various pre-training methods. While previous works focus on classification of 3D point clouds, we adapt a 3D point cloud feature extraction model for the regression of food portion.

3   Methodology

Our proposed MFP3D food portion estimation method derives fundamental quantitative attributes of food items such as shape, size, and texture from 3D point clouds and RGB images. The architecture of our three-stage pipeline is illustrated in Fig. 1. In **Stage 1**, given an RGB image, $x \in \mathbb{R}^{H \times W \times 3}$, we first separate the each food item from the background using Segment Anything [17] to obtain the mask. Next, we apply the mask to the original image, such that the processed image x_I contains only the food. This processed image is then fed into a point cloud reconstruction model. This model generates a 3D representation x_P of the food object from the single 2D image. In **Stage 2**, the image and its 3D representation are processed by two separate feature extractors: δ^I for the 2D image and δ^P for the 3D point clouds. These extractors produce feature maps f_I and f_P, each with dimensions of $C \times 1$. The feature maps are then concatenated along the second axis to form a comprehensive feature vector $f \in \mathbb{R}^{2C \times 1}$. In **Stage 3**, the concatenated feature vector f is fed into a deep regression module φ, which predicts the food portion $\hat{y}_t$. The attributes of y_t, such as energy content and volume, are defined by the ground truth labels used during training which are provided in the dataset. The pipeline is trained end-to-end in a supervised manner using the $\mathcal{L}1$ loss [18].

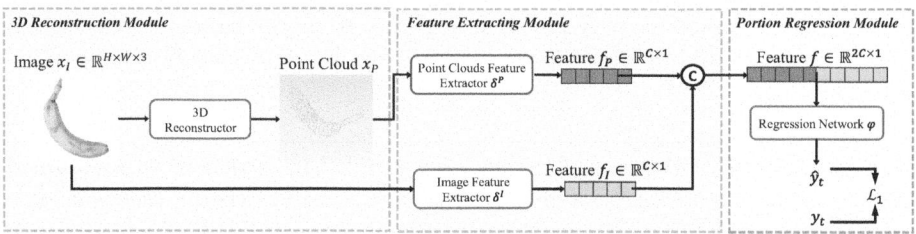

Fig. 1. An overview of the MFP3D framework: The input image x_I goes through a three-stage pipeline for accurate portion estimation. In **Stage 1**, a 3D reconstructor is used to generate the point clouds from the input image. In **Stage 2**, the 3D features (f_P) of the point cloud and the 2D features (f_I) of the input image are extracted using networks δ_P and δ_I, respectively. In **Stage 3**, these features are concatenated and passed through a regression network (φ) to estimate the food portion.

3.1   3D Point Cloud Reconstruction

To effectively leverage 3D information, it is essential to acquire accurate 3D representations. In our study, point clouds are chosen as the preferred 3D format due to their lightweight storage requirements and their rich encapsulation of shape and size information. We explore four different types of point clouds to assess their impact on the performance of the portion estimation model.

Ground Truth Point Clouds (GTPCs): GTPCs of food objects provide the most detailed and accurate representation of shape and size, enabling the network to achieve high precision in estimation results. We obtained these real point clouds by using a 3D scanner to capture the food items from multiple angles. From the original scans, we randomly sampled 1,024 points to derive the GTPCs, seen in Fig. 2(a). In contrast, reconstructed point clouds may lose some of this detailed information, leading to less accurate results. Therefore, the performance of models based on GTPCs is considered the upper bound in our experiments.

The true scaling information of 3D point clouds is crucial for accurate portion estimation. However, current 3D reconstruction methods cannot obtain actual size reconstruction from monocular images, thus focusing only on shape. To fairly compare with methods that estimate portions solely from monocular images, as described in Fig. 2(b), we **normalize GTPCs** to a range of $[0, 1]$, by rescaling all three dimensions of each point cloud to this range. This removes the true scaling information, allowing us to evaluate performance based on shape alone.

Reconstructed Point Clouds: Acquiring GTPCs requires specialized equipment, making it impractical for many applications. Therefore, we use point clouds reconstructed from monocular RGB images to simulate a more realistic scenario (as shown in Fig. 2(c)). Any point cloud reconstruction model that accepts single images as input can be utilized. In our method, we adopt two types of generated point clouds: Depth point clouds and TripoSR point clouds.

For the depth point clouds, we use ZoeDepth [13] to estimate the depth map from a monocular image. Next, we segment the food foreground using masks from MetaFood3D, generated by Segment Anything [17]. To reconstruct the 3D point cloud, we retain the two original dimensions from the 2D image and incorporate the estimated depth as the third dimension. Finally, we randomly sample 1,024 points from the food foreground region to create the depth point cloud reconstruction.

For the TripoSR point clouds, we use the masks from MetaFood3D to generate images that retain only the food foreground. Then, we apply the TripoSR model [14], which can directly reconstruct 3D meshes from monocular images and is widely used for this task. Finally, we randomly sample 1,024 points from the mesh to obtain the TripoSR point cloud reconstruction.

3.2 Feature Extraction

The point cloud provides stereoscopic shape and size while the image includes ingredients, edges, and textures. Neither the point cloud modality nor the image modality alone can fully represent the complex information associated with food portion estimation. In this work, we propose to leverage information from both 2D and 3D representations to enhance the understanding of different aspects of the eating occasion image. By concatenating features extracted from the original 2D RGB image and the reconstructed 3D point cloud, our model can capture a more comprehensive view of the food object for better portion estimation.

2D Feature Extraction: We use an image feature extraction model $\delta^I(\cdot)$, built upon ResNet50 [20] pre-trained on the ImageNet [21] dataset. We exclude the last

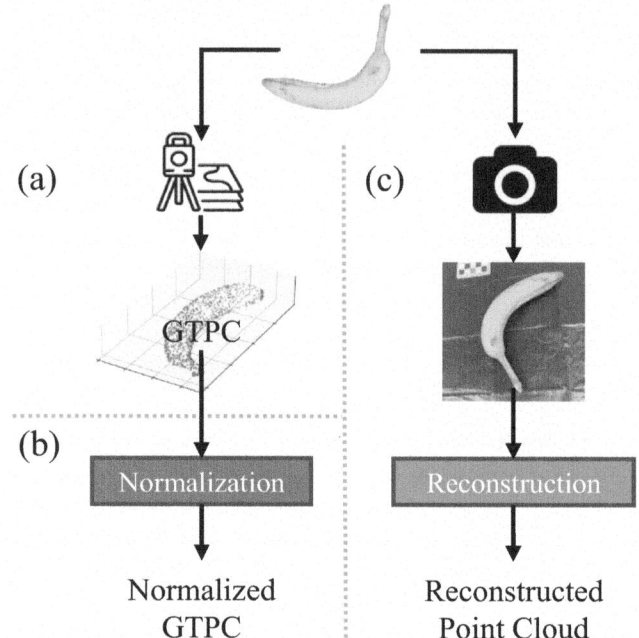

Fig. 2. An overview of (a) Ground Truth Point Clouds (GTPC), (b) Normalized GTPCs and (c) Reconstructed Point Clouds, utilized in our experiments.

two layers of original ResNet50 but introduce an additional fully connected layer that maps the high-dimensional output to a lower-dimensional feature vector of length 512. This ensures a coherent and efficient feature representation. The overall feature extraction process can be formalized as:

$$f_I^i = \delta^I(x_I^i) \tag{1}$$

where f_P^i represents the 2D feature of the ith sample x_I^i.

3D Feature Extraction: There exists many models designed for extracting features from point clouds. The pioneer network PointNet, known for its simplicity and efficiency, focuses on aggregating global features [15]. On the other hand, CurveNet's ability to capture local details makes it superior for tasks requiring intricate local feature extraction [16]. Therefore, CurveNet is selected as the backbone of the 3D feature extractor. The architecture of CurveNet consists of a Local Point Feature Aggregation (LPFA) module and a series of CurveNet Inception Convolutions (CIC). Firstly, LPFA aggregates local point features from the input point cloud, which is crucial for capturing fine-grained geometric details. Then CIC layers capture multi-scale features through point cloud down-sampling and feature extraction at various resolutions. After the CIC layers, convolutional and fully connected layers further process the aggregated features and map them to feature vector of the same size as the image features. The 3D feature f_P^i is formulated as:

$$f_P^i = \delta^P(x_P^i) \tag{2}$$

where δ^P is the 3D feature extractor and x_P^i is the reconstruction result of the ith sample x_I^i.

With features f_I^i and f_P^i, we combine them together and form the comprehensive feature f^i. This is achieved by concatenating the two feature vectors, as follows:

$$f^i = f_I^i \oplus f_P^i \tag{3}$$

where $\oplus$ denotes the concatenation of the two vectors along the second axis. In this way, the integrated extractor has the strengths of both modalities by leveraging the geometric details from point clouds and the rich visual features from images.

3.3 Portion Regression

For the portion estimation task, a numerical value is required to represent the final predictive result. To achieve this, we introduce a linear layer, denoted as $\varphi(\cdot)$, which maps the feature f^i to a scalar value. By modifying the ground truth labels in the training data, the model can learn different parameter distributions based on the relationship between inputs and attributes. The model is defined as follows:

$$\hat{y}_t^i = \varphi(f^i) \tag{4}$$

where $\hat{y}_t^i$ represents the estimated value of attribute t for the ith sample.

For the loss function, we use L1 loss to measure the distance between the ground truths and the outputs. The L1 loss is given by:

$$\mathcal{L}_1 = \frac{1}{N'} \sum_{i=1}^{N'} |\hat{y}_t^i - y_t^i| \tag{5}$$

where y_t^i is the ground truth value for attribute t of the ith sample and N' is the batch size.

4 Experiments

4.1 Experimental Setup

Dataset: For our experiments, we utilize the publicly available dataset MetaFood3D. This dataset includes 637 food objects across 108 categories. It is a comprehensive collection featuring 3D object meshes, 2D images, 3D point clouds, segmentation masks, RGBD video captures, nutritional information with weights, and blender renders with camera parameters for all the food items. We randomly select 510 food items for our training set, while 127 food items are reserved for the test set. Since the MetaFood3D dataset is still under review, especially for base experiments, we also train and test our model on Simple-Food45 [5] for a more comprehensive evaluation.

Implementation Details: In the base experiments, we take a monocular food image as the input to 3D reconstruction module. It reconstructs a 3D point cloud from the image. The feature extracting module can extract food features solely from the point cloud, or jointly from both the point cloud and the image itself. We compared our method with various existing image-based energy estimation and volume estimation methods.

Our feature extraction network is designed to accommodate relatively flexible input data, such as point clouds reconstructed by different methods (or GTPC), or the option to use images as input. Therefore, in the ablation study, we compared the impact of using different point clouds on the model's performance, and also the effect of incorporating images as the input modality.

Evaluation Metrics: We employ two evaluation metrics to assess the precision of the model's estimation results. The first metric, Mean Absolute Error (MAE) [22], calculates the average of the absolute errors in a set of predictions:

$$\text{MAE} = \frac{1}{N} \sum_{i=1}^{N} |\hat{y}_i - y_i| \tag{6}$$

where $\hat{y}_i$ is the prediction for the ith input, y_i is the corresponding ground truth, and N is the number of samples in the test batch. The second metric, Mean Absolute Percentage Error (MAPE) [26], expresses errors as a percentage, providing a clear depiction of the prediction error relative to the actual value:

$$\text{MAPE} = \frac{100\%}{N} \sum_{i=1}^{N} \frac{|\hat{y}_i - y_i|}{y_i} \tag{7}$$

4.2   Experimental Results

In this subsection, we compare our method MPF3D against existing image-based energy and volume estimation methods. We will also briefly introduce the key idea of each of the previous methods.

Energy Estimation Methods: The *baseline* model always predicts the mean volume and energy values from the dataset. The *RGB only* approach utilizes a ResNet50 backbone and two linear layers to regress the energy estimates from an input image. The *Density Map Only* method employs ground truth "Energy Density Maps" [4] as input to regress the energy estimates. Instead of a regression network, the *Density Map Summing* method sums up the values in the "Energy Density Maps" to estimate the energy. *3D Assisted Portion Estimation* estimates both food volume and energy from 2D images using a physical reference in the eating scene.

Results are shown in Table 1 and Table 2. By comparison, it can be observed that even without relying on the ground truth energy density map or physical reference as additional input or conditions, our method MPF3D still achieves the best results on both datasets, with the lowest MAE of 77.98 kCal and MAPE of 68.05%.

Table 1. Energy Estimation on MetaFood3D

Method	Energy	
	MAE(kCal)↓	MAPE (%)↓
Baseline	221.37	1,287.25
RGB Only [4]	1,932.01	1,124.90
Density Map Only [4]	1100.39	663.43
Density Map Summing [27]	436.12	142.44
3D Assisted Portion Estimation [5]	260.79	102.25
MPF3D (Ours)	**77.98**	**68.05**

Table 2. Energy Estimation on SimpleFood45

Method	Energy	
	MAE(kCal)↓	MAPE (%)↓
Baseline	120.09	547.34
RGB Only [4]	273.56	222.72
Density Map Only [4]	216.73	159.48
Density Map Summing [27]	192.76	93.16
3D Assisted Portion Estimation [5]	32.01	25.13
MPF3D (Ours)	**29.38**	**24.03**

Volume Estimation Methods: For volume estimation, we compare Stereo Reconstruction [7], Voxel Reconstruction [10], baseline method against our MFP3D method as shown in Table 3 and Table 4. The Voxel Reconstruction method [10] creates a voxel representation from the input image and corresponding depth maps, translating the number of occupied voxels into physical volume units. A regression network is trained to learn the relationship between voxel volume and ground truth volume, allowing for accurate volume estimation. Conversely, the Stereo Reconstruction method [7] estimates food volume by capturing two images from different angles, using feature matching and triangulation to calculate depth. This depth information is used to reconstruct a 3D model of the food item, which is then analyzed to estimate the volume.

Our method relies **solely on monocular images as the only input**, while other methods depend on additional information, such as binocular images, ground truth depth maps, or physical references. Through comparison, we found that our method can achieve performance close to or even surpassing other methods, despite using less information. On MetaFood3D, our method achieved the lowest MAE of 62.60 ml and MAPE of 41.43%, while on SimpleFood45, our method performed comparably to Voxel Reconstruction and 3D Assisted Portion Estimation.

Table 3. Volume Estimation on MetaFood3D

Method	Volume	
	MAE(ml)↓	MAPE(%)↓
Baseline	151.85	845.69
Stereo Reconstruction [7]	135.96	210.90
Voxel Reconstruction [10]	123.34	104.07
3D Assisted Portion Estimation [5]	195.92	79.33
MPF3D (Ours)	**62.60**	**41.43**

Table 4. Volume Estimation on SimpleFood45

Method	Volume	
	MAE(ml)↓	MAPE(%)↓
Baseline	83.28	170.37
Voxel Reconstruction [10]	**22.35**	24.51
3D Assisted Portion Estimation [5]	24.51	**14.01**
MPF3D (Ours)	25.83	16.15

Our results indicate that the MFP3D method holds significant advantages over existing methods for energy and volume estimation. This is reflected in either a lower estimation error or a reduced requirement for input data.

4.3   Ablation Studies

In the ablation studies, we design a series of comparative experiments on Metafood3D to analyze:

1. The impact of using different 3D point clouds as input to the feature extraction module on the model's portion estimation performance.
2. The effect of using RGB images as an additional input modality on the model's performance.

3. The critical information within the point cloud for portion estimation.

The various 3D point clouds used include GTPC (as described in Subsect. 3.1 and considered to be the upper bound), Normalized GTPC (without true scaling information), TripoSR [14], and Depth Point Clouds [13]. It is worth noting that we used GTPC and Normalized GTPC only as control groups in the ablation studies. We did not use them in the base experiments because they can not be retrieved from monocular images but rather from 3D scanners.

We trained 8 different MFP3D models, as shown in Table 5.

The main differences between these MPF3D models lie in: (1) the type of 3D point cloud used, and (2) whether 2D RGB images are also used as input. The top half of Table 5 displays the model performance with portion estimate using only the 3D point cloud as input, while the bottom half shows the model performance when both the 3D point cloud and 2D RGB image are used as input, as illustrated in Fig. 1. In Table 5, excluding the upperbound results from GTPC, the best result for each metric is bolded. In the bottom half of the table, we used small fonts to indicate the changes in MAPE for the models based on point cloud + RGB image compared to those based solely on the same point cloud.

Table 5. Ablation studies on different point clouds and the use of RGB images in **MPF3D**.

Input to Feature Extraction	Energy		Volume	
	MAE(kCal)↓	MAPE (%)↓	MAE(ml)↓	MAPE(%)↓
Point Cloud Only				
Upperbound - GTPCs	114.73	71.00	26.06	19.19
Normalized GTPCs	**135.61**	114.62	**79.93**	68.05
Depth Point Clouds [13]	155.24	**108.53**	80.41	**62.65**
TripoSR Point Clouds [14]	175.45	152.02	121.80	83.47
Point Cloud+RGB Image				
Upperbound - GTPCs	26.16	17.37 (-53.63)	26.68	15.59 (-3.6)
Normalized GTPCs	100.96	**62.65** (-51.97)	**49.26**	42.19 (-25.86)
Depth Point Clouds	**77.98**	68.05 (-40.48)	62.60	41.43 (-21.22)
TripoSR Point Clouds	109.64	98.45 (-53.57)	62.41	**39.45** (-44.02)

Observations

1. **Different point clouds:** We observed that GTPC achieved upper bound performance in both energy and volume estimation. Depth Point Clouds obtained the lowest Energy MAPE and volume MAPE among the point cloud-only methods. In the point cloud + RGB image methods, Depth Point Clouds

achieved the lowest Energy MAE, while TripoSR obtained the lowest MAPE. We can infer that normalized GTPC does not offer a significant advantage over Depth Point Clouds and TripoSR Point Clouds extracted from monocular images.

2. **Multimodality input:** We observed that adding RGB images as supplementary 2D input improved the performance of all models using the same point cloud across the board (as indicated by the small font in the table), though the degree of improvement varied. The percentage decrease in MAPE for volume estimation was less than that for energy estimation. For example, GTPC saw only a 3.6% decrease in volume MAPE after adding RGB images, but a 53.63% decrease in energy MAPE. We believe this may be because the point cloud data includes accurate volume information but lacks the food type, composition, and other energy-related information that might be present in RGB images. This suggests that incorporating multimodal information is crucial for accurate portion estimation.

3. **Important information within the point cloud:** We observed that GTPC performed significantly better than other point clouds reconstructed from monocular images, but normalized GTPC did not show a clear advantage over the above methods. The difference between the two lies in the inclusion of the ground truth scaling factor. Therefore, we can infer that, in addition to the shape of the point cloud, the true scaling factor also contains critical information for portion estimation.

Conclusion

In this paper, we introduce MFP3D for estimating food portions by leveraging the combined power of 3D point clouds and 2D RGB images. This approach enhances the accuracy of volume and energy estimations and simplifies the data acquisition process by utilizing existing 3D point cloud reconstruction methods. These methods reduce dependency on difficult-to-obtain real-world 3D point cloud data and enable the reconstruction of point clouds from monocular images without additional annotations, providing superior performance and demonstrating the practical applicability of our approach. For future work, we plan to improve existing 3D reconstruction algorithms to obtain point clouds that more accurately represent the actual size of objects and explore additional data modalities such as textual descriptions and videos. Our results demonstrate that our method significantly improves energy and volume estimates, showcasing its great potential for real-world applications deployment.

References

1. Liese, A.D., et al.: The dietary patterns methods project: synthesis of findings across cohorts and relevance to dietary guidance. J. Nutr. **145**(3), 393–402 (2015)
2. Boushey, C., Spoden, M., Zhu, F., Delp, E., Kerr, D.: New mobile methods for dietary assessment: review of image-assisted and image-based dietary assessment methods. Proc. Nutr. Soc. **76**(3), 283–294 (2017)

3. Poslusna, K., Ruprich, J., de Vries, J.H., Jakubikova, M., van't Veer, P.: Misreporting of energy and micronutrient intake estimated by food records and 24 hour recalls, control and adjustment methods in practice. Br. J. Nutr. **101**(S2), S73–S85 (2009)

4. Shao, Z., et al.: Towards learning food portion from monocular images with cross-domain feature adaptation. In: Proceedings of 2021 IEEE 23rd International Workshop on Multimedia Signal Processing, pp. 1–6 (2021)

5. Vinod, G., He, J., Shao, Z., Zhu, F.: Food portion estimation via 3D object scaling. In: Proceedings of the 2024 IEEE/CVF Conference on Computer Vision and Pattern Recognition, pp. 3741–3749 (2024)

6. Thames, Q., et al.: Nutrition5k: towards automatic nutritional understanding of generic food. In: Proceedings of the IEEE/CVF Conference on Computer Vision and Pattern Recognition, pp. 8903–8911 (2021)

7. Dehais, J., Anthimopoulos, M., Shevchik, S., Mougiakakou, S.: Two-view 3D reconstruction for food volume estimation. IEEE Trans. Multimedia **19**(5), 1090–1099 (2017)

8. Konstantakopoulos, F., Georga, E.I., Fotiadis, D.I.: 3D reconstruction and volume estimation of food using stereo vision techniques. In Proceedings of the 2021 IEEE 21st International Conference on Bioinformatics and Bioengineering, pp. 1–4 (2021)

9. Lo, F.P.-W., Sun, Y., Qiu, J., Lo, B.: Food volume estimation based on deep learning view synthesis from a single depth map. Nutrients **10**(12), 2005 (2018)

10. Shao, Z., Vinod, G., He, J., Zhu, F.: An end-to-end food portion estimation framework based on shape reconstruction from monocular image. In: Proceedings of 2023 IEEE International Conference on Multimedia and Expo, pp. 942–947 (2023)

11. He, J., Zhu, F.: Single-stage heavy-tailed food classification. In: Proceedings of the IEEE International Conference on Image Processing (2023)

12. Vinod, G., Shao, Z., Zhu, F.: Image based food energy estimation with depth domain adaptation. In: Proceedings of 2022 IEEE 5th International Conference on Multimedia Information Processing and Retrieval, pp. 262–267 (2022)

13. Bhat, S.F., Birkl, R., Wofk, D., Wonka, P., Müller, M.: ZoeDepth: Zero-shot transfer by combining relative and metric depth. arXiv preprint arXiv:2302.12288 (2023)

14. Tochilkin, D., et al.: TripoSR: Fast 3D object reconstruction from a single image. arXiv preprint arXiv:2403.02151 (2024)

15. Qi, C.R., Su, H., Mo, K., Guibas, L.J.: PointNet: deep learning on point sets for 3d classification and segmentation. In: Proceedings of the IEEE Conference on Computer Vision and Pattern Recognition, pp. 652–660 (2017)

16. Xiang, T., Zhang, C., Song, Y., Yu, J., Cai, W.: Walk in the cloud: learning curves for point clouds shape analysis. In: Proceedings of the IEEE/CVF International Conference on Computer Vision, pp. 915–924 (2021)

17. Kirillov, A., et al.: Segment anything. In: Proceedings of the IEEE/CVF International Conference on Computer Vision, pp. 4015–4026 (2023)

18. Barron, J.T.: A general and adaptive robust loss function. In: Proceedings of the IEEE/CVF Conference on Computer Vision and Pattern Recognition, pp. 4331–4339 (2019)

19. He, J., Lin, L., Eicher-Miller, H.A., Zhu, F.: Long-Tailed Food Classification. Nutrients (2023)

20. He, K., Zhang, X., Ren, S., Sun, J.: Deep residual learning for image recognition. In: 2016 IEEE Conference on Computer Vision and Pattern Recognition (CVPR), pp. 770–778 (2015)

21. Deng, J., Dong, W., Socher, R., Li, L.-J., Li, K., Fei-Fei, L.: ImageNet: a large-scale hierarchical image database. In: 2009 IEEE Conference on Computer Vision and Pattern Recognition, pp. 248–255 (2009)
22. Willmott, C.J., Matsuura, K.: Advantages of the mean absolute error (MAE) over the root mean square error (RMSE) in assessing average model performance. Climate Res. **30**(1), 79–82 (2005)
23. He, J., Shao, Z., Wright, J., Kerr, D., Boushey, C., Zhu, F.: Multi-task image-based dietary assessment for food recognition and portion size estimation. In: Proceedings of IEEE Conference on Multimedia Information Processing and Retrieval, pp. 49–54 (2020)
24. Pan, X., He, J., Zhu, F.: Muti-Stage Hierarchical Food Classification. arXiv preprint arXiv:2309.01075 (2023)
25. He, J., et al.: An end-to-end food image analysis system. Electron. Imaging **11**(4), 877 (2021)
26. De Myttenaere, A., Golden, B., Le Grand, B., Rossi, F.: Mean absolute percentage error for regression models. Neurocomputing **192**, 38–48 (2016)
27. Ma, J., He, J., Zhu, F.: An improved encoder-decoder framework for food energy estimation. In: Proceedings of the 8th International Workshop on Multimedia Assisted Dietary Management, pp. 53–59 (2023)
28. He, J., et al.: MetaFood CVPR 2024 Challenge on Physically Informed 3D Food Reconstruction: Methods and Results. arXiv preprint arXiv:2407.09285 (2024)
29. Shao, Z., Vinod, G., He, J., Zhu, F.: An end-to-end food portion estimation framework based on shape reconstruction from monocular image. In: 2023 IEEE International Conference on Multimedia and Expo (ICME), pp. 942–947 (2023)
30. He, J., Zhu, F.: Online continual learning for visual food classification. In: Proceedings of the IEEE International Conference on Computer Vision Workshop (2021)
31. Mao, R., He, J., Shao, Z., Yarlagadda, S.K., Zhu, F.: Visual aware hierarchy based food recognition. In: Proceedings of International Conference on Pattern Recognition Workshops (2020)
32. Chen, Y., et al.: MetaFood3D: Large 3D Food Object Dataset with Nutrition Values. arXiv preprint arXiv:2409.01966 (2024)
33. Min, W., et al.: Large scale visual food recognition. IEEE Trans. Pattern Anal. Mach. Intell. **45**(8), 9932–9949 (2023)

CalorieLLaVA: Image-Based Calorie Estimation with Multimodal Large Language Models

Hikaru Tanabe[ID] and Keiji Yanai[✉][ID]

The University of Electro-Communications, Chofu, Tokyo, Japan
{tanabe-h,yanai}@mm.inf.uec.ac.jp

Abstract. Multimodal large language models (MLLMs) have demonstrated remarkable capabilities in performing complex reasoning tasks by leveraging their language-based knowledge, including insights in the food domain. Building on this capability, we hypothesize that MLLMs can enhance calorie estimation from food images by incorporating the language-based reasoning, which is lacking in existing calorie estimation models. However, the effectiveness of these models, particularly when generating text-based outputs for calorie estimation, has not been fully explored. In this work, we present CalorieLLaVA, a model fine-tuned on paired food images and calorie data to exploit the reasoning potential of MLLMs in image-based calorie estimation. By fine-tuning the LLaVA model on the Nutrition5k dataset, we evaluate its performance in calorie estimation. Our experiments demonstrate that CalorieLLaVA surpasses the baseline models, including GPT-4V, GPT-4o, and FoodLMM, achieving superior results on the Nutrition5k dataset.

Keywords: Multimodal Large Language Models · Image-based Calorie Estimation · Nutrition5k

1 Introduction

Tracking daily food intake is essential for achieving health-related goals such as dieting and bodybuilding. In particular, accurate calorie estimation plays a crucial role in supporting these efforts. However, conventional methods, including Food Diaries, 24-hour Dietary Recalls (24HR), and Food Frequency Questionnaire (FFQ), are time-consuming and often introduce errors due to reliance on memory and subjective reporting.

In contrast, automated calorie estimation from food images offers a practical alternative, particularly suited for mobile and augmented reality (AR) applications. This approach facilitates convenient dietary monitoring, expanding accessibility for a wider range of users. Nonetheless, existing image-based calorie estimation methods have struggled with adaptability, often facing limitations when handling diverse food types accurately.

© The Author(s), under exclusive license to Springer Nature Switzerland AG 2025
S. Palaiahnakote et al. (Eds.): ICPR 2024 Workshops, LNCS 15617, pp. 63–75, 2025.
https://doi.org/10.1007/978-3-031-88217-3_5

The advent of Multimodal Large Language Models (MLLMs) presents new opportunities for overcoming these limitations. MLLMs possess strong reasoning abilities and can identify diverse food items from images, creating potential for high-quality calorie estimation. These models benefit from an integration of visual and textual insights, allowing for more contextual recognition on visual tasks and enhancing estimation accuracy.

In this study, we introduce CalorieLLaVA, a model that leverages MLLMs for image-based calorie estimation. By fine-tuning MLLMs on paired food image-calorie data, we aim to demonstrate the effectiveness of MLLMs in this domain and establish a baseline for MLLM-based calorie estimation.

The main contributions of this study are as follows:

- We propose CalorieLLaVA, a model that employs the reasoning capabilities of MLLMs to enhance image-based calorie estimation. Trained on the Nutrition5k dataset, CalorieLLaVA enables accurate calorie estimation from food images.
- We evaluate the performance of CalorieLLaVA, demonstrating its superiority over existing methods by achieving higher scores than both the original MLLM and previous calorie estimation models.
- We establish a baseline for MLLM-based calorie estimation, outperforming recent models such as GPT-4o and domain-specific models like FoodLMM, and discuss the impact of adjusting training configurations.

2   Related Work

2.1   Size-Based Methods for Calorie Estimation

There are two primary methods for estimating caloric content from food images: size-based methods and direct estimation methods.

In size-based methods, a pipeline is constructed that combines multiple image recognition modules to estimate caloric content. The basic procedure involves first extracting the food regions from the food image, then estimating the food category, and subsequently estimating the volume or mass of the food regions. Based on these results, the caloric content is estimated. By going through several stages prior to calorie estimation, this approach enables estimation that specifically takes the quantity of food into consideration.

As a method for obtaining the actual area of the food in the image, methods exist for estimating the actual size of objects included in the food image. To determine the actual size, Okamoto et al. [15] used a credit card or long wallet, Akpa et al. [8] used chopsticks, and Ege et al. [6] used rice grains as reference objects. Additionally, there is a method by Tanno et al. [20], which uses anchors placed in an AR space to obtain the actual size through interaction with the user.

To obtain the volume of food, there is DepthCalorieCam by Ando et al. [2]. This method significantly reduced the error in calorie estimation compared to existing methods by estimating the volume of food using a depth camera and a region segmentation model. Furthermore, Naritomi *et al.* [14] reconstructed high-quality 3D meshes of plates and food using an implicit surface representation.

However, these size-based methods have the limitation on the types of food that can be estimated. In particular, a noted issue with DepthCalorieCam is that the food types subject to estimation are limited to only three categories.

2.2   Direct Estimation Methods for Calorie Estimation

Direct estimation methods involve deep learning models that have achieved high performance in general image recognition are selected, and transfer learning related to caloric estimation is applied to achieve high-quality predictions.

Ege *et al.* [7] applied a multi-task learning approach based on VGG16 [19], to estimate not only the caloric content but also food category, ingredients, and cooking procedures. This method achieved higher quality estimation compared to simple transfer learning.

However, a challenge with the direct estimation methods is the difficulty in considering the quantity of food when estimating the caloric content. As a result, even with the same type of food, accurate estimation becomes difficult if the quantity differs. Furthermore, training calorie estimation models requires a large amount of training data, and the burden of data annotation remains a challenge.

In this study, we aim to address the limitations of both approaches by introducing MLLMs, which have recently seen significant improvements in performance. By leveraging their reasoning capabilities based on prior knowledge of food, we aim to achieve accurate calorie estimation. Additionally, we apply fine-tuning specific to caloric estimation to further enhance the model's performance in this task.

2.3   Large Language Models (LLMs)

In recent years, the field of natural language processing has seen the emergence of Large Language Models (LLMs), which are trained under conditions with large model parameters, extensive data, and substantial computational resources. These models have achieved high performance across various tasks. It has been reported that the performance of these models improves according to a power law with the scale of training conditions [10], and they exhibit emergent capabilities, where performance significantly improves at a certain scale [22], highlighting new aspects not observed in conventional language models.

2.4   Multimodal Large Language Models (MLLMs)

When LLMs are extended to multiple modalities such as vision, they are referred to as Multimodal Large Language Models (MLLMs). To extend these models to visual modalities, visual encoders that convert visual information, such as images

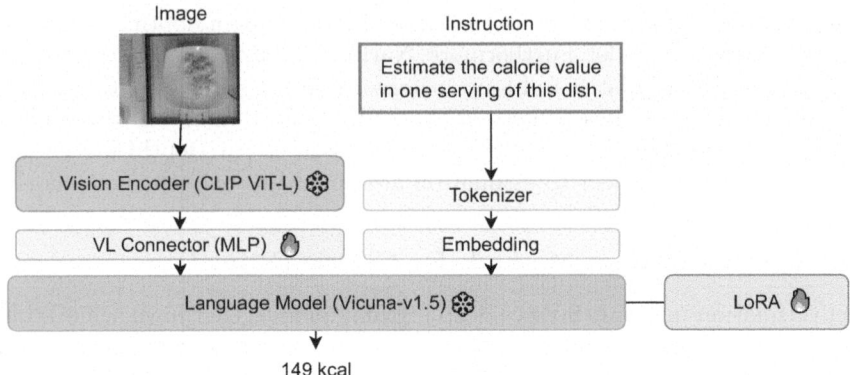

Fig. 1. Model architecture of CalorieLLaVA (based on LLaVA-v1.5)

or videos, into visual features are used. Flamingo [1] created a single model capable of handling various tasks related to images and videos by integrating visual features obtained from a visual encoder with textual features through a gated cross-attention layer. LLaVA [13] adopted a model structure that transforms visual features using a connector layer built with linear layers or MLPs, which are then fed into a LLM. It also employed a training framework called Visual Instruction Tuning, which used instruction-following data including visual information, to achieve high-quality task generalization performance related to images. Other models include BLIP-2 [11], which introduced Q-Former in the connector layer, and MiniGPT-4 [24] and InstructBLIP [4], which applied similar learning as Visual Instruction Tuning based on the same model structure.

In the domain of food, FoodLMM [23] has achieved SOTA performance across various food-related tasks, including caloric content estimation from food images. This study focuses specifically on improving the performance of caloric content estimation from food images.

3   Methods

In this study, we propose a framework called CalorieLLaVA. We first explain the method for estimating caloric content using MLLMs (Sect. 3.1), and then describe how to fine-tune them (Sect. 3.2).

3.1   Calorie Estimation Using MLLMs

We perform calorie estimation using MLLMs like LLaVA-v1.5 [12] (Fig. 1), and perform fine-tuning based on this model. The input image is encoded into visual features via the OpenAI CLIP ViT-L visual encoder [16]. These visual features are then transformed to match the dimension of text token embeddings through a two-layer MLP-based vision-language connector. Both the visual features and the text token embeddings are then fed into the LLM Vicuna-v1.5 [3], which produces the estimated calorie value as output. The content of the text instructions input to the LLM is designed to prompt the estimation of the calorie value from the food images.

3.2   Fine-Tuning MLLMs on Image-Caloric Data

In this study, we use the Nutrition5k [21] dataset for training and evaluating the model. This dataset, created by Google Research, is focused on nutritional understanding of food images and includes 3,265 top-down food images along with nutritional information, including caloric content. The dataset is split into 2,759 images for training and 506 images for testing, and we use the training split for this fine-tuning. To fine-tune the MLLM, we convert the training split of the dataset into an instruction-following format. The instruction-following format represents the instructions the model is supposed to follow and the expected responses. For this conversion, we prepare a text template that transforms the caloric content into an instruction-response format. We uniformly set the instruction as follows:

`Estimate the calorie value in one serving of this dish.`

The response is structured by enclosing the calorie value in [[]] followed by the word `calories`. By prompting the model to output calorie values in a single consistent format, we aim to make it easier to extract caloric content from text with regular expression.

The fine-tuning process involves training the vision-language connector and LLM using pairs of food images and calorie values converted into an instruction-response format. The LLM is fine-tuned using LoRA [9] for efficient adaptation with reduced computational overhead.

4   Experiments

4.1   Experiment Setting

We trained the LLaVA-7B and 13B models using the training set of the Nutrition5k and referred to the trained models as CalorieLLaVA-7B and 13B. The 6th and 5th epoch checkpoints were selected for CalorieLLaVA-7B and 13B respectively, based on monitoring the loss on the validation split using the model trained on the validation training split (Figs. 2 and 3).

During training, the AdamW optimization algorithm was used with a linear warmup and cosine decay of the learning rate, with a peak value of 2×10^{-4}. The rank for the LoRA matrix decomposition was set to 128, and the batch size was set to 64. The temperature parameter for text generation was set to 0, ensuring deterministic output of tokens. Additionally, data parallelism using the DeepSpeed [18] and memory optimization via ZeRO-3 [17] were implemented during training. The training was conducted on 4 × RTX 3090 for up to 10 epochs, taking approximately 5 h.

For models without fine-tuning including LLaVA and GPT-4o, we evaluated only the entries where the estimation was successfully completed, and the calorie value was correctly extracted. For cases where the calorie value could not be extracted with the temperature parameter set to 0, we adjusted the temperature parameter to 0.2 and repeated the same query up to five times to extract the calorie value. The entries that could not be extracted after these attempts were excluded from the evaluation. Specifically, 16, 4, and 28 entries were excluded from the evaluation datasets for LLaVA-7B, LLaVA-13B, and GPT-4V, respectively. Additionally, if the calorie estimation was output as a range, we used the average of the range as the estimated value.

4.2   Results of Calorie Estimation

Table 1 shows the results of calorie estimation on the test split of the Nutrition5k. The proposed model CalorieLLaVA achieved higher scores in mean absolute error (MAE) compared to the baseline Google-nutrition-monocular [21] and other MLLMs. It also achieved a better MAE score compared to the fine-tuned FoodLMM model. Furthermore, when comparing fine-tuned models, we observe that CalorieLLaVA-13B, with its larger number of parameters, outperforms the 7B model across all metrics.

According to the research on Nutrition5k [21], the mean absolute percentage error (MAPE) of nutritionists' estimations on Nutrition5k dataset is reported to be 41 %. In comparison, CalorieLLaVA-13B achieves a better score. This indicates that the estimation capability of CalorieLLaVA-13B surpasses that of human nutritionists. However, it should be noted that this result is based on evaluations conducted on a subset of the test split, and the test split used in this study does not perfectly match the one used in the Nutrition5k research.

4.3   Distribution of the Results

Figures 4 and 5 show the distribution of estimated calorie values by LLaVA-13B and CalorieLLaVA-13B. LLaVA-13B tends to make many inaccurate estimations, especially around 200 kcal. On the other hand, CalorieLLaVA-13B shows a significant reduction in incorrect estimations around that range, with more estimates concentrated in the intervals where the ground truth data is densely located. Figure 6 and Fig. 7 show that the correlation between estimated and actual values improved due to fine-tuning.

In these figures, the set of points where the true values and estimated values match is represented by red lines, while the 95 % confidence ellipses are shown in black. When comparing both the red lines and the confidence ellipses, we observe that the CalorieLLaVA-13B's predictions exhibit less variance. This is also supported by the higher correlation coefficient values for the CalorieLLaVA-13B. Additionally, in the scatter plot of LLaVA-13B, there are instances where the model estimates around 700 kcal and 180 kcal for true values of approximately 50 kcal and 900 kcal, respectively. In contrast, the scatter plot of the

Table 1. Results of calorie estimation

Method	MAE / kcal	MAPE / %	r
Google-nutrition-monocular [21]	70.6	26.1	-
LLaVA-7B	178.8	129.5	0.637
LLaVA-13B	177.1	92.8	0.656
GPT-4V	106.6	54.8	0.688
GPT-4o	82.7	46.7	0.817
FoodLMM FT [23]	67.3	**26.6**	-
CalorieLLaVA-7B (Ours)	74.2	41.5	0.927
CalorieLLaVA-13B (Ours)	**64.3**	39.8	**0.934**

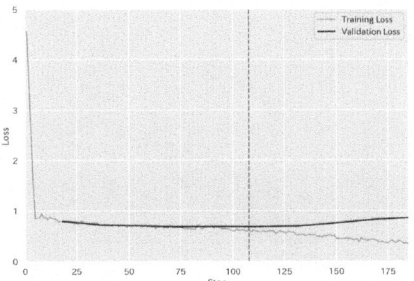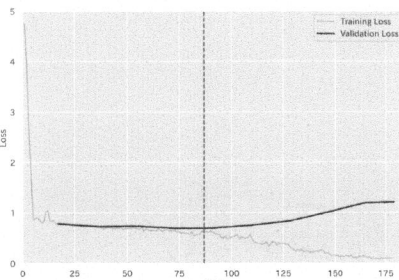

Fig. 2. Loss curves with respect to the number of training steps in CalorieLLaVA-7B training. Red line: selected checkpoint. (Color figure online)

Fig. 3. Loss curves with respect to the number of training steps in CalorieLLaVA-13B training. Red line: selected checkpoint. (Color figure online)

CalorieLLaVA-13B shows that such significant deviations, particularly in the lower true value ranges, are not present.

From these observations, we can conclude that the fine-tuned model provides more accurate calorie estimations.

Figures 8 to 10 represent the changes in the values of evaluation metrics on the test split as the number of training epochs increases. For MAE and MAPE, there is a tendency for the values to fluctuate and not decrease significantly even as the number of epochs increases. On the other hand, the correlation coefficient shows a tendency to decrease monotonically with the number of epochs up to about 5 epochs, which is particularly noticeable in CalorieLLaVA-13B. In contrast, the values of each evaluation metric for CalorieLLaVA-7B appear relatively unstable, with a temporary decline observed around the 5th epoch. Additionally, it is noted that CalorieLLaVA-7B achieves better scores in the first epoch (Fig. 9).

Figures 11 and 12 are examples of responses for calorie estimation by each model. For LLaVA-13B and GPT-4V without fine-tuning, the output includes both the process of calorie estimation and the estimated value. In contrast, for CalorieLLaVA-13B, the estimated value is directly outputted.

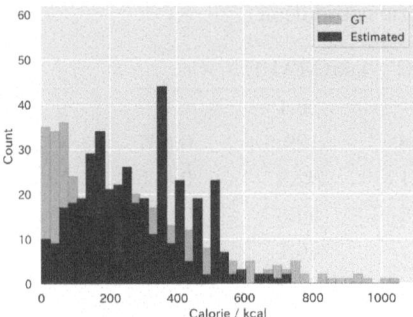

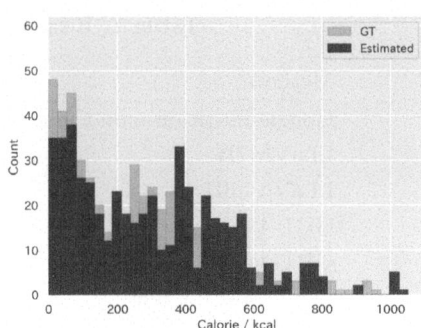

Fig. 4. Distribution of estimated calorie values by LLaVA-13B

Fig. 5. Distribution of estimated calorie values by CalorieLLaVA-13B

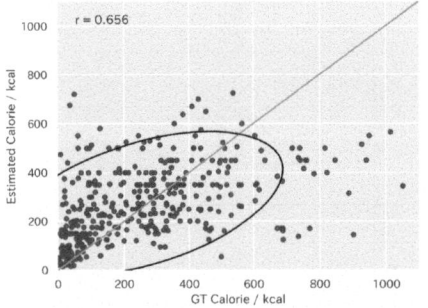

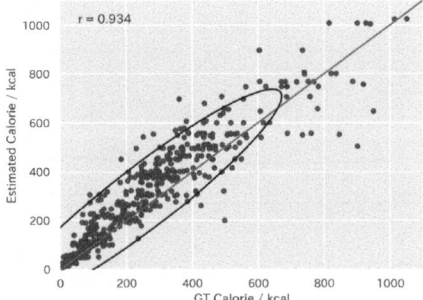

Fig. 6. Scatter plot of estimated calorie values by LLaVA-13B

Fig. 7. Scatter plot of estimated calorie values by CalorieLLaVA-13B

5   Discussion

In Sect. 4, we confirmed that increasing the number of training epochs during fine-tuning of MLLMs tends to improve or maintain the correlation coefficient scores. Additionally, the number of training samples in the Nutrition5k training split used in this study is around 2,700, which is relatively small compared to the number of data points used for Visual Instruction Tuning in the base model, LLaVA. Based on this, it can be said that when applying fine-tuning on a relatively small dataset for domain adaptation of MLLMs, increasing the number of training epochs is effective in improving the correlation between ground truth and estimated calories.

On the other hand, an excessive increase in the number of epochs was found to cause overfitting to the training split. In Figs. 2 and 3, the gap between the training and validation losses as the number of training steps increased was observed. Therefore, when increasing the number of epochs, it is important to monitor the validation loss during training and select appropriate checkpoints

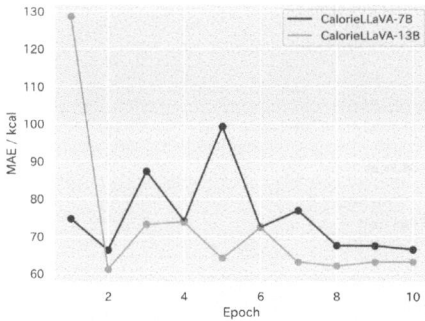
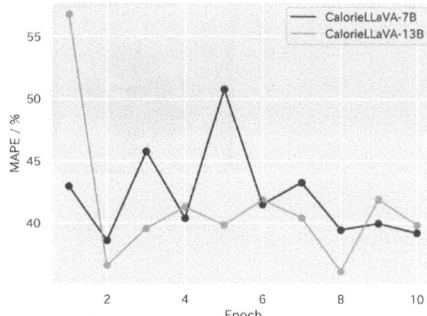

Fig. 8. Changes in MAE of calorie estimation results with the number of training epochs

Fig. 9. Changes in MAPE of calorie estimation results with the number of training epochs

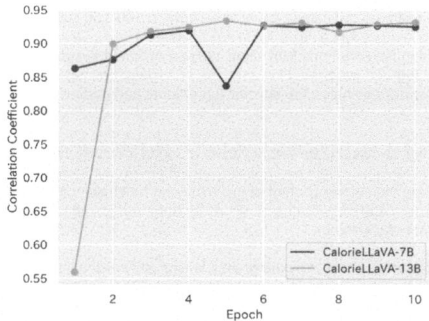

Fig. 10. Changes in correlation coefficient of calorie estimation results with the number of training epochs

using methods like early stopping to maintain the generalization performance of the model.

This trend is also confirmed by referencing other studies that applied fine-tuning to LLMs. Dinh *et al.* [5] applied LIFT (Language-Interfaced Fine-Tuning), a method for solving classification and regression tasks without changing the text interface, to LLMs and conducted analyses on their estimation performance and inductive bias. In this experiment, regression tasks on basic functions were evaluated. As a result, the relative absolute error (RAE) used as an evaluation metric improved or was maintained as the number of epochs increased. However, it was confirmed that from around 10 epochs, the validation error during training began to diverge from the training loss.

In this study, we referred to these results on training LLMs and selected checkpoints that did not exhibit overfitting to the training split during fine-tuning of MLLMs. As a future direction, it is promising to achieve higher performance by conducting a more extensive hyperparameter search, not limited

Answer: **164 kcal**

User | Estimate the calorie value in one serving of this dish.

LLaVA-13B | To estimate the calorie value of this dish, we need to consider the ingredients and their respective calorie counts. The dish consists of a salad, which typically contains a mix of vegetables, and a fruit salad with melon, strawberries, and blueberries.

1. Salad: The salad is made of lettuce, which is low in calories. Assuming the salad also contains other vegetables, we can estimate the calorie count to be around 100-200 calories.

2. Fruit salad: Melon is low in calories, while strawberries and blueberries are rich in nutrients and antioxidants. Assuming a serving of fruit salad contains 1\/2 cup of each fruit, we can estimate the calorie count to be around 100-150 calories.

Combining the salad and fruit salad, we can estimate the calorie value of one serving to be around **200-350 calories**. However, this is a rough estimate, and the actual calorie count may vary depending on the specific ingredients and portion sizes used in the dish.

GPT-4V | The image shows a plate with a variety of foods that include a leafy green salad, some fruit pieces (looks like melon and possibly strawberries), blueberries, and roasted potatoes. Estimating the calorie content of this meal can be challenging without knowing the exact quantities and any dressings or oils used, but I can provide a rough estimate based on typical serving sizes.

- Leafy greens: A cup of mixed greens is typically around [[10]] calories.
- Melon: A cup of diced melon is approximately [[60]] calories.
- Strawberries: A cup of strawberries is about [[50]] calories.
- Blueberries: A cup of blueberries comes to around [[85]] calories.
- Roasted potatoes: A half-cup of roasted potatoes can be roughly [[140]] calories, depending on the preparation.

Assuming this is a single serving and the fruits and potatoes are in half-cup portions, the total estimated calorie content for this plate might be around **[[345]] calories**. However, this is a rough estimate and the actual calorie content could be higher or lower.

CalorieLLaVA-13B (Ours) | **[[180]] calories**.

Fig. 11. Examples of responses by the MLLMs

to the number of epochs. Furthermore, verifying the impact of hyperparameter changes, including the number of epochs, on the performance of MLLMs in general domain adaptation is expected to accelerate the exploration of further methods.

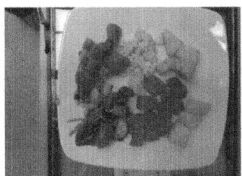

Answer: **339 kcal**

User	Estimate the calorie value in one serving of this dish.

LLaVA-13B

It is difficult to provide an accurate calorie estimate for this dish without knowing the specific ingredients and their quantities. However, we can make a rough estimate based on the types of food present in the image. The dish consists of a variety of foods, including fruits, vegetables, and possibly some meat.

Assuming that the dish contains a mix of fruits, vegetables, and meat, we can estimate the calorie value based on the average calorie content of each food group. For example, a serving of mixed vegetables might contain around 50-100 calories, a serving of mixed fruits might contain around 50-100 calories, and a serving of meat might contain around 100-200 calories.

Taking these estimates into account, a single serving of this dish could contain anywhere from **150 to 400 calories**. However, this is a rough estimate and the actual calorie value may vary depending on the specific ingredients and their quantities.

GPT-4V

The image shows a plate with a variety of foods that include what appears to be some bacon, scrambled eggs, pineapple, watermelon, honeydew melon, and a small salad with mixed vegetables such as carrots, tomatoes, and possibly some leafy greens.

To estimate the calorie content, I'll provide a rough estimate for each component:

- Bacon (2 strips): Approximately 80-100 calories
- Scrambled eggs (about 1 egg's worth): Approximately 90-100 calories
- Pineapple (1 small slice): Approximately 40 calories
- Watermelon (1 small slice): Approximately 30 calories
- Honeydew melon (1 small slice): Approximately 20 calories
- Mixed vegetables salad (small portion): Approximately 20-30 calories

Adding these up gives a total of approximately 280-320 calories. However, this is a rough estimate and actual calorie content can vary based on the exact serving sizes and preparation methods.

[[300]] calories

CalorieLLaVA-13B (Ours)

[[368]] calories.

Fig. 12. Examples of responses by the MLLMs

6 Conclusion

In this study, we verified the effectiveness of the approach using MLLMs for the task of estimating caloric content from food images. We created a model CalorieLLaVA by fine-tuning LLaVA, achieving performance that surpassed the baseline and contemporary MLLMs as evaluated on the Nutrition5k dataset.

Based on comparisons with recent methods, it is considered promising to introduce a monocular depth estimation model and apply multitask learning to models estimating caloric content based on special tokens and regression heads, like FoodLMM. Moreover, the Nutrition5k dataset used in this study includes only a limited range of food images within the food domain. The effectiveness of the method has not been fully verified for food domains representative of everyday meals, such as sushi or ramen, which are popular in Japan but not included in the dataset. Verification in these domains is crucial for the practical application of the method.

Acknowledgments. This work was supported by JSPS KAKENHI Grant Numbers, 22H00540 and 22H00548.

References

1. Alayrac, J.B., et al: Flamingo: a visual language model for few-shot learning. In: Advances in Neural Information Processing Systems, vol. 35, pp. 23716–23736 (2022)
2. Ando, Y., Ege, T., Cho, J., Yanai, K.: DepthCalorieCam: a mobile application for volume-based foodcalorie estimation using depth cameras. In: Proceedings of the 5th International Workshop on Multimedia Assisted Dietary Management, pp. 76–81 (2019)
3. Chiang, W.L., et al.: Vicuna: An open-source chatbot impressing GPT-4 with 90%* ChatGPT quality (2023). https://lmsys.org/blog/2023-03-30-vicuna/
4. Dai, W., et al.: InstructBLIP: Towards general-purpose vision-language models with instruction tuning. arXiv preprint arXiv:2305.06500 (2023)
5. Dinh, T., et al.: LIFT: Language-interfaced fine-tuning for non-language machine learning tasks. In: Advances in Neural Information Processing Systems, vol. 35, pp. 11763–11784 (2022)
6. Ege, T., Shimoda, W., Yanai, K.: A new large-scale food image segmentation dataset and its application to food calorie estimation based on grains of rice. In: Proceedings of ACMMM Workshop on Multimedia Assisted Dietary Management (2019)
7. Ege, T., Yanai, K.: Image-based food calorie estimation using knowledge on food categories, ingredients and cooking directions. In: Proceedings of the on Thematic Workshops of ACM Multimedia 2017, pp. 367–375 (2017)
8. Akpa, EAH., Suwa, H., Arakawa, Y., Yasumoto, K.: Smartphone-based food weight and calorie estimation method for effective food journaling. SICE J. Contr., Measure. Syst. Integr. **10**(5), 360–369 (2017)
9. Hu, E.J., et al.: LoRA: Low-rank adaptation of large language models. In: Proceedings of International Conference on Learning Representations (2022)
10. Kaplan, J., et al.: Scaling laws for neural language models. arXiv preprint arXiv:2001.08361 (2020)
11. Li, J., Li, D., Savarese, S., Hoi, S.: BLIP-2: bootstrapping language-image pretraining with frozen image encoders and large language models. In: Proceedings of International Conference on Machine Learning (2023)
12. Liu, H., Li, C., Li, Y., Lee, Y.J.: Improved baselines with visual instruction tuning. arXiv preprint arXiv:2310.03744 (2023)
13. Liu, H., Li, C., Wu, Q., Lee, Y.J.: Visual instruction tuning. In: Advances in Neural Information Processing Systems (2023)

14. Naritomi, S., Yanai, K.: Hungry Networks: 3d mesh reconstruction of a dish and a plate from a single dish image for estimating food volume. In: Proceedigns of the 2nd ACM International Conference on Multimedia in Asia (2021)
15. Okamoto, K., Yanai, K.: An automatic calorie estimation system of food images on a smartphone. In: Proceedings of the 2nd International Workshop on Multimedia Assisted Dietary Management (2016)
16. Radford, A., et al.: Learning transferable visual models from natural language supervision. In: Proceedings of International Conference on Machine Learning, pp. 8748–8763 (2021)
17. Rajbhandari, S., Rasley, J., Ruwase, O., He, Y.: ZeRO: Memory optimizations toward training trillion parameter models. In: SC20: International Conference for High Performance Computing, Networking, Storage and Analysis, pp. 1–16 (2020)
18. Rasley, J., Rajbhandari, S., Ruwase, O., He, Y.: DeepSpeed: System optimizations enable training deep learning models with over 100 billion parameters. In: Proceedings of the 26th ACM SIGKDD International Conference on Knowledge Discovery & Data Mining, pp. 3505–3506 (2020)
19. Simonyan, K., Zisserman, A.: Very deep convolutional networks for large-scale image recognition. arXiv preprint arXiv:1409.1556 (2014)
20. Tanno, R., Ege, T., Yanai, K.: AR DeepCalorieCam V2: Food calorie estimation with CNN and AR-based actual size estimation. In: Proceedings of the 24th ACM Symposium on Virtual Reality Software and Technology (2018)
21. Thames, Q., et al.: Nutrition5k: Towards automatic nutritional understanding of generic food. In: Proceedings of IEEE Computer Vision and Pattern Recognition, pp. 8903–8911 (2021)
22. Wei, J., et al.: Emergent abilities of large language models. arXiv preprint arXiv:2206.07682 (2022)
23. Yin, Y., et al.: FoodLMM: A versatile food assistant using large multi-modal model. arXiv preprint arXiv:2312.14991 (2023)
24. Zhu, D., Chen, J., Shen, X., Li, X., Elhoseiny, M.: MiniGPT-4: Enhancing vision-language understanding with advanced large language models. arXiv preprint arXiv:2304.10592 (2023)

Enhancing FKG.in: Automating Indian Food Composition Analysis

Saransh Kumar Gupta[1]([✉])(iD), Lipika Dey[1](iD), Partha Pratim Das[1](iD),
Geeta Trilok-Kumar[1](iD), and Ramesh Jain[2](iD)

[1] Ashoka University, Sonipat, India
{saransh.gupta,lipika.dey,partha.das,geeta.kumar}@ashoka.edu.in
[2] UCI Institute for Future Health, Irvine, UC, USA
jain@ics.uci.edu
https://www.ashoka.edu.in/, https://futurehealth.uci.edu/

Abstract. This paper presents a novel approach to compute food composition data for Indian recipes using a knowledge graph for Indian food (FKG.in) and LLMs. The primary focus is to provide a broad overview of an automated food composition analysis workflow and describe its core functionalities: nutrition data aggregation, food composition analysis, and LLM-augmented information resolution. This workflow aims to complement FKG.in and iteratively supplement food composition data from verified knowledge bases. Additionally, this paper highlights the challenges of representing Indian food and accessing food composition data digitally. It also reviews three key sources of food composition data: the Indian Food Composition Tables, the Indian Nutrient Databank, and the Nutritionix API. Furthermore, it briefly outlines how users can interact with the workflow to obtain diet-based health recommendations and detailed food composition information for numerous recipes. We then explore the complex challenges of analyzing Indian recipe information across dimensions such as structure, multilingualism, and uncertainty as well as present our ongoing work on LLM-based solutions to address these issues. The methods proposed in this workshop paper for AI-driven knowledge curation and information resolution are application-agnostic, generalizable, and replicable for any domain.

Keywords: Food Computing · Knowledge Engineering · Semantic Reasoning · Large Language Models · Nutrition Informatics · Indian Food

Supported by Ashoka Mphasis Lab.

Supplementary Information The online version contains supplementary material available at https://doi.org/10.1007/978-3-031-88217-3_6.

S. Palaiahnakote et al. (Eds.): ICPR 2024 Workshops, LNCS 15617, pp. 76–90, 2025.
https://doi.org/10.1007/978-3-031-88217-3_6

1   Introduction

Food is a fundamental necessity of life and greatly determines its quality. A healthy relationship with food develops when people enjoy their favorite dishes without compromising their health. However, too often, there is a wide gap between what people love to eat and what they are advised to consume for their well-being. This discrepancy can be traced to humans' multidimensional relationship with food, shaped by their evolutionary, social, and economic history. It reflects a view of food that extends beyond its role as a mere energy source and essential nutrients for sustenance. Historically, food choices have been largely affected by availability (climate, geography, water proximity), accessibility (political structures, legal frameworks, budget constraints), trade (industrialization, cultural exchange, economic status), customs (social hierarchies, religious practices, festivals), and technology (processing, preservation, transportation). However, with rising lifestyle diseases, there is a need to refocus on eating habits that support both mental and physical wellness. For holistic well-being, understanding the nutritional composition of preferred foods is essential. This has spurred the development of health applications with extensive food knowledge bases tailored to diverse ethnic groups.

While this tragedy of food affects most of the world, the situation in India is especially dire, with diverse malnutrition issues ranging from stunting and undernourishment to overweight and obesity, compounded by widespread nutritional insecurity [22]. Eating right remains a largely neglected challenge for most of the Indian population i.e. approximately one-fifth of the world's total. This is partly due to the country's historical struggle with severe food insecurity, where the focus has largely been on eating sufficiently rather than eating right. However, the larger issue lies in the absence of a consolidated, dynamic, and accessible knowledge base encompassing various aspects of Indian food. Although traditional Indian food, especially Indian meals, has a reputation for being balanced and sustainable, much of this knowledge remains undocumented or inadequately recorded. Additionally, there is a lack of comprehensive food composition tables necessary for accurate food composition analysis. As a result, most health applications used by the Indian population are unable to provide reliable, personalized, and balanced recommendations that cater to the Indian palette.

In this paper, we present our work on building a food knowledge graph using Indian recipes curated from diverse sources, enhancing it with nutrient information, and building an automated food composition analysis workflow. Engineering such a knowledge graph and sourcing information from recipe websites and cookbooks involves addressing several linguistic challenges - including multilingualism - such as entity and relationship name resolution, structural differences in the recipe information presented across sources, and uncertainties in it. Other major challenges arise from the gaps and incompleteness of food composition tables owing to the vast diversity and complexity of Indian food, inadequate recipe documentation of recipes, and the high cost of analytical experiments to empirically generate food composition data. This paper builds upon our earlier work [8], which introduced the knowledge graph (FKG.in) designed to store Indian recipes and their ingredients alongside numerous descriptive properties.

The novelty of the proposed work lies in the innovative use of Large Language Models (LLMs) to address structural and multilingual challenges, as well as the inherent uncertainties in recipes. A series of prompts are directed at the LLM, with the recipe provided as context, to extract reliable information about recipes, ingredients, their descriptors, and their measurements. This information is combined with food composition tables to determine the nutritional composition of recipes. While we have observed that the quality of results obtained can be further improved by incorporating additional details such as cooking techniques, cookware, and cooking time, the information curated thus far already provides a valuable source for knowledge discovery about Indian recipes. Additionally, we demonstrate how this knowledge graph can be leveraged to generate diet-based health recommendations and recipe suggestions.

The rest of the paper is organized as follows. Section 2 presents an overview of the work done in food knowledge graphs and personal digital health applications. Section 3 presents the unique challenges around consolidating and estimating nutritional information for Indian food, especially recipes. Section 4 briefly describes FKG.in for additional context. Section 5 compares three key sources of food composition data for Indian cuisine, their strengths, and gaps. Section 6 describes the Nutrition Data Aggregator (NDA) agent. Section 7 presents the challenges in analyzing recipe information along the lines of structure, multilingualism, and uncertainty and details the LLM-Augmented Information Resolution (LAIR) agent and its attempts to solve some of these challenges. Section 8 describes the automated food composition workflow and the Food Composition Analysis (FCA) agent. Section 9 presents some results. Section 10 concludes with a note on a few limitations of this work and future directions.

2 Related Work

Recently, individuals in urban regions in India (as in many other countries) have become more conscious of the nutritional composition of their food and have actively started adopting healthier lifestyles. This shift is driven by growing awareness of physical and mental well-being, as well as the rising prevalence and escalating threat of diet-related diseases such as obesity, hypertension, and diabetes in India [29]. This is increasingly being facilitated through technology and the application of scientific knowledge about food, health, nutrition, and behavior wherein notions like Personalized Health Navigators (PHN) [3,12,21] and Personalized Digital Health (PDH) [13,14] have emerged as key areas for research, development, and practical implementation.

Food composition refers to the nutritional information of food items, including macronutrients (carbohydrates, proteins, fats), micronutrients (vitamins, minerals), and other essential food components (fiber, water, bioactive compounds). Several applications and APIs, such as Edamam [5], Fitterfly [6], Healthify Me [10], My Fitness Pal [20], Nutritionix [23], Poshan Atlas [24], and

USDA FoodData Central [28] already provide nutritional information to their users. However, advances in food composition analysis technologies, personalized dietary recommendations, and the adoption of PHN/PDH are possible only with a digital representation of food, nutrients, and all their constituents. Hence, research at the intersection of food and health is gaining importance in areas like dietary management, precision nutrition, food safety, and food anthropology.

Many food ontologies and food knowledge graphs have been developed to support a variety of food computing applications [17–19]. However, with the ubiquitous rise of unreliable and unverified information on the Internet - further amplified by chatbots built on LLMs - it has become imperative to combat food and nutrition misinformation using the latest technological advances. In response, several initiatives have emerged to address issues related to food, nutrition, and health such as PIPS [2], FoodOn [4], FoodKG [9], FOODS [25], and WikiFCD [26]. In the Indian context, notable contributions include the Indian Food Composition Tables [16], the Indian Nutrient Databank [30], *Nutritional Profile Estimation in Cooking Recipes* [15], and *Dish detection in food platters* [7]. Building on this momentum, FKG.in [8] represents our effort to build a comprehensive, reliable, and granular knowledge graph for Indian food with associated intelligence, automation, and scalability to address some of these challenges.

3   Challenges in Indian Food Composition Analysis

India is a country of remarkable diversity. Climate, topography, culture, language, agricultural practices, availability of local ingredients, and economic conditions vary significantly every few kilometers, distinctly shaping food consumption patterns. It is also home to a vast array of cuisines, where the defining characteristics are often rooted in geographical, historical, religious, or economic contexts. Recipes from various Indian cuisines reflect some of these characteristics but not sufficiently. Designing an ontology and building a knowledge graph for Indian food necessitates careful consideration of these and other factors. Below, we outline key challenges in Indian food composition analysis:

1. **Structure:** Indian recipes typically lack a standard format for describing ingredients, their measures, size, state of processing, form, etc. This inconsistency makes it difficult to extract essential details and descriptors of ingredients accurately, which are crucial for precise food composition analysis.
2. **Multilingualism:** Ingredients are known by different names across the country, with recipes using English, vernacular, and colloquial terms. These names may appear in Roman or Indian scripts and often have varying phonetic spellings, regional dialects, and code-mixing. Such variations complicate straightforward lookups in static food composition tables. Additionally, homonyms and semantic ambiguities, such as *saag* meaning different greens across regions, require context-aware resolution in food composition analysis.

3. **Uncertainty in Ingredient Measures:** Indian cooking often eschews precise measurements, relying instead on ambiguous terms (e.g., one small *katori* (bowl), 2 large spoons). Sometimes, no measure is specified for common ingredients and spices assumed to be familiar and regularly used (e.g., ginger-garlic paste, *jeera* (cumin) powder). Such imprecision greatly impacts nutrient computation when key ingredient units and quantities are missing.
4. **Uncertainty in Nature of Ingredients:** Since recipes often lack standardized formats or guidelines, they frequently list generic ingredients (e.g., 1 cup oil for frying) rather than specifying their particular type. As different oils have different compositions, this also affects nutrition calculations. In this work, default labels are applied wherever possible, based on common knowledge of Indian cooking and cuisine. E.g., the knowledge that mustard oil is used for cooking fish in *Bengali* cuisine or groundnut oil is used in *Gujarati* cuisine can be assumed in the absence of more specific details.

4   FKG.in: A Knowledge Graph for Indian Food

Indian food, especially meals, primarily consists of cooked dishes. Hence, recipes serve as its core and are instrumental in building the Indian food knowledge graph (FKG.in) [8]. FKG.in draws inspiration from FoodOn [4] and FoodKG [9], adapting these frameworks wherever necessary to suit the Indian context. It aims to capture essential properties of Indian food in terms of culinary language, cooking variations, and precision nutrition, including, but not limited to, elements such as meals, recipes, ingredient details, cooking methods, cookware, and dietary labels. The design principles followed a modular and flexible approach to knowledge curation. To address linguistic challenges including multilingualism as well as inherent uncertainties in Indian recipes across diverse sources, we employed LLMs quite extensively. In the following sections, we discuss three verified food composition data sources and how FKG.in is enhanced by incorporating nutritional information from them through an automated workflow.

5   Sources of Nutritional Information for Indian Food

Since we could not find a single comprehensive and open-access source for obtaining nutritional information for Indian food items, we have used multiple sources as listed below along with their unique characteristics, strengths, and gaps:

1. **Indian Food Composition Table (IFCT, 2017):** This comprehensive resource [16] was developed by the *Indian Council of Medical Research-National Institute of Nutrition* (ICMR-NIN) in 2017 and provides detailed information about the nutritional composition of various food items commonly consumed in India. It also provides scientific names, food groups, dietary tags (e.g., vegetarian, eggetarian), over 150 nutrient and food component data points for 528 food items, and common names in 18 Indian vernacular languages for many of them. However, while it includes a wide array

of food items, it remains inconsistent and incomplete. E.g., 3 potato variants are found in IFCT viz. 'potato, brown skin, big', 'potato, brown skin, small', and 'potato, red skin' but the food composition data for 'boiled potatoes' is missing. Similarly, both regular and roasted variants of vermicelli are found in IFCT but the roasted variant for groundnuts and the milled variant of Bengal gram i.e. *besan* (Bengal gram flour) is missing. IFCT also misses out on some crucial ingredients that are commonly used in modern India such as cheese, tofu, butter, mayonnaise, noodles, broccoli, salt, etc., and misses some common nutrient data points such as Iodine and Vitamin B12. For all the oils and *ghee* (clarified butter), IFCT does not provide information about Energy, Cholesterol, and many important micronutrients.

2. **Indian Nutrient Databank (INDB, 2024):** This data repository [30] was built by *Anvaad Solutions* in 2024 and it builds on IFCT-2017 to fill in many of its gaps. For instance, it includes broccoli, roasted groundnuts, *besan*, cheese, noodles, salt, etc. It brings in food composition data for both raw ingredients and their variants from multiple sources viz. ICMR-NIN IFCT-2004 and nutrient databases from the United Kingdom [27] and the United States [28] in that order of priority making the total number of individual food items available in INDB 1095. INDB has also curated a vocabulary of common measurement units for both ingredients (e.g., tablespoon, pinch, sprig) and recipes (e.g., plate, bowl, slice) and their mapping to weights in grams for some of these common units. Notably, INDB also includes many complex ingredients such as *garam masala* (a blend of ground spices), tomato ketchup, and *rasam* (tamarind-tomato soup) powder which themselves follow recipe instructions and provides a detailed food composition table for 1014 unique and 'standard' Indian recipes which were sourced from 2 books on Indian cooking and selected recipe blogs. However, an issue with the INDB database is that many nutrient data points are not available for all the items. Only 38 out of the IFCT-2017's 150+ data points feature in INDB for all 1095 ingredients. INDB also does not include food composition information about branded or packaged food items yet. Additionally, while INDB provides some local names for recipes, it does not provide the scientific names, food groups, dietary tags, and vernacular names for the newly added ingredients.

3. **Nutritionix (2010):** This nutrition database [23] offers food composition details for thousands of branded, restaurant, and generic food items. While it caters primarily to the food items in the U.S., it includes a reasonable number of Indian food items as well, likely owing to the popularity of Indian cuisine. Most notably, it includes processed, form, and size variants of several ingredients that IFCT and INDB do not sufficiently include. E.g., chopped spinach and minced garlic are found in addition to spinach and garlic as well as boiled potato and steamed tofu are found in addition to potato and tofu in the Nutritionix database. It is important to note here that Nutritionix may not always give the most accurate results for Indian food as it is primarily built on top of USDA whereas the nutritional content of food varies depending on the geographic and climate conditions in which it is produced. In this light, only the IFCT data captures the nutrient information of Indian food items

accurately as it compositely samples each food item from six different regions covering the entire country and averages them [16].

The above discussion highlights the uniqueness and inadequacies of IFCT, INDB, and Nutritionix. In the next section, we present an automated workflow designed to dynamically aggregate the nutrient information for Indian food items (ingredients and recipes) from them. The proposed workflow enhances the previously described knowledge graph, FKG.in, by incorporating the food composition data into it at scale. Additionally, it creates an enhanced food composition table by consolidating the information from three reliable sources.

6   Nutrition Data Aggregation

In this section, we describe the design of the Nutrition Data Aggregator (NDA) agent, that enhances FKG.in with an aggregated food composition table, named FKG.in-FCT. For any recipe, once its ingredient names and measurements are extracted from the source, the NDA agent checks IFCT, INDB, and Nutritionix, in that order, to obtain nutritional information from them, if available. All ingredients newly encountered are added to FKG.in-FCT, resulting in a consolidated food composition table, that is also enriched with multilingual information about the ingredients. For each ingredient, it also stores information about its different variants along the axes of forms (e.g., seeds, powder, or paste), processing steps (e.g., boiled, roasted, or steamed), and size (e.g., small, medium, large). When an ingredient is missing from both IFCT and INDB, an API call to Nutritionix adds both the ingredient as well as its nutrient information to FKG.in-FCT. This allows FKG.in-FCT to include various ingredient variants commonly used in Indian recipes but not present in IFCT and INDB, significantly expanding the list of ingredients. The enhanced FKG.in-FCT ensures uniformity of scale across sources with the appropriate unit and serving size conversions.

Admittedly, significant limitations remain in achieving precise nutritional estimates. Firstly, the number of ingredients (with variants) used in Indian cuisine is countable but the number of recipes is virtually infinite, making a detailed analysis of numerous cooked samples impractical, especially in India's diverse culinary context. Secondly, many of Nutritionix's data points are accurate for American variants of ingredients but can only approximate their Indian counterparts. Additionally, in rare cases, approximations may arise because of the form in which an ingredient is used in a recipe. E.g., singhara (water chestnut) flour is missing from all three sources, so the nutrient values of the fruit are used as a proxy. Lastly, cooking is known to reduce nutrients, yet due to the lack of data on retention and yield factors for Indian ingredients and cooking methods, such adjustments could not be performed. The proposed workflow streamlines food composition analysis for the rapidly growing and continuously evolving repertoire of Indian recipes in FKG.in, adopting a trade-off in precision to enable large-scale automated calculations. Some of the challenges mentioned above, along with managing missing food items and leveraging LLMs to resolve uncertainties, are explored further in the next section.

7 LLM-Augmented Information Resolution

Despite using three reliable food composition tables, several ingredients used in Indian recipes could not be found in them. In some cases, ingredients were present in the databases but could not be found easily due to linguistic variations. Additionally, certain Indian food names could not be directly mapped to their equivalents in Nutritionix. LLMs were employed as a tool to navigate these difficulties. While it is well-known that LLMs may hallucinate, and our experience confirms that they cannot always be fully trusted for nutrient information, we assert that LLMs can play a crucial role in mitigating challenges of extracting information from unstructured recipe texts, resolving food or ingredient name ambiguities arising from multilingualism, and addressing quantitative uncertainties when recipe units and ingredient measures lack specificity and precision. With appropriate prompts, LLMs proved to be surprisingly effective at resolving many of these issues. We have developed an LLM-Augmented Information Resolution (LAIR) agent using OpenAI's GPT-3.5 Turbo[1] to process the recipe and ingredient information, leveraging prompt engineering to fine-tune the results as needed. The LAIR agent employs LLMs for both pre-processing as well as post-processing tasks to effectively carry out the following activities:

1. **Recipe Language Translation:** We collect recipes from a range of sources including recipe blogs, cookbooks, and Wikipedia, and also accept them as user inputs. Some of these recipes are written in vernacular Indian scripts such as *Hindi*, *Bengali*, or *Tamil* and require transliteration to Roman script for their assimilation into the FKG.in. The LAIR agent uses LLMs for transliteration as well as translation and gets reasonably good results.
2. **Recipe Format Normalization:** Recipe sources use varying formats for organizing recipes wherein cooking instructions may be presented and formatted differently, attributes may be mentioned using inconsistent or missing labels, and the recipe descriptions may contain information that could be useful for food composition analysis. We use LLMs to extract relevant information from recipes such as ingredient details, cooking instructions, category tags, cooking time, etc., and normalize them as per a standard format in JSON for them to be added to FKG.in in a streamlined manner.
3. **Ingredient Format Normalization:** Recipe sources also vary in detailing the list of ingredients. E.g., '2 cups boiled *aloo* (potatoes) (medium-sized), chopped' and ' kg chopped medium potatoes to be taken after boiling them' refer to the same ingredient referent approximately[2]. In this step, LLMs are instructed to singularize, normalize and segment the ingredient details such as their names, variant descriptors, quantities, and units, and store them in a unified JSON format as {"ingredient": "potato", "form": "chopped", "process": "boiled", "size": "medium", "quantity": "2", "unit": "cups"}.
4. **Ingredient Name Resolution:** Multilingualism leads to the same ingredients being mentioned across various sources with different identifiers. E.g., a

---

[1] https://platform.openai.com/docs/models.
[2] Assuming a cup is 240 ml and ignoring the ingredient density variations.

potato may be mentioned as *alu* (*Hindi*), *bateka* (*Gujarati*), and *oalu* (*Kashmiri*). Quantitative variations like 'whole ginger', and 'an inch of ginger' are also encountered, which add to the difficulty of food composition analysis. LLM helps us effectively remove the redundancies and normalize the non-vernacular aliases to the preferred label while ensuring that the important descriptors of form, processing, and size are not removed in the process.

5. **Ingredient Category Assignment:** FKG.in stores ingredients in hierarchical subcategories such as RootOrTuberousVegetable, MeatFromChicken, ProcessedMushroom, etc. For every unique ingredient, we infer their potential categories as per our ontology design using LLMs. E.g., potato will be assigned the category RootOrTuberousVegetable (Ingredient -> PlantOriginFood -> PrimaryFoodCommodityOfPlantOrigin -> Vegetable -> RootOrTuberousVegetable) whereas mushroom pickle will be assigned the category ProcessedMushroom (Ingredient -> FungusOrigin -> SecondaryFoodCommodityOfFungusOrigin -> ProcessedMushroom).

6. **Ingredient Unit Normalization:** Often same units are referred to by different identifiers. E.g., a tablespoon is commonly found to be written across sources such as *tablespoons*, *TABLESPOON*, *T.*, *TB. tbsp.*, *Tblsp.*, *tbs.*, *tbl.*, *tbls.*, *a large spoon*, etc. We prompt the LLM to normalize ingredient units by converting them to lowercase, singular form, and standard full names, exemplifying how all the above units should be normalized to *tablespoon*.

7. **Ingredient Measurement Resolution:** Often the units mentioned are associated with specific ingredients and refer to a specific weight per unit. E.g., garlic is commonly mentioned with the units 'clove' or 'segment' (3–7 g), as well as 'bulb' or 'head' (40–80 g) depending on the garlic size. On the other hand, certain units apply to multiple ingredients. E.g., 'pods' are

⊕ **Ingredients and Their Equivalent Measures in Grams**

1. केले का स्टेम: Banana stem - 1 stem - 200 grams (approximate)
2. काला चना: Black chickpeas - 1 cup - 200 grams
3. नारियल: Coconut, grated - 2 tbsp - 20 grams
4. जीरा: Cumin seeds - 2 tsp - 8 grams
5. धनिये के बीज: Coriander seeds - 2 tsp - 8 grams
6. लाल मिर्च पाउडर: Red chili powder - 1.5 tsp - 3 grams
7. प्याज: Onions - 2 (medium) - 150 grams
8. लहसुन: Garlic - 1 clove - 5 grams
9. कड़ी पत्ता: Curry leaves - to taste - 2 grams (approximate)
10. नमक: Salt - to taste - not converted
11. तेल: Oil - to taste - not converted
12. हरा धनिया: Fresh coriander - a little - 10 grams
13. हरी मिर्च: Green chili - 1 - 2 grams
14. निम्बू का रस: Lemon juice - 1 tsp - 5 grams

Sample Ingredient Information Processed by the LAIR Agent

Input:

2 cups boiled *aloo* (medium-sized), chopped

Output:

{
    "ingredient": "*aloo* (potato)",
    "form": "chopped",
    "process": "boiled",
    "size": "medium",
    "quantity": "2",
    "unit": "cup",
    "weight_in_grams": "480",
    "llm_estimated_weight_in_grams": "300"
}

Fig. 1. A sample ChatGPT response to a user prompt for translating ingredient names from Hindi to English and estimating their weights in grams

Fig. 2. A sample LAIR agent output for segmenting, formatting, and normalizing ingredient information, and estimating its weight in grams

frequently used with cardamom, vanilla, and tamarind. To resolve such issues with ingredient units, we use a combination of *Dietary Measurement Ontology* that contains mapping rules built on top of INDB's unit vocabulary and complemented by LLM. This helps us store standard unit conversions (e.g., 1 teaspoon = 5g, 1 cup = 48 teaspoon), map ingredient and variant-specific units (e.g., bulb/head for a whole garlic, clove/segment for a single section of garlic), and translate ingredient variant-specific units to other units (e.g., 1 bulb of garlic = 10 cloves, 1 clove of garlic (minced) = 1 teaspoon,). Such mapping rules help us convert both standard and inexact units to their respective weights in grams dynamically. We also use the unit information alongside ingredients in the recipes to extend the unit vocabulary by iteratively validating it with a human-in-the-loop. Occasionally, when an ingredient quantity is mentioned as a range such as 2–4 cups or 4–6 cloves, we average it, and if required, we convert the fractions to their decimal counterparts for smoother processing. It is important to note that when the recipe mentions the exact ingredient weight alongside measurements, we use it directly as it is already resolved. The running example JSON gets updated to { "ingredient": "potato", "form": "chopped", "process": "boiled", "size": "medium", "quantity": "2", "unit: "cup", "weight_in_grams": "480"}.

8. **Ingredient Weight Estimation:** Density is commonly ignored while calculating the weight of an ingredient in grams wherein the measurement containers often use milliliters and assume a convenient translation of 1gm = 1mL for all ingredients, including solids. We have found a more accurate representation in [1] but only for a few ingredients. The lack of a more complete data source often makes it difficult to estimate the weight of an ingredient from both the standard (cup, tablespoon) as well as inexact (glass, handful) measurement units to grams. We also use LLMs to estimate the weight in grams for each ingredient based on their quantity and unit such that the example JSON mentioned above gets updated to { "ingredient": "potato", "form": "chopped", "process": "boiled", "size": "medium", "quantity": "2", "unit": "cup", "weight_in_grams": "480", "llm_estimated_weight_in_grams": "300"}. We have observed that LLM mostly estimates this weight reasonably well by taking both the density and retention factor of the ingredient implicitly into account although with occasional errors. This helps calculate recipe nutritional information by deriving unit mapping-based weights when possible and using LLM-estimated weights as alternatives when necessary.

9. **Recipe Dietary Label Tagging:** In generating and improving diet-based health recommendations, it is often helpful to automatically infer whether certain dietary tags apply to recipes along the axes of dietary practices (e.g., vegetarian, pescatarian), health labels (e.g., keto-friendly, low-sugar), and allergen labels (e.g., contains-dairy, contains-peanuts). We have curated a list of 60+ such tags, formalized them into several rules, and designed a pipeline to assign these rule-based tags to recipes based on the presence, categories, and measurements of ingredients. This step extensively uses the earlier mentioned LLM-assigned category and the calculated or estimated ingredient weights to infer the appropriate dietary tags applicable to a recipe.

10. **Recipe Latent Information Inference:** Occasionally, it is useful to know which recipes are related and which ingredients are related in addition to knowing which ingredients can substitute other ones to recommend health-based food alternatives. We use LLMs to extract these and other latent details from recipe sources as they are often present in the recipe description and notes but not explicitly mentioned in the recipe cards. We prompt LLM to ensure that the information for these attributes is only extracted from the given recipe source and not inferred from elsewhere to ensure soundness although LLM tends to answer such questions quite well on its own also.

8   Automated Food Composition Analysis Workflow

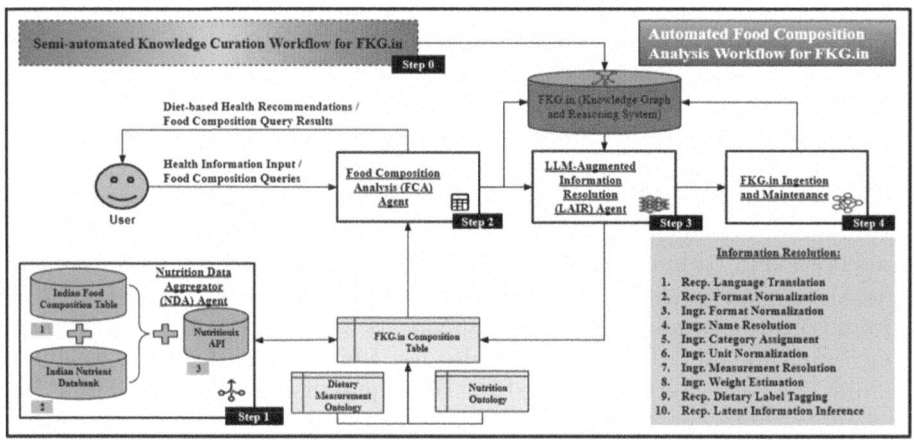

Fig. 3. Automated Food Composition Analysis Workflow for FKG.in

Figure 3 presents the automated food composition analysis system. At its heart is the Food Composition Analysis (FCA) agent which links the knowledge graph of Indian food i.e. FKG.in, the aggregated Indian food composition table i.e. FKG.in-FCT, and the LLM-Augmented Information Resolution (LAIR) agent, as well as provides an easy-to-use interface for interaction with users. The individual components and their roles in the workflow are explained below:

– **Step 0: Knowledge Curation -** This includes a set of steps for initializing FKG.in with data from reliable food ontologies, vocabularies, and various sources of recipes. The LLM-augmented information extraction process along with data validation, inconsistency resolution, and data ingestion steps are presented in detail in [8]. The resulting knowledge graph is stored in an OWL format and implemented using Ontotext's GraphDB. At the end of this workflow, FKG.in stores the list of ingredients with their respective descriptors and measurements for all the recipes exactly as mentioned in their sources. At this point, the recipes do not contain any information about their food composition unless it is explicitly given in the source.

– **Step 1: Nutrition Data Aggregation (NDA) Agent -** The NDA agent and the FKG.in-FCT creation process were described in the earlier section.

– **Step 2: Food Composition Analysis (FCA) Agent -** The primary role of the FCA agent is to derive the nutrient and food composition of a recipe based on its ingredients and their quantities. For each dish stored in FKG.in, it uses the FKG.in-FCT to look up ingredients, scale the nutrient values proportionally, and sum them up to calculate the recipe's food composition data. Cooking process transformations are not accounted for at this stage as [30] found the differences for Indian food with and without retention factors to be small, with notable losses in vitamin C, potassium, and phosphorus.

The FCA agent is also designed to provide on-demand nutritional information for food items not stored in the knowledge graph. Users can directly interact with the FCA agent via an intuitive interface. For a search involving a dish or recipe without ingredient details, the FCA agent first queries its local knowledge base FKG.in and FKG.in-FCT, using fuzzy matching techniques to find the closest match. It then outputs the nutritional information based on the stored recipe details. A recipe input with details of ingredients and their measures follows the same steps described earlier.

In addition to dynamically calculating food composition values, the FCA agent provides users with simple, diet-based health recommendations as per [11]. These recommendations are tailored based on inputs such as personal information (age, gender, weight, height), physiological stage (infant, child, adolescent, adult, elderly, pregnancy, lactation), activity (type, duration, frequency, intensity, calories burned), dietary preferences (food choices, 24-hour dietary recall, hydration, allergies), and weight goals (gain, lose, maintain).

– **Step 3: LLM-Augmented Information Resolution (LAIR) Agent -** Since recipes are curated from multiple sources, they are quite unstructured. From ingredient names to their units of measurement, nothing is assumed to be available in a standardized way. The LAIR agent works to take in an input, normalize it, handle multilingualism, resolve uncertainties, and obtain weight measurements to calculate nutrient and food composition information. In rare cases, when the FCA agent encounters recipes with ingredients missing from FKG.in-FCT, the LAIR agent also retrieves their nutritional information from public sources, marking it as LLM-sourced in FKG.in-FCT.

– **Step 4: FKG.in Ingestion and Maintenance -** This step ensures that all information obtained for the recipes and ingredients in Step 3, including the ones from public sources, is appropriately ingested in and appended to FKG.in. This is done by following the same soundness assessment and inconsistency resolution approaches that apply to the knowledge curation workflow in Step 0. Since the verification process is manual and time-consuming, there is a time lag between ingesting the information in the knowledge base and its availability for food composition analysis.

9 Current Status of FKG.in

Figure 4 illustrates a small sample of *chhole masala* (chickpea curry) variants and *samosa* (fried pastry with savory filling) alternatives, stored in FKG.in. These include selected nutrient information, enabling comparisons to support recipe recommendations tailored to dietary preferences, nutritional needs, and health objectives. As can be appreciated here, describing a 'standard' *samosa* or *chhole masala* is quite difficult as their recipes vary widely across regions, cultures, and preferences. Thus, it highlights the ambiguity in both defining 'standard' recipes for cooked food items as well as the complications in determining the food composition of purported 'standard' recipes. This led us to treat each recipe as a unique instance of the corresponding cooked food item. FKG.in currently includes information on 25,000+ unique recipe instances, sourced from 15+ recipe sites and 5+ cookbooks, with more recipes being added iteratively.

#	Recipe Blog	Recipe Name	Energy	Carbohydrate	Protein	Total Fat	Saturated Fat	Dietary Fiber	Sodium	Potassium	Calcium	Iron	Zinc	Phosphorus	Vitamin A	Vitamin B	Vitamin C	Vitamin D	Essential Fatty acids	Trans Fatty acids	Unsaturated Fatty acids	Moisture
1	archanaskitchen	Traditional Amritsari Chole Recipe | Punjabi Chole Masala	272.738	37.239	16.525	20.549	11.131	24.171	0.033	0.913	0.178	0.007	0.003	0.255	0.0002200	0.0054400	0.0013700	0.0000094	2.5653200	0.0660000	7.9666300	14.7429300
2	indianhealthyrecipes	Chole Recipe (Punjabi Chole Masala)	259.660	41.700	14.180	7.340	3.050	18.680	0.037	0.906	0.140	0.005	0.003	0.222	0.0014900	0.0045800	0.0231000	0.0000098	1.7100000	0.0165000	3.2400000	75.7800000
3	hookedonheat	Instant Pot Chole (Chickpea Curry)	189.638	26.476	11.974	10.954	7.113	16.152	0.020	0.649	0.111	0.005	0.002	0.177	0.0002357	0.0036915	0.0030255	0.0000025	1.6520972	0.0000025	2.9059961	14.8319373
4	vegrecipesofindia	Chole Recipe | Authentic Punjabi Chole Masala	214.441	26.426	11.438	6.492	0.448	15.390	0.023	0.801	0.287	0.006	0.003	0.192	0.0005300	0.0030400	0.0042700	0.0000036	2.0297400	0.0000004	5.2030500	14.7957900
5	masalakorb	Punjabi Style Amritsari Chole Masala	175.308	24.189	11.354	3.151	0.296	15.487	0.017	0.577	0.095	0.004	0.002	0.162	0.0001100	0.0034400	0.0000500	0.0000016	1.4346100	0.0000000	1.9766600	5.9581800

(a) *chhole masala* (chickpea curry) variants in decreasing order of protein

#	Recipe Blog	recipe	Energy	Carbohydrate	Protein	Total Fat	Saturated Fat	Dietary Fiber	Sodium	Potassium	Free Sugars	Cholesterol	Essential Fatty acids	Unsaturated Fatty acids	Monounsaturated Fatty acids	Polyunsaturated Fatty acids	Moisture
1	archanaskitchen	mushroom_paneer_and_soya_chunk_samosa	112.731	10.899	7.831	4.062	2.279	2.629	0.011	0.264	3.186	0.000	0.311	1.401	1.092	0.311	76.080
2	vegrecipesofindia	samosa_classic_punjabi_samosa	121.025	23.212	5.045	8.096	5.400	2.445	0.006	0.213	0.959	0.000	0.390	2.524	2.134	0.390	15.552
3	archanaskitchen	mutton_keema_samosa_mangsher_singara	264.575	30.843	13.645	8.915	3.237	4.248	0.061	0.282	0.911	0.034	0.703	1.036	3.867	0.834	6.565
4	archanaskitchen	gluten_free_samosa	264.575	30.843	13.645	8.915	3.237	4.248	0.061	0.282	0.911	0.034	0.703	1.036	3.867	0.834	6.565
5	indianhealthyrecipes	samosa_how_to_make_punjabi_samosa	272.824	48.467	12.218	10.523	6.746	10.503	0.068	1.366	14.253	0.007	0.793	2.786	2.561	0.820	95.120
6	archanaskitchen	moong_dal_mini_samosas_delicious_tea_time_snack	250.913	48.613	10.345	11.083	7.246	5.658	0.006	0.357	1.132	0.000	0.690	3.608	2.922	0.690	12.391

(b) *samosa* (fried pastry with savory filling) variants in increasing order of total fat

Fig. 4. Energy (kCal) and selected nutrients (g) comparison of recipe alternatives

10 Conclusions and Future Work

In this paper, we have presented the design of an automated workflow for enhancing the Indian food knowledge graph (FKG.in), which already contains an extensive collection of recipes and ingredients, with food composition information. The automated workflow facilitates the expansion of the FKG.in Food Composition Table (FCT) with detailed nutritional data for a vast number of ingredients. Additionally, this process results in an aggregated, validated, and comprehensive dataset of recipe nutrient compositions alongside the addition of new recipes from diverse sources. Most importantly, we demonstrated how the LLM-Augmented Information Resolution (LAIR) agent effectively addresses various structural, linguistic, and uncertainty-related challenges in parsing and analyzing recipe and ingredient information. This proposed approach is application-agnostic, supports dynamic computation of nutritional information for countless recipes, and enhances both the scope as well as the granularity of dietary recommendations.

Some limitations of this work and potential future improvements include:

1. Verified FCTs from neighboring countries like Bangladesh, Nepal, Pakistan, and Sri Lanka can be incorporated to represent Indian subcontinental cuisine better, scale FKG.in up, and improve FKG.in-FCT's completeness.
2. Nutritionix is not always accurate for Indian foods, as it relies on USDA data. However, the NDA agent calls the Nutritionix API only if an ingredient is missing from both IFCT and INDB, which occurs infrequently.
3. Without accounting for cooking retention and yield factors, our nutrition calculations may be slightly overestimated. We have retention factors from the USDA database in FKG.in-FCT but are currently not using them. Future updates to FKG.in will allow us to provide more accurate food composition results as it will utilize in-depth knowledge of Indian cooking styles as well.
4. The FCA agent doesn't suggest specific food items based on food group inadequacy. Incorporating dietary tag labels in the recommendation workflow can allow it to recommend food items to address dietary gaps as per [11].
5. The validation process for the LLM-generated information such as weight estimation, vernacular translation/transliteration, and category assignment needs to be improved. Currently, it is human-dependent and slow.

Acknowledgments. This research was supported by the Ashoka Mphasis Lab - a collaboration between Ashoka University and Mphasis Limited.

References

1. ArchanasKitchen: Weights & measurement chart — conversion table (2024). https://www.archanaskitchen.com/weights-measurement-chart-conversion-table
2. Cantais, J., Dominguez, D., Gigante, V., Laera, L., Tamma, V.: An example of food ontology for diabetes control, pp. 1–9 (2005)
3. Cooper, T.: Personalized health navigation (phn) (2024). https://confluence.hl7.org/pages/viewpage.action?pageId=171443414, pre-PSS. 31 Jan 31 2024
4. Dooley, D.M., et al.: FoodOn: a harmonized food ontology to increase global food traceability, quality control and data integration. npj Sci. Food **2** (2018). https://doi.org/10.1038/s41538-018-0032-6
5. Edamam: Edamam. https://www.edamam.com/, Accessed 8 Aug 2024
6. Fitterfly: Fitterfly. https://www.fitterfly.com
7. Goel, M., et al.: Dish detection in food platters: A framework for automated diet logging and nutrition management (2023). https://arxiv.org/abs/2305.07552
8. Gupta, S.K., Dey, L., Das, P.P., Jain, R.: Building fkg.in: a knowledge graph for Indian food (2024). https://ceur-ws.org/Vol-3882/ifow-4.pdf
9. Haussmann, S., et al.: FoodKG: a semantics-driven knowledge graph for food recommendation. In: Ghidini, C., et al. (eds.) ISWC 2019. LNCS, vol. 11779, pp. 146–162. Springer, Cham (2019). https://doi.org/10.1007/978-3-030-30796-7_10

10. HealthifyMe: Healthifyme. https://www.healthifyme.com/in/
11. ICMR-NIN: National institute of nutrition: Dietary guidelines for indians (2024). https://www.nin.res.in/dietaryguidelines/index.html
12. International Organization for Standardization (ISO): Iso/cd 9472-10000: Health informatics - personalized health navigation: Part 10000: Architecture (2021). https://www.iso.org/standard/83497.html
13. International Organization for Standardization (ISO): Iso/tr 11147:2023: Health informatics - personalized digital health - digital therapeutics health software systems (2023). https://www.iso.org/standard/83767.html
14. Jain, R.: Empowering individual health through technology (2023). https://medium.com/@jain49/empowering-self-health-through-technology-4c48b7aeaf54
15. Kalra, J., Batra, D., Diwan, N., Bagler, G.: Nutritional profile estimation in cooking recipes. In: 2020 IEEE 36th International Conference on Data Engineering Workshops, pp. 82–87 (202https://doi.org/10.1109/ICDEW49219.2020.000-3
16. Longvah, T., Ananthan, R., Bhaskar, K., Venkaiah, K.: Indian food composition tables (Jan 2017)
17. Min, W., Jiang, S., Jain, R.: Food recommendation: framework, existing solutions, and challenges. IEEE Trans. Multimedia 22(10), 2659–2671 (2020). https://doi.org/10.1109/TMM.2019.2958761
18. Min, W., Jiang, S., Liu, L., Rui, Y., Jain, R.: A survey on food computing. ACM Comput. Surv. 52(5), 1–36 (2019). https://doi.org/10.1145/3329168
19. Min, W., Liu, C., Xu, L., Jiang, S.: Applications of knowledge graphs for food science and industry. Patterns 3(5) (2022). https://doi.org/10.1016/j.patter.2022.100484
20. MyFitnessPal: Myfitnesspal. https://www.myfitnesspal.com/en/
21. Nag, N., Jain, R.: A navigational approach to health: actionable guidance for improved quality of life. IEEE Comput. 52(4), 12–20 (2019). https://doi.org/10.1109/MC.2018.2883280
22. Nguyen, P.H., et al.: The double burden of malnutrition in india: trends and inequalities (2006–2016). PLoS ONE 16(2), e0247856 (2021). https://doi.org/10.1371/journal.pone.0247856
23. Nutritionix: Nutritionix. https://www.nutritionix.com/, Accessed 8 Aug 2024
24. Poshan Atlas: Poshanatlas. https://www.poshanatlas.wcd.gov.in/
25. Snae, C., Bruckner, M.: Foods: a food-oriented ontology-driven system. In: 2008 2nd IEEE Int'l Conf. on Digital Ecosystems & Technologies, pp. 168–176 (2008). https://doi.org/10.1109/DEST.2008.4635195
26. Thornton, K., Seals-Nutt, K., Matsuzaki, M.: Introducing wikifcd: many food composition tables in a single knowledge base. In: Joint Ontology Workshops (2021). https://api.semanticscholar.org/CorpusID:240005417
27. UK-GOV: Composition of foods integrated dataset (cofid) (2015)
28. USDA: Fooddata central. https://fdc.nal.usda.gov/, Accessed 6 Sep 2024
29. Vennu, V., Abdulrahman, T.A., Bindawas, S.M.: The prevalence of overweight, obesity, hypertension, and diabetes in India: analysis of the 2015–2016 national family health survey. Int. J. Environ. Res. Public Health 16(20), 3987 (2019). https://doi.org/10.3390/ijerph16203987
30. Vijayakumar, A., Dubasi, H.B., Awasthi, A., Jaacks, L.M.: Development of an Indian food composition database. Current Develop. Nutrition 8(7), 103790 (2024). https://doi.org/10.1016/j.cdnut.2024.103790, https://www.sciencedirect.com/science/article/pii/S2475299124017244

W12

Advancing Image Registration with Multi-angle Projection Keypoint Descriptors

Yen-Fu Lai and Daw-Tung Lin[✉][iD]

Department of Computer Science and Information Engineering,
National Taipei University, New Taipei City, Taiwan
dalton@mail.ntpu.edu.tw

Abstract. Keypoint detection is a well-established technique in computer vision that finds applications in various domains, particularly in tasks such as image registration and scene stitching, where high accuracy is crucial. One prominent challenge in these applications is the accurate handling of object rotation. The standard image registration process involves keypoint detection, description, and matching. Recent advancements in hardware capabilities have spurred research efforts to enhance keypoint detection by applying deep learning methodologies. However, relying solely on deep learning falls short of addressing rotations in three-dimensional space. To tackle this, we present a novel algorithm focused on keypoint matching. The process involves keypoint detection, descriptor computation, and the formulation of multi-angle descriptors using a three-dimensional projection technique. In empirical evaluations, our proposed method demonstrates significant improvements in accuracy, ranging between 5% and 20%, across various keypoint detection models and datasets. Impressively, these enhancements come without substantial computational overhead, making our approach compatible with diverse keypoint detection models and hardware configurations.

Keywords: Keypoint Detection · Rotation Object Matching · Multi-angle Descriptor · Three-dimensional Projection

1 Introduction

Image registration, a fundamental technique within computer vision, seeks to precisely align and correlate multiple images, ensuring their consistent spatial orientation within a shared coordinate system. The primary goal of image registration is to determine an optimal transformation (rotation, translation, scaling, etc.) that minimizes discrepancies between images. This process involves the comparison of features, edges, textures, and other visual cues, followed by the calculation of transformation parameters that effectively align the images. Essentially, image registration establishes precise correspondences between images, enabling a wide range of applications. In an image registration system consists

© The Author(s), under exclusive license to Springer Nature Switzerland AG 2025
S. Palaiahnakote et al. (Eds.): ICPR 2024 Workshops, LNCS 15617, pp. 93–105, 2025.
https://doi.org/10.1007/978-3-031-88217-3_7

of three key steps: (1) Keypoint Detection; (2) Keypoint Description; and (3) Keypoint Matching.

Following these keypoint detection and matching steps, the bounding box of the target object in the image is successfully computed. A bounding box represents a rectangular frame surrounding the target object, and this information can be utilized in subsequent augmented reality applications.

Keypoint-related techniques have diverse applications across various fields, including face detection, motion detection, image stitching, building reconstruction, and augmented reality (AR). Moreover, addressing the multitude of possible angle combinations in three-dimensional space requires AR technology with high hardware requirements, rapid computational speed, and high accuracy to ensure a positive user experience. Consequently, deep learning models may not be proficient in learning all conceivable angles, rendering them unsuitable for universal application in augmented reality. For instance, we utilized the NVIDIA RTX 3090 as our training GPU. The R2D2 [17] deep-learning-based keypoint detection model comprises approximately 5 million parameters. When training the model with 100,000 images (such as those in POT (see Sect. 4.2)), the most efficient training speed is about 10 min per epoch, resulting in a total training time of 8 to 9 h for 50 epochs. While it is possible to incorporate additional angles into the training, doing so would significantly increase the training time. Furthermore, many images would be duplicated when we apply rotation. In conclusion, learning from all conceivable angles would require excessive time, and the expected returns do not justify the effort. The main focus of this study is to propose a method that fulfills the aforementioned requirements and effectively improves accuracy in augmented reality applications.

This study makes significant contributions that can be summarized as follows: (1) Novel Keypoint Matching: The use of multi-angle descriptors in 3D projection technique; (2) Improved Accuracy: Our approach markedly enhances keypoint matching accuracy, outperforming traditional techniques like SIFT and ASIFT; (2) Seamless Plugin Integration: It seamlessly integrates with various keypoint detection architectures without requiring extensive modifications to their original structures; (3) Efficient Hardware Utilization: Through the systematic generation of multi-angle descriptors, our method reduces hardware resource requirements while either maintaining or enhancing accuracy; (4) Addressing Rotation Challenges: Our approach excels in tackling challenges posed by substantial object rotations, resulting in accuracy improvements of up to 12%; and (5) Practical Applicability: Empirical validation demonstrates consistent effectiveness across diverse scenarios, highlighting the real-world applicability of our method.

2   Related Work

2.1   Deep Learning Based Keypoint Detection

Due to the rapid growth in deep learning and advancements in hardware performance, a multitude of strategies based on deep learning for acquiring keypoints have emerged. Keypoints derived from deep learning are more adaptable and, when combined with other techniques, can result in more comprehensive findings. For example, Barroso-Laguna et al. [3] introduced a keypoint detector that integrated deep learning and artificial intelligence techniques. They devised a loss function for keypoints at various scales, minimizing the risk of overfitting by utilizing fewer detector parameters, thereby requiring less training data. In contrast to pointwise training, Yang et al. [24] employed an unsupervised framework trained on the entire image. Lu et al. [14] utilized random sampling for determining keypoints and mitigated data loss with a random expansion clustering strategy, significantly enhancing processing speed. Samet et al. [19] generated regions using log-polar coordinates, selecting keypoints based on scores within the regions, and proposed a voting-based method for obtaining keypoints applicable for both short and long distances. Zhao et al. [26] introduced a differentiable keypoint detector that produces subpixel keypoints trained using reprojection and dispersity peak losses, achieving a balance between accuracy and execution speed in a lightweight network. By employing a Generative Adversarial Network (GAN) to compute the Kullback-Leibler divergence, You et al. [25] introduced an adversarial keypoint detector. This method creates adversarial keypoint distributions, resulting in improved keypoints with fewer samples. Liu et al. [12] developed a pixel-by-pixel keypoint detection network integrating depth images and extended object semantic segmentation into three dimensions. Yang et al. [23] presented Click-Pose, an end-to-end neural keypoint detection model with a self-correction ability for pose reconstruction. This model utilizes an interactive human-feedback loop to efficiently update keypoints based on user selections. Bai [1] introduced a contrastive learning keypoint detection model that effectively distinguishes keypoints from non-keypoint features, demonstrating robustness in clutter and occlusion scenarios.

2.2   Keypoint Description

Creating an effective feature descriptor is challenging due to its substantial impact on picture matching accuracy. The descriptor must handle variations in views, lighting conditions, occlusions, and disparities in camera positions affecting the matching process. Simultaneously, it must meet processing speed and hardware performance requirements. Invariant region descriptors like SIFT, SURF, HOG, DAISY, ORB, LIOP, etc. [4,5,13,18,21,22] have been extensively explored. Tian et al. [6] directly sampled logarithmic polar coordinates, suitable for deep network learning. Hausler et al. [7] introduced region-global feature descriptors, amplifying the impact of local descriptors by describing keypoints with multiple blocks, achieving superior results in scale variations compared to single-block descriptors. However, the high-dimensional output increases memory requirements, rendering it unsuitable for real-time detection. Jun et al. [8] proposed a strategy that combines various global descriptors for flexible outcomes and more comprehensive feature point descriptions by switching the descriptor model used. Ng et al. [16] used an adversarial learning framework to construct descriptors capable of concealing the input image using minimal effective information, addressing privacy concerns and preventing image reconstruction.

3 Methodology

3.1 System Architecture

Figure 1 presents the proposed system's flowchart in this study, offering a visual representation of the processes applied to both query and training images. For the training image, the three main steps are as follows: (1) employing an existing model for keypoint detection, (2) calculating keypoint descriptors, and (3) conducting keypoint matching following the standard keypoint detection process. Additionally, for the query image, Step 2 is divided into two sub-steps: (2.1) simulating the three-dimensional projection of the image and (2.2) calculating descriptors of the same keypoints at different angles, concatenating them into multi-angle descriptors. We assessed our method's performance using two existing keypoint-detection architectures, evaluating both algorithmic and deep-learning-based keypoint detectors. Specifically, we utilized SIFT [13] as the algorithmic keypoint detector and R2D2 [17] as the deep-learning-based keypoint detector. We intend to explore the most general methods to evaluate the usefulness of our approach. SIFT is a classic keypoint detection technique and serves as our initial introduction to keypoint learning. While R2D2 performs well with repeatable objects, it struggles with rotations. We believe that our method can provide a more efficient solution, enhancing performance in rotational challenges. In conclusion, we aim to maximize the impact of our research on models that are weak in handling rotations.

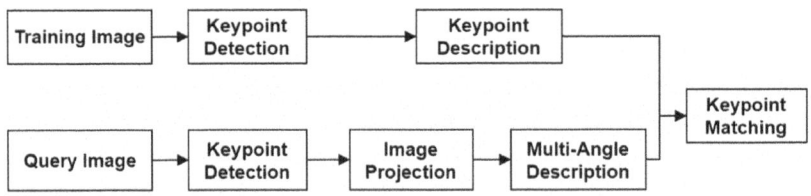

Fig. 1. Flowchart of the proposed multi-angle descriptor and matching system.

3.2 Image 3D Projection

To model the three-dimensional rotation of real-world objects in simulations, this study employs three-dimensional rotation matrices for image computations. Initially, we formulate rotation matrices for each axis, as represented by Eq. (1), where θ_x, θ_y and θ_z denote the rotation angles around the X, Y, and Z axes, respectively.

$$Rx(\theta x) = \begin{bmatrix} 1 & 0 & 0 & 0 \\ 0 & \cos\theta x & -\sin\theta x & 0 \\ 0 & \sin\theta x & \cos\theta x & 0 \\ 0 & 0 & 0 & 1 \end{bmatrix}, Ry(\theta y) = \begin{bmatrix} \cos\theta y & 0 & -\sin\theta y & 0 \\ 0 & 1 & 0 & 0 \\ \sin\theta y & 0 & \cos\theta y & 0 \\ 0 & 0 & 0 & 1 \end{bmatrix}, Ry(\theta z) = \begin{bmatrix} \cos\theta z & -\sin\theta z & 0 & 0 \\ \sin\theta z & \cos\theta z & 0 & 0 \\ 0 & 0 & 1 & 0 \\ 0 & 0 & 0 & 1 \end{bmatrix}.$$

$$(1)$$

Following that, the image distance was computed using $F = \sqrt{h^2 + w^2}/(2 * \sin(\theta_z \times \pi \div 180))$, where h denotes the image height, and w represents the image width. Afterward, three matrices T, A1, and A2 were formulated, as presented in Eq. (2). The rotation matrix M is obtained through the computation described in Eq. (3).

$$T = \begin{bmatrix} 1 & 0 & 0 & 5 \\ 0 & 1 & 0 & 0 \\ 0 & 0 & 1 & F \\ 0 & 0 & 0 & 1 \end{bmatrix}, A1 = \begin{bmatrix} 1 & 0 & -w/2 \\ 0 & 1 & -h/2 \\ 0 & 0 & 1 \\ 0 & 0 & 1 \end{bmatrix}, A2 = \begin{bmatrix} F & 0 & w/2 & 0 \\ 0 & F & h/2 & 0 \\ 0 & 0 & 1 & 0 \end{bmatrix} \qquad (2)$$

$$M = A2(T((RxRyRz)A1)) \qquad (3)$$

To tackle the challenge of minimal differences between descriptors before and after rotation, this study intentionally avoided common rotation angles in trigonometry, such as 30° and 45°, as well as angles resulting in minimal image alterations, like 90° or 180°. Additionally, considering the need for the rotated projection of the image to remain visible, positive and negative values of 50° were chosen for the rotation. This implies rotations of 0°, 50°, and 310° on the X-, Y-, and Z-planes, respectively. The selection of 50° and -50° as rotation angles is based on the practical need to evaluate the algorithm's performance under significant but manageable transformations. These angles were chosen to simulate realistic scenarios where objects might undergo moderate rotation, allowing us to assess the robustness of our keypoint detection and matching methods.

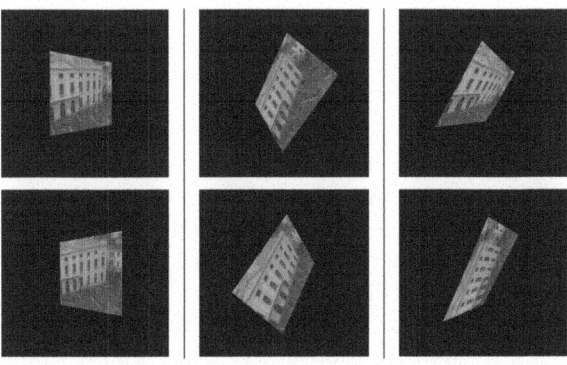

Fig. 2. Image 3D projection.

Subsequently, these angles were arranged in various combinations, resulting in 27° rotational angles. The final outcome is illustrated in Fig. 2.

An ablation study of this parameter could indeed be beneficial. By systematically testing a range of rotation angles, we could identify the optimal values that maximize matching accuracy while minimizing computational costs. This would provide insights into how different angles impact performance and could lead to further refinements in our method.

3.3   Multi-angle Descriptor and Matching

To acquire descriptors at various angles, our approach commences by initially computing the keypoints of a rotated image. This process involves projecting keypoints K onto the rotation matrix M, resulting in new keypoints k', as depicted in Fig. 3. Following this, the rotated image and the keypoints k' are fed into descriptor extractors (such as SIFT [13] or R2D2 [17]) to extract descriptors. We iterated this procedure 27 times to generate 27 sets of descriptors, in addition to the descriptors corresponding to the original image keypoints K. In total, we obtained 28 sets of descriptors, which were then combined to create a unified set of multi-angle descriptors.

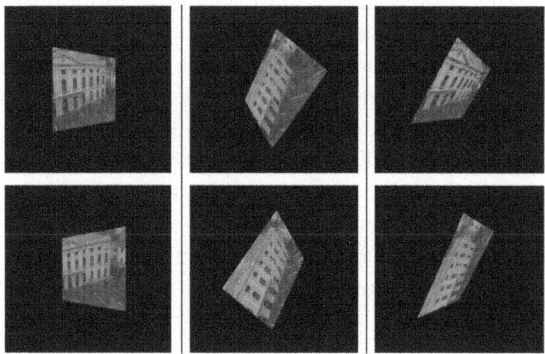

Fig. 3. Image 3D projection and keypoints detection results after rotation calculations.

The keypoint matching process employs brute-force matching, where the multi-angle descriptors of the query image are sequentially compared with the descriptors of the training image. The aim is to discover the highest number of matches between the two sets of descriptors. Once the set of descriptors with the best match is identified, it is utilized to calculate the bounding box of an object in the training image. Figure 4a illustrates the matching results under normal conditions, involving a small rotation angle, while Fig. 4b showcases matching outcomes when dealing with a larger rotation angle, presenting a notably more challenging task. We aim to employ the most common matching methods to demonstrate that our research is both viable and scalable. We anticipate achieving greater efficiency by utilizing more advanced matching techniques.

(a)   (b)

Fig. 4. Matching results with (a) small rotation angles, and (b) large rotation angles.

4   Experimental Results

4.1   Experimental Setup and Comparison Protocol

In this study, we conducted a comparison of two keypoint detection frameworks: SIFT [13] and R2D2 [17]. Furthermore, we subjected our proposed enhancement method, the 3D Projective Descriptor (3D-PD), to testing on both the SIFT and R2D2 [17] algorithms. SIFT [13] a widely adopted keypoint detection system known for its balance of speed and accuracy, is selected as the primary keypoint detector in this study. We enhance its capabilities using our proposed 3D Projective Descriptor (3D-PD) technique, resulting in a multi-angle descriptor named SIFT-3D-PD. In contrast, ASIFT [15], a derivative of SIFT, applies affine transformations to images at 42 different angles, creating a total of 43 images for both query and training images. All 43 sets of keypoints are then matched, making ASIFT suitable for comparison with our 3D-PD approach. Another keypoint detector is R2D2, a deep-learning-based method designed for repetitive patterns in images. In this study, we use the R2D2 architecture to handle substantial-angle rotations by integrating our method, referred to as R2D2-3D-PD. For comparison, we modify ASIFT by replacing the SIFT keypoint detector with R2D2's detector, resulting in the architecture named AR2D2. To assess these methodologies, experiments were conducted on benchmark datasets: POT [10] and HPatches [2]. The evaluation involved matching keypoints between query and training images, followed by scoring to measure matching accuracy.

4.2   POT Benchmark and Performance Comparison

The POT [10] dataset, designed for object tracking, features 30 sets of video sequences with specific tracking targets. Challenges include scale change, rotation, perspective distortion, motion blur, occlusion, out-of-view, and unconstrained scenarios. Each sequence has 501 frames, totaling 105,210 images. Accuracy is assessed by comparing bounding boxes from matched keypoints with ground truth boxes. Successful tracking requires an overlap error below a set threshold, measured as precision in Eq. 4. Figure 5a shows performance results, with 3D-PD in red, ASIFT and AR2D2 in green, and the original architectures in blue (SIFT as dotted lines, R2D2 as solid lines). The legend ranks scores based on a five-pixel alignment error threshold.

$$precsion = \frac{number\ of\ tracked\ frames}{number\ of\ total\ frames} \tag{4}$$

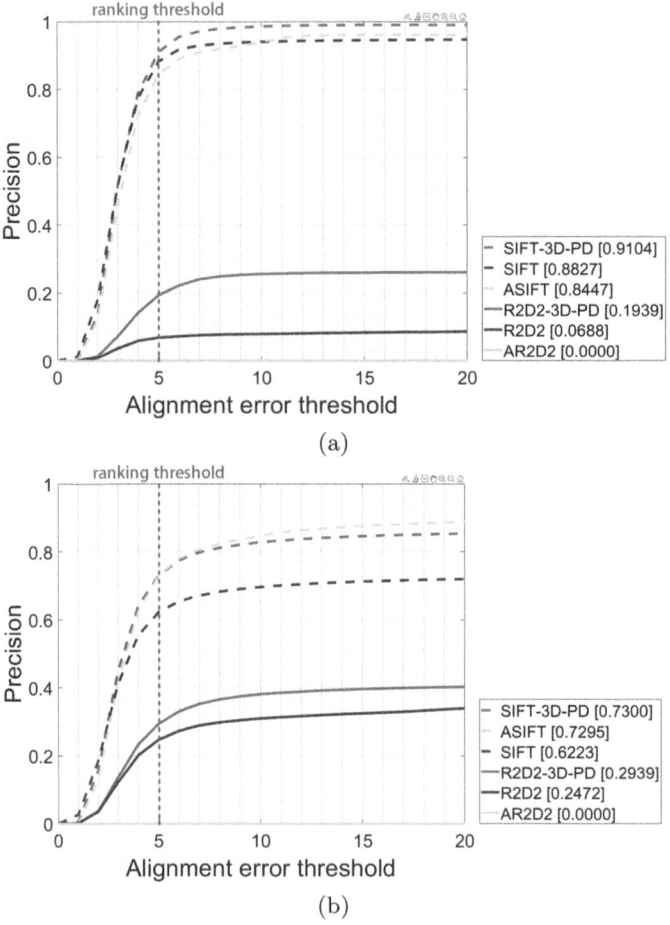

Fig. 5. POT: (a) All sequences results, (b) Rotation results.

In Fig. 5a, differences are notable between SIFT and SIFT-3D-PD when the error threshold exceeds 5 pixels, favoring SIFT-3D-PD below 5 pixels. SIFT keypoint detection typically ranges between 1000 and 2000 keypoints on this dataset. While our method enhances individual keypoints, ASIFT achieves stability by providing numerous keypoints. Originally unsuitable for POT, R2D2-3D-PD improves accuracy by around 5%. However, AR2D2 faces challenges due to increased keypoints, leading to excessive hardware requirements. To address this, we use R2D2 to retain higher-scoring keypoints, introducing difficulties in drawing bounding boxes. The POT comparison focuses on ASIFT and SIFT-3D-PD. In Fig. 5b, emphasizing rotation, SIFT-3D-PD consistently outperforms SIFT and ASIFT, showing a robust enhancement. R2D2 encounters limitations with rotation, and R2D2-3D-PD exhibits significant advancement with an approximately 13% accuracy improvement.

The AR2D2 consistently generates a large number of keypoints. In challenges such as motion blur, it still produces many keypoints. However, many of these keypoints are unstable, preventing them from being paired effectively. This instability can result in errors exceeding 20 pixels, which are not reflected in our plot. Therefore, we consider these instances as scoring 0 points.

4.3 HPatches Benchmark and Performance Comparison

The HPatches [2] dataset evaluates illumination and viewpoint changes with 116 image sets, including one query image and variations for training. For accuracy, Mean Matching Accuracy (MMA) (Eq. 5)is measured with a nearest-neighbor threshold (nnThreshold) from 1 to 10 pixels. Figure 6a, 6b, and 6c show results with 3D-PD in red, ASIFT and AR2D2 in green, and the original architecture in blue. SIFT-based architectures are dashed, and R2D2-based architectures are solid.

$$MMA = \frac{number\ of\ matched\ keypoints}{number\ of\ total\ keypoints} \tag{5}$$

In Fig. 6a, R2D2-3D-PD and SIFT-3D-PD excel, with SIFT-3D-PD outperforming SIFT by over 20%, and R2D2-3D-PD achieving about 2% higher accuracy than R2D2. AR2D2 and ASIFT face challenges with viewpoint changes and affine transformations, resulting in more unusable keypoints. Figure 6b indicates an initial increase and stabilization of keypoints for SIFT, while ASIFT outperforms SIFT in viewpoint changes. R2D2's fixed count of 5000 keypoints leads to many unusable keypoints in scenarios with substantial deformation. Figure 6c demonstrates the effects of illumination variations, where R2D2 outperforms SIFT due to a consistent keypoint count. AR2D2 excels over ASIFT, especially in acquiring keypoints before and after affine transformation. R2D2-3D-PD remains congruous with the original R2D2 version, focusing on rotation rather than lighting changes. AR2D2 performs optimally below nnThreshold 5 pixels, with its overall score closely mirroring R2D2 and R2D2-3D-PD.

4.4 Computation Cost Performance Comparison

Although our method involves generating a larger number of descriptors compared to the original version, resulting in increased processing time, this process

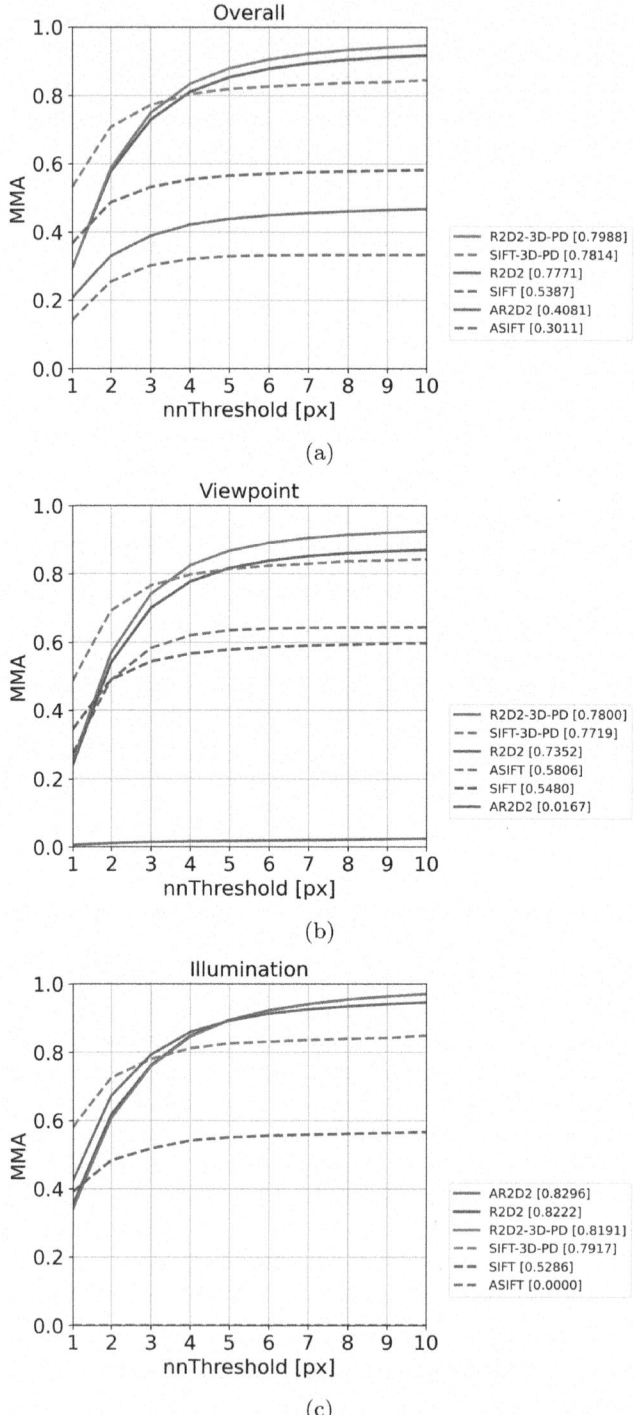

Fig. 6. HPatches: (a) Overall results, (b) Viewpoint results, (c)Illumination results.

is required only at the beginning of multi-angle descriptors generation for query images. As can be observed from the computation cost performance comparison with that of R2D2 shown on Table 1, the proposed method improved matching performance (284.46 ms) offsets this additional time, resulting in comparable overall processing time for keypoint matching. Additionally, since query images are processed only once for each dataset, any extra time spent is significantly minimized when there are a sufficient number of training images. Ultimately, this trade-off results in significantly improved matching accuracy.

Table 1. Keypoint Matching Computation Cost (ms)

Method	Load Descriptors	Descriptors Matching	Overall
Ours	20.51	**284.46**	304.97
R2D2	0.82	298.66	299.48

5 Conclusion and Future Work

This study introduces an innovative technique focusing on three-dimensional projection multi-angle descriptors. This approach aims to seamlessly enhance keypoint matching accuracy across various architectures without extensive framework modifications. It proves effective for both conventional algorithms and machine learning-based models, systematically generating multi-angle descriptors to balance computational strain and resource requirements while improving accuracy. Through rigorous empirical testing on multiple datasets and keypoint detection models, our approach consistently outperforms existing methodologies, demonstrating notable performance improvement without significant computational overhead. While effective, the sequential approach leads to a linear increase in computation time, prompting future developments to focus on computational efficiency, time complexity, and a state-of-the-art comparison.

Considering the simulation of three-dimensional projections through a range of positive and negative 50-degree angles, future efforts will prioritize efficiency, exploring a deep learning approach for obtaining specific angles to reduce unnecessary descriptors and improve overall matching time. Our comparative analysis extends to include additional cutting-edge matching techniques such as Super-Glue [20], Key.Net [3], and PlanarTrack [11], providing a comprehensive evaluation against our innovative proposal.

Acknowledgments. This work was partially supported by the National Science and Technology Council in Taiwan grants MOST 108-2221-E-305-009-MY3 and MOST 111-2221-E-305-008. This paper is a major revision of the first author's master thesis presented in February 2023 and a local conference short paper [9].

References

1. Bai, Y., Wang, A., Kortylewski, A., Yuille, A.: Coke: contrastive learning for robust keypoint detection. In: Proceedings of the IEEE/CVF Winter Conference on Applications of Computer Vision, pp. 65–74 (2023)
2. Balntas, V., Lenc, K., Vedaldi, A., Mikolajczyk, K.: Hpatches: a benchmark and evaluation of handcrafted and learned local descriptors. In: Proceedings of the IEEE CVPR, pp. 5173–5182 (2017)
3. Barroso-Laguna, A., Mikolajczyk, K.: Key. net: keypoint detection by handcrafted and learned cnn filters revisited. IEEE Trans. Pattern Anal. Mach. Intell. **45**(1), 698–711 (2022)
4. Bay, H., Ess, A., Tuytelaars, T., Van Gool, L.: Speeded-up robust features (surf). Comput. Vis. Image Underst. **110**(3), 346–359 (2008)
5. Dalal, N., Triggs, B.: Histograms of oriented gradients for human detection. In: CVPR, vol. 1, pp. 886–893. IEEE (2005)
6. Ebel, P., Mishchuk, A., Yi, K.M., Fua, P., Trulls, E.: Beyond cartesian representations for local descriptors. In: Proceedings of the IEEE ICCV, pp. 253–262 (2019)
7. Hausler, S., Garg, S., Xu, M., Milford, M., Fischer, T.: Patch-netvlad: multi-scale fusion of locally-global descriptors for place recognition. In: Proceedings of the IEEE CVPR, pp. 14141–14152 (2021)
8. Jun, H., Ko, B., Kim, Y., Kim, I., Kim, J.: Combination of multiple global descriptors for image retrieval. arXiv preprint arXiv:1903.10663 (2019)
9. Lai, Y.F., Lin, D.T.: Exploring 3d projection and multi-angle descriptors for robust keypoint matching. In: Proceedings of CVGIP (2023)
10. Liang, P., et al.: Planar object tracking benchmark in the wild. Neurocomputing **454**, 254–267 (2021)
11. Liu, X., et al.: Planartrack: a large-scale challenging benchmark for planar object tracking. arXiv preprint arXiv:2303.07625 (2023)
12. Liu, Y., et al.: Deep learning based 3d target detection for indoor scenes. Appl. Intell. **53**(9), 10218–10231 (2023)
13. Lowe, D.G.: Distinctive image features from scale-invariant keypoints. Int. J. Comput. Vision **60**, 91–110 (2004)
14. Lu, F., Chen, G., Liu, Y., Qu, Z., Knoll, A.: Rskdd-net: random sample-based keypoint detector and descriptor. Adv. Neural. Inf. Process. Syst. **33**, 21297–21308 (2020)
15. Morel, J.M., Yu, G.: Asift: a new framework for fully affine invariant image comparison. SIAM J. Imag. Sci. **2**(2), 438–469 (2009)
16. Ng, T., et al.: Ninjadesc: content-concealing visual descriptors via adversarial learning. In: Proceedings of the IEEE CVPR, pp. 12797–12807 (2022)
17. Revaud, J., et al.: R2d2: repeatable and reliable detector and descriptor. arXiv preprint arXiv:1906.06195 (2019)
18. Rublee, E., Rabaud, V., Konolige, K., Bradski, G.: Orb: an efficient alternative to sift or surf. In: 2011 ICCV, pp. 2564–2571. IEEE (2011)
19. Samet, N., Hicsonmez, S., Akbas, E.: Houghnet: integrating near and long-range evidence for visual detection. IEEE Trans. Pattern Analy. Mach. Intell. **45**(4), 4667–4681 (2022)
20. Sarlin, P.E., DeTone, D., Malisiewicz, T., Rabinovich, A.: Superglue: learning feature matching with graph neural networks. In: Proceedings of the IEEE CVPR, pp. 4938–4947 (2020)

21. Tola, E., Lepetit, V., Fua, P.: A fast local descriptor for dense matching. In: 2008 IEEE CVPR, pp. 1–8. IEEE (2008)
22. Wang, Z., Fan, B., Wu, F.: Local intensity order pattern for feature description. In: 2011 ICCV, pp. 603–610. IEEE (2011)
23. Yang, J., Zeng, A., Li, F., Liu, S., Zhang, R., Zhang, L.: Neural interactive keypoint detection. In: Proceedings of the IEEE CVPR, pp. 15122–15132 (2023)
24. Yang, T.Y., Nguyen, D.K., Heijnen, H., Balntas, V.: Ur2kid: unifying retrieval, keypoint detection, and keypoint description without local correspondence supervision. arXiv preprint arXiv:2001.07252 (2020)
25. You, Y., Liu, W., Ze, Y., Li, Y.L., Wang, W., Lu, C.: Ukpgan: a general self-supervised keypoint detector. In: Proceedings of the IEEE CVPR, pp. 17042–17051 (2022)
26. Zhao, X., Wu, X., Miao, J., Chen, W., Chen, P.C., Li, Z.: Alike: accurate and lightweight keypoint detection and descriptor extraction. IEEE Trans. Multimedia (2022)

Smart Phone Sensor Data Fusion: A Joint Learning Approach to Activity Recognition

Devraj Jhala[1], Bhargav Nadiadra[1], Chintan Bhatt[1(✉)], Alessandro Bruno[2(✉)], and Salvatore Sorce[3]

[1] Department of Computer Science and Engineering, School of Technology, Pandit Deendayal Energy University, 382007 Gandhinagar, GJ, India
{devraj.jce20,bhargav.nce20,chintan.bhatt}@sot.pdpu.ac.in
[2] Department of Business, Law, Economics, and Consumer Behaviour 'A. Ricciardi', IULM University, 20143 Milan, Italy
alessandro.bruno@iulm.it
[3] Department of Engineering and Architecture, University of Enna "Kore", 94100 Enna, Italy
salvatore.sorce@unikore.it

Abstract. This study introduces a novel method for classifying human activities on wearable smart devices using joint fusion learning. The paper commences with a comprehensive review of the existing literature on human activity classification based on several deep learning methods and the challenges encountered in this field. The article concludes with a detailed discussion of the results and the potential future lines of research in this area. Overall, this paper provides valuable insights into the use of wearable sensors and several deep learning techniques for human activity recognition, and contributes to the growing body of literature on this topic.

Keywords: Activity Recognition · Full Transformer · Multi-Head CNN

1 Introduction

Classifying activities based on sensor data is a concept that has gained prominence with the advent of wearable technology and the internet of things (IoT) [1]. In the era of rapidly advancing technology and the increasing prevalence of sedentary lifestyles, the need for accurate and convenient methods of monitoring physical activity has never been more pronounced. Sedentary lifestyles, driven by modern conveniences and digital distractions, have led to an alarming decline in physical activity levels. With approximately 80% of adults failing to meet recommended guidelines for physical activity, the repercussions on public health are profound. Sedentary behavior and insufficient physical activity are contributing factors to a global health crisis, leading to a surge in chronic diseases, obesity,

S. Palaiahnakote et al. (Eds.): ICPR 2024 Workshops, LNCS 15617, pp. 106–116, 2025.
https://doi.org/10.1007/978-3-031-88217-3_8

and diminished overall well-being. In our ever-changing world, the emergence of smartwatches has been truly extraordinary. These elegant devices, worn not only for their fashionability but also for their practicality, are demonstrating their worth as invaluable partners in our pursuit of a more wholesome way of living.

The primary objective of this paper is to bridge these gaps in knowledge and to examine the accuracy, reliability, and effectiveness of smartwatch sensors in monitoring physical activity, including walking, running, and cycling. Machine learning and deep learning techniques are then used to recognize patterns in the sensor data and classify them into corresponding activities [2].

Furthermore, we aim to explore the user experience, usability, and motivation aspects related to the adoption of smartwatches for physical activity tracking. By conducting a rigorous analysis, this paper seeks to offer practical insights into the current capabilities and potential improvements of this technology, with implications for individuals, healthcare providers, and the broader public health landscape.

The structure of the rest of this paper unfolds as follows: Sect. 2 presents the literature review, then Sect. 3 describes the methodology, including a subsection on dataset description and on the model's architecture. This study compares two architectures: Full Transformer and a Joint Learning Architecture between multi-head CNN and Transformer. Section 4 discusses the achieved results and Sect. 5 draws conclusions from the conducted research.

2 Literature Review

Yin, X. et al. proposed a novel CNN with Bi-long short term memory units along with parallel attention mechanism (ConvBLSTM-PmwA) which was tested on both publicly available datasets namely UCI HAR [3] and WISDM [4] thereby achieving an impressive accuracy of 96.71% and 95.86% respectively [5].

Khan, Z.N., Ahmad, J. developed a novel attention induced mechanism (AIM) along with multi-head convolutional neural network having 3 heads each to extract specicific patterns and features. This model (AIM-CNN) was tested on both datasets UCI HAR and WISDM and achieved accuracy of 95.38% and 98.18% respectively [6].

Thakur, D. et al. utilized combination of multi-head convolutional neural network with attention mechanism along with long short term memory architecture to extract and retain important features and to solve the issues from data heterogeneity. The model is tested on publicly available datasets UCI HAR and WISDM achieving an accuracy of 97.07%. on both respectively. [7]

Benhaili, Z. et al. proposed a novel light-weight deep stacked long short memory network to directly extract all important features from sensor data. This model is tested on both publicly available datasets namely UCI HAR and WISDM thereby achieving accuracy of 96.5% and 94.5% respectively [8].

Thakur, D., Biswas, S., Ho, E.S., Chattopadhyay, S. proposed an innovative deep learning approach named ConvoAE-LSTM which is a combination of convolutional auto-encoder along with long short term memory units. This model was tested on four datasets namely UCI HAR, OPPORTUNITY, PAMPA2, WISDM achieving impressive accuracies of 98.14%, 95.69%, 94.33% and 95.86% respectively [9].

Abdel-Basset, M., Hawash, H., Chakrabortty, R.K., Ryan, M., Elhoseny, M., Song, H. proposed supervized dual channel ST-deepHAR along with LSTM and CNN for spatial fusion of sensor data tested on datasets namely UCI and WISDM datasets thereby achieving accuracy of 97.70% and 98.90% respectively [10].

Bi, H., Perello-Nieto, M., Santos-Rodriguez, R., Flach, P. proposed a novel dynamic active learning (DAL) where a two-stage pipeline where-in first step focusses on discovering new features and second step focuses on selection of most informative samples to assist classifier tested on UCI dataset achieving accuracy of 96.50% [11].

Khan, I.U., Afzal, S., Lee, J.W. developed a hybrid approach integrating CNN and LSTM architecture tested on custom created dataset achieving accuracy of 90.89% on 30 frames. This model was aimed to extract temporal features comprising of 12 activities involving 20 participants [12].

Xia, K., Huang, J., Wang, H. developed convolutional layers with long short term architecture tested on three publicly available datasets namely UCI HAR, OPPORTUNITY, WISDM achieving 95.78%, 92.63% and 95.85% respectively [13].

Wang, H., Zhao, J., Li, J., Tian, L., Tu, P., Cao, T., An, Y., Wang, K., Li, S. developed a mixed learning architecture that is a combination of CNN and LSTM architecture tested on custom datasets developed by the researchers. This model achieved an accuracy of 95.87% [14].

Table 1. Comprehensive analysis of human activity recognition.

References	Dataset	Models	Accuracy
[3]	UCI HAR and WISDM	1-D CNN based bi-directional LSTM parallel model with attention mechanism (ConvBLSTM-PMwA)	UCI is 96.71%. WISDM is 95.86%
[4]	UCI HAR and WISDM	multi-Head CNN model with attention	UCI is 95.38%. WISDM is 98.18%
[5]	UCI HAR and WISDM	multi-head CNN, an attention mechanism LSTM network	UCI is 97.07%. WISDM is 97.07%
[6]	UCI HAR and WISDM	Deep Stacked LSTM network	UCI is 96.5%. WISDM is 94.5%

(*continued*)

Table 1. (*continued*)

References	Dataset	Models	Accuracy
[7]	UCI, OPPORTUNITY [15], PAMPA2 [16], and WISDM	ConvAE-LSTM, which combines a convolutional autoencoder and a long short-term memory network	UCI is 98.14%. OPPORTUNITY is 95.69%. PAMPA2 is 94.33%. WISDM is 95.86%
[8]	UCI HAR and WISDM	ST-deepHAR, a supervised dual-channel model that combines LSTM and attention mechanism for temporal fusion, and a convolutional residual network for spatial fusion of sensor data	UCI is 97.70%. WISDM is 98.90%
[9]	UCI HAR	HAR based on Dynamic Active Learning (DAL)	UCI is 96.5%
[10]	Authors created a custom dataset	Hybrid approach that integrates CNN and LSTM networks	90.89% on 30 frames
[11]	UCI HAR, OPPORTUNITY, and WISDM	Convolutional layers with long short-term memory	UCI is 95.78%. OPPORTUNITY is 92.63%. WISDM is 95.85%
[12]	Custom dataset	Combination of CNN and LSTM	95.87% on the custom dataset

3   Methodology

3.1   Dataset Description

The dataset used here is a publicly available dataset [17] which goes by the name of UCI-HAR dataset available under UCI repository. The dataset was chosen because of its balanced nature and ample number of samples for training the model. The dataset contains 7352 entries and 562 columns including the target column having sensor data of six activities. The details about number of entries of each records are given in the below table:

Figure 1 shows a concise flow diagram to reach the desired result, ensuring a systematic and efficient approach.

The dataset was taken from UCI-HAR repository and first was standardized using StandardScaler from scikit-learn [18]. Then the dataset was split in 70:30 ratio and passed to both the models whose architectures are given below. The model performance was evaluated using parameters like Classification Report, Confusion Matrix, ROC curves etc.

Table 2. Activity distribution count in the dataset

Activity Name	Number of Entries
LAYING	1407
STANDING	1374
SITTING	1286
WALKING	1226
WALKING UPSTAIRS	1073
WALKING DOWNSTAIRS	986

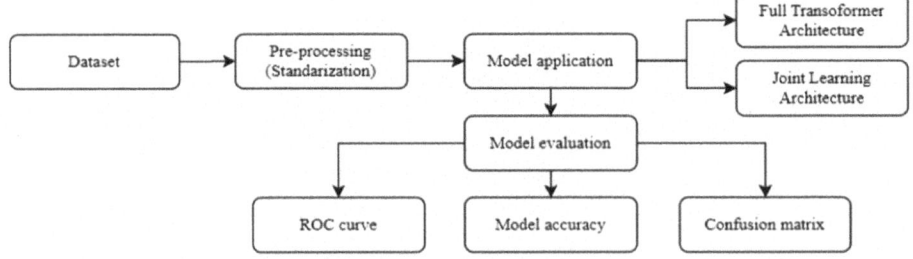

Fig. 1. Proposed methodology.

3.2   Model Architecture

Full Transformer Architecture. The custom PositionalEncoding1D layer was defined, implementing the positional encoding mechanism essential for transformer architectures. Positional encoding helps the model understand the sequential order of input data, crucial for tasks involving time series or sequences. The layer was applied to the input data, allowing the model to capture the positional information of each feature in the sequence.

The features were then reshaped to match the expected input shape of the model, which was 561 features in a sequence of length 1. The neural network architecture was defined using the Keras functional API. It started with an input layer, followed by the PositionalEncoding1D layer to incorporate positional information. The model then featured six parallel CNN branches. These branches captured different aspects of the input data through convolutional operations.

The outputs from the CNN branches were concatenated, and a multi-head self-attention layer was applied to capture global dependencies in the data. The attention mechanism enhanced the model's ability to focus on relevant information across the entire sequence. A residual connection was then established to preserve the information from the original input.

Subsequently, two LSTM layers with 256 units each were applied to capture sequential dependencies in the data. Batch normalization was applied to stabilize the training process. Global average pooling was used to reduce the spatial dimensions of the data, creating a more compact representation. The output was then fed through fully connected layers with dropout regularization for classification. The final output layer used softmax activation for multi-class classification with six output classes.

Finally, this full transformer architecture was compiled using the Adam optimizer. The model was trained on the training data for 50 epochs, and the training history was stored. The model was then evaluated on the validation data, and the validation loss and accuracy were printed. Overall, the architecture combines convolutional, attention, and recurrent layers to effectively capture both local and global patterns in sequential data for the classification task at hand.

Figure 2 gives the flow-diagram of the full-transformer architecture.

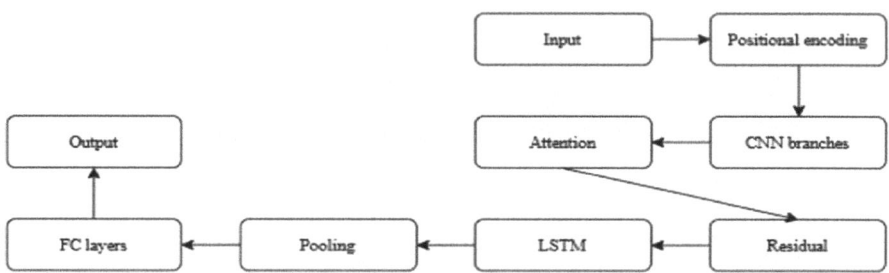

Fig. 2. Full transformer architecture

Joint Learning Architecture. The merged dataset (merged_train) was loaded and the features (X_train) and labels (y_train) were separated. The features were reshaped to match the input shape (561 features in a sequence of length 1), and the data was split into training and validation sets using the train_test_split function.

Two separate input layers were defined for the CNN-LSTM and Transformer architectures. The CNN-LSTM architecture starts with six parallel Conv1D branches, each consisting of a convolutional layer, batch normalization, and ReLU activation. The outputs from these 11 branches were concatenated and passed through two LSTM layers with 256 units each. Batch normalization was applied to stabilize the training process. Global Average Pooling was used to create a condensed representation of the data.

The transformer architecture starts with a positional encoding layer, followed by a multi-head self-attention layer. A residual connection was established, and global Average Pooling was applied to create a representation of the transformer output.

The outputs from both architectures were concatenated, and fully connected layers with dropout regularization were applied for classification. The final output layer used softmax activation for multi-class classification with six output classes.

This joint learning architecture has been created using the Keras functional API, taking both CNN-LSTM and transformer inputs and producing a single output. It has been compiled using the Adam optimizer, sparse categorical cross entropy loss, and accuracy as the evaluation metric. The model has been trained on the data for 50 epochs and batch size. Finally, the model has been evaluated on the validation data, and the validation loss and accuracy were printed. This composite architecture leverages both CNN-LSTM and transformer components to capture both local and global patterns in the sequential data, providing a more comprehensive representation for the classification task.

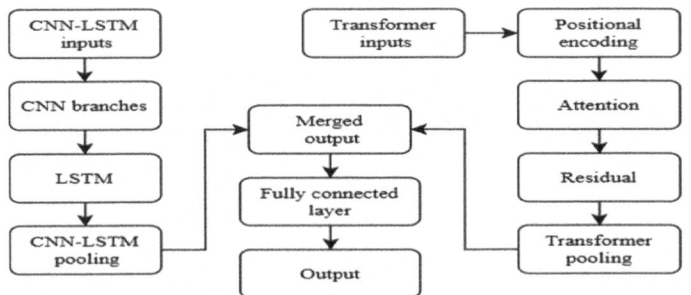

Fig. 3. Joint learning model architecture

4   Results and Discussions

Figure 4, on the left side, shows classification report of the full transformer architecture whereas Fig 5, on the right side, shows the classification report of the joint learning architecture.

We conclude that the main outcome of this study was to prove the effectiveness of deep learning as well as joint learning mechanisms in complex classification problems. The study demonstrated that joint learning mechanism outperformed the conventional transformer architecture in accuracy by 2%. The

```
Classification Report:
              precision   recall  f1-score   support

           0       1.00     1.00      1.00       361
           1       1.00     1.00      1.00       315
           2       1.00     1.00      1.00       280
           3       1.00     0.77      0.87       406
           4       0.81     1.00      0.90       409
           5       1.00     1.00      1.00       435

    accuracy                          0.96      2206
   macro avg       0.97     0.96      0.96      2206
weighted avg       0.96     0.96      0.96      2206
```

```
                precision   recall  f1-score   support

     Class 0       1.00     0.99      0.99       361
     Class 1       0.99     1.00      1.00       315
     Class 2       1.00     1.00      1.00       280
     Class 3       0.98     0.90      0.94       406
     Class 4       0.91     0.99      0.94       409
     Class 5       1.00     1.00      1.00       435

    accuracy                          0.98      2206
   macro avg       0.98     0.98      0.98      2206
weighted avg       0.98     0.98      0.98      2206
```

Fig. 4. Classification report of Full transformer model

Fig. 5. Classification report of Joint learning model

results show that the accuracy of the joint learning model turned out to be 98% as compared to the 96% of transformer model along with a very good F1-Score.

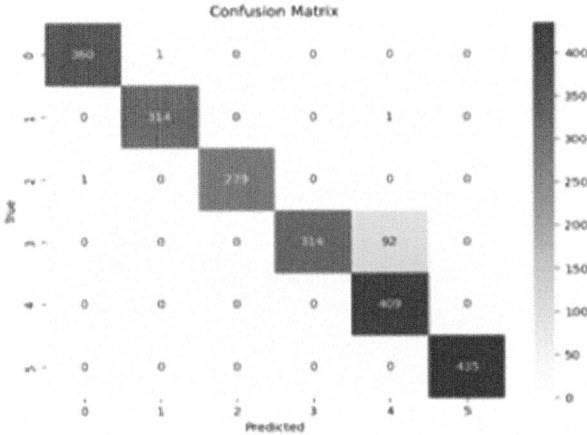

Fig. 6. Confusion matrix of Full transformer model

Figure 6 and Fig. 7 show the confusion matrix of the full transformer architecture and the joint learning architecture.

Henceforth, we compare the performance of our joint fusion learning model having an accuracy of 98%, surpassing the accuracy of 97.07% achieved by Fig. 5 with the approach of multi-head CNN, and a LSTM network with an overall F1 score of 96.6% which is less than 98% achieved in this study. This result

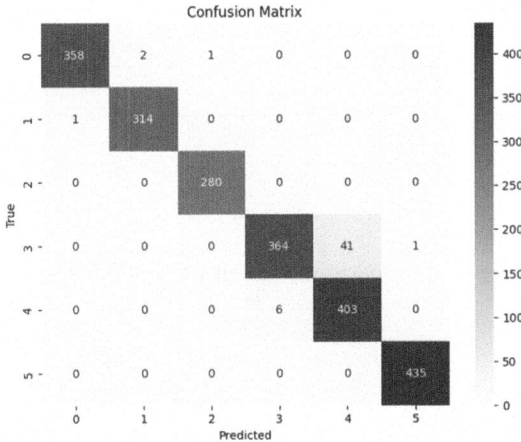

Fig. 7. Confusion matrix of Joint learning

highlights the efficacy of our approach in achieving both high precision and recall.

Furthermore, the results of Fig. 7 had a slightly higher accuracy of 98.14, in comparison to the 98% that was achieved in this study. Nevertheless, the F1-Score remained at 97.67% in 7 which is lower than the 98% achieved in this study.

The bar graphs in Fig. 8 and Fig. 9 provide a comparative of the performance of the proposed method and the methods described in the literature review.

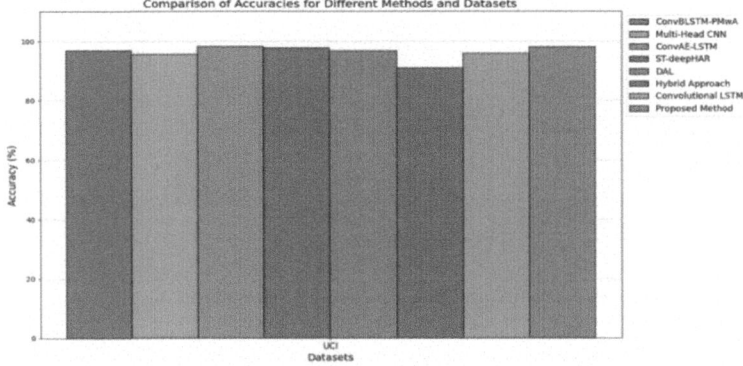

Fig. 8. Comparison of the accuracy for different methods and datasets.

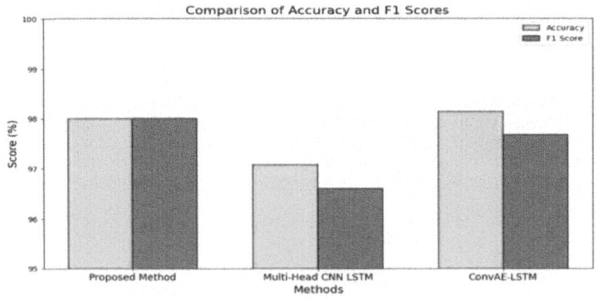

Fig. 9. Comparison of accuracy and F1 score.

5   Conclusion

In conclusion, this study has focused on two main approaches: a full transformer learning and a joint fusion learning approach consisting of 6 head CNN-LSTM learning mechanism and full transformer learning mechanism were implemented and their results were duly evaluated and analysed. It was discovered that the joint learning approach produced better results than existing literature with an accuracy of 98% along with a 98% F1-score thereby proving that joint deep learning models are better suited for complex problems such as classification and recognition of activities on wearable devices.

The performance of Joint learning approach proved its ability to solve complex classification problems. CNNs are effective in capturing spatial patterns in data while Transformers excel at capturing sequential dependencies in data. By combining both of these in such architecture, we are able to retain and capture patterns more effectively thereby boosting the performance.

In the future, we intend to test different joint learning approaches, such as the gated recurrent unit (GRU) and transformer architecture. We also intend to develop a larger dataset to test the models more accurately. Also, it is yet to be tested how the behavior of such approaches changes upon increasing the number of CNN heads for feature extraction.

Acknowledgments. This research has been supported by the AgrarIA project (I+D Mission Program in Artificial Intelligence of the Secretary of State of Digitalization and Artificial Intelligence (SEDIA) from the Ministry of Economic Affairs and Digital Transformation (File No. MIA.2021.M01.0004), corresponding to funds from the Recovery, Resilience, and Transformation Plan).

References

1. Al-Khamees, H.A. et al.: Classifying the human activities of sensor data using Deep Neural Network. Commun. Comput. Inform. Sci., 107-118 (2022)
2. Saha, S., Bhattacharya, R.: Human activity recognition systems based on sensor data using machine learning. Smart Comput. Intell. 121-150 (2022)
3. Reyes-Ortiz, J., Anguita, D., Ghio, A., Oneto, L., Parra, X.: Human activity recognition using smartphones. UCI Machine Learning Repository (2013). https://doi.org/10.24432/C54S4K
4. Kwapisz, J.R., Weiss, G.M., Moore, S.A.: Activity recognition using cell phone accelerometers. ACM SIGKDD Explorations Newsl **12**(2), 74–82 (2011). https://doi.org/10.1145/1964897.1964918
5. Yin, X., et al.: A novel CNN-based BI-LSTM parallel model with attention mechanism for human activity recognition with noisy data. Sci. Rep. **12**, 1 (2022)
6. Khan, Z.N., Ahmad, J.: Attention induced multi-head convolutional neural network for human activity recognition. Appl. Soft Comput. **110**, 107671 (2021)
7. Thakur, D., et al.: Attention-based Multihead deep learning framework for online activity monitoring with smartwatch sensors. IEEE Internet Things J. **10**(20), 17746–17754 (2023)
8. Benhaili, Z., et al.: Basic activity recognition from wearable sensors using a lightweight deep neural network. J. ICT Standardization (2022)
9. Thakur, D., Biswas, S., Ho, E.S., Chattopadhyay, S.: Convae-LSTM: convolutional autoencoder long short-term memory network for smartphone-based human activity recognition. IEEE Access. **10**, 4137–4156 (2022)

10. Abdel-Basset, M., Hawash, H., Chakrabortty, R.K., Ryan, M., Elhoseny, M., Song, H.: St-DeepHAR: deep learning model for human activity recognition in IOHT applications. IEEE Internet Things J. **8**, 4969–4979 (2021)
11. Bi, H., Perello-Nieto, M., Santos-Rodriguez, R., Flach, P.: Human activity recognition based on dynamic active learning. IEEE J. Biomed. Health Inform. **25**, 922–934 (2021)
12. Khan, I.U., Afzal, S., Lee, J.W.: Human activity recognition via hybrid deep learning based model. Sensors **22**, 323 (2022)
13. Xia, K., Huang, J., Wang, H.: LSTM-CNN architecture for human activity recognition. IEEE Access **8**, 56855–56866 (2020)
14. Wang, H., et al.: Wearable sensor-based human activity recognition using hybrid deep learning techniques. Sec. Commun. Netw. **2020**, 1–12 (2020)
15. Roggen, D., Calatroni, A., Nguyen-Dinh, L., Chavarriaga, R., Sagha, H.: Opportunity Activity Recognition. UCI Machine Learning Repository (2010). https://doi.org/10.24432/C5M027
16. Reiss, A.: PAMAP2 Physical Activity Monitoring. UCI Machine Learning Repository (2012) https://doi.org/10.24432/C5NW2H
17. https://www.kaggle.com/code/reemasolan/human-activity-recognition-feature-selection
18. Fabian, P., et al.: SciKit-Learn: Machine Learning in Python. J. Mach. Learn. Res. (2011). https://doi.org/10.5555/1953048.2078195.

Multimodal Emotion Recognition System Leveraging Decision Fusion with Acoustic and Visual Cues

Md. Tanvir Rahman⬤, Shawly Ahsan⬤, Jawad Hossain⬤,
Mohammed Moshiul Hoque^(✉)⬤, and M. Ali Akber Dewan⬤

Chittagong University of Engineering and Technology, Chittagong 4349, Bangladesh
{u1804002,u1704057,u1704039}@student.cuet.ac.bd, moshiul_240@cuet.ac.bd,
adewan@athabascau.ca

Abstract. Multimodal emotion recognition (MER) involves detecting and understanding human emotions by analyzing multiple modalities, such as images, audio, videos, and texts. MER is a challenging problem due to the complexities of multiple modalities and fusing their information to interpret and classify human emotions accurately. This paper introduces an intelligent framework (**MEmoR**) for multimodal emotion recognition leveraging audio-visual fusion. It focuses on the challenging domain of emotion detection within a Bengali audio-visual dataset. A vital aspect of this work involves creating a new dataset, a multimodal emotion recognition dataset (**MERD**), tailored to specific task requirements. The MERD encompasses 1937 annotated multimodal data across four categories: happy, sad, angry, and neutral. The proposed framework utilizes various machine learning (ML), deep learning (DL), and transformer-based models for audio and visual modalities. This work explores and integrates audio and visual modalities through feature-level and decision-level fusion. The results demonstrate that the multimodal approach of decision fusion combining TimeSformer and DistilHuBERT achieved the highest accuracy of **80%**.

Keywords: Natural Language Processing · Multimodal Emotion Recognition · Visual Features · Acoustic Features · Decision Fusion

1 Introduction

Emotions are fundamental elements within human communication, intricately woven into everyday interactions through various channels such as written discourse, spoken language, and non-verbal cues. Multimodal emotion recognition (MER) involves identifying and understanding human emotions by integrating information from multiple modalities or sources. These modalities can include facial expressions, vocal intonations, body language, gestures, physiological signals (such as heart rate or skin conductivity), and even textual content in some cases. Exploration of emotions through these diverse channels fuels advancements in human-computer interaction, affective computing, virtual reality, mental health monitoring, and practical computing. It fosters deeper insights into psychological processes, guiding ongoing research and innovation.

To decipher and understand the nuances of a user's emotional state, researchers have delved into various input modalities, such as speeches, facial expressions, videos, and texts, offering unique insights into the human emotional experience. However, the MER is challenging due to the complexities of multiple modalities, data heterogeneity, temporal misalignment, and contextual dependency. Therefore, the integration and fusion of information from different modalities are complicated to classify human emotion effectively. By combining data from various modalities, multimodal emotion recognition systems aim to improve the accuracy and robustness of emotion detection compared to systems that rely on a single modality. For example, analyzing facial expressions and speech patterns can provide more comprehensive insights into a person's emotional state than analyzing either modality in isolation. Among the many languages spoken worldwide, Bengali is one of the most widely used, with a staggering populace of over 280 million speakers. Despite its prominence, scholarly attention toward understanding and recognizing emotions within the Bengali linguistic framework is conspicuously limited. This need for more research poses a significant impediment to comprehensively understanding the nuances of emotional expression within Bengali-speaking communities. Previous research has focused on refining the unimodal method of Bengali emotion recognition, including speech, text, and multimodal (image+text) approaches [18]. However, multimodal investigations combining visual and acoustic features must be more conspicuously present within the Bengali language and culture domain, leaving a critical gap in our understanding of emotion recognition in this linguistic context. This work thus addresses this gap by systematically exploring emotion recognition utilizing a Bengali audio-visual dataset. Central to our inquiry is examining two primary modalities: audio and visual cues through which emotions are communicated within Bengali-speaking communities.

This research leverages a range of machine learning (ML), deep learning (DL) baselines, and transformer-based models for emotion recognition using speech signals from audio and image sequences from video. ConvLSTM, 3D CNN, LRCN, TimeSformer, and ViViT models are employed for visual analysis. BiLSTM, LSTM, CLSTM, CNN, DistilHuBERT, and Wav2Vec2 models are utilized for audio analysis. Furthermore, traditional ML models such as RF, LR, KNN, MLP, and XGBoost are explored for both modalities. The visual and acoustic features are fused for final classification using decision and feature-level fusion techniques. The critical contributions of this work are illustrated in the following:

- Developed a new dataset **MERD (Multimodal Emotion Recognition Dataset)** comprising 1937 audios and 1937 videos. The multimodal data are labeled into four distinct classes: happy, sad, angry, and neutral.

- Proposed **MEmoR**, a multimodal framework to identify emotion from multiple modalities (speech and image) leveraging fusion of visual and acoustic features.

2   Related Work

While extensive research exists on multimodal approaches for MER, predominantly in English and other high-resourced languages (HRLs), it is in the primary stage in low-resourced languages (LRLs), including Bengali. Ito et al. [9] presented an audio-visual speech emotion recognition (AV-SER) model that effectively disentangles emotion and identity attributes using a co-attention module, achieving an f1 score of 40.4% on the CMU-MOSEI dataset. Paluzo et al. [10] introduced a novel approach for emotion recognition from talking-face videos, achieving promising results with an average accuracy of 95.97%. Few studies have been conducted on emotion recognition in Bengali, mainly concentrated on a single modality (text, speech, or audio). Sultana et al. [17] contributed a Bengali emotional speech corpus comprising over 7 h of audio; each recording simulates seven targeted emotions. Evaluation involving 50 participants demonstrated recognition rates above 70%. Das et al. [7] introduced a Bangla language-based emotional speech-audio recognition dataset. This dataset comprises 1467 recordings from 34 speakers, covering five emotional states. Sadaf et al. [15] developed an LR-based model with an accuracy of 68.8%. Purba et al. [11] introduced a novel dataset comprising Bengali documents annotated with three emotions: happy, sad, and angry. They utilized BoW and word embedding for feature extraction, with the multinomial Naive Bayes classifier emerging as the top performer with an accuracy of 68.27%. Rayhan et al. [13] introduced two deep learning models, BiGRU and CNN-BiLSTM, for detecting emotions in Bengali text, catering to native and non-native speakers. CNN-BiLSTM outperforms BiGRU (64.96%) with a slightly higher accuracy of 66.62%. Rahman et al. [12] conducted a benchmark investigation on classifying emotion in Bengali texts, and they found the highest accuracy (86.52%) with Bidirectional GRU. Ayon et al. [2] explained the ensemble of ML techniques for emotion recognition from speech. Their work achieved 84.37% accuracy with bootstrap aggregation and voting ensemble method.

Taheri et al. [18] pioneered multimodal emotion classification in Bengali social media content, leveraging image and text data. Their study achieved a significant weighted f1-score of 77.50% through feature fusion techniques. Investigating past literature, it is evident that there remains a noticeable gap in MER, including utilizing audio-visual multimodal features, specifically Bengali datasets. This work addresses this gap and develops an intelligent MER system through audio and visual modalities within the Bengali linguistic context.

3   MERD: A New Benchmark Dataset

Emotion recognition emerges as a formidable challenge in our research endeavor due to a lack of a comprehensive dataset involving video and audio modalities.

To address this gap, we have developed **MERD**, a multimodal emotion recognition dataset that includes various emotions, incorporating visual and acoustic modalities. We followed the guidelines provided by Ahsan et al. [1] to develop MERD.

3.1 Data Collection

Between June 2023 and January 2024, we manually gathered publicly available YouTube videos encompassing various domains, including movies, dramas, and video blogs (vlogs). We collected data from a diverse range of domains to ensure a variety of emotions and scenarios were represented in the dataset. Figure 1 depicts a detailed distribution of domains in the dataset.

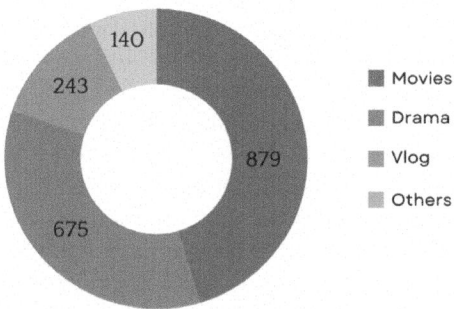

Fig. 1. Distribution of domains of the dataset. Each cell represents the number of samples collected from the corresponding domain.

We searched for videos using keywords such as *"Bengali Movie Clips," "Bengali Drama Clips," 'Bengali News Clips," "Bengali Natok," "Bengali Funny Videos," "Bengali Vlogs," "Bengali Videos,"*. We extracted 2000 short clips from this collection, meticulously screening them for quality and relevance to ensure the creation of a robust dataset for emotion recognition research. We manually reviewed each video and removed the ones that met the following criteria: i) videos with low audio or visual quality, ii) videos have unclear audio, iii) videos with excessive background noise, and iv) videos with missing audio clips. Ultimately, we curated a final dataset comprising 1937 high-quality videos portraying diverse emotions. To convert videos into mp3 audio format, we utilized MoviePy[1], a Python library.

3.2 Data Annotation and Class Definition

The dataset was manually annotated into four categories: happy, sad, angry, and neutral. The annotators were provided with definitions of each category to

---

[1] https://pypi.org/project/moviepy/.

ensure consistency in the annotation process. We decided on the following class definitions after analyzing existing works on emotion analysis [14]:

- **Happy:** A multimodal content can express a positive emotional state characterized by joy, contentment, and satisfaction. It is expressed through smiling facial expressions, relaxed posture, and upbeat vocal tones.
- **Sad:** A multimodal sad content expressing sorrow, grief, or unhappiness characterizes a negative emotional state. It manifests through facial expressions such as down-turned mouth corners, drooping eyelids, and a pensive or withdrawn demeanor.
- **Angry:** This data expressed displeasure, irritation, or hostility. It is often characterized by facial expressions such as furrowed brows, a clenched jaw, narrowed eyes, and vocal cues such as a raised voice or harsh tones.
- **Neutral:** It refers to a lack of emotional solid expression or neutrality. It is characterized by a calm facial expression, relaxed posture, and neutral vocal tones without significant displays of emotion.

Figure 2 portrays a sample from each class.

Audio In Bengali: কলার ছেড়ে দে, ওসি, কলার ছেড়ে দে।
English Translation: Drop the collar, OC, drop the collar.

(a) Angry

Audio In Bengali: বাহ, কন্ত ভালো মানুষ তুমি, জামাই।
English Translation: Wow, what a good person you are, son-in-law.

(b) Happy

Audio In Bengali: আমি বাঁচব না, সজল বাবু।
English Translation: I will not live, Sajal Babu.

(c) Sad

Audio In Bengali: আমার তো কারো জন্য খারাপ লাগে না।
English Translation: I don't feel bad for anyone.

(d) Neutral

Fig. 2. Image sequences with associated audio transcript from different emotion categories

Process of Annotation: During the initial annotation phase, two groups of three annotators were engaged to label each audio and video clip separately with

Table 1. Summary of multimodal emotion recognition dataset (MERD)

Dataset	Angry	Happy	Sad	Neutral	T_{avg}	T_{min}	T_{max}
Train	381	328	416	424	2.94	0.91	7.76
Validation	48	41	52	53	2.89	0.91	5.56
Test	48	41	52	53	2.80	1.02	6.76
Total	477	410	520	530	–	–	–

the expressed emotion. The initial labeling process relied on a majority voting method. The annotators were trained with a small subset of data to ensure consistency in their labeling process. They were asked to follow the definitions of the classes provided and note down the reasoning for their annotations. In cases of disagreement among annotators, an expert with over 20 years of experience in NLP was consulted to resolve discrepancies and determine the final label. This thorough procedure was implemented to maintain the accuracy and consistency of emotion labels throughout the dataset. We used Cohen's Kappa score [6] to assess annotation quality. The dataset had a high inter-annotator agreement of 82.7%, indicating the validity of the assigned emotion labels.

3.3 Dataset Statistics

The MERD is partitioned into three subsets: a training set comprising 80% (1549 out of 1937) of the data, a test set comprising 10% (194 out of 1937), and a validation set comprising 10% (194 out of 1937). Table 1 illustrated the distribution of MERD.

After the curation process, we ran a thorough statistical analysis to determine the duration of the videos and audios. We calculated the minimum duration (T_{min}), maximum duration (T_{max}), and average duration (T_{avg}) of MERD's video/audio as 0.91 sec, 7.76 sec and 2.92 sec, respectively. The dataset can be accessed through the following link: https://github.com/tanvir000002/MERD.

4   Methodology

This work proposed a framework, **MEmoR** for recognizing emotion by integrating visual and acoustic features. Initially, the input visual and acoustic data underwent preprocessing, applying various techniques to extract features from both modalities. These features were then combined using fusion techniques to facilitate multimodal training.

4.1   Preprocessing

We extracted frames from video clips for the video data, selecting five frames of 128×128 pixels for ML and DL models and eight frames of 224×224 pixels for transformer-based models. Due to computational limitations, we experimented with a small number of frames. We investigated several configurations and found that five frames yielded the best results for machine learning and deep learning models, while eight frames yielded the best results for transformer-based models (Table 2). Normalized these frames to adjust pixel values, ensuring consistency in subsequent analysis. The audio files are resampled to a consistent sample rate 16000 Hz for the acoustic data and applied zero padding or truncation to achieve a fixed length.

4.2   Feature Level Fusion

We extracted audio features from preprocessed acoustic data using MFCC, mel-spectrogram, chroma, and spectral contrast, resulting in a vector $F_A = [A_1, A_2, ..., A_{48}]$. For video features, we used ResNet50 to process each frame, yielding for each frame t the vectors $F_v^t = [v_1^t, v_2^t, ..., v_m^t]$. We combined the frames by taking the mean of five frames. Subsequently, we employed Principal Component Analysis [8] to reduce the dimensionality. From this PCA transformation, we selected 96 features, forming the vector $F_V = [V_1, V_2, ..., V_{96}]$. Finally, we concatenated these video features with the audio feature vector to produce the final fused feature vector F, as represented by Eq. 1.

$$F = [A_1, A_2, ..., A_{48}, V_1, V_2, ..., V_{96}] \tag{1}$$

The fused vector was then passed to several machine learning models (LR, RF, MLP, and XGB) and deep learning models (CNN, LSTM, BiLSTM, and CLSTM) for multimodal training.

4.3   Decision Level Fusion

The architecture employing decision-level fusion consists of three components: acoustic feature extraction, visual feature extraction, and decision fusion. The overview of the architecture is depicted in Fig. 3.

Acoustic Features Extraction: We employed ML, DL, and transformer-based models for acoustic feature extraction. For ML and DL models, we extracted features from preprocessed audio signals segmented into 2.75-second intervals. We utilized various techniques, including Mel-Frequency Cepstral Coefficients (MFCCs), which generated 13 coefficients; Chroma Features, which generated 12 coefficients; Mel-scaled Spectrogram, which generated 16 coefficients; and Spectral Contrast, which generated 7 coefficients. The number of Mel filter banks was set to 16 to closely align with the number of features produced by other feature extraction techniques, ensuring consistency in the feature space across different methods. These 48 features were then input into ML models (RF, XGB) and DL models (CLSTM, BiLSTM).

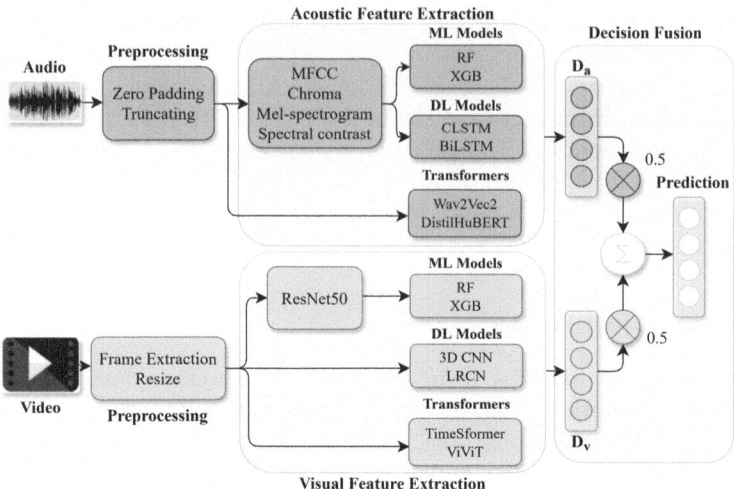

Fig. 3. Overview of decision level fusion based framework for multimodal emotion recognition (MEmoR)

For transformers, the preprocessed audio signals were first resampled at a sampling rate 16000 Hz and processed using the transformer's feature extractor obtained from HuggingFace. The extracted features were then normalized and passed to the transformers, also obtained from HuggingFace, for fine-tuning using our corpus. We explored two transformers for this task: Wav2Vec2 and DistilHuBERT.

Visual Features Extraction: We explored several ML, DL, and transformer-based models for visual feature extraction. For ML models, preprocessed frames were first processed by ResNet-50 to extract features. We took the mean of the features from five frames to represent each video sample. Subsequently, we employed Principal Component Analysis (PCA) to reduce the dimensionality of the extracted features. This PCA transformation yielded 96 features, which were then input into ML models (RF and XGB).

For DL models, we passed the preprocessed frames to 3D CNN and LRCN models for visual model training. For transformers, the preprocessed frames were initially processed by their respective image processors obtained from Hugging-Face. We then fine-tuned the transformer models, also sourced from Hugging-Face, using our corpus. Specifically, we explored two transformer models for this task: ViViT and TimeSformer.

Decision Fusion: We combined the softmax values obtained from unimodal models by averaging or using a weighted sum in the decision fusion approach. In this work, we employed a weighted sum approach, where we multiplied the softmax values obtained from each model by 0.5 and then summed the results to obtain the final prediction. Specifically, we obtained a softmax vector D_a from the acoustic modality and a softmax vector D_v from the visual modality, where $D_a(i)$ and $D_v(i)$ represent the softmax probabilities of the i-th class from the acoustic and visual modalities, respectively. The final prediction for each class $D(i)$ was obtained using Eq. 2.

$$D(i) = 0.5 \times D_a(i) + 0.5 \times D_v(i) \tag{2}$$

Table 2. Hyperparameters for DistilHuBERT and TimeSformer

Model	Hyperparameter	Hyperparameter Space	Value
DistilHuBERT	Batch Size	8, 16, 32, 64	8
	Learning Rate	$1e^{-5}$, $2e^{-5}$, $3e^{-5}$, $5e^{-5}$	$2e^{-5}$
	Number of Epochs	10, 20, 30, 50	20
TimeSformer	Batch Size	2, 4, 8, 16, 32	2
	Learning Rate	$1e^{-4}$, $2e^{-4}$, $3e^{-4}$, $5e^{-4}$	$3e^{-4}$
	Number of Epochs	10, 20, 30, 50	10
	Number of Frames	2, 4, 8	8

4.4 MEmoR

We explored two fusion approaches in this work. For the feature fusion approach, we experimented with eight models and for the decision fusion approach 20 models. Of all the multimodal models we investigated, the TimeSformer + DistilHuBERT architecture using the decision fusion approach, referred to as MEmoR, demonstrated superior performance compared to the others. The MEmoR system leverages state-of-the-art pre-trained models, specifically TimeSformer [3] and DistilHuBERT [5]. We utilized the "facebook/timesformer-base-finetuned-k400" version of TimeSformer and the "ntu-spml/distilhubert" version of DistilHuBERT. These models have been fine-tuned using a meticulous approach that involves adjusting key hyperparameters such as learning rates, batch sizes, and epochs as depicted in Table 2.

5 Experiments

This work investigates seven visual and eight acoustic baselines to evaluate the performance of multimodal emotion recognition tasks. We conducted experiments on Google Colab, utilizing its GPU-backed environment, which included NVIDIA Tesla T4 hardware for accelerated computing. TensorFlow, Keras, and PyTorch were used to implement the model architectures. The scikit-learn and matplotlib libraries were used to evaluate and visualize. We used a validation set to determine the optimal hyperparameters empirically and select the best model during training. We used the weighted f_1-score (WF) as the primary evaluation metric. However, other performance metrics such as accuracy (A), weighted recall (R), and weighted precision (P) were also measured.

5.1 Visual Baseline Models

We used ResNet50 to extract features from the preprocessed frames and fed the extracted features to four ML baseline models (KNN, RF, MLP, and XGB). Additionally, we passed the preprocessed frames to three DL models (ConvLSTM, 3D CNN, and LRCN).

- **ConvLSTM:** The ConvLSTM architecture comprises blocks of ConvLSTM layers followed by batch normalization and max-pooling layers. Each block has increasing filter sizes (64, 128, 256) with a dropout rate of 0.6. After flattening, dense layers with ELU activation and dropout are used for feature extraction. The final layer is a time-distributed dense layer with softmax activation for classification.
- **3D CNN:** The 3D CNN architecture consists of three blocks of convolution layers. Each block has two convolution layers with a ReLU activation function, followed by a batch normalization layer. The final layer in each block is a MaxPooling layer. The convolution layer in the three blocks consists of 64, 128, and 256 filters, respectively, followed by a Flatten layer. The Flatten layer is followed by a dense layer with a 0.6 dropout rate and then a dense layer with softmax activation for classification.
- **LRCN:** The LRCN model comprises four blocks, each with a convolution layer and a MaxPooling layer. The four blocks' convolution layers contain 16, 32, 64, and 64 filters, respectively. The final block is followed by a Flatten layer and an LSTM layer with 32 units. The output of the LSTM layer is then fed into a dense layer for classification.

5.2 Acoustic Baseline Models

To train the acoustic baseline models, the extracted audio features were fed into four ML classifiers (LR, RF, MLP, and XGB) and four DL classifiers (CNN, CLSTM, LSTM, and BiLSTM).

- **CNN:** The CNN model begins with a 1D convolutional layer with 64 filters and a kernel size of 3, followed by a max pooling layer. The resulting feature maps are flattened to be fed into a dense layer with 128 units and a dropout rate of 0.3. Finally, a dense layer with softmax activation was added for classification.
- **LSTM:** The LSTM architecture consists of a single LSTM layer with 128 units and a dropout layer of 0.3. The final layer is a dense layer with softmax activation.

- **BiLSTM:** The BiLSTM model starts with a Bidirectional LSTM layer containing 128 units and a dropout rate of 0.3. A dense layer with softmax activation follows the BiLSTM layer.
- **CLSTM:** The CLSTM network consists of three blocks of convolution layers. Each block contains a convolution layer with a kernel size of 5, followed by a max pooling layer, batch normalization layer, and dropout layer with a dropout rate of 0.3. The three blocks have convolution layers with 1024, 512, and 256 filters, respectively. Subsequently, three stacked LSTM layers with 128 units and a dropout rate of 0.3 are employed. The LSTM layers are followed by three dense layers with 128, 64, and 32 units, respectively. Finally, a dense layer with softmax is added.

Table 3. Performance of unimodal baseline models on the test set

Visual Baseline Models					Acoustic Baseline Models				
Approach	A	P	R	WF	Approach	A	P	R	WF
KNN	0.53	0.53	0.53	0.52	LR	0.51	0.51	0.51	0.51
RF	0.63	0.64	0.63	0.62	**RF**	0.62	0.62	0.62	**0.62**
MLP	0.54	0.54	0.54	0.54	MLP	0.55	0.55	0.55	0.53
XGB	0.62	0.62	0.62	0.62	XGB	0.61	0.61	0.61	0.61
ConvLSTM	0.58	0.58	0.58	0.58	CNN	0.53	0.52	0.53	0.52
3D CNN	0.61	0.61	0.61	0.61	LSTM	0.48	0.49	0.48	0.48
LRCN	0.65	0.66	0.65	**0.65**	BiLSTM	0.54	0.52	0.54	0.53
–	–	–	–	–	CLSTM	0.60	0.59	0.60	0.59

6 Results

Table 3 demonstrates the results of the unimodal baseline models. Among the visual baseline models, the LRCN model achieved the highest WF-score of 0.65, outperforming other models such as RF (0.62), XGB (0.62), and 3D CNN (0.61). Among the acoustic baseline models, RF emerged as the top-performing model with a WF-score of 0.62, followed closely by XGB (0.61), CLSTM (0.59), and BiLSTM (0.53). Table 4 presents the performance of multimodal models, revealing that the multimodal approach using the decision-level fusion yielded the best performance. In particular, the TimeSformer + DistilHuBERT model achieved the highest WF-score (0.80). Other combinations closely follow the best-performed models, such as ViViT + DistilHuBERT (0.79) and TimeSformer + Wav2Vec2 (0.75). Feature fusion exhibited poorer performance than decision fusion due to challenges such as feature alignment issues, high dimensionality, and redundancy. Feature-level fusion runs the risk of losing critical modality-specific information, whereas decision-level fusion preserves the distinctive characteristics of each modality. This preservation enhances overall performance by effectively combining their respective decisions.

Table 4. Performance of multimodal models, where WV, DH, TS denote Wav2Vec2, DistilHuBERT, and TimeSformer, respectively

Feature Level Fusion

Approach	A	P	R	WF	Approach	A	P	R	WF
LR	0.48	0.49	0.48	0.48	CNN	0.47	0.51	0.47	0.48
RF	0.57	0.57	0.57	**0.57**	LSTM	0.26	0.25	0.26	0.25
MLP	0.46	0.46	0.46	0.46	CLSTM	0.45	0.47	0.45	0.45
XGB	0.55	0.55	0.55	0.55	Bi-LSTM	0.53	0.52	0.53	0.52

Decision Level Fusion

Approach	A	P	R	WF	Approach	A	P	R	WF
LRCN + BiLSTM	0.71	0.71	0.71	0.71	RF + RF	0.73	0.73	0.73	0.73
LRCN + CLSTM	0.69	0.68	0.69	0.68	RF + XGB	0.68	0.67	0.68	0.67
LRCN + RF	0.69	0.69	0.69	0.68	XGB + BiLSTM	0.70	0.70	0.70	0.69
LRCN + XGB	0.72	0.72	0.72	0.72	XGB + CLSTM	0.66	0.66	0.66	0.65
3D CNN + BiLSTM	0.69	0.69	0.69	0.69	XGB + RF	0.69	0.70	0.69	0.68
3D CNN + CLSTM	0.66	0.66	0.66	0.66	XGB + XGB	0.74	0.74	0.74	0.74
3D CNN + RF	0.66	0.66	0.66	0.66	ViViT + WV	0.74	0.75	0.74	0.74
3D CNN + XGB	0.69	0.68	0.69	0.68	ViViT + DH	0.79	0.79	0.79	0.79
RF + BiLSTM	0.63	0.62	0.63	0.62	TS + WV	0.76	0.77	0.76	0.75
RF + CLSTM	0.62	0.61	0.62	0.61	**TS + DH (MEmoR)**	0.80	0.80	0.80	**0.80**

6.1   Ablation Study

Our ablation study further confirms the effectiveness of our approach by demonstrating that the removal of certain components leads to a decrease in performance. As shown in Table 5, the performance of the system drops by 11% when the acoustic modality is removed and by 15% when the visual modality is removed.

6.2   Efficiency Evaluations

We conducted an in-depth analysis to evaluate the efficiency of transformer-based approaches. Table 6 presents the number of trainable parameters and

Table 5. Results of the ablation study showing the impact of acoustic (AM) and visual (VM) modalities

Approach	Model	A	P	R	WF
MEmoR w/o AM	TimeSformer	0.70	0.71	0.70	**0.69**
MEmoR w/o VM	DistilHuBERT	0.65	0.65	0.65	**0.65**
MEmoR (proposed)	TimeSformer + DistilHuBERT	0.80	0.80	0.80	**0.80**

execution time of these approaches. Our proposed approach, MEmoR, has significantly fewer parameters than ViViT + Wav2Vec2 and TimeSformer + Wav2Vec2. Despite this, MEmoR achieves superior performance compared to both models. This advantage may be attributed to the use of DistilHuBERT, a distilled version of HuBERT, which allows for a more efficient model without sacrificing performance.

Table 6. The computational complexity of transformer-based multimodal models

Model	Parameters	Execution Time
ViViT + Wav2Vec2	181, 412, 744	3 h 49 min 5 s
ViViT + DistilHuBERT	110, 533, 000	3 h 32 min 54 s
TimeSformer + Wav2Vec2	215, 831, 432	4 h 12 min 36 s
TimeSformer + DistilHuBERT (**MEmoR**)	144, 951, 688	3 h 56 min 25 s

6.3   Classwise Models Performance:

To better understand the model's performance, we assessed the class-wise performance of the proposed multimodal architecture, MEmoR, and its components (Fig. 4). The visual model consistently outperformed the acoustic model across all classes. However, MEmoR consistently outperformed the unimodal models in every class. It achieved the highest f_1-score of 0.85 for the classes *angry* and *sad*, while the *happy* class had the lowest f_1-score of 0.73. This lower performance for this class may be due to a smaller amount of training data.

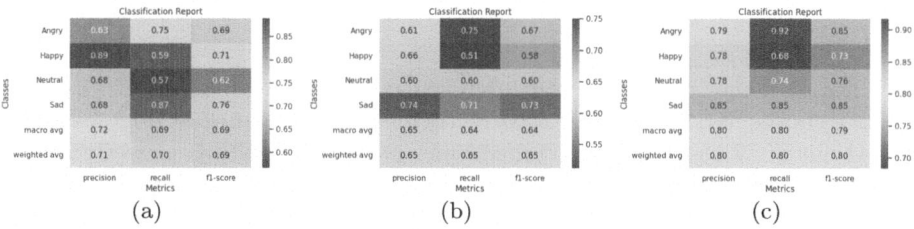

Fig. 4. Classwise performance comparison: (a) TimeSformer (visual) (b) DistilHu-BERT (acoustic) (c) TimeSformer + DistilHuBERT (MEmoR)

6.4   Comparison with Existing Techniques

We compared our proposed method, MEmoR, with existing techniques to evaluate the performance of our system (Table 7). For consistency and comparative analysis, we implemented methods from previous studies on our dataset (MERD) and compared their performance with our proposed technique.

Table 7. Comparison between proposed and existing techniques

Technique	WF
Byun et al. [4]	0.76
Sultana et al. [16]	0.71
MEmoR (proposed)	**0.80**

6.5   Error Analysis

We further conducted both quantitative and qualitative error analyses to gain a deeper understanding of the model's performance.

Quantitative Analysis: To conduct a quantitative error analysis, we utilized a confusion matrix (Fig. 5) to evaluate MEmoR and its components, TimeSformer and DistilHuBERT.

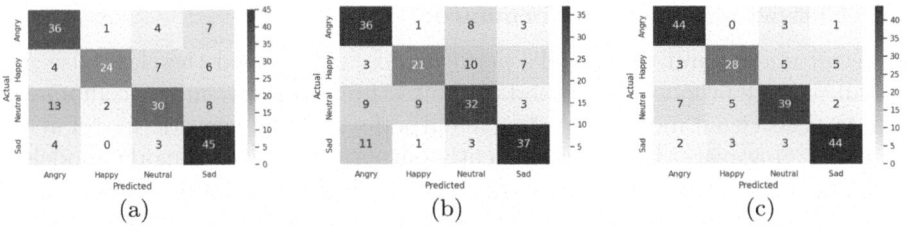

Fig. 5. Confusion matrix: (a) TimeSformer (visual) (b) DistilHuBERT (acoustic) (c) TimeSformer + DistilHuBERT (MEmoR)

MEmoR demonstrated overall improved performance compared to its individual components. Specifically, it correctly identified 44 out of 48 *angry* samples and 44 out of 52 *sad* samples. TimeSformer performed well by correctly identifying 45 out of 48 samples in the *angry* class. However, MEmoR exhibited lower accuracy in identifying *neutral* samples, correctly classifying only 39 out of 53, and in identifying *happy* samples, correctly classifying 28 out of 41. Interestingly, DistilHuBERT outperformed TimeSformer in recognizing the *happy* class, highlighting the difficulty in identifying happy expressions based solely on visual cues. The *happy* class had the highest misclassification rate for MEmoR, indicating challenges in accurately distinguishing happy expressions within the dataset. This could be due to the smaller amount of data available for the happy class or the features in happy samples being harder to differentiate from other classes. For instance, subtle movements in happy expressions may closely resemble the neutral class, leading to potential overlap.

Qualitative Analysis. We analyzed correct and incorrect emotion predictions depicted in Fig. 6 to further evaluate the effectiveness of the proposed MEmoR method. In Fig. 6(a), MEmoR made a perfect prediction, correctly identifying an angry face, consistent with its classification. Conversely, in Fig. 6(b), MEmoR's prediction was inaccurate. Classifying the emotion as happy posed challenges due to minimal changes in facial expressions compared to the neutral class. Consequently, the model incorrectly predicted it as neutral.

Audio In Bengali: আমার মায়ের স্বপ্নটা এক বছর পিছিয়ে দিয়েছিস।
English Translation: You delayed my mother's dream by a year.

Audio In Bengali: আরে, দেখতে হবে না? কার বউ, ননদ টা কার।
English Translation: Hey, don't you want to see? Whose wife, whose sister-in-law.

(a) Actual: *Angry*, Predicted: *Angry*   (b) Actual: *Happy*, Predicted: *Neutral*

Fig. 6. Sample prediction made by MEmoR: (a) correct prediction (b) incorrect prediction

7   Conclusion

This study introduces a novel multimodal dataset, MERD, designed for emotion recognition from videos, comprising 1937 samples. Using state-of-the-art feature extraction methods, a decision-level fusion framework named MEmoR, was developed to classify multimodal emotions into four categories (sad, happy, angry, and neutral). Visual feature extraction employed TimeSformer, while acoustic feature extraction utilized DistilHuBERT. Experimental results demonstrate the effectiveness of the decision-level fusion strategy, with the TimeSformer + DistilHuBERT model achieving the highest weighted f_1-score of 0.80. While our proposed model demonstrated reasonable performance overall, it exhibited poor performance in specific classes, attributable to several factors, including limited training data and the absence of advanced fusion methods. Future research will focus on expanding the dataset, both in size and diversity, to improve the generalizability of results. In addition, future directions include integrating advanced hybrid architectures to enhance accuracy and robustness in audio-visual emotion recognition. More sophisticated multimodal fusion techniques, such as attention-based mechanisms and hierarchical fusion strategies, will also be explored to effectively capture the complex interactions between audio and visual modalities.

Acknowledgment. This work is supported by the Directorate of Research & Extension, Chittagong University of Engineering & Technology (CUET), Chittagong, Bangladesh.

References

1. Ahsan, S., Hossain, E., Sharif, O., Das, A., Hoque, M.M., M. Ali, A.D.: A multimodal framework to detect target aware aggression in memes. In: Proceedings of 18th EACL, vol. 1, pp. 2487—2500 (2024)
2. Ayon, R., Rabbi, M.S., Habiba, U., Hasana, M.: Bangla speech emotion detection using machine learning ensemble methods. Adv. Sci. Technol. Eng. Syst. J. **7**(6), 70–76 (2022)
3. Bertasius, G., Wang, H., Torresani, L.: Is space-time attention all you need for video understanding? In: ICML, vol. 2, p. 4 (2021)
4. Byun, S.W., Lee, S.P.: Human emotion recognition based on the weighted integration method using image sequences and acoustic features. Multimedia Tools Appli. **80**(28), 35871–35885 (2021)
5. Chang, H.J., Yang, S.w., Lee, H.y.: DistilHuBERT: speech representation learning by layer-wise distillation of hidden-unit BERT. arXiv preprint: arXiv: 2110.01900 (2021)
6. Cohen, J.: A coefficient of agreement for nominal scales. Educ. Psychol. Measur. **20**(1), 37–46 (1960)
7. Das, R.K., Islam, N., Ahmed, M.R., Islam, S., Shatabda, S., Islam, A.M.: Banglaser: a speech emotion recognition dataset for the bangla language. Data Brief **42**, 108091 (2022)
8. Hasan, B., Abdulazeez, A.M.: A review of principal component analysis algorithm for dimensionality reduction. J. Soft Comput. Data Mining **2**(1), 20–30 (2021)
9. Ito, K., Fujioka, T., Sun, Q., Nagamatsu, K.: Audio-visual speech emotion recognition by disentangling emotion and identity attributes. In: Interspeech, pp. 4493–4497 (2021)
10. Paluzo-Hidalgo, E., Aguirre-Carrazana, G., Gonzalez-Diaz, R.: Emotion recognition in talking-face videos using persistent entropy and neural networks. arXiv preprint arXiv:2110.13571 (2021)
11. Purba, S.A., Tasnim, S., Jabin, M., Hossen, T., Hasan, M.K.: Document level emotion detection from bangla text using machine learning techniques. In: Proceedings of ICICT4SD, pp. 406–411. IEEE (2021)
12. Rahman, R., Hasan, S.A., Rubel, F.A.: Identifying sentiment and recognizing emotion from social media data in bangla language. In: Proceedings of 12th ICECE, pp. 36–39. IEEE (2022)
13. Rayhan, M.M., Al Musabe, T., Islam, M.A.: Multilabel emotion detection from bangla text using bigru and cnn-bilstm. In: Proceedings of 23rd ICCIT, pp. 1–6 (2020)
14. Russell, J.A.: Core affect and the psychological construction of emotion. Psychol. Rev. **110**(1), 145 (2003)
15. Sadaf, F., Muntakim, A., Azharul Hasan, K.: Building an affective database for emotion detection from natural bangla text. In: International Conference on Big Data, IoT and Machine Learning, pp. 621–635. Springer (2023). https://doi.org/10.1007/978-981-99-8937-9_42

16. Sultana, S., Iqbal, M.Z., Selim, M.R., Rashid, M.M., Rahman, M.S.: Bangla speech emotion recognition and cross-lingual study using deep CNN and BLSTM networks. IEEE Access **10**, 564–578 (2021)
17. Sultana, S., Rahman, M.S., Selim, M.R., Iqbal, M.Z.: Sust bangla emotional speech corpus (subesco): an audio-only emotional speech corpus for bangla. Plos one **16**(4) (2021)
18. Taheri, Z.S., Roy, A.C., Kabir, A.: Bemofusionnet: a deep learning approach for multimodal emotion classification in bangla social media posts. In: Proceedings of 26th ICCIT, pp. 1–6. IEEE (2023)

M-SAM: Multimodal Sentiment Analysis Exploiting Textual and Visual Features of Social Media Memes

Tanzin Ahammad⦿, Shawly Ahsan⦿, Jawad Hossain⦿,
and Mohammed Moshiul Hoque(✉)⦿

Chittagong University of Engineering and Technology, Chittagong 4349, Bangladesh
{u1704003,u1704057,u1704039}@student.cuet.ac.bd, moshiul_240@cuet.ac.bd

Abstract. The prevalence of memes in social media communication underscores their role in information dissemination. However, the potential for memes to spread negativity through offensive or harmful content is a significant concern. This negativity poses a challenge for sentiment analysis, mainly due to the multimodal nature of memes. To address this issue, this paper presents an intelligent multimodal framework (named M-SAM) for classifying Bengali memes into three sentiment categories: *positive*, *negative*, and *neutral*. Moreover, this work introduces new a corpus (**M-SAD**), encompassing 8361 memes. The proposed framework integrates visual and textual models, leveraging deep learning (DL) and transformer-based architectures. This work explored various DL (CNN, BiLSTM) and transformer-based models (Bangla-Bert-Base, m-BERT, XLM-R, BanglaBERT, and Indic-DistilBERT) to assess their efficacy in extracting textual features. Additionally, pre-trained visual models such as VGG16, VGG19, and ResNet50 were employed for extracting visual features. Furthermore, we investigated the late fusion method to integrate textual and visual features for multimodal training. The experimental results demonstrate that the proposed multimodal model (m-BERT + VGG16), leveraging m-BERT for textual features and VGG16 for visual features, achieves the highest weighted f_1-score of 0.749 among all multimodal methods, indicating its effectiveness in sentiment classification of Bengali memes.

Keywords: Natural language processing · Sentiment analysis · Transformers · Multimodal classification · Meme corpus

1 Introduction

Social media memes are humorous, catchy, or culturally significant content that spreads rapidly across social media platforms. They often take the form of images, videos, or text accompanied by a caption. Users share and remix them to express ideas, opinions, or emotions concisely and relatable. Social media memes shape online discourse, reflect societal trends, and foster community engagement. They can convey complex ideas or critiques in a lighthearted and accessible manner, making them particularly effective for spreading information, promoting

S. Palaiahnakote et al. (Eds.): ICPR 2024 Workshops, LNCS 15617, pp. 134–150, 2025.
https://doi.org/10.1007/978-3-031-88217-3_10

social commentary, or engaging in online activism. Detecting memes on social media platforms is crucial for maintaining a positive user experience, protecting against harmful content, and gaining insights into online trends and behavior. Memes are often created with the intent to be sarcastic or satirical; however, they can also become violent, threatening, and abusive [20]. Despite the significant increase in meme usage, meme sentiment analysis in low-resource languages, including Bengali, has received little attention. Sentiment analysis is among the extensively researched domains in Natural Language Processing (NLP). It has been thoroughly investigated in only one modality, like text or image. Combining two modalities to find sentiment is still a new research concern in LRLs. Memes make it even more difficult because they implicitly communicate humor and sarcasm. Therefore, accurately evaluating a meme may require an analysis of both the image and the accompanying text.

Although some research studies have explored sentiment analysis of social media memes in high-resource languages (HRLs) [11,17], this area remains in a rudimentary stage. To our knowledge, no prior work has addressed sentiment classification of multimodal memes in Bengali. This gap motivated us to design a system that leverages deep learning (DL) and transformer-based architectures to automatically detect whether a meme is positive, negative, or neutral based on its multimodal content. The critical contributions of the work are demonstrated in the following:

- We developed **M-SAD**, a dataset for multimodal sentiment analysis of memes, which includes 8361 Bengali memes labeled as positive, negative, or neutral. This corpus serves as a valuable resource for training and evaluating multimodal frameworks.
- We have developed M-SAM, a multimodal framework for sentiment analysis of Bengali social media memes. This framework leverages both textual and visual features, incorporating transformer architecture (m-BERT) and deep learning model (VGG16).

2   Related Work

Multimodal sentiment analysis has received less attention from NLP experts than text-based sentiment analysis. Studies on social media meme's sentiment analysis are scarce in LRLs. Kiela et al. [13] introduced a dataset comprising 10,000 memes for multimodal hateful meme detection. They investigated various unimodal and multimodal models, employing different fusion strategies. Among these, visual BERT COCO with multimodal pretraining achieved the highest AUROC score of 75.44%. Suryawanshi et al. [20] developed a MultiOFF dataset for objectionable content detection that contains 743 memes. Despite having a 0.50 f_1-score, the combined model fared worse than the text-based CNN model. Pranesh et al. [17] introduced a multimodal framework (MemeSem) for sentiment analysis of memes and achieved the highest accuracy of 67.12%. Jannat et al. [12] proposed an empirical framework for sentiment analysis of memes. They created a dataset of 1671 memes, focusing on two classes: positive and negative sentiments. Their proposed model (BiLSTM+VGG19) has the highest f_1-score (0.68). Suryawanshi et al. [21] created the Tamil memes dataset for identifying troll memes. Their approach utilized image-based features but achieved suboptimal performance, yielding an f_1-score of 0.58. Kumari et al. [15] proposed a hybrid model that extracted image and textual features using VGG16 and layered CNN. They achieved a weighted f_1-score of 0.74. Du et al. [7] developed a model to detect offensive, hateful, or false information in memes. They achieved an accuracy of 78% using the IWT meme classifier.

Sharma et al. [19] organized a shared task examining humor and sentiment in memes. Their findings demonstrated the effectiveness of merging visual and textual features using multimodal fusion approaches. Hasan et al. [8] investigated DL models to identify troll memes in the Tamil language. Their CNN-Text+VGG16 model outperformed other approaches, achieving the highest F1-score (0.49). Ahsan et al. [1] developed a novel dataset MIMOSA in Bengali and presented the MAF (Multimodal Attentive Fusion) model, which obtained 0.742 f_1-score. Hossain et al. [10] proposed a multimodal framework (MCA-SCF) which was evaluated on two publicly available datasets, MUTE and MultiOFF. Their proposed approach achieved f_1-scores of 69.7% and 70.3% for the MUTE and MultiOFF datasets, respectively, demonstrating improvement over the state-of-the-art systems on these datasets. Cao et al. [4] introduced a model to classify hateful memes utilizing pre-trained language models, achieving an AUC of 90.96. However, it faced challenges in interpreting complex contexts to produce exact predictions. In another study, Kiela et al. [14] designed a dataset to identify hate speech in multimodal memes. Their findings demonstrated that multimodal approaches outperformed unimodal counterparts. A recent study [3] utilized a frozen PVLM to generate image captions by posing questions on hateful content, which helped catch vital details for hate identification. However, some of the questions in their experiment may not have been optimal for gaining the best outcomes. Naseem et al. [16] proposed a transformer-based technique that utilizes contextual embeddings for Twitter sentiment analysis. They utilized BiLSTM to extract sentiment from Bengali texts. Their suggested model revealed significant performance advancements on US airlines (1.49%), airlines (0.95%), and Emirates Airlines (1.80%). Most past studies have primarily explored unimodal techniques (either text or image) for sentiment detection. However, both modalities (text and images) have been less explored for sentiment analysis of memes in LRLs, particularly in Bengali. This work introduces a multimodal framework that leverages deep learning and transformer-based architectures, integrating visual and textual features for improved sentiment analysis.

3   M-SAD: A New Benchmark Dataset

Due to a lack of comprehensive coverage of diverse scenarios and sufficient sample size in existing datasets for multimodal sentiment analysis, we developed **M-SAD**, a novel multimodal dataset for sentiment analysis from social media memes. To develop **M-SAD** we followed the guidelines provided by Hossain et al. [9].

Throughout seven months (from July 2022 to January 2023), 8400 memes were collected from various social media, including Facebook, Instagram, and Twitter. Approximately 88.2% of the data was gathered from Facebook. Twitter, Instagram, and Google Images each contributed 1.8%, 2.2% and 7.8% of the total, respectively. We thoroughly reviewed the memes and removed any blurry, ambiguous, or unimodal (only images or text). The filtering process produced 8361 memes. An OCR (Pytesseract[1]) was used to extract embedded text from memes. However, we manually checked and corrected the extracted captions for missing or incorrect words and phrases due to the lack of a standard OCR. After extracting text, we chose not to remove it from the images to avoid losing valuable visual and semantic information. Removing the text could potentially eliminate essential parts of the image, negatively impacting the performance of the system.

3.1   Data Annotation and Class Definition

Each data is annotated manually. The annotators were asked to adhere to the following definitions of sentiment in a meme, which we arrived at after researching existing works in this area [9]:

- **Negative:** A meme is classified as negative if its primary purpose is to degrade, insult, or dismiss an entity based on its social, personal, or organizational status or if it contains inappropriate content, such as offensive visuals or language.
- **Positive:** A meme is considered to convey positive sentiment if it expresses feelings of joy, appreciation, admiration, or amusement or if it has a humorous context without subtly intending to denigrate, mock, or demonize an entity.
- **Neutral:** A meme is termed neutral if it indicates a lack of strong positive or negative feelings, suggesting indifference, neutrality, or objectivity.

Process of Annotation: Three undergraduate students were assigned to carry out the initial annotation. To ensure consistency and accuracy during annotation, annotators were asked to explain why they assigned a sentiment to a meme. A majority vote decided the initial label. In cases of conflict, an expert with over 20 years of NLP experience thoroughly reviewed and resolved the situation. We attempted to assemble a diverse group of annotators to ensure impartiality and avoid bias toward any particular community, ethnicity, culture, or religion. Cohen's kappa was used to assess the quality of the annotation. Table 1 shows the three annotators' pairwise kappa scores (P_1, P_2, and P_3).

The average kappa value for our dataset is 0.840, indicating nearly perfect agreement among the annotators. Figure 1 depicts some memes' samples in each sentiment class.

---

[1] https://pypi.org/project/pytesseract/.

Table 1. Pairwise Cohen's kappa scores of annotators

Annotator Pair	Kappa Score
P_1 (annotators 1 and 2)	0.842
P_2 (annotators 1 and 3)	0.849
P_3 (annotators 2 and 3)	0.830
Average	**0.840**

English Translation: Happiness is casting the first vote of life

(a) Positive

English Translation: In this era, upon seeing boys and girls, one feels the urge to beat.

(b) Negative

English Translation: Everyone stays on Facebook but keeps chat offline.

(c) Neutral

Fig. 1. Sample memes from different sentiment classes: (a) Shows funny humor (b) Shows conflict (c) Shows neither positive nor negative sentiment (i.e., neutral)

3.2   Dataset Statistics

Table 2 summarizes the class-wise distribution of M-SAD, where T_w, T_{uw}, T_{mw}, and $T_{aw/c}$ denote total words, total unique words, maximum number of words, and average number of words per caption, respectively.

Table 2. M-SAD Statistics

Class	Train	Test	T_w	T_{uw}	T_{mw}	$T_{aw/c}$
Positive	2173	510	36779	9702	114	17.36
Negative	2511	695	39304	11846	74	15.41
Neutral	2004	468	32876	8745	43	15.65
Total	6688	1673	108959	17836	114	15.32

The dataset was divided into two sets: training (80%) and testing (20%). We also used 20% of the training data to create the validation set. After analyzing the dataset, we discovered that the *positive* class has 2683 samples and 9702 unique words, while the *negative* class has 3206 documents and 11846 unique words. The *neutral* class contains 2472 documents and 8745 unique words. The maximum word length in our dataset is 114. The positive class had an average of 17 words per caption, whereas the negative and neutral classes had an average of ≈15 words per caption. The developed dataset can be accessed through the following link: https://github.com/TanzinAhammad/M-SAD.

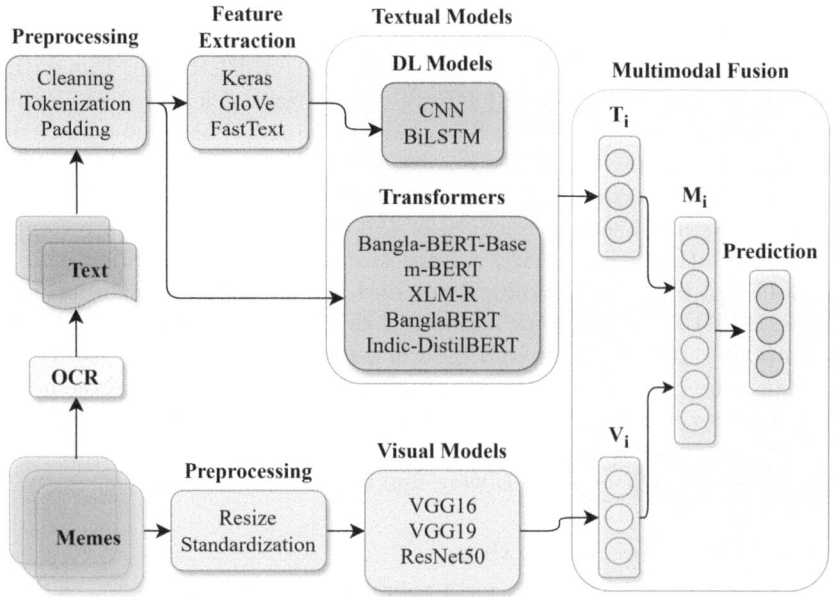

Fig. 2. Abstract view of the proposed multimodal framework (M-SAM)

4   Methodology: Development of M-SAM

This work aims to present a multimodal architecture to classify sentiment from social media memes in Bengali. We first preprocess the text and image inputs before extracting textual and visual features using various DL and transformer-based architectures. Textual and visual features are then combined to determine the sentiment of a multimodal meme. Figure 2 depicts the abstract view of the proposed architecture.

4.1   Preprocessing

Memes incorporate various modalities, such as images and text, which require distinct preprocessing techniques due to their inherent disparities. All images are resized to a uniform size of 256×256 pixels with 3 color channels to ensure consistency in the visual data processing. The input images are also preprocessed using the Keras image preprocessing function to ensure compatibility with the selected image models. Text preprocessing consists of several steps: text cleaning, sentence tokenization, sequence vectorization, etc. Initially, unwanted symbols such as punctuation and special characters were removed from the text. The BNLP toolkit was then used to compile a list of Bengali stopwords. The raw text was cleaned by removing these stopwords, which were then tokenized and padded.

4.2   Textual Features Extraction

We used CNN, BiLSTM, Bangla-BERT-Base [18], m-BERT [6], BanglaBERT [2], XLM-R [5], and Indic DistilBERT to extract textual features. We explored Keras, along with pretrained FastText and pretrained GloVe embedding methods, to extract features, which were subsequently input into DL-based textual models. For the Keras embedding method, we employed an embedding dimension of 64 and a maximum sequence length of 150. The CNN architecture comprises a single convolutional layer with a filter size of 128 and a window size of 5. This is followed by a max pooling layer and a dense layer containing 64 neurons. The BiLSTM architecture includes a single BiLSTM layer with 64 units and a dropout rate of 0.2, followed by a dense layer with 32 neurons. The final layer of both the CNN and BiLSTM models is a dense layer with three neurons. The preprocessed texts were initially tokenized for transformer-based models using the corresponding pre-trained transformer's tokenizer. Subsequently, the transformer-based textual models were fine-tuned using our corpus.

4.3   Visual Features Extraction

To extract visual features, we utilized VGG16, VGG19, and ResNet50 models. These models were pre-trained on large image datasets and then adapted to our specific corpus using the transfer learning method. For fine-tuning, we removed the top layers of each pre-trained model and added a global average pooling layer, followed by a flattened layer. Finally, we incorporated a dense layer with softmax activation function to facilitate classification.

4.4   Multimodal Fusion

For multimodal training, we concatenate the softmax outputs of the visual and textual models along the feature dimension. This involves taking the output vectors from both models and combining them side-by-side to form a more significant vector. If we denote the softmax outputs of the textual and visual models for the i-th sample as $T_i = \{t_1, t_2, ..., t_n\}$ and $V_i = \{v_1, v_2, ..., v_n\}$, respectively, then the concatenated vector M_i can be obtained using Eq. 1.

$$M_i = \{v_1, v_2, ..., v_n, t_1, t_2, ..., t_n\} \tag{1}$$

The concatenated vector was passed through a dense layer with three neurons and a softmax activation function for classification.

4.5   Model Training

We trained the multimodal model using the '*categorical_crossentropy*' loss function and the '*adam*' optimizer, with a learning rate of $4e^{-5}$ and a batch size of 16. We experimented with 11 textual feature extractors and 3 visual feature extractors to determine the best architecture for sentiment analysis. Among all the framework variations we investigated, the m-BERT+VGG16 architecture, referred to as M-SAM, demonstrated superior performance compared to the others.

5   Experiments

Google Colaboratory platform is used to conduct the experiments. All experiments employed Python 3, with access to 12 GB of RAM and GPU acceleration. The dataset was 976 MB in size. For DL, we operated several essential libraries, including Pandas, NumPy (version 1.18), Keras (version 2.3), and TensorFlow (version 2.2). The models were created and trained using the TensorFlow framework and the Keras library. Pre-trained transformers were downloaded and fine-tuned utilizing the Hugging Face library. This work employed the BNLP toolkit for text preprocessing, while model evaluation was executed using the Scikit-Learn library (version 0.22). The models were trained with the '*categorical_crossentropy*' loss function and '*adam*' optimizer. We ran extensive experiments on the models before selecting the best model using the validation set. To evaluate the performance of our proposed architecture, we investigated eleven textual baseline models and three visual baseline models. We adopted the weighted f_1-score (WF) as the primary evaluation metric. Besides, the individual class performance is measured through accuracy (A), precision (P), and recall (R).

5.1   Textual Baseline Models

We explored various textual baseline models, encompassing CNN and BiLSTM variants employing diverse embedding techniques such as Keras, GloVe, and FastText. Additionally, we examined transformer models, including Bangla BERT Base, m-BERT, XLM-R, Bangla BERT, and Indic DistilBERT.

- **CNN:** We used a single-layer CNN architecture to construct the model. The convolution layer included 256 filters, each with a kernel size of five. After the convolution layer, a max-pooling layer was used to extract the most important features. The output of the max-pooling layer was then fed into a dense layer of 64 neurons. Finally, for classification, a softmax layer of three neurons was added.
- **BiLSTM:** The BiLSTM architecture consisted of a single-layer bidirectional LSTM with 64 hidden units and a dropout rate of 0.3. A dense layer with 32 neurons was added after the BiLSTM layer. A softmax layer was used for classification.
- **Transformers:** We investigated transformer-based baseline models, which have gained popularity in natural language processing tasks due to their ability to capture long-range sequence dependencies. Bangla BERT and Bangla BERT Base are transformers that process Bengali language text. The Indic DistilBERT is another transformer model explicitly created for processing Bengali language text. It is based on a simplified version of the original BERT model that is more computationally efficient while maintaining high performance. Multilingual BERT (m-BERT) is a multilingual transformer model trained in various languages, whereas XLM-R is a cross-lingual transformer model trained in 100 languages. We trained the transformers with a batch size of 16.

Table 3. Performance of visual baseline models on the test set

Modality	Classifier	A	P	R	WF
Visual	**VGG16**	0.751	0.761	0.751	**0.750**
	VGG19	0.725	0.737	0.725	0.730
	ResNet50	0.626	0.659	0.626	0.635

5.2   Visual Baseline Models

Visual baseline models were constructed using the pre-trained image models
VGG16, VGG19, and ResNet50. These models were trained on large-scale image
datasets such as ImageNet, enabling them to extract high-level features from
images. The top layers of the pre-trained models were removed, and the models were fine-tuned using the developed corpus. The VGG16 model comprises
16 layers, including 13 convolutional layers and three fully connected layers.
Each convolutional layer is followed by a max pooling layer to reduce the spatial
dimension of the feature maps. The VGG19 model comprises 19 layers, including
convolutional layers and max pooling layers for downsampling. The ResNet50
comprises 50 layers and utilizes skip connections to address the vanishing gradient problem, allowing for more accessible training of deep networks. These
pre-trained models have been widely used in various computer vision tasks due
to their feature extraction and classification effectiveness. We added a global
average pooling layer, a flattened layer, and a softmax layer on top of the base
models to train the visual baseline models.

6   Results

Table 3 illustrates the evaluation results of the visual baseline models on the
test set. The VGG16 achieved the highest WF score of 0.750 among the visual
baseline models. VGG19 also demonstrated good performance with a WF score
of 0.730, outperforming ResNet50.

The textual baseline model, BiLSTM, outperformed the CNN model for
Keras and FastText embedding methods (Table 4). However, the CNN model
outperformed the BiLSTM model for the GloVe embedding method. The m-
BERT model demonstrated superior performance compared to other textual
models. It achieved a WF score of 0.791, precision of 0.794, recall of 0.791, and
accuracy of 0.791. Indic-DistilBERT achieved the second-highest WF score of
0.782.

Table 5 demonstrates the performance of DL-based multimodal models, confirming that the BiLSTM+VGG16 model with keras embedding achieved the
highest WF score of 0.720 among all the DL-based multimodal models. Table 6
shows the performance of transformer-based multimodal models. The results
revealed that the m-BERT+VGG16 model outperformed all multimodal models, achieving the maximum WF score (0.749). However, multimodal models

Table 4. Performance of textual baseline models on the test set

Embedding	Classifier	A	P	R	WF
Keras	CNN	0.728	0.745	0.728	0.733
	BiLSTM	0.763	0.778	0.763	**0.768**
FastText	CNN	0.672	0.710	0.672	0.686
	BiLSTM	0.682	0.715	0.682	0.694
GloVe	CNN	0.699	0.716	0.699	0.705
	BiLSTM	0.692	0.720	0.692	0.702
-	Bangla-Bert-Base	0.756	0.761	0.756	0.753
	m-BERT	0.791	0.794	0.791	**0.791**
	XLM-R	0.748	0.752	0.748	0.745
	BanglaBERT	0.750	0.754	0.750	0.751
	Indic-DistilBERT	0.781	0.790	0.781	0.782

sometimes fail to beat unimodal models for several reasons. Primarily, images and text frequently represent opposing or conflicting sentiments. For instance, an image may have a positive visual appeal, while the accompanying text might express a negative sentiment, or vice versa. This disparity raises noise and confusion in the multimodal approach, making it hard for the model to incorporate and analyze these conflicting signals effectively. Besides, the features extracted from images and text may not always align appropriately, problematizing the fusion process. Enriching the fusion process or investigating alternative feature representations could aid in mitigating these concerns and improve the overall performance of multimodal approaches. Moreover, further research into optimizing the integration of diverse modalities may yield better performance in sentiment analysis tasks.

Summary of Best-Performed Models: Table 7 presents the performance comparison between the best multimodal and unimodal models. The analysis indicates that the multimodal model (M-SAM), which integrates deep learning and transformer-based techniques (m-BERT+VGG16), performed worse than the unimodal models, specifically the visual (VGG16) and textual (m-BERT) models. This suggests there may be challenges in effectively combining different modalities for sentiment analysis. Future studies could explore ways to improve the performance of multimodal models by addressing these challenges and optimizing the integration process.

6.1   Class-Wise Performance

To comprehensively evaluate the model's performance, we examined the class-wise performance of the best textual baseline, visual baseline, and multimodal models (Table 8). The analysis reveals significant improvements, notably with

Table 5. Performance of DL-based multimodal models on the test set

Embedding	Classifier	A	P	R	WF
Keras	CNN+VGG16	0.692	0.731	0.692	0.706
	BiLSTM+VGG16	0.706	0.742	0.706	**0.720**
	CNN+VGG19	0.698	0.729	0.698	0.710
	BiLSTM+VGG19	0.687	0.719	0.687	0.699
	CNN+ResNet50	0.676	0.702	0.676	0.686
	BiLSTM+ResNet50	0.620	0.656	0.620	0.630
FastText	CNN+VGG16	0.692	0.733	0.692	0.707
	BiLSTM+VGG16	0.684	0.732	0.684	0.702
	CNN+VGG19	0.606	0.655	0.606	0.624
	BiLSTM+VGG19	0.621	0.670	0.621	0.640
	CNN+ResNet50	0.615	0.679	0.615	0.639
	BiLSTM+ResNet50	0.659	0.691	0.659	0.671
GloVe	CNN+VGG16	0.650	0.701	0.650	0.669
	BiLSTM+VGG16	0.664	0.712	0.664	0.682
	CNN+VGG19	0.646	0.696	0.646	0.665
	BiLSTM+VGG19	0.656	0.705	0.656	0.674
	CNN+ResNet50	0.677	0.690	0.677	0.682
	BiLSTM+ResNet50	0.680	0.711	0.680	0.691

Table 6. Performance of transformer-based multimodal models on the test set

Classifier	A	P	R	WF
Bangla-Bert-Base+VGG16	0.734	0.745	0.734	0.733
m-BERT+VGG16 (proposed)	0.752	0.757	0.752	**0.749**
XLM-R+VGG16	0.730	0.740	0.730	0.729
BanglaBERT+VGG16	0.731	0.736	0.731	0.728
Indic-DistilBERT+VGG16	0.736	0.741	0.736	0.734
Bangla-Bert-Base+VGG19	0.713	0.741	0.713	0.723
m-BERT+VGG19	0.739	0.751	0.739	0.740
XLM-R+VGG19	0.676	0.704	0.676	0.687
BanglaBERT+VGG19	0.723	0.727	0.723	0.724
Indic-DistilBERT+VGG19	0.736	0.740	0.736	0.737
Bangla-Bert-Base+ResNet50	0.704	0.731	0.704	0.714
m-BERT+ResNet50	0.735	0.744	0.735	0.734
XLM-R+ResNet50	0.697	0.704	0.697	0.696
BanglaBERT+ResNet50	0.723	0.724	0.723	0.723
Indic-DistilBERT+ResNet50	0.731	0.733	0.731	0.732

Table 7. Performance summary of the best-performed multimodal and unimodal models

Modality	Classifier	A	P	R	WF
Visual	VGG16	0.751	0.761	0.751	0.750
Textual	m-BERT	0.791	0.794	0.791	0.791
Textual + Visual	**m-BERT+VGG16 (M-SAM)**	0.752	0.757	0.752	**0.749**

the best multimodal model (M-SAM), achieving the highest accuracy and recall for the *negative* class and the highest precision for the *positive* class. However, m-BERT performed better than mBERT+VGG16 across all the classes in terms of weighted f_1-score. The M-SAM performed best for the *negative* class (0.796) while it performed worst for the *neutral* class (0.711).

Table 8. Class-wise performance of the best textual baseline (m-BERT), visual baseline (VGG16), and multimodal (m-BERT+VGG16) models

Class	Method	A	P	R	WF
Positive	mBERT	**0.792**	0.729	0.792	0.759
	VGG16	0.770	0.682	0.770	0.723
	mBERT+VGG16	0.647	0.814	0.647	0.721
Negative	mBERT	0.833	0.809	0.833	0.821
	VGG16	0.812	0.751	0.812	0.781
	mBERT+VGG16	**0.873**	0.731	0.873	0.796
Neutral	mBERT	**0.729**	0.844	0.729	0.782
	VGG16	0.637	0.864	0.637	0.733
	mBERT+VGG16	0.688	0.735	0.688	0.711

6.2 Comparison with Existing Works

The performance of the proposed m-BERT+VGG16 model was evaluated by comparing it with existing multimodal meme classification methods. We implemented these existing approaches using our dataset and presented the comparative performance of the models in Table 9. The results indicate that the proposed model surpassed previous techniques regarding weighted F1-score.

6.3 Error Analysis

We conducted quantitative and qualitative error analyses to understand the proposed model's performance comprehensively.

Table 9. Comparison between M-SAM and existing studies

Approach	WF
BERT+VGG16 [17]	0.73
BiLSTM+VGG16 [12]	0.72
CNN+ResNet50 [9]	0.68
m-BERT+VGG16 (**proposed**)	0.74

Quantitative Analysis: We performed an in-depth error analysis of the best visual baseline, textual baseline, and multimodal models using a confusion matrix to gain further insight (Fig. 3).

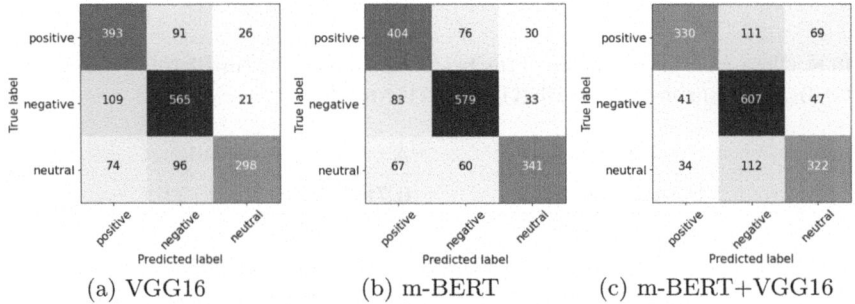

(a) VGG16   (b) m-BERT   (c) m-BERT+VGG16

Fig. 3. Confusion matrix for: (a) best visual baseline, (b) best textual baseline, and (c) best multimodal model (M-SAM)

The VGG16 model successfully predicted 565 negative memes, 393 positive memes, and 298 neutral memes, but it misclassified 130 memes as negative, 117 memes as positive, and 170 as neutral. The m-BERT model performed significantly better than VGG16 by correctly classifying 404 instances out of 510 positive memes. It only made incorrect predictions for 106 memes, reducing the error rate by 2%. Out of 510 positive memes, the M-SAM model correctly recognized 330 memes and misclassified the remaining 180 as negative or neutral. However, the M-SAM model significantly improved over the visual and textual baseline models in correctly classifying negative memes. It accurately identified 607 out of 695 negative memes. It showed notable improvement in detecting neutral memes compared to the visual baseline model, accurately identifying 332 out of 468 neutral memes.

Qualitative Analysis: Figure 4 depicts sample predictions on the test set by the visual model (VGG16), textual model (m-BERT), and M-SAM. The m-BERT model accurately predicted two memes (first and third). The VGG16 model accurately predicted two memes (second and third). The M-SAM model accurately predicted all four memes. Due to the multimodal nature of the memes, the unimodal models encountered challenges in prediction. In contrast, the multimodal model successfully predicted the four memes by leveraging visual and textual modalities.

Meme	True Label	Visual Model (VGG16)	Textual Model (m-BERT)	M-SAM
 (পরিবারের সবাই:সেহেরী করতে ঘুম থেকে উঠার জন্য এলার্ম দেয় না ঘুমিয়ে একবারে সেহরী করা আমি:)	Neutral	Negative	Neutral	Neutral
 (আগে মানুষ গরুর সাথে কাউকি তুলতো আর এখন গরুর সাথে লাইভে আসে!)	Negative	Negative	Positive	Negative
 (সুখ হল জীবনের প্রথম ভোট দেওয়া)	Positive	Positive	Positive	Positive
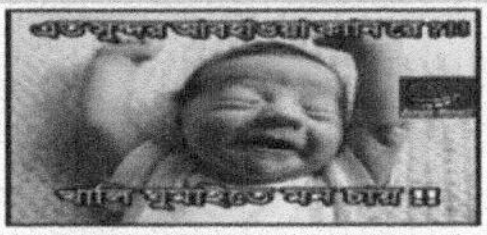 (এত সুন্দর আবহাওয়া ক্যান রে ?!! থালি ঘুমাইতে মন চায়!)	Positive	Negative	Negative	Positive

Fig. 4. Few predicted outcomes by the best-performed models

7 Discussion

Our multimodal approach occasionally demonstrated inferior performance compared to unimodal approaches. The current model's absence of advanced fusion methods may hinder the effective integration of text and image data. Concatenating high-level features from both modalities may inadequately capture their intricate interactions, resulting in suboptimal performance. Additionally, the computational expense of combining BERT and VGG poses significant challenges in memory usage and processing power, limiting scalability and practical deployment. Moreover, this study classified sentiments into three primary categories: positive, negative, and neutral. However, this classification schema lacks the granularity of systems incorporating benign confounders, essential for effectively leveraging textual and visual information, capturing complex multimodal interactions, enhancing generalization to real-world data, and mitigating biases towards any single modality. In this work, we employed straightforward feature extraction methods and fusion strategies. In future work, we plan to explore more novel approaches, such as developing custom architectures that seamlessly integrate multimodal data and employing advanced techniques like attention mechanisms, transformer-based fusion strategies, and intermediate fusion strategies to enhance the synergy between textual and visual features. Additionally, we will focus on optimizing models and reducing computational overhead. We plan to incorporate benign confounders in future studies to enrich multimodal interaction, leading to deeper insights and improved performance.

8   Conclusion

This study introduced a multimodal approach to classifying sentiment in Bengali social media memes into positive, negative, and neutral classes. This work developed a framework called M-SAM that leverages multimodal features, including visual and textual data, utilizing deep learning and transformer-based techniques. Experimental evaluation on a newly created dataset (M-SAD) showcased superior performance, achieving the highest WF-score (0.749) when M-SAM utilized m-BERT for textual features and VGG16 for visual features. We plan to explore other fusion strategies to merge image and text sentiment analysis in future work. Specifically, we aim to improve the fusion process by including early fusion, hybrid fusion, and other advanced techniques to enhance overall performance. Future directions include expanding the dataset across diverse domains and incorporating benign confounders. Moreover, further exploring advanced techniques such as MMBT, ViLBERT, and VisualBERT could enhance performance.

Acknowledgment. This work was supported by Directorate of Research & Extension (DRE), CUET.

References

1. Ahsan, S., Hossain, E., Sharif, O., Das, A., Hoque, M.M., Dewan, M.: A multimodal framework to detect target aware aggression in memes. In: Proceedings of the 18th EACL, pp. 2487–2500 (2024)
2. Bhattacharjee, A., et al.: BanglaBERT: language model pretraining and benchmarks for low-resource language understanding evaluation in Bangla. In: Findings of the ACL: NAACL 2022, pp. 1318–1327. ACL (2022)
3. Cao, R., Hee, M.S., Kuek, A., Chong, W.H., Lee, R.K.W., Jiang, J.: Pro-cap: leveraging a frozen vision-language model for hateful meme detection (2023). https://arxiv.org/abs/2308.08088

4. Cao, R., Lee, R.K.W., Chong, W.H., Jiang, J.: Prompting for multimodal hateful meme classification. In: Goldberg, Y., Kozareva, Z., Zhang, Y. (eds.) Proceedings of the 2022 Conference on Empirical Methods in Natural Language Processing, pp. 321–332. Association for Computational Linguistics, Abu Dhabi, United Arab Emirates (2022). https://doi.org/10.18653/v1/2022.emnlp-main.22. https://aclanthology.org/2022.emnlp-main.22

5. Conneau, A., et al.: Unsupervised cross-lingual representation learning at scale. CoRR **abs/1911.02116** (2019). http://arxiv.org/abs/1911.02116

6. Devlin, J., Chang, M.W., Lee, K., Toutanova, K.: BERT: pre-training of deep bidirectional transformers for language understanding. arXiv:1810.04805 (2018)

7. Du, Y., Masood, M.A., Joseph, K.: Understanding visual memes: an empirical analysis of text superimposed on memes shared on Twitter. In: Proceedings of the International AAAI Conference on Web and Social Media, vol. 14, pp. 153–164 (2020)

8. Hasan, M., Jannat, N., Hossain, E., Sharif, O., Hoque, M.M.: CUET-NLP@ DravidianLangTech-ACL2022: investigating deep learning techniques to detect multimodal troll memes. In: Proceedings of the 2nd DravidianLangTech, pp. 170–176 (2022)

9. Hossain, E., Sharif, O., Hoque, M.M.: MemoSen: a multimodal dataset for sentiment analysis of memes. In: Proceedings of the 13th LREC, pp. 1542–1554 (2022)

10. Hossain, E., Sharif, O., Hoque, M.M., Preum, S.M.: Align before attend: aligning visual and textual features for multimodal hateful content detection. In: Falk, N., Papi, S., Zhang, M. (eds.) Proceedings of the 18th EACL: SRW, pp. 162–174. ACL (2024)

11. Hu, A., Flaxman, S.: Multimodal sentiment analysis to explore the structure of emotions. In: Proceedings of the 24th ACM SIGKDD International Conference on Knowledge Discovery & Data Mining, pp. 350–358 (2018)

12. Jannat, N., Das, A., Sharif, O., Hoque, M.M.: An empirical framework for identifying sentiment from multimodal memes using fusion approach. In: Proceedings of the 25th ICCIT, pp. 791–796. IEEE (2022)

13. Kiela, D., et al.: The hateful memes challenge: detecting hate speech in multimodal memes. Adv. Neural. Inf. Process. Syst. **33**, 2611–2624 (2020)

14. Kiela, D., et al.: The hateful memes challenge: detecting hate speech in multimodal memes (2021). https://arxiv.org/abs/2005.04790

15. Kumari, K., Singh, J.P., Dwivedi, Y.K., Rana, N.P.: Multi-modal aggression identification using convolutional neural network and binary particle swarm optimization. Futur. Gener. Comput. Syst. **118**, 187–197 (2021)

16. Naseem, U., Razzak, I., Musial, K., Imran, M.: Transformer based deep intelligent contextual embedding for twitter sentiment analysis. Futur. Gener. Comput. Syst. **113**, 58–69 (2020)

17. Pranesh, R.R., Shekhar, A.: MemeSem: a multi-modal framework for sentimental analysis of meme via transfer learning. In: 4th Lifelong Machine Learning Workshop at ICML 2020 (2020)

18. Sarker, S.: BanglaBERT: Bengali mask language model for Bengali language understanding (2020). https://github.com/sagorbrur/bangla-bert

19. Sharma, C., et al.: SemEval-2020 task 8: Memotion analysis-the visuo-lingual metaphor! In: Proceedings of the 14th Workshop on SemEval, pp. 759–773 (2020)

20. Suryawanshi, S., Chakravarthi, B.R., Arcan, M., Buitelaar, P.: Multimodal meme dataset (multiOFF) for identifying offensive content in image and text. In: Proceedings of the 2nd Workshop TRAC, pp. 32–41. ELRA (2020)
21. Suryawanshi, S., Chakravarthi, B.R., Verma, P., Arcan, M., McCrae, J.P., Buitelaar, P.: A dataset for troll classification of tamilmemes. In: Proceedings of the 5th WILDRE5, pp. 7–13. ELRA (2020)

Dynamic Modality and View Selection for Emotion Recognition: An Experimental Study on Missing Modality Evaluation

Luciana Trinkaus Menon[1(✉)], Luiz Carlos Ribeiro Neduziak[1],
Jean Paul Barddal[1], Alessandro Lameiras Koerich[2],
and Alceu de Souza Britto Jr.[1]

[1] Graduate Program in Informatics (PPGIa), Pontifical Catholic University
of Parana (PUCPR), Curitiba, PR, Brazil
`luciana.menon@ppgia.pucpr.br`
[2] École de Technologie Supérieure (ÉTS), Montreal, Canada

Abstract. Multiple channels, such as speech (voice) and facial expressions (image), are crucial in understanding human emotions. However, AI's journey in multimodal emotion recognition (MER) is marked by substantial technical challenges. One significant hurdle is how AI models manage the absence of a particular modality - a frequent occurrence in real-world situations. This study's central focus is assessing the performance and resilience of two strategies when confronted with the lack of one modality: a novel multimodal dynamic modality and view selection and a cross-attention mechanism. Results on the RECOLA dataset show that dynamic selection-based methods are a promising approach for MER. In the missing modalities scenarios, most dynamic selection-based methods outperformed the baseline. The study concludes by emphasizing the intricate interplay between audio and video modalities in emotion prediction, showcasing the adaptability of dynamic selection methods in handling missing modalities.

Keywords: Multimodal Emotion Recognition · Missing Modalities · Dynamic Modal Selection

1 Introduction

The world we live in is multimodal. In this context, modality refers to how we perceive and interact with our environment. Such a concept is crucial in advancing artificial intelligence (AI), as it underlines the AI systems' need to understand and integrate these different modalities effectively. The study of the complementary relationships between modalities such as visual (video), auditory (audio), textual (text), and sensory signals (e.g., heart rate variability) is essential for developing more sophisticated and context-aware AI systems [2,9].

Most current multimodal approaches assume that multiple modalities are always available and they carry complementary information [9]. This perspective is crucial in understanding how combining these modalities can lead to a richer and more comprehensive interpretation of underlying data. Each modality - visual, audio, textual, or otherwise - is believed to contribute unique insights. When merged, these insights form enhanced representations that are often more informative and accurate than any modality could achieve alone [15].

However, the ideal scenario of having all expected modalities available for a given task is not always possible [5,8,21,23]. In many situations, data from certain modalities may be missing or corrupted due to technical issues, privacy concerns, or other constraints. Therefore, addressing missing modalities in multimodal learning is critical, as it reflects the challenges of dealing with real-world data that may not always conform to ideal settings.

This work evaluates two possible strategies to model the interaction of modalities (video+audio) in the context of emotion recognition. The first is a novel approach based on dynamic selection across the multimodal space. The second employs a well-known strategy using a neural network with an attention-based mechanism to jointly learn the modalities inspired by the method proposed in [16]. We focus on assessing the impact of one modality's absence on model performance within these distinct multimodal AI approaches. Thus, two research questions (RQ) guided our experiments. RQ1: "Could dynamic selection of modalities and views be a promising approach for a multimodal AI method?", assessing the proposed dynamic selection method; RQ2: "What is the impact on emotion recognition performance when one modality (video or audio) is missing?", concerning the impact of a missing modality on each evaluated multimodal approach. To this end, we simulate the loss of a modality by replacing the corresponding features with zeros

This work examines the challenges faced by AI in multimodal emotion recognition (MER). By mitigating the impact of missing data through intelligent selection strategies, our methods lead to more accurate and resilient models capable of maintaining performance even in challenging conditions. Additionally, it explores innovative methodologies and contributes to advancing the state of the art in emotion recognition regarding strategies to integrate different modalities.

The remainder of this paper is structured into seven sections. Section 2 discusses related works on MER and missing modalities. Section 3 outlines the proposed method for dynamic modality and view selection. Section 4 explains the cross-attention method. Section 5 details the strategies employed to assess the impact of missing modalities on the proposed methods and the baseline. Section 6 presents the experimental results and corresponding analysis. Finally, our conclusions and avenues for further research are presented in Sect. 7.

2   Related Works

The field of MER has been the subject of extensive research, given its applicability in various domains [1,3,4,9,14–16]. This section highlights relevant works addressing the importance of emotion recognition through multiple modalities and dealing with missing modalities during inference.

Multiple modalities are essential in emotion recognition because humans simultaneously express emotions through various channels. Multimodal emotion recognition leverages both verbal and non-verbal cues, enhancing reliability and accuracy compared to unimodal models [4,9]. However, multimodal data present challenges such as choosing the most suitable data representations, addressing misalignment between elements of different modalities, and managing intramodal and cross-modal data correlation and fusion approaches [4].

Dealing with missing data is one of the most critical challenges in multimodal fields [9]. Several factors can contribute to the absence or unavailability of specific modalities in MER approaches at inference time, such as hardware malfunctions, privacy restrictions, and environmental conditions [1,3,8]. Addressing these challenges is critical for developing robust MER systems.

Handling missing modalities in multimodal approaches often involves three strategies to adapt to such situations [1,3,7,8,21]: (i) imputing or filling in missing modalities using data imputation or leveraging information from other available modalities; (ii) designing models that can gracefully handle scenarios where certain modalities are missing, potentially by learning to rely more on available modalities; (iii) developing models that can adapt to varying modalities or different data distributions, allowing for better generalization when faced with missing modalities.

Several works propose innovative approaches to the absence of modalities during inference. When dealing with missing modalities, common approaches often perform imputations to address the absence of modalities before proceeding with additional computations. Simple imputation methods, such as filling missing values with zeros, are straightforward but may lead to considerable inaccuracies.

Da Silva-Filarder et al. [19] studied multimodal variational autoencoders and stated that a critical property of multimodal generative models is to have efficient approaches to deal with missing modalities and to enable cross-generation. The authors introduced latent component dropout and exhaustive cross-generation methods to handle missing modalities. Li et al. [5] also address the issue of missing modalities. According to the authors, these missing data harm extracting features of multimodal data, resulting in a decline in model performance and inaccurate results. Therefore, a multi-head attention network is proposed to enhance feature extraction and association between missing and non-missing modalities.

Zhu et al. [23] developed an invariant feature for a missing modality imagination network, using two encoders to extract high-level and modality-invariant features. Vazquez-Rodriguez et al. [21] proposed a transformer-based architecture for continuous prediction of arousal and valence with missing modalities; a multimodal transformer is used as an encoder to obtain representations from the different modalities, and a transformer decoder is used to process those representations and make predictions. An encoder-decoder attention mechanism (cross-attention) of the transformer decoder is used to weigh the importance of different modalities.

Concerning the techniques used to solve the emotion recognition task, LSTM networks have proven effective in handling time-series data and capturing temporal dependencies, critical aspects of emotion recognition. Their ability to retain long-term dependencies makes them suitable for modeling sequences of emotional expressions over time and are widely used in arousal and valence regression problems [6,7,9]. Other interesting works present multimodal frameworks based on Transformer architecture and attention mechanisms for MER [3,8,10]. Despite the impressive performance of transformer-based approaches, their computation of attention weights does not consider the complementary relationship between audio and video features [16]. Additionally, recent work shows that Transformers fail at capturing sequential dependencies in time series [22].

3 Proposed Dynamic Modality and View Selection Method

The proposed dynamic selection-based method considers features from AVEC'16 [20], encompassing audio and video modalities. As shown in Fig. 1, the audio features include acoustic features, MFCCs, and Mel spectrograms. On the video side, we incorporate appearance features and geometric features. Each regressor is trained independently, resulting in a pool of regressors denoted as $F = f_1, f_2, \ldots, f_N$, where N is the total number of regressors. Two LSTM layers with 256 cells each are employed to consider the temporal structure of the data. For the recurrent layers, the input is segmented into sequences of 6 s, corresponding to 150 time steps (frames) at a sampling rate of 16 kHz.

The LSTM models are initially evaluated in the dynamic modal selection (DMS) phase. DMS is performed by training a meta-classifier with concatenated outputs from each regressor (a vector of dimension N). Training is conducted on the validation set, and the ideal output is defined as the modal (audio or video) with the best mean Concordance Correlation Coefficient (CCC), the modal whose predictions are closest to the proper labeling.

After the modal is selected, intra-modal dynamic view selection (DVS) is performed. Each model from the selected modal receives a weight to assess each test case $\mathbf{x}_j$ based on its performance in the competence region Ψ - set composed of the K-nearest neighbors of $\mathbf{x}_j$ in the validation set. The distance metric used to find Ψ, denoted as $dist_k$, is defined as the Euclidean distance between two sets of features. For each test instance $\mathbf{x}_j$, we find Ψ by calculating the distances $dist_k(\mathbf{x}_j, \mathbf{x}_i)$ with all instances $\mathbf{x}_i$ in the validation set. We then sort these distances in ascending order and define Ψ as the set of the K nearest neighbors of $\mathbf{x}_j$, which are the K smallest distances.

$$\Psi = \{\mathbf{x}_{(1)}, \mathbf{x}_{(2)}, \ldots, \mathbf{x}_{(k)}\} \tag{1}$$

where $\mathbf{x}_{(1)}, \mathbf{x}_{(2)}, \ldots, \mathbf{x}_{(k)}$ are the feature instances in the validation set. The DVS selects the regressor with the smallest accumulated error in the competence region or combines all the regressors or a subset using weighted averaging according to a calculated weight α_i of regressor f_i.

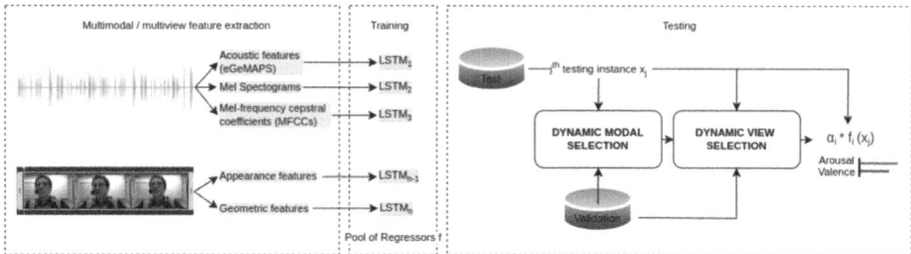

Fig. 1. Dynamic modality and view selection method. The audio features include acoustic features, MFCCs, and Mel spectrograms. The video features include appearance features and geometric features. All regressors are trained separately, and a pool of regressors is obtained. The best modal is selected in the dynamic modal selection phase. After that, in the intra-modal dynamic view selection, each model receives a weight to evaluate each test case according to its assertiveness in the competence zone.

The impact of the absence of a modality was accessed using traditional dynamic selection techniques [11], adapted here for the multimodal problem: dynamic selection (DS), dynamic weighting (DW) and dynamic weighting selection (DWS). In the **DS**, we select the regressor from the previously chosen modal with the smallest accumulated error in the competence region. **DW** combines all regressors from a pre-selected modal using weighted averaging. For each test pattern $\mathbf{x}_j$, its competence region Ψ is calculated. For each item in Ψ, a weight d_k is calculated using Eq. (2), where $dist_k$ is the distance measure between the item in the competence region $t_k \in \Psi$ and the test pattern x_j. The vector $d_1, d_2, ..., d_k$ is used to calculate the weight α_i of regressor f_i using Eq. (3), where N is the size of the selected modal regressors pool, k represents the neighbor index, and $sqe_{k,i}$ is the squared error of regressor i calculated using the item $t_k \in \Psi$. Finally, **DWS** combines a subset of regressors, and regressors with the accumulated error in the upper half of the error interval $E_i > (E_{max} - E_{max})/2$ are discarded. The method for calculating the weights of the regressors and the strategy for combining the models are the same as the **DW** algorithm (Eqs. (2) and (3)).

$$d_k = \frac{(\text{dist}_k)^{-1}}{\sum_{j=1}^{K} (\text{dist}_j)^{-1}} \tag{2}$$

$$\alpha_i = \frac{\left[\sum_{k=1}^{K} (d_k * sqe_{k,i})\right]^{-1}}{\sum_{n=1}^{N} \left[\sum_{k=1}^{K} (d_k * sqe_{k,i})\right]^{-1}} \tag{3}$$

It is important to emphasize that tests were conducted using the standard methods of dynamic selection, DS, DW, and DWS, with K varying from 5 to 150. All results presented in this work are with $K = 100$. In addition, as baselines, we compute the simple average of the regressors' outputs and utilize the cross-attention architecture described in the next section.

4   Cross-Attention Architecture

The current work utilizes the cross-attention architecture proposed by Praveen et al. [16]. In general terms, the cross-attention model is set to receive two data sequences representing audio and video modalities, which are combined and processed to generate a single prediction of arousal or valence.

Let the feature vector sets X_a and X_v be extracted from the audio (A) and video (V) modalities from a fixed-size subsequence S, where $X_a = \{x_a^1, x_a^2, \ldots, x_a^L\} \in \mathbb{R}^{d_a \times L}$ and $X_v = \{x_v^1, x_v^2, \ldots, x_v^L\} \in \mathbb{R}^{d_v \times L}$. Here, L denotes the number of non-overlapping clips taken uniformly from S. In turn, d_a and d_v represent the dimensions of the audio and video features, respectively, where x_a^l and x_v^l are audio and video vectors for $l = 1, 2, \ldots, L$ clips.

The joint representation of audio and video features ($\mathbf{J}$) is obtained from the concatenation of audio and video feature vectors $\mathbf{J} = [\mathbf{X_a}; \mathbf{X_v}] \in \mathbb{R}^{d \times L}$, where $d = d_a + d_v$ denotes the dimension of the concatenated features. The joint representation $\mathbf{J}$ of a subsequence $\mathbf{S}$ is used to focus attention on the unimodal representations $\mathbf{X_a}$ and $\mathbf{X_v}$. In this regard, the joint correlation matrix for the audio features $\mathbf{C_a}$ between the audio features $\mathbf{X_a}$ and the representation $\mathbf{J}$ will be given by Eq. (4).

$$\mathbf{C_a} = \tanh\left(\frac{\mathbf{X}_a^T \mathbf{W}_{ja} \mathbf{J}}{\sqrt{d}}\right) \tag{4}$$

where $\mathbf{W}_{ja}$ represents the trainable weight matrix of dimension $L \times L$. Similarly, the joint correlation matrix for the video features ($\mathbf{C_v}$) will be given by the expression Eq. (5).

$$\mathbf{C_v} = \tanh\left(\frac{\mathbf{X}_v^T \mathbf{W}_{jv} \mathbf{J}}{\sqrt{d}}\right) \tag{5}$$

The matrices C_a and C_v represent the joint correlation between the input vectors $\mathbf{X}_a$ and $\mathbf{X}_v$ and the joint representation $\mathbf{J}$. It is important to highlight that the correlation matrices C_a and C_v have a semantic meaning where higher values of C_a and C_v imply high correlation between the audio and video modalities and within each modality.

In turn, the audio modality $\mathbf{X}_a$ and video modality $\mathbf{X}_v$ are combined with the joint correlation matrices C_a and C_v to compute the attention maps H_a and H_v (Eqs.(6), (7)).

$$\mathbf{H_a} = \text{ReLU}(\mathbf{W}_a \mathbf{X}_a + \mathbf{W}_{ca} C_a^t) \tag{6}$$

$$\mathbf{H}_v = \text{ReLU}(\mathbf{W}_v\mathbf{X}_v + \mathbf{W}_{cv}C_v^t) \tag{7}$$

The attention maps are used to capture attention in each modality, as shown in Eqs. (8), (9).

$$\mathbf{X}_{\text{att},a} = \mathbf{W}_{ha}\mathbf{H}_a + \mathbf{X}_a \tag{8}$$

$$\mathbf{X}_{\text{att},v} = \mathbf{W}_{hv}\mathbf{H}_v + \mathbf{X}_v \tag{9}$$

Finally, the attention matrices $\mathbf{X}_{\text{att},a}$ and $\mathbf{X}_{\text{att},v}$ are concatenated to obtain the attention matrix (Eq. (10)).

$$\mathbf{X}_{\text{att}} = [\mathbf{X}_{\text{att},a}; \mathbf{X}_{\text{att},v}] \tag{10}$$

which is fed into a densely connected layer that will predict values of arousal or valence.

5 Missing Modality Analysis

The experimental approach was structured in three distinct phases. The first phase involved training the models using both audio and video modalities. In the second phase, a portion the audio modality was disabled, and the relative contribution of the video modality to the regression task was assessed. Finally, in the third phase, a portion of the video modality was disabled, allowing for the evaluation of the audio modality's relative contribution to the regression task. The proportions of missing data analyzed were 25%, 50%, and 100%.

This approach was inspired by sensitivity analysis methods used in [12, 13]. In these studies, sensitivity analysis was conducted at the feature level, examining the impact of subsets of features on the overall performance of a machine learning model. In the present work, however, the sensitivity analysis was performed by generating a zero feature vector for the portion of the modality intended to be disabled. Subsequently, the model was tested with a fusion of this feature vector from the disabled modality and the active feature vector from the other modality.

Such analysis provided us valuable insights into how each modality independently influences the model's performance and how the strategies employed by dynamic selection and cross-attention handle the absence of specific modalities. By comparing the results from each phase, one could discern the individual and combined effects of audio and video modalities. Moreover, this analysis sheds light on the sensitivity of the proposed methods when confronted with missing modalities.

6 Experiments

The remote collaborative and affective interactions (RECOLA) dataset [17] represents an extensive source of multimodal data, encompassing extracted features and raw data from various modalities, including audio, video, and physiological recordings (electrocardiogram and electrodermal activity). The labeling of the first five minutes of interaction for 18 participants is available.

The data is labeled within the repository, adhering to a continuous emotional scale. This labeling is mapped into a two-dimensional space, a psychologically grounded method for describing emotions through the linear combination of arousal and valence. The concept of representing emotions in arousal and valence follows the circumplex model proposed by Russell [18].

The official metric for evaluating the performance of the problem is the CCC [20], which captures the co-variation relationship between predictions and ground truth and accounts for any deviation. As a result, it offers a more accurate representation of the alignment between predictions and ground truth [6]. Several studies have used CCC as a standard metric [14, 16, 21], demonstrating its relevance and applicability in multimodal emotion recognition tasks. Higher CCC values signify excellent performance in terms of consistency and accuracy. The calculation process for CCC is as follows:

$$CCC = \frac{2 * \rho * \sigma_y * \sigma_{\hat{y}}}{\sigma_y^2 + \sigma_{\hat{y}}^2 + (\mu_y - \mu_{\hat{y}})^2} \tag{11}$$

where ρ is the Pearson correlation coefficient, σ_y and $\sigma_{\hat{y}}$ are the standard deviations and μ_y and $\mu_{\hat{y}}$ are the means of actual and predicted emotional state.

This experiment emphasized two primary modalities: audio and video. The eGeMAPS acoustic feature set was employed for the audio component, which was extracted using the OpenSmile software and is available within the RECOLA dataset. Additionally, feature sets based on Mel-frequency cepstral coefficients (MFCCs) and Mel spectrograms, both of which were extracted by the authors of this work, were utilized. The video component, on the other hand, has been focused solely on extracted features from the RECOLA dataset, including geometric features derived from 49 distinct facial landmarks and appearance features obtained by a principal component analysis from 50,000 LGBP-TOP features.

6.1 Experimental Protocol

An experimental protocol based on the k-fold cross-validation method has been implemented to ensure the robustness and reliability of our findings.

The dataset comprised data from 18 individuals. To balance training and testing and ensure that our model was tested on unseen data, we allocated three individuals for testing and three for validation. The remaining participants were used for training. The experimental setup was repeated ten times, each time with a different configuration, to enhance the generalization of our results. In each iteration of the experiment, the participants were randomly shuffled.

We deliberately introduced a modality-absent condition to simulate a real-world scenario. These simulations are essential for assessing the robustness and adaptability of our model under less-than-ideal conditions. A zero input vector was used to simulate the absence of a modality. In practical terms, this meant that for any given instance where a particular modality was supposed to be missing, its feature values were replaced with zeros. This approach effectively mimics scenarios where a modality's data is entirely or partially unavailable, allowing us to observe how the model performs when deprived of information from one of the modalities. Tests were conducted with proportions of missing data at 25%, 50%, and 100%. When only part of the data was missing, the central portion of the feature vector was zeroed out.

6.2   Results

This section offers an in-depth analysis of the outcomes achieved by employing the proposed techniques of dynamic modal and view selection and cross-attention mechanism under ideal conditions and modality-absent conditions.

Table 1 displays the arousal and valence results, in terms of CCC, for the pool of regressors F. The findings reveal that the audio modality better represents the arousal dimension, with acoustic features, MFCCs, and Mel spectrograms, achieving CCC values of 0.69, 0.64, and 0.68. Conversely, valence is more accurately represented by the video modality, with its appearance features and geometric features representations, achieving CCC values of 0.48 and 0.56.

Figure 2 shows the arousal prediction of all models for the same test case, considering scenarios where both modalities are available and when each modality is 50% unavailable. Under ideal conditions, all models exhibit a consistent pattern with similar predictions. However, at certain moments, one model aligns more closely with the gold standard, while another performs better at other times. When a modality is absent, the imputation technique used to handle the missing values by replacing features with zeros enables the model to continue making predictions. However, a noticeable decline in performance is observed among models relying on representations of that particular modality, highlighting the importance of having both modalities available or using methods capable of effectively dealing with missing modalities, such as those proposed in this work.

For arousal, under ideal conditions, with all modalities available - video and audio, the highest performance with $CCC = 0.72$ was observed when employing DW, DWS, and a simple mean of all regressors' outputs. DW and DWS yielded the best outcomes in the valence dimension with $CCC = 0.54$ and $CCC = 0.53$, surpassing DS and the mean of regressors' outputs, which registered $CCC = 0.46$. Cross-attention results included $CCC = 0.46$ for arousal and $CCC = 0.41$ for valence. Detailed results are shown in Table 2.

Regarding arousal, methods based on dynamic selection (DW and DWS, $CCC = 0.72$) outperformed the top-performing regressor alone, relying solely on acoustic features, $CCC = 0.69$. It shows that dynamic selection of modalities can be a promising approach for a multimodal AI method. Valence achieved its peak performance with geometric features, $CCC = 0.56$, and none of the proposed methods managed to surpass this benchmark in valence prediction.

Table 1. CCC for arousal and valence encompassing models based on acoustic features, MFCCs, Mel spectrograms, appearance features, and geometric features. Models were trained with two layers of LSTM with 256 cells and a time window of 6 s.

Features	Arousal	Valence
Acoustic	**0.69 ± 0.06**	0.18 ± 0.07
MFCCs	0.64 ± 0.06	0.35 ± 0.08
Mel Spectrograms	0.68 ± 0.06	0.22 ± 0.09
Appearance	0.42 ± 0.09	0.48 ± 0.06
Geometric	0.41 ± 0.09	**0.56 ± 0.14**

6.3   Impact of Missing Modalities

Our second research question is related to how the different approaches (dynamic selection and cross-attention) respond to the absence of a specific modality.

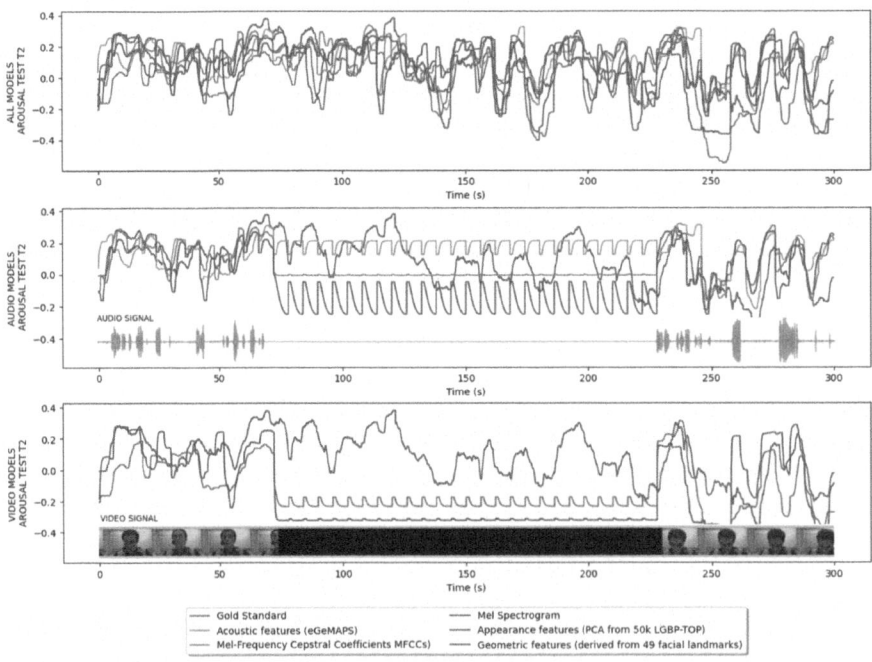

Fig. 2. Arousal gold standard and prediction of models based on acoustic features, MFCCs, Mel spectrograms, appearance features, and geometric features. The image was generated using test case T2 (second person from the test set) of the second cross-validation fold (k = 2). From top to bottom, we have (i) predictions with all active modalities, (ii) audio models predictions with the absence of 50% of audio modality and the corresponding audio signal, and (iii) video models predictions with the absence of 50% of video modality and the corresponding sequence of video frames.

Table 2. CCC for arousal and valence encompassing the mean of the regressors' outputs, dynamic selection (DS, DW, DWS), and cross-attention-based methods. The DS, DW, and DWS results were generated with K = 100.

Approach	Arousal	Valence
DS	0.67 ± 0.06	0.46 ± 0.08
DW	$\mathbf{0.72 \pm 0.04}$	$\mathbf{0.54 \pm 0.10}$
DWS	$\mathbf{0.72 \pm 0.04}$	0.53 ± 0.10
Cross-Attention	0.46 ± 0.13	0.41 ± 0.17
Mean	$\mathbf{0.72} \pm 0.04$	0.46 ± 0.08

Tables 3 and 4 display the arousal and valence results, in terms of CCC, of all comparison methods - encompassing mean of the regressors' outputs, dynamic selection (DS, DW, DWS), and cross-attention. Figure 3 compares the arousal gold standard, prediction with all active modalities, and with the absence of each modality.

Table 3. Arousal results, in terms of CCC, encompassing the mean of the regressors' outputs, dynamic selection (DS, DW, DWS), and cross-attention-based methods. The results are presented in the following scenarios: audio (A) and video (V) available, audio disabled, and video disabled. The proportions of missing data analyzed were 25%, 50%, and 100%.

Modalities	Mean	DS	DW	DWS	Cross-Attention
A and V available	$\mathbf{0.72 \pm 0.04}$	0.67 ± 0.06	$\mathbf{0.72 \pm 0.04}$	$\mathbf{0.72 \pm 0.04}$	0.46 ± 0.13
25% V disabled	$\mathbf{0.68 \pm 0.05}$	0.62 ± 0.03	0.65 ± 0.05	0.65 ± 0.05	0.42 ± 0.11
25% A disabled	$\mathbf{0.60 \pm 0.04}$	0.51 ± 0.07	0.54 ± 0.07	0.54 ± 0.08	0.36 ± 0.15
50% V disabled	0.66 ± 0.06	0.65 ± 0.03	$\mathbf{0.68 \pm 0.04}$	$\mathbf{0.68 \pm 0.04}$	0.41 ± 0.09
50% A disabled	0.50 ± 0.04	0.48 ± 0.07	$\mathbf{0.52 \pm 0.07}$	0.51 ± 0.07	0.21 ± 0.14
100% V disabled	0.61 ± 0.09	0.67 ± 0.06	$\mathbf{0.71 \pm 0.05}$	$\mathbf{0.71 \pm 0.05}$	0.49 ± 0.12
100% A disabled	0.31 ± 0.05	0.35 ± 0.15	$\mathbf{0.41 \pm 0.17}$	0.40 ± 0.17	0.23 ± 0.12

In the context of arousal, the cross-attention method demonstrated heightened robustness in terms of sensitivity, exhibiting a 6.52% increase in CCC when the video modality was unavailable (100% disabled), compared to the ideal scenario where both audio and video modalities were available. Contrarily, the remaining methods either sustained their performance or experienced some loss. Among the dynamic selection-based methods, DS exhibited no performance lowering, while DW and DWS showed a minimal decrease of 1.39%. The mean method observed the most substantial decline, recording a significant loss of 15.28%.

Table 4. Valence results, in terms of CCC, encompassing the mean of the regressors' outputs, dynamic selection (DS, DW, DWS), and cross-attention-based methods. The results are presented in the following scenarios: audio (A) and video (V) available, audio disabled and video disabled, simulating the absence of a modality with a zero vector. The proportions of missing data analyzed were 25%, 50%, and 100%.

Modalities	Mean	DS	DW	DWS	Cross-Attention
A and V available	0.46 ± 0.08	0.46 ± 0.08	$\mathbf{0.54 \pm 0.10}$	$\mathbf{0.54 \pm 0.10}$	0.41 ± 0.17
25% V disabled	0.44 ± 0.07	0.41 ± 0.07	$\mathbf{0.46 \pm 0.06}$	$\mathbf{0.46 \pm 0.06}$	0.34 ± 0.11
25% A disabled	0.44 ± 0.08	0.46 ± 0.07	$\mathbf{0.52 \pm 0.07}$	$\mathbf{0.52 \pm 0.07}$	0.37 ± 0.14
50% V disabled	0.40 ± 0.07	0.40 ± 0.08	$\mathbf{0.42 \pm 0.07}$	$\mathbf{0.42 \pm 0.07}$	0.25 ± 0.07
50% A disabled	0.39 ± 0.07	0.45 ± 0.06	$\mathbf{0.52 \pm 0.07}$	0.51 ± 0.07	0.38 ± 0.16
100% V disabled	0.27 ± 0.08	0.28 ± 0.18	$\mathbf{0.30 \pm 0.17}$	$\mathbf{0.30 \pm 0.17}$	0.13 ± 0.15
100% A disabled	0.32 ± 0.06	0.49 ± 0.09	$\mathbf{0.59 \pm 0.09}$	0.56 ± 0.09	0.40 ± 0.14

More pronounced performance losses were observed when the audio modality was unavailable. Several approaches witnessed a decline of over 50% in performance, which is understandable as the audio modality most effectively represents the arousal dimension. DW emerged as the most robust approach in scenarios without audio, experiencing a performance decline of 43.06% compared to the scenario with all available modalities. Following closely, DWS and DS demonstrated a CCC decline of 44.44% and 47.76%, respectively.

A contrasting pattern was observed in valence, where disabling the audio modality yields superior results. When the video modality is unavailable, DS proves to be the least sensitive approach with a performance decline of 39.13%. In the same scenario, when the audio modality is missing, DW and DS emerged as the most robust methods, showcasing a 9.26% and 6.52% increase in CCC, respectively.

In the cross-attention method, concerning arousal, there was a notable 6.52% increase in CCC when the video modality was unavailable but a substantial 50% decline in performance when the audio modality was disabled. Regarding valence, promising outcomes were observed when the video modality was turned off, with a performance lowering of 2.44%. However, turning off the video modality resulted in a significant decline of 68.29% in performance compared to the ideal scenario where both audio and video modalities were available.

When examining scenarios with 25% and 50% missing data, similar patterns were observed. An interesting observation is that for arousal, the higher the proportion of audio disabled, the worse the results. This underscores the greater importance of audio data for arousal detection. Conversely, as we increase the proportion of video disabled, the results improve, as the solution relies more on audio features. For valence, the patterns were opposite. The higher the proportion of video disabled, the worse the results, whereas increasing the proportion of audio disabled improved the results, indicating that the video modality is more significant for valence detection.

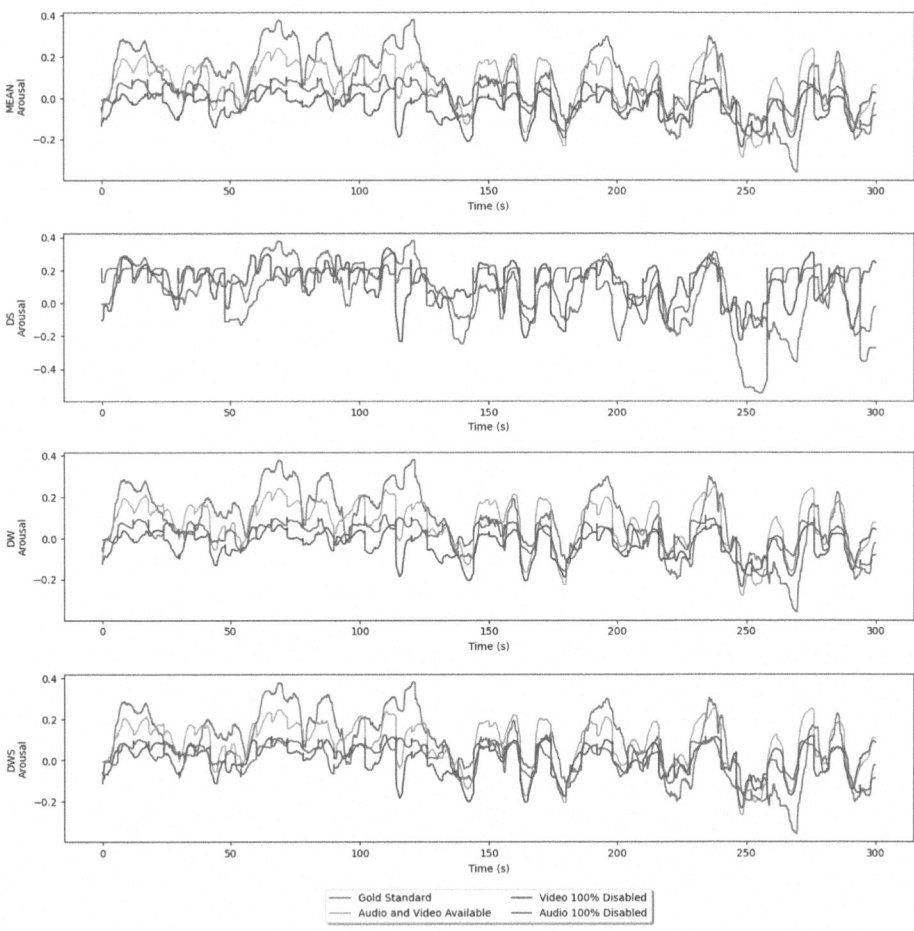

Fig. 3. Comparison of arousal gold standard, prediction with all active modalities, prediction with the absence of audio modality, and prediction with the absence of video modality of the mean of the regressors' outputs and dynamic selection-based methods (DS, DW, DWS). The image was generated using test case T2 (second person from the test set) of the second cross-validation fold (k = 2).

Considering the scenarios of missing modalities in arousal and valence dimensions, the dynamic selection-based methods DW and DWS consistently outperformed the baselines, mean of all regressors' output, and cross-attention-based method. The only exception was with 25% of missing data for arousal, where the simple mean of the regressors achieved the best result. These findings emphasize the robustness of dynamic selection-based methods, especially DW and DWS, in handling partial data loss.

6.4   Discussion

The proposed approach performs better in arousal than valence, especially when the audio features are available. It may be related to the fact that arousal, which relates to the emotional intensity or activation level, might be more distinctly captured in tone of voice, volume, and speech rate, even without visual cues. For example, screams or high intonations may indicate a more excited emotional state. Elements like rhythm and timbre in speech also reflect emotional excitement; rapid rhythm or timbre changes can indicate more intense emotional states. Audio data carry significant information about the emotional state and can be quite effective in capturing the subtleties of arousal levels.

Auditory cues might be less effective in conveying valence levels. Valence, associated with the positivity or negativity of emotions, is often reflected in facial expressions and might be more nuanced and complex to discern from audio alone. Visual cues are critical in identifying the valence levels, making video a more informative modality for this dimension.

MER using dynamic modality and view selection appears to be an effective strategy for combining audio and video modalities, showing promising results under ideal conditions. The highest performances were observed when employing DW, with arousal $CCC = 0.72$ and valence $CCC = 0.54$.

Furthermore, dynamic modality and view selection techniques exhibit notable robustness when confronted with the absence of specific modalities. In scenarios where the audio modality was absent, DW also demonstrated heightened robustness in terms of sensitivity, exhibiting a performance decline of 43.06% in arousal and an increase of 9.26% in valence, compared to the ideal scenario where both audio and video modalities were available. The cross-attention method emerged as the most robust approach when the video modality was absent, exhibiting a 6.52% increase in CCC in arousal (DW demonstrated a decline of 1.39%). In the valence dimension, DS proves to be the least sensitive approach in scenarios without video with a performance decline of 39.13% (DW demonstrated a decline of 44.44%).

For (RQ1) – "Could dynamic selection of modalities and views be a promising approach for a multimodal AI method?", the results affirmatively show that dynamic selection-based methods are promising. However, the outcome of missing modalities revealed interesting nuances, addressing the research question (RQ2) – "What is the impact on emotion recognition performance when one modality (video or audio) is missing?", several approaches witnessed a decline of over 50% in performance when a modality is absent, emphasizing the importance of each modality in contributing to accurate predictions.

7   Conclusion

Our investigation into the representation of time-continuous emotions, particularly in arousal and valence dimensions, through different dynamic selection approaches has yielded valuable insights. Even under less-than-ideal conditions, MER systems have demonstrated their versatility and reliability.

The findings reveal that DW shows the highest performance in arousal and valence predictions under ideal conditions, with both modalities available. In the missing modalities scenarios, DW and DWS outperformed the baselines, mean of all regressors' output and cross-attention-based method. The study concludes by emphasizing the intricate interplay between audio and video modalities in emotion prediction, showcasing the adaptability of dynamic selection methods in handling missing modalities.

Finally, it is essential to highlight that we have employed simple two-layer LSTMs to compose the pool of regressors to represent each modality. This choice sets the stage for future work to explore more advanced LSTM architectures and evaluate more complex architectures, such as Transformers and large language models.

Acknowledgment. Thanks to the Brazilian funding agencies CNPq (grants 306688/2018-2, 406030/2023-5 and 441610/2023-4) and CAPES SticAmSud (023-STIC-13).

References

1. Aslam, M.H., Zeeshan, O., Pedersoli, M., Koerich, A.L., Bacon, S., Granger, E.: Privileged knowledge distillation for dimensional emotion recognition in the wild. In: CVPRw 2023: IEEE/CVF CVPR, Vancouver, Canada (2023)
2. Baltrusaitis, T., Ahuja, C., Morency, L.P.: Multimodal machine learning: a survey and taxonomy. IEEE Trans. Pattern Anal. Mach. Intell. **41**(2), 423–443 (2019)
3. Cheng, C., Fan, Z., Feng, L., Jia, Z.: A novel transformer autoencoder for multimodal emotion recognition with incomplete data. Neural Netw., 106111 (2024)
4. Gladys, A.A., Vetriselvi, V.: Survey on multimodal approaches to emotion recognition. Neurocomputing **556**, 126693 (2023)
5. Li, J., Li, L., Sun, R., Yuan, G., Wang, S., Sun, S.: MMAN-M2: multiple multi-head attentions network based on encoder with missing modalities. Patt. Recogn. Lett. **177**, 110–120 (2024)
6. Lian, H., Lu, C., Li, S., Zhao, Y., Tang, C., Zong, Y.: A survey of deep learning-based multimodal emotion recognition: speech, text, and face. Entropy **25**(10) (2023)
7. Lin, R., Hu, H.: MissModal: increasing robustness to missing modality in multimodal sentiment analysis. Trans. Assoc. Comput. Ling. **11**, 1686–1702 (2023)
8. Lin, W.C., Goncalves, L., Busso, C.: Enhancing resilience to missing data in audio-text emotion recognition with multi-scale chunk regularization. In: 25th ICMI, pp. 207–215 (2023)
9. Liu, S., Gao, P., Li, Y., Fu, W., Ding, W.: Multi-modal fusion network with complementarity and importance for emotion recognition. Inf. Sci. **619**, 679–694 (2023)
10. Liu, Z., Zhou, B., Chu, D., Sun, Y., Meng, L.: Modality translation-based multimodal sentiment analysis under uncertain missing modalities. Inf. Fusion **101**, 101973 (2024)
11. Moura, T.J., Cavalcanti, G.D., Oliveira, L.S.: MINE: a framework for dynamic regressor selection. Inf. Sci. **543**, 157–179 (2021)
12. Naik, D., Kiran, R.: A novel sensitivity-based method for feature selection. J. Big Data **8** (2021)

13. Nunes, C., Britto, A., Kaestner, C., Sabourin, R.: An optimized hill climbing algorithm for feature subset selection: evaluation on handwritten character recognition. In: 9th IWFHR, pp. 365–370 (2004)
14. Ortega, J.D.S., Cardinal, P., Koerich, A.L.: Emotion recognition using fusion of audio and video features. In: IEEE International Conference on SMC, pp. 3827–3832 (2019)
15. Praveen, R.G., Cardinal, P., Granger, E.: Audio-visual fusion for emotion recognition in the valence-arousal space using joint cross-attention. IEEE Trans. Biom. Behav. Identity Sci. **5**(3), 360–373 (2023)
16. Praveen, R.G., et al.: A joint cross-attention model for audio-visual fusion in dimensional emotion recognition. In: 2022 IEEE/CVF CVPRw, pp. 2485–2494 (2022)
17. Ringeval, F., Sonderegger, A., Sauer, J., Lalanne, D.: Introducing the RECOLA multimodal corpus of remote collaborative and affective interactions. In: 10th IEEE International Conference FG, pp. 1–8 (2013)
18. Russell, J.A.: A circumplex model of affect. J. Pers. Soc. Psychol. **39**(6), 1161 (1980)
19. Silva-Filarder, M.D., Ancora, A., Filippone, M., Michiardi, P.: Multimodal variational autoencoders for sensor fusion and cross generation. In: 20th IEEE ICMLA, pp. 1069–1076 (2021)
20. Valstar, M., et al.: AVEC 2016: depression, mood, and emotion recognition workshop and challenge. In: 6th AVEC, pp. 3–10 (2016)
21. Vazquez-Rodriguez, J., Lefebvre, G., Cumin, J., Crowley, J.L.: Accommodating missing modalities in time-continuous multimodal emotion recognition. CoRR **abs/2311.10119** (2023)
22. Zeng, A., Chen, M., Zhang, L., Xu, Q.: Are transformers effective for time series forecasting? (2023). https://doi.org/10.1609/aaai.v37i9.26317
23. Zhu, Y., Sun, X., Zhou, X.: Exploiting multi-modal fusion for robust face representation learning with missing modality. In: ICANN 2023, pp. 283–294 (2023)

Image Fusion Survey: A Novel Taxonomy Integrating Transformer and Recent Approaches

Bernardi Gwendal[1,2]($\boxtimes$), Strubel David[1], Brisebarre Godefroy[1],
Garin Jean-François[1], Ardabilian Mohsen[2], and Dellandréa Emmanuel[2]

[1] Tiama, Saint-Genis-Laval, France
g.bernardi@tiama.com
[2] Ecole Centrale de Lyon, CNRS, INSA Lyon, Universite Claude Bernard Lyon 1,
Université Lumiére Lyon 2, LIRIS, UMR5205, 69130 Ecully, France

Abstract. Research progress in multi-modal information fusion, particularly in Image Fusion, has experienced significant advancements over the last decade. By integrating information from multiple sources or modalities, image fusion enables the extraction of comprehensive insights and facilitates more accurate analysis and decision-making processes. The inherent complexity of image fusion, stemming from its unstructured nature, necessitates high levels of abstraction and intricate data representation. The utilization of deep learning, notably CNN and more recently introduced Vision Transformer, has yielded substantial enhancements in image fusion methodologies. This paper presents a comprehensive survey of image fusion methodologies, focusing on recent advancements and introducing a novel taxonomy based on supervised, unsupervised, and task-driven approaches. The survey encompasses recent contributions, including the integration of transformer architectures, which have emerged as powerful tools for image fusion tasks. This classification is supported by a distinction of methods by architecture type (CNN, GAN, Transformer) for a better understanding of the relationships between methods. Through the synthesis of existing literature and the introduction of a new classification paradigm, this survey aims to provide researchers and practitioners with a comprehensive overview of image fusion techniques and guide future research directions in this rapidly evolving field.

Keywords: Image Fusion · Multi-modal · Task-driven · Fusion Transformer

1 Introduction

Image fusion represents a critical area within computer vision with broad applicability spanning domains such as autonomous driving, medicine, industry and military operations. Traditional image processing including learning techniques

S. Palaiahnakote et al. (Eds.): ICPR 2024 Workshops, LNCS 15617, pp. 167–180, 2025.
https://doi.org/10.1007/978-3-031-88217-3_12

applied to individual images often prove inadequate, particularly when confronted with complex scenarios. Utilizing data from a single sensor capturing a specific light spectrum or a singular angle of view results in a partial scene or object representation. Image fusion appears to be an eloquent and effective solution to improve the performance of systems by ensuring the completeness of crucial information for perception, object detection, saliency detection and segmentation. Image fusion encompasses a variety of usage, including multi-focus fusion which integrates images with different scales of object representation, multi-exposure fusion dealing with images captured in various lighting conditions, and multi-modal fusion involving images acquired from sensors operating in different wavelength spectra [11,33]. This paper defines a new taxonomy divided into three learning-based categories: Supervised, Unsupervised, and Task-Driven paradigms. Supervised approaches use a ground truth to compute a cost function, which requires knowing the result of the merge. Task-Driven approaches rely on an image fusion paradigm that uses the ground truth of a task (detection, classification, segmentation ...) to calculate the error of the fused part. Unsupervised approaches use an unsupervised strategy to solve learning problems, such as image processing metrics or adversarial learning. The Table 1 presents the most representative approaches studied in this paper, classified according to these three paradigms. On the other hand, non-learning methods suffer from finite fusion rules and intricate manual design requirements, constraining the complexity of fusion techniques. These methods are based on image processing and require expertise to design, and are task-specific. Examples of non-learning fusion methods include multiscale transforms [17], sparse representation [40], hybrid [22], subspace [38] methods or others methods [28]. The advent of deep learning has exceeded these limitations by offering heightened abstraction capabilities and superior data representation.

This paper presents a comprehensive review of deep learning-based image fusion methodologies, encompassing diverse surveys addressing methods, applications, emerging trends, modalities, and future prospects within the field. Compared to the different state-of-the-art image fusion already available [2,3,9–11], this analysis provides three main contributions: a comparison of the most representative Transformer methods with other methods, a recent review of the latest approaches to the image fusion problem and a new taxonomy of fusion methods: Supervised, Unsupervised and Task-Driven.

As shown in Fig. 1, Unsupervised fusion methods generally follow a similar structure. These methods fuse information from two or more images to produce an output image that contains the essential features from the input images. A loss function based on image quality metrics, information quantity, etc., is used to refine the fusion process. Task-Driven fusion methods employ a similar approach to Unsupervised methods for image fusion. However, they also incorporate a loss function calculated from the error of a task executed on the fused image, such as classification, detection, or segmentation.

This categorization approaches offers valuable insights for understanding similarities and dissimilarities between the approaches. Moreover, the article

Supervised Fusion Method

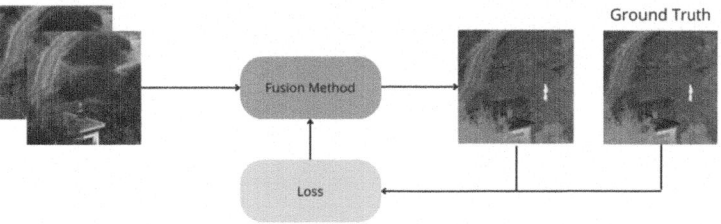

Unsupervised Fusion Method

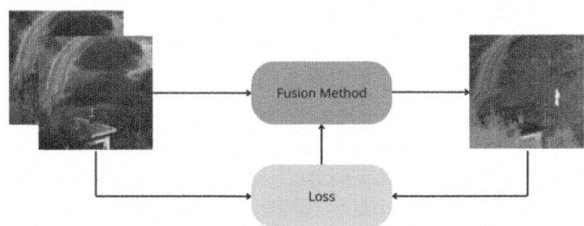

Task-Driven Fusion Method

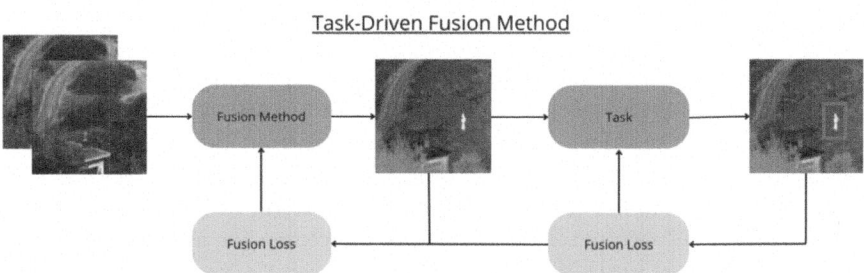

Fig. 1. Common architecture for image fusion: Unsupervised and Task-Driven

also organizes methods based on CNN, GAN and Transformers to maintain a clear understanding of their operational mechanisms. This complementary approach aims to elucidate the fundamental principles and distinctive features of each method, making it easier to compare and understand image fusion methodologies.

2   Image Fusion Methods

Image fusion techniques with deep learning offer a superior performance without the need for manual design based on fusion rules, contrasting with conventional methods. Image fusion can be categorized in three groups according to the fusion process in the pipeline: Early, Late or Intermediate presented in [2,9]. Another designation for these categories reflects the level of abstraction for fusion level: pixel-level, feature-level, and decision-level [11]. This classification of methods provides a simplified summary of how fusion methods work, and highlights the advantages and disadvantages of each type of methodology [11]. The classification presented in the paper primarily relies on the nature of the methods and their training paradigm.

2.1 Convolutional Neural Network Based Method

CNNs are key architectures in image processing, particularly in tasks like image fusion, where they extract spatial representations and highlight inter-feature relationships. However, the traditional approach involves applying CNNs independently to extract feature maps for each image.

For instance, MVMM-Net [24] encodes each image's features independently, which are then concatenated for further processing. Nonetheless, this method has limitations, including a fixed fusion system and an isolated feature extraction that overlooks inter-image correlations. A possible approach of the strictly defined fusion system problem is the Gated Information Fusion cell, GIF [12].

GIF, a Task-Driven method, utilizes multiple images for object detection and concatenates information with a learned weighting mechanism. During training, the GIF cell assigns weights through a learned process, enabling the fusion of features from each image. The disadvantage of GIF is provided information fusion at a single level only. To address this, a multi-layer information fusion architecture named CentralNet [29] presents a solution. The architecture is a feature extractor for each modality and a feature fusion model. At each layer of the extraction models, the information is sent to a central model, which merges the data but also takes into account the information from these N-1 layers. A classifier model then determines the desired output according to the task in progress, it is a Task-Driven learning. Task-Driven architectures for image segmentation are generally inspired by U-Net [23].

Image fusion methods such as MFNet [6] or RTFNet [25] use this U-Net-inspired to offer a fusion solution like CentralNet [29], which uses different stages of feature extraction to combine information. RTFNet [25] is closer to CentralNet [29] in its design, as the encoder part is composed of a model for each image. At each stage of the lateral model, the features are fused using a fusion layer in one of the feature extraction models.

MFNet [6] architecture is much closer to U-Net, with one encoder per image and a common decoder. Each encoder incorporates skip connections that concatenate the encoders' features to the decoder. These multi-layer information fusion methods provide an in-depth relationship between the features of each image. GMFNet [1] is a method inspired by the CentralNet, with a dedicated network for each modality and a central network dedicated to information fusion. The architecture of each model is also inspired by U-Net-based methods and is used to encode a ResNet [7] and to decode an MFNet [6]. The central model generates a segmented image by fusing input modalities. Fusion layers utilize the

Table 1. An Overview of Representative Image Fusion Methods Studied in this Paper.

Methods	Categories	Learning approach	Dataset/Images	Advantages/Disadvantages
GMFNet [1]	CNN	Task-Driven	MFNet Dataset	+ learning resulting in a robust method - complex method with 3 models for 1 useful output
U2Fusion [33]	CNN	Unsupervised	TNO, RS, Harvard, EMPA HDR, public Dataset	+ generalist methods (multiple fusion problems) - only captures local relationships in images (no long-range relationships)
DDcGAN [19]	CNN, GAN	Unsupervised	TNO	+ unsupervised method, includes multiscale support - possible artifact generation, unstable GAN training
MEF-GAN [35]	CNN, Attention	GAN, Supervised, Unsupervised	HDR-Eye, Fairchild, public Dataset	+ applies attention to GAN - partially based on supervised learning
TarDAL [15]	CNN, GAN	Task-Driven	TNO, INO, RS, M3FD, MS	+ dual path discriminator, task-driven - focus on Infrared/visible only, uses image processing extraction
SCGRFuse [31]	CNN, Transformer	Task-Driven	MSRS, TNO, RS	+ includes Transformer, task-driven learning - not very generalizable to other contexts, hyperparameters only based on other related literature
IFT [30]	CNN, Transformer	Unsupervised	KAIST, TNO, Harvard and PET Dataset	+ spatial and Transformer path (extract local and long-distance information) - complex architecture
STFNet [16]	CNN, Transformer	Unsupervised	KAIST, LLVIP, M3FD, MSRS, VLIRVDIF	+ feature align network, cross-attention model - need stronger detail constrain, complex architecture

Gated Fusion Module, akin to GIF [12], employing convolution-based principles for Task-Driven learning.

Supervised methods can be used when the ground truth of the fusion objective is known. Datasets can thus be built to specialize learning on the data fusion. IFCNN [41] is a supervised image fusion method. A CNN is used for each modality, and convolution blocks are used between the two models to interconnect features. At output, the features are concatenated and then reconstructed as a fused image using another convolution block. The output is then compared with a ground truth.

Both Task-Driven and supervised approaches require labelled data for a specific task or a known ground truth to perform image fusion, posing a disadvantage. However, these methods have the advantage of easily to calculate and interpret error metrics. However, in real-world applications, it is not always possible to have such complete datasets. This is why some image fusion methods use unsupervised approaches. Such case with DenseFuse [13], an unsupervised image fusion method based on an encoder-decoder architecture and convolution blocks. DenseFuse compare the fused and original image using a cost function SSIM [32]. The disadvantage of DenseFuse is the pixel-by-pixel comparison metric imposes very strong constraints on similarity with input images.

FusionDN [34] proposes a solution capable of generating an image from several others, containing an agglomeration of all the features of the input images. The method is unsupervised and works with a DenseNet [13]. The main originality of this method is the use of a retention system. The cost function uses a combination of SSIM, Entropy and a network which plays the role of a metric for evaluating the image quality assessment. U2Fusion [33] is also based on a metric composed of an image quality and quantity analysis. This information is recovered through feature extraction. The special aspect of the method is that it learns from several tasks simultaneously: multi-modal, multi-exposure and multi-focus. It implies the different tasks can be addressed together, while at the same time taking advantage of the specific learning gained globally, with each task helping to improve the others. This specific training workflow designed to learn across multiple tasks by conducting sequential training sessions while retaining a portion of the data and information between each train. Beyond CNNs, the focus extends to the generative methods, especially GANs, and their role in image fusion. GANs offer unique capabilities for generating high-quality synthetic images, thus enriching fused representations.

2.2   Generative Adversarial Based Methods

GAN-based architecture [5] enables images to be generated from noise in an unsupervised way. To generate images from several other images by fusion, GAN fusion methods use images from several modalities as input instead of noise. FusionGAN [20] is the precursor method in this field, offering an architecture with a discriminator and a convolution-based generator to generate images fused between an infrared and a visible images. The generator takes two visible and infrared images as inputs to generate a new image. A cost function is designed for the generator to help the learning process converge towards a solution that comes close to the image fusion objective. The loss is based on a loss content which aims to preserve both the thermal radiation information contained in the infrared image and the gradient information contained in the visible image. Dense-FG [37] uses almost the same system with a different loss. Moreover, this method adds the use of dense connection blocks for convolutional model architecture to improve the performance of the system.

The two-part content loss system for each of the modalities is further developed in GANMcc [21]. The generator has two branches for each image modality: the contrast path for infrared and the gradient path for visible. These two branches are concatenated encoders to reconstruct an image. In this way, loss gradient is more accurate for the gradient path and loss contrast is more precise for the contrast path. The input to each path is a concatenation per channel of two images of the path type and one of the other type (e.g. for contrast, there are two infra-red images and one visible). The loss of the adversarial system is used with a gradient and contrast loss. Supervised learning approach is possible when the ground truth of the fusion result is known.

It is then possible to integrate a Mean Square Error into the generator loss in addition to the adversarial system loss, as MEF-GAN [35] does. To achieve ground truth, the dataset is constructed from an image with its underexposed and overexposed equivalents. A pixel-by-pixel comparison is used because the image must be perfectly faithful to ground truth. The generator consists of three blocks: self-attention, local detail and a merge block of the two systems. It is rare to have a dataset with ground truth, and comparing a fused image with its infrared or visible equivalent (or other type of modality) is not necessarily efficient. This is why solutions with two discriminator branches are used.

GAN-FM [39] uses an architecture with full-scale skip connection and dual Markovian discriminators to accomplish image fusion. The full-scale skip generator extracts and fuses deep features of different scales. The two Markovian discriminators allow the network to focus attention on local regions and generate the fused results. The generator architecture is similar to a UNet [43]. Beside the adversarial system, a loss content is used, consisting of intensity and gradient loss. DDcGAN [19] (Dual-Discriminator Conditional GAN) also uses a two-branch architecture, but to handle the case of images with different resolutions. The images are pre-processed to have the same resolution. The discriminator has two branches to handle the two resolutions: one branch with the fused image and one branch with the low-resolution fused image. The cost function uses the two adversarial system with a content loss. Finally, the dual branch system can be used to handle different image modalities by associating a specific discriminator.

Another approach to the use of a two-branch model is proposed with CMAFusion [18]. The architecture consists of two main components: a feature extractor and an image reconstructor. The feature extractor includes five convolutional layers for each modality, incorporating fusion blocks from layer C2 onwards. Fusion information is added to the outputs of the feature extraction layers via element-wise addition. The fusion module, called the Cross-Modal Feature Fusion module, performs element-wise subtraction. A Global Average Pooling (GAP) operation is then applied, followed by a Fully Connected Model. The infrared information is element-wise added with the visible information, and vice versa. The two channels are finally concatenated for the image reconstruction part, which consists of four convolutional layers. The cost function is a combination of SSIM, texture loss, and pixel intensity loss. TarDAL [15] uses a discriminator branch for the infrared and the visible by associating a cost function based on contrast and texture, furthermore to the adversarial system. A distinctive aspect of this method is its cooperative training, which uses a detection network on the fused image to additionally correct the fusion system. After the advancements with GAN, attention has shifted to transformer architectures for image fusion tasks. Known for capturing long-range dependencies and contextual interactions within images, transformers promise to refine fusion methodologies.

GAN have been extensively used in image fusion literature. However, other promising generative architectures are emerging. One such method is DDFM (Denoising Diffusion Model for Multi-Modality Image Fusion) [42], an unsupervised approach designed to integrate multiple modalities such as infrared and visible images. The core architecture leverages the principles of denoising diffusion models [8], iteratively refining the fused image through a series of denoising steps. The model consists of two main components: a diffusion process that gradually adds noise to the images, and a denoising process that removes this noise while preserving and enhancing critical features from each modality. Two additional modules are integrated into the DDPM framework: the Unconditional Diffusion Sampling (UDS) module, which aims to recreate a natural-looking image, and the Expectation Maximization (EM) module, which strives to retain the maximum amount of information in the image.

2.3   Transformer Based Methods

Attention mechanisms have revolutionized NLP and extended their influence across domains. Initially proposed for sequence-to-sequence learning in machine translation, attention mechanisms enable models to focus selectively on input sequence elements, improving performance on tasks involving sequential data. Transformers, introduced by Vaswani et al. [27], rely on attention mechanisms for sequence modelling. Transformers use self-attention to capture global dependencies across input sequences in parallel, enhancing efficiency and scalability in modelling. Visual transformers, an extension tailored for computer vision, have gained prominence. Dosovitskiy et al. [4] introduced Vision Transformers, applying transformers directly to images and revolutionizing conventional convolutional approaches. Integrating attention mechanisms into computer vision via visual transformers allows models to grasp global context and long-range dependencies, enhancing visual understanding.

The approach of SCGRFuse [31] is to use a feature extractor for each of the modalities based on convolution blocks and to use a Visual Transformer block to fuse the information. The architecture is inspired by SeAFusion [26]. The convolutional feature extraction part, composed of residual blocks and dense residual blocks, is used as an encoder. There is one encoder per image that transmits the information to the fusion layer. The fusion layer is made up of two attention systems: a channel attention system and a spatial attention system. These two attention systems feed the feature map to a Pooling Fusion Block for segmentation. The segmentation network decodes and solves the segmentation task; the method is Task-Driven. The segmentation loss is used to calculate the system error, with a loss content composed of a texture loss to maximize texture in the image and an intensity loss that measures the pixel-level difference between the source and fused images. The visual fidelity of the image and the information it contains decreases in the absence of the spatial channel's attention module. This underlines the importance of the attention mechanism in preserving the details of the original image, and highlights the need to focus on its structure and edges to retain relevant information.

NestFuse [14] also uses a fusion layer based on channel and spatial attention systems. It is used directly for fusion, rather than using a Pooling Fusion Block, which makes full use of the attention systems for fusion. The encoder and decoder architecture is also convolution-based, but based on the UNet++ architecture [43]. This architecture allows for shorter skip connections and therefore better information preservation. This unsupervised method employs a loss function that assesses pixel-level differences between output and input images, augmented with SSIM to enhance learning. However, using a pixel-level cost function makes the system highly sensitive to slight variations or artefacts, prompting exploration of feature-level approaches.

Image Fusion Transformer [30] is an unsupervised infrared and visible image fusion architecture based on transformers. Each image has its own encoder composed of four blocks that operate at multiple scales, and a decoder similar to a U-Net++ [43] decoder. In U-Net++, nested and dense skip connections involve linking feature maps from the encoder to multiple intermediate layers within the decoder, enhancing information flow and gradient propagation. These connections allow each decoder block to receive inputs from all preceding layers, improving feature reuse and segmentation accuracy. The goal is to create an image that integrates the fused features from the input images. Fusion occurs between the encoder and decoder through a Spatio-Transformer Fusion block for each scale of the multi-scale architecture. This module comprises a transformer branch based on multi-head attention methods to capture global context, and a spatial branch made up of convolutional layers to capture local context. The cost function used combines SSIM [32] and a feature similarity loss that calculates the difference in information content between the output image and the two input images.

STFNet [16] uses a (DSA) detail self-attention and (SCA) saliency cross-attention: this category of method improves the contextual relationships between infrared and visible images. DSA is used for each feature map of the input images, and the queries from each DSA are combined in two SCA with the values and keys of the DSA output. A last SCA is used to merge the two branches and forward the feature map to a convolution-based decoder. A convolution-based encoder is used for each input image, and a feature alignment module is implemented to reduce artefacts using deformable convolution. The method is unsupervised, and its cost function is calculated from a SSIM, a frequency consistency loss and a Fourier spectral consistency loss.

A different two-stage unsupervised approach is proposed by the MDAN method [36]. First, an encoder-decoder architecture, composed of dense convolutional layers and skip connections similar to U-Net [43], is used to learn image encoding. The aim is to encode an image and decode it to reproduce an identical image, with a separate encoder for each input image. The learned architecture and weights are then reused, incorporating fusion blocks between each dense layer of the encoder. These fusion blocks are based on spatial-channel attention and feature aggregation, utilizing dual-branch fusion mechanisms. The two decoders receive fused information, and their outputs are concatenated via element-wise addition to produce the fused image. The fusion system's cost function comprises a SSIM [32], a pixel loss, and an algebra loss.

3   Synthesis

The methods presented in this paper are the main methods of image fusion by learning. The methods highlighted in the Table 1 are the most representative in terms of performance and specificity. These approaches are often presented as the most efficient in the state of the art, and their operation is a synthesis of the previous methods. Categorization by learning approach enables context-specific method selection. If the dataset has a fusion ground truth, then a supervised approach is the most appropriate. If the fusion is associated with a task and the dataset is labelled, then a Task-Driven approach enables efficient learning. Otherwise, if no data other than images is available, an unsupervised approach is the most suitable. The selection of the method type depends on the context and needs of the fusion. Convolution-based image fusion methods capture spatial features for precise fusion, while Transformer-based methods capture long-range dependencies for contextual fusion. Generative algorithms enable creative fusion by generating new information from source images, but can generate artefacts and unstable learning. Each approach offers unique advantages to meet specific image fusion needs. These methods are not complete and improvements are required to be fully effective.

4   Challenges and Future Research Areas

Future research should focus on developing robust fusion methods capable of handling missing data within the image ensemble. Techniques need to be devised to effectively incorporate incomplete information without compromising fusion quality or robustness. GMFNet [1] choose the direction by using data augmentation and noise addition method. This direction can be further explored to increase the robustness.

There is a growing need for fusion methods that generalize across various problem domains, including multi-exposure, multi-modal, and multi-focus scenarios, while mitigating over-fitting risks. These methods should exhibit adaptability to different fusion contexts without excessive reliance on specific training data. U2Fusion [33] is an interesting first approach that could be applied to more generalist methods.

With the increasing demand for applications such as autonomous driving, future research should focus on methods capable of integrating multi-view and multi-modal data. These methods must address the unique challenges posed by diverse data sources to enhance the effectiveness of fusion techniques in complex environments. MVMM-Net [24] includes an early processing of multi-view information, although in a naive way. Using 3D representation can improve understanding of multi-view scene, for example. Given the industrial implications of image fusion, there is a need for methods capable of achieving real-time fusion while maintaining high accuracy and efficiency. To facilitate the deployment of fusion methods in practical settings, research efforts should prioritize techniques capable of training with limited data. Methods that effectively leverage small datasets without sacrificing fusion quality are essential for widespread adoption and implementation, particularly considering Transformer architectures [16,30,31], which are costly in terms of processing for inference, training time and training data needs.

5   Conclusion

The current exploration of image fusion techniques using deep learning methodologies, encompassing CNN, GAN and transformers, highlights a diverse landscape of approaches with distinct advantages and limitations. CNN demonstrate capabilities in extracting spatial features and learning hierarchical representations, making them well suited to image fusion tasks. However, their dependence on their limitations in capturing long-range dependencies impedes their effectiveness in certain contexts. GANs generate high-quality synthetic images, which benefits image fusion by improving information richness. However, problems such as learning instability impact their practical deployment, affecting the fidelity of fused images. In addition, GANs tend to create visual artefacts due to their generative nature. On the other hand, Transformer, with their self-attention mechanism, excels at capturing long-range dependencies and contextual interactions within images, underlining their potential for precise fusion tasks. However, they can be very resource-intensive to train, and scalability problems pose practical obstacles.

The methods reviewed in this study have been classified into supervised, unsupervised and task-oriented approaches, offering a new taxonomy for understanding their conceptual similarities and to help choose the right strategy depending on the context. Supervised methods are based on labelled data for training, while unsupervised techniques learn autonomously from data structures and custom metrics. Task-Driven approaches prioritize specific goals in the fusion process. While recent advances in techniques such as Transformer have shown promise for improving image fusion capabilities, further research is needed to refine these methods for optimum performance and wider applicability in a variety of fields.

References

1. Balit, E., Chadli, A.: GMFNet: gated multimodal fusion network for visible-thermal semantic segmentation. In: Proceedings of the 16th European Conference on Computer Vision, pp. 1–4 (2020)
2. Baltrušaitis, T., Ahuja, C., Morency, L.P.: Multimodal machine learning: a survey and taxonomy. IEEE Trans. Pattern Anal. Mach. Intell. **41**(2), 423–443 (2018)
3. Bayoudh, K., Knani, R., Hamdaoui, F., Mtibaa, A.: A survey on deep multimodal learning for computer vision: advances, trends, applications, and datasets. Vis. Comput. **38**(8), 2939–2970 (2022)
4. Dosovitskiy, A., et al.: An image is worth 16x16 words: transformers for image recognition at scale. In: International Conference on Learning Representations (2020)
5. Goodfellow, I., et al.: Generative adversarial networks. Commun. ACM **63**(11), 139–144 (2020)
6. Ha, Q., Watanabe, K., Karasawa, T., Ushiku, Y., Harada, T.: MFNet: towards real-time semantic segmentation for autonomous vehicles with multi-spectral scenes. In: 2017 IEEE/RSJ International Conference on Intelligent Robots and Systems (IROS), pp. 5108–5115 (2017)
7. He, K., Zhang, X., Ren, S., Sun, J.: Deep residual learning for image recognition. Proceedings of the IEEE Conference on Computer Vision and Pattern Recognition, pp. 770–778 (2016)
8. Ho, J., Jain, A., Abbeel, P.: Denoising diffusion probabilistic models. Adv. Neural. Inf. Process. Syst. **33**, 6840–6851 (2020)
9. Huang, S.C., Pareek, A., Seyyedi, S., Banerjee, I., Lungren, M.P.: Fusion of medical imaging and electronic health records using deep learning: a systematic review and implementation guidelines. NPJ Digit. Med. **3**(1), 136 (2020)
10. Kalamkar, S., et al.: Multimodal image fusion: a systematic review. Decis. Anal. J., 100327 (2023)
11. Karim, S., Tong, G., Li, J., Qadir, A., Farooq, U., Yu, Y.: Current advances and future perspectives of image fusion: a comprehensive review. Inf. Fusion **90**, 185–217 (2023)
12. Kim, J., Koh, J., Kim, Y., Choi, J., Hwang, Y., Choi, J.W.: Robust deep multimodal learning based on gated information fusion network. In: Asian Conference on Computer Vision, pp. 90–106 (2018)
13. Li, H., Wu, X.J.: DenseFuse: a fusion approach to infrared and visible images. IEEE Trans. Image Process. **28**(5), 2614–2623 (2018)
14. Li, H., Wu, X.J., Durrani, T.: NestFuse: an infrared and visible image fusion architecture based on nest connection and spatial/channel attention models. IEEE Trans. Instrum. Meas. **69**(12), 9645–9656 (2020)
15. Liu, J., et al.: Target-aware dual adversarial learning and a multi-scenario multi-modality benchmark to fuse infrared and visible for object detection. In: IEEE/CVF Conference on Computer Vision and Pattern Recognition, pp. 5802–5811 (2022)

16. Liu, Q., Pi, J., Gao, P., Yuan, D.: STFNet: self-supervised transformer for infrared and visible image fusion. IEEE Trans. Emerg. Top. Comput. Intell. (2024)
17. Liu, Z., Tsukada, K., Hanasaki, K., Ho, Y.K., Dai, Y.: Image fusion by using steerable pyramid. Pattern Recogn. Lett. **22**(9), 929–939 (2001)
18. Liu, Z., Geng, K., Cheng, X., Shen, K., Li, A., Cheng, S.: CMAFusion: cross modal attention based end-to-end infrared and visible image fusion network. In: 2023 7th CAA International Conference on Vehicular Control and Intelligence (CVCI), pp. 1–6. IEEE (2023)
19. Ma, J., Xu, H., Jiang, J., Mei, X., Zhang, X.P.: DDcGAN: a dual-discriminator conditional generative adversarial network for multi-resolution image fusion. IEEE Trans. Image Process. **29**, 4980–4995 (2020)
20. Ma, J., Yu, W., Liang, P., Li, C., Jiang, J.: FusionGAN: a generative adversarial network for infrared and visible image fusion. Inf. Fusion **48**, 11–26 (2019)
21. Ma, J., Zhang, H., Shao, Z., Liang, P., Xu, H.: GANMcC: a generative adversarial network with multiclassification constraints for infrared and visible image fusion. IEEE Trans. Instrum. Meas. **70**, 1–14 (2020)
22. Paramanandham, N., Rajendiran, K.: Multi sensor image fusion for surveillance applications using hybrid image fusion algorithm. Multimedia Tools Appl. **77**, 12405–12436 (2018)
23. Ronneberger, O., Fischer, P., Brox, T.: U-Net: convolutional networks for biomedical image segmentation. In: Navab, N., Hornegger, J., Wells, W.M., Frangi, A.F. (eds.) MICCAI 2015. LNCS, vol. 9351, pp. 234–241. Springer, Cham (2015). https://doi.org/10.1007/978-3-319-24574-4_28
24. Song, J., et al.: Multiview multimodal network for breast cancer diagnosis in contrast-enhanced spectral mammography images. Int. J. Comput. Assist. Radiol. Surg. **16**(6), 979–988 (2021). https://doi.org/10.1007/s11548-021-02391-4
25. Sun, Y., Zuo, W., Liu, M.: RTFNet: RGB-thermal fusion network for semantic segmentation of urban scenes. IEEE Robot. Autom. Lett. **4**(3), 2576–2583 (2019)
26. Tang, L., Yuan, J., Ma, J.: Image fusion in the loop of high-level vision tasks: a semantic-aware real-time infrared and visible image fusion network. Inf. Fusion **82**, 28–42 (2022)
27. Vaswani, A., et al.: Attention is all you need. Adv. Neural Inf. Process. Syst. **30** (2017)
28. Veshki, F.G., Ouzir, N., Vorobyov, S.A., Ollila, E.: Multimodal image fusion via coupled feature learning. Signal Process. **200**, 108637 (2022)
29. Vielzeuf, V., Lechervy, A., Pateux, S., Jurie, F.: CentralNet: a multilayer approach for multimodal fusion. In: Proceedings of the European Conference on Computer Vision (ECCV) Workshops (2018)
30. Vs, V., Valanarasu, J.M.J., Oza, P., Patel, V.M.: Image fusion transformer. In: 2022 IEEE International Conference on Image Processing (ICIP), pp. 3566–3570 (2022)
31. Wang, Y., Pu, J., Miao, D., Zhang, L., Zhang, L., Du, X.: SCGRFuse: an infrared and visible image fusion network based on spatial/channel attention mechanism and gradient aggregation residual dense blocks. Eng. Appl. Artif. Intell. **132**, 107898 (2024)
32. Wang, Z., Bovik, A.C., Sheikh, H.R., Simoncelli, E.P.: Image quality assessment: from error visibility to structural similarity. IEEE Trans. Image Process. **13**(4), 600–612 (2004)
33. Xu, H., Ma, J., Jiang, J., Guo, X., Ling, H.: U2Fusion: a unified unsupervised image fusion network. IEEE Trans. Pattern Anal. Mach. Intell. **44**(1), 502–518 (2020)

34. Xu, H., Ma, J., Le, Z., Jiang, J., Guo, X.: FusionDN: a unified densely connected network for image fusion. Proc. AAAI Conf. Artif. Intel. **34**(07), 12484–12491 (2020)
35. Xu, H., Ma, J., Zhang, X.P.: MEF-GAN: multi-exposure image fusion via generative adversarial networks. IEEE Trans. Image Process. **29**, 7203–7216 (2020)
36. Xu, L., Wang, Z., Wu, B., Lui, S.: MDAN: multi-level dependent attention network for visual emotion analysis. In: Proceedings of the IEEE/CVF Conference on Computer Vision and Pattern Recognition, pp. 9479–9488 (2022)
37. Xu, X., Shen, Y., Han, S.: Dense-FG: a fusion GAN model by using densely connected blocks to fuse infrared and visible images. Appl. Sci. **13**(8), 4684 (2023)
38. Yang, L., Guo, B., Ni, W.: Multifocus image fusion algorithm based on contourlet decomposition and region statistics. In: Fourth International Conference on Image and Graphics (ICIG 2007), pp. 707–712 (2007)
39. Zhang, H., Yuan, J., Tian, X., Ma, J.: GAN-FM: infrared and visible image fusion using GAN with full-scale skip connection and dual Markovian discriminators. IEEE Trans. Comput. Imaging **7**, 1134–1147 (2021)
40. Zhang, Q., Liu, Y., Blum, R.S., Han, J., Tao, D.: Sparse representation based multi-sensor image fusion for multi-focus and multi-modality images: a review. Inf. Fusion **40**, 57–75 (2018)
41. Zhang, Y., Liu, Y., Sun, P., Yan, H., Zhao, X., Zhang, L.: IFCNN: a general image fusion framework based on convolutional neural network. Inf. Fusion **54**, 99–118 (2020)
42. Zhao, Z., et al.: DDFM: denoising diffusion model for multi-modality image fusion. In: Proceedings of the IEEE/CVF International Conference on Computer Vision, pp. 8082–8093 (2023)
43. Zhou, Z., Rahman Siddiquee, M.M., Tajbakhsh, N., Liang, J.: UNet++: a nested U-net architecture for medical image segmentation. In: Deep Learning in Medical Image Analysis and Multimodal Learning for Clinical Decision Support: 4th International Workshop, DLMIA 2018, and 8th International Workshop, ML-CDS 2018, Held in Conjunction with MICCAI 2018, Granada, Spain, 20 September 2018, Proceedings 4, pp. 3–11 (2018)

Comprehensive Perceptual Analysis and Rating of Material Properties from Video Data

Jiri Filip[1]([✉]), Filip Dechterenko[2], Jiri Lukavsky[2], Roland W. Fleming[3,4], and Filipp Schmidt[3,4]

[1] The Czech Academy of Sciences, Institute of Information Theory and Automation, Prague, Czech Republic
`filipj@utia.cas.cz`
[2] The Czech Academy of Sciences, Institute of Psychology, Prague, Czech Republic
{`dechterenko,lukavsky`}`@praha.psu.cas.cz`
[3] Experimental Psychology, Justus Liebig University of Giessen, Giessen, Germany
{`roland.w.fleming,filipp.schmidt`}`@psychol.uni-giessen.de`
[4] Centre for Mind, Brain and Behaviour, Universities of Marburg, Giessen and Darmstadt, Germany

Abstract. The real world is abundant with a diverse array of materials, each possessing unique surface appearances that play a crucial role in our daily perception and understanding of their properties. Despite advancements in technology enabling the realistic reproduction of material appearances for visualization and quality control, the interoperability of material property information across various measurement representations and software platforms remains a complex challenge. A key to overcoming this challenge lies in the automatic identification of materials' perceptual features, enabling intuitive differentiation of properties stored in disparate material data formats. This paper introduces a novel approach to material identification by encoding perceptual features obtained from dynamic visual stimuli. We conducted a psychophysical experiment to identify and validate 16 particularly significant perceptual attributes across 347 materials. Subsequently, we gathered attribute ratings from 20–24 participants for each material, creating a 'material signature' that encodes the perceptual properties of each material.

Keywords: material · appearance · perception · feature · identifier

1 Introduction

The digital representation of materials plays a pivotal role in numerous applications, ranging from virtual reality to industrial design. However, accurately

Supplementary Information The online version contains supplementary material available at https://doi.org/10.1007/978-3-031-88217-3_13.

predicting the perceived properties of these materials from a human vision perspective remains a significant challenge in contemporary research. This difficulty in mapping visual appearance to intuitive properties results both from the variety and complexity in material appearances as well as the rich space of human perceptual inferences. Here, we aim to identify some of the most critical appearance attributes of a diverse set of real-world materials including, but not limited to, fabric, leather, wood, plastic, metal, and paper, and use these to characterize the space of appearances. We selected the samples to cover a broad spectrum of textures, colors, and reflective properties, and use them to produce standardized video sequences, to provide a comprehensive overview of material appearances typically encountered in both everyday life and specialized industries. We opted for captured videos showing the genuine material appearance of flat specimens under different viewing conditions [5]. These dynamic material appearance data allowed us to obtain reliable identification of the most important appearance attributes as well as their human ratings. We collected ratings for 347 materials spanning wide range of categories as shown in Fig. 1.

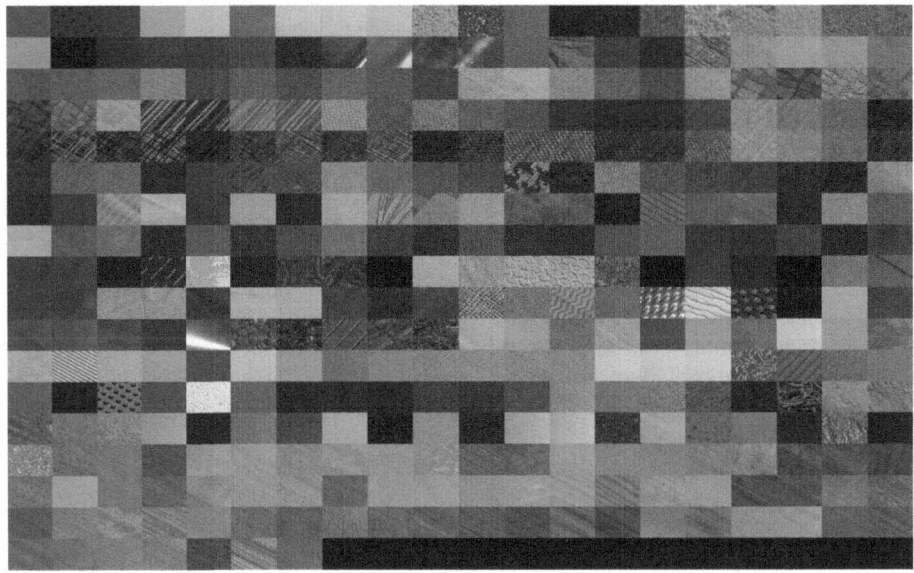

Fig. 1. Frame 30 from a video sequences of the 347 materials in the study.

The primary contributions of our paper are:

- Determination of key perceptual features – through rigorous analysis, we have identified sixteen crucial perceptual attributes of these materials, providing a foundational understanding of material perception.
- Extensive public collection of human observer ratings – we have amassed a substantial dataset by obtaining over 110,000 ratings from human observers

for the sixteen attributes across all material samples, offering a rich basis for further analysis.
- Evaluation of the proposed features' performance in material retrieval task and providing their ratings publicly.

2   Related Work

Our work is related to human visual perception of comprehensive aspects of real material appearance as a function of illumination and viewing conditions. Namely identification of appearance visual attributes and their changes for different material categories have been a subject of research interest for decades. Researchers attempted to establish a connection between perceptual texture space and computational statistics. Tamura et al. [28] suggested a computational form of six basic texture properties and evaluated their performance in a psychophysical experiment on 56 gray-scaled textures of Brodatz's catalogue [1]. Rao and Lohse [19] identified a perceptual texture space by grouping Brodatz's textures and using hierarchical cluster analysis, non-parametric multi-dimensional scaling (MDS), classification and regression tree analysis, discriminant analysis, and principal component analysis. They concluded that the perceptual texture space can be represented by a three-dimensional space with axes describing repetitiveness, contrast/directionality, and coarseness/complexity. [16] performed an experiment with human subjects to obtain a pattern vocabulary governed by grammar rules. Malik and Perona [13] presented a model of human preattentive texture perception based on low-level human perception. Vanrell and Vitria [29] suggested a texton-based four-dimensional texture space with perceptual textons' attributes along each of the dimensions. Long and Leow [11] presented an approach attempting to solve the missing link between the perceptual texture space and the space of computational texture features, by reduction of Gabor features represented by a convolutional neural network a four-dimensional texture space. Schwartz et al. [22] proposed so called visual material traits encoding appearance of characteristic material properties by means of convolutional features of train image patches. In follow up work, researchers discovered space of locally-recognizable material attributes from perceptual material distances by training classifiers to reproduce this space from image patches [26]. Sawayama et al. [21] created dataset of synthetic images with variable illumination and geometries and conducted psychophysical experiments (an oddity task) discriminating materials on one of six dimensions. Schwartz and Nishino [23] avoided fixed set of attributes by proposing a method deriving material attributes annotation based on probing the human visual perception of materials by asking simple yes/no questions comparing pairs of small image patches. Filip et al. [5] analyzed perceptual dimensions of 30 wood materials were analyzed in by means of a combination of similarity and rating studies and compared them to basic image statistics.

Many studies represented textureless material appearance by means of bidirectional reflectance distribution function (BRDF) [17] and its parametric models. Matusik et al. [14] psychophysically evaluated large sets of BRDFs, and showed that there are consistent transitions in perceived properties between different BRDFs. They analyzed whether they possess any of the 16 perceptual predefined attributes. They used the observers ratings to build a model in both the linear and non-linear embedding spaces. Such a manifold is then used for editing/mixing between the measured BRDFs. Serrano, et al. [25] psychophysically analyzed isotropic BRDFs to identify smooth and intuitive material appearance transition between different visual attributes. Lagunas et al. [10] presented a deep learning model measuring the similarity in appearance between different BRDFs, which correlates with human similarity judgments. Serrano et al. [24] collected a large-scale dataset of perceptual ratings of five appearance attributes for combinations of material, shape, and illumination, to analyze the effects of illumination and geometry on material perception across such a large collection of varied BRDFs. Recently, and nad Lagunas [27] proposed a single-image appearance editing generative framework that allows to intuitively modify the material appearance of an object by increasing or decreasing high-level perceptual attributes describing such appearance (e.g., plastic, rubber, metallic, glossy, bright, rough, and the strength and sharpness of reflections).

Related research also investigated angle-dependent material appearance represented by more advanced texture models. Jarabo et al. [9] ran perceptual experiments to investigate the visual equivalence [18] of rendered images for different levels of bidirectional texture function (BTF) [2] filtering, and found that blur in a spatial domain is less tolerable than in its angular counterpart. Filip et al. [4] assessed accuracy of advanced material appearance representation using BTF on 16 diverse physical material samples, by comparing human judgements of material attributes made when viewing a computer graphics rendering to those made when viewing a physical sample of the same material. Deschaintre et al. [3] introduced a novel dataset that links free-text descriptions to various fabric materials. The dataset comprises 15,000 natural language descriptions associated to 3,000 corresponding images of fabric materials. Authors identified a compact lexicon, set of attributes and key structure that emerge from the descriptions explaining how people describe fabrics.

What sets our study apart from the previous work is (1) identification of interpretable appearance attributes derived from user studies rather than non-interpretable visual features, and (2) the use videos capturing dynamic light interaction with real materials samples rather than static or synthetic stimuli.

3   Capturing Material Data

We collected 347 material samples, with a focus on capturing a broad variety of visual appearances but also the most common material categories.

For many material categories with spatially homogeneous appearances, such as metal, plastic, and paper, we can relatively accurately represent individual materials using parametric reflectance models, which encapsulate these materials with compact, physically-related parameters. In contrast, our analysis focuses on more visually complex materials that cannot be easily represented by such models due to local physical effects like shadowing, masking, or subsurface scattering. Therefore, the majority of materials in our collection come from fabric and wood, which are categories with a wide range of appearances due to different fiber types and thread weaving patterns. For the remaining categories, we focus mainly on material samples with specific non-homogeneous structures. Our dataset consists of 347 samples distributed to the following major categories: fabric (157), wood (67), coating (30), paper (23), plastic (17), metal (14), leather (11), and others (28) (see Fig. 1 showing one frame from the image sequence). Our dataset contains, among others, materials from UTIA BRDF database [6] and MAM 2014 benchmark [20].

As real-world illumination is important for correct matching of material properties especially in interactions between lighting and object geometry [8], we decided to use dynamic stimuli showing material appearance from different observation directions. For each material sample, we produced a video sequence showcasing the material's non-specular and specular characteristics by a slow rotation. These sequences featured close-up views of approximately 42×42 mm areas of the samples, captured using the UTIA goniometer [7]. In line with industry standards [15], we maintained a constant polar angle of $45°$ for both the camera and the light source, varying only the azimuthal angle of the camera to facilitate more rapid measurements. Each sequence commenced with the light and camera azimuthal angles differing by $90°$, followed by a 90-degree camera movement, resulting in a final difference of $180°$ between the azimuthal angles probing specular reflection of the material. Comprising 60 image frames of resolution 632×412, each 4-s sequence was played in reverse order after completion, creating an 8-second continuous loop that effectively illustrates the dynamic behavior of the rotating material.

4   Selection of Main Perceptual Attributes

In this section, we describe two studies to identify key visual features for describing the appearance of the material videos in our dataset. The scheme depicting our psychophysical assessment of materials is shown in Fig. 2-a.

4.1   Study 1 – Attributes Identification

First, we performed an online free naming study. For this, we created three arrangements of 70 material videos each, randomly selected from our full dataset. Participants were then asked to type and rank at least five most visually distinguishing features, in the order of their importance, that they thought sets apart all the materials presented within each arrangement. We collected a total of 451 valid text responses from 32 participants with a mean response duration per arrangement of 2.8 min. Subsequently, we grouped synonyms and equivalent terms into clusters, and removed all responses with occurrences $< 0.45\%$ (i.e. with less than two responses) - obtaining a condensed set of 21 visual material attributes. In Fig. 2, the plot on the left shows the probability a_p for each

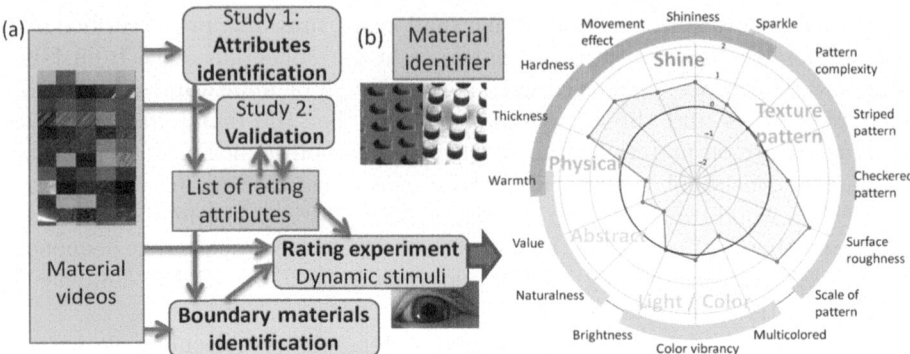

Fig. 2. (a) Scheme of the proposed approach to obtain human ratings of visual attributes. (b) visualization of the attributes for a given material using a polar plot grouping related visual properties.

attribute (calculated across participants and three trials), as well as the average ranking a_o by participants, and the combination of both, $a_p \cdot (\max(a_o) - a_o)$ (Fig. 3).

As two of the most frequent terms *texture* and *patterns* are vague without further elaboration we replaced them with the more specific attributes *pattern complexity, striped pattern, checkered patterns*. The clusters*gritty, physical,* and *opacity* were removed as they were rarely mentioned (less than five responses). In total, we did not account only for 1.5% responses.

The most prominent attributes that participants used to describe the visual appearances of our material videos include common optical attributes such as color variability, saturation, roughness, brightness, shininess, texture, and pattern, but also tactile or subjective attributes like warmth, hardness, naturalness, and attractiveness. The final set of sixteen perceptual attributes used in our rating study is shown in Table 1, together with the boundary materials and the instructive questions for all attributes that were given to the participants.

4.2   Study 2 – Attributes Validation

As the clustering of attributes might have been subject to experimenter bias, we performed a second study to validate the 16 attributes. We asked six participants to cluster all 451 valid text responses into the 16 predefined attributes (Table 1). Overall, the inter-rater agreement was notably high (Fleiss' Kappa score of 0.786) and for 198 out of 451 responses (43.9%), all six raters reached a unanimous decision. For 254 (56.3%) of responses at least three raters agreed, and for 396 (87.8%) responses at least two raters did.

4.3   Study 3 – Boundary Materials Identifications

To create a representative visual anchor for the rating study, we asked 9 online participants to pick from the three arrangements of 70 material videos, the mate-

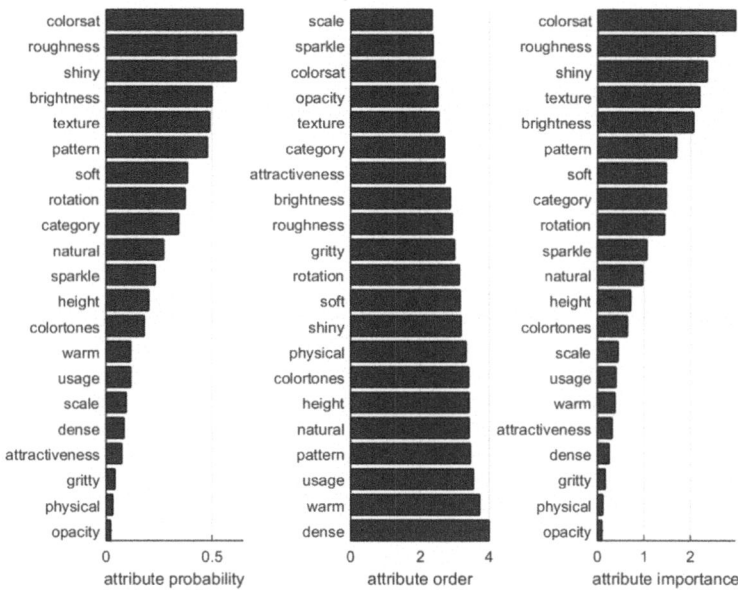

Fig. 3. Attribute statistics obtained from the psychophysical experiment: attribute probability (left), attribute order (middle), and their combination attribute importance (right).

rial exhibiting the lowest and the highest value of a specified visual attribute (e.g., Which of the materials displays the greatest level of brightness?). Participants completed 96 responses each (3 arrangements × 16 attributes × 2 extrema). Out of 9 participants, the same material video was perceived to express the lowest value of an attribute by 3.6 participants on average, and the highest value by 2.8 on average. We removed double occurrences, yielding the arrangement of 25 materials in Fig. 4, which were used as fixed anchor materials in the following rating study helping observers to adjust visual scales.

5   Rating Study

In each trial, we showed a material video stimulus on the left, together with a fixed set of the anchor materials on the right. For each perceptual attribute (Table 1), we showed all material videos in random order and online participants provided their evaluation with a slider (Fig. 4). Anchor materials were the same for all tested videos and attributes. We collected a total of 111 040 ratings (20–24 participants/attribute). Data were normalized at the participant level by Z-scoring and then computing mean rating scores across all participants. We excluded participants' ratings from the analysis, when their values had a negative correlation with the mean (typically 1–2 participants per attribute). Finally, we obtained mean opinion score values for 16 attributes and 347 materials.

Table 1. A list of 16 perceptual attributes evaluated in the rating study and their description.

ID	attribute	extreme values	instructions
1.	**color vibrancy**	dull, vibrant	How richly colored is the material, ranging from monochromatic or neutral-colored materials to vibrantly colored materials?
2.	**surface roughness**	smooth, rough	How rough is the material, ranging from fine or smooth to coarse or grainy?
3.	**pattern complexity**	plain, complex	How complex are the patterns on the material, ranging from simple to intricate?
4.	**striped pattern**	no, pronounced stripes	To what extent does the material exhibit stripy patterns?
5.	**checkered pattern**	no, pronounced checks	To what extent does the material exhibit checkered patterns?
6.	**brightness**	black, white	How bright is the material, ranging from dim or subdued to bright or luminous?
7.	**shininess**	matt, mirror	How shiny is the material, ranging from dull or non-reflective to highly reflective?
8.	**sparkle**	none, sparkling	To what extent does the material exhibit sparkling and glittery effects?
9.	**hardness**	soft, hard	How hard is the material, ranging from soft or plush to firm or rigid?
10.	**movement effect**	none, extreme	To what extent does the appearance change due to camera movement?
11.	**pattern scale**	fine, large	How large are the pattern elements, ranging from fine-grained or uniform to large or blotchy patterns?
12.	**naturalness**	manmade, natural	How natural is the material, ranging from manmade to natural origin?
13.	**thickness**	flat, thick	How deep is the material structure, ranging from flat or thin to thick?
14.	**multicolored**	single, many	How multicolored is the material, ranging from a single or uniform color to colorful or many colors?
15.	**value**	cheap, luxurious	How valuable is the material, ranging from low-cost or cheap to extravagant or luxurious?
16.	**warmth**	cold, warm	How warm is the material to the touch, ranging from cool or cold to pleasant or warm?

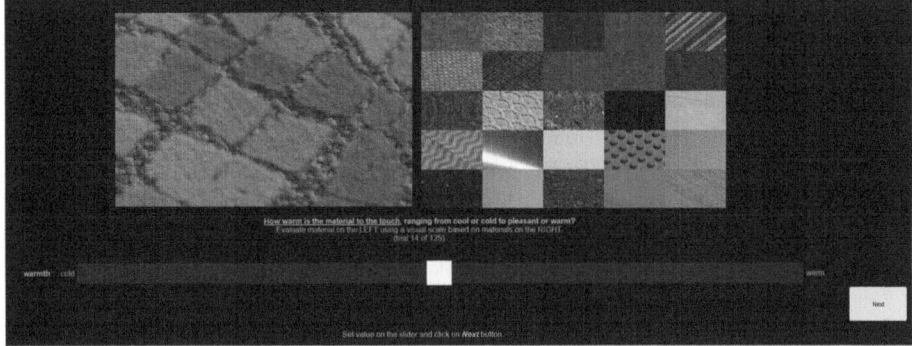

Fig. 4. An example of the rating stimulus with boundary materials on the left.

We can use the obtained ratings of our attributes in various scenarios, such as directly comparing the visual similarity of materials. For instance, during material retrieval, one can filter materials by using only selected attributes. As a similarity measure for comparing sets of attributes of two material samples, we used Pearson correlation; however, other metrics are also possible. Figure 5 shows rank ordering of materials based on their rating values for individual attributes, where samples are shown in non-specular and specular conditions. Each image illustrates the material appearance under non-specular (left) and specular (right) conditions.

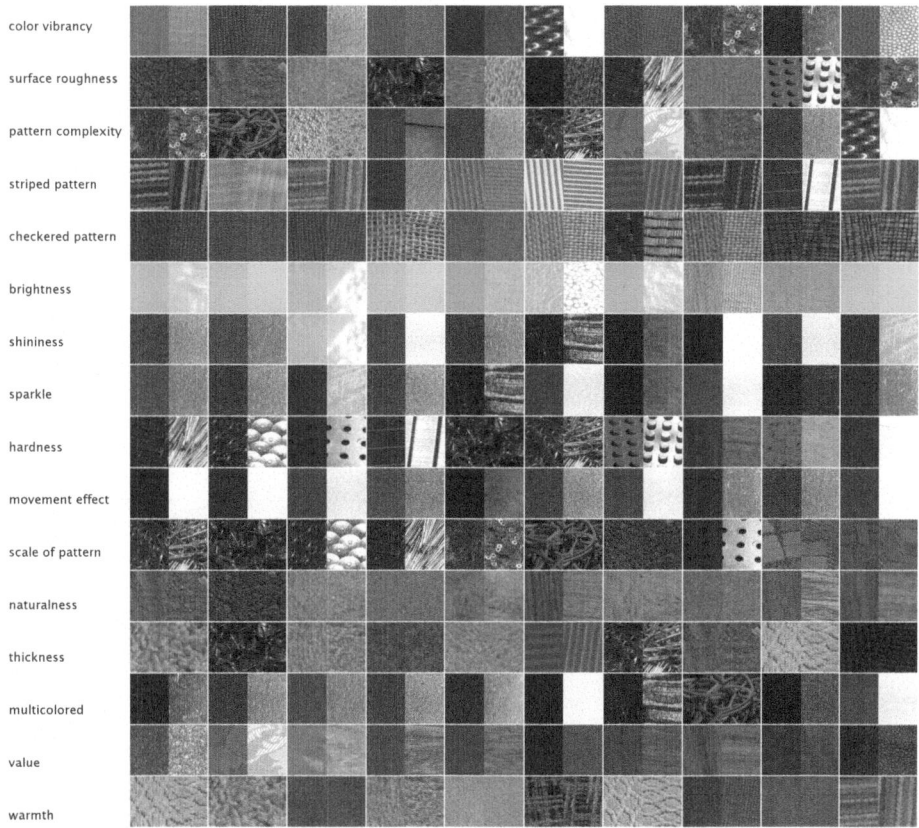

Fig. 5. Ten materials having the highest ranking along individual attributes.

To obtain insight in two dimensional embedding of the material samples, we also performed t-distributed stochastic neighbor embedding (t-SNE) [12] as shown in Fig. 6. For classes *wood*, *fabric*, *carpet*, and *coating* we observe coherent clusters while for other categories we can see considerable overlaps. This is due to high variability in sample appearance withing this class, e.g. metal in a form of sheet or pins.

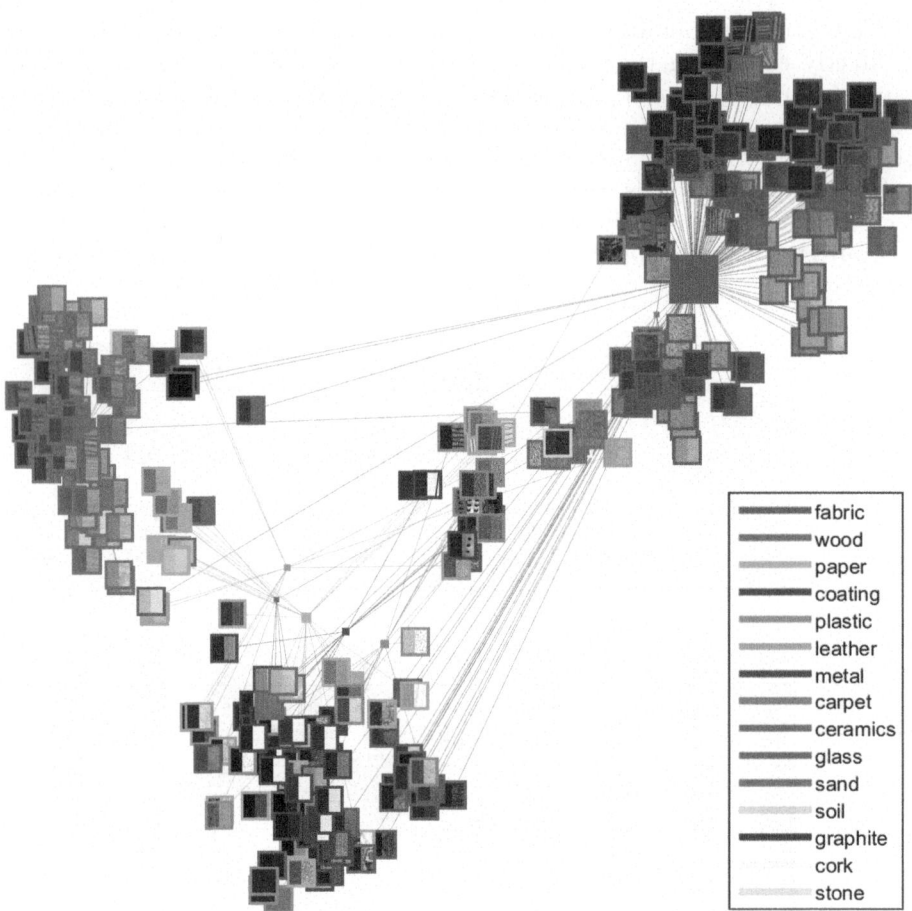

Fig. 6. Material samples proximity obtained as their two-dimensional embedding using t-SNE.

This finding is supported by clustering of the similarity matrix between materials' attributes computed using Pearson correlation shown in Fig. 7.

6   Application to Material Retrieval

The material attributes for each material can be visualized in a polar plot, creating a unique visual signature of the material's appearance, as illustrated in Fig. 2-b. The azimuthal ordering of attributes is based on their relationships, forming five clusters loosely related to gloss, texture and pattern, light and color, and both physical and abstract properties. The most significant attributes having higher values are positioned near the plot's boundary, while the less important ones are closer to its center. Figure 8 displays the visual attributes computed

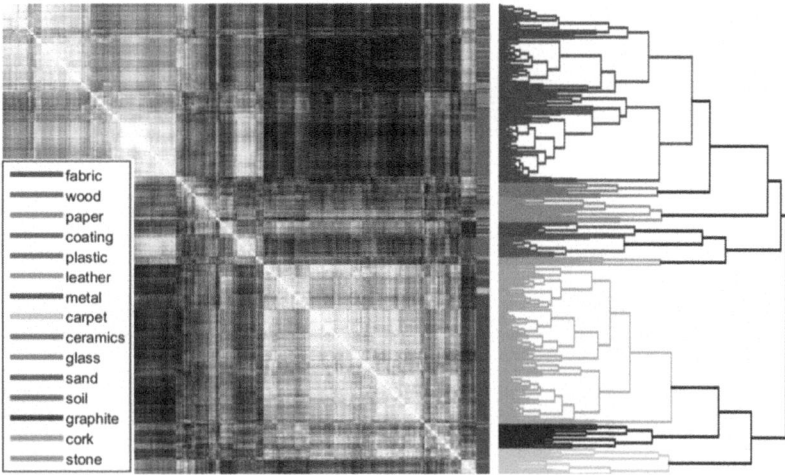

Fig. 7. Material samples proximity obtained as a similarity matrix between the materials with corresponding clustering dendrogram.

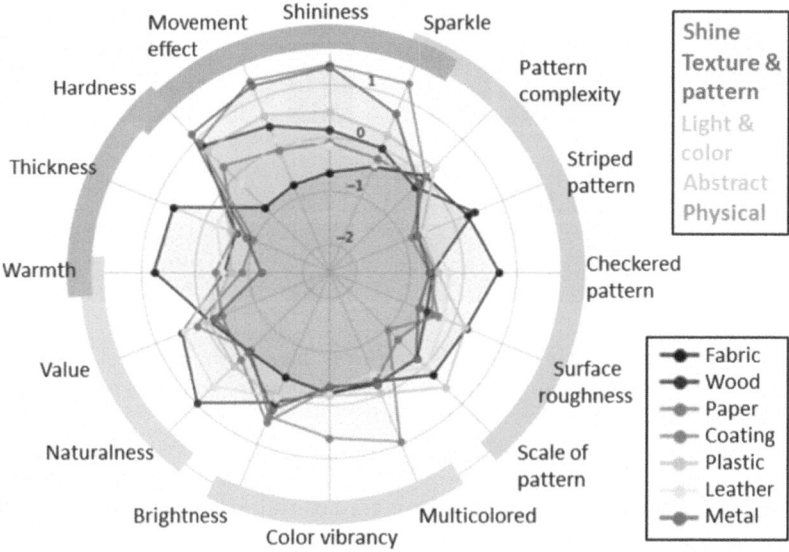

Fig. 8. A comparison of typical visual attributes for major material categories in our dataset.

as the median value across all samples in seven major material categories. This allows us to clearly distinguish between categories; for example, fabric is characterized as thick and warm, whereas coatings and leather are identified as hard and shiny.

Fig. 9. Examples of similar materials retrieval based on a correlation between attributes' values: material in query, its visual signature and five retrieved images from our dataset having the closest appearance.

We utilized Pearson correlation between material attributes as a measure for retrieving materials with similar appearance and presented the results in Fig. 9, where the three materials most similar to the query are displayed. Size of the retrieved images indicate their correlation to the query image and can serve as approximate measure of material typicality in the dataset. We observe that the retrieval is highly effective when similar materials are present in the category, such as carpet (013), fabric (067, 093), leather (114), sand (176), or wood (210). However, even in the absence of similar materials in the dataset, the retrieval system suggests plausible materials, such as fancy fabric (103), crinkled paper (123), or paper clips (137). Retrieval performance for all materials can be found in a supplementary material.

7   Discussion

The main contribution of this paper is definition of the crucial visual attributes for identification of material visual properties. Although our study uses one of the largest sets of material samples used in a psychophysical analysis to date, and we carefully selected this set from a portfolio of real-world materials, the number of samples per material category varies. The highest number of samples is in the categories of fabric and wood due to their inherited high visual variability. This could potentially impact selection of our visual attributes and skew their generalization towards these categories. On the other hand, including more samples would have made our similarity experiment much more demanding.

Our current study is limited to a fixed level-of-detail of the material surface. It analyzes the sample area of 40×40 mm and thus is limited to materials with relatively fine and stationary textures and cannot describe visual behavior of materials beyond our sample size, i.e., textures with too low spatial frequencies or slow gradient changes over the sample. Also our dynamic stimuli represented a limited subset of all possible lighting-sample-viewer configurations. We had to limit camera and light trajectories so that movies were of reasonable duration. Therefore, we do not account for specific retroreflective, goniochromatic, or anisotropic behavior of materials due to changes in viewing and lighting angles which are not present in our stimuli.

We consider this work as a proof-of-concept study, which can be extended in the future by collecting ratings of even wider range of materials. To support future research in this area, we have made all stimuli data and rating responses available in a public repository accessible from https://staff.utia.cas.cz/filip/pub.html.

8   Conclusions

In a series of psychophysical studies involving 347 materials across various categories, we identified a set of sixteen material attributes and had them rated by twenty observers. Our findings indicate that these attributes perform well in facilitating intuitive, human-centered comparisons and retrievals of material appearances, thereby creating a unique visual signature for each material. This signature enables effective material retrieval based on perception-related features. In future work, we aim to predict human ratings of these attributes using image statistics derived from photographs of the materials, which would allow for the automatic computational identification of the material appearance fingerprint.

Acknowledgments. We would like to thank all volunteers taking part in the psychophysical experiments. This research has been supported by the Czech Science Foundation grant GA22-17529S. This work was also partially funded by the Deutsche Forschungsgemeinschaft (DFG, German Research Foundation)-No. 222641018-SFB/TRR 135 TP C1, by the ERC Consolidator Award 'SHAPE'-project number ERC-CoG-2015-682859, by the ERC Advanced Award 'STUFF'-project number ERC-ADG-2022-101098225 and by the Research Cluster "The Adaptive Mind" funded by the Hessian Ministry for Higher Education, Research, Science and Arts.

References

1. Brodatz, P.: A Photographic Album for Artists and Designers (Brodatz Texture Database). Dover Publications (1966)
2. Dana, K., van Ginneken, B., Nayar, S., Koenderink, J.: Reflectance and texture of real-world surfaces. ACM Trans. Graph. **18**(1), 1–34 (1999). https://doi.org/10.1145/300776.300778
3. Deschaintre, V., Guerrero-Viu, J., Gutierrez, D., Boubekeur, T., Masia, B.: The visual language of fabrics. ACM Trans. Graph. **42**(4) (2023). https://doi.org/10.1145/3592391
4. Filip, J., Kolafová, M., Havlíček, M., Vávra, R., Haindl, M., Rushmeier, H.: Evaluating physical and rendered material appearance. Vis. Comput., 805–816 (2018). https://doi.org/10.1007/s00371-018-1545-3
5. Filip, J., Lukavský, J., Děchtěrenko, F., Schmidt, F., Fleming, R.W.: Perceptual dimensions of wood materials. J. Vis. **5**, 12 (2024)
6. Filip, J., Vávra, R.: Template-based sampling of anisotropic BRDFs. Comput. Graph. Forum **33**(7), 91–99 (2014)
7. Filip, J., Vavra, R., Haindl, M., Zid, P., Krupicka, M., Havran, V.: BRDF slices: accurate adaptive anisotropic appearance acquisition. In: Conference on Computer Vision and Pattern Recognition, CVPR, pp. 4321–4326 (2013). https://doi.org/10.1109/CVPR.2013.193
8. Fleming, R.W.: Visual perception of materials and their properties. Vision. Res. **94**, 62–75 (2014)
9. Jarabo, A., Wu, H., Dorsey, J., Rushmeier, H., Gutierrez, D.: Effects of approximate filtering on the appearance of bidirectional texture functions. IEEE Trans. Visual Comput. Graphics **20**(6), 880–892 (2014). https://doi.org/10.1109/TVCG.2014.2312016
10. Lagunas, M., Malpica, S., Serrano, A., Garces, E., Gutierrez, D., Masia, B.: A similarity measure for material appearance. ACM Trans. Graph. (TOG) **38**(4), 1–12 (2019)
11. Long, H., Leow, W.: A hybrid model for invariant and perceptual texture mapping. In: 16th International Conference on Pattern Recognition. Proceedings, vol. 1, pp. 135–138. IEEE (2002)
12. Van der Maaten, L., Hinton, G.: Visualizing data using t-SNE. J. Mach. Learn. Res. **9**(11), 2579–2605 (2008)
13. Malik, J., Perona, P.: Preattentive texture discrimination with early vision mechanisms. JOSA A **7**(5), 923–932 (1990)
14. Matusik, W., Pfister, H., Brand, M., McMillan, L.: A data-driven reflectance model. ACM Trans. Graph. **22**(3), 759–769 (2003)
15. McCanny, C.S.: Observation and measurement of the appearance of metallic materials. Part. 1. Macro appearance. COLOR Res. Appl. **21**(4), 292–304 (1996)
16. Mojsilovic, A., Kovacevic, J., Kall, D., Safranek, R., Kicha Ganapathy, S.: The vocabulary and grammar of color patterns. IEEE Trans. Image Process. **9**(3), 417–431 (2000)

17. Nicodemus, F., Richmond, J., Hsia, J., Ginsburg, I., Limperis, T.: Geometrical considerations and nomenclature for reflectance. NBS Monogr. **160**, 1–52 (1977)
18. Ramanarayanan, G., Ferwerda, J., Walter, B., Bala, K.: Visual equivalence: towards a new standard for image fidelity. ACM Trans. Graph. **26**(3), 76:1–76:10 (2007)
19. Ravishankar Rao, A., Lohse, G.: Towards a texture naming system: identifying relevant dimensions of texture. Vision. Res. **36**(11), 1649–1669 (1996). https://doi.org/10.1016/0042-6989(95)00202-2
20. Rushmeier, H.: The MAM2014 sample set. In: Proceedings of the Eurographics 2014 Workshop on Material Appearance Modeling: Issues and Acquisition, MAM 2014, pp. 25–26 (2014)
21. Sawayama, M., et al.: Visual discrimination of optical material properties: a large-scale study. J. Vis. **22**(2), 17 (2022)
22. Schwartz, G., Nishino, K.: Visual material traits: Recognizing per-pixel material context. In: 2013 IEEE International Conference on Computer Vision Workshops, pp. 883–890 (2013)
23. Schwartz, G., Nishino, K.: Recognizing material properties from images. IEEE Trans. Pattern Anal. Mach. Intell. **42**(8), 1981–1995 (2019)
24. Serrano, A., et al.: The effect of shape and illumination on material perception: model and applications. ACM Trans. Graph. (TOG) **40**(4), 1–16 (2021)
25. Serrano, A., Gutierrez, D., Myszkowski, K., Seidel, H.P., Masia, B.: An intuitive control space for material appearance. ACM Trans. Graph. (TOG) **35**(6), 1–12 (2018)
26. Sharan, L., Liu, C., Rosenholtz, R., Adelson, E.H.: Recognizing materials using perceptually inspired features. Int. J. Comput. Vision **103**(3), 348–371 (2013)
27. Subias, J.D., Lagunas, M.: In-the-wild material appearance editing using perceptual attributes. Comput. Graph. Forum **42**(2), 333–345 (2023)
28. Tamura, H., Mori, S., Yamawaki, T.: Textural features corresponding to visual perception. IEEE Trans. Syst. Man Cybernet. **8**(6), 460–473 (1978). https://doi.org/10.1109/TSMC.1978.4309999
29. Vanrell, M., Vitria, J.: A four-dimensional texture representation space. In: Pattern Recognition and Image Analysis, vol. 1, pp. 245–250 (1997)

SD-SORT - Self Driving SORT for Autonomous Vehicle

Omkar Shinde[1]([✉]) and Azim Eskandarian[2]

[1] Virginia Tech University, Blacksburg, VA 24060, USA
omkarshinde@vt.edu
[2] Virginia Commonwealth University, Richmond, VA 23284, USA

Abstract. Effective multi-object tracking is crucial for autonomous vehicles to navigate safely and efficiently in dynamic environments. Three challenges in implementation of multi object tracking in autonomous vehicles are: 1) In these vehicles, sensors like cameras are not static, which can cause motion blur in the frames and make tracking inefficient. 2) Traditional methods for motion compensation, such as those used in Kalman Filter-based Multi-Object Tracking, require extensive parameter tuning to match features between consecutive frames accurately. 3) Simple intersection over union (IoU) metric is insufficient for reliable identification in such environments. This paper explores new methodology for 2D multi-object tracking using cameras, introducing three primary modules in a Tracking-by-Detection (TBD) approach: 1) Real-time deblurring module mitigates motion blur, ensuring clearer frames for more accurate detection; 2) Deep learning based motion compensation dynamically adjusts to varying motion patterns, enhancing robustness; 3) Adaptive cost function for association using bounding boxes, incorporating factors such as object appearance and temporal consistency, improves upon traditional IoU metrics. While keeping it Simple Online and Realtime (SORT), we enhance detection by fine-tuning YOLOv8 on the KITTI dataset, tailored for autonomous driving scenarios. Our evaluations show that this methodology significantly outperforms previous state-of-the-art methods while maintaining the same inference rate as the baseline. These improvements increase the accuracy and reliability of multi-object tracking and reduce the computational overhead associated with parameter tuning and motion compensation, advancing robust, tracking systems for autonomous vehicles.

Keywords: 2D Object Tracking · Multi Object Tracking · Autonomous Driving

1 Introduction

Autonomous driving systems rely on robust perception capabilities to safely interpret and navigate complex environments. A critical component of this perception is the real-time tracking of multiple objects, which poses significant chal-

© The Author(s), under exclusive license to Springer Nature Switzerland AG 2025
S. Palaiahnakote et al. (Eds.): ICPR 2024 Workshops, LNCS 15617, pp. 196–210, 2025.
https://doi.org/10.1007/978-3-031-88217-3_14

lenges due to variations in object appearance, frequent occlusions, and unpredictable motion patterns. In recent years, there have been significant advancements in enhancing the safety and reliability of autonomous driving systems, particularly in the field of multi-object tracking. Accurately identifying and tracking multiple objects is essential for the vehicle's decision-making process, ensuring it can navigate safely through dynamic and intricate environments. However, achieving this task is complicated by limited computational resources within the autonomous system, which hinder effective utilization of sensor fusion techniques such as combining LiDAR and camera data. Moreover, the dynamic nature of both the camera and the objects being tracked adds further complexity to the tracking process.

In scenarios where computational power limits the integration of sensors like LiDAR, and when dealing with dynamic cameras and objects, tracking becomes notably challenging. Consequently, systems often resort to 2D multi-object tracking methods. These methods primarily involve creating and maintaining 2D bounding boxes with unique tracking identifications (IDs). In 2D multi object tracking there are two approaches Tracking-by-Detection (TBD) and Joint Detection and Tracking (JDT). The TBD paradigm has separate detection and tracking components, whereas the JDT paradigm works on detection and tracking simultaneously. JDT, sharing the network, causes it to focus on either detection or tracking only, making it less robust. In the case of TBD, separate detection and tracking components make it more robust in improving both detection and tracking. Our study is mainly focused on tackling these challenges by using the TBD paradigm rather than the JDT paradigm. Recent advancements in camera-only TBD paradigms [1,4,10,35,36] have focused on datasets like the MOT dataset [8,23] and DANCETRACK dataset [31], where the camera is static and limited for autonomous systems. In autonomous systems, both the camera and objects can move leading to decrease accuracy of detection and tracking. Moreover, movement in the camera results in blurred frames, decreasing the quality of detections.

In the improvement of 2D object detection, there has been significant improvement. In terms for using detection for tracking, YOLO series [5,13,15,33] has been widely adopted due to its high speed processing capabilities and high detection accuracy. YOLOv8 [16], introduces several enhancements over its predecessor, YOLOv7 [33]. YOLOv8 incorporates a more advanced backbone network, which improves feature extraction by leveraging deeper and more complex convolutional layers. This results in a more refined detection of objects with higher precision and recall rates. Additionally, YOLOv8 integrates improved anchor-free mechanisms, which eliminate the need for predefined anchor boxes, allowing for more flexible and efficient detection across varying object scales and aspect ratios. This is particularly advantageous in tracking scenarios where objects can undergo significant size and shape changes.

In previous methodologies, a primary focus was placed on the motion deblurring module to achieve clearer images, employing deep learning techniques. However, these methods often proved inefficient for real-time applications. Classical approaches for motion compensation, such as ORB [30], SIFT [21], and Lucas-Kanade sparse Optical Flow [6], were utilized due to their efficiency. Despite their effectiveness, these approaches involve numerous parameters, complicating fine-tuning. Additionally, the cost matrix for associating tracklets was primarily based on Intersection over Union (IoU), which introduced further limitations. To address these challenges, we introduce SD-SORT, a novel framework designed to enhance tracking accuracy while maintaining near real-time performance. This paper proposes the following advancements:

– We propose utilizing the LightGlue [20] deep learning method to enhance feature matching between adjacent frames. Traditional methods like sparse optical flow often struggle with accuracy and require extensive parameter tuning. LightGlue, on the other hand, leverages advanced deep learning algorithms to significantly improve feature matching accuracy. This method reduces the necessity for exhaustive parameter adjustments, facilitating more robust and efficient motion compensation in dynamic scenes.
– To improve the association of tracks, we adapt and expand the conventional cost matrix. In addition to the standard IoU, we incorporate AspectRatioIoU (AR-IoU). These enhancements provide a more nuanced evaluation of object overlap and spatial alignment, leading to more accurate track associations. AR-IoU accounts for the aspect ratio consistency between predicted and ground truth boxes, thereby improving tracking precision.
– We enhance the detection model by implementing YOLOv8, a state-of-the-art object detection algorithm known for its superior accuracy and speed. To tailor this model for driving datasets, we fine-tune it using the KITTI [14] dataset. This specialized training ensures that YOLOv8 can effectively detect objects in complex driving environments, further augmenting the overall performance of our tracking system. The YOLOv8 model's multi-scale feature fusion and efficient prediction heads make it particularly suitable for real-time applications.

2   Related Works

2.1   Camera Motion Compensation

The primary purpose of camera motion compensation is to identify and align key feature points between consecutive frames, ensuring accurate motion estimation and object tracking. Classical methods such as SIFT [21], ECC [11] and ORB [30] have been widely used to detect and describe these local feature keypoints. Once keypoints are identified, RANSAC [12] (Random Sample Consensus) is typically employed to remove outliers and establish a robust model for the transformation between frames. While more sophisticated methods like MAGSAC [2] (Maximum A Posteriori Sample Consensus) have been developed to enhance outlier removal by incorporating probabilistic models and maximum likelihood estimation, these come at the cost of increased computational complexity, making them less suitable for real-time applications. Therefore, RANSAC remains the preferred choice for outlier removal due to its balance of effectiveness and computational efficiency, maintaining real-time performance in camera motion compensation.

In recent advancements aimed at enhancing keypoint matching for applications like image registration and object tracking, the traditional Lucas-Kanade sparse optical flow [6] method has faced challenges due to its reliance on numerous parameters, making precise tuning complex and time-consuming. To address these limitations, LightGlue [20], proposed by Lindenberger, Sarlin, and Pollefeys, introduces a deep learning-based approach to feature keypoint matching. This work represents a lightweight method that leverages deep learning frameworks to achieve more robust and efficient results compared to traditional methods. By integrating deep learning models, LightGlue aims to enhance the accuracy and reliability of keypoint matching while maintaining real-time performance.

2.2   Object Detection in 2D and Tracking by Detection

Most the works previously [1, 4, 35, 36] have used YOLOX [13] or YOLOv7 [33] as the detection in their Tracking-by-Detection method as they primarily focused on tracking and kept the same detector. But as YOLO series has shown significant improvement over the years in terms of accuracy and inference speed, the choice of YOLOX or YOLOv7 as the detection backbone underscores a commitment to leveraging state-of-the-art deep learning architectures to achieve robust object detection performance, thereby enhancing the overall tracking capabilities of these systems.

Tracking by Detection method in recent years has found significant progress because of independent improvement in detection and tracking complimenting each other. Moreover due to the ability of plug and play makes it easy for different applications. With Initial approach by SORT [4], it introduces detection by FasterRCNN [29] and tracking is done by IoU cost matrix between association of detection and predicted bounding box from Kalman filter. In improvement BYTETRACK [36] uses YOLOX detector as well as using a second association for the low detection score but still use IoU as the cost matrix.

Therefore, incorporating YOLOv8, with its more robust performance, enhanced accuracy, and efficient inference speed within the YOLO series, is intended to significantly augment object detection capabilities. This strategic adoption is critical for advancing the overall efficacy of our tracking systems. As well as, we use BOT-SORT [1] as the baseline method to improve association of ID.

2.3   Frame Restoration

There have been numerous approaches to address the challenge of deblurring images and videos, with recent strides leveraging deep learning networks to significantly enhance quality. In DC-MOT [7], the CDVD module (CNN-based) [25] is utilized for deblurring, although it falls short in terms of real-time processing capability. Meanwhile, Tsai and Peng [32] have made strides with BANet, achieving real-time video deblurring; however, the inclusion of additional modules has resulted in inference times remaining relatively high at around 23 ms.

In response to these challenges, our approach opts for a classical method for image deblurring. This approach allows to maintain minimal computational overhead while ensuring efficient processing as well as improving the performance.

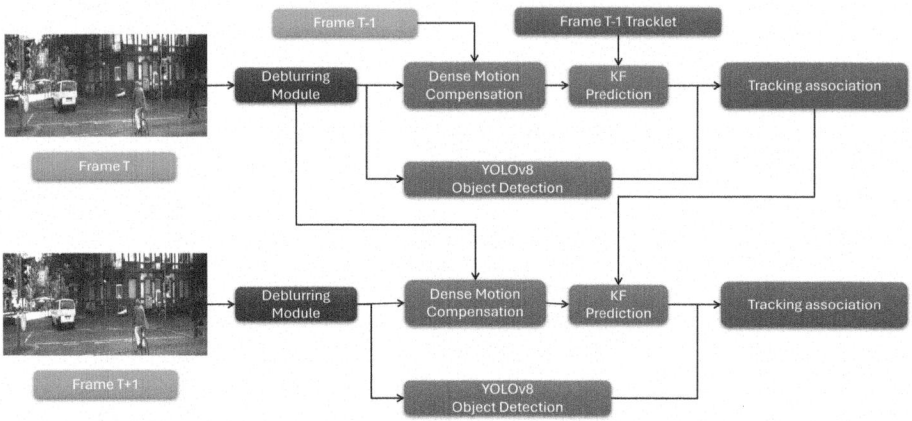

Fig. 1. The proposed framework of SD-SORT. There are three modules shown in different colors: 1) (*green*) Deblurring module to assist in better object detection. 2) (*blue*) Detection Module which consist of YOLOv8 for detecting object and dense motion compensation creating homography matrix assisting Kalman filter to predict the future state of the bounding box. 3) (*pink*) Tracking module which uses a approach to cost matrix (Color figure online)

3   Proposed Method

In this section, we introduce our proposed method. In our model as shown Fig. 1, we go through frame by frame where the frame passes through a signal-to-noise ratio evaluation. For ratio values less than a given threshold, it passes through a Laplacian filter to sharpen the image. Then the sharpened image is processed by YOLOv8 for object detection and deep learning-based motion compensation to find the homography matrix (rotation and translation) between the previous and current frame's feature keypoints. This matrix, along with the previous frame's track information, is passed through a Kalman filter to predict future bounding boxes. With YOLO detected and Kalman Filter (KF) detected boxes, an association is made, and an ID is assigned to each bounding box using a cost function defined by the aspect ratio and intersection-over-union (IoU) of the bounding box. For lower detection confidence cases, a second association is done through IoU. The combination of both the first and second associations constitutes the final tracking for that frame.

3.1   Laplace Deblurring Module

In the context of autonomous driving, the motion of the vehicle often results in the production of blurred images, especially during diverse road conditions that may induce vertical oscillations or sudden movements. This phenomenon significantly impedes the effectiveness of object detection models, even those trained with extensive data augmentation techniques. From previous work [7], used deep neural network models for image deblurring, at the expense of computational efficiency. Moreover, the evaluation of deblurring efficacy through Peak Signal-to-Noise Ratio (PSNR) values necessitated ground truth images, rendering the method impractical for real-time deployment scenarios lacking such references.

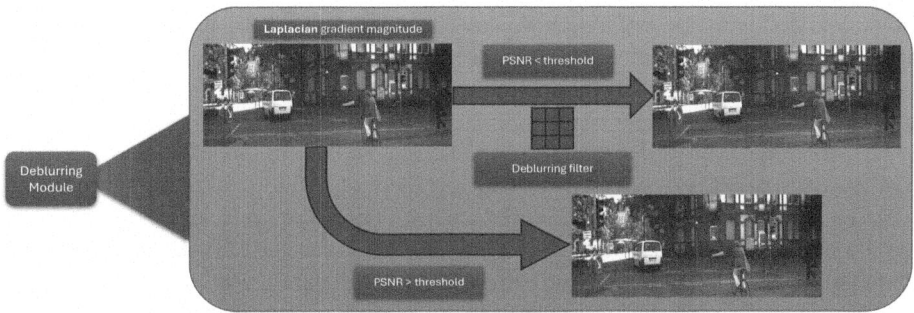

Fig. 2. This shows a detailed outline of the deblurring module where the frame is passed through Laplace gradient magnitude to find PSNR and if the value is below the threshold then the image is passed through a 2D kernel for deblurring.

Therefore, a deblurring module is introduced that determines whether a frame should be deblurred based on its PSNR (Peak Signal-to-Noise Ratio) value. The PSNR is calculated using the blur gradient method, which assesses the image sharpness by computing the second derivative with the Laplacian operator, a robust technique for noise resilience. Figure 2 shows the working of this module. As we are going frame-by-frame without giving a ground truth, we experimentally find a threshold to identify if frame is considered blurry. If the PSNR value falls below a threshold value, indicating significant blur, the frame undergoes a deblurring process using a sharpening filter. This filter is a 2D kernel in the form of a 3×3 matrix designed to enhance the center pixel's intensity relative to its neighboring pixels, effectively accentuating edges and details. The filter works by amplifying the center pixel's value while subtracting the values of the surrounding pixels, thus enhancing the image's overall sharpness. By applying this sharpening kernel, the blurred image is transformed into a clearer and more defined version. The integration of this real-time deblurring module ensures that frames with lower PSNR values are effectively sharpened.

3.2   AspectRatio + IoU

In driving datasets like KITTI [14], a combination of pedestrians and vehicles is annotated using bounding boxes, where the height dimension is particularly significant for pedestrians and the width dimension is critical for vehicles. In recent work, such as Hybrid-SORT [35], have focused exclusively on the height of bounding boxes due to their primary application to the DANCETRACK [31] dataset, which consists solely of pedestrians and exhibits abrupt variations in width. However, for applications in autonomous driving, it is imperative to incorporate both the height and width dimensions of bounding boxes to achieve accurate detection and tracking of diverse objects. Therefore, the concept of Aspect ratio can be applied. Utilizing the aspect ratio, defined as the ratio of the width to the height of the bounding box, facilitates a more comprehensive representation of the object's dimensions. This enhances the precision of object localization and classification. The consideration of both height and width ensures that tracking algorithms can effectively manage a variety of objects. Figure 3 shows the detailed perspective of the tracking association.

To enhance object detection and tracking in autonomous driving, we propose the incorporation of Aspect-ratio Intersection over Union (ARIoU). In the adaptive approach both height and width of bounding box is used depending on the dimension of the box as shown in Eq. 2. In ARIoU, the aspect ratio between the predicted bounding box from Kalman filter, box_1 with $width = w_1$ and $height = h_1$, and bounding box from YOLOv8 [16] object detection, box_2 with $width = w_2$ and $height = h_2$. The minimum over maximum ratio as shown in Eq. 3 between both the bounding boxes aspect ratio provides a normalized score providing a robust approach in using of the size of the bounding boxes. By adding IoU (Intersection over Union) to Aspect-Ratio (AR) (Eq. 3), the effective cost balances the shape similarity and spatial overlap. Here are equation for finding the ARIoU:

$$IoU = \frac{|box_1 \cap box_2|)}{|box_1 \cup box_2|)} \tag{1}$$

$$AR_1 = \frac{w_1}{h_1}, \quad AR_2 = \frac{w_2}{h_2} \tag{2}$$

$$Aspect - ratio = \frac{\min(AR_1, AR_2)}{\max(AR_1, AR_2)} \tag{3}$$

$$ARIoU = AR \cdot IoU \tag{4}$$

The inclusion of Aspect-ratio IoU in the cost matrix addresses the variations in object shapes, leading to more robust tracking. This approach ensures that both size and shape attributes are considered, thereby enhancing the performance of object association algorithms in complex driving environments.

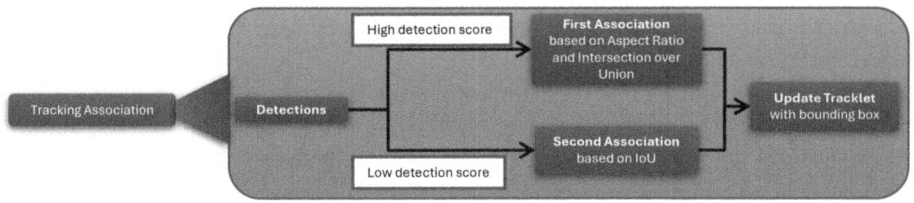

Fig. 3. Tracking module where using prediction from Kalman filter, first association using cost function based on AspectRatioIoU is created. Matched tracklets are updated and unmatched tracklets are passed through second association which uses IoU as the cost function.

3.3 Deep Motion Compensation

The motion compensation pre-processes the previous and current frame to extract key feature points and align them assisting in predicting stage of Kalman filter. In previous works like BOT-SORT, have primarily focused on scenarios with static cameras, neglecting dynamic camera setups, as commonly encountered in driving datasets.

To address this, we propose the integration of a deep neural network feature matching algorithm—LightGlue, which better performs and pairs key feature points between adjacent frames, which improves efficiency, accuracy, adding adaptability by having to the parameters for specific task and keeping inference speed close the optical flow estimation.

For each frame f_t and previous frame f_{t-1}, we employ a key feature point extractor, SUPERPOINT [9], followed by feature matching utilizing LightGlue. By establishing correspondences between key points in both frames, we compute an affine homography matrix using the RANSAC algorithm to robustly estimate translation and rotation, thereby filtering out outliers. This homography matrix serves as the basis for predicting the future state of the system using a Kalman Filter [18].

3.4 2D Object Detection Module

In previous works, object detection algorithms such as YOLOX, YOLOv5, and YOLOv7 have been extensively utilized due to their balance of accuracy and computational efficiency. However, recent advancements in the YOLO series have led to the development of YOLOv8, which demonstrates significant improvements in both accuracy and speed. With increase in speed of detection, deep learning modules can be added to tracker to improve the accuracy and speed. Consequently, we adopt the YOLOv8 model, implemented using the ultralytics [16] framework, to enhance detection performance in our study.

For this research, we specifically focus on driving datasets, which present unique challenges due to the diverse and dynamic nature of road environments. To address these challenges, we train the YOLOv8 model on the KITTI dataset.

The training process involves fine-tuning the YOLOv8 model to optimize its performance for the specific characteristics of the KITTI dataset. This includes adjusting the model's hyperparameters, data augmentation techniques, and training strategies to ensure that the model can effectively generalize to various driving situations. The integration of the Aspect-ratio Intersection over Union (Aspect-ratio IoU) into the cost matrix further enhances the model's ability to accurately associate bounding boxes, accounting for both size and shape variations of detected objects.

Overall, the adoption of YOLOv8, combined with specialized training on the KITTI dataset and the introduction of Aspect-ratio IoU, represents a significant advancement in object detection for autonomous driving applications. This approach promises to deliver higher accuracy and faster detection, ultimately contributing to the development of safer and more reliable autonomous vehicles.

4 Experiments Setup

4.1 Datasets

In our research, we conducted an in-depth evaluation of multi-object tracking performance using the KITTI dataset [14], a widely recognized benchmark and provides test set for 2D tracking in the field of autonomous driving. The dataset's 2D object tracking benchmark encompasses 21 training sequences and 29 testing sequences, providing a robust framework for assessing tracking algorithms under various real-world driving scenarios. Initially, we fine-tuned a pretrained model on the complete set of eight annotated object classes available in KITTI. However, our primary emphasis was on refining our model for the specific classification of two important classes: 'Car' and 'Pedestrian'. These classes were prioritized due to their high occurrence in the dataset, reflecting their critical relevance in autonomous driving applications. The dataset captures scenes using a camera operating at 10 frames per second (FPS), ensuring that our evaluations are aligned with real-time processing constraints typically encountered in autonomous vehicle systems.

4.2 Evaluation Metrics

Our study uses three standards: CLEAR MOT [3], HOTA (Higher Order Tracking Accuracy) [22], and IDSW (Identity Switch). These metrics measure how well tracking algorithms work in different situations. The KITTI benchmark primarily uses HOTA as its main evaluation metric. Unlike MOTA (Multi Object Tracking Accuracy, from CLEAR MOT), which focuses more on detection, HOTA balances detection quality with identity association. This means it looks at both how accurately objects are detected and how correctly their identities are tracked over time. IDSW measures how well a tracking algorithm keeps the same identity for objects as they move. This is important for seeing if the algorithm can consistently track objects correctly.

4.3   Implementation Details

For the detection component, we utilize the YOLOv8 network, leveraging its advanced capabilities. We start with a pretrained model on the COCO dataset [19] and fine-tune it using the KITTI dataset to enhance performance for our specific application. The training process is conducted over 200 epochs, with each image resized to 640×380 pixels to ensure consistency and efficiency. To further improve detection quality, we apply various data augmentation techniques. Additionally, we employ a copy-paste strategy by overlaying images to increase the frequency of objects and introduce occlusions, thereby making the model more robust in handling diverse and complex scenarios. During inference, we implement detection confidence of 0.5 and apply non maximum suppression.

In the tracking phase of the pipeline, for the deblurring filter, through experimentation, we found the best value of λ to be 9. For camera motion compensation, parameters in LightGlue were set to 'None' for maximum number of keypoints, with a filter threshold set at 1%. No depth confidence or width confidence was added. For both training and inference (including tracking), an NVIDIA Tesla V100 was used.

Table 1. Comparison between algorithms on the KITTI-Test Set

CLASS	METHOD	HOTA (%)↑	DetA (%)↑	AssA (%)↑	MOTA (%)↑	IDSW↓
Car	IMMDP [34]	68.66	68.02	69.76	82.75	**211**
	Quasi-Dense [27]	68.45	72.44	38.10	84.55	313
	PNAS-MOT [28]	67.32	**77.69**	58.99	**89.59**	751
	MO-YOLO [26]	72.08	71.02	73.84	83.19	275
	SRK_ODESA [24]	64.25	74.87	55.70	88.50	491
	SORT [4]	42.52	44.01	41.31	53.15	370
	SD-SORT(OURS)	**73.08**	71.07	**75.57**	82.72	416
Pedestrian	IMMDP [34]	-	-	-	-	-
	Quasi-Dense [27]	41.12	44.81	38.10	55.55	487
	PNAS-MOT [28]	-	-	-	-	-
	SRK_ODESA [24]	43.73	**53.73**	36.05	**67.31**	683
	MO-YOLO [26]	**51.46**	45.59	**58.39**	56.84	**164**
	SORT [4]	-	-	-	-	-
	SD-SORT(OURS)	49.62	45.05	54.96	56.25	435

4.4   Tracking Comparison

From the Table 1, it can be seen that we have compared our method with other state-of-the-art published method on KITTI test set with object classes: 'CAR'

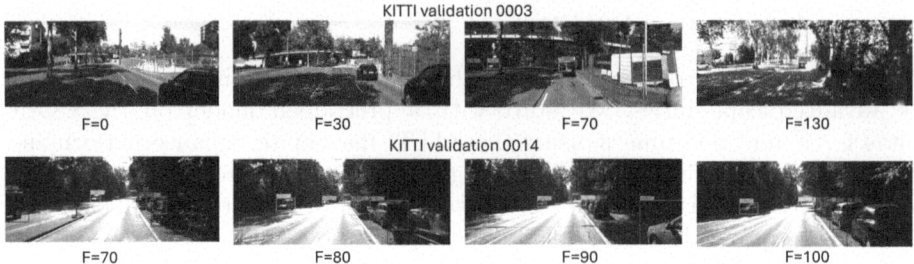

Fig. 4. Example output of tracking with 2D bounding boxes and tracking ID from KITTI Validation Set and F is Frame Number

Table 2. Comparing to the baseline method on KITTI validation set

CLASS	METHOD	HOTA (%)↑	DetA (%)↑	AssA(%)↑	MOTA (%)↑	IDSW↓	FPS↑
Car	BOT-SORT [1]	64.71	69.71	61.95	68.43	435	**9.70**
	SD-SORT	**85.00**	**90.68**	**81.87**	**80.74**	429	8.37
Pedestrian	BOT-SORT [1]	44.10	32.37	42.20	47.24	**425**	**9.70**
	SD-SORT	**59.84**	**77.50**	**68.58**	**52.37**	429	8.37

and 'PEDESTRIAN'. The ground truth for test set is not given and is submitted to the KITTI evaluation server. The bold text represents highest rank compared to other methods. We compared with other 2D realtime tracking algorithms. Our method outperforms all other method with respect to HOTA and AssA indicating that the accuracy of tracking. While it is lower in terms of MOTA is due to the metric being highly biased on detection. For 'PEDESTRAIN', for HOTA, DetA and AssA our method comes second best. We have not included inference rate because different methods use different computing system and only tracking inference rate are published. Therefore, we run inference speed on ablation study.

As KITTI does not provide ground truth for test set, we evaluated BOT-SORT on the validation dataset. From Table 2, we observe that our method consistently outperforms BOT-SORT in all evaluation metrics, indicating significant improvements in both tracking and detection accuracy while decreasing the speed by 1.33 fps. Our method demonstrates superior performance in handling various challenges such as motion blur, object occlusion, and varying object scales. Furthermore, Fig. 4 illustrates the qualitative results of our method, showcasing its ability to accurately track multiple objects in dynamic environments.

5   Ablation Studies

In ablation study we do comparison of each module on KITTI validation and see how they tracking metrics differ from each other. For comparing on validation set, TrackEval [17] is used where the tracking result from the algorithm is taken and compared with the ground truth to give the results shown in the tables for following ablation studies.

Effect of Detection Module. In this part of ablation we train different size of YOLOv8 [16] models (Yolov8-X: 68.2M parameters, Yolov8-M: 25.9 parameters, Yolov8-N: 3.2 parameters) on KITTI and compare the affect of the accuracy with our tracking. Table 3 shows comparison with the tracking accuracy metrics. Yolov8-X shows highest accuracy with least inference speed because of the size.

Table 3. Comparison between different YOLOv8 models [16] on KITTI validation dataset

CLASS	METHOD	HOTA(%)↑	DetA(%)↑	AssA (%)↑	MOTA (%)↑	IDSW↓	FPS↑
Car	YOLOv8n [16]	79.1	79.68	78.84	89.42	340	**8.91**
	YOLOv8m [16]	84.87	85.64	84.32	94.19	**203**	8.67
	YOLOv8-x [16]	**86.30**	**86.79**	**86.02**	**95.21**	429	8.37
Pedestrian	YOLOv8n [16]	54.66	55.73	53.71	64.43	**316**	**8.91**
	YOLOv8m [16]	62.76	68.61	57.51	79.03	347	8.67
	YOLOv8x [16]	**63.76**	**68.90**	**59.10**	**79.75**	429	8.37

Table 4. Comparison between different PSNR values from deblurring filter on KITTI-validation dataset

CLASS	Threshold(%)	HOTA(%)↑	DetA(%)↑	AssA(%)↑	MOTA(%)↑	IDSW↓	FPS↑
Car	0	85.7	86.35	85.23	94.40	195	**8.61**
	1	**85.73**	**86.4**	**85.31**	**94.97**	192	8.50
	3	83.01	83.40	82.86	92.31	236	8.52
	5	75.37	75.08	75.98	83.99	314	6.70
Pedestrian	0	63.21	69.37	57.71	**79.63**	367	**8.61**
	1	**63.58**	**69.43**	**58.34**	79.58	365	8.50
	3	63.34	69.26	58.05	79.52	**359**	8.52
	5	50.33	53.43	47.64	61.95	411	6.70

Effect of PSNR Threshold. In this section, different PSNR thresholds are compared on KITTI validation dataset. From Table 4 it can be seen that we perform test for PSNR values from 0% to 5% and it shows best performance at PSNR = 1%.

Effect of Camera Compensation. In terms of motion compensation, we apply non-learning-based methods used to find the feature key points and compare them to see that applying LightGlue has outperformed other methods for accuracy of tracking (HOTA, DetA, AssA and MOTA) as shown in Table 5.

In this comparison we have kept all other parameters same.

Table 5. Comparison between different camera motion compensation on KITTI-validation dataset

CLASS	METHOD	HOTA(%)↑	DetA(%)↑	AssA(%)↑	MOTA(%)↑	IDSW↓	FPS↑
Car	(OURS)+ecc [11]	42.96	85.20	21.77	50.499	11118	2.27
	(OURS)+sift [21]	85.52	81.19	85.52	94.22	425	5.79
	(OURS)+orb [30]	85.91	86.35	85.74	84.89	**224**	10.44
	(OURS)+opticalflow [6]	80.83	81.08	80.85	89.54	290	**14.50**
	(OURS)+lightglue [20]	**86.29**	**86.79**	**86.07**	**95.21**	429	8.37
Pedestrian	(OURS)+ecc [11]	36.42	69.53	19.18	38.22	5079	2.27
	(OURS)+sift [21]	63.05	69.38	57.43	79.49	**246**	5.79
	(OURS)+orb [30]	63.83	**69.80**	58.48	80.11	353	10.44
	(OURS)+opticalflow [6]	62.46	68.45	57.11	78.84	319	**14.50**
	(OURS)+lightglue [20]	**63.76**	68.90	**59.09**	**79.74**	429	8.37

6   Conclusion

In this paper, we use BOT-SORT [1] as the baseline, a Tracking-by-Detection method, and introduce a multi-object tracking method tailored for an autonomous vehicles dataset using various modules to enhance detection and tracking. Compared to previous methods, we first improve detection by applying YOLOv8, which provides state-of-the-art accuracy and efficiency. Secondly, we propose using a deblurring filter based on the Laplace operator to assist in better detection, effectively handling motion blur caused by camera movement. Thirdly, we introduce a deep learning-based feature matching technique to improve prediction accuracy in the Kalman Filter, allowing for more robust tracking. Lastly, we enhance the association process by incorporating aspect ratio into the IoU for the cost matrix, improving the reliability of object identification. Through extensive experiments, we find that our method significantly outperforms previous state-of-the-art methods in terms of tracking accuracy and robustness, demonstrating its effectiveness for autonomous vehicle applications.

References

1. Aharon, N., Orfaig, R., Bobrovsky, B.Z.: BoT-SORT: robust associations multi-pedestrian tracking. arXiv preprint arXiv:2206.14651 (2022)
2. Barath, D., Matas, J., Noskova, J.: MAGSAC: marginalizing sample consensus. In: Proceedings of the IEEE/CVF Conference on Computer Vision and Pattern Recognition, pp. 10197–10205 (2019)
3. Bernardin, K., Stiefelhagen, R.: Evaluating multiple object tracking performance: the CLEAR MOT metrics. EURASIP J. Image Video Process. **2008**, 1–10 (2008)
4. Bewley, A., Ge, Z., Ott, L., Ramos, F., Upcroft, B.: Simple online and realtime tracking. In: 2016 IEEE International Conference on Image Processing (ICIP), pp. 3464–3468. IEEE (2016)
5. Bochkovskiy, A., Wang, C.Y., Liao, H.Y.M.: YOLOv4: optimal speed and accuracy of object detection. arXiv preprint arXiv:2004.10934 (2020)

6. Bouguet, J.Y., et al.: Pyramidal implementation of the affine Lucas Kanade feature tracker description of the algorithm. Intel Corporation **5**(1–10), 4 (2001)
7. Cheng, S., Yao, M., Xiao, X.: DC-MOT: motion deblurring and compensation for multi-object tracking in UAV videos. In: 2023 IEEE International Conference on Robotics and Automation (ICRA), pp. 789–795 (2023). https://doi.org/10.1109/ICRA48891.2023.10160931
8. Dendorfer, P., et al.: MOT20: a benchmark for multi object tracking in crowded scenes. arXiv preprint arXiv:2003.09003 (2020)
9. DeTone, D., Malisiewicz, T., Rabinovich, A.: SuperPoint: self-supervised interest point detection and description. In: Proceedings of the IEEE Conference on Computer Vision and Pattern Recognition Workshops, pp. 224–236 (2018)
10. Du, Y., et al.: StrongSORT: make DeepSORT great again. IEEE Trans. Multimedia **25**, 8725–8737 (2023)
11. Evangelidis, G.D., Psarakis, E.Z.: Parametric image alignment using enhanced correlation coefficient maximization. IEEE Trans. Pattern Anal. Mach. Intell. **30**(10), 1858–1865 (2008)
12. Fischler, M.A., Bolles, R.C.: Random sample consensus: a paradigm for model fitting with applications to image analysis and automated cartography. Commun. ACM **24**(6), 381–395 (1981)
13. Ge, Z., Liu, S., Wang, F., Li, Z., Sun, J.: YOLOX: exceeding YOLO series in 2021. arXiv preprint arXiv:2107.08430 (2021)
14. Geiger, A., Lenz, P., Urtasun, R.: Are we ready for autonomous driving? The KITTI vision benchmark suite. In: Conference on Computer Vision and Pattern Recognition (CVPR) (2012)
15. Jocher, G.: Ultralytics YOLOv5 (2020). https://doi.org/10.5281/zenodo.3908559. https://github.com/ultralytics/yolov5
16. Jocher, G., Chaurasia, A., Qiu, J.: Ultralytics YOLOv8 (2023). https://github.com/ultralytics/ultralytics
17. Jonathon Luiten, A.H.: TrackEval. https://github.com/JonathonLuiten/TrackEval (2020)
18. Kalman, R.E.: A new approach to linear filtering and prediction problems (1960)
19. Lin, T.-Y., et al.: Microsoft COCO: common objects in context. In: Fleet, D., Pajdla, T., Schiele, B., Tuytelaars, T. (eds.) ECCV 2014. LNCS, vol. 8693, pp. 740–755. Springer, Cham (2014). https://doi.org/10.1007/978-3-319-10602-1_48
20. Lindenberger, P., Sarlin, P.E., Pollefeys, M.: LightGlue: local feature matching at light speed. In: ICCV (2023)
21. Lowe, D.G.: Distinctive image features from scale-invariant keypoints. Int. J. Comput. Vision **60**, 91–110 (2004)
22. Luiten, J., et al.: HOTA: a higher order metric for evaluating multi-object tracking. Int. J. Comput. Vis. (IJCV) (2020)
23. Milan, A., Leal-Taixé, L., Reid, I., Roth, S., Schindler, K.: MOT16: a benchmark for multi-object tracking. arXiv preprint arXiv:1603.00831 (2016)
24. Mykheievskyi, D., Borysenko, D., Porokhonskyy, V.: Learning local feature descriptors for multiple object tracking. In: ACCV (2020)
25. Pan, J., Bai, H., Tang, J.: Cascaded deep video deblurring using temporal sharpness prior. In: Proceedings of the IEEE/CVF Conference on Computer Vision and Pattern Recognition, pp. 3043–3051 (2020)
26. Pan, L., Feng, Y., Di, W., Bo, L., Xingle, Z.: MO-YOLO: end-to-end multiple-object tracking method with YOLO and MOTR. arXiv preprint arXiv:2310.17170 (2023)

27. Pang, J., et al.: Quasi-dense similarity learning for multiple object tracking (2021)
28. Peng, C., et al.: PNAS-MOT: multi-modal object tracking with pareto neural architecture search. IEEE Rob. Autom. Lett., 1–8 (2024). https://doi.org/10.1109/LRA.2024.3379865
29. Ren, S., He, K., Girshick, R., Sun, J.: Faster R-CNN: towards real-time object detection with region proposal networks. In: Advances in Neural Information Processing Systems, vol. 28 (2015)
30. Rublee, E., Rabaud, V., Konolige, K., Bradski, G.: ORB: an efficient alternative to sift or surf. In: 2011 International Conference on Computer Vision, pp. 2564–2571. IEEE (2011)
31. Sun, P., et al.: DanceTrack: multi-object tracking in uniform appearance and diverse motion. In: Proceedings of the IEEE/CVF Conference on Computer Vision and Pattern Recognition, pp. 20993–21002 (2022)
32. Tsai, F.J., Peng, Y.T., Tsai, C.C., Lin, Y.Y., Lin, C.W.: BANet: a blur-aware attention network for dynamic scene deblurring. IEEE Trans. Image Process. **31**, 6789–6799 (2022)
33. Wang, C.Y., Bochkovskiy, A., Liao, H.Y.M.: YOLOv7: trainable bag-of-freebies sets new state-of-the-art for real-time object detectors. In: Proceedings of the IEEE/CVF Conference on Computer Vision and Pattern Recognition (CVPR) (2023)
34. Xiang, Y., Alahi, A., Savarese, S.: Learning to track: online multi- object tracking by decision making. In: International Conference on Computer Vision (ICCV), pp. 4705–4713 (2015)
35. Yang, M., et al.: Hybrid-SORT: weak cues matter for online multi-object tracking. In: Proceedings of the AAAI Conference on Artificial Intelligence, vol. 38, pp. 6504–6512 (2024)
36. Zhang, Y., et al.: ByteTrack: multi-object tracking by associating every detection box. In: Avidan, S., Brostow, G., Cissé, M., Farinella, G.M., Hassner, T. (eds.) ECCV 2022. LNCS, vol. 13682, pp. 1–21. Springer, Cham (2022). https://doi.org/10.1007/978-3-031-20047-2_1

Vision-Language Multimodal Fusion in Dermatological Disease Classification

Moreno La Quatra$^{(\boxtimes)}$ (ID), Nicole Dalia Cilia (ID), Vincenzo Conti (ID), Salvatore Sorce (ID), Giovanni Garraffa (ID), and Valerio Mario Salerno (ID)

Kore University of Enna, Piazza dell'Università, 94100 Enna, EN, Italy
{moreno.laquatra,nicoledalia.cilia,vincenzo.conti,salvatore.sorce, giovanni.garraffa,valeriomario.salerno}@unikore.it

Abstract. Accurate diagnosis of dermatological diseases traditionally depends on expert analysis of visual data, which can be both resource-intensive and difficult to scale. In response to these challenges, this study explores the use of pre-trained Vision-Language Models (VLMs) to automate the annotation of dermatological images. These models generate detailed text descriptions that mimic expert dermatological assessments, providing an additional modality for disease classification. While visual data remains the primary factor for high accuracy, the inclusion of VLM-generated text annotations leads to a measurable improvement in classification performance. We experimented with several late-fusion strategies to combine visual and textual data, demonstrating that this multimodal approach enhances the overall effectiveness of disease classification systems. The results indicate that although VLM-generated descriptions are secondary to visual information, they add valuable context that improves diagnostic accuracy when combined with image-based models. This approach contributes to making automated disease classification more effective and accessible. We release the automatically generated annotations to support further research in this domain.

Keywords: Multimodal Learning · Vision-Language Models · Dermatological Disease Classification

1 Introduction

Accurate diagnosis of dermatological diseases is crucial in clinical practice, as it directly impacts patient outcomes and treatment plans. Traditionally, dermatological diagnosis has relied on the visual inspection of skin lesions by expert dermatologists. This process is often challenging due to the vast variety of skin conditions and their overlapping visual symptoms. The diagnostic process heavily depends on the expertise of dermatologists, who must apply their specialized knowledge to differentiate between subtle visual cues. However, this reliance on human expertise introduces several challenges. Firstly, the manual interpretation of visual data can lead to inconsistencies in diagnosis, as different dermatologists

© The Author(s), under exclusive license to Springer Nature Switzerland AG 2025
S. Palaiahnakote et al. (Eds.): ICPR 2024 Workshops, LNCS 15617, pp. 211–225, 2025.
https://doi.org/10.1007/978-3-031-88217-3_15

might have varying levels of experience and interpret the same images differently. Secondly, the availability of skilled dermatologists is limited, particularly in remote or underserved areas, leading to delays in diagnosis and treatment. In an effort to overcome these challenges, artificial intelligence (AI) and deep learning have emerged as powerful tools in medical imaging. Deep learning models have demonstrated high accuracy in classifying various medical images, including those of skin-related conditions. By processing large datasets of images, it is possible to specialize them to recognize patterns that might not be immediately apparent to human observers [8, 19].

Despite their success, these models are generally limited to analyzing visual data alone, which can be insufficient for the complex and variable nature of dermatological diseases. In many cases, the visual inspection of a skin lesion is only part of the diagnostic process. Dermatologists often complement visual assessment with detailed descriptions that incorporate their expert knowledge and clinical observations. These textual descriptions can provide critical context that enhances the accuracy of diagnosis. However, generating such detailed reports requires time and expertise, resources that are not always available.

The combination of heterogeneous sources of information can improve accuracy in various domains [7, 9]. Multimodal models have been introduced as a means of combining visual data with textual descriptions. Modern Vision Language Models (VLMs) are capable of interpreting images and producing descriptive captions that can mimic the detailed reports typically generated by dermatologists. These models leverage large-scale datasets to learn the associations between visual features and their corresponding textual descriptions, making them valuable tools in medical diagnostics [16, 18, 26]. In dermatology, VLMs have the potential to significantly enhance the diagnostic process by providing both visual analysis and contextual descriptions, thus mimicking the dual approach used by human experts. These models are particularly useful in scenarios where expert dermatologists are not available, as they can generate informative text that supports the visual data, potentially improving the accuracy of automated diagnosis [4].

In our study, we explore the integration of VLM-generated text with visual data to improve the classification of dermatological diseases. We utilize Transformer-based models for image analysis [6, 22] and experiment with various strategies to combine the visual and textual information generated by VLMs, including attention pooling, feature concatenation, and gating mechanisms. Our goal is to evaluate the impact of these multimodal fusion techniques on the performance of classification models and to identify the most effective approach. By improving the capability of AI-driven tools through the integration of VLMs, our goal is to advance the field of dermatological diagnosis, making it more reliable and accessible, particularly in resource-limited settings.

The main contributions of this work are as follows:

- We propose a multimodal approach to dermatological disease classification, integrating text and visual modalities to enhance diagnostic accuracy.

- We investigate and compare multiple fusion strategies to determine their effectiveness in combining visual and textual data.
- We demonstrate that the inclusion of VLM-generated textual descriptions, in addition to visual data, can improves the performance of classification models, making them more robust in real-world applications.
- Given the importance of data availability in this domain, we enrich an existing dataset of dermatological images with automatically generated text descriptions, which are open-sourced to support further research in this area[1].

2   Related Work

The use of deep learning and multimodal approaches in medical diagnostics has gained considerable attention in recent years. With the growing availability of large datasets and the development of advanced models, researchers have explored various strategies to improve the accuracy and reliability of automated diagnostic systems. In dermatology, where accurate diagnosis often requires both visual and contextual information, these models are particularly valuable.

2.1   Deep Learning and Multimodal Approaches in Medical Imaging

Deep learning has significantly advanced the field of medical imaging, with Convolutional Neural Networks (CNNs) traditionally being the primary choice for image classification tasks. CNN-based architectures, such as ResNet [12], have been widely applied in image classification tasks, including the diagnosis of skin diseases [10]. However, while these models have proven effective, they focus primarily on visual data, which can limit their performance in complex diagnostic tasks.

Recent developments have introduced Transformer-based models, which have shown significant improvements in handling complex visual data. Vision Transformers (ViTs) [6] and Data-efficient Image Transformers (DeiT) [22] are examples of these advancements, offering a more comprehensive understanding of the global context within images. This capability is particularly crucial in dermatology, where subtle visual differences must be accurately identified to make correct diagnoses. These advancements suggest that Transformer-based approaches may be better suited for tasks requiring a deep analysis of image features, thereby enhancing diagnostic accuracy.

Although visual data has traditionally been the primary focus, relying solely on it can be limiting, especially in fields such as dermatology, where contextual information is critical. Multimodal learning, which integrates various data modalities such as visual and textual data, has emerged as a promising approach to address this limitation. For example, multimodal approaches have shown effectiveness in tasks that require modeling complex interactions between different

---

[1] https://github.com/MorenoLaQuatra/vl-dermnet-annotations.

modalities [24,25]. In the medical field, integrating visual and textual data can provide richer insights, which is particularly valuable for diagnostic tasks [17].

Vision-Language Models (VLMs) combine the advanced language generation capabilities of large language models with the visual understanding of image transformers [13]. In the medical domain, these models can generate detailed captions that mimic the reports typically produced by dermatologists, adding an additional layer of information that can enhance diagnostic accuracy. The integration of VLMs into dermatological diagnostics has the potential to significantly improve automated systems, especially in scenarios where expert dermatologists are not readily available and visual data alone might be insufficient.

2.2 Vision-Language Models and Multimodal Fusion in Medical Diagnostics

The evolution of Vision-Language Models (VLMs) has brought significant advancements in handling tasks that require a combination of visual and textual understanding. Large Language Models (LLMs) as Llama [23] or GPT [1] have established themselves as powerful tools in natural language processing, capable of capturing complex linguistic patterns. Building on these foundations, VLMs have been developed to address more complex multimodal tasks. For example, models like LLaVA [18] and LLaVA-Med [16] demonstrate the effectiveness of VLMs in general and medical domains, respectively, by focusing on both visual and textual reasoning.

In dermatology, the recently introduced SkinGPT-4 [27] has demonstrated the potential of VLMs in automating the diagnostic process. SkinGPT-4 is an interactive diagnostic system that leverages an advanced visual large language model fine-tuned on a vast collection of skin disease images, clinical concepts, and doctors' notes. This model is trained to analyze skin disease images, interpret their medical features, and generate detailed, patient-friendly diagnostic reports. By integrating visual analysis with contextual understanding, SkinGPT-4 addresses critical challenges in dermatology, such as the shortage of dermatologists and the difficulty of accurately interpreting complex skin conditions.

In our study, we take a different approach by leveraging annotated text descriptions generated by Vision-Language Models (VLMs) to enhance the classification of dermatological diseases. We employ InternVL [4], a state-of-the-art VLM that is particularly well-suited for tasks requiring detailed image understanding and robust descriptive capabilities. InternVL is designed to handle a wide range of visual-linguistic tasks, making it suitable for multimodal diagnostic applications. The model has been scaled up to incorporate a large vision encoder aligned with an LLM using web-scale image-text data from diverse sources. This extensive training and alignment process allows InternVL to achieve state-of-the-art performance across numerous visual-linguistic benchmarks, demonstrating its potential in multimodal reasoning.

2.3   Transformers and Multimodal Fusion Techniques

Transformers have become the standard architecture in NLP due to their effectiveness in handling various language understanding tasks [3,14,15]. Models like BERT [5] and its variants like RoBERTa [20] are widely used for text encoding, proving highly effective in capturing complex contextual relationships. Given their success in general NLP tasks, researchers have adapted these models to specialized fields. In the biomedical domain, for instance, domain-specific variants such as BioMed-RoBERTa [11] have been pre-trained on large datasets of biomedical text, enhancing their ability to process medical language.

The integration of these transformer-based language models with visual models like Vision Transformers (ViTs) represents a significant advancement in multimodal learning. This approach allows for the combination of textual and visual data, enabling models to leverage the strengths of both modalities. In dermatological diagnostics, where both image interpretation and clinical information are essential, this integration can lead to more comprehensive and accurate assessments.

In our work, we explore the potential of combining transformer-based language models with ViTs through various multimodal late-fusion strategies. By leveraging the detailed image understanding provided by ViTs and the rich contextual information encoded by transformer-based language models, we aim to develop more robust and reliable multimodal diagnostic tools.

3   Methodology

This study proposes a multimodal late-fusion architecture for the classification of dermatological diseases, leveraging both visual and textual data. The architecture consists of three main components: two modality-specific backbones, a fusion network that integrates the outputs of these backbones, and a classification head that processes the fused representation to produce the final prediction. An overview of this architecture is illustrated on the left side of Fig. 1.

3.1   Multimodal Late-Fusion Architecture

The architecture employs two backbones: a Vision Backbone (VB) for extracting visual features and a Text Backbone (TB) for obtaining textual features. Each backbone generates a sequence of vectors: one vector per image patch in the case of the VB, and one vector per token in the case of the TB. Additionally, each backbone produces a special CLS token that is typically used to summarize the content of the image or text, respectively.

Let $\mathbf{V} \in \mathbb{R}^{L_v \times d_v}$ represent the sequence of visual feature vectors, where L_v is the number of patches and d_v is the dimension of each patch embedding. Similarly, let $\mathbf{T} \in \mathbb{R}^{L_t \times d_t}$ represent the sequence of textual feature vectors, where L_t is the number of tokens and d_t is the dimension of each token embedding. The CLS tokens, denoted as $\mathbf{V}_{\text{CLS}}$ and $\mathbf{T}_{\text{CLS}}$, serve as condensed representations of the entire image and text, respectively.

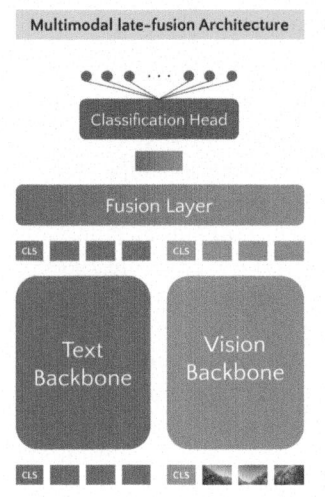
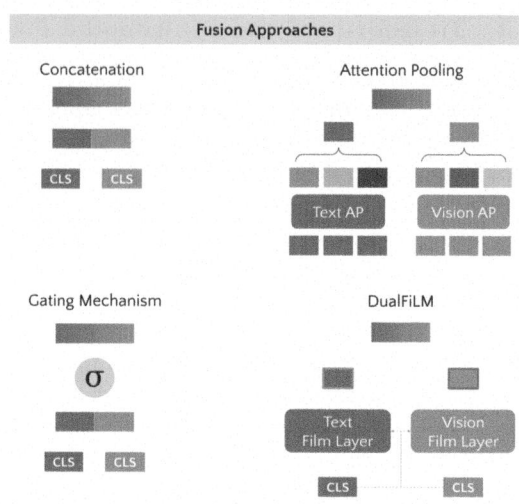

Fig. 1. Overview of the proposed multimodal late-fusion architecture and the different fusion approaches. AP stands for Attention Pooling, σ indicates the sigmoid activation function, and `CLS` indicates special tokens used for classification.

Once the fusion network has integrated the visual and textual inputs, the resulting fused representation $\mathbf{F}$ is passed through a classification head to produce the final output logits $\mathbf{y} \in \mathbb{R}^C$, where C is the number of classes:

$$\mathbf{y} = \text{ClassificationHead}(\mathbf{F})$$

3.2 Fusion Techniques

We experimented with several fusion strategies designed to effectively combine visual and textual information. These include advanced techniques such as Attention Pooling, Gating, and Dual Feature-wise Linear Modulation (FiLM), each offering different approaches to combine multimodal information. A visual depiction of each method is provided on the right side of Fig. 1.

Attention Pooling. Attention Pooling is designed to dynamically weigh the importance of different parts of the input sequence for both visual and textual modalities. Each backbone produces a sequence of feature vectors: one vector per image patch from the Vision Backbone (VB) and one vector per token from the Text Backbone (TB). To extract a single representative vector for each modality, attention pooling is applied separately to the visual and textual sequences.

For the visual modality, the sequence of visual vectors $\mathbf{V} \in \mathbb{R}^{L_v \times d_v}$ is processed to compute attention scores $\mathbf{W}_v \in \mathbb{R}^{L_v \times 1}$, which indicate the importance of each image patch. These scores are obtained using a learned weight matrix $\mathbf{W}_a^v \in \mathbb{R}^{d_v \times 1}$:

$$\mathbf{W}_v = \text{softmax}(\mathbf{V}\mathbf{W}_a^v)$$

The final pooled visual feature $\mathbf{V}_p \in \mathbb{R}^{d_v}$ is then computed as a weighted average of the visual vectors:

$$\mathbf{V}_p = \mathbf{W}_v^\top \mathbf{V}$$

Similarly, for the textual modality, the sequence of textual vectors $\mathbf{T} \in \mathbb{R}^{L_t \times d_t}$ is processed to compute attention scores $\mathbf{W}_t \in \mathbb{R}^{L_t \times 1}$, using a learned weight matrix $\mathbf{W}_a^t \in \mathbb{R}^{d_t \times 1}$:

$$\mathbf{W}_t = \text{softmax}(\mathbf{T}\mathbf{W}_a^t)$$

The final pooled textual feature $\mathbf{T}_p \in \mathbb{R}^{d_t}$ is then obtained as a weighted average of the textual vectors:

$$\mathbf{T}_p = \mathbf{W}_t^\top \mathbf{T}$$

The fused feature vector $\mathbf{F}$ is obtained by concatenating these pooled features from both modalities:

$$\mathbf{F} = [\mathbf{V}_p; \mathbf{T}_p]$$

This process ensures that the most informative parts of the image and text sequences contribute more significantly to the final fused representation, enhancing the model's ability to make accurate classifications.

Gating Mechanism. The Gating Mechanism controls the flow of information between the visual and textual features. It combines the CLS tokens of both modalities into a single vector, applies a sigmoid gate to modulate the contributions of each modality, and dynamically balances the importance of visual and textual inputs. This approach is inspired by the work of Arevalo et al. [2].

$$\mathbf{G} = \sigma(\mathbf{W}_g[\mathbf{V}_{\text{CLS}}; \mathbf{T}_{\text{CLS}}])$$

where $\mathbf{W}_g \in \mathbb{R}^{(d_v+d_t) \times (d_v+d_t)}$ is a learned weight matrix, and σ is the sigmoid function. The gated features $\mathbf{F}_g$ are then computed as:

$$\mathbf{F}_g = \mathbf{G} \odot [\mathbf{V}_{\text{CLS}}; \mathbf{T}_{\text{CLS}}]$$

where $\odot$ represents element-wise multiplication.

Dual Feature-Wise Linear Modulation (Dual FiLM). Dual FiLM modulates the features of one modality based on the information from the other, creating a sophisticated interaction between visual and textual data. This bidirectional modulation enhances the feature representations by incorporating cross-modal influences, where vision modulates text features and vice versa. This technique is inspired by the FiLM approach proposed by Perez et al. [21]. The modulation is defined as:

$$\gamma_{v \to t} = \mathbf{W}_\gamma^{vt} \mathbf{V}_{\text{CLS}}, \quad \beta_{v \to t} = \mathbf{W}_\beta^{vt} \mathbf{V}_{\text{CLS}}$$

$$\gamma_{t \to v} = \mathbf{W}_\gamma^{tv} \mathbf{T}_{\text{CLS}}, \quad \beta_{t \to v} = \mathbf{W}_\beta^{tv} \mathbf{T}_{\text{CLS}}$$

where $\mathbf{W}_\gamma^{vt}, \mathbf{W}_\beta^{vt} \in \mathbb{R}^{d_t \times d_v}$ and $\mathbf{W}_\gamma^{tv}, \mathbf{W}_\beta^{tv} \in \mathbb{R}^{d_v \times d_t}$ are learned weight matrices. The modulated features are computed as:

$$\mathbf{T}_{\text{mod}} = \mathbf{T}_{\text{CLS}} \odot (1 + \gamma_{v \to t}) + \beta_{v \to t} \quad \text{and} \quad \mathbf{V}_{\text{mod}} = \mathbf{V}_{\text{CLS}} \odot (1 + \gamma_{t \to v}) + \beta_{t \to v}$$

The final fused feature vector $\mathbf{F}_{\text{FiLM}}$ is obtained by concatenating the modulated vision and text features:

$$\mathbf{F}_{\text{FiLM}} = [\mathbf{V}_{\text{mod}}; \mathbf{T}_{\text{mod}}]$$

3.3 Classification Head

After obtaining the fused feature vector $\mathbf{F}$, it is passed through a classification head. The classification head is a fully connected network (MLP) that processes the fused representation further. It typically consists of one or more hidden layers, each followed by ReLU activation functions, and aims to refine the combined features before outputting the final logits.

$$\mathbf{y} = \text{MLP}(\mathbf{F})$$

The MLP processes the fused representation to produce the final classification output, predicting the likelihood of each class.

4   Experiments

We conducted a series of experiments to assess the effectiveness of the proposed multimodal fusion techniques in classifying dermatological diseases. These experiments focus on evaluating how different fusion strategies, combining visual and textual data, impact the accuracy and reliability of automated diagnostics.

4.1   Dataset

For our experiments, we utilized the DermNet dataset[2], which contains images categorized into 23 different classes of skin conditions. The dataset is split into training and test sets, as summarized in Table 1. The dataset does not contain any extremely imbalanced classes, with a reasonable distribution of samples across different skin condition categories.

---

[2] https://www.kaggle.com/datasets/shubhamgoel27/dermnet.

Table 1. DermNet Dataset Statistics. Min, Max and Avg indicate the minimum, maximum and average number of samples per class in the corresponding split.

Split	Min	Max	Avg	Total
Training	212	1405	676.39	15,557
Testing	53	352	174.00	4,002
Overall	265	1757	850.39	19,559

Textual Annotations with InternVL. To enhance the dataset with textual annotations, we used the InternVL2 8B parameters version [4][3]. The model was prompted with the following system message to generate objective and medically relevant descriptions for each image:

> "You are a doctor. You are seeing photos for dermatological reports. Please describe the image from a medical perspective in an objective manner. Ignore any overlaying text or any other information. Just describe what you see in the image. Use a single paragraph, without newlines or numbering, and keep the description within 5 sentences max."

We specifically asked the model to generate objective and medically relevant descriptions to ensure that the annotations were consistent with the clinical context. Additional instructions aim at guiding the model in generating descriptions that were concise, informative, and relevant to the medical domain. Here is an example of a typical generated caption:

> "The image depicts a skin lesion characterized by a central ulcerated area with a raised, irregular border. The lesion appears to have a granular texture with a mix of dark and lighter pigmentation. The surrounding skin shows erythema, indicating inflammation. The lesion's appearance suggests a possible malignancy, warranting further clinical evaluation."

Please note that the reference image is not included in the paper to avoid potential exposure to sensitive medical content. The generated annotations were integrated into our multimodal model to assess the impact of combining visual and textual data on classification performance.

4.2 Experimental Setup

In our experiments, we evaluated several pre-trained models tailored for textual and visual data processing. For the textual modality, we evaluated BioMed-RoBERTa[4], BERT[5], and RoBERTa[6], while for the visual modality, we tested

---

[3] https://huggingface.co/OpenGVLab/InternVL2-8B.
[4] https://huggingface.co/allenai/biomed_roberta_base.
[5] https://huggingface.co/google-bert/bert-base-uncased.
[6] https://huggingface.co/FacebookAI/roberta-base.

DeiT[7] and ViT[8] models. All experiments were executed on a single A100 80 GB GPU, which was also utilized to generate textual annotations.

Evaluation Metrics. We assessed the model's performance using accuracy, precision, recall, and F1-score. Accuracy reflects the proportion of correctly classified instances overall, though it can be affected by class imbalances in a multi-class scenario. Precision measures the model's ability to minimize false positives, while recall indicates how well it captures all relevant instances. The F1-score, which is the harmonic mean of precision and recall, provides a balanced metric that considers both the accuracy and completeness of the model's predictions.

The training procedure involved a learning rate of 0.0001, with each model fine-tuned for 10 epochs. We employed a batch size of 32 and used a linear warmup followed by a linear decay scheduler, with the warmup phase accounting for 10% of the total training steps. The training set was divided into training and validation subsets using a 90/10 split, and the best model was selected according to the highest validation accuracy achieved during training.

Following modality-specific evaluation, the best-performing models-ViT for visual data and BERT for textual data-were chosen as the backbones for the multimodal fusion experiments. These selected models were integrated into our fusion strategies, ensuring that the strongest representations from each modality were utilized for the multimodal model.

4.3   Results

Table 2 presents the performance metrics for different models across various training configurations and fusion strategies. The results highlight several important observations about the effectiveness of text, vision, and multimodal approaches.

Comparison of Text and Vision Models. Vision-based models clearly outperform text-based counterparts. The best vision model, ViT, achieves an accuracy of 0.7059 when fine-tuned, while the best text model, BERT, reaches an accuracy of 0.3566. This indicates that visual information is much more critical for accurate dermatological diagnosis than text alone, which is expected given the visual nature of skin conditions.

Interestingly, despite BioMed-RoBERTa being pre-trained on biomedical data, it does not perform better than general models like BERT or RoBERTa. This suggests that the specific biomedical pre-training of BioMed-RoBERTa does not provide a significant advantage for this particular task, possibly because the dermatological text does not differ substantially from general language in ways that would benefit from such specialized pre-training.

---

[7] https://huggingface.co/facebook/deit-base-distilled-patch16-384.
[8] https://huggingface.co/google/vit-base-patch16-384.

Table 2. Performance of different models on dermatological disease classification. T indicates Text modality, V indicates Vision modality, and T + V indicates a combination of both modalities. Frozen refers to models where the backbone weights are not trained during the experiment, while Fine-tuned refers to models where the backbone weights are trained end-to-end with the classification head. C, G, DF, and AP represent Concat, Gating, DualFiLM, and Attention Pooling fusion strategies, respectively.

Model	Modality	Training	Accuracy	Precision	Recall	F1-Score
BioMed-RoBERTa	T	Frozen	0.2094	0.0709	0.1178	0.0806
RoBERTa	T	Frozen	0.1797	0.0634	0.0998	0.0617
BERT	T	Frozen	0.2526	0.1978	0.1745	0.1622
BioMed-RoBERTa	T	Fine-tuned	0.3463	0.2817	0.2883	0.2817
RoBERTa	T	Fine-tuned	0.3316	0.2663	0.2804	0.2692
BERT	T	Fine-tuned	0.3566	0.2986	0.3031	0.2992
DeiT	V	Frozen	0.4905	0.4652	0.4177	0.4219
ViT	V	Frozen	0.5055	0.4776	0.4404	0.4467
DeiT	V	Fine-tuned	0.7004	0.6713	0.6619	0.6648
ViT	V	Fine-tuned	0.7059	0.6779	0.6670	0.6648
ViT + BERT (C)	T + V	Frozen	0.5650	0.5307	0.5069	0.5135
ViT + BERT (G)	T + V	Frozen	0.5687	0.5316	0.5111	0.5171
ViT + BERT (DF)	T + V	Frozen	0.5722	0.5406	0.5114	0.5192
ViT + BERT (AP)	T + V	Frozen	0.5705	0.5303	0.5127	0.5179
ViT + BERT (C)	T + V	Fine-tuned	0.7044	0.6805	0.6629	0.6696
ViT + BERT (G)	T + V	Fine-tuned	0.7039	0.6768	0.6613	0.6671
ViT + BERT (DF)	T + V	Fine-tuned	0.7041	0.6846	0.6625	0.6702
ViT + BERT (AP)	T + V	Fine-tuned	**0.7131**	**0.6901**	**0.6725**	**0.6794**

Impact of Fine-Tuning vs. Frozen Models. Fine-tuning the models leads to substantial improvements in performance compared to using frozen weights. This is evident in both text and vision models. For example, the fine-tuned ViT model achieves an accuracy of 0.7059, compared to 0.5055 for the frozen version. Fine-tuning allows the models to better adapt to the specific characteristics of the dermatological dataset, leading to better performance across all metrics. This highlights the importance of training the backbone models on the specific dataset, particularly when a relatively large dataset like DermNet is available.

Multimodal Fusion Strategies. Multimodal fusion strategies generally perform comparably to the best single-modality vision models, with certain configurations achieving better results. Notably, the Attention Pooling fusion strategy achieves the highest overall accuracy of 0.7131 when combining ViT and BERT. This indicates that while multimodal fusion can enhance performance, its effectiveness is closely tied to the method used for integrating visual and textual information. The Attention Pooling strategy in fine-tuned settings achieves the best overall results and proves to be the most effective fusion approach. It dynamically selects the most relevant features from both modalities. Unlike other fusion strategies, Attention Pooling specializes feature extraction by assigning specific weights to different elements of the input sequences, allowing the model to focus on the most informative parts of both the image and text data. This approach likely contributes to its superior performance, as it better captures the complementary nature of the two modalities.

4.4   Discussion

The experimental results highlight the potential of multimodal fusion techniques to improve the classification of dermatological diseases. While vision-based models like ViT show strong performance in single-modality settings, combining visual and textual data through multimodal fusion provide additional benefits. This suggests that textual information, when effectively integrated with visual data, can enhance the overall accuracy of automated diagnostic systems.

The effectiveness of multimodal fusion largely depends on the choice of fusion strategy. Our findings show that Attention Pooling, which dynamically prioritize relevant features from both visual and textual inputs, achieve the highest accuracy. This highlights the importance of selecting fusion strategies that can dynamically adapt to the strengths of each modality while minimizing the influence of noise or irrelevant information.

The quality of the textual descriptions also affects the performance of multimodal models. The relevance and clarity of these automatically generated annotations are crucial for improving model performance. Given the computational demands of VLMs, this pilot study utilized the InternVL-2 8B model to generate the descriptions. Future research could explore the use of larger VLMs with enhanced reasoning capabilities to produce higher-quality textual descriptions, which could provide better context for the multimodal fusion process.

5   Conclusion

In this study, we explored a multimodal approach for the classification of dermatological diseases by integrating visual data with textual annotations generated by Vision-Language Models (VLMs). We demonstrated that while visual information from deep learning models like Vision Transformers (ViTs) remains critical for accurate diagnosis, the inclusion of VLM-generated textual descriptions provides valuable contextual information that enhances overall classification performance. By experimenting with various fusion strategies, we found that Attention Pooling was the most effective in dynamically weighting and combining visual and textual features, leading to the highest accuracy.

Our results show that multimodal fusion, particularly when using an effective fusion strategy, can leverage the complementary strengths of visual and textual modalities to enhance the robustness and reliability of automated diagnostic systems. This approach is particularly valuable in dermatology, where both visual inspection and clinical context are crucial for accurate diagnosis. The ability to automatically generate and integrate textual descriptions mimicking expert annotations allows the system to provide a more comprehensive analysis, potentially bridging the gap in areas where expert dermatological resources are scarce. The findings from this study have may have relevant implications for both future research and clinical practice, underscoring the role of multimodal learning in enhancing the performance of AI-driven diagnostic tools. Future research could investigate the use of more advanced VLMs with enhanced reasoning capabilities to generate higher-quality annotations, potentially leading to greater diagnostic accuracy. The proposed approach can be extended to other areas of medical imaging, where integrating multimodal information could provide a more comprehensive diagnostic perspective.

Limitations. While the DermNet dataset provides a comprehensive resource for common skin conditions, it may not fully represent the diversity of real-world clinical settings, especially across different skin types and rare conditions. Future research could explore additional datasets to improve the generalizability of our approach.

Acknowledgments. The work by Moreno La Quatra, Vincenzo Conti, Salvatore Sorce, and Valerio Mario Salerno was conducted as part of the "D.A.R.E. - Digital Lifelong Prevention" project (code: PNC0000002, CUP: B53C22006450001), co-funded by the Italian Complementary National Plan PNC-I.1 Research initiatives for innovative technologies and pathways in the health and welfare sector (D.D. 931 of 06/06/2022).

The work by Nicole Dalia Cilia and Valerio Mario Salerno was conducted as part of the "LifeMap: Dalla Patologia Pediatrica alle Malattie Cardiovascolari e Neoplastiche nell'Adulto: Mappatura Genomica per la Medicina e Prevenzione Personalizzata" project (CUP: G33C22000460001).

References

1. Achiam, J., et al.: GPT-4 technical report. arXiv preprint arXiv:2303.08774 (2023)
2. Arevalo, J., Solorio, T., Montes-y Gómez, M., González, F.A.: Gated multimodal units for information fusion. arXiv preprint arXiv:1702.01992 (2017)
3. Benedetto, I., La Quatra, M., Cagliero, L., Vassio, L., Trevisan, M.: Transformer-based prediction of emotional reactions to online social network posts. In: Proceedings of the 13th Workshop on Computational Approaches to Subjectivity, Sentiment, & Social Media Analysis, pp. 354–364 (2023). https://doi.org/10.18653/v1/2023.wassa-1.31
4. Chen, Z., et al.: InternVL: scaling up vision foundation models and aligning for generic visual-linguistic tasks. In: Proceedings of the IEEE/CVF Conference on Computer Vision and Pattern Recognition, pp. 24185–24198 (2024)
5. Devlin, J., Chang, M.W., Lee, K., Toutanova, K.: BERT: pre-training of deep bidirectional transformers for language understanding. In: Burstein, J., Doran,

C., Solorio, T. (eds.) Proceedings of the 2019 Conference of the North American Chapter of the Association for Computational Linguistics: Human Language Technologies, Volume 1 (Long and Short Papers), pp. 4171–4186. Association for Computational Linguistics, Minneapolis, Minnesota, June 2019. https://doi.org/10.18653/v1/N19-1423. https://aclanthology.org/N19-1423

6. Dosovitskiy, A., et al.: An image is worth 16x16 words: transformers for image recognition at scale. In: International Conference on Learning Representations (2021). https://openreview.net/forum?id=YicbFdNTTy

7. D'Ippolito, F., Garraffa, G., Sferlazza, A., Zaccarian, L.: A hybrid observer for localization from noisy inertial data and sporadic position measurements. Nonlinear Anal. Hybrid Syst **49**, 101360 (2023)

8. Esteva, A., et al.: Dermatologist-level classification of skin cancer with deep neural networks. Nature **542**(7639), 115–118 (2017)

9. Garraffa, G., Sferlazza, A., D'Ippolito, F., Alonge, F.: Localization based on parallel robots kinematics as an alternative to trilateration. IEEE Trans. Industr. Electron. **69**(1), 999–1010 (2022). https://doi.org/10.1109/TIE.2021.3050354

10. Gouda, N., Amudha, J.: Skin cancer classification using ResNet. In: 2020 IEEE 5th International Conference on Computing Communication and Automation (ICCCA), pp. 536–541. IEEE (2020)

11. Gururangan, S., et al.: Don't stop pretraining: adapt language models to domains and tasks. In: Jurafsky, D., Chai, J., Schluter, N., Tetreault, J. (eds.) Proceedings of the 58th Annual Meeting of the Association for Computational Linguistics, pp. 8342–8360. Association for Computational Linguistics, Online, July 2020. https://doi.org/10.18653/v1/2020.acl-main.740. https://aclanthology.org/2020.acl-main.740

12. He, K., Zhang, X., Ren, S., Sun, J.: Deep residual learning for image recognition. In: Proceedings of the IEEE Conference on Computer Vision and Pattern Recognition, pp. 770–778 (2016)

13. Ji, J., Hou, Y., Chen, X., Pan, Y., Xiang, Y.: Vision-language model for generating textual descriptions from clinical images: model development and validation study. JMIR Formative Res. **8**, e32690 (2024)

14. Koudounas, A., et al.: Towards comprehensive subgroup performance analysis in speech models. IEEE/ACM Trans. Audio Speech Lang. Process. (2024)

15. La Quatra, M., Cagliero, L.: Transformer-based highlights extraction from scientific papers. Knowl.-Based Syst. **252** (2022). https://doi.org/10.1016/j.knosys.2022.109382

16. Li, C., et al.: LlaVA-med: training a large language-and-vision assistant for biomedicine in one day. In: Advances in Neural Information Processing Systems, vol. 36 (2024)

17. Li, Y., et al.: A review of deep learning-based information fusion techniques for multimodal medical image classification. Comput. Biol. Med., 108635 (2024)

18. Liu, H., Li, C., Wu, Q., Lee, Y.J.: Visual instruction tuning. In: Advances in Neural Information Processing Systems, vol. 36 (2024)

19. Liu, X., et al.: A comparison of deep learning performance against health-care professionals in detecting diseases from medical imaging: a systematic review and meta-analysis. Lancet Digit. Health **1**(6), e271–e297 (2019)

20. Liu, Y.: RoBERTa: a robustly optimized BERT pretraining approach. arXiv preprint arXiv:1907.11692 (2019)

21. Perez, E., Strub, F., De Vries, H., Dumoulin, V., Courville, A.: Film: visual reasoning with a general conditioning layer. In: Proceedings of the AAAI Conference on Artificial Intelligence, vol. 32 (2018)

22. Touvron, H., Cord, M., Douze, M., Massa, F., Sablayrolles, A., Jégou, H.: Training data-efficient image transformers & distillation through attention. In: International Conference on Machine Learning, pp. 10347–10357. PMLR (2021)
23. Touvron, H., et al.: LlaMA: open and efficient foundation language models. arXiv preprint arXiv:2302.13971 (2023)
24. Vaiani, L., La Quatra, M., Cagliero, L., Garza, P.: Leveraging multimodal content for podcast summarization. In: Proceedings of the 37th ACM/SIGAPP Symposium on Applied Computing, pp. 863–870 (2022)
25. Vaiani, L., La Quatra, M., Cagliero, L., Garza, P.: ViPER: video-based perceiver for emotion recognition. In: Proceedings of the 3rd International on Multimodal Sentiment Analysis Workshop and Challenge, pp. 67–73 (2022)
26. Zhang, J., Huang, J., Jin, S., Lu, S.: Vision-language models for vision tasks: a survey. IEEE Trans. Pattern Anal. Mach. Intell. (2024)
27. Zhou, J., et al.: Pre-trained multimodal large language model enhances dermatological diagnosis using SkinGPT-4. Nat. Commun. **15**(1), 5649 (2024)

Plastic Waste Detection Using YOLOv5 Deep Learning Object Detection Algorithm

Rima Prasad[✉], Jitendra Musale, Dewendra Bharambe, Pranil Dhanke, Dhanashri Nagare, and Pratiksha Nale

Department of Computer Engineering, ABMSP's Anantrao Pawar College of Engineering and Research, Pune, India
reemavarma830@gmail.com, {jitendra.musale, dewendra.bharambe}@abmspcoerpune.org

Abstract. Plastic waste poses a vast danger to the surroundings and human health. Effective detection and control are vital for mitigating this problem. This study introduces about plastic waste detection using YOLOv5 algorithm by using this we can detect the objects. We advanced a device that makes use of YOLO to correctly identify plastic waste in various environments, along with seashores, oceans, and concrete regions. The gadget became skilled in a numerous dataset of categorized images containing distinct kinds of plastic waste. Data augmentation strategies have been employed to improve the version's robustness. Our consequences reveal that the YOLO-primarily based system achieves high accuracy and outperforms conventional methods. This research aims to offer automatic solutions for tracking plastic pollution, with plans to integrate actual-time tracking and support waste management initiatives.

The research paper offers a unique technique for identifying and categorizing primary assets of plastic waste via the utilization of the YOLOv5 deep studying object detection set of rules. The proliferation of plastic waste has emerged as a full-size environmental subject because of its destructive impact on ecosystems and human health. Accurate and efficient detection of plastic waste is important for effective waste control and pollution management. The assessment of the overall performance is carried out the use of overarching criteria, inclusive of the counseled common precision (mAP) and frames consistent with 2nd (FPS), showcasing its efficacy in figuring out and classifying plastic waste with precision and performance. The research paper contributes to the sphere of laptop imaginative and prescient and environmental technological know-how imparting a practical and efficient answer for plastic waste detection. The proposed technique can be included in automatic.

Keywords: Deep learning · yolov5 object detection algorithm · Plastic waste detection · Computer vision · Image processing

1 Introduction

Plastic waste has been diagnosed as a prime environmental hassle. The predominant resources of plastic waste are various industries, public littering, and home rubbish. Since plastics aren't biodegradable, the hazard is increasing with populace increase. Unlike

S. Palaiahnakote et al. (Eds.): ICPR 2024 Workshops, LNCS 15617, pp. 226–238, 2025.
https://doi.org/10.1007/978-3-031-88217-3_16

other material plastic cannot decompose or biodegrade easily that causes human life, wildlife, marine life etc. Effective strong waste management is required to ensure environmental conservation [1]. There are many conventional techniques for tracking solid waste, together with sweepers and street lifting, however, their predominant limitations consist of excessive preservation expenses, disruption of human sports, and inefficiency. With the development of image evaluation and machine studying generation, the far-flung sensing era has been used to screen plastic waste and other strong waste materials in massive areas. The accuracy of conventional gadget mastering algorithms depends closely on characteristic engineering. Meanwhile, deep mastering (DL) algorithms have made incredible progress in photo reputation, object detection, and semantic segmentation during the last few years. The key advantage of DL algorithms is their avoidance of guide function engineering. Due to the use of convolutional neural networks, they can learn the hierarchical features of input visible information. Plastic waste has turned out to be a sizeable environmental situation because of its sturdiness, big use, and improper disposal. Accurate and efficient detection of plastic waste in numerous environments is essential for powerful waste management and pollution control. Deep knowledge of item detection algorithms, such as YOLOv5, offers a promising way to this undertaking [2]. In modern days by using Yolov5 we can discover the real time objects which offers higher speed and correctness. It excels at real-time detection of more than one gadget inside a picture or video. By practicing YOLOv5 on a dataset of plastic waste pictures, we can create a model capable of appropriately figuring out and localizing plastic waste gadgets in real-international scenarios.

We can find plastic and trash with the help of object detection algorithm. These have been studied in gadgets getting to know and quantifying plastic waste are critical. Deep getting to know, a subset of artificial intelligence, has emerged as a powerful device for item detection tasks, including the identity of plastic waste in diverse environments [3].

YOLOv5, the latest object detection version, has gained a reputation for its velocity, accuracy, and simplicity of use. By leveraging the capabilities of YOLOv5, researchers, and practitioners can broaden strong systems for detecting plastic waste in pixels and motion pictures. This introduction will delve into the essential ideas of deep mastering and object detection, explore the architecture and advantages of YOLOv5, and talk about the capacity packages of plastic waste detection and the use of this effective algorithm. In the area of Deep mastering, item detection take part in identifying and localizing specific real time objects within an image or video. This task calls for the version to no longer understand the presence of objects but additionally correctly decide their bounding packing containers. YOLOv5 achieves this by using a single-degree detector structure, because of this it performs both item category and localization in a single bypass. This method allows accurate time in processing, making it appropriate for programs that call for speedy detection.

The YOLOv5 structure consists of several key components, which include a spine community for characteristic extraction, a neck network for feature pyramid enhancement, and a head community for item detection. The backbone network, regularly primarily based on a pre-educated model like Darknet, extracts features from the enter image. The neck community combines capabilities from one-of-a-kind degrees of the spine to create a multi-scale function representation. Finally, the top community predicts bounding boxes and class chances for each detected item.

By leveraging the energy of deep studying and the efficiency of YOLOv5, researchers, and practitioners can expand innovative answers to cope with the plastic waste crisis. Automated systems geared up with YOLOv5 may be deployed in various settings, consisting of recycling centers, waste management websites, and coastal areas, to facilitate the green detection, sorting, and removal of plastic waste. This generation has the potential to seriously enhance waste control practices, reduce environmental pollution, and sell an extra sustainable destiny.

2   Importance of Technology

The importance of plastic waste detection and the use of the YOLOv5 deep learning object detection set of rules is profound. This generation offers a sizable jump forward in addressing the global plastic pollution crisis. It empowers green waste management techniques by enabling fast, correct, and autonomous identity of plastic waste in various environments. From accelerating cleanup efforts on land and in water our bodies to informing coverage choices and guiding recycling initiatives, YOLOv5-based total detection is instrumental. It not simplest mitigates environmental damage but additionally contributes to the circular economy by facilitating the restoration of precious plastic sources. Furthermore, by offering statistics on plastic waste distribution and brands, it supports medical research and informs the improvement of preventive measures. Essentially, this technology is a cornerstone in constructing a sustainable future unfastened by the pervasive problem of plastic pollution [4].

The contents and import the text document you have got generated. You can now use the scroll-down window on the left of the Microsoft Word formatting toolbar to layout your paintings. Effective trash Management: Timely and specific identity of plastic trash is essential to green waste management procedures. YOLOv5 can assist automate the technique of identifying and locating plastic waste, lowering manual hard work and growing performance. Environmental Protection: Plastic pollutants are a main environmental problem by identifying and disposing of plastic waste, we will help reduce its devastating impact on ecosystems and wildlife. Resource Recovery: Plastic waste may be recycled and reused, lowering the call for new materials. YOLOv5 can assist in figuring out recyclable plastic waste, enabling more efficient recycling applications [5].

Public Health Research and Monitoring: YOLOv5 can be used to display plastic waste accumulation in specific areas, offering valuable records for research and coverage improvement.

3   Literature Survey

Be Dr. K. Soumya [1] This research investigates YOLOv5 deep learning for plastic detection and discover. Given the significant environmental impact of plastic pollution, accurate and efficient detection methods are crucial. By leveraging a dataset of plastic photographs and employing photograph augmentation strategies, we have a look at evaluating the performance of YOLOv5. The outcomes, measured through Mean Average

Precision, display the set of rules' effectiveness in identifying and categorizing plastic waste, imparting a promising solution for addressing this pressing environmental difficulty.

Jiajia Meng [2] This paper presents a new method for real-time water waste analysis using the YOLOv5 algorithm. By combining YOLOv5 with a PyQt5-based detection interface, the system enables efficient and convenient detection of floating garbage in images, videos, and live camera feeds. The YOLOv5 model, trained on a custom dataset of 4591 images, achieves impressive performance with an average precision of 99.5% and 82.5% at different IoU thresholds. This system offers a valuable tool for 24/7 water waste monitoring, supporting timely garbage cleaning and improved water environment management.

Bhanumathi M [3] This study explores the utility of YOLOv4 and YOLOv5 deep mastering algorithms for finding and figuring out plastics inside the zone quarter. Given the substantial environmental effect of plastic pollutants, accurate and green detection methods are vital. By utilizing a dataset of ocean plastic images and incorporating image augmentation, the study evaluates the performance of both YOLO algorithms. The results, measured by Mean Average Precision, demonstrate their effectiveness in identifying marine plastics, providing a valuable tool for addressing this pressing environmental concern.

Andrii Marusk [4] The paper investigates the application of CNNs for automatically detecting plastic waste on water surfaces. It compares the performance of different YOLO architectures trained on a dataset of plastic waste images. Preprocessing steps included image categorization and data augmentation. The models were trained using PyTorch and CUDA, incorporating analytical parameters like a accurateness, MAP, recollect, and F1 scores. The study highlights the effectiveness of several YOLO models in detecting plastic waste, provides insight into their positive and negative, and identifies areas for further study.

Jansi Rani S.V. [5] The abstract discusses the challenges of waste handling and disposal in urban areas and the potential of deep learning to address these issues. It highlights the need for a multi-class dataset and compares the execution of YOLOv5 and Faster R-CNN for object detection and classification. The results show that both models achieve high mAP scores, suggesting their effectiveness in this domain.

Yugia Li [6] The abstract discusses the challenges of garbage detection in complex environments and proposes an improved YOLOv5 model, YOLOv5-OCDS. The model incorporates ODConv, C3DCN, decoupled head, and Soft NMS to enhance detection performance. Experimental results demonstrate the superior performance of YOLOv5-OCDS compared to the original YOLOv5, succeeding suitable for garbage detection in complex scenarios.

Yizhe Li [7] The abstract discusses the MRS-YOLOv5 waste disposal. The model incorporates enhancements like Slide Loss IOU, RepViT, and unusual removal plan to upgrade correctness and efficiency. Exploratory outcomes on a data record of 12,072 samples show that MRS-YOLO outperforms YOLOv8 in terms of mAP and volume. The model is also effective in detecting small targets and is suitable for various detection scenarios. The source code and dataset are publicly available on GitHub.

Qiuhong Sun [8] The abstract discusses the challenges of garbage detection in complex environments and proposes an improved YOLOv5 model, YOLOv5-OCDS. The model incorporates ODConv, C3DCN, decoupled head, and Soft NMS to enhance detection performance. Experimental results demonstrate the superior performance of YOLOv5-OCDS compared to the original YOLOv5, succeeding suitable for actual garbage detection in complex scenarios.

Jingyang Wang [9] The abstract discusses the challenges of plastic waste observation with probable of AI techniques to contacting issues. The study proposes a YOLOv5-based model that utilizes both RGB and RGNIR images for detecting the plastic waste.. The model is analyze using a 10-fold cross-validation method and a proposed performance metric, WMS. The solution indicate the benefit of the model in detecting plastic waste, particularly when using fused RGB and RGNIR data. This research suggests that combining visible light and near-infrared spectrum can improve plastic waste detection performance, opening new avenues for automated plastic detection systems.

Jitendra. C. Musale [10] The abstract discusses the use of satellite imagery and machine learning for forest fire detection. The proposed method utilizes Inception-v3 and local binary patterns to classify satellite images into fire and non-fire categories. The study aims to improve fire detection accuracy and prevent large-scale fires.

4   Research Methodology

The study's method involves collecting a diverse dataset of photographs containing numerous plastic waste gadgets in exceptional environments, observed by labeling these photos with bounding containers across the plastic waste objects. This annotated dataset is then used to train the YOLOv5 item detection model. The version's overall performance is evaluated using metrics like precision, do not forget, and MAP. Once optimized, the version is deployed for actual international testing and capacity integration into structures (Fig. 1).

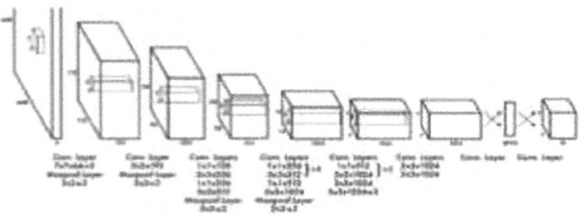

Fig. 1. YOLO algorithm architecture.

Examples of unmarried-shot object detection algorithms consist of YOLO (You Only Look Once) and SSD (Single Shot Multi Box Detector). YOLO divides the input photo into a grid and for each grid mobile, predicts a positive variety of bounding containers and class chances. SSD, then again, predicts bounding packing containers and class chances at more than one scale in specific function maps.

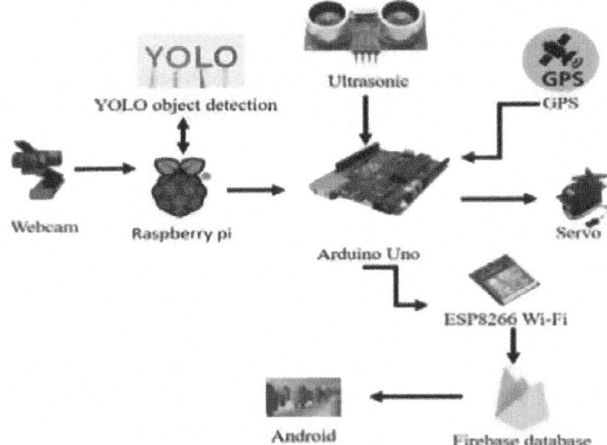

Fig. 2. System architecture.

The proposed machine can be categorized into two main components: hardware and software. The hardware includes a webcam for video capture, a Raspberry Pi 4 developed by the Raspberry Pi Foundation in Pencoed, South Wales, United Kingdom, an Arduino Uno produced by Arduino in Scarmagno, Italy, an ultrasonic sensor from Kuongshun Electronic in Shenzhen, China, a servo manufactured by TowerPro in Florida, United States, a GPS module created by Ublox in Surendranagar, India, and an ESP8266 Wi-Fi module produced by Espress if Systems in Shanghai, China. The choice of Raspberry Pi as the primary computing device is due to its compact size, allowing it to be easily installed in a standard trash bin. Additionally, Raspberry Pi is readily available and cost-effective, providing sufficient computing power compared to alternatives such as the NVIDIA Jetson Nano, Odroid XU4, and Asus Tinker Board. The software component consists of a Firebase Database for data storage and a mobile application for displaying information related to the trash bin's capacity. The Raspberry Pi 4, webcam, and servo are utilized for object detection and classification, while the ultrasonic sensor, GPS, and ESP8266 Wi-Fi are employed for capacity monitoring. The system architecture is depicted in Fig. 2.

Webcam: Webcams are virtual cameras that capture actual-time video and transmit it over the internet. They are widely used for diverse functions, consisting of video conferencing, stay streaming surveillance, and far-off tracking. Webcams come in one-of-a-kind resolutions, frame costs, and functions, including autofocus, integrated microphones, and privacy shutters. They can be included in laptops, computers, or standalone gadgets, and can be linked to computer systems or different gadgets via USB, Bluetooth, or Wi-Fi.

YOLO Object Detection: YOLO (You Only Look Once) is the latest item exposure set of rules to revolutionized the sector. Unlike traditional strategies that scan pictures in more than one instance, YOLO v5 detects the real time object by bouding each image by boxces the image will be devided into grids and inside each grid it will detect the object. This unmarried-pass technique makes it appreciably faster than different techniques. YOLO excelsat detecting several objects at time, making it available for real-time applications like video surveillance and self-sustaining driving. While YOLO is exceedingly efficient, it can on occasion struggle with smaller gadgets and can have obstacles in detecting items that might be very near together. Overall, YOLO's velocity, accuracy, and capacity to discover more than one item make it a powerful tool in the subject of laptop vision.

Raspberry Pi: The Raspberry Pi is a card-area computer (SBC) that has become popular with enthusiasts, developers, and educators. It is designed to be affordable and accessible, making it ideal for instructional programming, electronic workflows, and even standard computers. Its GPIO pins (General-Purpose Input/Output) permit the Raspberry Pi to interface with a variety of components, from sensor motors to LED displays. Its versatility has led to a verity of applications including home automation, robotics, and retro gaming.

Ultrasonic: Sound waves with frequencies higher than the upper reaches of human hearing (usually around 20,000 Hz) is called Ultrasonic. These wavelengths have a variety of applications, such as medical imaging (ultrasound), non-destructive testing of materials, and cleaning of delicate materials Ultrasonic waves can be used to make visualizations of materials, detect defects in materials to remove dirt and grime from surfaces without damage

Arduino Uno: The Arduino Uno is one of the famous microcontroller board for prototyping and developing electronic projects. It is depend on the ATmega328P microcontroller and provides a simple interface for beginners to learn programming and electronics. With its 14 digital input/output pins, 6 analog inputs, and built-in USB connectors, the Arduino Uno can be used to control a vast array of electronic components such as LEDs, motors, sensors, and more and it helps it immensely and a huge array of libraries and tutorials here Available, making it a great option for amateurs and professionals alike.

Servo: Servos are a form of electromechanical actuator that can be used to exactly control the angular role of a shaft. They are extensively utilized in various packages, which include robotics, RC vehicles, and automatic systems.

ESP8266 Wi-Fi: The ESP8266 is a low-cost, excessive-overall performance Wi-Fi microcontroller module. It's a famous desire for IoT tasks because of its affordability, ease of use, and flexibility.

YOLO Model:

The initial step towards training the YOLO model is gathering images of recyclable waste. A primary dataset would be collected by downloading images from a data repository like Kaggle or getting images from the search engine, although it should not be done using Google because collecting data this way takes such a long time to collect a sufficient amount of data. As an alternative to this approach, web crawling can be used to gather images via the internet efficiently. The YOLO model is known for being fast as well as very efficient in real-time applications or real time objects. The yolov5 is a object detection algorithm, It will detect the object from an image and divide the image into an grid and inside each grid it will detect the object. The YOLOv5 is a famous algorithm for its speed and accuracy which detects the real time objects from an image in a faster and efficient way. By using yolov5 we can detect real-time objects inside in any video or images (Fig. 3).

5   Flowchart

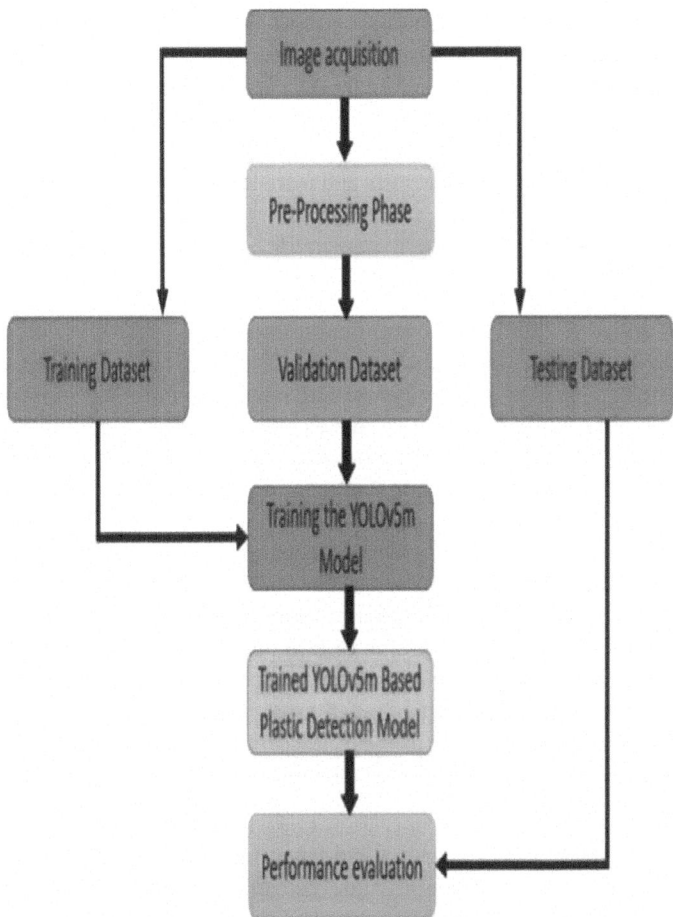

Fig. 3. Flowchart of the Proposed Method.

The images obtained were divided in a number of ways: one set was used for the model training, while the other was used for the model testing. The ratio of separation may vary in other situations, in this case however, the training and validation sets were respectively 80% and 20% out of the total. To Increase the final accuracy and efficiency of the trained model with foundation yourself on YOLO, Melting Pot of crisp images also becomes a necessity by applying the data probalistic approach. This augmentation can be realized through two methods, namely traditional (white box) methods and deep learning based (black box) techniques. This study preferred to use the traditional method as it is more common. Data augmentation extension of training data is achieved by transforming all the images in the training set in many random ways, such as in rotation, scaling, inversion, and adding noise, allowing the model to have a better perspective of the data. The models within the YOLOv5 series has an architecture which can be described in terms of three components – the feature extraction backbone, the feature fusion neck and the detection head. In the model of YOLOv5, there are five subcategories, namely: YOLOv5n, YOLOv5s, YOLOv5m, YOLOv5l and YOLOv5x, from smallest to largest.. YOLOv5 is a pc imaginative and prescient version that is used for object detection. It is a more advantageous model of preceding YOLO fashions and operates at an excessive inference velocity, making it powerful for real-time programs. It makes use of PyTorch for faster and extra correct deployment.

YOLOv5 is available in different sorts and is mainly proper at detecting small items.

6 Algorithm

YOLOv5 was added in 2020 via the identical group that advanced the primary YOLO set of rules as an extend-supply challenge and is preserved by Ultralytic. YOLOv5 construct for the prosperity of preceding adaptation and provides variety of new functions and upgrades. Unlike YOLO, YOLO v5 makes use of additional complicated planning known as Efficient Det (structure proven below), based on the Efficient Net community planning. By using a greater composite architecture in YOLO v5 lets it to attain higher precision and higher induction to a much long range of various object categories Another distinction between YOLO and YOLO v5 is the schooling facts used to examine the item search version. YOLO turned into trained on the PASCAL VOC dataset, which includes 20 item classes. YOLO v5, then again, became trained on a larger and more varied dataset known as D5, which incorporates a some of 600 item classes…YOLOv5 uses a brand new technique for producing the anchor bins, known as "dynamic anchor containers." It entails the use of a clustering set of rules to organize the ground reality bounding containers into clusters and then the usage of the centroids of the clusters because of the anchor bins. This permits the anchor bins to be more carefully aligned with the detected gadgets' length and form.

1. Data Preparation: YOLOv5 statistics guidance involves several key steps to make certain the version can accurately locate gadgets in snapshots. First, a dataset of photographs with labeled bounding containers for the objects of the hobby is collected. These labels specify the area and size of every object in the image. Second, the dataset is split into schooling, declaration, and check sets to analyze the version's overall performance during education and trying out. Third, the snapshots are resized and normalized to a constant size and layout, typically 640×640 pixels. Finally, the labels are transformed right into a format well suited to YOLO v5, which entails specifying the center coordinates, width, and peak of every bounding field relative to the photograph size. This organized dataset is then used to teach the YOLO v5 version, which learns to apprehend and find items inside pictures.

2. Model Architecture: YOLOv5 is a trendy object detection version recognized for its speed and accuracy. Its architecture is characterized using a sequence of convolutional layers, observed using a feature pyramid community (FPN) and a head. The convolutional layers extract functions from the enter image, at the same time as the FPN merges features from distinct scales to enhance detection overall performance. The head is chargeable for predicting bounding containers and class possibilities for each item in the photograph. YOLOv5 introduces numerous innovations, together with a new backbone structure (CSPDarknet53), a novel neck layout (PAN), and various loss capabilities to optimize schooling. These enhancements contribute to YOLOv5's potential to detect objects efficiently and accurately in actual international packages.

3. Training: YOLOv5 is very famous model used for object detection which offers higher speed and accuracy. During education, the model is fed with a large dataset containing photographs and corresponding annotations (bounding containers and labels). The model learns to discover and locate objects within pix through a procedure of iterative optimization. The schooling manner entails modifying the version's load and diagonal to limit the difference between its anticipated outputs and the ground reality labels. This is commonly carried out with the usage of back propagation, which calculates gradients to update the version parameters. The training process continues the model reaches a first-class degree of overall performance, as measured using metrics such as imply common precision (mAP).

4. Inference: YOLOv5 is innovative object recognition model known for its fast speed and. During on point. During evaluation, the model processes an input image at a time, dividing it into gridded cells. Each cell predicts bounding boxes, item confidence scores, and a set of class probabilities. Minimum limitation is then separate out to filter out the irrelevant choices and select the most likely ones. The final result consists of known objects, their bounding boxes, and class labels. The design of YOLOv5 is optimized for real-time applications, making it suitable for a several types of uses such as monitoring, autonomous driving, and industrial monitoring

5. Output: YOLOv5 is a trendy item detection model known for its velocity and accuracy. Its output normally includes a list of detected items, every with related bounding bins, confidence ratings, and sophistication labels. The bounding packing containers define the spatial extent of the detected item, whilst the self-assurance ratings Suggest the version's fact within the detection. The magnificence labels specify the category of the item, along with "character," "vehicle," or "dog." YOLOv5's output format is regularly well-matched with various downstream responsibilities, which include image category, item tracking, and example segmentation.

7   Advantages of Proposed Model Over Existing Model

1. It provides valuable knowledge and contributes to the modifying of more accurate and efficient plastic detection methods
2. It can process images and videos at high frame rates, enabling efficient detection in dynamic environments
3. YOLOv5 achieves high accuracy in object detection tasks, including plastic waste detection.

4. YOLOv5 is highly customizable, allowing you to adapt it to specific plastic waste detection requirements
5. The framework is relatively easy to use, making it reachable to developers with different levels of skills.
6. YOLOv5 can effectively handle large datasets, making it suitable for training models on extensive plastic waste images.

8 Results and Discussion

YOLOv5 has validated significant potential in accurately and correctly detecting plastic waste within pictures and video frames. By training the model on a numerous dataset of plastic waste photographs, it learns to recognize diverse plastic items and their locations. The set of rules excels in actual-time performance, making it suitable for applications like waste sorting centers and environmental tracking. The version processes input images and generates bounding bins around detected plastic items, alongside confidence rankings indicating the chance of accurate identification. While the precise effects can vary based on dataset quality and version structure, studies have stated high mean common precision (mAP) values, suggesting unique detection. YOLOv5's capability to handle multiple gadgets inside a body and its velocity make it a promising tool for addressing the global plastic pollution crisis The YOLOv4 and YOLOv5 algorithms were trained on hundreds of datasets, among which the most prominent was the COCO dataset; however, they were both retrained on specifically collected marine plastic images in the epipelagic zone of the oceans. Because this is a limited number of images, in effect, a dataset was created through image augmentations [8].

The datasets demanded careful hyper parameter fine-tuning with multiple epochs to achieve the best possible weights, which will prove to be the key to increasing the mAP values for the algorithms. The weights were saved at every epoch of one thousand, which gave room for the creation of better weights for both the YOLOv4 and YOLOv5 algorithms. At first, images as well as videos containing marine plastics were used in the evaluation of the algorithms. It will happen to be among the decisive factors that led to high-quality weights and precision metrics. The models are tested in real-time on simulation of different scenarios set up in the epipelagic ocean layer. A live camera feed is integrated into the system, which enables its ability to detect plastics with an accuracy ranging from a minimum of forty percent to a maximum of eighty percent. The performances of YOLOv4 and YOLOv5 with regards to the accuracy of real-time predictions might be improved by infusing more images of marine plastic into the dataset while accounting for a broader range of environmental conditions that might affect the clarity of the image and plastic properties. A comparison of the performances of YOLOv4 and YOLOv5 demonstrated that the YOLOv4 model reached about mean Average Precision 80–82%. In addition, the average precision and frames per second estimated in this experiment with the help of YOLOv4 were 8–10% more significant as compared to YOLOv3. The algorithm also proved to be highly precise and fast for input videos. It was able to identify nearly all the marine plastics under real-time conditions.

9 Conclusion

YOLOv5 has been verified to be quite effective tool for actual-time plastic waste detection, demonstrating exquisite accuracy and pace. Its potential to pick out and localize various plastic items within complex environments positions it as a cornerstone for developing superior waste management structures. While demanding situations such as occlusions and ranging light conditions persist, ongoing research and improvements in deep studying techniques promise to further enhance the version's abilities. By integrating YOLOv5 into broader environmental tracking and cleanup tasks, we can substantially make contributions to mitigating the plastic pollution crisis and fostering a sustainable destiny. YOLOv5 has emerged as an impressive device for actual-time plastic waste detection, demonstrating remarkable accuracy and velocity in identifying and localizing various plastic objects inside complex environments. Its ability to correctly technique snap shots and motion pictures makes it a cornerstone for developing advanced waste control systems. While challenges which include occlusions and varying lighting conditions persist, ongoing research and advancements in deep mastering strategies are poised to in addition decorate the model's performance. By integrating YOLOv5 into broader environmental tracking and cleanup projects, we can considerably make contributions to mitigating the plastic pollution crisis and promoting a sustainable future. Additionally, YOLOv5's versatility and scalability make it adaptable to numerous applications, such as self-sustaining robots for waste collection and real-time environmental monitoring structures. As deep getting to know continues to evolve, YOLOv5 is likely to play an increasingly more pivotal role in addressing the worldwide plastic pollution task.

References

1. Song, G., Cao, H., Liu, L., Jin, M.: Analysis of marine microplastic pollution of disposable masks under COVID-19 Epidemic-A DPSIR FRAMEWORK. Int. J. Environ. Res. Public Health **19**(23), 16299 (2022)
2. Lin, F., et al.: Improved YOLO based detection algorithm for floating debris in waterway. Entropy (Basel, Switzerland) **23**(9), 1111 (2021). https://doi.org/10.3390/e23091111
3. Bhanumathi M, et al.: Marine plastic detection using deep learning. Mar. Pollut. Bull. **178**, 113527 (2022). https://doi.org/10.1016/j.marpolbul.2022.113527
4. Zailan, N.A., et al.: An automated solid waste detection using the optimized YOLO model for riverine management. Front. Public Health **10**, 907280 (2022). https://doi.org/10.3389/fpubh.2022.907280
5. Böer, G., Gröger, J.P., Badri-Höher, S., et al.: A deep-learning based pipeline for estimating the abundance and size of aquatic organisms in an unconstrained underwater environment from continuously captured stereo video. Sensors (Basel) **23**(6), 3311 (2023). https://doi.org/10.3390/s23063311
6. Musale, J.C.: Survey on forest wildfire detection using deep learning. Int. J. Res. Appl. Sci. Eng. Technol. (IJRASET). ISSN: 2321-9653; IC Value: 45.98; SJ Impact Factor: 7.538 Volume 11 Issue V May 2023. www.ijraset.com. Pages 6SJ Impact Factor 7.538 I ISRA Journal Impact Factor 7.894 Link. https://doi.org/10.22214/ijraset.2023.52164
7. Ye, Z., Liang, H., Lan, C.: Applied to YOLOv5s algorithm model of underwater target detection. J. TV Technol. **47**(2), 39–43 (2023). https://doi.org/10.16280/j.videoe

8. Lei, L., Yin, Y., Liang, M., et al.: Research on elderly fall recognition algorithm based on improved YOLOv5s. J. Chongqing Univ. Sci. Technol. (Nat. Sci. Edn.) **25**(01), 85–90 2023. https://doi.org/10.19406/j.cnkicqkjxyxbzkb.2023.01.002

9. Xue, B., Huang, B., Chen, G., Li, H., Wei, W.: Deep-sea debris identification using deep convolutional neural networks. IEEE J. Sel. Top. Appl. Earth Observations Remote Sens. **14**, 8909–8921 (2021). https://doi.org/10.1109/JSTARS.2021.3107853

10. Wu, Z., et al.: Using YOLOv5 for garbage classification. In: 2021 4th International Conference on Pattern Recognition and Artificial Intelligence (PRAI), pp. 35–38 (2021). https://doi.org/10.1109/PRAI53619.2021.9550790

11. Boominathan, M., Uthayakumar, R.: Automatic detection and classification of plastic objects using deep learning. J. Clean. Prod. **258**, 120916 (2020)

12. Wang, D., Wang, J., Xu, K.: Deep learning for object detection, classification, and tracking in industry applications. Sensors **21**(21), 7349 (2021)

13. Musale, J.C.: Suspicious movement detection and tracking of human behavior and object with fire detection using a closed circuit TV (CCTV) cameras. Int. J. Res. Appl. Sci. Eng. Technol. **5**(XII) (2017). ISSN: 2321 9653. Paper ID: IJRASET12179. www.ijraset.com

W13

Multi-modal Fusion of LiDAR and PRISMA Data for Cobalt Mapping: A Case Study from the Áramo Mine, Spain

Fahimeh Farahnakian[1,2]([⊠])(ID), Farshad Farahnakian[2](ID), Javad Sheikh[2](ID), Steven Downey[3](ID), Vaughan Williams[3](ID), and Jukka Heikkonen[2](ID)

[1] Geological Survey of Finland (GTK), 02151 Espoo, Finland
[2] Department of Computing, University of Turku, 20500 Turku, Finland
{fahfar,farfar,javshe,jukhei}@utu.fi
[3] Aurum Exploration Limited (Aurum), Kells, Ireland
{sdowney,vwilliams}@aurumexploration.com

Abstract. This paper presents a framework for combining airborne LiDAR and hyperspectral PRISMA data to create a more comprehensive input for the Machine Learning (ML) models. To predict Cobalt concentration, we apply three well-known ML methods: Random Forest (RF), Support Vector Regression (SVR), and Multi-Layer Perceptron (MLP). A key challenge in this application is the limited availability of labeled data, which we address by employing three data augmentation techniques, ranging from traditional methods to deep learning-based approaches, to generate synthetic data points. Experiments were conducted on a mineralization site at the Áramo mine in Asturias, Spain. The results demonstrate that these data augmentation techniques significantly enhance the ML models' ability to accurately predict the minority class, which is crucial for mineral exploration. Combining data from LiDAR and PRISMA improves model performance compared to using a single modality.

Keywords: mineral prospectivity mapping · machine learning · data augmentation · Lidar · PRISMA · remote sensing · satellite imagery

1 Introduction

Nowadays, Remote Sensing (RS) technologies play a crucial role in various real-world applications, including maritime and natural resource monitoring [1,2], agriculture [3], and disaster management [4]. RS data, which includes satellite and aircraft images and land-based sensors, provides valuable information about the Earth's surface and specific research areas. This information is essential for

This work is part of the Secure and Sustainable Supply of raw materials for EU Industry (S34I) project funded by European Union.

stakeholders when making critical decisions. The growing use of RS technology in different applications does not only connect to the sensor progress. The growing use of RS technology is largely due to recent advancements in Machine Learning (ML) and improved access to high-quality data. ML algorithms have the potential to automatically explore different types of RS data and extract patterns to perform various tasks, such as classification and prediction without human intervention.

Mineral prospectivity mapping (MPM) using RS data is a novel research topic that has attracted much attention among researchers and data scientists over the last decade. MPM is a crucial process in geosciences, enabling the identification of areas with potential mineral deposits, which is vital for efficient resource exploration. In the past, MPM was done manually and required a lot of effort, such as drilling and sample collection, which made the MPM task very challenging and costly. However, the data-driven technique has emerged not only to save time and energy but also to map mineral deposits with higher accuracy and reliability. The data-driven approaches that are mostly based on ML models can learn from labeled datasets including mineral deposits data points that are already known. After training the models, they can answer a vital question 'How close are the unknown or unlabelled data points to the known mineral deposits based on their geological, geophysical, and geochemical features?'

ML-based methods used for the MPM application have been explored to capture more complex relationships between explanatory variables and deposit locations, offering improved predictive accuracy compared to non-ML methods techniques. Previous MPM research has employed models such as Artificial Neural Network (ANN) [5,6], Support Vector Machine (SVM) [7], Random Forest (RF) [8], and Gradient Boosting (GB) [9]. Among these algorithms, decision tree-based approaches have been particularly popular. These methods are capable of modeling non-linear relationships and evaluating the significance of explanatory features across all predictions.

Cobalt (Co) powers our lives and is a critical mineral for green technologies, has garnered significant attention due to its increasing demand in renewable energy technologies, particularly in battery production. According to the Huge Centre for Strategical Studies (HCSS), co-mining within Europe could assist the region become more independent when it comes to securing its own resources [10]. At the moment, most of the world's Co is mined in the Democratic Republic of Congo (70%), and most of it is refined in China (also 70%) [10]. If Europe starts mining more Co locally, it could meet about 3.1% of its demand by the year 2035 [10]. This would help reduce Europe's reliance on other countries for Co. Therefore, identifying Co-rich areas with high precision is vital for EU (European Union) members. Figure 1 displays 509 identified Co-bearing deposits and occurrences across 25 European nations.

While several advanced ML algorithms and remote sensing data show great potential, challenges persist in the availability of labeled datasets to train ML models. Supervised ML models' performance highly relies on labeled datasets, requiring enough labeled data to be trained for extracting patterns. This limi-

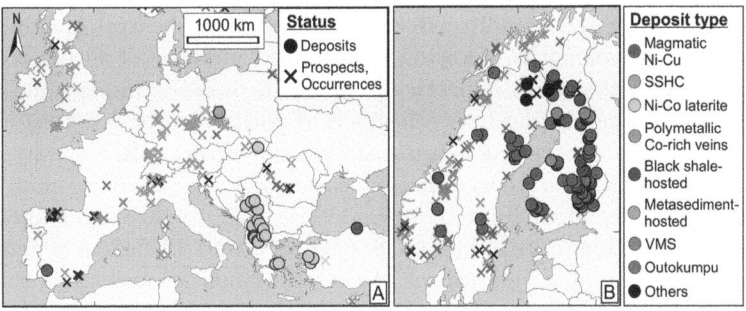

Fig. 1. The location of cobalt-bearing deposits and occurrences in EU [11].

tation can hinder the effectiveness of ML models in classification and prediction tasks [12]. Several studies were conducted in the field of MPM to address the lack of enough labeled data or imbalanced data for training prediction models. In [12], geological map knowledge graphs with exploration data have been integrated to enhance accuracy in predicting gold ore occurrences in China. They first employed the Gaussian mixture model (GMM) for spatial feature classification to expand the number of positive samples, and then two Deep Learning (DL)-based classification methods: 1-dimensional convolutional neural network (CNN1D) and graph convolutional network to extract spatial pattern and prediction. To further address imbalanced data issues in MPM, various generative models have been proposed. In another [13], Conditional Generative Adversarial Network (CTGAN), a generative model designed for tabular data, utilizes a conditional generator and mode-specific normalization to handle mixed data types and imbalanced categorical variables.

In [13], Tabular Variational Autoencoder (TVAE) extends the traditional VAE to better capture mixed data types and complex distributions. It uses preprocessing techniques like mode-specific normalization and one-hot encoding to model joint distributions accurately, making it a robust option for generating realistic synthetic data, particularly in the context of tabular datasets. In another [14], Gaussian Copula Synthesizer (GCS), introduced in the Synthetic Data Vault (SDV), generates synthetic data by modeling statistical properties and dependencies within a single table. It standardizes columns to a normal distribution, capturing covariances to replicate realistic patterns and correlations efficiently.

Although previous research has demonstrated several advantages of using data augmentation techniques to solve imbalanced data in MPM applications, their ability to integrate and utilize geochemical information with Light Detection and Ranging (LiDAR) and PRISMA data has still not been proven. LiDAR data provides detailed topographical information, making it a valuable resource for identifying subtle geological features that may indicate the presence of minerals such as those containing Co. Another useful data type for monitoring and studying environmental phenomena is hyperspectral data from satellites like

PRISMA. The PRISMA satellite offers high-resolution spectral imaging across a wide range of wavelengths, allowing for detailed analysis of surface compositions. This capability makes it particularly useful in detecting specific mineral signatures and distinguishing between different rock types or vegetation.

In this study, we proposed a framework to integrate PRISMA hyperspectral imagery, LiDAR, and geochemical data for Co prospectivity mapping. To overcome the challenge of limited labeled data, we employed advanced data augmentation techniques, including GCS, CTGAN, and TVAE, to generate synthetic data. We evaluated the impact of these augmentation techniques on the performance of three ML models including MLP [15], RF [16], SVR [17], with hyperparameter tuning to optimize model performance. The main contributions of this paper are summarized as follows:

- Integration of PRISMA and high-resolution airborne LiDAR data to improve the accuracy of Co prospectivity mapping.
- Application of multiple ML models for Co concentration prediction in the MPM field, allowing for a comprehensive comparison of model performance.
- Use three different data augmentation approaches, ranging from traditional methods to deep learning models, to enhance the performance of supervised ML models and mitigate the limitations of labeled data.
- Experiments conducted on a mineralization site at the Áramo mine in Asturias, Spain, with a scalable framework that can be adapted to other regions and mineral deposits for future prospectivity studies.

2   Study Area and Data

The Aramo land exploration pilot site, is located in the Sierra del Aramo in northern Spain (Fig. 2), and encompasses the Saint Patrick Exploration License, known historically for its cobalt, copper, and nickel mineralization at the historical Aramo Mine. This mineralization is linked to Late-Variscan structures associated with the principal Aramo Fault [18]. The mineralization is focussed within an allochthonous unit known as the Aramo Unit, which is part of the Cantabrian Zone stratigraphy [19]. The mineralization is predominantly associated with Upper Carboniferous limestones, which are often karstified and have undergone multiple stages of hydrothermal alteration, followed by a later supergene stage [20,21]. These distinct characteristics of the alteration zones in the lithologies related to mineralization make the Aramo mine and the greater area of the licence close to the historical mine an intriguing site for developing RS technology as an exploration technique applied to cobalt mapping.

2.1   PRISMA

The PRISMA (PRecursore IperSpettrale della Missione Applicativa)[1] is a hyperspectral satellite that provides hyperspectral imagery in 250 bands with continuous spectral coverage (66 bands in the VNIR, covering 400–1010 nm and 173

---

[1] https://www.asi.it/en/earth-science/prisma/.

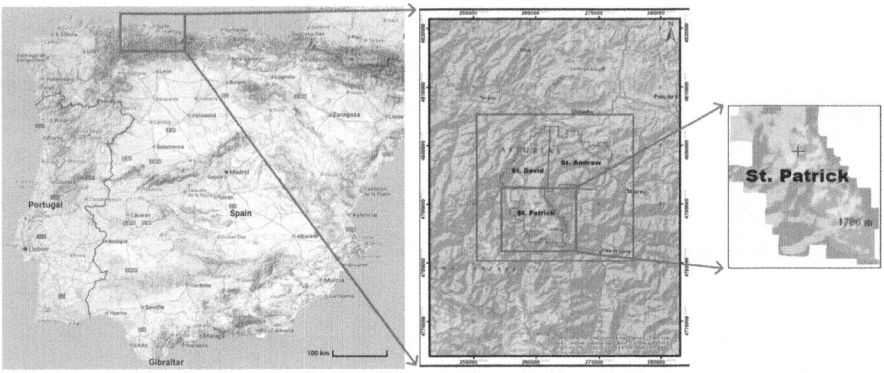

Fig. 2. Location of the Aramo pilot site for the land exploration study area which is covered by the St. Patrick Licence, central Asturias, northern Spain.

bands in the SWIR, covering 920–2505 nm). VNIR and SWIR have a spatial resolution of 30 m. In addition, a panchromatic camera is also onboard PRISMA that provides a single band (400–700 nm) image at 5 m spatial resolution. A PRISMA image of the study area with 5.1% cloud coverage was obtained on May 10, 2022 (Fig. 3). The image was provided at the L2D processing level. We resampled all bands into 5 m resolution. To reduce the dimensional of PRISM data and noise, we used Principal Component Analysis (PCA) which has been effectively applied for mineral exploration using satellite imagery [22,23]. We used PCA to compress the information contained in a given set of bands into three number of bands called principal components (PCs). Each resulting PC is influenced by contributions from all input image bands, and the PCs are ordered according to the descending percentage of variance they explain [22].

2.2 Airborne Light Detection and Ranging (LiDAR)

In this study, high-resolution airborne LiDAR data was collected by the Eurosense[2] to capture detailed topographic information of the study area. The LiDAR survey was conducted at an altitude of approximately 2,450 m above mean sea level (AMSL) and 1,450 m above ground level (AGL). To ensure comprehensive coverage, the LiDAR strips were flown with an overlap of 70–80%, minimizing gaps between flight paths and enhancing the data's spatial continuity.

The average LiDAR point density exceeded 10 points per square meter, providing fine-grained spatial resolution, with each LiDAR spot having a 36 cm diameter on the ground. This high-density data was instrumental in generating accurate Digital Terrain Models (DTM) and Digital Surface Models (DSM). Both the DTM and DSM were produced using a 0.5-m grid resolution, ensuring that the terrain and surface details were captured at a high level of accuracy. To

---

[2] https://www.eurosense.com/.

interpolate the ground elevation values between LiDAR points, Inverse Distance Weighting (IDW) interpolation [24] was applied, which assigns greater weight to points closer to the target location, thereby ensuring smooth and accurate surface modeling.

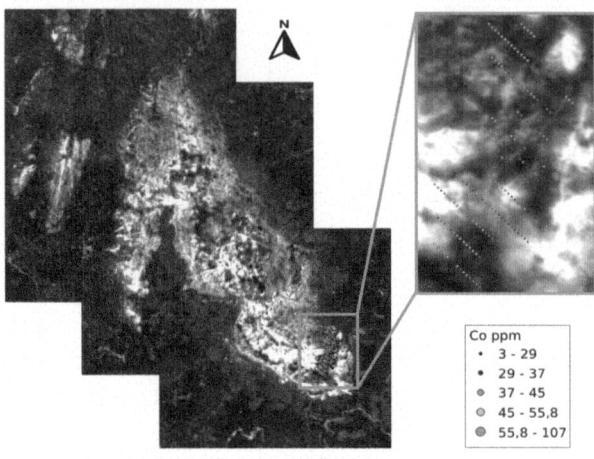

Fig. 3. Soil geochemistry exploration samples analysed for cobalt and used for PRISMA sensor data calibration on the Aramo pilot site.

2.3 Geochemical Data

The pilot study area comprising of the historical Aramo Mine (Texeo) and the surrounding Saint Patrick Exploration License, is currently being explored for copper, cobalt and nickel, by Aurum Global Exploration6, on behalf of the licence holder Asturmet Recursos S.L.

An exploration dataset of shallow soil geochemical samples collected by the company was made available for the RS study. A subset of this data comprising of 214 samples collected on a closely spaced grid over one of the prospective areas has been used in this study. The analytical results for cobalt ranged from as low as 3 parts per million (ppm) to a maximum of 107 ppm on certain parts of the grid. The mean cobalt concentration for all of the samples is 42 ppm, indicating that while the background geochemical values for cobalt are quite low the anomalous values are very significant from an exploration perspective. Figure 3 illustrates the cobalt deposits and their concentration on the PRISMA image.

3   Methodology

This study aims to enhance the performance of ML techniques for predicting Co deposits and generating an accurate MPM using a limited labeled dataset. To achieve our goal, we proposed a framework, as illustrated in Fig. 4. The main tasks in the framework are as follows:

- Dataset creation: As described in the previous section, we used three types of data: PRISMA hyperspectral, LiDAR, and geochemical data. The obtained dataset includes five features (DEM, DSM, and the first three PCs (PC1, PC2, and PC3) from PRISMA) and comprises 247 samples. It is split into training and test sets in a 70:30 ratio.
- Data augmentation: Synthetic data is generated from the training dataset using three augmentation techniques, which are described in Subsect. 3.1.
- ML modeling: Multiple regression models are applied, with cross-validation used to determine the optimal hyperparameters.
- Evaluation: Model performance is assessed on the test set using metrics such as RMSE and MAE.
- Co mapping: A predictive Co-occurrence map is generated based on the trained models, visualizing Co distribution across the study area.

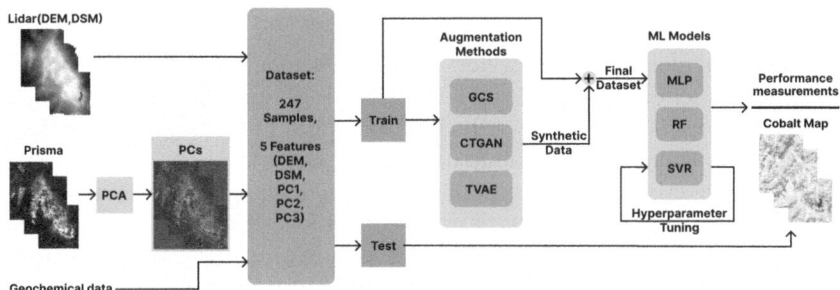

Fig. 4. Overall framework.

3.1 Data Augmentation Methods

To improve the performance of ML methods and address imbalanced data, we employed several advanced data augmentation techniques, including CTGAN, TVAE, and GCS. These methods generate synthetic data that preserve the statistical properties and dependencies of the original data, enhancing model robustness and generalization.

CTGAN [13] is a generative model designed to handle the complexities of tabular data, including mixed data types and imbalanced categorical variables. It uses a conditional generator and mode-specific normalization to accurately capture data patterns and generate high-quality synthetic data. CTGAN is computationally efficient and stable during training, outperforming other models by addressing the unique challenges of tabular data, making it ideal for applications requiring data privacy, augmentation, and reliable ML performance.

TVAE is a generative model designed for tabular data, extending the traditional Variational Autoencoder (VAE) by adapting the network structure and loss function to better capture mixed data types and complex distributions. It uses preprocessing techniques like mode-specific normalization and one-hot encoding to model joint distributions accurately. TVAE learns latent representations and reconstructs data through a decoder network, offering competitive performance in generating realistic synthetic data, particularly in scenarios requiring privacy, data augmentation, and robust handling of complex tabular datasets [13].

GCS introduced in the Synthetic Data Vault (SDV), generates synthetic data by modeling statistical properties and dependencies within a single table [14]. It standardizes columns to a normal distribution to capture covariances, ensuring realistic replication of patterns and correlations. Compared to complex models like GANs, it is computationally efficient, scalable, and easier to implement, making it ideal for scenarios requiring high-quality synthetic data with minimal computational overhead.

3.2   ML Methods

This section provides a brief overview of ML methods employed in this study. These methods include RF, SVR, and MLP. RF is an ensemble learning method that builds multiple decision trees during training and aggregates their predictions to improve accuracy and robustness.

RF [16] is effective for large, high-dimensional datasets and provides estimates of feature importance. Its design reduces overfitting by combining the predictions of multiple trees, enhancing generalization. Recent advancements focus on reducing overfitting and improving computational efficiency.

SVR [17] seeks to find a function that approximates target values within a specified tolerance margin while minimizing complexity to prevent overfitting. A key strength of SVR is its ability to balance model complexity and error tolerance, which helps in achieving good generalization on unseen data.

MLP [15] is a feedforward neural network consisting of an input layer, one or more hidden layers, and an output layer. MLPs are known for their universal approximation capability, making them versatile for tasks like regression and classification. However, they are prone to overfitting, especially with too many neurons or layers, which can be mitigated using techniques such as dropout and regularization.

The best hyper-parameters of the proposed ML models are selected by the greedy forward search algorithm. For RF, the optimal number of estimators was 50, and the maximum depth of the trees was set to 10. For SVR, the best kernel was identified as linear, and the regularization parameter c was set to 0.1. For MLP, the best configuration for the hidden layer size was 100, and the regularization term alpha was set to 0.001. We also used the 10-fold Stratified Cross Validation (SCV) [25] technique to divide the dataset into training and validation datasets during training. SCV is one of the standard methods in order to evaluate the generalization accuracy of a classifier. Compared with the standard CV, SCV ensures that each fold of a dataset has the same distribution of classes.

4   Results and Discussion

4.1   Performance vs. Number of Synthetic Data Points

Different amounts of synthetic data are systematically tested and combined with real data to enhance model robustness. The original dataset is split into training and test sets, with synthetic data generated from the training set and model performance evaluated on the test set. Figure 5 illustrates the performance metrics (MAE and RMSE) versus the number of synthetic data points for three different augmentation methods including CTGAN, GCS, and TVAE. In each case, the performance of RF, SVR, and MLP is compared. In Fig. 5 (a), which corresponds to the CTGAN augmentation method, RF and SVR exhibit consistently low values for all performance metrics across the increasing number of synthetic data points. Both models show very minimal variation, indicating robust performance regardless of dataset size. MLP, however, starts with the highest error metrics and performs significantly worse than RF and SVR. While MLP's performance does improve slightly as the dataset grows, it remains less stable compared to RF and SVR. In Fig. 5 (b), using the GCS augmentation method, RF and SVR maintain similarly low error values, with RF consistently outperforming SVR across most metrics. MLP exhibits higher error values than the other two models but shows variability, with a general downward trend as the synthetic data points increase, though it remains less stable than RF and SVR.

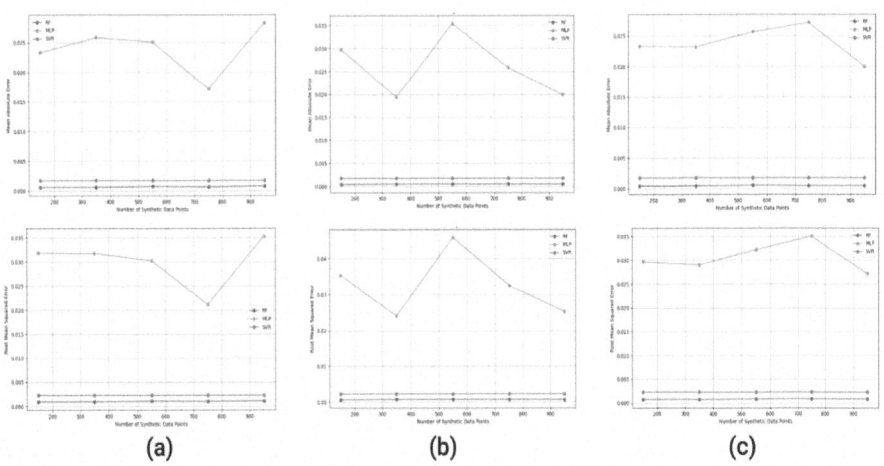

(a)   (b)   (c)

Fig. 5. MAE and RMSE vs the number of synthetic data points for three augmentation methods: (a) CTGAN, (b) GCS, and (c) TVAE.

In Fig. 5 (c), the performance of the TVAE augmentation method is shown. RF and SVR maintain consistently low error values across all metrics, with RF slightly outperforming SVR as the dataset size increases. MLP exhibits similar behavior to its performance in (a) and (b), starting with relatively high error metrics. It shows variability, with a peak in error around 700 synthetic data points, indicating some instability before improving as the dataset size further increases. In summary, across all three augmentation methods, RF is the most effective model in minimizing error metrics, demonstrating stable and low values regardless of the number of synthetic data points or the augmentation method used. In contrast, MLP struggles the most, showing higher error metrics and greater variability, particularly with small to moderate datasets.

Table 1. Performance Metrics (RMSE, MAE, R^2) for ML models across three augmentation methods.

Model	Without			CTGAN			TVAE			GCS		
	RMSE	MAE	R^2	RMSE	MAE	R^2	RMSE	MAE	R^2	RMSE	MAE	R^2
RF	0.0007	0.0004	0.9057	0.0007	0.0004	0.905	0.00067	0.0004	0.9057	0.0006	0.0003	0.9819
SVR	0.0023	0.0416	−0.0042	0.0023	0.0018	−0.0042	0.0271	0.0200	−142.837	0.0271	0.0200	−142.837
MLP	0.0523	0.0018	−533.760	0.0271	0.0200	−142.837	0.0023	0.0018	−0.0042	0.0023	0.0018	−0.0042

4.2   Performance of ML Models

Table 1 summarizes the performance metrics for each applied ML model across four conditions: Without synthetic data, and with synthetic data generated using CTGAN, TVAE, and GCS models. RF demonstrates consistently strong performance compared to the other models (SVR and MLP) across all three data augmentation techniques (CTGAN, TVAE, and GCS). The R^2 values are significantly positive, indicating that RF explains the variance well, and the errors (RMSE and MAE) are quite low. RF is the most consistent and best-performing model, especially with GCS augmentation. The R^2 values for RF are consistently positive, especially for TVAE (0.9057) and GCS (0.9819), which shows that RF can explain a significant proportion of the variance in the data. This is critical for reliable mapping in Co data where understanding patterns and relationships is key. SVR and MLP both have much higher RMSE and MAE values, and their R^2 values are negative, indicating poor fit and unreliable predictions. To compare the performance of RF without data augmentation and with the GCS method, the RMSE and MAE are improved by 17% and 33%, respectively. In addition, R^2 increased from 0.9057 to 0.9819, indicating that the model can explain almost all the variance in the data, which is a major improvement. These improvements, especially in R^2, are substantial and suggest that the GCS model significantly enhances RF's performance in this case.

4.3   Performance of Data Augmentation

We visualized (Fig. 6) the distribution data before and after data augmentation only for the best number of synthetic data in each data augmentation method where RF achieved the lowest RMSE. The number of synthetic data points is 350 by all CTGAN, TVAE and GCS, respectively. The synthetic data (turquoise) generated by CTGAN closely follows the distribution of the real data (dark blue), especially around the mean values (Fig. 6 (a)). CTGAN seems to have effectively captured the underlying distribution of the real data with 1500 synthetic points. Figure 6 (b) shows that TVAE also generates a distribution that aligns well with the real data, but there is a notable shift in the synthetic data, especially at higher Co percentages. The synthetic data distribution seems to have a slightly broader spread than the real data, and the peak in the real data distribution is somewhat sharper. The GCS method in Fig. 6 (c) generates a synthetic distribution that is generally aligned with the real data but shows noticeable deviation at the tails. Each of the data augmentation methods (CTGAN, TVAE, GCS) shows a reasonable level of alignment with the real data distribution. However, CTGAN appears to be the most effective at reproducing the distribution, particularly in the mid-range values, while GCS shows more smoothing of the real data.

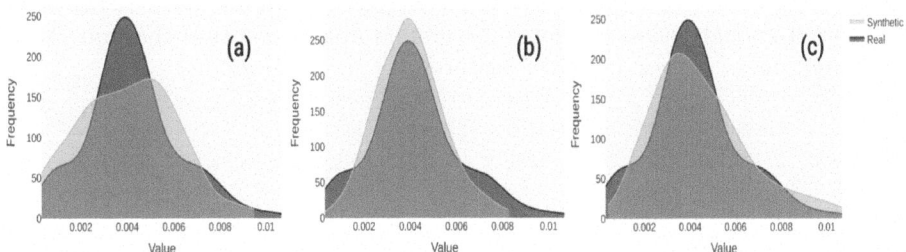

Fig. 6. Distribution of real and synthetic data where RF achieved the lowest RMSE (a) CTGAN, (b) TVAE, and (c) GCS.

In addition, the evaluation metrics used for data augmentation include the Column Shapes Score and the Column Pair Trends Score, which assess the quality of synthetic data. The Column Shapes Score measures the similarity between real and synthetic data using Kolmogorov-Smirnov (KS) Complement statistic.

The Column Pair Trends Score evaluates how well the synthetic data preserves relationships between pairs of columns, using the Pearson correlation coefficient. For a given pair of columns, such as A and B, this metric computes correlation coefficients for both the real and synthetic datasets, denoted as $R_{A,B}$ and $S_{A,B}$ respectively. The score is then calculated using the formula:

$$\text{score} = 1 - \frac{|S_{A,B} - R_{A,B}|}{2}$$

A higher score means a closer match in correlations. This evaluation is done across all column pairs to ensure that multivariate dependencies are maintained. The overall evaluation combines these two metrics, providing a comprehensive measure of how well the synthetic data replicates both individual distributions and relationships between columns.

Figure 7 shows the comparison of these models based on the scoring metric for different amounts of synthetic data. From the result, we can observe that Gaussian tends to have consistently higher scores across different synthetic sample sizes. TVAE also performs well, with scores that are often close to those of the GCS model, particularly for larger sample sizes. CTGAN has lower scores compared to the other two models but shows improvement as the number of synthetic samples increases. The fact that the GCS model is outperforming the more complex deep learning models (TVAE and CTGAN) can be explained by the following reasons:

- Deep learning models like TVAE and CTGAN might overfit the training data. This might result in poorer performance on quality metrics like the Column Shapes Score or Column Pair Trends Score. In contrast, the GCS model is less prone to overfitting because it assumes a well-known distribution and doesn't try to capture overly complex relationships.
- TVAE and CTGAN typically require a large amount of training data to perform well. If the dataset used for generating synthetic data is not large or varied enough, these models may not be able to capture the underlying distribution as well as a simpler method like the GCS model.

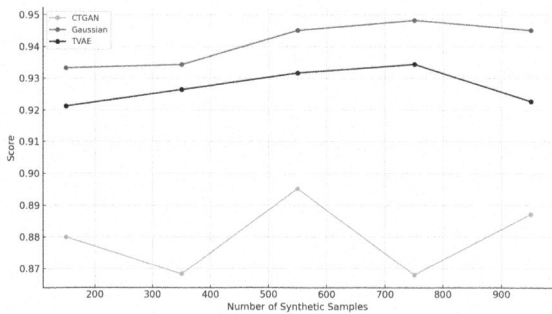

Fig. 7. Comparison of data augmentation methods.

4.4   Uni-modal vs Multi-modal

To demonstrate the ability of fusing two data sources, PRISMA hyperspectral data or LiDAR data, we evaluated RF model using each input source individually as well as in combination for Co mapping. Table 2 compares the performance of unimodal (single-source) and multimodal (dual-source) frameworks. From the results, we observe the multi-modal approach (LiDAR + PRISMA) significantly improves performance across all metrics compared to using LiDAR or PRISMA alone. This result indicates that the multi-model outperforms both uni-modal frameworks, achieving the lowest RMSE and MAE, and the highest R^2 value. The uni-modal PRISMA framework performs much better than LiDAR (uni-modal). LiDAR (uni-modal) has the worst performance, with a negative R^2, meaning it fails to explain the variance in the data.

Table 2. Performance comparison between uni-modal vs multi-modal RF frameworks.

Framework	Input Source	RMSE	MAE	R^2
Uni-modal	LiDAR	0.0024	0.0019	−0.1856
Uni-modal	PRISMA	0.0007	0.0004	0.90297
Multi-modal	LiDAR+ PRISMA	0.0006	0.0003	0.9819

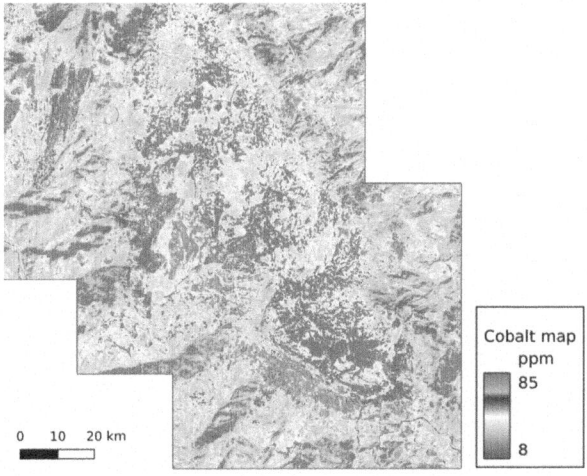

Fig. 8. Cobalt distribution map generated using the trained RF model with Lidar and PRISMA data.

4.5 Cobalt Maps

The map in Fig. 8 illustrates the spatial distribution of Co, generated using a trained RF model. The model integrates data from LiDAR and PRISMA sensors, combining them to predict Co-occurrence. The color gradients on the map represent varying concentrations of Co, with higher intensities indicating areas of greater Co presence. This map provides a detailed visualization of the predicted Co distribution across the study area, offering valuable insights for further exploration and resource management.

5   Conclusion

This study presents the application of three well-known supervised ML techniques for cobalt mapping, offering an innovative approach to mineral exploration. To address the challenge of limited labeled data, we explored the performance of three data augmentation methods: traditional and deep learning-based approaches, which generated synthetic data to enhance the performance of the ML models. Additionally, we fused data from two sources-LiDAR and PRISMA-to improve classification performance. The experimental results from the Áramo mine site in Spain demonstrate that multi-modal data fusion outperforms single-modal approaches in enhancing model performance. In conclusion, this research highlights the potential of integrating LiDAR and hyperspectral data with ML, combined with data augmentation, to improve mineral prospectivity mapping.

In future works, we plan to focus on improving the scalability of the framework by applying it to other mineral deposits and diverse geological settings to validate its generalizability. Additionally, refining the data augmentation techniques or incorporating more advanced generative models could address limitations in labeled data, particularly in regions with sparse geological sampling.

References

1. Farahnakian, F., Zelioli, L., Middleton, M., Seppä, I., Pitkänen, T.P., Heikkonen, J.: CNN-based boreal peatland fertility classification from Sentinel-1 and Sentinel-2 imagery. In: IEEE International Symposium on Robotic and Sensors Environments (ROSE), pp. 1–7. IEEE (2023)
2. Farahnakian, F., Heikkonen, J., Nevalainen, P.: Abnormal behaviour detection by using machine learning-based approaches in the marine environment: a literature survey. In: 2022 International Conference on Electrical, Computer and Energy Technologies (ICECET), pp. 1–11. IEEE (2022)
3. Shanmugapriya, P., Rathika, S., Ramesh, T., Janaki, P.: Applications of remote sensing in agriculture-a review. Int. J. Curr. Microbiol. Appl. Sci. 8(01), 2270–2283 (2019)
4. Tran, D.Q., Park, M., Jung, D., Park, S.: Damage-map estimation using UAV images and deep learning algorithms for disaster management system. Remote Sens. 12(24), 4169 (2020)
5. Brown, W.M., Gedeon, T.D., Groves, D.I., Barnes, R.G.: Artificial neural networks: a new method for mineral prospectivity mapping. Aust. J. Earth Sci. 47(4), 757–770 (2000)
6. Rodriguez-Galiano, V., Sanchez-Castillo, M., Chica-Olmo, M., Chica-Rivas, M.J.O.G.R.: Machine learning predictive models for mineral prospectivity: an evaluation of neural networks, random forest, regression trees and support vector machines. Ore Geol. Rev. 71, 804–818 (2015)

7. Abedi, M., Norouzi, G.-H., Bahroudi, A.: Support vector machine for multi-classification of mineral prospectivity areas. Comput. Geosci. **46**, 272–283 (2012)
8. Parsa, M., Maghsoudi, A.: Assessing the effects of mineral systems-derived exploration targeting criteria for random forests-based predictive mapping of mineral prospectivity in Ahar-Arasbaran area, Iran. Ore Geol. Rev. **138**, 104399 (2021)
9. Ibrahim, B., Majeed, F., Ewusi, A., Ahenkorah, I.: Residual geochemical gold grade prediction using extreme gradient boosting. Environ. Challenges **6**, 100421 (2022)
10. Cobalt mining in the EU: securing supplies and ensuring energy justice, October 2022. https://hcss.nl/report/cobalt-mining-in-the-eu-securing-supplies-and-ensuring-energy-justice/. Accessed 20 Sept 2024
11. Horn, S., et al.: Cobalt resources in Europe and the potential for new discoveries. Ore Geol. Rev. **130**, 103915 (2021)
12. Yan, Q., et al.: Mineral prospectivity mapping based on spatial feature classification with geological map knowledge graph embedding: case study of gold ore prediction at Wulonggou, Qinghai province (Western China). Nat. Resources Res., 1–22 (2024)
13. Xu, L., Skoularidou, M., Cuesta-Infante, A., Veeramachaneni, K.: Modeling tabular data using conditional GAN. In: Advances in Neural Information Processing Systems, vol. 32 (2019)
14. Patki, N., Wedge, R., Veeramachaneni, K.: The synthetic data vault. In: IEEE International Conference on Data Science and Advanced Analytics (DSAA) 2016, pp. 399–410 (2016)
15. Haykin, S.: Neural Networks and Learning Machines, Prentice Hall (2009)
16. Genuer, R., Poggi, J.-M., Tuleau, C.: Random forests: some methodological insights (2008)
17. Drucker, H., Burges, C.J.C., Kaufman, L., Smola, A.J., Vapnik, V.: Support vector regression machines. In: Advances in Neural Information Processing Systems, vol. 9 (1997)
18. Paniagua, A., Loredo, J., Garcia Iglesias, J.: Epithermal (Cu-Co-Ni) mineralization in the Aramo mine (Cantabrian Mountains, Spain): correlation between paragenetic and fluid inclusion data. Bulletin de Minéralogie **111**(3), 383–391 (1988)
19. Aller, J.: La estructura geológica de la sierra del aramo (zona cantábrica, no de españa). Trabajos De Geología **19**(19), 3–15 (1983)
20. Álvarez, R., Ordóñez, A., Pérez, A., De Miguel, E., Charlesworth, S.: Mineralogical and environmental features of the Asturian copper mining district (Spain): a review. Eng. Geol. **243**, 206–217 (2018)
21. Archibald, S.M.: Technical report on the LRH Resources Limited, Asturmet Cu-Co-Ni project, Asturias, NW Spain. Technical report, LRH Resources Limited (2021)
22. Carvalho, M., Azzalini, A., Cardoso-Fernandes, J., Santos, P., Lima, A., Teodoro, A.C.: Multi-sensor approach for cobalt exploration in Asturias (Spain) using machine learning algorithms. In: IGARSS 2024 - 2024 IEEE International Geoscience and Remote Sensing Symposium, pp. 2122–2126, July 2024
23. Adiri, Z., Lhissou, R., El Harti, A., Jellouli, A., Chakouri, M.: Recent advances in the use of public domain satellite imagery for mineral exploration: a review of Landsat-8 and Sentinel-2 applications. Ore Geol. Rev. **117**, 103332 (2020)
24. Shepard, D.S.: A two-dimensional interpolation function for irregularly-spaced data. In: Proceedings of the 1968 23rd ACM National Conference (1968)
25. Zeng, X., Martinez, T.R.: Distribution-balanced stratified cross-validation for accuracy estimation. J. Exp. Theor. Artif. Intell. **12**(1), 1–12 (2000)

Adapting SAM 2 for Visual Object Tracking: 1st Place Solution for MMVPR Challenge Multi-modal Tracking

Cheng-Yen Yang[1]([✉]), Hsiang-Wei Huang[1], Pyong-Kun Kim[2], Chien-Kai Kuo[1], Jui-Wei Chang[1], Kwang-Ju Kim[2], Chung-I Huang[3], and Jenq-Neng Hwang[1]

[1] University of Washington, Seattle, WA, USA
cycyang@uw.edu
[2] Electronics and Telecommunications Research Institute, Daejeon, South Korea
[3] National Center for High-performance Computing, Hsinchu, Taiwan

Abstract. We present an effective approach for adapting the Segment Anything Model 2 (SAM2) to the Visual Object Tracking (VOT) task. Our method leverages the powerful pre-trained capabilities of SAM2 and incorporates several key techniques to enhance its performance in VOT applications. By combining SAM2 with our proposed optimizations, we achieved a first place AUC score of 89.4 on the 2024 ICPR Multi-modal Object Tracking challenge, demonstrating the effectiveness of our approach. This paper details our methodology, the specific enhancements made to SAM2, and a comprehensive analysis of our results in the context of VOT solutions along with the multi-modality aspect of the dataset.

Keywords: Visual Object Tracking · Multi-modal Object Tracking · Segment Anything Model

1 Introduction

Visual Object Tracking (VOT) is a core problem in computer vision, where the objective is to detect and continuously track the position of a target object in a sequence of video frames. Despite notable advancements in the field, VOT still faces significant challenges due to various factors such as occlusion, where the object becomes temporarily hidden from view; motion blur, caused by rapid movement of the object or camera; and target deformation, where the object changes shape, size, or appearance over time. These factors make maintaining robust and accurate tracking throughout the video sequence highly difficult.

Traditional tracking approaches, such as discriminative correlation filters (DCF) and Siamese networks, have contributed to significant progress in the field. However, these methods often fail in handling complex scenarios like long-term occlusion or severe target appearance changes. To address these issues,

---

C.-Y. Yang, H.-W. Huang and P.-K. Kim—These authors are the core members of the challenge team: uwipl and consider equal contribution to the work.

S. Palaiahnakote et al. (Eds.): ICPR 2024 Workshops, LNCS 15617, pp. 256–266, 2025.
https://doi.org/10.1007/978-3-031-88217-3_18

hybrid methods that combine tracking and segmentation, such as SiamMask [3], have been introduced. These approaches refine the object's boundaries frame by frame but still suffer from inconsistencies when objects reappear after occlusion or undergo dramatic appearance shifts.

Recent developments in segmentation models, particularly the Segment Anything Model 2 (SAM2) [11], have opened new possibilities for enhancing the robustness and efficiency of VOT systems. SAM2, developed by Meta AI, builds upon its predecessor by incorporating real-time video segmentation capabilities, memory modules for tracking, and the ability to handle occlusions and appearance variations with minimal user input. This makes SAM2 a strong candidate for addressing some of the most pressing challenges in VOT.

In this report, we explore the adaptation of SAM2 for the VOT task, leveraging its superior segmentation capabilities to handle complex tracking scenarios. SAM2's ability to consistently track objects even in occluded or fast-moving scenes makes it highly suitable for VOT. However, the basic segmentation functionality of SAM2 is not sufficient for optimal performance in real-world tracking applications, which often involve variable conditions and dynamic environments. Therefore, we introduce a series of novel techniques specifically designed to enhance SAM2's performance in VOT.

The proposed tricks include backward tracking and tracklet interpolation. Specifically, our approach achieved an AUC score of 89.4 on the 2024 ICPR Multi-modal Object Tracking Challenge, earning first place among the participants. This demonstrates the potential of advanced segmentation models like SAM2, combined with task-specific adjustments, to push the boundaries of VOT performance.

2   Related Work

2.1   Visual Object Tracking

Visual Object Tracking (VOT) is a long-standing challenge in computer vision, where the goal is to detect and follow a target object in consecutive video frames. Traditional tracking algorithms include discriminative correlation filters (DCF) and tracking-by-detection approaches. DCF methods, such as KCF (Kernelized Correlation Filters) and ECO (Efficient Convolution Operators), excel in tracking by applying correlation between frames. However, these approaches are often vulnerable to occlusion, scale variation, and deformation. In contrast, learning-based models, particularly those utilizing convolutional neural networks (CNNs), have significantly advanced VOT performance. Models like SiamFC [1] and SiamRPN [9] introduced the use of Siamese networks, where a template image of the target is matched with candidate regions in the search frame. While these methods have improved robustness, they still struggle when significant appearance changes occur or when objects leave and re-enter the scene. And other post-processing methods leveraging appearance [5,12,17], motion [4], or meta-data [16] are required to enhance the tracking performance.

To tackle these challenges, hybrid method such as SAMURAI [15], SiamMask [3] combined tracking with segmentation. These approaches refined the tracked object's boundaries frame-by-frame but still faced issues in handling complex backgrounds and long-term tracking.

Recent advancements in transformer-based architectures have further improved tracking. Methods like TransT [2] and STARK [14] integrate attention mechanisms to capture long-range dependencies in video sequences, enhancing robustness against occlusion and appearance variation. However, these methods are computationally expensive and may struggle in real-time applications.

2.2 Multi-modal Tracking

Multi-modal tracking involves leveraging data from multiple sensor modalities, such as RGB, thermal, or depth cameras, to enhance object tracking in challenging environments. Traditional object tracking systems often rely solely on RGB data, which can struggle under poor lighting conditions, heavy occlusion, or when the object's appearance changes significantly. Multi-modal systems aim to overcome these limitations by fusing complementary information from different sensors, thereby improving robustness and accuracy.

In recent years, various approaches have emerged for multi-modal visual object tracking. Many of these methods utilize deep learning architectures that incorporate cross-modal fusion, where the features extracted from different modalities are combined. For example, CRAFT [8] proposed the fusion of radar and camera to boost the tracking performance. DiMP [18] introduced an end-to-end framework that achieves strong performance in RGB-T tracking, while ViPT [19] proposed a multi-modal object tracking framework that achieves decent performance across multiple multi-modal tracking tasks.

Multi-modal tracking has become increasingly important in real-world applications, such as autonomous driving, surveillance, and medical imaging. For instance, in autonomous vehicles, integrating data from LiDAR, RGB cameras, and radar helps maintain accurate tracking even in adverse weather conditions, where certain sensors may become unreliable.

In the context of the 2024 ICPR Multi-modal Object Tracking challenge, the dataset features RGB, depth and infrared imagery, pushing participants to develop techniques that can intelligently fuse these data streams. Models that effectively combine information from both modalities have shown superior performance, especially in scenarios involving low-light environments or occluded objects.

2.3 SAM2

The Segment Anything Model 2 [11] is an evolution of the original SAM model, designed for both image and video segmentation. SAM2 builds on the concept of Promptable Visual Segmentation, allowing the user to interactively guide the segmentation process with simple clicks or bounding boxes. This makes SAM2 highly versatile, capable of segmenting a wide variety of objects across different scenarios.

Compared to its predecessor, SAM2 introduces several key innovations that improve its performance in video segmentation, particularly in tracking applications. It integrates a memory module that enables it to track objects consistently across frames, even when objects are temporarily occluded or undergo significant appearance changes.

Additionally, SAM2's ability to work on diverse video datasets, such as DAVIS [10] and YouTubeVOS [13], makes it well-suited for the VOT task. This capability is enhanced by training on the SA-V dataset [7], which contains over 50,000 videos and millions of frames, providing a rich set of object appearances and transformations.

By integrating SAM2 into the VOT pipeline and introducing task-specific modifications, this work demonstrates the potential for SAM2 to push the boundaries of performance in multi-modal tracking environments (Fig. 1).

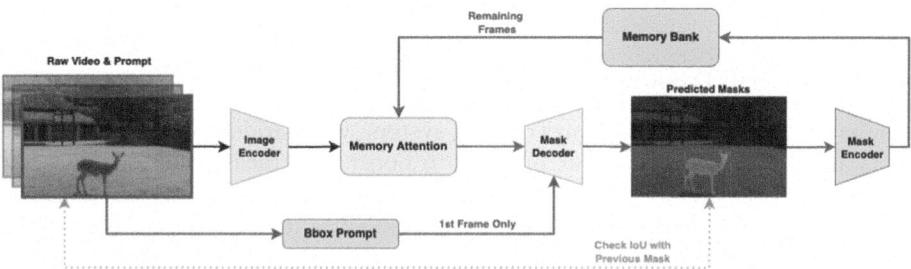

Fig. 1. An example illustration of adapting SAM2 [11] on VOT task. This pipeline leverages SAM2's powerful segmentation capabilities by using an initial bounding box prompt on the first frame, then utilizes its memory bank feature to propagate and refine object masks through subsequent video frames, enabling efficient and accurate object tracking.

3   Method

3.1   SAM2 for Visual Object Tracking

In this work, we adapt the Segment Anything Model 2 (SAM2), originally designed for image and video segmentation tasks, to perform Visual Object Tracking (VOT). SAM2's ability to generate high-quality object masks provides a strong foundation for accurate and robust object tracking. By leveraging its advanced segmentation capabilities, we can consistently detect and localize target objects across a sequence of video frames, even in complex scenarios such as occlusion or rapid movement.

To adapt SAM2 for VOT, we utilize its video object segmentation (VOS) capabilities to segment the target object in each frame. Specifically, SAM2 outputs a segmentation mask that delineates the object of interest. However, VOT traditionally operates with bounding boxes, not segmentation masks. To address this, we extract the bounding box from the segmentation mask by calculating the minimum and maximum coordinates of the mask in each frame.

This approach efficiently translates the pixel-level precision of SAM2's segmentation masks into the bounding box format typically used in VOT benchmarks, allowing us to achieve high tracking accuracy while maintaining computational efficiency. Through this method, SAM2's strong segmentation performance is directly leveraged for visual object tracking, making it suitable for a variety of real-world applications.

In addition, the bounding box extraction technique ensures that we can apply SAM2 seamlessly to existing VOT pipelines, without requiring significant modifications to handle segmentation outputs. This combination of segmentation precision and tracking flexibility underpins our approach's success in achieving state-of-the-art performance on multi-modal visual object tracking benchmarks.

3.2   Backward Tracking

To enhance the robustness of our tracking system, we introduce Backward Tracking as an additional step in our pipeline to boost the tracking performance for those sequence with poor tracking results. This method involves running the tracking process in reverse after completing the initial forward pass through the video sequence. The rationale behind this approach is that running SAM2 with the final bounding box from the last frame and processing the video in reverse allows the model to leverage different memory states and object features, which may lead to better tracking results in certain challenging frames. The process works as follows:

1. Forward Tracking: Initially, we run SAM2 in the normal forward direction on the video, producing a sequence of bounding boxes based on the object's location in each frame.
2. Backward Initialization: After obtaining the forward tracking results, we take the last bounding box from the forward pass as the initial object state for the backward pass. This bounding box is used to reinitialize the tracker in reverse.
3. Backward Tracking Process: We re-run SAM2, but this time we traverse the video frames backward, from the last frame to the first. Since SAM2 operates with a memory module that influences its understanding of the object's position and appearance over time, running the tracker in reverse allows it to have a chance to retrieve missed detections, recover from errors, and achieve improved tracking in certain sequences where the forward pass struggled (e.g., due to occlusion, motion blur, or changes in object appearance).

3.3   Tracklet Interpolation

In our adaptation of SAM2 for visual object tracking, we treat each frame as a new instance of object detection. SAM2 identifies the best mask by selecting the prediction with the maximum Intersection over Union (IoU) out of N_{max} predictions for the subsequent frame $t+1$ with the current frame t. However, this approach can lead to certain challenges in tracking consistency. Most objects in the dataset exhibit limited deformation and maintain relatively stable bounding box ratios and sizes, given the frame rate and annotation characteristics of the data. Despite this, the frame-by-frame predictions from SAM2 can sometimes result in jittery or inconsistent segmentations, particularly in cases of occlusion or camera movement.

Interestingly, SAM2's memory attention mechanism allows it to successfully track objects with similar appearances across extended sequences of frames. Leveraging this capability, we have developed a post-processing interpolation method to refine these findings and improve tracking stability.

Our tracklet interpolation method operates on the initial results from SAM2. Let's denote the first pass of SAM2 results as $B = \{b_1, b_2, ..., b_n\}$, where $b_i = (x_i, y_i, w_i, h_i)$ represents the bounding box for frame i, with x_i, y_i as the top-left coordinates and w_i, h_i as the width and height respectively.

We calculate the percentage change in the bounding box ratio between consecutive frames:

$$\Delta r_i = \left| \frac{(w_i/h_i) - (w_{i-1}/h_{i-1})}{w_{i-1}/h_{i-1}} \right| \times 100\% \tag{1}$$

Next, we compute the mean ratio as a thresholding value t:

$$t = \frac{1}{n-1} \sum_{i=2}^{n} \Delta r_i. \tag{2}$$

We identify sections where the bounding box ratios exhibit extreme changes and label them as "frames to interpolate". These are frames where $\Delta r_i > \alpha t$, where α is a tunable parameter. For each section of frames to interpolate, we use the nearest unaffected frames (frames where $\Delta r_i \leq \alpha t$) as anchor points. Let's denote these anchor frames as b_a and b_b. We then interpolate the bounding boxes for frames i where $a < i < b$ using:

$$b_i' = b_a + \frac{i-a}{b-a}(b_b - b_a) \tag{3}$$

This process can be repeated multiple times until convergence or until a satisfactory level of smoothness is achieved. The convergence criterion can be defined as:

$$\max_{i=2}^{n} \Delta r_i < \beta t \tag{4}$$

where β is another tunable parameter (typically set slightly higher than α). This approach allows us to progressively smooth out extreme variations in the bounding box ratios while preserving the overall trajectory of the tracked object (Fig. 2).

Fig. 2. Sample of the multi-modal videos from the testing sequence.

4 Experiments

4.1 Dataset

For our experiments, we utilized the track1 visual object tracking dataset provided by the 2024 ICPR Multi-Modal Visual Pattern Recognition Workshop. This dataset is specifically designed to tackle the challenges of tracking objects across different modalities, including RGB, infrared thermal, depth, and event data. It consists of 500 multi-modal videos, which are divided into 400 videos for training and 100 videos for testing.

It's important to note that although the challenge description mentions 400 videos in the training set, the actual data provided consists of 10 images each along with the annotations for the three modalities (RGB, infrared thermal, and depth). These 10 images appear to be selected randomly from the original videos, which are not provided to the participants. For the testing set, the length of the sequences varies from 100 to 600 frames. Each test sequence is provided with the ground-truth bounding box for the very first frame, which serves as the initial target location for tracking algorithms (Fig. 3).

4.2 Metrics

We utilized the Area Under the Curve (AUC) as our primary evaluation metric. The AUC is calculated based on the success rates at various thresholds of bounding box IoU between groundtruth box and predict box. This metric provides a comprehensive measure of tracking performance across different scenarios.

Fig. 3. Visualization of our tracking results on the ICPR multi-modal tracking dataset. We selected three different tracking cases with different level of difficulties, caused by the moving speed of object, occlusion, and distractor in the environment.

We calculate the overlap rate between the predicted bounding box (P_t) and the ground truth bounding box (G_t) in frame t:

$$R_t = \frac{|P_t \cap G_t|}{|P_t \cup G_t|} \tag{5}$$

When the target is visible, R_t measures the IoU value. If the target is out of view or occluded (G_t is empty), R_t is set to 0. We then compute success rates at different thresholds θ_i:

$$SR(\theta_i) = \frac{1}{N} \sum_{t=1}^{N} u_t(\theta_i) \tag{6}$$

where $u_t(\theta_i)$ is 1 if $R_t > \theta_i$, and 0 otherwise. Finally, we calculate the AUC by averaging the success rates across all thresholds (Table 1):

$$AUC = \frac{1}{n} \sum_{i=1}^{n} SR(\theta_i) \tag{7}$$

This comprehensive evaluation approach allows us to assess the overall performance of our tracking method across various scenarios and difficulty levels. For the challenge, the AUC is setting the $\theta_i \in \{0, 0.05, 0.10, ..., 1.0\}$, providing a fine-grained analysis of the tracking performance across a wide range of overlap thresholds.

Table 1. Leaderboard of Track 1 in the Multi-Modal Visual Pattern Recognition 2024: Multi-Modal Tracking. Our method obtained an AUC score of 89.4, ranking in the first-place.

Ranking	Team Name	AUC score (%)
1	UWIPL_ETRI (ours)	89.4
2	xxxxl	86.9
3	Weidlnu	86.8
4	Peace	86.8
5	ylh	85.9
6	hubulai	83.1
7	xxxxxjjjjjxxxx	81.1
8	yyy	78.5
9	xuanwang	77.8
10	huxiantao	75.9
Baseline	ViPT [6]	74.1

Table 2. The performance of using SAM2 with different input modality on the 2024 ICPR multi-modal tracking dataset.

Modality	Model	AUC score (%)
Depth	SAM2-l	19.8
Infrared	SAM2-l	56.5
RGB	SAM2-l	88.6

4.3 Performance

We tested different input modalities with SAM2 on the 2024 ICPR multi-modal tracking dataset. Including RGB image, infrared and depth. Among all the modalities, RGB achieve the highest performance. Results are shown in Table 2. Incorporating SAM2 and our tricks resulted in 89.4 AUC score on the 2024 ICPR multi-modal tracking dataset, ranking 1st place among all the participants.

5   Conclusion

In this paper, we presented an adaptation of the Segment Anything Model 2 for visual object tracking. By leveraging SAM2's advanced segmentation capabilities and integrating task-specific enhancements such as bounding box extraction, backward tracking, and tracklet interpolation. SAM2's inherent strength in maintaining object focus, even in challenging conditions like occlusion or motion blur, allowed us to achieve superior results on the 2024 ICPR Multi-modal Tracking challenge, securing first place with an AUC score of 89.4%.

Acknowledgement. This work was supported by Electronics and Telecommunications Research Institute (ETRI) grant funded by the Korean government: 24ZD1120, Regional Industry ICT Convergence Technology Advancement and Support Project in Daegu-GyeongBuk (AI).

References

1. Bertinetto, L., Valmadre, J., Henriques, J.F., Vedaldi, A., Torr, P.: Fully-Convolutional Siamese Networks for Object Tracking. In: Hua, G., Jégou, H. (eds.) ECCV 2016. LNCS, vol. 9914, pp. 850–865. Springer, Cham (2016). https://doi.org/10.1007/978-3-319-48881-3_56
2. Chen, X., Yan, B., Zhu, J., Wang, D., Yang, X., Lu, H.: Transformer tracking. In: Proceedings of the IEEE/CVF Conference on Computer Vision and Pattern Recognition, pp. 8126–8135 (2021)
3. Hu, W., Wang, Q., Zhang, L., Bertinetto, L., Torr, P.H.: Siammask: a framework for fast online object tracking and segmentation. IEEE Trans. Pattern Anal. Mach. Intell. 45(3), 3072–3089 (2023)
4. Huang, H.W., Yang, C.Y., Chai, W., Jiang, Z., Hwang, J.N.: Exploring learning-based motion models in multi-object tracking. arXiv preprint arXiv:2403.10826 (2024)
5. Huang, H.W., et al.: Enhancing multi-camera people tracking with anchor-guided clustering and spatio-temporal consistency id re-assignment. In: Proceedings of the IEEE/CVF Conference on Computer Vision and Pattern Recognition, pp. 5239–5249 (2023)
6. Jiawen, Z., Simiao, l., Xin, C., Wang, D., Lu, H.: Visual prompt multi-modal tracking. In: CVPR (2023)
7. Kirillov, A., et al.: Segment anything. In: Proceedings of the IEEE/CVF International Conference on Computer Vision, pp. 4015–4026 (2023)
8. Kuan, S.Y., et al.: Boosting online 3d multi-object tracking through camera-radar cross check. In: 2024 IEEE Intelligent Vehicles Symposium (IV), pp. 2125–2132. IEEE (2024)
9. Li, B., Yan, J., Wu, W., Zhu, Z., Hu, X.: High performance visual tracking with SIAMESE region proposal network. In: Proceedings of the IEEE Conference on Computer Vision and Pattern Recognition, pp. 8971–8980 (2018)
10. Perazzi, F., Pont-Tuset, J., McWilliams, B., Van Gool, L., Gross, M., Sorkine-Hornung, A.: A benchmark dataset and evaluation methodology for video object segmentation. In: Proceedings of the IEEE Conference on Computer Vision and Pattern Recognition, pp. 724–732 (2016)
11. Ravi, N., et al.: Sam 2: segment anything in images and videos. arXiv preprint arXiv:2408.00714 (2024)
12. Sun, J., Huang, H.W., Yang, C.Y., Jiang, Z., Hwang, J.N.: GTA: global tracklet association for multi-object tracking in sports. In: Proceedings of the Asian Conference on Computer Vision, pp. 421–434 (2024)
13. Xu, N., et al.: Youtube-VOS: a large-scale video object segmentation benchmark. arXiv preprint arXiv:1809.03327 (2018)
14. Yan, B., Peng, H., Fu, J., Wang, D., Lu, H.: Learning spatio-temporal transformer for visual tracking. In: Proceedings of the IEEE/CVF International Conference on Computer Vision, pp. 10448–10457 (2021)

15. Yang, C.Y., Huang, H.W., Chai, W., Jiang, Z., Hwang, J.N.: Samurai: adapting segment anything model for zero-shot visual tracking with motion-aware memory. arXiv preprint arXiv:2411.11922 (2024)
16. Yang, C.Y., et al.: Sea you later: metadata-guided long-term re-identification for UAV-based multi-object tracking. In: Proceedings of the IEEE/CVF Winter Conference on Applications of Computer Vision, pp. 805–812 (2024)
17. Yang, C.Y., et al.: An online approach and evaluation method for tracking people across cameras in extremely long video sequence. In: Proceedings of the IEEE/CVF Conference on Computer Vision and Pattern Recognition, pp. 7037–7045 (2024)
18. Zhang, L., Danelljan, M., Gonzalez-Garcia, A., Van De Weijer, J., Shahbaz Khan, F.: Multi-modal fusion for end-to-end RGB-T tracking. In: Proceedings of the IEEE/CVF International Conference on Computer Vision Workshops (2019)
19. Zhu, J., Lai, S., Chen, X., Wang, D., Lu, H.: Visual prompt multi-modal tracking. In: Proceedings of the IEEE/CVF Conference on Computer Vision and Pattern Recognition (CVPR), pp. 9516–9526 (2023)

Tracking Model gdi-SAM2 for RGB, Depth, and Infrared Data

Xinglin Xie[✉], Kehuan Song, and Kefan Chen

Xidian University, Xi'an, China
663136057@qq.com
http://github.com

Abstract. In the ICPR 2024 Multi-Modal Visual Pattern Recognition Challenge-Track 1 (Tracking), we proposed a multi-modal tracking method gdi-SAM2, based on the SAM2 algorithm, which significantly improves the accuracy and robustness of target tracking by fusing RGB, depth, and infrared data. Our method first converts the bounding box (bbox) annotations in the fused dataset into pixel-level mask images, then inputs these mask images into the SAM2 tracking model. The tracking results are outputted in the form of mask images, which are then converted back to bbox for performance evaluation. Our solution achieved second place in the competition with an AUC of 0.869, demonstrating the potential of multi-modal tracking technology in handling complex scenarios.

Keywords: Multi-modal Tracking · RGB-D Data Fusion · Object Tracking

1 Introduction

Visual object tracking is one of the most fundamental problems in computer vision, aimed at estimating the trajectory of objects in videos. It has been successfully applied in numerous applications such as intelligent traffic control, artificial intelligence, and autonomous driving [1]. Despite significant achievements in the research of visual object tracking, there are still many challenges in effectively tracking targets in practical applications [2–6]. For instance, tracking objects remains quite difficult under conditions such as frequent occlusions, appearance changes, complex object motion, and lighting variations [7]. The main drawback of tracking methods that use only RGB data [8, 9] is their lack of robustness to appearance changes, and they are still prone to failure in complex and corner scenarios, such as extreme lighting, background clutter, and motion blur [10–13].

Therefore, multimodal tracking is gaining more attention as it can provide complementary information between different modalities, helping trackers deal with challenging situations that cannot be resolved through RGB input alone. The multimodal tracking in this paper focuses on the fusion of RGB, depth, and infrared data. RGB data captures color and texture information, depth data provides the geometric layout of the scene, and infrared data performs well under poor lighting conditions [14]. By leveraging the combined advantages of RGB images, depth maps, and infrared data to

S. Palaiahnakote et al. (Eds.): ICPR 2024 Workshops, LNCS 15617, pp. 267–273, 2025.
https://doi.org/10.1007/978-3-031-88217-3_19

advance the field of tracking, addressing key challenges such as feature heterogeneity, data alignment, and fusion is crucial for achieving robust and accurate tracking in complex environments [15]. This approach can provide a more comprehensive understanding of dynamic scenes, thereby improving tracking performance where a single mode may be insufficient.

The dataset provided for this challenge includes 500 multimodal videos, with 400 for training and 100 for testing. The main challenges include effectively fusing different modalities and ensuring precise tracking under various conditions. We track the data of RGB, depth, and infrared modalities by improving the SAM2 algorithm and achieve multimodal data fusion.

2 Method

Under the framework of multi-modal tracking, feature extraction is the cornerstone of the entire process, involving the extraction of key information from RGB, depth, and infrared data [16]. The fused features are used for tracking prediction, which is implemented through our tracking model SAM2, leveraging this rich information to predict the position and movement of the target object in the video sequence [17–19]. This process not only improves the accuracy of tracking but also enables the tracking system to maintain stable and reliable performance in variable environments [20].

2.1 Multi-modal Fusion

Multi-modal tracking provides a more comprehensive understanding of dynamic scenes by combining RGB images, depth maps, and infrared data, thereby achieving more accurate tracking in complex environments [21]. This approach allows us to utilize the complementary information provided by each modality [22], as each provides unique visual cues: RGB data captures color and texture information, depth data offers geometric layout of the scene, and infrared data performs well in poor lighting conditions. These features are then sent to the feature fusion stage, the purpose of which is to integrate data from different modalities to take advantage of their complementary information [23, 24].

We explored the use of Modality-complementary prompter (MCP), which can generate effective visual prompts for task-oriented multimodal tracking. This method simplifies auxiliary modality input into a few prompts instead of designing an additional network branch, thereby achieving more efficient feature fusion and information representation.

In experiments, our method's comparison on the RGBT234 and LasHeR datasets shows superiority over state-of-the-art methods in terms of accuracy and success rate. This proves that our dual-stream tracking framework with bidirectional Adapters successfully tracked most targets in complex environments and adaptively extracted effective information from dynamically changing dominant-auxiliary modalities, achieving state-of-the-art performance (Table 1).

Table 1. .

Deep Features	AUC
Only RGB	0.809
RGB + Depth	0.842
RGB + infrared	0.801
Depth + infrared	0.768
RGB + Depth + infrared	**0.869**

2.2   Video Tracking

When working on this task, our team used a total of three methods: the first was the baseline provided by the competition officials, as well as the Cutie model and the SAM2 model.

The Cutie model introduced an object query mechanism, using an object transformer to facilitate bidirectional interaction between object-level memory and pixel-level features. This mechanism enables the capture of higher-level semantic information in video object segmentation, enhancing performance in complex scenes. To better distinguish between foreground objects and the background, Cutie employed an extended mask attention mechanism. Some object queries focus only on the foreground, while others concentrate on the background, achieving cleaner semantic separation. This mechanism helps to enhance the model's robustness in the presence of distractions. In addition to pixel memory, Cutie also introduced object memory, which serves as a high-level feature summary of the target object. This memory information is re-read during segmentation, further improving the expression of specific features of the target object. The Cutie model ensures interaction between high-resolution features and object-level features through bidirectional top-down and bottom-up information transfer, thereby enhancing segmentation accuracy.

SAM2 is a natural extension of the Segment Anything Model, suitable for segmentation tasks in images and videos. It specifically targets spatiotemporal segmentation in videos, capable of handling the continuity of video frames and the complex changes in object motion. By introducing Promptable Visual Segmentation (PVS), SAM2 can input prompts in the form of clicks, boxes, or masks, and then generate segmentation masks for target objects throughout the entire video. SAM2 uses a memory-based architecture that maintains object memory across frames when processing videos. The model adjusts and corrects segmentation results on subsequent frames through a memory attention mechanism, achieving accurate object tracking in videos. SAM2 uses an interactive data engine to collect and process video segmentation data, ultimately building the world's largest Segment Anything Video (SA-V) dataset. This dataset contains over 50,000 videos and millions of segmentation masks, making it one of the largest datasets for similar tasks. The data engine allows for model performance improvement through user interaction, ensuring that the model can be applied to different types of objects without category restrictions. SAM2 achieves higher segmentation accuracy than its predecessor, with a threefold reduction in interaction and a sixfold increase in speed. This efficient stream-ing processing capability ensures real-time video object segmentation and outstanding performance in various benchmark tests. Additionally, SAM2 demonstrates stronger robustness and precision in addressing segmentation issues in low-quality videos and complex environments.

Processing the fused data first involves converting annotations from bbox to png image representations of masks. The converted mask images are input into the SAM2 tracking model. The tracking results are outputted in the form of png images, which include the masks of the target objects. To evaluate tracking performance, we need to convert these mask images back to bbox form (Fig. 1).

Fig. 1. The execution process of SAM2.

3   Experimental Results

We compared our results with other state-of-the-art tracking algorithms and found that our multi-modal method outperforms single-modal systems. The fusion of RGB, depth, and infrared data significantly improves tracking accuracy and robustness, especially in challenging situations such as low light or occlusion. In the Multi-Modal Visual Pattern Recognition Challenge-Track 1: Tracking, we achieved second place with an AUC of 0.869 (Table 2).

Figure 2 displays the visualization results of our gdi-SAM2 model, indicating that our model has a high level of accuracy.

Our work in the multi-modal tracking challenge demonstrates that the fusion of RGB, depth, and infrared data can significantly enhance target tracking performance. Our SAM2 solution, integrating advanced feature extraction and multi-modal data fusion, achieved second place in the competition. This result highlights the potential of multi-modal tracking technology in addressing complex real-world scenarios.

Table 2. Our method achieved second place in the Multi-Modal Visual Pattern Recognition Challenge-Track 1.

User	AUC
uwipl	0.894 (1)
ours	**0.869 (2)**
Weidlnu	0.868 (3)
Peace	0.868 (3)
ylh	0.859 (4)
hubulai	0.831 (5)
xxxxxjjjjjxxxx	0.811 (6)
yyy_	0.785 (7)
xuanwang	0.778 (8)
huxiantao	0.759 (9)
oracle_su	0.745 (10)
hi_1	0.745 (10)
zzr678	0.742 (11)
grindelwald	0.741 (12)
MMVPR_BASELINE	0.741 (12)
xionggeng	0.738 (13)
zzzyt	0.737 (14)

Fig. 2. Examples of visualization results.

References

1. Ravi, N., Gabeur, V., Hu, Y.-T., Hu, R., Ryali, C., et al.: SAM 2: segment anything in images and videos. In: CVPR (2024)
2. Zhu, J., Lai, S., Chen, X., Wang, D., Lu, H.: Visual prompt multi-modal tracking. In: CVPR (2023)
3. Bahng, H., Jahanian, A., Sankaranarayanan, S., Isola, P.: Exploring visual prompts for adapting largescale models. arXiv preprint arXiv:2203.17274 **1**(3), 4 (2022)
4. Jia, M., et al.: Visual prompt tuning. In: ECCV (2022)
5. Chen, K., Tao, W., Han, S.: Visual object tracking via enhanced structural correlation filter. Inf. Sci. **394–395**, 232–245 (2017)
6. Jiang, M., Wang, D., Qiu, T.: Multi-person detecting and tracking based on RGB-D sensor for a robot vision system. Int. J. Embedded Syst. **9**(1), 54–60 (2017)
7. Song, S., Xiao, J.: Tracking revisited using RGBD camera: unified benchmark and baselines. In: Proceedings of the 2013 IEEE International Conference on Computer Vision (ICCV), Sydney, Australia, December 2013, pp. 233–240 (2013)
8. An, N., Zhao, X.-G., Hou, Z.-G.: Online RGB-D tracking via detection-learning-segmentation. In: Proceedings of the 23rd International Conference on Pattern Recognition, ICPR 2016, Mexico, December 2016, pp. 1231–1236 (2016)
9. Michel, D., Qammaz, A., Argyros, A.A.: Markerless 3D human pose estimation and tracking based on RGBD cameras: an experimental evaluation. In: Proceedings of the 10th ACM International Conference on PErvasive Technologies Related to Assistive Environments, PETRA 2017, Greece, June 2017, pp. 115–122 (2017)
10. Wang, A., Cai, J., Lu, J., Cham, T.-J.: Modality and component aware feature fusion for RGB-D scene classification. In: Proceedings of the 2016 IEEE Conference on Computer Vision and Pattern Recognition, CVPR 2016, USA, July 2016, pp. 5995–6004 (2016)
11. Hou, S., Wang, Z., Wu, F.: Object detection via deeply exploiting depth information. Neurocomputing **286**, 58–66 (2018)
12. Dosovitskiy, A., Fischery, P., Ilg, E., et al.: FlowNet: learning optical flow with convolutional networks. In: Proceedings of the 15th IEEE International Conference on Computer Vision, ICCV 2015, Chile, December 2015, pp. 2758–2766 (2015)
13. Gkioxari, G., Malik, J.: Finding action tubes. In: Proceedings of the IEEE Conference on Computer Vision and Pattern Recognition, CVPR 2015, USA, June 2015, pp. 759–768 (2015)
14. Karen, S., Andrew, Z.: Two-stream convolutional networks for action recognition in videos. In: Andrew Z. Two-Stream Convolutional Networks for Action Recognition in Videos. NIPS (2014)
15. Spinello, L., Luber, M., Arras, K.O.: Tracking people in 3D using a bottom-up top-down detector. In: Proceedings of the 2011 IEEE International Conference on Robotics and Automation (ICRA), Shanghai, China, May 2011, pp. 1304–1310 (2011)
16. Meshgi, K., Maeda, S.-I., Oba, S., Skibbe, H., Li, Y.-Z., Ishii, S.: An occlusion-aware particle filter tracker to handle complex and persistent occlusions. Comput. Vis. Image Underst. **150**, 81–94 (2016)
17. Xiao, J., Stolkin, R., Gao, Y., Leonardis, A.: Robust fusion of color and depth data for RGB-D target tracking using adaptive range-invariant depth models and spatio-temporal consistency constraints. IEEE Trans. Cybernet. (2017)
18. Camplani, M., Hannuna, S., Mirmehdi, M., et al.: Real-time RGBD tracking with depth scaling kernelised correlation filters and occlusion handling. In: Proceedings of the British Machine Vision Conference 2015, pp. 145.1–145.11, Swansea (2015)

19. Luber, M., Spinello, L., Arras, K.O.: People tracking in RGBD data with on-line boosted target models. In: Proceedings of the 2011 IEEE/RSJ International Conference on Intelligent Robots and Systems: Celebrating 50 Years of Robotics, IROS'11, USA, September 2011, pp. 3844–3849 (2011)
20. Zheng, W.-L., Shen, S.-C., Lu, B.-L.: Online depth imagebased object tracking with sparse representation and object detection. Neural Process. Lett. **45**(3), 745–758 (2017)
21. Li, H., Li, Y., Porikli, F.: DeepTrack: learning discriminative feature representations online for robust visual tracking. IEEE Trans. Image Process. **25**(4), 1834–1848 (2016)
22. Bertinetto, L., Valmadre, J., Henriques, J.F., Vedaldi, A., Torr, P.H.S.: Fully-convolutional SIAMESE networks for object tracking. In: Lecture Notes in Computer Science (including subseries Lecture Notes in Artificial Intelligence and Lecture Notes in Bioinformatics): Preface, vol. 9914, pp. 850–865 (2016)
23. Wang, L., Ouyang, W., Wang, X., Lu, H.: Visual tracking with fully convolutional networks. In: Proceedings of the 15th IEEE International Conference on Computer Vision, ICCV 2015, Chile, December 2015, pp. 3119–3127 (2015)
24. Ma, C., Huang, J.-B., Yang, X., Yang, M.-H.: Hierarchical convolutional features for visual tracking. In: Proceedings of the 15th IEEE International Conference on Computer Vision, ICCV 2015, Chile, December 2015, pp. 3074–3082 (2015)

Visual Prompt with Larger Model for Multi-modal Tracking

Simiao Lai[1(✉)], Yuntao Wei[2], Dong Wang[1], and Huchuan Lu[1]

[1] Dalian University of Technology, Dalian, China
laisimiao@mail.dlut.edu.cn
[2] Dalian Minzu University, Dalian, China

Abstract. The multi-modal tracking focusing on RGB, Depth, and Infrared fusion aims to advance the field of tracking by leveraging the combined strengths of RGB images, depth maps, and infrared data. In this paper, an end-to-end large visual prompt multi-modal object tracker, named **VPLMMT**, is proposed to achieve robust and accurate tracking in complex environments. For the limited three-modal training data, we employ a prompt tuning paradigm to fine-tune a large foundational model pre-trained on RGB data. This approach not only leverages the advantages of pre-trained feature representations but also significantly reduces training costs and memory requirements. We utilize depth maps and thermal infrared images as visual prompts for the RGB images, enabling the original foundational model to adapt to multi-modal tasks. The performance of the framework is evaluated through its application to the multi-modal (RGB, Depth and Thermal Infrared modalities) video dataset released for the competition. The results verifies that the proposed method achieves the 3rd overall tracking performance on the track of this competition.

Keywords: Multi-modal object tracking · Vision transformers · Prompt tuning

1 Introduction

Multi-modal object tracking [16,23] aims to leverage information from various modalities, such as RGB images, thermal infrared images, and depth maps, to provide comprehensive information fusion. This allows for more robust and accurate tracking of specific targets. Given the initial position of the target, multi-modal tracking algorithms integrate this multi-modal information to accurately locate the target's position in subsequent frames. Generally, these multi-modal images are aligned both spatially and temporally, which mean that their relative spatial positions are coordinated, and their temporal steps are synchronized. Leveraging multi-modal information expands the perceptual boundaries of tracking algorithms, addressing challenges that cannot be effectively resolved by relying solely on RGB image data, even with the design of dedicated network

© The Author(s), under exclusive license to Springer Nature Switzerland AG 2025
S. Palaiahnakote et al. (Eds.): ICPR 2024 Workshops, LNCS 15617, pp. 274–283, 2025.
https://doi.org/10.1007/978-3-031-88217-3_20

structures. For instance, in conditions of darkness, low light, or backlighting, RGB images may lose texture and detail due to overexposure. In contrast, thermal infrared images can effectively distinguish targets by their thermal radiation, as they are unaffected by lighting conditions. Moreover, when two similar targets appear simultaneously and their visual features are insufficient to differentiate them, a depth camera can capture the depth variations between objects, providing essential distinguishing information.

Before this challenge, the multi-modal tracking research [16–19,22,26,32,33, 35] focuses largely on bimodal tracking, combining modalities like RGB with thermal infrared images or RGB with depth maps. This competition, however, introduces for the first time a multi-modal tracking dataset in which three modalities are spatially aligned and temporally synchronized. Current multi-modal tracking algorithms can be broadly divided into two categories. The first involves fully fine-tuning the model's parameters, with an emphasis on designing multi-modal fusion modules to enhance the efficiency of information integration. The second approach, visual prompt tuning, keeps the large foundation model fixed, adjusting only a small subset of training parameters. Here, multi-modal information is treated as prompts and injected into the pre-trained model, allowing it to adapt to multi-modal data. Considering the insufficient training data volume, we adopt the second paradigm to develop our solution. Specifically, we select the state-of-the-art RGB tracker LoRAT-Giant [20] as our large foundation model for providing the powerful object discriminative capability. Experimental results demonstrate that a good foundation model shows great generalization ability even without any fine-tuning using the MMVPR Challenge training data. We also follow the pioneer work ViPT [34] to delve the visual prompt branch fitted for the extra bimodal input. Since we choose the largest variant of LoRAT as our foundation model, the visual prompt paradigm helps us fuse the multi-modal information for tracking in a GPU-affordable and time-efficient manner. With the extra bimodal images as visual prompts, the foundation tracker gains further performance improvement, achieving top three rankings without bells and whistles.

2   Related Work

In this section, we show the recent development of related multi-modal tracking tasks: RGBT tracking and RGBD Tracking.

2.1   RGBT Tracking

RGBT tracking seeks to utilize the complementary data from visible light (RGB) and thermal infrared (TIR) images to estimate an object's position and size. Benefiting from the strong nocturnal photosensitivity and penetration ability of thermal infrared data, RGBT tracking has been widely applied in various fields such as video surveillance processing [1], intelligent robotics [3], and autonomous driving [4].

The key challenges in RGBT tracking task lie in alignment and fusion. Early typical works mainly were developed to foster the more effective and deeper bimodal information interaction and complementarity. For example, [31] proposed mfDiMP and investigated three end-to-end fusion architectures, consisting of pixel-level fusion, featurelevel fusion, and response-level fusion, enabling the optimal use of information from both modalities. [21] explored the challenge-aware neural network to model the target appearance under the modality-shared challenges and the modality-specific challenges. Since the prevalence of prompt-tuning, this effective paradigm quickly swept arcoss the RGBT tracking field and gave rise to many related algorithms, such as ProTrack [28], ViPT [34], SDSTrack [7], OneTracker [6], TATrack [24], and so on. The benchmark datasets commonly used in this field include GTOT [16], RGBT210 [19], RGBT234 [17], LasHeR [18], and VTUAV [32], to name a few. Precision rate and success rate [25] are two widely used metrics to evaluate RGBT tracking algorithms.

2.2   RGBD Tracking

Similar to RGBT tracking, RGBD tracking gains more research attention due to the popularization of accessible depth sensors. RGBD tracking can more effectively handle with the challenges faced by traditional RGB object tracking in complex environments, such as target and background interference and low-light conditions, which are limitations of color-only sensors.

Early RGBD trackers [2,8,9] were developed from RGB-only trackers by incorporating depth information as an auxiliary modality, primarily due to the lack of large-scale labeled data for model development and training at the time. With the release of RGBD tracking training datasets, [5] proposed a dual-fused modality-aware tracker (DMT) integrating modality-shared features and modality-specific features in a modality-aware scheme. [26] not only introduced a diverse and large RGBD benchmark DepthTrack for training and evaluation, but also proposed an end to-end offline tracker DeT, which is pre-trained on DepthTrack data with two-stream backbone. [15] proposed the DepthRefiner for adapting RGB Trackers to RGBD Scenes via depth-fused refinement. ViPT [34] and VADT [30] both utilized the visual prompt tuning to adapt foundation model to RGBD tracking scenes. The benchmark datasets commonly used in this field include CDTB [22], DepthTrack [26], RGBD1K [35], ARKitTrack [33], D2Cube [27], and VOT-RGBD series [10–14] to name a few. One-Pass Evaluation (OPE) is a common evaluation protocol to test trackers' performance. Pr, Re and F_{score} are metrics to evaluate RGBD tracking algorithms.

3   Proposed Methods

3.1   Foundation Model

Through preliminary experiments, we have decided to choose the sota RGB tracker LoRAT-giant [20] with the 378 input resolution as our foundation model. LoRAT-giant is the largest variant model of LoRAT, which totally has 1296 M

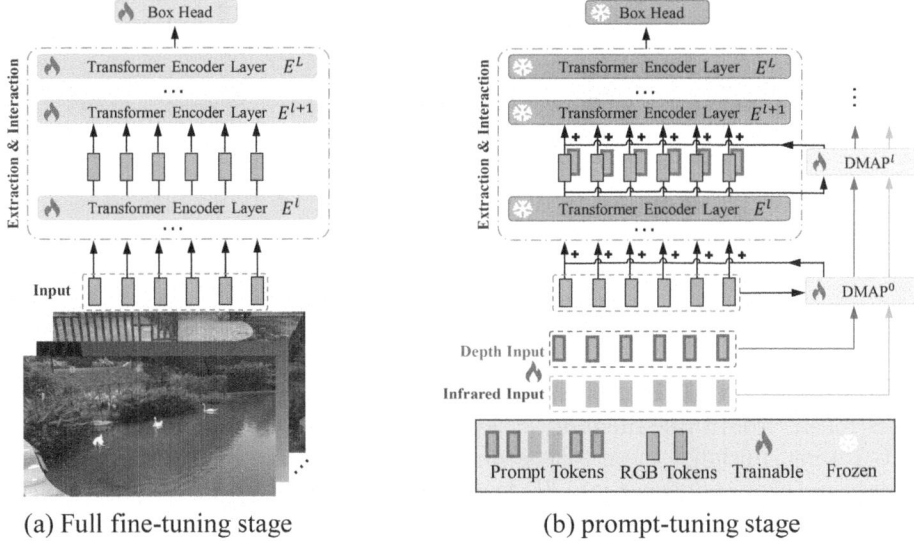

(a) Full fine-tuning stage   (b) prompt-tuning stage

Fig. 1. The framework of VPLMMT, which adopts LoRAT as our foundation model.

parameters, achieving the best and generalized feature and out-of-distribution performance. As illustrated in the Fig. 1 (a), LoRAT model consists of standard vision transformer encoder layers $E^l(l = 1, 2, \ldots, L)$ for feature extraction and relation interaction, and the bounding box prediction head H for coordination prediction. The head network encompasses the regression branch for regressing the size of targets and classification branch for positioning the center of targets. LoRAT-giant has $L = 40$ encoder layers and its embedding dimension is 1536. In Multi-head Self-Attention (MHSA), there are 24 split heads. To the best of our knowledge, this is the first attempt in the field of multi-modal tracking to utilize a giant-scale foundation model, whereas previous research has typically focused on tuning base-scale models.

3.2 Visual Prompt with Larger Model

Dual-Modal Auxiliary Prompter. Inspired by the ViPT [34], we design the dual-modal auxiliary prompter (DMAP) for the depth and infrared data flows. As shown in the Fig. 1 (b), the input flow of each DMAP contains the RGB tokens from the output of the last transformer encoder layer and depth and infrared tokens from the output of the last DMAP block. Mathematically, the collaborative process betwwen the foundation model and DMAP is depicted as:

$$\mathcal{T}^l = \mathcal{T}^l_{RGB} + \hat{\mathcal{T}}^l_{RGB}, \hat{\mathcal{T}}^l_{RGB} = DMAP^l(\mathcal{T}^l_{RGB}, \mathcal{T}^l_D, \mathcal{T}^l_T), \quad l = 1, 2, \ldots L \quad (1)$$

where $\mathcal{T}^l$ is the prompted tokens that will be injected into the next layer of the foundation model. $\mathcal{T}^l_{RGB}$ is the output of last $i - 1$th encoder layer. $\hat{\mathcal{T}}^l_{RGB}$ is the RGB token part of the output from the ith DMAP block. The detailed

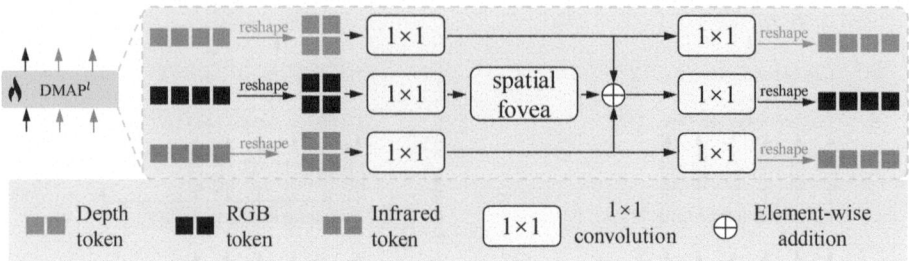

Fig. 2. The detail of DMAP.

architecture of DMAP block can be seen in the Fig. 2. Each block's input comprises tokens from three modalities: depth tokens, thermal infrared tokens, and RGB tokens. Initially, these tokens undergo a reshaping operation, converting them from token sequences into 2D features. Subsequently, a 1×1 convolution is applied. Specifically, the RGB tokens, after undergoing a spatial fovea operation, are added to the features of the other two modalities. Finally, the features of each modality are passed through another 1×1 convolution and then reshaped back into the token sequences.

Two-Stage Training Pipeline. As illustrated in Fig. 1, the training pipeline of our entire model is divided into two stages. (a) The first stage involves full fine-tuning on the RGB single-modality image training set. During this phase, we fine-tune all parameters of the LoRAT model. The initial learning rate is set to 0.0001, with a total of 2 epochs, each comprising 60,000 samples. In the second training stage, in addition to incorporating data from the other two modalities to prompt-tune the corresponding DMAP modules, the training volume and configurations such as the learning rate remain the same as the first phase.

4   Experiments

4.1   Tri-Modality Tracking Dataset

The dataset was obtained from the Multi-Modal Visual Pattern Recognition Challenge 2024-Multi-Modal Tracking Track, employing three modality cameras that encompass RGB, Depth, and Infrared images. The entire dataset contains a variety of complex real-world scenarios, covering challenging attributes such as tissues and trash bins with similar appearances, frequently occluded dolls, swiftly swinging pendants, and pedestrians crossing paths at night. The complete dataset for this task includes 500 multi-modal videos, with 400 allocated for training and the remaining 100 for testing. Each video comprises sequences from three modalities with an equal number of frames, all sharing the same ground truth annotations due to their spatiotemporal alignment. However, due to alignment errors, the bounding boxes in some modalities may not strictly enclose the target, resulting in slight offsets.

4.2   Evaluation Protocols

A common indicator to evaluate whether the predicted bounding box encloses the object is the the Intersection over Union (IoU) that is the overlap rate between the predicted bounding box (P_T) and the ground truth bounding box (G_T) in frame t. It can be described mathematically as following:

$$R_T = \begin{cases} \frac{\text{area}(P_T \cap G_T)}{\text{area}(P_T \cup G_T)}, & \text{if } P_T \neq \emptyset \text{ and } G_T \neq \emptyset \\ 1 & \text{if } P_T = \emptyset \text{ and } G_T = \emptyset \\ 0 & \text{otherwise} \end{cases} \tag{2}$$

where P_T and G_T are the predicted bounding box and the ground truth bounding box in frame t, respectively. When the target is visible in frame t, R_T measures the IoU value between the prediction and the ground truth bounding box. And a good tracker should also predict the absence status of target when the target goes out of view or is completely occluded, resulting in G_T being empty. Otherwise, the R_T is assigned a value of 0. Therefore, this metric guide us to empower tracking algorithms with the ability to determine whether targets are lost or not.

After obtaining R_T, they further need to be calculated at different thresholds $\theta_i \in \{0, 0.05, 0.10, 0.15, \ldots, 0.95, 1\}$ to get the success rates (SR):

$$u_t(\theta_i) = \begin{cases} 1, & \text{if } R_T > \theta_i \\ 0, & \text{otherwise} \end{cases}, SR(\theta_i) = \frac{1}{\text{T}} \sum_{1}^{T} u_t(\theta_i) \tag{3}$$

where R_T is calculated according to the Eq. 2, θ_i is the current threshold, and u_t is an indicator that denotes whether the prediction in frame t is successful. If R_T is greater than θ_i, then $u_t(\theta_i)$ takes the value of 1, otherwise 0. Finally, the last metric Area Under the Curve (AUC) can be determined as following:

$$AUC(\theta_i) = \frac{1}{21} \sum_{i=1}^{21} SR(\theta_i) \tag{4}$$

where $SR(\theta_i)$ is the success rate at the corresponding threshold θ_i. And we can calculate the success rates at each threshold and further compute the average of these success rates (AUC) through the above steps.

4.3   Experiments Results

Baseline Results. We have tested some state-of-the-art RGB trackers and multi-modal RGBT trackers in the testing set without any retraining for selecting a foundation tracker as our powerful baseline solution. As shown in Table 1, OSTrack256 [29] achieves 0.764 score in terms of AUC metric, indicating relying solely on information of the single RGB modality can not deal with this dataset consisting of many complex and real-word challenging scenes. And we try several different LoRAT [20] variants, from LoRAT-B224 to LoRAT-g378, and find that

Table 1. The evaluated AUC results of different sota RGB and RGBT trackers on the testing set of competition benchmark.

Method	Modality	AUC↑
OSTrack$_{256}$	RGB	0.764
LoRAT-B$_{224}$	RGB	0.765
LoRAT-L$_{378}$	RGB	0.848
LoRAT-g$_{224}$	RGB	0.839
LoRAT-g$_{378}$	RGB	**0.853**
SeqTrackV2-L$_{384}$	RGB; T	0.790

Table 2. Baseline improvement schemes and expriment results.

Method	Modality	AUC↑
LoRAT-g$_{378}$	RGB	0.853
LoRAT-g$_{378}$ + full fine-tuning	RGB	0.856
LoRAT-g$_{378}$ + full fine-tuning + DMAP	RGB; D; T	**0.868**

the LoRAT one with larger scale and more parameters has more superior AUC performance, demonstrating larger models indeed has greater capability to capture more discriminative features and provide more unambiguous representation, even with complicated environment. The expriment results reveal that LoRAT has better generalization ability than OSTrack, even using a smaller resolution. We also observed that LoRAT-g378, utilizing only the RGB modality, outperforms the SeqTrackV2-Large384 method, which uses RGBT modalities, by 6.3% in AUC. Therefore, we finally choose LoRAT-g378 as our baseline model.

Improved Results. Moreover, we incorporate the visual prompt design to further improve the overall performance on the basis of our baseline model. Specifically, we firstly attempt to fine-tune the RGB tracker LoRAT-g378 only using the MMVPR Challenge training data. What'more, inspiring by ViPT [34], we investigate the dual-modal auxiliary prompter (DMAP) to conduct the multi-modal communication between the RGB modality and Depth and Infrared modalities. As demonstrated in Table 2, fine-tuning on the competition's training set just yields a slight improvement, indicating that the baseline has already acquired a highly generalized and excellent feature representation through pre-training on a large-scale RGB image dataset. The integration of data from two additional modalities significantly enhances model performance from 0.856 to 0.868. We perceive that this performance improvement stems from the model's superior adaptation to challenging sequences that require complementary information from multiple modalities to be resolved.

5   Conclusion

In this paper, the proposed VPLMMT framework demonstrates the effectiveness of leveraging RGB, Depth, and Infrared fusion for robust multi-modal tracking in complex environments. By employing a prompt tuning paradigm, the framework successfully adapts a large pre-trained foundational model to accommodate the limited three-modal training data. The integration of depth maps and thermal infrared images as visual prompts proves to be an effective strategy for enhancing the model's adaptability to the Multi-Modal Visual Pattern Recognition Challenge. In conclusion, we achieves the 3rd place overall tracking performance.

References

1. Alldieck, T., Bahnsen, C.H., Moeslund, T.B.: Context-aware fusion of RGB and thermal imagery for traffic monitoring. Sensors **16**, 1947 (2016)
2. Camplani, M., ET AL.: Real-time RGB-D tracking with depth scaling kernelised correlation filters and occlusion handling. In: BMVC. vol. 3, pp. 01–12 (2015)
3. Chen, L., Sun, L., Yang, T., Fan, L., Huang, K., Xuanyuan, Z.: RGB-T slam: a flexible slam framework by combining appearance and thermal information. In: 2017 IEEE International Conference on Robotics and Automation (ICRA), pp. 5682–5687. IEEE (2017)
4. Dai, X., Yuan, X., Wei, X.: Tirnet: object detection in thermal infrared images for autonomous driving. Appl. Intell. **51**, 1244–1261 (2021)
5. Gao, S., Yang, J., Li, Z., Zheng, F., Leonardis, A., Song, J.: Learning dual-fused modality-aware representations for RGBD tracking. In: European Conference on Computer Vision, pp. 478–494. Springer (2022)
6. Hong, L., et al.: Onetracker: unifying visual object tracking with foundation models and efficient tuning. In: CVPR, pp. 19079–19091 (2024)
7. Hou, X., et al.: SDstrack: self-distillation symmetric adapter learning for multi-modal visual object tracking. In: CVPR, pp. 26551–26561 (2024)
8. Kart, U., Kamarainen, J.K., Matas, J.: How to make an RGBD tracker? In: Proceedings of the European Conference on Computer Vision (ECCV) Workshops (2018)
9. Kart, U., Lukezic, A., Kristan, M., Kamarainen, J.K., Matas, J.: Object tracking by reconstruction with view-specific discriminative correlation filters. In: Proceedings of the IEEE/CVF Conference on Computer Vision and Pattern Recognition, pp. 1339–1348 (2019)
10. Kristan, M., et al.: The tenth visual object tracking vot2022 challenge results. In: European Conference on Computer Vision, pp. 431–460. Springer (2022)
11. Kristan, M., et al.: The eighth visual object tracking VOT2020 challenge results. In: Bartoli, A., Fusiello, A. (eds.) ECCV 2020. LNCS, vol. 12539, pp. 547–601. Springer, Cham (2020). https://doi.org/10.1007/978-3-030-68238-5_39
12. Kristan, M., et al.: The sixth visual object tracking vot2018 challenge results. In: Proceedings of the European Conference on Computer Vision (ECCV) Workshops (2018)
13. Kristan, M., et al.: The ninth visual object tracking vot2021 challenge results. In: Proceedings of the IEEE/CVF International Conference on Computer Vision. pp. 2711–2738 (2021)

14. Kristan, M., et al.: The seventh visual object tracking vot2019 challenge results. In: Proceedings of the IEEE/CVF International Conference on Computer Vision Workshops (2019)
15. Lai, S., Wang, D., Lu, H.: Depthrefiner: adapting RGB trackers to RGBD scenes via depth-fused refinement. In: 2024 IEEE International Conference on Multimedia and Expo (ICME), pp. 1–6. IEEE (2024)
16. Li, C., Cheng, H., Hu, S., Liu, X., Tang, J., Lin, L.: Learning collaborative sparse representation for grayscale-thermal tracking. IEEE Trans. Image Process. **25**(12), 5743–5756 (2016)
17. Li, C., Liang, X., Lu, Y., Zhao, N., Tang, J.: RGB-T object tracking: benchmark and baseline. Pattern Recogn. **96**, 106977 (2019)
18. Li, C., et al.: Lasher: a large-scale high-diversity benchmark for RGBT tracking. IEEE Trans. Image Process. **31**, 392–404 (2021)
19. Li, C., Zhao, N., Lu, Y., Zhu, C., Tang, J.: Weighted sparse representation regularized graph learning for RGB-T object tracking. In: ACM MM, pp. 1856–1864 (2017)
20. Lin, L., Fan, H., Zhang, Z., Wang, Y., Xu, Y., Ling, H.: Tracking meets Lora: faster training, larger model, stronger performance. In: ECCV (2024)
21. Liu, L., Li, C., Xiao, Y., Ruan, R., Fan, M.: RGBT tracking via challenge-based appearance disentanglement and interaction. IEEE Trans. Image Process. (2024)
22. Lukezic, A., et al.: CDTB: a color and depth visual object tracking dataset and benchmark. In: Proceedings of the IEEE/CVF International Conference on Computer Vision, pp. 10013–10022 (2019)
23. Song, S., Xiao, J.: Tracking revisited using RGBD camera: Unified benchmark and baselines. In: Proceedings of the IEEE International Conference on Computer Vision, pp. 233–240 (2013)
24. Wang, H., Liu, X., Li, Y., Sun, M., Yuan, D., Liu, J.: Temporal adaptive RGBT tracking with modality prompt. In: AAAI, vol. 38, pp. 5436–5444 (2024)
25. Wu, Y., Lim, J., Yang, M.H.: Object tracking benchmark. IEEE Trans. Pattern Anal. Mach. Intell. **37**(09), 1834–1848 (2015)
26. Yan, S., et al.: Depthtrack: unveiling the power of RGBD tracking. In: Proceedings of the IEEE/CVF International Conference on Computer Vision, pp. 10725–10733 (2021)
27. Yang, J., Gao, S., Li, Z., Zheng, F., Leonardis, A.: Resource-efficient RGBD aerial tracking. In: Proceedings of the IEEE/CVF Conference on Computer Vision and Pattern Recognition, pp. 13374–13383 (2023)
28. Yang, J., Li, Z., Zheng, F., Leonardis, A., Song, J.: Prompting for multi-modal tracking. In: ACM MM, pp. 3492–3500 (2022)
29. Ye, B., Chang, H., Ma, B., Shan, S., Chen, X.: Joint feature learning and relation modeling for tracking: a one-stream framework. In: ECCV, pp. 341–357 (2022)
30. Zhang, G., Liang, Q., Mo, Z., Li, N., Zhong, B.: Visual adapt for RGBD tracking. In: ICASSP 2024-2024 IEEE International Conference on Acoustics, Speech and Signal Processing (ICASSP), pp. 9391–9395. IEEE (2024)
31. Zhang, L., Danelljan, M., Gonzalez-Garcia, A., Van De Weijer, J., Shahbaz Khan, F.: Multi-modal fusion for end-to-end RGB-T tracking. In: ICCV Workshops (2019)
32. Zhang, P., Zhao, J., Wang, D., Lu, H., Ruan, X.: Visible-thermal UAV tracking: a large-scale benchmark and new baseline. In: Proceedings of the IEEE/CVF Conference on Computer Vision and Pattern Recognition, pp. 8886–8895 (2022)

33. Zhao, H., Chen, J., Wang, L., Lu, H.: Arkittrack: a new diverse dataset for tracking using mobile RGB-D data. In: Proceedings of the IEEE/CVF Conference on Computer Vision and Pattern Recognition, pp. 5126–5135 (2023)
34. Zhu, J., Lai, S., Chen, X., Wang, D., Lu, H.: Visual prompt multi-modal tracking. In: CVPR, pp. 9516–9526 (2023)
35. Zhu, X.F., et al.: RGBD1K: a large-scale dataset and benchmark for RGB-D object tracking. In: Proceedings of the AAAI Conference on Artificial Intelligence, vol. 37, pp. 3870–3878 (2023)

Enhancing Multi-modal Object Detection with Data Augmentation, Focal Loss, and Model Ensembling

Junyu Wu[iD], Yuhao Chao[iD], and Jie Liu$^{(\boxtimes)}$[iD]

State Key Laboratory for Novel Software Technology, Nanjing University, Nanjing,
NKG 210023, China
{221870052,221240013}@smail.nju.edu.cn, liujie@nju.edu.cn

Abstract. This article discusses our team's success in securing first place in ICPR 2024 Multi-Modal Visual Pattern Recognition Challenge-Track 2 by applying data augmentation, focal loss, and model ensemble techniques. Data enhancement improves training data diversity, focal loss addresses class imbalance by focusing on challenging examples, and model ensembling combines predictions from multiple models for better performance. Together, these strategies lead to significant improvements in model accuracy and robustness, contributing to our high-ranking result. Code at https://github.com/chaoyuhao/ICPR24_competition.git.

Keywords: Multi-modal · recognition · data augmentation · focal loss · ensemble

1 Introduction

The ICPR 2024 Multi-Modal Visual Pattern Recognition Challenge-Track 2: Detection has garnered significant interest among researchers in the computer vision community. This track aims to investigate advanced methodologies for detecting objects of interest within multi-modal data streams. The dataset employed for this purpose, the ICPR_JNU_MMDetection_v1, includes a total of 5000 multi-modal image pairs spanning 13 distinct categories, with 4000 image pairs designated for training and the remaining 1000 reserved for testing. Each pair comprises an RGB image, a depth image, and an infrared image, all consistently sized at a resolution of 1920 × 1080. It is noteworthy that this dataset features three classes of objects, namely signs, balls, and lights, which pose particular challenges for detection algorithms. The difficulties in learning each of these classes differ. The challenge with signs does not stem from a lack of samples but rather from their similarity to another class (traffic signs), which makes them hard to distinguish. Balls are difficult to detect due to the small number of samples and their small size. Despite having a relatively large number

---

J. Wu and Y. Chao—These authors contributed equally to this work.

S. Palaiahnakote et al. (Eds.): ICPR 2024 Workshops, LNCS 15617, pp. 284–292, 2025.
https://doi.org/10.1007/978-3-031-88217-3_21

of samples, lights are hard to learn, likely due to their unique optical characteristics. First, lights can vary significantly in intensity, color, and size, depending on the source and environmental conditions. Second, the presence of reflections, glare, and dynamic lighting conditions can confuse detection algorithms, especially in real-world scenarios. Third, lights often appear in varied and complex backgrounds, which can complicate their localization and identification. These factors together create challenges for accurate and consistent detection of lights in images.

2 Related Work

2.1 Computer Vision in Pattern Recognition

Pattern recognition is the scientific discipline whose goal is the classification of objects into a number of categories or classes [7,12]. With the development of society, the demand for processing and retrieving various types of information has become increasingly important across different industries. This trend has pushed pattern recognition to the forefront of today's engineering applications and research. Pattern recognition is an integral part of most machine intelligence systems designed for decision-making.

Computer vision has long been a foundational area in the development of pattern recognition algorithms. With the rise of deep learning, particularly Convolutional Neural Networks (CNNs) [17], the field underwent a significant shift. CNN-based models, such as AlexNet [3], VGG [9], and ResNet [2], demonstrated superior performance by learning hierarchical feature representations directly from data, thereby surpassing the limitations of handcrafted features.

2.2 Multi-modal Object Detection

There are two main approaches to fusing multi-modal information: decision-level fusion (result-level fusion) and feature-level fusion. Both approaches have distinct advantages and are widely studied in the context of multi-modal object detection [11].

Decision-level fusion operates by processing each modality independently through separate detection models, followed by combining the detection results. This method leverages the individual strengths of different modalities without requiring deep integration. One common technique is to apply non-maximum suppression (NMS) or voting mechanisms to merge the final object detection outputs. Decision-level fusion is relatively straightforward to implement and allows the use of modality-specific architectures. It also provides flexibility, as it enables the combination of modalities even if they have vastly different characteristics or resolutions. However, the independent processing of each modality may lead to suboptimal performance, as it does not fully exploit the potential for early interaction and collaboration between modalities [4].

Feature-level fusion, on the other hand, involves integrating multi-modal data at an earlier stage in the detection pipeline. This approach typically combines features extracted from different modalities before making object detection predictions. By fusing information at the feature level, this method allows the model to learn richer and more discriminative representations, effectively capturing correlations and complementarities between modalities. Feature-level fusion can be achieved through various techniques, such as concatenating feature maps, attention mechanisms, or more sophisticated neural network architectures designed for multi-modal fusion. While this method often leads to better performance due to the more integrated processing of data, it also requires more complex model designs and careful tuning to handle the discrepancies between modalities.

Recent works have explored both fusion strategies in depth, with numerous models demonstrating the benefits of combining RGB and depth information for enhanced object detection accuracy. For instance, decision-level fusion has been successfully applied in autonomous driving scenarios, where RGB and LiDAR data are combined to detect objects in dynamic environments. On the other hand, feature-level fusion has been particularly effective in indoor settings where RGB and depth data complement each other, enhancing the detection of objects in cluttered or occluded scenes.

3   Our Solution

3.1   Model

We have ultimately chosen the YOLOv5-P6 model [8] for this competition. Like the original YOLOv5-P5, the YOLOv5-P6 model features a backbone based on Cross Stage Partial (CSP) networks [15], which enhances gradient flow and reduces computational cost. It also employs the Path Aggregation Network (PANet) [6] in the neck to facilitate Feature Pyramid Networks (FPN) with improved feature representation. Components such as Focus layers and SiLU activation functions contribute to enhanced detection accuracy and speed. The key advantage of YOLOv5-P6 over YOLOv5-P5 is the additional output layer (P6) it introduces to the existing YOLOv5 framework, enhancing its ability to detect larger objects like cars, as shown in Fig. 1. Additionally, the YOLOv5-P6 model is trained at a higher resolution (1280 pixels) compared to the P5 models (640 pixels), allowing small objects to be more prominently represented in the image, thereby improving the detection of small objects such as balls, as illustrated in Fig. 2. While there have been subsequent advancements in object detection models, such as YOLOv8 [13], YOLOv9 [16], and YOLOv10 [14], these newer iterations primarily target optimizing the trade-off between processing speed and detection accuracy. Consequently, in scenarios where processing time is not constrained, the YOLOv5-P6 model, boasting a higher pretrained resolution, a more extensive architecture, and a deeper network, may exhibit performance advantages over these newer models.

Fig. 1. An example of large objects in ICPR_JNU_MMDetection_v1 dataset.

Fig. 2. An example of small objects in ICPR_JNU_MMDetection_v1 dataset.

3.2 Data Augmentation

Mixup Data Augmentation. Mixup is a data augmentation technique that involves creating new training samples by combining two images and their corresponding labels [18]. By introducing Mixup, we increase the diversity of the training data. This helps the model learn smoother decision boundaries between classes, thereby reducing overfitting and improving its ability to make predictions, especially in ambiguous cases (Fig. 3).

Copy-Paste Data Augmentation. Copy-Paste is another augmentation technique where objects are directly copied from one image and pasted into another [1]. This method is particularly useful for generating complex scenes with multiple objects, which enhances the model's ability to handle occlusions and challenging backgrounds. In our implementation, we first identify objects in certain images using semantic segmentation or contour detection. We then randomly select background images and paste these objects onto them. This approach not only increases the number of training samples but also enhances the variety and complexity of visual scenarios, thus improving the model's detection capabilities.

Mosaic Augmentation. This technique involves combining four different images into one during training. It allows the model to see objects at different scales and contexts, which enhances its ability to generalize across diverse scenes and improves detection performance on small objects.

Random Affine Transformations. This includes translations, rotations, scaling, and shearing applied randomly to the images. These transformations help

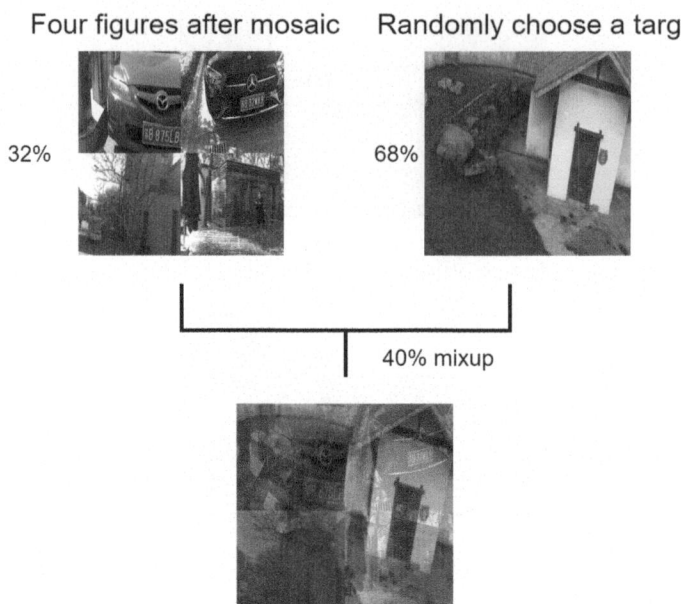

Fig. 3. Main data augmentation process

the model become invariant to these alterations, improving its robustness in real-world applications.

Color Jittering. This technique involves randomly changing the brightness, contrast, saturation, and hue of the images. It helps the model to better handle variations in lighting conditions across different environments.

Summary of Data Augmentation Techniques. These augmentation techniques collectively enhance the diversity of the training data without actually collecting more images, enabling our model to achieve better generalization and performance across a range of different object detection tasks. The baseline already incorporates the last three data augmentation techniques, and we introduce additional MixUp and Copy-Paste data augmentation methods. The application of these two data augmentation techniques results in an increase of approximately 4.0% in AP. However, these two methods primarily benefit the detection of classes that are relatively straightforward to identify. The performance of the model on the three classes that are challenging to classify demonstrates minimal improvement.

3.3   Focal Loss

Focal Loss is a loss function designed to address the class imbalance challenge often encountered in object detection tasks. Proposed by Lin [5] et al. in the context of the RetinaNet object detection framework, Focal Loss modifies the conventional Cross Entropy Loss by adding a factor that reduces the loss contribution from well-classified examples. This allows the model to focus more on hard-to-classify examples, thereby improving the detection of objects that are sparse and difficult to recognize.

We employ Focal Loss to train our model, resulting in a significant enhancement in detection performance for the three classes that are challenging to classify. However, the performance for other classes exhibits a slight decline due to the heightened focus on challenging examples. To address this, we integrate the detection outcomes of our models trained on Binary Cross-Entropy Loss and Focal Loss, which will be discussed in detail in Sect. 3.5.

3.4 Weighted Box Fusion (WBF)

In this competition, the models are evaluated using the mean average precision (mAP) at different intersection-over-union (IoU) values. The IoU is a ratio of overlap between two objects to the total area of the two objects combined. The bounding box of two models (A and B) can be calculated as:

$$IoU(box_A, box_B) = \frac{box_A \cap box_B}{box_A \cup box_B}$$

According to Solovyev's research [10], the WBF method performs better than NMS and soft-NMS when used with a set of trained models. The score is calculated as the average result across IoU thresholds from 0.5 to 0.95, with a step size of 0.05. This method can improve the accuracy of the bounding box predictions.

In the traditional method of WBF, the algorithm will sort the bounding boxes by their confidence. Then the algorithm will merge different bounding boxes by their confidence.

One of our approaches to applying WBF is selecting models from a single training session. Specifically, we choose six models from epochs 130 to 135. In our method, we use the best model as the main predictor and merge the bounding boxes with IoU over 0.75. For the result of models with corresponding bounding boxes with IoU lower than 0.75, we choose the best model as the replacement for this model.

$$B_{1,2} = \frac{\sum_{i=1}^{n} \left(\mathbf{1}_{\text{IoU}(B_i, B_0) > 0.75} \cdot B_{1,2_i} + \mathbf{1}_{\text{IoU}(B_i, B_0) \leq 0.75} \cdot B_{1,2_0} \right)}{n+1}$$

Therefore, we can fuse those bounding boxes that are easier to detect and highly similar. In our experiment, there are 85.08% bounding boxes of all those models have IoU higher than 0.75.

3.5 Model Ensemble

We employ two types of model ensemble methods. The first type involves ensembling models trained on different image modalities, specifically RGB images, depth images, and infrared images. We utilize WBF to merge predictions from these models, maximizing the information extracted from each modality. The second type of ensemble combines models trained with different loss functions. As discussed in Sect. 3.3, the use of focal loss enhances the model's ability to detect three particularly challenging classes, albeit at the expense of decreased performance on other classes. To address this, we integrate the prediction results from a model trained with Focal Loss with those from a model trained with the original Binary Cross-Entropy Loss. Ultimately, we achieve a 1.0% improvement in AP.

4   Experiment

4.1   Training Approach

In our training approach, we employed a Stochastic Gradient Descent (SGD) optimizer, initializing the learning rate at 0.01, with a final learning rate set to 0.0005 as per the OneCycleLR learning schedule. The momentum is configured at 0.937 to facilitate smoother convergence. We incorporate a weight decay of 0.0005 to mitigate overfitting by penalizing large weights. The training regimen includes 3.0 warmup epochs to gradually adjust the model parameters, starting with an initial momentum of 0.8 and a warmup bias learning rate of 0.1.

For loss optimization, the model is configured with a box loss gain of 0.05 and a classification loss gain of 0.5. The object loss gain is standard at 1.0, ensuring balanced emphasis across different loss components. The Intersection over Union (IoU) training threshold is set at 0.20, aiding in the effective filtering of predictions, while an anchor-multiple threshold of 4.0 is used to optimize anchor box selection.

Data augmentation plays a crucial role, incorporating techniques such as HSV augmentation for hue (0.015), saturation (0.7), and value (0.4) adjustments, alongside image translation (0.1), scaling (0.5), and mixup with a probability of 0.4. This diverse augmentation strategy aims to bolster the model's robustness by exposing it to a wide variability of input conditions. Additionally, probabilities of 0.5 and 0.1 are set for horizontal flipping and copy-paste augmentation, respectively, further enhancing generalization capabilities. Through these comprehensive strategies, the training process is optimized for achieving high performance and generalizability in diverse object detection scenarios.

We utilize four NVIDIA GeForce RTX 3090 GPUs, configuring the batch size to 4, effectively assigning one batch per GPU. This configuration is chosen due to the considerable memory demands of the large model size, and based on our observations that smaller batch sizes tend to yield enhanced model performance. Initially, we load the weights pretrained on the COCO dataset, to leverage transfer learning benefits. The model is trained for a total of 180 epochs; however, we observe signs of overfitting beginning to manifest after approximately 150 epochs. This indicates a need for careful monitoring of model performance metrics and potential early stopping in future iterations to prevent degradation of generalization capabilities.

5   Result

The detection track stands out as particularly competitive among all three tracks in the ICPR 2024 Multi-Modal Visual Pattern Recognition Challenge, with largest number of participants. To facilitate a comprehensive comparison of our final submission with those of other participants, we present the leaderboard for the ICPR 2024 Multi-Modal Visual Pattern Recognition Challenge-Track 2: Detection in Table 1. The results clearly demonstrate that our detection system achieves exceptional performance, securing the 1st place ranking among all competitors.

Table 1. Leaderboard of the ICPR 2024 Multi-Modal Visual Pattern Recognition Challenge-Track 2: Detection, where we only list the top-5 entries.

Team Name	mAP50_95
idiotgoose (Ours)	0.5344
archaea	0.5321
hxxiao	0.5282
daicver	0.5255
siyitracy	0.5237

6   Conclusion

In this paper, we present a state-of-the-art detection system for the ICPR_JNU_MMDetection_v1 dataset. Specifically, we utilize data augmentation, focal loss and model ensembling to yield robust detections. Our overall detection system achieved the 1st place in the detection track of the ICPR 2024 Multi-Modal Visual Pattern Recognition Challenge.

References

1. Ghiasi, G., et al.: Simple copy-paste is a strong data augmentation method for instance segmentation. In: 2021 IEEE/CVF Conference on Computer Vision and Pattern Recognition (CVPR), Los Alamitos, CA, USA, pp. 2917–2927. IEEE Computer Society (2021). https://doi.org/10.1109/CVPR46437.2021.00294, https://doi.ieeecomputersociety.org/10.1109/CVPR46437.2021.00294
2. He, K., Zhang, X., Ren, S., Sun, J.: Deep residual learning for image recognition. In: Proceedings of the IEEE Conference on Computer Vision and Pattern Recognition (CVPR), pp. 770–778 (2016). https://doi.org/10.1109/CVPR.2016.90
3. Krizhevsky, A., Sutskever, I., Hinton, G.E.: Imagenet classification with deep convolutional neural networks. Commun. ACM **60**(6), 84–90 (2017). https://doi.org/10.1145/3065386

4. Li, H., Wu, X.J., Kittler, J.: Infrared and visible image fusion using a deep learning framework. In: 2018 24th International Conference on Pattern Recognition (ICPR), pp. 2705–2710. IEEE (2018)

5. Lin, T.Y., Goyal, P., Girshick, R., He, K., Dollár, P.: Focal loss for dense object detection. IEEE Trans. Pattern Anal. Mach. Intell. **42**(2), 318–327 (2020). https://doi.org/10.1109/TPAMI.2018.2858826

6. Liu, S., Qi, L., Qin, H., Shi, J., Jia, J.: Path aggregation network for instance segmentation (2018). https://arxiv.org/abs/1803.01534

7. Paolanti, M., Frontoni, E.: Multidisciplinary pattern recognition applications: a review. Comput. Sci. Rev. **37**, 100276 (2020). https://doi.org/10.1016/j.cosrev.2020.100276, https://www.sciencedirect.com/science/article/pii/S1574013719300899

8. Redmon, J., Divvala, S., Girshick, R., Farhadi, A.: You only look once: unified, real-time object detection (2016). https://arxiv.org/abs/1506.02640

9. Simonyan, K., Zisserman, A.: Very deep convolutional networks for large-scale image recognition. In: Proceedings of the International Conference on Learning Representations (ICLR) (2015). https://arxiv.org/abs/1409.1556, arXiv preprint arXiv:1409.1556

10. Solovyev, R., Wang, W., Gabruseva, T.: Weighted boxes fusion: Ensembling boxes from different object detection models. Image Vis. Comput. 1–6 (2021)

11. Tang, L., Zhang, H., Xu, H., Ma, J.: Deep learning-based image fusion: a survey. J. Image Graphics **28**(1), 3–36 (2023)

12. Theodoridis, S., Koutroumbas, K.: Pattern Recognition. Academic Press, 4th edn. (2009). https://doi.org/10.1016/B978-1-59749-272-0.X0001-2

13. Varghese, R., M., S.: Yolov8: a novel object detection algorithm with enhanced performance and robustness. In: 2024 International Conference on Advances in Data Engineering and Intelligent Computing Systems (ADICS), pp. 1–6 (2024) https://doi.org/10.1109/ADICS58448.2024.10533619

14. Wang, A., et al.: Yolov10: real-time end-to-end object detection. arXiv:abs/2405.14458 (2024). https://api.semanticscholar.org/CorpusID:269983404

15. Wang, C.Y., Liao, H.Y.M., Yeh, I.H., Wu, Y.H., Chen, P.Y., Hsieh, J.W.: CSPNet: a new backbone that can enhance learning capability of CNN (2019). https://arxiv.org/abs/1911.11929

16. Wang, C.Y., Yeh, I.H., Liao, H.: Yolov9: learning what you want to learn using programmable gradient information. arXiv:abs/2402.13616 (2024). https://api.semanticscholar.org/CorpusID:267770251

17. Yamashita, R., Nishio, M., Do, R., Togashi, K.: Convolutional neural networks: an overview and application in radiology. Insights Imaging **9**(4), 611–629 (2018). https://doi.org/10.1007/s13244-018-0639-9

18. Zhang, H., Cisse, M., Dauphin, Y.N., Lopez-Paz, D.: Mixup: beyond empirical risk minimization. In: International Conference on Learning Representations (2018)

Advancing Multi-modal Visual Pattern Recognition: Object Detection

Arjun J. Nair[1(✉)], Swathi Jayakumar[1], Varalekshmy M. Mohan[1],
Jyothisha J. Nair[1], Vishnu Thooprath Subran[2], and Hrishikesh Puthuvamana[2]

[1] Department of Computer Science and Engineering, Amrita School of Computing,
Amrita Vishwa Vidyapeetham, Amritapuri, Kerala, India
arjunjnair01@gmail.com
[2] Founding Minds Software, Kochi, India

Abstract. Recently, the integration of multimodal data systems has emerged as a critical area of research and development, significantly improving the robustness and accuracy of visual pattern recognition systems. In this paper, we propose a novel approach by creating a hybrid model architecture that leverages the detection capabilities of YOLOv8. Our data set consists of 5000 multimodal image pairs, encompassing 13 distinct classes: RGB, depth, and infrared, processed separately. The outputs of each are fused using late fusion techniques, and Non-Maximum Suppression (NMS) is applied to increase accuracy. We utilized stratified test-train split algorithms to validate the datasets. Our evaluations produced results demonstrating significant improvements in detection performance, with mean Average Precision (mAP) as the primary metric. An accuracy of 0.2048 was obtained by testing our model. Our findings suggest that improved multimodal detection can enhance the impact of real-world applications, creating new avenues for scrutiny in visual pattern recognition.

Keywords: Multi-Modal Data Integration · YOLO · Late Fusion · NMS

1 Introduction

Multimodal data integration has become one of the most powerful approaches toward enriching visual pattern recognition, especially in object detection tasks. Conventional object detection models tend to only use RGB images, which do not make use of all information, and can often be improved by integrating with other related modalities. For this reason, using depth and infrared images combined with RGB data would better serve the purpose of gaining a more unified and accurate detection result. Each of these types of image has unique properties: RGB captures the color and texture of an image, depth images provide information about distance to objects, and infrared gives thermal data, which is often more important in applications involving infrared vision. We introduce a

---

The original version of the chapter has been revised. The author name has been corrected as "Jyothisha J. Nair". A correction to this chapter can be found at https://doi.org/10.1007/978-3-031-88217-3_33

S. Palaiahnakote et al. (Eds.): ICPR 2024 Workshops, LNCS 15617, pp. 293–301, 2025.
https://doi.org/10.1007/978-3-031-88217-3_22

hybrid architecture here and apply the above for processing RGB, Depth, and Infrared images with YOLOv8 models, then train each modality. Late-fusion techniques are applied to improve the general detection performance. We take advantage of the integration of the outputs of models trained with RGB, depth, and infrared data. These fusion processes help to combine the strengths of the respective modality predictions based on complementary information provided. Using weights for the outputs based on their reliability and context ensures that the final detection results obtained by the late fusion technique are more robust and accurate, especially in more complicated or challenging scenarios.

Upon obtaining the fused results, we apply Non-Maximum Suppression (NMS) as a post-processing step. NMS allows for redundancy elimination by selecting the most confident prediction for each object, suppressing overlapping bounding boxes of lower confidence scores. This step refines the detection outcomes, reducing noise, and ensuring that only the most accurate and relevant predictions are retained. Together, the late-fusion and NMS processes significantly enhance the precision and overall effectiveness of the detection system, making it suitable for a wide range of practical applications.

1.1 Related Works

Recent advancements in Artificial Intelligence have proposed that combining different types of sensor data, such as RGB and thermal images, can significantly enhance detection accuracy, particularly under challenging conditions like reduced visibility [1]. Conventional detection models, like YOLO, are designed to utilize multimodal data, but their efficiency decreases in the presence of environmental factors such as haze. Dehazing images has been a well-known practice to overcome this disadvantage. Techniques have been researched to address this issue, ranging from classical atmospheric scattering models to modern deep learning-based networks. While these methodologies can aid object detection and improve visibility, their performance remains underwhelming in dense haze, where visibility is severely limited [2]. Furthermore, these methods often do not provide real-time object detection, which is crucial for applications like autonomous driving [3].

The depth estimation approach called Monodepth may be combined with the given RGB data under challenging conditions. Two YOLO object detectors process the dehazed RGB and thermal images and apply Non-Maximum Suppression (NMS) to extract optimal bounding boxes from the detections. However, the fusion of depth estimation with dehazing to enhance object detection in low visibility conditions has hardly been explored [4]. Strategies like late fusion have been implemented to combine strengths from different modalities, enhancing the effectiveness of feature synthesis [5]. A major challenge persists: as detection accuracy improves, computational demands increase, hampering real-time applications. Investigations indicate a dire need for effective fusion techniques in extremely dense haze. Therefore, developing a deep multimodal object detection model that integrates advanced dehazing, depth estimation, and efficient fusion strategies is vital for reliable detection under adverse conditions.

Among these advancements, a noteworthy proposal is M2FNet, introduced by Jiang et al. (2024), which fuses visible (VIS) and thermal infrared (TIR) images to achieve efficient object detection under low light conditions. Traditional models typically train the VIS and TIR data separately, resulting in poor performance, especially when the training data is limited. M2FNet utilizes the Transformer architecture and incorporates two new modules: Union-Modal Attention (UMA) for collecting multispectral features and Cross-Modal Attention (CMA) for enhancing feature learning from paired VIS and TIR data. The experimental results demonstrate significant improvements in detection accuracy, with mAP increasing by 10.71 and 2.97 compared to the baseline models. Furthermore, M2FNet shows robustness against different illumination conditions, indicating its practical potential. This aligns with other work that emphasizes the importance of integrating multiple modalities for successful object detection.

Additionally, the paper "Enhancing Object Detection in Dense Images: Adjustable Non-Maximum Suppression for Single-Class Detection" by Noh et al. discusses an innovative approach to improve object detection in dense images through an Adjustable NMS technique. Traditional NMS struggles with overlapping objects, leading to missed detections in dense environments. The proposed method adjusts parameters based on object density, improving the detection accuracy for single-class objects. This advancement addresses limitations in existing algorithms, showcasing superior performance, particularly in scenarios with a high density of small objects [6].

Another relevant work is the paper "Multimodal Object Detection by Channel Switching and Spatial Attention" by Cao et al., which proposes a lightweight fusion module to enhance the efficiency of multimodal object detection. The Channel Switching and Spatial Attention (CSSA) method improves detection performance while decreasing computational costs. Experimental results suggest that CSSA significantly outperforms existing models, increasing accuracy and demonstrating robustness across various illumination conditions. Thus, this research opens exciting avenues for new fusion paradigms in multimodal systems.

Amrutha J. M., Sankarabukta Nandini, and Anjali T. proposed the real-time litter detection system for moving vehicles using YOLO object detection models that can be used to detect objects in environmental monitoring tasks [7]. M. Sai Sree Akshitha Reddy and Aishwarya N. proposed a deep learning framework exploiting YOLO to classify fresh and stale fruits and vegetables, which demonstrates the framework's applicability to the quality and safety of food [8]. Sudharson S., Priyanka Kokil, Annamalai R., and Sai Manoj N. V. published an advanced food classification using YOLO models where they emphasized accuracy and robustness in object detection algorithms to classify food items [9]. Kumar et al. used transfer learning-based object detection models to diagnose tomato leaf diseases to demonstrate the applicability of YOLO frameworks for crop health management [10]. Priya et al. presented a study on breast mass classification that combined the best of both worlds from the classic neural network architectures along with SVM, and insight into the hybrid approaches toward medical diagnosis [11]. Venugopal et al. developed an ensemble deep learning model for the classification of breast histopathology images that achieved high accuracy and validated the worth of combining different neural network architectures to produce accurate medical image analysis [12].

2 Methodology

2.1 Proposed Solution

The process begins with data preparation for three modalities: RGB, infrared, and depth. For RGB, images are prepared and annotated with bounding boxes; dataset paths and object classes are defined within rgb.yaml. Infrared images are prepared and annotated similarly; dataset paths and object classes are specified in infrared.yaml, tailored to single-channel data. Dataset paths and object classes defined in depth.yaml are also applicable for single-channel inputs; depth images are prepared and annotated. To train the model, initialize a pre-trained YOLOv8 model using yolov8s.pt weights. The You Only Look Once (YOLO) detection system simplifies the task by framing it as a regression problem from pixel coordinates of an image to bounding box coordinates and class probabilities [1].

More recent approaches like R-CNN use region proposal methods to first generate potential bounding boxes in an image and then run a classifier on these proposed boxes. After classification, post-processing is used to refine the bounding boxes, eliminate duplicate detections, and rescore the boxes based on other objects in the scene. These complex pipelines are slow and hard to optimize because each individual component must be trained separately.

In object detection, the confidence C of a bounding box prediction is computed as the product of the probability that an object is present in the bounding box and the Intersection over Union (IoU) between the predicted bounding box and the ground truth bounding box. Mathematically, this can be expressed as:

$$C = \Pr(\text{object}) \times \text{IOU}_{\text{truth, pred}} \tag{1}$$

where $\Pr(\text{object})$ represents the probability that the bounding box contains the object, and $\text{IOU}_{\text{truth, pred}}$ denotes the IoU, which measures the overlap between the predicted and the actual bounding boxes [2]. If the central coordinates of the predicted bounding box match the ground truth, $\Pr(\text{object})$ is set to 1; otherwise, it is set to 0.

To determine the probability that a specific class i is present within the bounding box, this can be further expressed as:

$$C \cdot \Pr(\text{Class}_i|\text{object}) = \Pr(\text{object}) \times \text{IOU}_{\text{truth, pred}} \times \Pr(\text{Class}_i|\text{object}) \tag{2}$$

which simplifies to:

$$C \cdot \Pr(\text{Class}_i|\text{object}) = \Pr(\text{Class}) \times \text{IOU}_{\text{truth, pred}} \tag{3}$$

The configurations in rgb.yaml will be used to fine-tune the model for detecting RGB images. It trains for 1000 epochs, with a batch size of 8, so that the model picks up the objects optimally and classifies them. For infrared image detection, the model trains using the infrared.yaml configurations. The initial convolutional layer of the customyolov8.yaml is changed and reduced to a filter size of 1 from 3, as we're dealing with single-channel images. For the depth image, a similar process is applied that reduces the filter size with the aid of depth.yaml. After training, the multi-modal fusion process starts. Every single trained YOLOv8 model then detects RGB and IR images as well as a depth image. From the respective detections, bounding boxes, confidence scores, and class predictions are extracted for each of the three modalities. In late fusion, these results are combined using techniques such as concatenating feature vectors, averaging or weighting confidence scores, and other strategies to merge results from the different modalities [3].

Late fusion is a technique used in multimodal machine learning where information from multiple modalities (e.g., RGB images, depth images, audio, or text) is combined at a later stage in the model pipeline, typically after each modality has been independently processed [1]. In late fusion, each modality is passed through separate feature extraction networks to capture distinct characteristics, and the outputs (features) are then fused together in the final layers of the model for decision-making. This method allows each modality to be treated independently, ensuring that modality-specific features are preserved before combining them. One key advantage of late fusion is its flexibility, as it enables the model to process different modalities using tailored networks best suited to each input type (e.g., convolutional neural networks for images, recurrent networks for text or audio) [5]. The separate feature extraction process allows the network to capture and maintain specific nuances from each modality before merging, leading to potentially richer representations. Late fusion is often used in tasks such as object detection, action recognition, or autonomous driving, where integrating information from various sources (e.g., RGB, infrared, depth) can improve overall performance and decision accuracy [4].

Subsequently, non-maximum suppression (NMS) is applied to refine the detection results. The procedure involves the following steps:

- First, the bounding box with the highest class probability for a particular class is selected and added to the final list of bounding boxes.
- Second, the Intersection over Union (IoU) of the selected bounding box is compared with all other predicted boxes, and any box with an IoU exceeding the threshold is removed.
- Third, from the remaining boxes, the one with the next highest class probability is selected and added to the final list. This comparison and removal process based on IoU is repeated until no bounding boxes remain in the list.

Finally, in the post-processing stage, the refined bounding boxes are overlaid on the original images for visualization and analysis. The performance of the detection system is evaluated using metrics such as precision, recall, and mean average precision (mAP).

Evaluation Metrics. The Mean Average Precision (mAP) is calculated by averaging the Average Precision (AP) for each class:

$$mAP = \frac{1}{C} \sum_{i=1}^{C} AP_i \tag{4}$$

where C is the number of classes and AP_i is the Average Precision for class i.

For optimal performance in our research, we target an mAP range between 50 and 90. This range reflects a strong balance between precision and recall, ensuring that the model effectively addresses both false positives (FP) and false negatives (FN) across various detection scenarios.

2.2 Dataset

The objective of this research is to advance and develop techniques for the detection of objects within multimodal data streams. The dataset in use consists of 5000 multimodal image sets, sourced from the Multi-Modal Visual Pattern Recognition Challenge at ICPR 2024, encompassing 13 distinct classes (Table 1).

Table 1. Class IDs with Corresponding Class Names and Instances

Class_ID	Class_Name	Instances
0	Person	5766
1	Boat	270
2	Traffic Sign	435
3	Animal	2582
4	Seat	1500
5	Bird	2276
6	Sign	900
7	Cyclist	445
8	Bicycle	901
9	Car	2085
10	Ball	156
11	Light	1136
12	Garbage Can	456

Each group includes an RGB image, a Depth image, and an Infrared image, which had been passed at 1920 × 1080 pixels. Preliminary alignment has already been done to avoid inconsistencies. Further research into the data set revealed noise in it, which might affect the precision of detection. The issue, therefore, needs to be resolved for improvement in model performance and for successful reliable results in multimodal object detection (Fig. 1).

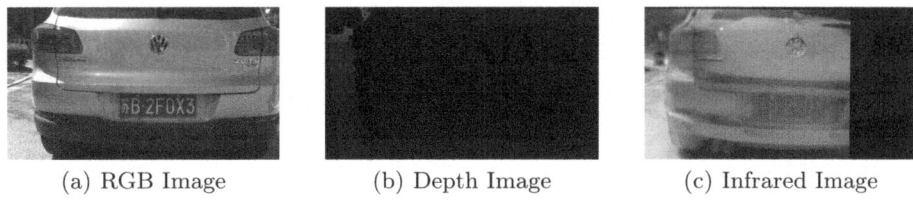

(a) RGB Image   (b) Depth Image   (c) Infrared Image

Fig. 1. Some sample RGB, Depth, and Infrared Images from our dataset.

3 Implementation

3.1 Architecture

We pursued the YOLOv8 detector pre-trained on RGB images (yolov8s.pt) and proceeded to fine-tune it on a custom RGB dataset, incorporating specifications defined in rgb.yaml. Training was conducted for 1000 epochs, utilizing a batch size of 8 samples, with the aim of improving detection of persons, boats, and traffic signs [1]. For infrared image detection, the model was trained using the infrared.yaml dataset, but a single channel was used for processing infrared images. The main convolutional layer of the YOLOv8 backbone was altered to work with single-channel infrared images by reducing the filter size from 3 to 1 [2]. Similarly, the depth image detection model, covered in depth.yaml, was trained with analogous modifications to accommodate depth data [4]. Both the depth and infrared models were implemented with moderate changes, fixing the number of object classes at 13 (Fig. 2).

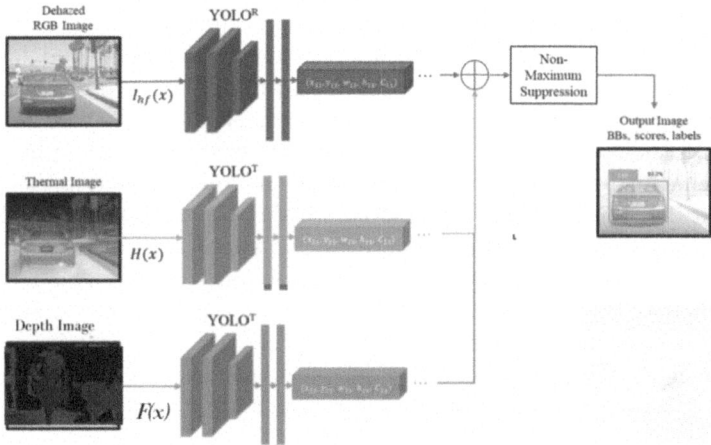

Fig. 2. Block diagram of YOLO object detection method based on late fusion and NMS

Scaling parameters of the YOLOv8 were adjusted to maintain the ratio of depth to width on dual datasets, and the head of the network was trained for three scales: P3, P4, and P5, enhancing the quality of detection for objects of varying sizes [3]. Moreover, training was performed across several epochs, with batch increments made to achieve optimal results.

4   Result

In the multimodal object detection task, we utilized three different modalities, each contributing equally, with a total of 1000 weights incorporated in the model. The Intersection over Union (IoU) threshold was set to 0.7, and a confidence threshold of 0.5 was used to filter out low-confidence predictions. The resulting detection score was 0.2048. Here we have provided a table that shows mAPs obtained for different modalities (Table 2):

Table 2. Average mAP scores for different types of data

Type of Data	Average mAP Score
Color	60.691
Depth	27.8
Infrared	40.581

5   Conclusion

In this work, we mainly focus on the multimodal approach in object detection through the use of YOLOv8 and Non-Maximum Suppression and late fusion techniques when combining RGB, infrared and depth images. The aim was to integrate detection accuracy in any format of image. It used a late fusion approach, where their detection results are merged from different approaches on modality, which helps them exploit their complementary strengths. Using an IoU threshold of 0.7, the confidence threshold was kept at 0.5, and a total of 1000 weights were used in the final fusion process, which produced a detection score of 0.2048. The score will reflect the baseline level of performance for the fusion strategy whereas the necessity of further optimization to reach desired values of accuracy will be noted. Future efforts may then try to optimize the fusion mechanism along with adjusting the detection parameters for each modality in a manner to be able to have improved overall system performance.

References

1. Redmon, J., Divvala, S., Girshick, R., Farhadi, A.: You only look once: unified, real-time object detection. In: CVPR, pp. 779–788 (2016). https://www.cv-foundation.org/openaccess/content_cvpr_2016/papers/Redmon_You_Only_Look_CVPR_2016_paper.pdf

2. Yoon, S., Cho, J.: Deep multimodal detection in reduced visibility using thermal depth estimation for autonomous driving. Sensors **22**(14), 5084 (2022). https://www.mdpi.com/1424-8220/22/14/5084

3. Jiang, C., et al.: M2FNet: multi-modal fusion network for object detection from visible and thermal infrared images. Int. J. Appl. Earth Obs. Geoinf. **130**, 103918 (2024). https://doi.org/10.1016/j.jag.2024.103918

4. Wang, D., Chen, X., Yi, H., Zhao, F.: Improvement of non-maximum suppression in RGB-D object detection. IEEE Access **7**, 144134–144143 (2019). https://ieeexplore.ieee.org/stamp/stamp.jsp?tp=&arnumber=8863938

5. Cao, Y., Bin, J., Hamari, J., Blasch, E., Liu, Z.: Multimodal object detection by channel switching and spatial attention. In: Proceedings of the IEEE/CVF Conference on Computer Vision and Pattern Recognition (CVPR) Workshops, pp. 403–411 (2023). https://openaccess.thecvf.com/content/CVPR2023W/PBVS/papers/Cao_Multimodal_Object_Detection_by_Channel_Switching_and_Spatial_Attention_CVPRW_2023_paper.pdf

6. Noh, K., Hong, S.K., Makonin, S., Lee, Y.: Enhancing object detection in dense images: adjustable non-maximum suppression for single-class detection. IEEE Access **12**, 130253–130263 (2024). https://doi.org/10.1109/ACCESS.2024.3459629

7. Amrutha, J.M., Sankarabukta, N., Anjali, T.: Real-time litter detection system for moving vehicles using YOLO. In: Proceedings of the 2022 4th International Conference on Smart Systems and Inventive Technology (ICSSIT), pp. 1311–1315 (2022). https://doi.org/10.1109/ICSSIT53264.2022.9716512

8. Reddy, M.S.S.A., Aishwarya, N.: A deep learning approach to identify fresh and stale fruits and vegetables with YOLO. In: Proceedings of the 2023 International Conference on Advances in Electronics, Communication, Computing and Intelligent Information Systems (ICAECIS), pp. 606–610 (2023). https://doi.org/10.1109/ICAECIS58353.2023.10170163

9. Sudharson, S., Kokil, P., Annamalai, R., Manoj, S.N.V.: Enhanced food classification system using YOLO models for object detection algorithm. In: Proceedings of the 2023 14th International Conference on Computing Communication and Networking Technologies (ICCCNT), pp. 1–6 (2023). https://doi.org/10.1109/ICCCNT56998.2023.10307943

10. Kumar, N.S., Sony, J., Premkumar, A.R., Meenakshi, R., Nair, J.J.: Transfer learning-based object detection models for improved diagnosis of tomato leaf disease. Procedia Comput. Sci. **235**, 3025–3034 (2024). In: ICMLDE 2023. https://doi.org/10.1016/j.procs.2024.04.286

11. Priya, R., Sreelekshmi, V., Nair, J.J., Gopakumar, G.: Breast mass classification using classic neural network architecture and support vector machine. In: Thampi, S.M., Gelenbe, E., Atiquzzaman, M., Chaudhary, V., Li, K.-C. (eds.) Advances in Computing and Network Communications. LNEE, vol. 736, pp. 435–448. Springer, Singapore (2021). https://doi.org/10.1007/978-981-33-6987-0_36

12. Venugopal, A., Sreelekshmi, V., Nair, J. J.: Ensemble deep learning model for breast histopathology image classification. In: Tuba, M., Akashe, S., Joshi, A. (eds.) ICT Infrastructure and Computing, pp. 607–612. Springer, Singapore (2023). https://doi.org/10.1007/978-981-19-5331-6_51

Action Recognition Using Temporal Shift Module and Ensemble Learning

Anh-Kiet Duong[1]([✉])[iD] and Petra Gomez-Krämer[2][iD]

[1] University of Limoges, Limoges, France
anh-kiet.duong@etu.unilim.fr
[2] L3i Laboratory, La Rochelle University, La Rochelle, France
petra.gomez@univ-lr.fr

Abstract. This paper presents the first-rank solution for the Multi-Modal Action Recognition Challenge, part of the Multi-Modal Visual Pattern Recognition Workshop at the International Conference on Pattern Recognition (ICPR) 2024. The competition aimed to recognize human actions using a diverse dataset of 20 action classes, collected from multi-modal sources. The proposed approach is built upon the Temporal Shift Module (TSM), a technique aimed at efficiently capturing temporal dynamics in video data, incorporating multiple data input types. Our strategy included transfer learning to leverage pre-trained models, followed by meticulous fine-tuning on the challenge's specific dataset to optimize performance for the 20 action classes. We carefully selected a backbone network to balance computational efficiency and recognition accuracy and further refined the model using an ensemble technique that integrates outputs from different modalities. This ensemble approach proved crucial in boosting the overall performance. Our solution achieved a perfect top-1 accuracy on the test set, demonstrating the effectiveness of the proposed approach in recognizing human actions across 20 classes. Our code is available online (https://github.com/ffyyytt/TSM-MMVPR).

Keywords: Multi-Modal Action Recognition · Thermal Infrared Data · Ensemble Learning

1 Introduction

Human action recognition is a computer vision task with the aim of recognizing and classifying human activities in images or videos. The objective is to analyze, understand human behavior and to classify the actions performed in the image or video into a predefined set of action classes. It is important for many applications such as video indexing, biometrics, surveillance and security. Human action

A.-K. Duong—The master program pursued by the first author is sponsored by the "Vingroup Science and Technology Scholarship Program for Overseas Study for Master's and Doctoral Degrees".

S. Palaiahnakote et al. (Eds.): ICPR 2024 Workshops, LNCS 15617, pp. 302–313, 2025.
https://doi.org/10.1007/978-3-031-88217-3_23

recognition is a complex task due to the difficulty of extracting information about person's identity and their psychological states [4]. Moreover, ambiguities in recognizing actions does not only come from the difficulty to define the motion of body parts, but also from many other challenges related to real world problems such as camera motion, dynamic background, and bad weather conditions [7].

Human action recognition can be achieved using different sensors such as RBG or RGB-D cameras, but also depth sensors, infrared or thermal cameras. 2D RGB data have attracted huge attention as visual data are rich in features and less computational expensive than 3D data. Furthermore, RGB cameras are very common and affordable. However, combining modalities like depth or thermal can enhance recognition by providing complementary information, especially in challenging environments.

The Multi-Modal Action Recognition Challenge, part of the Multi-Modal Visual Pattern Recognition Workshop at International Conference on Pattern Recognition (ICPR) 2024, focuses on the complex task of recognizing human actions from multi-modal data sources. This track presents a unique opportunity to explore the integration of multiple data modalities–namely RGB, Depth, and thermal infrared (IR) to improve the accuracy and robustness of action recognition systems. The challenge dataset comprises 2,500 videos, featuring 20 different action classes such as "shake hands," "ride a bike," "rope skipping," and potentially confusing pairs like "up the stairs" vs. "down the stairs," and "swivel" vs. "twist waist." With 2,000 videos designated for training and 500 for testing, each video spans a duration of 2 to 13 s and is captured in varying resolutions for different modalities, posing additional challenges for multi-modal fusion and feature extraction.

The objective of the competition is to advance the state-of-the-art in multi-modal action recognition by encouraging participants to develop innovative solutions that leverage the strengths of each modality while addressing the technical hurdles posed by feature heterogeneity and data fusion. To evaluate performance, the challenge uses the Top-1 and Top-5 accuracy metrics, which are commonly adopted benchmarks in the action recognition field. The organizers have provided a baseline model to guide participants, yet the competition aims to push beyond this baseline, setting new standards for multi-modal action recognition techniques.

This paper presents the 1st place solution for Track 3, which achieved a perfect score of 1.000 on the test set. Unlike typical multi-modal approaches, our solution focused solely on the thermal IR modality, as it yielded the highest accuracy during experimentation. We utilized the Temporal Shift Module (TSM) [9] for efficient video understanding and applied transfer learning along with fine-tuning techniques specifically optimized for the thermal IR data. This targeted approach proved effective in overcoming the challenges of action recognition, even for closely related classes. By prioritizing a single modality, we simplified the model architecture while still surpassing the provided baseline and establishing a new benchmark for the challenge. The results highlight the potential of thermal IR data in this task's dataset, demonstrating its robustness and capability in accurately recognizing complex human actions.

The reminder of the article is organized as follows. We review related work in Sect. 2. Section 3 presents our methods for action recognition based on TSM and ensemble learning. Section 4 presents and discusses our results. Finally, we conclude our work in Sect. 5 and outlines future work.

2 Related Work

We discuss below related work on video action recognition, deep learning architectures for video action recognition and ensemble learning.

2.1 Video Action Recognition

Video action recognition has been a key area of research in computer vision, evolving significantly with the advent of deep learning. Traditional approaches often relied on hand-crafted features, such as Histogram of Oriented Gradients (HOG) [2], Motion History Images (MHI) and optical flow, for capturing motion information, which were effective but limited by their inability to learn features directly from data in an end-to-end fashion [15]. However, these methods struggled to generalize across complex datasets due to their inability to learn data-driven representations.

With the introduction of deep learning, convolutional neural networks (CNNs) emerged as powerful tools for learning features directly from raw video data. Various architectures have been proposed, each with different strategies for capturing temporal and spatial information. These include:

- 2D models: Methods like Temporal Segment Networks (TSN) [14] extend 2D CNNs by applying temporal sampling and aggregation strategies across video frames, allowing them to capture long-range temporal dependencies. While the Temporal Shift Module (TSM) shifts part of the feature channels along the temporal dimension, enabling the model to capture temporal dependencies without the computational cost of full 3D convolutions.
- 3D models: Approaches such as Convolutional 3D (C3D) [13] and Inflated 3D CNN (I3D) [1] extend traditional 2D convolution to the temporal dimension, enabling joint spatial-temporal feature learning. These models have demonstrated superior performance on benchmark datasets but often require substantial computational resources.
- Two-Stream models: The two-stream architecture [15] consists of separate RGB and optical flow streams, which are later fused to combine spatial and motion information. Although effective, this approach relies heavily on the quality of optical flow estimation.

2.2   Deep Learning Architectures

Deep learning architectures have significantly advanced video action recognition. One of the foundational models is ResNet, introduced by He et al. [6]. ResNet employs skip connections to facilitate the training of very deep networks, effectively addressing the vanishing gradient problem and enabling improved feature learning through residual learning. Its effectiveness in extracting rich features has made it a popular choice for various computer vision tasks.

Building on ResNet, ResNeXt [16] enhances the model capacity through a split-transform-merge strategy. This design allows ResNeXt to learn complex patterns more efficiently without a substantial increase in computational cost, making it particularly effective for high-accuracy tasks such as action recognition.

Another notable architecture is ResNeSt [17], which extends ResNeXt by incorporating split-attention mechanisms. This enhancement improves the model's ability to capture rich feature representations by dynamically focusing on different parts of the input data, further boosting performance in action recognition tasks.

Recent developments in transformer architectures, including the Vision Transformer (ViT) [3] and Swin Transformer [10], have also shown promise in video analysis. ViT [3] treats video frames as sequences of patches, allowing it to capture long-range dependencies and global context more effectively than traditional CNNs. Meanwhile, the Swin Transformer [10] introduces a hierarchical architecture that operates at multiple scales, demonstrating strong performance across various benchmarks. Together, these transformer-based models highlight the potential for innovative approaches in enhancing action recognition tasks.

2.3   Ensemble Learning

Ensemble learning has been widely used in action recognition to improve the accuracy and the robustness by combining predictions from multiple models. Techniques like Bagging, Stacking, and weighted averaging are popular, with more advanced methods such as AdaBoost and Gradient Boosting also explored [11]. These approaches help to address individual model limitations by merging outputs from different modalities or architectures.

In this work, we chose weighted averaging for its simplicity and effectiveness, as well as time constraints, allowing us to efficiently combine predictions without adding excessive complexity.

3   Action Recognition Method

In Fig. 1, we illustrate the methodology employed in our solution for predicting human actions. Our method is centered around the Temporal Shift Module (TSM) [9]. Specifically utilizing the ResNeSt-269 [17] variant, which is trained exclusively on RGB images, and also takes RGB data as input for prediction

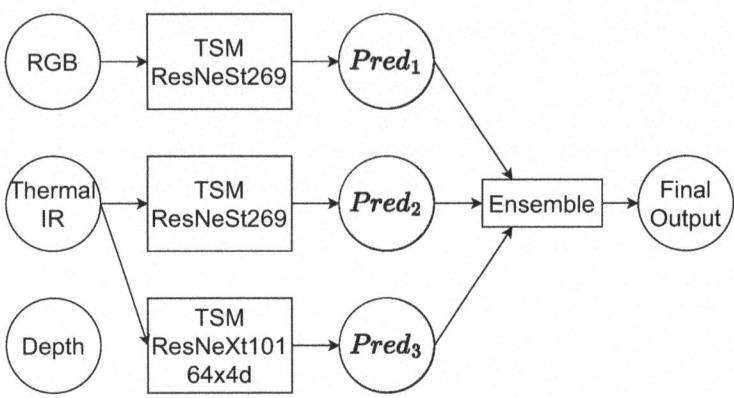

Fig. 1. Overview of the prediction process in the proposed solution.

pharse. Additionally, we incorporate two TSM models trained on thermal IR images: one is the ResNeSt-269, and the other is the ResNeXt101 $64 \times 4d$ [16], both of which also take thermal IR data as input. Notably, we opted not to use depth images in our approach due to their large size. We also tested other backbone models, such as ResNet [6] and Inception [12], but the results were not high on the leaderboard. Therefore, we decided to use ResNeSt-269 and ResNeXt101 $64 \times 4d$ for our final solution since it provide higher score on the leaderboard. And we use both for ensemble learning because both have very high and almost perfect results on the test set.

The outputs from these three distinct models are subsequently ensembled to produce the final predictions. This strategy not only streamlines the computational resources required for training and inference but also enhances the overall performance of our system. By allowing each model to focus on a specific type of data input (RGB or thermal IR) we reduce the computational burden, as it eliminates the need to process all three data modalities simultaneously. This approach significantly decreases the resources needed for training and utilizing the models for prediction, enabling us to achieve more efficient results while maintaining high accuracy in action recognition.

3.1   Temporal Shift Module (TSM)

Following the baseline provided by the organizers, we continued to use the TSM as the core of our solution for action recognition. To enhance performance, we explored different backbone models and input data modalities, as detailed in the following subsections.

Backbone Models. Due to the public code provided by the authors of TSM [9], which is compatible with ResNet architectures, we experimented with various models, including ResNet [6], ResNeXt [16], and ResNeSt [17]. Among these, ResNeXt and ResNeSt demonstrated superior performance compared to ResNet. Consequently, we selected ResNeXt and ResNeSt for the ensemble process, as they provided better accuracy and robustness for action recognition tasks.

Data Modality. In our experiments, we utilized both RGB and thermal IR data. We opted not to explore depth data due to its substantial file size and the time constraints we faced during the challenge. Notably, our findings revealed that thermal IR images yielded better classification performance than RGB images. When using identical backbone architectures, models processing thermal IR input consistently outperformed those using RGB, highlighting the advantages of leveraging different data modalities for improved action recognition.

3.2   Training Strategy

Initially, we split the dataset into two distinct subsets: a training set and a validation set, consisting of 80% and 20% of the data, respectively. This partitioning results in 1,600 videos used for training and 400 videos reserved for validation. During the training phase, we train the models using the training set for 100 epochs, while the validation set is employed to evaluate the models' performance and to select the most suitable hyperparameters. The validation process allows us to select the backbone model and fine-tune parameters such as learning rate, dropout rate, and number of segments,... thereby optimizing the models for the task of action recognition.

Given the limited size of the dataset, comprising only 2,000 videos in total, we take an additional step to improve model generalization. After identifying the optimal hyperparameters based on the validation set, we retrain the models using the entire dataset for 200 epochs, including all 2,000 videos without the validation. This final training step aims to enhance the models' ability to learn from the complete set of available data, thereby maximizing their capacity to capture the underlying patterns within the action sequences.

By employing this two-step training strategy, we ensure that our models are well-calibrated and capable of achieving high performance despite the small dataset size. This approach allows us to make the most effective use of the available data, balancing the need for hyperparameter tuning with the advantages of training on the full dataset.

3.3   Configuration

As detailed in Sect. 3.2, we selected our hyperparameters by training the models for a limited number of epochs on the validation set. This method allowed us to efficiently identify suitable configurations. In addition to the hyperparameters we fine-tuned, we retained several default settings from the strong public implementation of the TSM[1], such as image size and augmentation techniques.

---

[1] https://github.com/mit-han-lab/temporal-shift-module.

Ultimately, the hyperparameters we converged on include an average type for ensemble weighting, a segment count of 8, and a learning rate of 0.01. These choices reflect our commitment to optimizing the model's performance.

3.4 Ensemble Learning

In our solution, we employ a basic ensemble learning method as follows in [8] by combining the softmax outputs of each model, applying a specific weight w_i to each model i. This approach allows us to leverage the strengths of each individual model while mitigating their weaknesses, leading to improved overall performance. The final prediction P is computed using the following formula:

$$P = \sum_{i=1}^{n} w_i \cdot Pred_i \tag{1}$$

where $Pred_i$ represents the softmax output of model i and n denotes the total number of models in the ensemble. By adjusting the weights w_i, we can fine-tune the contribution of each model to the final prediction, thereby optimizing the ensemble's performance based on their respective accuracies and confidence levels.

This weighted ensemble strategy not only enhances the robustness of our predictions but also provides a means to effectively manage the trade-off between computational efficiency and predictive accuracy. Ultimately, this methodology enables us to achieve superior results in action recognition tasks, as the combined predictions from diverse models yield a more comprehensive understanding of the input data across different modalities.

Looking toward the future, our ensemble methodology could be expanded to incorporate more sophisticated ensemble techniques. For instance, algorithms such as AdaBoost [5], which focuses on converting weak learners into a strong learner by adjusting weights iteratively, could be implemented to further enhance prediction accuracy. Additionally, more advanced techniques like Bagging and Stacking could also be explored [11]. These ensemble methods have shown promise in various machine learning tasks and may provide further improvements in the context of multi-modal action recognition. By integrating these approaches, we aim to refine our ensemble strategy and explore new avenues for enhancing model performance in future research.

4   Results

In this section, we present our results on our validation sub-set and on the test set of the competition.

4.1 Task Description

The competition provided the participants with two datasets: a labeled training set consisting of 2,000 videos across 20 action classes, and an unlabeled test set of 500 videos. The goal was to predict the labels of the test videos, with each video allowing up to five ranked predictions for evaluation. The competition metrics used were Top-1 and Top-5 accuracy, based on the highest-ranked correct prediction and any correct prediction within the top five, respectively.

For model training, we initially split the training set into 80% for training (1,600 videos) and 20% for validation (400 videos) to optimize hyperparameters and evaluate performance. After this step, we retrained the models using the entire training set of 2,000 videos for 200 epochs to maximize the utilization of the available data. The dataset consisted of 20 action labels:

switch light	up the stairs	pack backpack	ride a bike	turn around
fold clothes	hug somebody	long jump	move the chair	open the umbrella
orchestra conducting	rope skipping	shake hands	squat	swivel
tie shoes	tie hair	twist waist	wear hat	down the stairs

In Fig. 2 we show two samples taken from the same video and frame of the "ride a bike" class, but displayed in different formats: RGB and thermal IR. It is evident that the RGB image appears quite dark, making it difficult to discern details. In contrast, the thermal IR image clearly highlights the subject and action, offering better visibility. This observation helps explain why models with thermal IR input consistently outperformed those using RGB, as the IR modality provides more reliable information in low-light conditions, leading to better classification performance.

4.2   Validation

In Fig. 3, we present the validation accuracy results on 20% of the dataset for validation, while training was conducted on the remaining 80%. The figure illustrates the performance of the ResNeSt-269 and ResNeXt101 64 × 4d backbone models with thermal IR and RGB input, respectively. This step was primarily used to evaluate the models and determine suitable hyperparameters. After this preliminary validation phase, we retrained the models for 200 epochs on the full set of 2,000 videos without a separate validation set, to make full use of the available data and maximize model performance.

4.3   Test Set

Table 1 presents the results obtained on the test set of the competition. The results illustrate the effectiveness of different TSM configurations, backbones, and input modalities, highlighting the superior performance of the ensemble method. Notably, the TSM-ResNeSt-269 model stands out as the highest-performing single model, achieving a Top-1 accuracy of 0.9860 and a perfect Top-5 accuracy, showcasing its exceptional capability in action recognition tasks. However, it is important to note that ResNeSt-269 is also a backbone with

(a) RGB image

(b) Thermal IR image

Fig. 2. Comparison of RGB and thermal IR images from the same frame of the "ride a bike" class.

very high computational complexity, which may pose challenges in terms of resource requirements during training and inference. This trade-off between performance and computational efficiency is a critical consideration in model selection for real-world applications.

The baseline model, which combines TSM with a ResNet50 backbone and incorporates all three input modalities (RGB, IR, and Depth), achieved an impressive Top-1 accuracy of 0.8643 and a Top-5 accuracy of 0.9940. It is particularly surprising that such high performance can be attained with the ResNet50 backbone, significantly outperforming configurations that rely solely on a RGB input. This result highlights the substantial benefits of integrating multiple data modalities for action recognition. However, the trade-off is that this approach demands significantly higher computational resources due to the need to process all three input types simultaneously.

Finally, our ensemble method achieved a perfect Top-1 accuracy of 1.0000 and a Top-5 accuracy of 1.0000, demonstrating the effectiveness of our approach

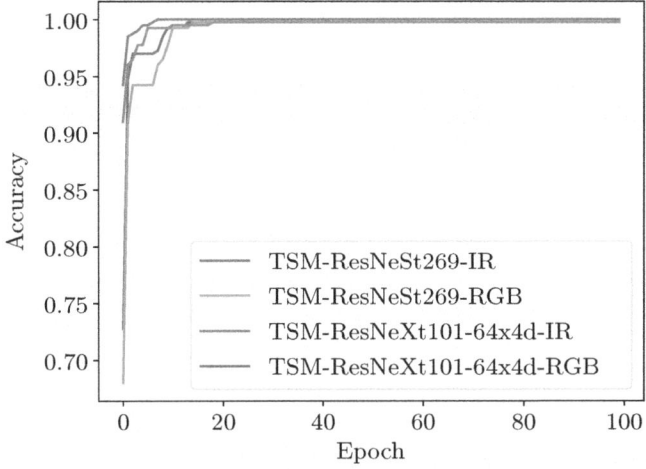

Fig. 3. Validation accuracy of the ResNeSt269 and ResNeXt101 $64 \times 4d$ backbone models with thermal IR and RGB input on the validation set.

in integrating multiple models to enhance overall performance. All the results show a clear trend: increasing computational complexity tends to improve model accuracy, whether by using larger backbone architectures or incorporating multiple input modalities. Based on this observation, we decided to maximize the size of our backbones while training each model on a single input type, and then combine them using ensemble learning. This strategy allowed us to achieve the highest performance without the need to train on all three input types simultaneously, thus optimizing both accuracy and computational efficiency.

Table 1. Performance comparison of various methods on the test set.

Method	Accuracy	
	Top-1	Top-5
TSM-ResNet50-RGB	0.5600	0.9260
TSM-ResNeXt50-RGB	0.6660	0.8760
Baseline	0.8643	0.9940
TSM-ResNeXt101-64×4d-RGB	0.8620	0.9700
TSM-ResNeSt269-RGB	0.9620	1.0000
TSM-ResNeXt101-64×4d-IR	0.9820	1.0000
TSM-ResNeSt269-IR	0.9860	1.0000
Ensemble	**1.0000**	1.0000

5   Conclusion

In conclusion, our solution for the Multi-Modal Action Recognition Challenge at ICPR 2024 demonstrated that focusing on thermal IR data and leveraging the Temporal Shift Module (TSM) with an ensemble learning of selected models can achieve state-of-the-art results. The approach not only maximized accuracy but also highlighted the potential of using single-modality data in complex recognition tasks. Future research should explore advanced ensemble methods and additional modalities to further enhance performance and robustness in multimodal action recognition systems.

References

1. Carreira, J., Zisserman, A.: Quo vadis, action recognition? A new model and the kinetics dataset. In: Proceedings of the IEEE Conference on Computer Vision and Pattern Recognition, pp. 6299–6308 (2017)
2. Dalal, N., Triggs, B.: Histograms of oriented gradients for human detection. In: 2005 IEEE Computer Society Conference on Computer Vision and Pattern Recognition (CVPR 2005), vol. 1, pp. 886–893. IEEE (2005)
3. Dosovitskiy, A.: An image is worth 16x16 words: transformers for image recognition at scale. arXiv preprint arXiv:2010.11929 (2020)
4. Elharrouss, O., Almaadeed, N., Al-Maadeed, S.: A review of video surveillance systems. J. Vis. Commun. Image Represent. **77**, 103116 (2021). https://doi.org/10.1016/j.jvcir.2021.103116. https://www.sciencedirect.com/science/article/pii/S1047320321000729
5. Freund, Y., Schapire, R.E.: A decision-theoretic generalization of on-line learning and an application to boosting. J. Comput. Syst. Sci. **55**(1), 119–139 (1997)
6. He, K., Zhang, X., Ren, S., Sun, J.: Deep residual learning for image recognition. In: Proceedings of the IEEE Conference on Computer Vision and Pattern Recognition, pp. 770–778 (2016)
7. Jegham, I., Ben Khalifa, A., Alouani, I., Mahjoub, M.A.: Vision-based human action recognition: an overview and real world challenges. Forensic Sci. Int. Digit. Invest. **32**, 200901 (2020). https://doi.org/10.1016/j.fsidi.2019.200901. https://www.sciencedirect.com/science/article/pii/S174228761930283X
8. Jeon, S.: 1st place solution to google landmark retrieval 2020. arXiv preprint arXiv:2009.05132 (2020)
9. Lin, J., Gan, C., Han, S.: TSM: temporal shift module for efficient video understanding. In: Proceedings of the IEEE International Conference on Computer Vision (2019)
10. Liu, Z., et al.: Swin transformer: hierarchical vision transformer using shifted windows. In: Proceedings of the IEEE/CVF International Conference on Computer Vision, pp. 10012–10022 (2021)
11. Mienye, I.D., Sun, Y.: A survey of ensemble learning: concepts, algorithms, applications, and prospects. IEEE Access **10**, 99129–99149 (2022)
12. Szegedy, C., Vanhoucke, V., Ioffe, S., Shlens, J., Wojna, Z.: Rethinking the inception architecture for computer vision. In: Proceedings of the IEEE Conference on Computer Vision and Pattern Recognition, pp. 2818–2826 (2016)

13. Tran, D., Bourdev, L., Fergus, R., Torresani, L., Paluri, M.: Learning spatiotemporal features with 3D convolutional networks. In: Proceedings of the IEEE International Conference on Computer Vision, pp. 4489–4497 (2015)

14. Wang, L., et al.: Temporal segment networks: towards good practices for deep action recognition. In: European Conference on Computer Vision, pp. 20–36. Springer (2016)

15. Wu, F., et al.: A survey on video action recognition in sports: datasets, methods and applications. IEEE Trans. Multimedia **25**, 7943–7966 (2022)

16. Xie, S., Girshick, R., Dollár, P., Tu, Z., He, K.: Aggregated residual transformations for deep neural networks. In: Proceedings of the IEEE Conference on Computer Vision and Pattern Recognition, pp. 1492–1500 (2017)

17. Zhang, H., et al.: Resnest: split-attention networks. In: Proceedings of the IEEE/CVF Conference on Computer Vision and Pattern Recognition, pp. 2736–2746 (2022)

Modality Fusion Adaptor-Enhanced Vision Transformer for Multimodal Action Recognition

Xin Hu[1,2], Yunan Li[1,2,3](✉)(iD), Yulang Xu[1,2], Wei Chen[1], Yihao Zhang[1,2], Shoude Li[1,2], and Qiguang Miao[1,2,3](iD)

[1] School of Computer Science and Technology, Xidian University, Xi'an, China
{xinhu123,yulangxu,cw,zhangyihao,shoulderlee}@stu.xidian.edu.cn,
{yunanli,qgmiao}@xidian.edu.cn
[2] Xian Key Laboratory of Big Data and Intelligent Vision, Xi'an, China
[3] Key Laboratory of Smart Human-Computer Interaction and Wearable Technology of Shaanxi Province, Xi'an, China

Abstract. Multimodal action recognition is a critical task for understanding complex human behaviors across different data sources. In this paper, we focus on Track 3 of the Multimodal Visual Pattern Recognition Challenge, which emphasizes recognizing human actions or activities from multimodal data streams. However, traditional methods have not sufficiently considered the complementarity of different modalities, thereby failing to fully leverage the valuable information from each. In this paper, we propose a Modality Fusion Vision Transformer (MF-ViT) network, in which we design a Modality Fusion Adaptor module that significantly enhances the model's ability to capture complex cross-modal relationships and fine-grained features by strengthening inter-modality interactions. Our approach achieved 1st place in the MMVPR Challenge Track 3, and the experimental results demonstrate its effectiveness, achieving 100% Top-1 accuracy on the RGB-T modality, 99% Top-1 accuracy on the RGB-D modality, and 97.4% Top-1 accuracy on the RTD modality. These results demonstrate the effectiveness and superiority of our approach in the multimodal action recognition task. The code of our method is available at: https://github.com/caicai211/MF-ViT.

Keywords: Multimodal Action Recognition · Modality Fusion Adaptor · Vision Transformer

1 Introduction

In an increasingly interconnected world, understanding human behavior through multimodal data has become a critical research area across various fields, including surveillance [5], healthcare [12], and robotics [3]. Multimodal action recognition requires the accurate identification of human activities by integrating information from diverse sources, such as visible light (RGB) cameras, depth (Depth)

© The Author(s), under exclusive license to Springer Nature Switzerland AG 2025
S. Palaiahnakote et al. (Eds.): ICPR 2024 Workshops, LNCS 15617, pp. 314–323, 2025.
https://doi.org/10.1007/978-3-031-88217-3_24

sensors, and thermal Infrared (TIR) imaging. This capability not only enhances the robustness of recognition systems but also provides a more comprehensive understanding of human behavior in complex environments.

Integrating multimodal data faces challenges such as background interference, illumination variations, and the inherent differences between data types, as well as the need for effective fusion techniques. These factors bring unique difficulties when combining multiple modalities. In multimodal action recognition tasks, there are significant feature differences between different modalities (such as RGB, depth, and thermal imaging), making it crucial to effectively fuse this multimodal information. Additionally, complex human behaviors often have diverse temporal and spatial dependencies, which are difficult to fully capture using a single modality. Therefore, leveraging the complementary information from multimodal data becomes a key issue. Researchers have proposed effective solutions in areas such as action recognition [8,11,15] and low-light action recognition [9,14] to address these challenges, and the Multimodal Visual Pattern Recognition Challenge Track 3 provides an excellent platform for further exploring these complexities.

To address these challenges, we propose the Modality Fusion Vision Transformer (MF-ViT) network, which achieves multimodal fusion through the Modality Fusion Adaptor module. This module is a novel modality fusion adaptor embedded within the Vision Transformer (ViT) framework, designed to seamlessly integrate information from multiple data streams. By efficiently aligning cross-modal features, the Modality Fusion Adaptor enables the model to fully exploit complementary information, enhancing its ability to recognize complex human behaviors. By combining the strengths of RGB, depth, and thermal imaging data, the Modality Fusion Adaptor significantly improves the model's ability to capture intricate cross-modal relationships and fine-grained features, thereby greatly enhancing the performance of multimodal action recognition.

2 Methodology

2.1 Overall Network Framework

The overall network structure is shown in Fig. 1(a), We employed the ViT [4] as the backbone network to process video inputs. The video is composed of T sampled frames, forming a four-dimensional tensor $V \in \mathbb{R}^{(T \times H \times W \times C)}$, where T represents the number of frames in the temporal dimension, H and W denote the height and width of the video frames, respectively, and C is the number of channels. To efficiently extract spatiotemporal features from the video, we adopted the tubelet embedding method [1,13]. This approach segments the input video V into a series of non-overlapping spatiotemporal fragments, referred to as tubelets, each with a size of $t \times h \times w$, where t indicates the temporal length, and h and w represent the spatial height and width, respectively. Each tubelet is then linearly projected into a D-dimensional feature vector space, generating tokens $H_0^M \in \mathbb{R}^{N \times D}$. Where, M can represent the RGB, TIR, or Depth modalities, and $N = \lfloor \frac{T}{t} \rfloor \times \lfloor \frac{H}{h} \rfloor \times \lfloor \frac{W}{w} \rfloor$. Given the large amount of data in the RGB modality, we

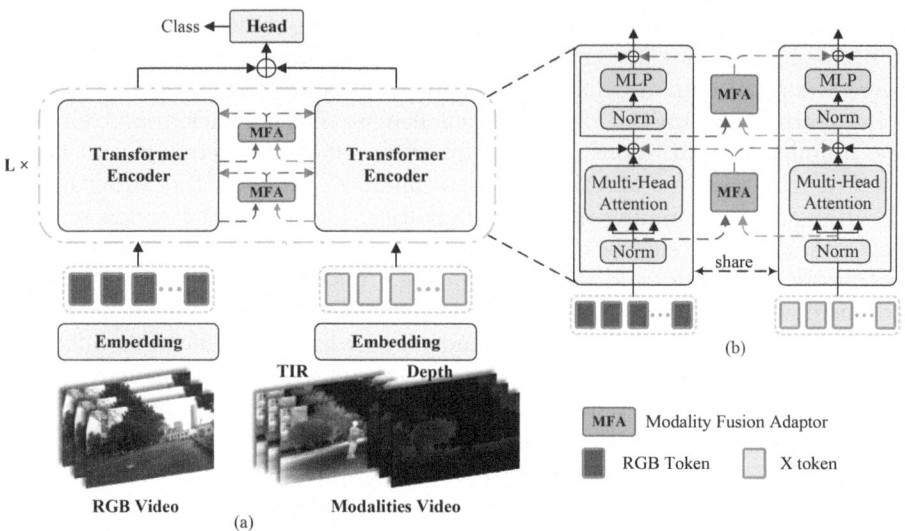

Fig. 1. Our proposed MF-ViT network framework, which converts RGB and X modality videos into tokens processed by L-layer Transformer encoders with the Modality Fusion Adaptor, and finally concatenates the outputs and passes them to the prediction head.(a) The overall network structure. (b) The architecture of the Transformer with Modality Fusion Adaptor.

choose RGB as the mandatory modality to be fused with other modalities. After obtaining the tokens from both the RGB and modality X, they are fed into the Transformer Encoder layer with the embedded Modality Fusion Adaptor module to achieve global modeling and efficient multimodal fusion.

2.2 Feature Extraction

After obtaining the tokens $H_0^{RGB} \in \mathbb{R}^{(N \times D)}$ and $H_0^X \in \mathbb{R}^{(N \times D)}$, where X represents either the TIR or Depth modality, they are fed into an L-layer Transformer Encoder equipped with the Modality Fusion Adaptor. The Transformer Encoder consists of Layer Normalization (LN) [2], Multi-head Self-Attention (MSA), and a Multi-layer Perceptron (MLP). All modalities share the same Transformer Encoder parameters.

Taking the TIR or Depth modality as an example, where X represents TIR or Depth, the computation process of the Transformer Encoder is as follows:

$$H_i^{X'} = \text{MSA}(\text{LN}(H_{i-1}^X)) + F_i^{RGBX} + H_{i-1}^X \tag{1}$$

$$H_i^X = \text{MLP}(\text{LN}(H_i^{X'})) + F_i^{RGBX'} + H_i^{X'} \tag{2}$$

where F_i^{RGBX} represents the fused features obtained from the RGB modality and the X modality after passing through the Modality Fusion Adaptor module, which will be detailed in Sect. 2.3.

Finally, the fusion feature is computed as:

$$H^{Fusion} = \text{Mean}(H_L^{RGB} + H_L^T + H_L^D, \dim = 0) \tag{3}$$

The resulting H^{Fusion} is then sent to a linear layer (Head) to obtain the final class predictions.

2.3   Modality Fusion Adaptor

To integrate the differences between different modalities, we have embedded the proposed Modality Fusion Adaptor module into the Transformer Encoder for efficient feature fusion of two modalities. In each Transformer Encoder layer, the Modality Fusion Adaptor operates in a modular manner and is divided into two stages. The first stage processes in parallel with the Multi-Head Self-Attention (MSA), while the second stage processes in parallel with the Multi-Layer Perceptron (MLP) to further enhance the representation of the fused features. Given the large volume of RGB data, we selected RGB as the intermediary modality for fusion with other modalities. By aligning and fusing the features of other modalities based on RGB, we can better preserve rich detail information, thereby improving the effectiveness of multimodal feature fusion. Consequently, we only apply the Modality Fusion Adaptor to the combinations of RGB with TIR and Depth modalities, respectively. The overall framework is illustrated in Fig. 1(b), where we exemplify the fusion of RGB with modality X, where X can be either TIR or Depth modality.

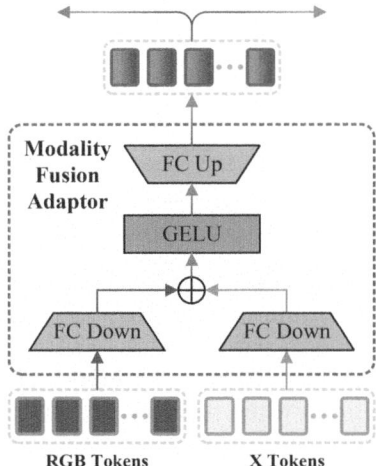

Fig. 2. The structure of the Modality Fusion Adaptor accepts tokens from the RGB modality and tokens from modality X. After processing, it generates the fused tokens.

Assume that H_{i-1}^{RGB} and H_{i-1}^X represent the input features of the RGB modality and X modality, respectively, to the i-th layer of the Transformer Encoder. The feature fusion in the i-th layer is performed as follows:

$$H_i^{\text{RGB}'} = \text{MSA}(\text{LN}(H_{i-1}^{\text{RGB}})) + F_i^{\text{RGBX}} + H_{i-1}^{\text{RGB}} \tag{4}$$

$$H_i^{X'} = \text{MSA}(\text{LN}(H_{i-1}^{X})) + F_i^{\text{RGBX}} + H_{i-1}^{X} \tag{5}$$

where MSA denotes the, Multi-head Self-Attention, LN represents the Layer-Norm layer, and F_i^{RGBX} is the fused feature obtained through the first stage using the Modality Fusion Adaptor. The RGB modality H_{i-1}^{RGB} is processed by LayerNorm before being input to the, Multi-head Self-Attention, and the resulting output is added to H_{i-1}^{RGB} and F_i^{RGBX} to produce $H_i^{\text{RGB}'}$. The X modality follows a similar process. Specifically, the calculation of F_i^{RGBX} is as follows:

$$F_i^{\text{RGBX}} = \text{MFA}(\text{LN}(H_{i-1}^{X}), \text{LN}(H_{i-1}^{\text{RGB}})) \tag{6}$$

In the above equation, the structure of Modality Fusion Adaptor is depicted in Fig. 2 and consists of three fully connected (FC) layers and a GELU activation layer [6]. The inputs are the LayerNorm-processed features of the RGB and X modalities. The first two FC layers project the input features into a lower-dimensional space, and the resulting features are summed. After being activated by the GELU layer, the features are projected back to their original dimension through the third FC layer, resulting in the fused representation F_i^{RGBX}.

After the initial fusion in the first stage, the process moves to the second stage, which runs in parallel with the MLP for deeper integration of information from the RGB and X modalities. Specifically, $H_i^{\text{RGB}'}$ and $H_i^{X'}$ are input into Modality Fusion Adaptor to obtain the fused representation $F_i^{\text{RGBX}'}$, which is then added to the MLP output:

$$H_i^{\text{RGB}} = \text{MLP}(\text{LN}(H_i^{\text{RGB}'})) + F_i^{\text{RGBX}'} + H_i^{\text{RGB}'} \tag{7}$$

$$H_i^{X} = \text{MLP}(\text{LN}(H_i^{X'})) + F_i^{\text{RGBX}'} + H_i^{X'} \tag{8}$$

$$F_i^{\text{RGBX}'} = \text{MFA}(H_i^{\text{RGB}'}, H_i^{X'}) \tag{9}$$

The Modality Fusion Adaptor is embedded in parallel within the Transformer Encoder, facilitating efficient information exchange and fusion between different modalities. By processing in parallel with MSA and MLP, MFA effectively leverages the characteristics of multiple modalities, enhancing the model's performance in cross-modal tasks while maintaining computational efficiency and scalability.

2.4   Network Training

During training, we utilize only the cross-entropy loss function relevant to the action recognition task to guide the classification training of the model. Specifically, the overall loss function can be expressed as:

$$L = L_{ce} \tag{10}$$

where L_{ce} represents the cross-entropy loss, which serves as the sole task-specific loss for the model in the action recognition task.

3 Experimental Setup

3.1 Implementation Details

Our model is implemented using Python and the PyTorch framework and trained on two NVIDIA RTX 4090 GPUs. We use the base version of the ViT-Base model, with a tubelet size set to $t \times h \times w = 2 \times 16 \times 16$. The intermediate layer dimension of the Modality Fusion Adaptor is set to 8.

The input data is first resized to a spatial resolution of 256×256. During training, the data is randomly cropped to 224×224, while for inference, a center crop of 224×224 is used. In the temporal domain, video sequences are randomly sampled to 16 frames during training and uniformly sampled to 16 frames during inference.

We use the AdamW optimizer [10] with a weight decay of 0.05 and an initial learning rate of 2×10^{-5}. The learning rate follows a cosine decay schedule, with a minimum value of 2×10^{-6}. The model is trained on the Track3 dataset for 10 epochs with a batch size of 4. To initialize our model, we use a ViT model pre-trained and fine-tuned on the Kinetics-400 [7] dataset using VideoMAE [13].

Model. We trained three different types of modality interactions: RGB-T, RGB-D, and RTD.

- **RGB-T**: The interaction between RGB images and TIR information.
- **RGB-D**: The interaction between RGB images and Depth information.
- **RTD**: The interaction between RGB, TIR, and Depth information.

The frameworks for RGB-T and RGB-D interactions are illustrated in Fig. 1, where the X modality corresponds to the T and D modalities, respectively. The RTD framework is an extended version based on Fig. 1(a), as shown in Fig. 3.

3.2 Datatsets

MMVPR Challenge Track 3 Dataset. The multimodal action recognition dataset is designed to evaluate the model's ability to recognize human actions from multiple modality data sources. The dataset contains a total of 2,500 multimodal video clips, including RGB, TIR, and Depth modalities, with 2,000 clips used for training and 500 clips reserved for testing. The videos cover 20 different action categories, offering a diverse range of scenarios for action recognition.

3.3 Evaluation Metrics

The evaluation for the MMVPR Challenge Track 3 test set is based on Top-1 and Top-5 accuracy. Top-1 accuracy measures the percentage of times the model's most confident prediction matches the correct action label. Top-5 accuracy assesses whether the correct action label is among the model's top 5 predictions, providing a broader perspective on the model's ability to recognize relevant action categories.

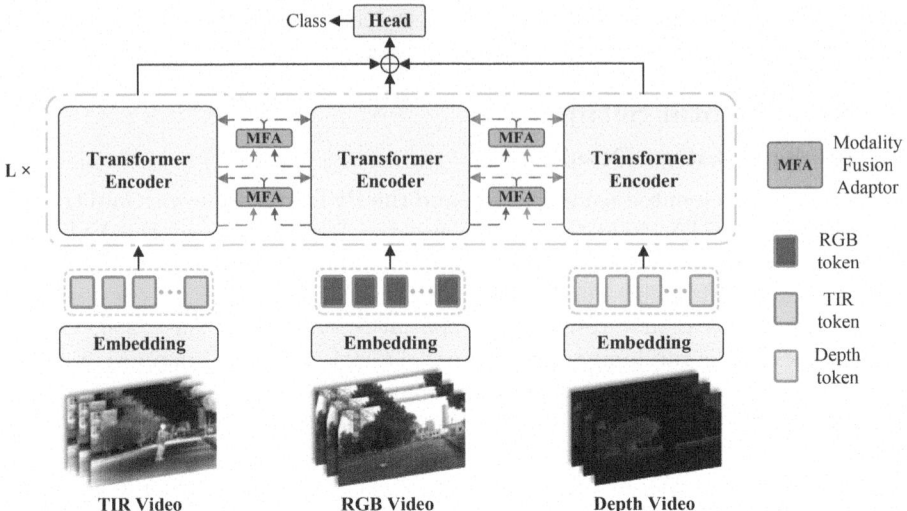

Fig. 3. The multimodal fusion network architecture processes tri-modal (RGB, TIR, Depth) video inputs, using RGB as the intermediate modality to interact with both TIR and Depth modalities.

Table 1. Final ranking in MMVPR Challenge Track 3 test set.

User	Rank	Top-1(%)	Top-5(%)
baseline	–	86.43	99.40
dee	3	99.00	**100.00**
zzz222	3	99.00	**100.00**
NPU_Dragons	2	99.40	**100.00**
dakiet	1	**100.00**	**100.00**
Aw_universe(Ours)	**1**	**100.00**	**100.00**

4   Results and Analysis

4.1   Comparison with Other Entries

Table 1 presents the final top 3 results of the MMVPR Challenge Track 3. Our method (Ours) achieved a Top-1 accuracy of 100% and a Top-5 accuracy of 100%, tying for first place with dakiet. Both teams outperformed other participants. The NPU_Dragons team ranked second with a Top-1 accuracy of 99.40%. The dee and zzz222 teams tied for third, each with a Top-1 accuracy of 99.00%. Lastly, the baseline performance was relatively low, with a Top-1 accuracy of 86.43% and a Top-5 accuracy of 99.40%. This comparison highlights the superior performance of our approach, achieving the highest accuracy in the competition.

4.2   Ablation Studies

In the MMVPR Challenge Track 3 test set, our method demonstrated outstanding performance across multiple modalities, as shown in Table 2. When trained with RGB-T modality, the model achieved 100.00% accuracy in both Top-1 and Top-5 accuracy, representing the best performance. With the RGB-D modality, the model achieved a Top-1 accuracy of 99.00% and a Top-5 accuracy of 100.00%, slightly lower than the RGB-T modality but still at a high level. With the RTD modality, the model achieved a Top-1 accuracy of 97.4%, while the Top-5 accuracy remained at 100.00%. Although the Top-1 accuracy was slightly lower, the Top-5 performance remained consistent with other modalities. Overall, our method maintained a consistent 100.00% Top-5 accuracy, indicating that the model can reliably recognize the correct action classes across multiple modalities. The Top-1 accuracy varies slightly across modalities, with the RGB-T modality performing the best.

Performance Comparison of Different Modalities. As shown in Table 2, the experiment indicates that the RGB-T modality slightly outperforms the RGB-D modality in terms of Top-1 accuracy. This suggests that fusing RGB and TIR information contributes to improving the model's performance in action recognition tasks. This may be due to the fact that thermal infrared can supplement the missing details in visible light data under low-light or complex background conditions. For instance, in low-light environments, thermal infrared provides additional discriminative power, helping the model capture action details. In contrast, depth information (Depth) primarily captures object distance and three-dimensional spatial structure features, making it sensitive to spatial positioning but unable to perceive changes in texture, color, and temperature as thermal infrared does. Therefore, its performance under complex lighting conditions is relatively limited. Although the RGB-D modality effectively captures spatial features, its ability to compensate for details in low-light or occluded scenarios is still inferior to that of the RGB-T modality.

Validation of MFA Module Effectiveness. In theory, the RTD modality, which includes RGB, TIR, and Depth information, should enhance the model's action recognition capabilities by leveraging multimodal features. However, experimental results show that the Top-1 accuracy of the RTD modality is lower than that of the combinations of RGB-T and RGB-D modalities. To verify the effectiveness of the Modality Fusion Adaptor module, we also conducted additional comparative experiments. Specifically, during the training of the RTD model, we removed the MFA module and, after obtaining the corresponding Tokens for each modality, simply concatenated all the tokens and fed them into a ViT block for training. As shown in the last row of Table 2, the Top-1 accuracy was merely 91.20%, which was 6.2% lower than the approach of introducing the MFA module. This finding indicates that simple feature concatenation fails to fully exploit the correlation and complementarity between multimodal information. In contrast, by using the MFA module, we enhanced the complementary utilization of the different modalities, allowing the model to better capture action features in multimodal scenarios, which significantly improved recognition performance.

Table 2. Performance comparison of our proposed method on the MMVPR Challenge Track 3 test set using different modalities.

Modality	Method	Top-1(%)	Top-5(%)
RGB-T	MF-ViT	**100.00**	**100.00**
RGB-D	MF-ViT	99.00	**100.00**
RTD	MF-ViT	97.40	**100.00**
RTD	ViT	91.20	96.20

5   Conclusion

In this paper, we propose a novel network called Modality Fusion Vision Transformer (MF-ViT) for multimodal action recognition tasks. Addressing the limitations of traditional methods that fail to fully exploit the complementarity between different modalities, we designed a Modality Fusion Adaptor module that enhances the interaction mechanism between modalities. This effectively improves the model's ability to capture complex cross-modal relationships and fine-grained features. Our approach achieved 1st place in MMVPR Challenge Track 3. The experimental results on the MMVPR Challenge Track 3 dataset demonstrate the effectiveness and superiority of the proposed MF-ViT model, showcasing its strong capability in multimodal action recognition tasks.

Acknowledgements. The work is jointly supported by the National Natural Science Foundation of China under grants No. 62472342, and 62272364, the National Science and Technology Major Project under grant No. 2022ZD0117103, the provincial Key Research and Development Program of Shaanxi under grant No. 2024GH-ZDXM-47, the Research Project on Higher Education Teaching Reform of Shaanxi Province under grant No. 23JG003.

References

1. Arnab, A., Dehghani, M., Heigold, G., Sun, C., Lučić, M., Schmid, C.: Vivit: a video vision transformer. In: Proceedings of the IEEE/CVF International Conference on Computer Vision, pp. 6836–6846 (2021)
2. Ba, J.L.: Layer normalization. arXiv preprint arXiv:1607.06450 (2016)

3. Bandi, C., Thomas, U.: Skeleton-based action recognition for human-robot interaction using self-attention mechanism. In: 2021 16th IEEE International Conference on Automatic Face and Gesture Recognition (FG 2021), pp. 1–8. IEEE (2021)
4. Dosovitskiy, A.: An image is worth 16x16 words: transformers for image recognition at scale. arXiv preprint arXiv:2010.11929 (2020)
5. Elharrouss, O., Almaadeed, N., Al-Maadeed, S., Bouridane, A., Beghdadi, A.: A combined multiple action recognition and summarization for surveillance video sequences. Appl. Intell. **51**, 690–712 (2021)
6. Hendrycks, D., Gimpel, K.: Gaussian error linear units (gelus). arXiv preprint arXiv:1606.08415 (2016)
7. Kay, W., et al.: The kinetics human action video dataset. arXiv preprint arXiv:1705.06950 (2017)
8. Li, Y., Miao, Q., Tian, K., Fan, Y., Xu, X., Li, R., Song, J.: Large-scale gesture recognition with a fusion of RGB-D data based on the C3D model. In: 2016 23rd International Conference on Pattern Recognition (ICPR), pp. 25–30. IEEE (2016)
9. Li, Y., et al.: Watching it in dark: a target-aware representation learning framework for high-level vision tasks in low illumination. In: European Conference on Computer Vision (2022)
10. Loshchilov, I.: Decoupled weight decay regularization. arXiv preprint arXiv:1711.05101 (2017)
11. Miao, Q., et al.: Multimodal gesture recognition based on the resc3d network. In: Proceedings of the IEEE International Conference on Computer Vision Workshops, pp. 3047–3055 (2017)
12. Serpush, F., Menhaj, M.B., Masoumi, B., Karasfi, B.: Wearable sensor-based human activity recognition in the smart healthcare system. Comput. Intell. Neurosci. **2022**(1), 1391906 (2022)
13. Tong, Z., Song, Y., Wang, J., Wang, L.: VideoMAE: masked autoencoders are data-efficient learners for self-supervised video pre-training. In: Advances in Neural Information Processing Systems (2022)
14. Xu, Y., Cao, H., Mao, K., Chen, Z., Xie, L., Yang, J.: Aligning correlation information for domain adaptation in action recognition. IEEE Trans. Neural Netw. Learn. Syst. (2022)
15. Zhou, B., et al.: Decoupling and recoupling spatiotemporal representation for RGB-D-based motion recognition. In: Proceedings of the IEEE/CVF Conference on Computer Vision and Pattern Recognition, pp. 20154–20163 (2022)

An Effective End-to-End Solution for Multimodal Action Recognition

Songping Wang[1], Haoxiang Rao[1], Xiantao Hu[2], Yueming Lyu[1(✉)], and Caifeng Shan[1(✉)]

[1] School of Intelligence Science and Technology, Nanjing University, Nanjing, China
ymlv@nju.edu.cn
[2] PCA-Lab, School of Computer Science and Engineering, Nanjing University of Science and Technology, Nanjing, China

Abstract. Recently, multimodal tasks have strongly advanced the field of action recognition with their rich multimodal information. However, due to the scarcity of tri-modal data, research on tri-modal action recognition tasks faces many challenges. To this end, we have proposed a comprehensive multimodal action recognition solution that effectively utilizes multimodal information. First, the existing data are transformed and expanded by optimizing data enhancement techniques to enlarge the training scale. At the same time, more RGB datasets are used to pre-train the backbone network, which is better adapted to the new task by means of transfer learning. Secondly, multimodal spatial features are extracted with the help of 2D CNNs and combined with the Temporal Shift Module (TSM) to achieve multimodal spatial-temporal feature extraction comparable to 3D CNNs and improve the computational efficiency. In addition, common prediction enhancement methods, such as Stochastic Weight Averaging (SWA), Ensemble and Test-Time augmentation (TTA), are used to integrate the knowledge of models from different training periods of the same architecture and different architectures, so as to predict the actions from different perspectives and fully exploit the target information. Ultimately, we achieved the Top-1 accuracy of 99% and the Top-5 accuracy of 100% on the competition leaderboard, demonstrating the superiority of our solution.

Keywords: Multimodal Action Recognition · Temporal Shift Module · Spatial-temporal feature

1 Introduction

In recent years, Deep Neural Networks (DNNs) have achieved significant success in various tasks [13,14,19,28,30,33,34]. Earlier work focused on tasks in a single modality; however, as technology continues to advance and real-world needs become more complex, research on multimodal fusion is gradually becoming a hot area. By integrating multimodal data from different sensors, a more

S. Palaiahnakote et al. (Eds.): ICPR 2024 Workshops, LNCS 15617, pp. 324–338, 2025.
https://doi.org/10.1007/978-3-031-88217-3_25

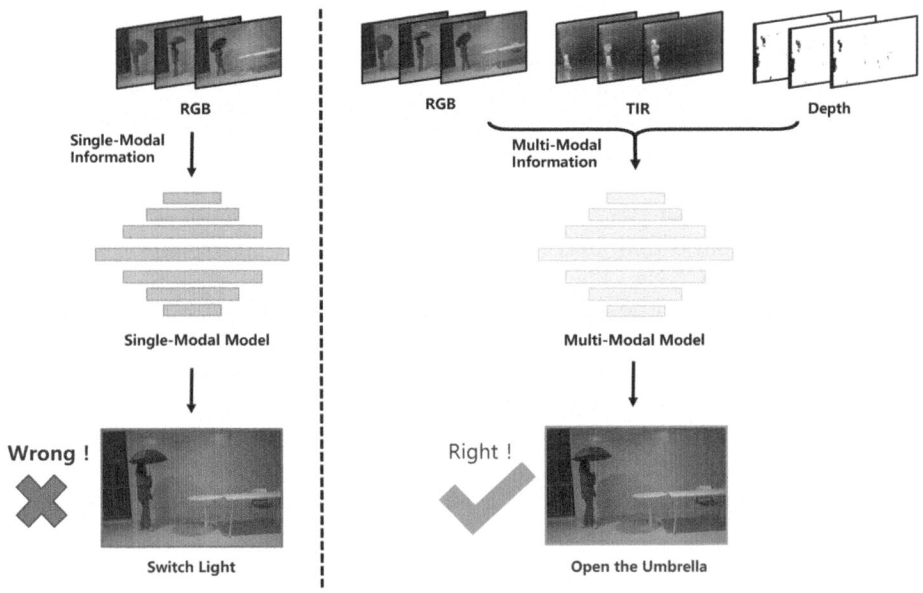

Fig. 1. Comparison between single-modal action recognition and multi-modal action recognition.

comprehensive and robust understanding of complex real-world scenes can be achieved [1,22] (Fig. 1).

To promote the development of this technology, the ICPR 2024 Multimodal Action Recognition competition provides a platform for researchers to apply the latest algorithms and techniques to multimodal pattern recognition tasks. This not only offers researchers the opportunity to showcase and share their achievements but also fosters the emergence of new technologies and solutions to address various challenges in this domain [35]. This competition focuses on multimodal action recognition, aiming to classify human actions using data from multiple modalities such as RGB, depth images, and thermal infrared images (TIR). However, the limited number of samples in that challenge undoubtedly adds difficulties to the training of deep learning models, greatly elevating the risk of overfitting [20].

To address these issues, we introduce the data enhancement methods of Group Multi-Scale Cropping and Group Random Horizontal Flip to improve the diversity of the data. Group Multi Scale Crop increases the model's ability to adapt to objects of different sizes. Group Random Horizontal Flip expands the amount of data so that the model can learn features from different viewpoints. Second, better pre-training quality tends to result in better model initialization. In this way, the model can converge faster in the subsequent fine-tuning phase and is more likely to achieve better performance. With this in mind, we introduce knowledge of the ImageNet [8], Kinetics400 [17], and Something-somethingV2 [10] datasets to adequately pretrain the model.

The architecture of the model plays a key role in predicting robustness. We choose Temporal Shift Module (TSM) [18] as our base model. TSM is an efficient spatio-temporal modeling approach that shifts part of the feature map channels along the temporal dimension, achieving time modeling with zero additional computation cost [18]. It retains the computational efficiency of 2D CNNs while achieving spatio-temporal feature extraction with performance comparable to that of 3D CNNs. The model is not only capable of processing RGB video data but can also be extended to multimodal inputs, such as optical flow and depth images, further improving action recognition performance [23]. Additionally, to enhance model performance, we adopted several powerful backbone models on top of TSM, including ResNet50, ResNet50 NL (Non-Local Module), and ResNext101 [11]. These models excel at capturing complex spatio-temporal dependencies in videos. We also designed a multimodal fusion strategy to ensure that information extracted from different modalities can be effectively integrated [7].

In addition, we use commonly used prediction enhancement methods. SWA [15] enhances the model's generalization by randomly averaging its weights across various training phases, effectively amalgamating the strengths from different stages of training. Ensemble combines different models to predict actions from different perspectives by using their diversity to improve the overall performance. TTA enhances the input data in the testing phase to analyze the actions from multiple perspectives to make full use of the target information to obtain more reliable predictions. At the same time, we conduct secondary sampling of the delineated sampling area. Through secondary sampling, the diversity of data can be further enriched, so that the model can be exposed to more different sample features, thus increasing the accuracy of prediction and enabling the model to give more accurate results in different kinds of complex situations.

2   Related Work

Action Recognition. In recent years, action recognition has undergone a significant shift from convolutional neural network (CNN)-based approaches to transformer-based models. Early research primarily relied on 2D or 3D convolutional neural networks to extract features by processing video frames independently or introducing convolution operations in the spatio-temporal dimension [5,9,24,27]. For example, 2D CNN-based methods like TSN (Temporal Segment Networks) and the two-stream network reduced computational costs by averaging features across video frames but struggled to effectively capture complex temporal relationships [21,27].

In contrast, within video recognition frameworks, 3D CNNs (such as C3D, I3D, R3D) can effectively extract spatio-temporal features, but their large number of parameters and high computational costs hinder their large-scale deployment in practical applications [5,9,24]. To address this issue, some studies have proposed hybrid architectures combining 2D and 3D convolutional networks, where 3D convolutions are decomposed into 2D spatial convolutions and 1D temporal convolutions to reduce computational complexity [31,32].

Recently, transformer-based models have emerged in the field of action recognition. These models often incorporate new temporal modules on top of pre-trained image models or extend 2D convolutions to 3D to handle video data [2,4]. However, the fine-tuning process of these models demands large-scale video datasets, resulting in high training costs [25,32].

In our method, we adopt the Temporal Shift Module (TSM) model as our base model. In contrast to these methods, TSM network, with fewer parameters and faster inference speeds, saves memory and training time while maintaining comparable performance. By shifting feature maps along the temporal dimension, TSM enables effective spatio-temporal modeling while preserving the computational efficiency of 2D CNNs [18].

Multimodal Action Recognition. In recent years, significant progress has been made in multimodal action recognition, particularly in the fusion of RGB, depth (Depth), and thermal infrared (TIR) modalities. By leveraging the complementary strengths of these modalities, researchers have enhanced the performance of action recognition systems. Studies combining RGB and depth modalities have shown that depth information can effectively supplement the 3D spatial information missing in RGB videos, enhancing the accuracy of action recognition [6]. The thermal infrared modality, due to its robustness in low-light conditions, has also been widely applied in surveillance systems [16]. Regarding fusion strategies, both early and late fusion methods have been widely used, with late fusion proving more effective in handling the discrepancies between modalities [26]. Additionally, cross-modal fusion methods based on self-attention mechanisms have shown great potential in recent years, enabling the efficient capture of correlated information between different modalities [23]. To tackle the challenge of limited data availability, techniques such as transfer learning, few-shot learning, and data augmentation have been widely adopted to improve model generalization [3]. Despite these advances, the scarcity of samples continues to pose significant challenges in this field.

3   Methodology

3.1   Preprocessing

Compared to traditional single-modal data processing, the complexity of multimodal data significantly increases. This complexity arises because multimodal datasets typically contain data from different sources (such as RGB, TIR, Depth, etc.), which may have significant differences in feature space, sampling rates, and data distribution. To effectively handle these data and make the most of limited training samples, we have adopted a series of data preprocessing and augmentation techniques. The steps and descriptions of our multimodal data processing operations includes dynamic group temporal sampling strategy, group batch augmentation processing and group regularization techniques.

Dynamic Group Temporal Sampling Strategy. We simultaneously load data from different modalities, such as RGB (color images), TIR (thermal infrared images), and Depth (depth images). To improve training efficiency and reduce the interference of a large number of redundant frames, each modality's data is evenly divided into multiple groups, and then frames are randomly selected from each group to form a video frame sequence for training. In actual training, we divide each video of each modality into eight groups, randomly select one frame from each group, and these frames are combined to form the multimodal video frames used for training.

Group Batch Augmentation Processing. Considering the limited number of training samples, how to effectively augment the data is a key strategy for expanding the training dataset, improving model generalization ability, and reducing overfitting. We perform various efficient batch augmentations on multimodal video frames, including: (1) Group Multi-scale Cropping: Randomly crop images at different scales to increase data diversity, simulating visual effects under different perspectives and fields of view. (2) Group Random Horizontal Flipping: Randomly horizontally flip images to increase data symmetry, forcing the model to learn to correctly recognize objects even under left-right flipped conditions.

Group Normalization Techniques. Group Normalization techniques are used to standardize multimodal data by subtracting the mean and dividing by the variance for each data point, normalizing the data. This improves the training speed and stability of the model and reduces overfitting phenomena.

Through the above steps, we can effectively process multimodal data, make the most of the knowledge from limited training samples, and enhance the performance and generalization ability of multimodal models.

3.2 Proposed Method

As illustrated in Fig. 2, the architecture of our proposed method includes two multimodal action recognition models, namely the TSM-Res50 and the TSM-Res101. These models are both based on the TSM framework [18] and utilize ResNet-50 and ResNet-101 [11] as their backbones, respectively. Through these architectures, multimodal spatial features are extracted using 2D CNNs and then combined with the Temporal Shift Module (TSM) to achieve multimodal spatial-temporal feature extraction. This approach not only improves performance but also enhances computational efficiency. Details of the model training and inference processes are provided in the following sections.

Training of Multimodal Video Recognition Models. An individual video input can be represented as $X \in \mathbb{R}^{T \times W \times H \times C}$. The symbols T, W, H, C denote the number of video frames, frame width, frame height, and the number of

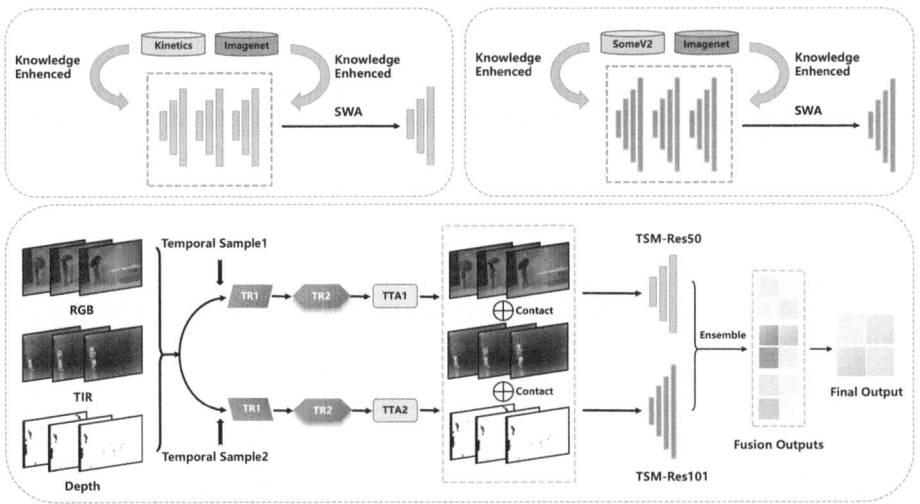

Fig. 2. The framework of our proposed solution. Temporal Sample1 and Temporal Sample2 represent two temporal samplings of multimodal videos, TR1 and TR2 represent different data augmentation methods, TTA1 and TTA2 represent Test-Time augmentation techniques, SWA represents stochastic weight averaging technique, Kinetics400 and ImageNet, SomeV2 correspond to different pre-training knowledge, where SomeV2 is the abbreviation for the Something-SomethingV2 dataset.

video channels respectively. Similarly, we denote the RGB modality video as $X^R \in \mathbb{R}^{T \times W \times H \times C}$, the TIR modality video as $X^I \in \mathbb{R}^{T \times W \times H \times C}$, and the Depth modality video as $X^D \in \mathbb{R}^{T \times W \times H \times C}$. We set Y as ground truth label.

To effectively utilize the multimodal information, we adopt a simple and effective approach. Specifically, we concatenate the preprocessed multimodal video frames along the channel dimension and input them into the model TSM-Res50. Finally, we perform a weighted fusion of the model's output along different modal channels, which can be expressed by the following formula:

$$Logits^R, Logits^I, Logits^D = F_\theta(Cat(X^R, X^I, X^D)), \tag{1}$$

$$\min_\theta(J(\gamma * Logits^R + \beta * Logits^I + \alpha * Logits^D, Y)), \tag{2}$$

where F_θ denotes the model that is to be trained, parameterized by θ. The function $Cat(\cdot)$ represents the concatenation operation, while β, γ, and α are the weight coefficients. $Logits^R$, $Logits^I$, and $Logits^D$ represent the logits from different modalities, respectively. Lastly, $J(\cdot)$ signifies the cross-entropy loss function.

In the training phase of TSM-Res50, we employed a finely tuned hyperparameter configuration, including dividing the input video frame data into 8 groups, setting 30 training epochs, a batch-size of 6, and an initial learning rate of 0.01, with a decaying learning rate. Additionally, we used a momentum of 0.9 to accelerate the optimization process and controlled overfitting with a weight decay of 5e-4. To prevent gradient explosion, we implemented a gradient clipping strategy and ensured that Batch Normalization was fully calculated in each mini-batch, which guaranteed the efficiency and stability of model training. Considering the limited training dataset, we utilize the pre-trained knowledge from Kinetics400 [17] and ImageNet [8] to enhance the model's performance on downstream tasks. We also trained the model TSM-Res101 with different pre-training knowledge and architectures. Specifically, we utilized pre-trained knowledge from Something-somethingV2 [10] and ImageNet, and fine-tuned TSM-Res101 on the training set with similar training configurations. In the subsequent inference process, we employed these two well-trained models with different architectures and distinct pre-training knowledge for model ensembling, thereby further enhancing the recognition performance.

Inference Process. In the inference phase, we employed a suite of effective techniques to maximize the knowledge extracted from our meticulously trained models for more accurate predictions on multimodal videos during the testing phase. The specific techniques adopted are as follows:

Preprocessing in the Inference Phase. We selected a set of enhancement strategies to preprocess multimodal video data in the inference phase, including Group Scale and Group Center Crop techniques. These methods enhance the model's robustness to input data by scaling and cropping images at different scales.

Test-Time Augmentation (TTA) Technique. We implemented an efficient TTA technique that encompasses horizontal flipping of images, among others. This strategy allows the model to assess video content from different perspectives, thereby improving the model's adaptability to changes in viewpoint.

Stochastic Weight Averaging (SWA) Technique. For the TSM-Res50 and TSM-Res101 models, we saved multiple sets of weights at different stages during the training process. By selecting the top three performing weights from different training stages for each model, we performed SWA processing, ultimately obtaining two sets of optimized TSM-Res50 and TSM-Res101 model weights for subsequent model ensembling.

Model Ensembling Technique. To further enhance model performance, we conducted model ensembling with TSM-Res50 and TSM-Res101 models that possess different architectures and pre-training knowledge. This strategy effectively improves the model's generalization capability by integrating the prediction results of different models.

Multiple Temporal Sampling Strategy. We adopted a multiple temporal sampling strategy, which involves repeatedly sampling the multimodal data temporally and fusing the inference results obtained from these samples. This method has been proven to significantly enhance the model's recognition accuracy.

Full-Resolution Inference Strategy. We employed a full-resolution inference strategy, feeding multimodal video frames with a resolution of 256*256 into the video recognition model. Although this approach increases computational complexity, it significantly enhances the accuracy of recognition.

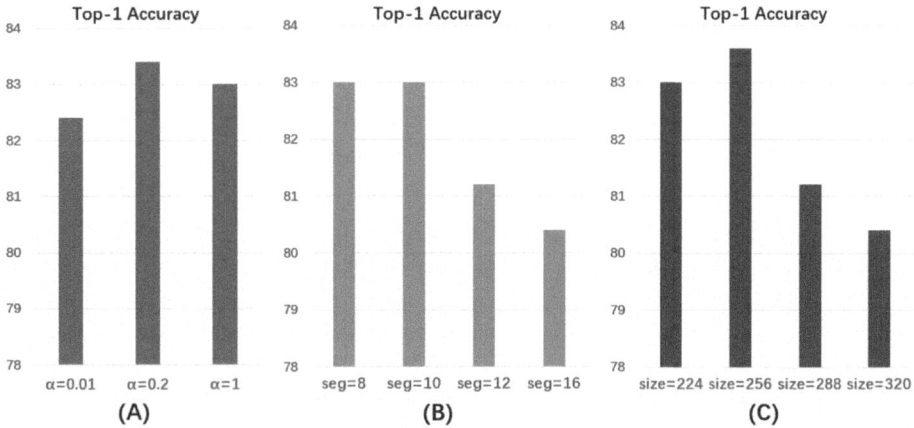

Fig. 3. The results of Top-1 accuracy under three different parameter adjustments. Subplot (A) shows the impact of varying the output coefficient (α) on model performance. Subplot (B) illustrates how the number of video segments (seg) affects accuracy. Subplot (C) demonstrates the effect of different input sizes (size) on the model's performance.

4   Experiments

4.1   Setups

Dataset. The ICPR 2024 workshop officially provided a multimodal video dataset for model training and testing. The dataset includes RGB, thermal infrared (TIR), and depth modality information, covering twenty action categories. The training set contains 2,000 video samples, with each modality having over 32,000 frames, which contain twenty categories. The video modalities have the following resolutions: Depth at 640Œ360, TIR at 320Œ256, and RGB at 455Œ256 pixels. The test set includes 500 video samples, with each modality containing over 8,300 frames, maintaining the same resolution as the training set. All videos range from 2 to 13 s in duration. Depth data is stored in PNG format, while thermal TIR and RGB data are stored in JPEG format.

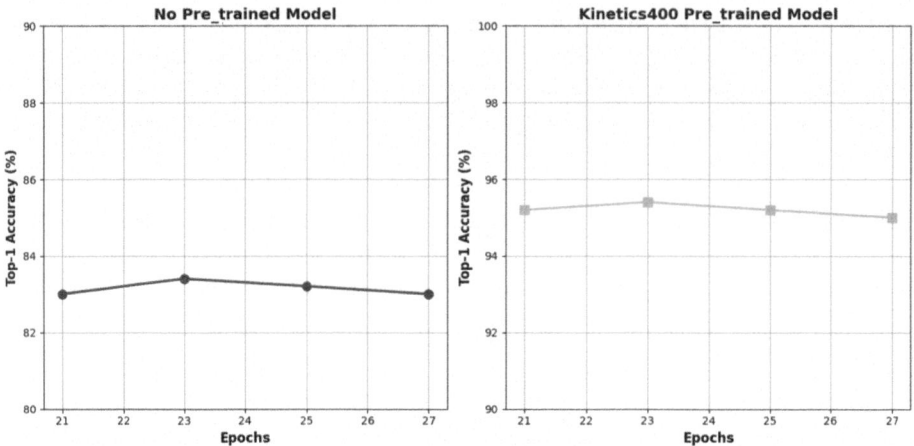

Fig. 4. The figure presents the impact of training epochs on the Top-1 accuracy for two scenarios: without pretraining (left) and with Kinetics400 pretraining (right).

Evaluation Metrics. The ICPR 2024 workshop employs Top-1 and Top-5 accuracy metrics for performance evaluation. Top-1 accuracy denotes the model's precision in correctly classifying actions, aligning the predicted class with the ground truth. Conversely, Top-5 accuracy measures the model's robustness by considering instances where the true class appears within the top five predictions. These metrics offer insights into the model's classification efficacy under strict and relaxed conditions, respectively, providing a nuanced assessment of its action recognition capabilities. In the experiments, we primarily utilize Top-1 accuracy as the metric for evaluating model performance.

4.2   Parameter Tuning

In this section, we embark on a detailed examination of hyperparameter optimization, which is crucial for the exceptional performance of our multimodal action recognition model. This chapter offers a thorough investigation into the key factors that enhance our model's predictive capabilities, encompassing the allocation of weights to multimodal logits, the determination of training epochs, the number of video segments, and the selection of inference input sizes. Through a series of meticulous experiments, we have calibrated these parameters to achieve a harmonious balance between computational efficiency and the precision of recognition.

Weights for Multimodal Logits. As shown in Eq. (2), The allocation of weights to multimodal logits constrains the contribution of the model's output for different modalities in determining the final prediction, thereby impacting the accuracy of multimodal video recognition. Considering the limited number of submissions allowed in the competition, we conducted experiments only on the output weights of the depth modality, denoted as α. We first adjusted the output coefficient α to find the optimal weight allocation for the final predictions across different modalities. The results shown in Fig. 3(A) indicate that a smaller output coefficient (e.g., $\alpha = 0.2$) slightly improved model accuracy, whereas an extremely small coefficient ($\alpha = 0.01$) led to a performance drop. Therefore, we set the value of α to 0.2.

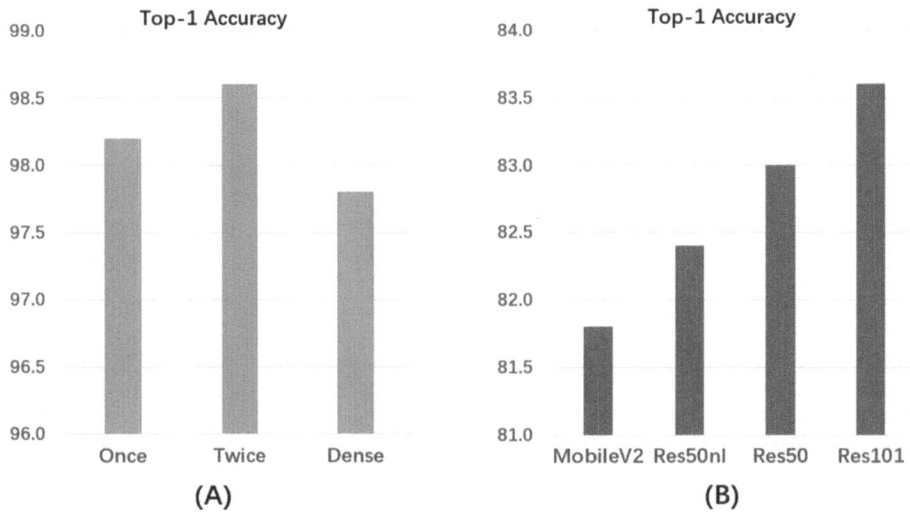

Fig. 5. Subplot (A) presents the effect of different sampling strategies on the model's performance. Subplot (B) compares the accuracy of various backbone network architectures.

Training Epochs. We conducted experiments on The influence of training epochs both with and without the use of Kinetics400 pre-train knowledge. As shown in Fig. 4, Experiments indicate that the model's accuracy on the test set fluctuates with the number of epochs. Through this experimental process, we have identified a set of superior weights. These weights were subsequently integrated using Stochastic Weight Averaging (SWA) to enhance the model's performance.

Number of Video Segments. Next, we experimented with different numbers of video segments. The results shown in Fig. 3(B) demonstrated that model accuracy remains unchanged at first, but decreased with more segments. The model performed best when the number of segments was set to 8 or 10, achieving an accuracy of 0.83. The decrease by increased segments may be due to the introduction of redundant information, increasing computational complexity and degrading model performance. Therefore, we set the Number of Video Segments to 8.

Inference Input Size. Finally, we conducted an evaluation to determine the impact of varying inference input sizes on the model's recognition accuracy. As depicted in Fig. 3(C), the highest accuracy of 0.836 was achieved when the input size was slightly increased to 256. Although larger input sizes offer more image details, deviating significantly from the input size used during training may adversely affect the model's performance.

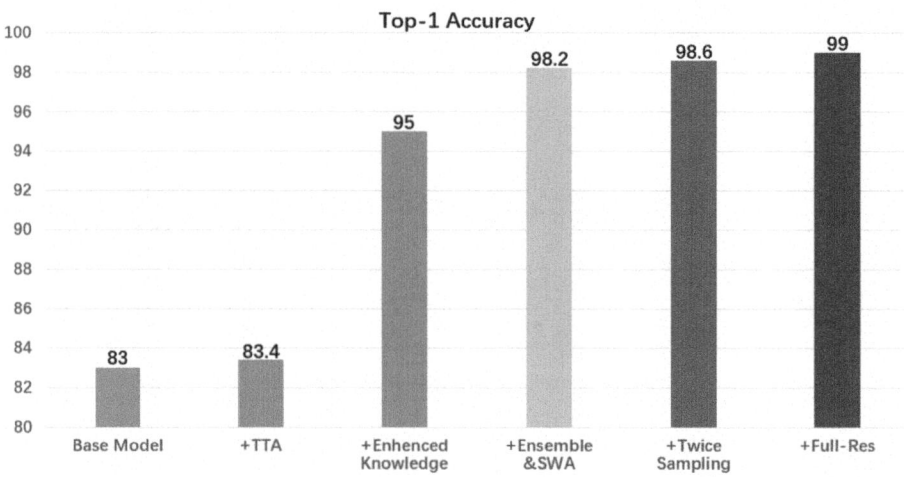

Fig. 6. The figure illustrates the performance improvements of the model under different strategies. Starting from the base model, various enhancements such as Test-Time Augmentation (TTA), Enhanced knowledge (pre-training knowledge), ensemble technique combined with stochastic weight averaging (SWA), twice sampling strategy, and full-resolution strategy are applied to progressively refine the model's accuracy.

4.3   Ablation Study

We conducted ablation studies to examine the impact of different backbone networks, sampling strategy, and scoring strategy on the performance of multimodal action recognition.

Backbone Network Selection. We report the ablation analysis performed on several backbone networks, including ResNet50, ResNet50 NL (with a Non-Local module) [29], ResNet101, and MobileNetV2 [12]. The results shown in Fig. 5(B) illustrate that ResNet50 offers a balanced trade-off between accuracy and computational efficiency, while ResNet50 NL exhibits a modest decline. ResNet101, on the other hand, shows significant advantages in deeper feature extraction, particularly in handling complex spatio-temporal action sequences. Although MobileNetV2 excels in computational efficiency, it exhibits a slight drop in recognition accuracy. Ultimately, we selected the ResNet50 and ResNet101 models as

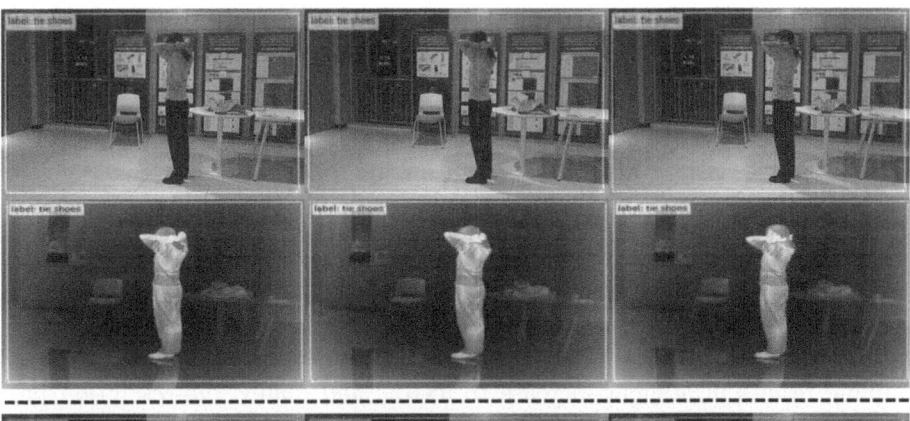

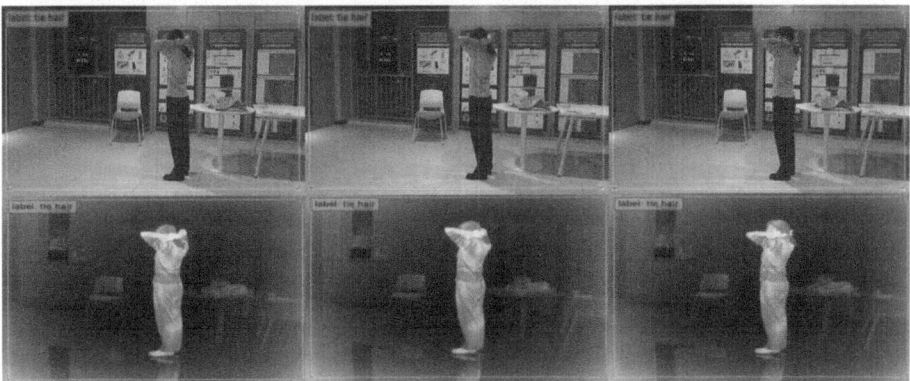

Fig. 7. Our proposed method compared to the baseline method in the identification visualization results on a multimodal video. The first and second rows show the prediction results of the base method on the RGB and TIR modalities, respectively, while the last two rows display the prediction results of our method on the RGB and TIR modalities, respectively. On some more challenging multimodal video samples, our method is still able to correctly predict the multimodal video samples, whereas the baseline method makes incorrect predictions.

Backbone for TSM, which demonstrated the most outstanding performance, for subsequent model ensembling.

Sampling Strategy. In the inference phase, we evaluated three temporal sampling strategies: once sampling, twice sampling, and dense sampling. Our results demonstrated that twice sampling achieved the highest Top-1 accuracy among all strategies. This method enables the model to capture a more comprehensive set of temporal cues, leading to a more holistic inference. Although dense sampling can gather additional information, the presence of substantial redundancy in high-frame-rate videos can impede the model's precision in judgment.

Twice sampling effectively reduces this redundancy and optimizes performance, thus we opted for it as our strategy for further experiments.

Scoring Strategy. In the experiment, we tried a variety of strategies to enhance the model's performance in multimodal video recognition as much as possible, and Fig. 6 shows the results of the experiment. Initially, the Base multimodal Model achieves a performance of 83%. By incorporating Test-Time Augmentation (TTA), the performance slightly improves to 83.4%. The addition of pre-training knowledge leads to a significant performance boost, reaching 95%. Further improvements are seen when ensemble learning and Stochastic Weight Averaging (SWA) are combined, pushing the metric to 98.2%. Twice sampling results in a slight increase to 98.6%, and finally, full-resolution processing brings the performance to its peak at 99%. Figure 7 demonstrates the visual prediction results of our method and the base method on a multimodal video, highlighting the superiority of our approach. By employing these effective scoring strategies, we ultimately achieved the Top-1 accuracy of 99% and the Top-5 accuracy of 100 % on the competition's leaderboard.

5 Conclusion

Multimodal tasks have significantly advanced the field of action recognition by harnessing rich multimodal information. However, the limited number of training samples and the significant differences between different modalities present substantial challenges to research in this area. In this workshop, we adopted a straightforward yet effective multimodal fusion method, concatenating different modal information and utilizing the Temporal Shift Module (TSM) to efficiently extract multimodal spatio-temporal features from multimodal video data, followed by weighted fusion of multimodal output results. Specifically, during the preprocessing stage, we employed various data processing and augmentation techniques. In the training phase, we fine-tuned two heterogeneous models, TSM-Res50 and TSM-Res101, using pre-training knowledge from Kinetics, Something-somethingV2, and ImageNet datasets for downstream multimodal recognition tasks. During the inference phase, we applied a series of effective scoring strategies, including Test-Time Augmentation (TTA), Stochastic Weight Averaging (SWA), model ensembling, Twice temporal sampling, and full-resolution processing strategies. Through our comprehensive solution for preprocessing-model training-inference process, we effectively improved the model's generalization and accuracy in multimodal task scenarios. Ultimately, the proposed method achieved the Top-1 accuracy of 99%and the Top-5 accuracy of 100 % on the competition leaderboard, demonstrating the superiority of our solution.

References

1. Ardianto, S., Hang, H.M.: Multi-view and multi-modal action recognition with learned fusion. In: APSIPA ASC, pp. 1601–1604. IEEE (2018)
2. Arnab, A., Dehghani, M., Heigold, G., Sun, C., Lučić, M., Schmid, C.: Vivit: a video vision transformer. In: ICCV, pp. 6836–6846 (2021)
3. Avola, D., Bernardi, M., Foresti, G.L.: Fusing depth and colour information for human action recognition. Multimedia Tools Appl. **78**(5), 5919–5939 (2019)
4. Bertasius, G., Wang, H., Torresani, L.: Is space-time attention all you need for video understanding? In: ICML, vol. 2, p. 4 (2021)
5. Carreira, J., Zisserman, A.: Quo vadis, action recognition? A new model and the kinetics dataset. In: CVPR, pp. 6299–6308 (2017)
6. Chen, C., Jafari, R., Kehtarnavaz, N.: A survey of depth and inertial sensor fusion for human action recognition. Multimedia Tools Appl. **76**, 4405–4425 (2017)
7. Cheng, Q., Liu, Z., Ren, Z., Cheng, J., Liu, J.: Spatial-temporal information aggregation and cross-modality interactive learning for rgb-d-based human action recognition. IEEE Access **10**, 104190–104201 (2022)
8. Deng, J., Dong, W., Socher, R., Li, L.J., Li, K., Fei-Fei, L.: ImageNet: a large-scale hierarchical image database. In: CVPR (2009)
9. Feichtenhofer, C., Fan, H., Malik, J., He, K.: Slowfast networks for video recognition. In: ICCV, pp. 6202–6211 (2019)
10. Goyal, R., et al.: The "something something" video database for learning and evaluating visual common sense. In: ICCV, pp. 5842–5850 (2017)
11. He, K., Zhang, X., Ren, S., Sun, J.: Deep residual learning for image recognition. In: CVPR, pp. 770–778 (2016)
12. Howard, A.G.: Mobilenets: efficient convolutional neural networks for mobile vision applications. arXiv preprint arXiv:1704.04861 (2017)
13. Hu, X., Zhong, B., Liang, Q., Zhang, S., Li, N., Li, X.: Towards modalities correlation for rgb-t tracking. TCSVT (2024)
14. Hu, X., et al.: Transformer tracking via frequency fusion. TCSVT **34**(2), 1020–1031 (2023)
15. Izmailov, P., Podoprikhin, D., Garipov, T., Vetrov, D., Wilson, A.G.: Averaging weights leads to wider optima and better generalization. arXiv preprint arXiv:1803.05407 (2018)
16. Jiang, Z., Rozgic, V., Adali, S.: Learning spatiotemporal features for infrared action recognition with 3d convolutional neural networks. In: CVPRW, pp. 115–123 (2017)
17. Kay, W., et al.: The kinetics human action video dataset. arXiv preprint arXiv:1705.06950 (2017)
18. Lin, J., Gan, C., Han, S.: TSM: temporal shift module for efficient video understanding. In: ICCV, pp. 7083–7093 (2019)
19. Lyu, Y., Jiang, Y., He, Z., Peng, B., Liu, Y., Dong, J.: 3d-aware adversarial makeup generation for facial privacy protection. TPAMI (2023)
20. Palmero, C., Clapés, A., Bahnsen, C., Møgelmose, A., Moeslund, T.B., Escalera, S.: Multi-modal rgb-depth-thermal human body segmentation. IJCV **118**, 217–239 (2016)
21. Simonyan, K., Zisserman, A.: Two-stream convolutional networks for action recognition in videos. NIPS **27** (2014)
22. Song, S., Lan, C., Xing, J., Zeng, W., Liu, J.: Skeleton-indexed deep multi-modal feature learning for high performance human action recognition. In: ICME, pp. 1–6. IEEE (2018)

23. Sun, Z., Ke, Q., Rahmani, H., Bennamoun, M., Wang, G., Liu, J.: Human action recognition from various data modalities: a review. TPAMI **45**(3), 3200–3225 (2022)
24. Tran, D., Wang, H., Torresani, L., Ray, J., LeCun, Y., Paluri, M.: A closer look at spatiotemporal convolutions for action recognition. In: CVPR, pp. 6450–6459 (2018)
25. Vu, D.Q., Le, N., Wang, J.C.: Self-supervised learning via multi-transformation classification for action recognition. In: ICMEW, pp. 1–6. IEEE (2024)
26. Wang, C., Yan, J.: A comprehensive survey of rgb-based and skeleton-based human action recognition. IEEE Access **11**, 53880–53898 (2023)
27. Wang, L., et al.: Temporal segment networks: towards good practices for deep action recognition. In: Leibe, B., Matas, J., Sebe, N., Welling, M. (eds.) ECCV 2016. LNCS, vol. 9912, pp. 20–36. Springer, Cham (2016). https://doi.org/10.1007/978-3-319-46484-8_2
28. Wang, S., Liu, H., Zhao, H.: Public-domain locator for boosting attack transferability on videos. In: ICME, pp. 1–6. IEEE (2024)
29. Wang, X., Girshick, R., Gupta, A., He, K.: Non-local neural networks. In: CVPR, pp. 7794–7803 (2018)
30. Wei, X., Wang, S., Yan, H.: Efficient robustness assessment via adversarial spatial-temporal focus on videos. TPAMI (2023)
31. Xie, S., Sun, C., Huang, J., Tu, Z., Murphy, K.: Rethinking spatiotemporal feature learning: speed-accuracy trade-offs in video classification. In: ECCV, pp. 305–321 (2018)
32. Zhai, X., et al.: A large-scale study of representation learning with the visual task adaptation benchmark. arXiv preprint arXiv:1910.04867 (2019)
33. Zhao, C., Cai, W., Dong, C., Hu, C.: Wavelet-based fourier information interaction with frequency diffusion adjustment for underwater image restoration. In: CVPR, pp. 8281–8291 (2024)
34. Zhao, C., Cai, W., Hu, C., Yuan, Z.: Cycle contrastive adversarial learning with structural consistency for unsupervised high-quality image deraining transformer. Neural Netw., 106428 (2024)
35. Zhu, X., Zhu, Y., Wang, H., Wen, H., Yan, Y., Liu, P.: Skeleton sequence and rgb frame based multi-modality feature fusion network for action recognition. TOMM **18**(3), 1–24 (2022)

Evolution of Hybrid Multi-modal Action Recognition: From DA-CNN+Bi-GRU to EfficientNet-CNN-ViT

Adars Thazhayamkotath Mana Subramanian[1]([✉]), Anagha S. Menon[1],
Vaishnav Reghunath[1], Jyothisha J. Nair[1],
Akhil Kalathiparambil Asokakumar[2], and Nandagopal Jayagopal[2]

[1] Department of Computer Science and Engineering, Amrita School of Computing,
Amrita Vishwa Vidyapeetham, Amritapuri, Kerala, India
adars.nambootiri@gmail.com
[2] Founding Minds Software, Kochi, India

Abstract. Multi-modal action recognition, which leverages spatial and temporal information from various data streams, has become crucial in computer vision. This paper traces the evolution of our research from a model employing Dual Attention Convolutional Neural Networks (DA-CNNs) with Bidirectional Gated Recurrent Units (Bi-GRUs) to a sophisticated hybrid architecture integrating EfficientNet for feature extraction, custom CNN layers for feature refinement, and Vision Transformers (ViTs) for temporal modeling. This work was developed for the ICPR 2024 Multi-Modal Visual Pattern Recognition Challenge (Track 3: Multi-Modal Action Recognition). The dataset comprises 2,500 multi-modal videos (2,000 for training and 500 for testing) across 20 action classes, each including synchronized RGB, Infrared (IR), and Depth streams with varying resolutions and durations. Our final model processes these diverse data streams to achieve robust action recognition. We present a thorough analysis of both our initial and advanced architectures, including detailed mathematical formulations and experimental results. Notably, our approach attained an accuracy of 87.8%, surpassing the baseline model's performance of 86.43%. This research contributes significantly to the ongoing development of multi-modal action recognition techniques, with potential applications in various domains like surveillance, human-computer interaction, and autonomous systems.

Keywords: Multi-modal action recognition · DA-CNN · Bi-GRU · EfficientNet · CNN · Vision Transformer · RGB-IR-Depth fusion · Spatial-temporal modeling

1 Introduction

Action recognition in computer vision has become increasingly crucial for applications in surveillance, human-computer interaction, and autonomous systems. However, traditional approaches relying solely on RGB video data often struggle with real-world challenges such as poor lighting, occlusions, and complex environments. The Multi-Modal Visual Pattern Recognition Challenge, specifically Track 3: Multi-Modal Action Recognition, addresses these limitations by incorporating multiple data modalities including RGB, infrared (IR), and depth information. This multi-modal approach aims to enhance robustness and accuracy in diverse scenarios, from low-light conditions to crowded spaces. The challenge encourages researchers to develop innovative algorithms that can effectively fuse and interpret these varied data streams, capturing both spatial and temporal aspects of human actions. By leveraging complementary information from different sensors, multi-modal systems have the potential to overcome the shortcomings of single-modality approaches, leading to more reliable and versatile action recognition capabilities.

2   Proposed Solution

Our research contributes to this field by exploring advanced architectures that efficiently combine these modalities, progressing from a Dual Attention CNN with Bi-GRU model to a novel hybrid approach integrating EfficientNet, custom CNN layers, and Vision Transformers for improved performance in this challenging domain.

3   Related Work

Multi-modal action recognition has seen significant advancements in recent years, leveraging the complementary information from different data streams to improve performance. Simonyan and Zisserman [1] proposed a two-stream convolutional network architecture, setting a foundation for future work in this domain. Building on this, Wang et al. [2] introduced non-local neural networks to capture long-range dependencies in video data. Carreira and Zisserman [3] further advanced the field with their I3D model and the introduction of the Kinetics dataset. Temporal modeling has been a key focus, with Lin et al. [4] proposing the Temporal Shift Module (TSM) for efficient video understanding. Feichtenhofer et al. [5] introduced SlowFast networks, which process video at multiple temporal resolutions. The advent of transformer architectures, as presented by Vaswani et al. [6], has opened new avenues for action recognition research. In the realm of efficient architectures, Tan and Le proposed EfficientNet, which has shown promise in various computer vision tasks. Recent work has also explored hybrid models that combine multiple deep learning techniques. Ullah and Munir [7] proposed a computationally efficient framework combining a dual attentional CNN with a bi-directional GRU for human activity recognition, achieving significant improvements in execution time. Our work builds upon these foundations, integrating multi-modal data processing with efficient feature extraction and advanced temporal modeling to push the boundaries of action recognition performance. Building upon prior multi-modal action recognition research, recent medical imaging studies have similarly explored advanced deep learning techniques for complex classification tasks. Pillai et al. [8] demonstrated nuclei segmentation using UNet with EfficientNetV2, while Sreelekshmi et al. [9] proposed SwinCNN, integrating Swin Transformer and CNN for breast cancer grade classification. Complementary work by Venugopal et al. [10] developed an ensemble deep learning model for breast histopathology image classification, with earlier foundational research by Shastri et al. [11] exploring machine learning techniques for breast cancer diagnosis.

4   Dataset

This research utilizes the dataset from the ICPR 2024 Multi-Modal Visual Pattern Recognition Challenge (Track 3: Multi-Modal Action Recognition). This comprehensive dataset is specifically designed for multi-modal action recognition tasks, providing a rich source of synchronized data across multiple modalities (Table 1).

Table 1. Dataset Overview

Characteristic	Value
Total Videos	2,500
Training Set	2,000 videos
Test Set	500 videos
Action Classes	20
Modalities	RGB, Thermal IR, Depth

This multi-modal approach enables our models to leverage diverse and complementary information streams, potentially leading to more robust and accurate action recognition across various environmental conditions. The dataset comprises three synchronized modalities: RGB, Infrared (IR), and Depth. The videos in the dataset exhibit the following properties: training set contains more than 32,000 frames per modality, while the test set includes over 8,300 frames per modality. The duration of the videos varies between 2 to 13 s per video and dataset encompasses 20 diverse action categories, as listed in Table 2.

This diverse set of actions provides a challenging benchmark for multi-modal action recognition algorithms, encompassing a wide range of human activities and movements. To better understand the distribution of action classes in our dataset, Fig. 1 presents a bar chart showing the number of occurrences for each class.

As evident from Fig. 1, there is some variation in the frequency of different action classes. The majority of classes appear to have between 100 and 120 occurrences, with a few exceptions. Notably, classes such as "down the stairs" (class 19) and "twist waist" (class 17) have fewer occurrences, while classes like "hug

Table 2. Action Categories

1. Switch light	11. Orchestra conducting
2. Up the stairs	12. Rope skipping
3. Pack backpack	13. Shake hands
4. Ride a bike	14. Squat
5. Turn around	15. Swivel
6. Fold clothes	16. Tie shoes
7. Hug somebody	17. Tie hair
8. Long jump	18. Twist waist
9. Move the chair	19. Wear hat
10. Open the umbrella	20. Down the stairs

somebody" (class 6) and "open umbrella" (class 9) are more frequent. This distribution provides insight into the balance of our dataset and may inform strategies for handling potential class imbalance during model training and evaluation.

5   Methodology

Our research in multi-modal action recognition evolved from the baseline Temporal Shift Module (TSM) model, which achieved 0.8643 top-1 and 0.9940 top-5 accuracy. We initially developed a model combining a Dual Attention Convolutional Neural Network (DA-CNN) with a Bidirectional Gated Recurrent Unit (Bi-GRU). The DA-CNN selectively focused on crucial spatial features across RGB, IR, and depth modalities, while the Bi-GRU captured bidirectional temporal relationships. Building on insights from this approach, we then shifted to a more advanced architecture leveraging EfficientNet for efficient feature extraction and Vision Transformers for temporal modeling. This progression aimed to enhance the model's ability to process multi-modal data and capture complex spatio-temporal patterns, potentially surpassing both the TSM baseline and our initial DA-CNN + Bi-GRU approach in challenging action recognition scenarios.

5.1   Data Preprocessing

We apply a series of data augmentation techniques to improve model generalization:

- Random Horizontal Flip: $p(flip) = 0.5$
- Random Rotation: $\theta \sim Uniform(-15, 15)$
- Random Resized Crop: $size = (224, 224)$, $scale = (0.08, 1.0)$, $ratio = (3/4, 4/3)$
- Color Jitter: brightness $\pm 40\%$, contrast $\pm 40\%$, saturation $\pm 40\%$, hue $\pm 10\%$

These augmentations are applied consistently across all frames in a video clip to maintain temporal coherence.

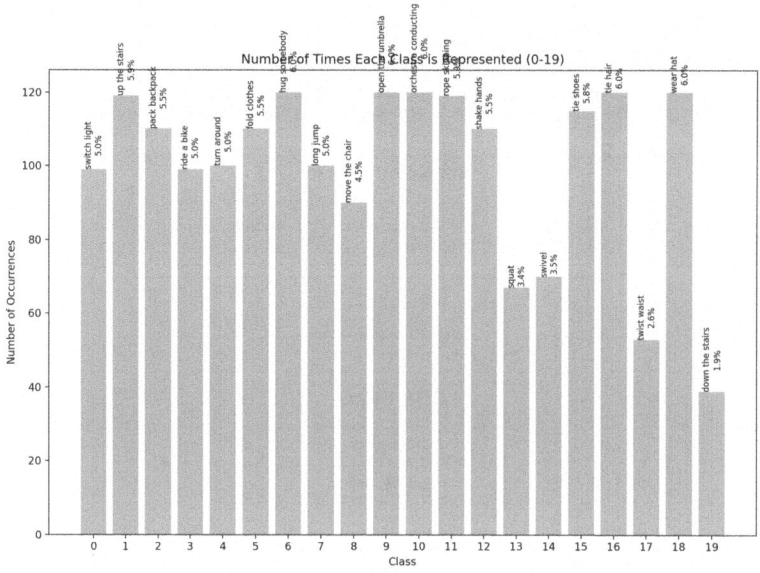

Fig. 1. Number of Times Each Class is Represented in the Dataset

5.2   DA-CNN+Bi-GRU: Initial Approach

Dual Attention CNN. The DA-CNN architecture incorporates two attention mechanisms:

1) Spatial Attention: This mechanism generates a spatial attention map M_s for each input feature map F:

$$M_s = \sigma(f^{7\times7}([\text{AvgPool}(F); \text{MaxPool}(F)])) \tag{1}$$

where $f^{7\times7}$ represents a convolutional layer with a 7×7 kernel, σ is the sigmoid activation function, and $[;]$ denotes concatenation.

2) Channel Attention: This mechanism generates a channel attention vector M_c:

$$M_c = \sigma(MLP(AvgPool(F)) + MLP(MaxPool(F))) \tag{2}$$

where MLP represents a multi-layer perceptron.
The final output of the DA-CNN is computed as:

$$F_{out} = M_c \otimes (M_s \otimes F) \tag{3}$$

where $\otimes$ represents element-wise multiplication (Fig. 2).

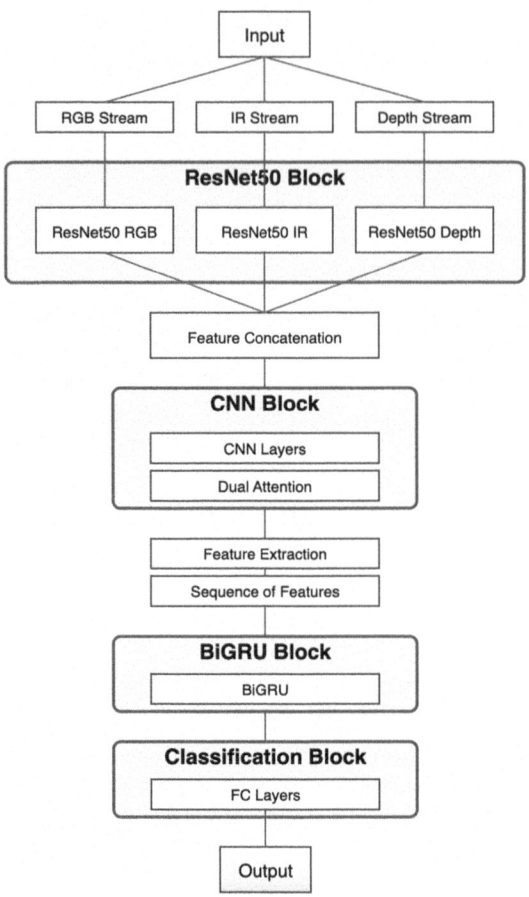

Fig. 2. DA-CNN Bi-GRU Architecture

Bi-GRU. The Bi-GRU processes sequential data from multiple frames, capturing forward and backward temporal dependencies. For a given input sequence $x = (x_1, ..., x_T)$, the Bi-GRU computes:

$$\overrightarrow{h_t} = GRU(x_t, \overrightarrow{h_{t-1}}) \tag{4}$$

$$\overleftarrow{h_t} = GRU(x_t, \overleftarrow{h_{t+1}}) \tag{5}$$

The final output is the concatenation of forward and backward hidden states:

$$h_t = [\overrightarrow{h_t}; \overleftarrow{h_t}] \tag{6}$$

We employ a late fusion strategy to combine information from multiple modalities:

$$y = softmax(W_f[h_{RGB}; h_{IR}; h_{depth}] + b_f) \tag{7}$$

where h_{RGB}, h_{IR}, and h_{depth} are the final hidden states from the Bi-GRU for each modality, W_f and b_f are learnable parameters, and y is the final classification output.

5.3   EfficientNet-CNN-ViT: Advanced Hybrid Architecture

While the DA-CNN+Bi-GRU model showed promising results, it struggled with increased complexity of spatial details in large datasets and the need for better temporal sequence modeling. To address these limitations, we developed a hybrid model that combined EfficientNet's superior feature extraction with custom CNN layers for feature refinement and the temporal modeling capabilities of Vision Transformers (ViTs) (Fig. 3).

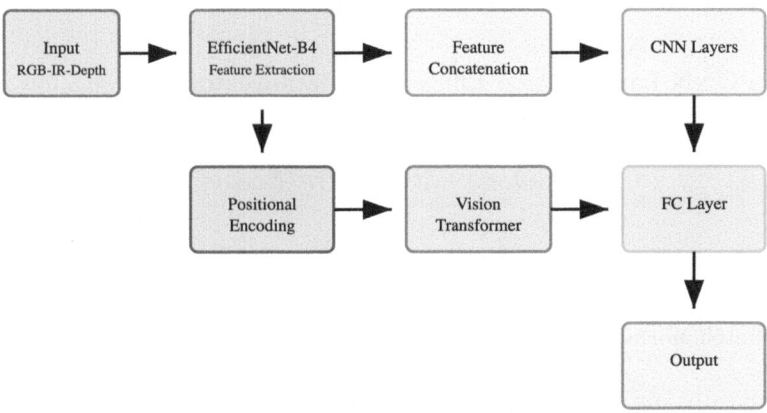

Fig. 3. EfficientNet-B4 CNN-ViT Architecture

Our proposed architecture consists of three main components: EfficientNet-based feature extractors, custom CNN layers, and a Vision Transformer for temporal modeling.

EfficientNet Feature Extraction. We employ EfficientNet-B4 as the backbone for feature extraction from each modality (RGB, IR, and Depth). EfficientNet-B4 is chosen for its balanced trade-off between model size and performance.

For the RGB stream, we use a standard pre-trained EfficientNet-B4:

$$F_{RGB} = EfficientNet_{RGB}(X_{RGB}) \tag{8}$$

For the IR and Depth streams, we modify the input layer to accept single-channel data:

$$F_{IR} = EfficientNet_{IR}(X_{IR}) \tag{9}$$

$$F_{Depth} = EfficientNet_{Depth}(X_{Depth}) \tag{10}$$

where X_{RGB}, X_{IR}, and X_{Depth} are the input tensors for each modality, and F_{RGB}, F_{IR}, and F_{Depth} are the corresponding feature maps.

To optimize training, we fine-tune only the last two stages of each Efficient-Net, freezing the earlier layers to leverage pre-trained weights:

$$\theta_{EfficientNet} = \{\theta_i | i > N - 150\} \tag{11}$$

where $\theta_{EfficientNet}$ represents the trainable parameters, and N is the total number of parameters in EfficientNet.

Custom CNN Layers. After EfficientNet feature extraction, we apply custom CNN layers to refine and combine features from all modalities:

$$F_{combined} = [F_{RGB}; F_{IR}; F_{Depth}] \tag{12}$$

$$F_{refined} = CNN_2(ReLU(BN(CNN_1(F_{combined})))) \tag{13}$$

where $[;]$ denotes concatenation, CNN_1 and CNN_2 are convolutional layers, BN is batch normalization, and $ReLU$ is the rectified linear unit activation function.

Specifically, our CNN layers are defined as:

$$CNN_1 : \mathbb{R}^{5376 \times H \times W} \rightarrow \mathbb{R}^{2688 \times H \times W} \tag{14}$$

$$CNN_2 : \mathbb{R}^{2688 \times H \times W} \rightarrow \mathbb{R}^{d_{model} \times H \times W} \tag{15}$$

where H and W are the spatial dimensions of the feature maps, and d_{model} is the dimension of the model (set to 512 in our experiments).

Positional Encoding. Before feeding the refined features into the Vision Transformer, we add positional encoding to provide temporal information:

$$PE_{(pos,2i)} = sin(pos/10000^{2i/d_{model}}) \tag{16}$$

$$PE_{(pos,2i+1)} = cos(pos/10000^{2i/d_{model}}) \tag{17}$$

where pos is the position in the sequence and i is the dimension.

Vision Transformer (ViT). The Vision Transformer processes the sequence of frame features to model temporal relationships:

$$Z = ViT(F_{refined} + PE) \tag{18}$$

Our ViT consists of multiple transformer encoder layers, each comprising multi-head self-attention and feed-forward networks:

$$Attention(Q, K, V) = softmax(\frac{QK^T}{\sqrt{d_k}})V \tag{19}$$

where Q, K, and V are query, key, and value matrices, respectively, and d_k is the dimension of the key vectors.

Classification Layer. The final classification is performed using a linear layer on the output of the last transformer encoder layer:

$$y = softmax(W \cdot Z_{[-1]} + b) \tag{20}$$

where $Z_{[-1]}$ is the final time step of the transformer output, W and b are learnable parameters, and y is the predicted class probabilities.

6   Evaluation Metrices

Our evaluation metrics encompass several key components for optimizing model performance. We employ cross-entropy loss for training, which measures the dissimilarity between predicted and true class probabilities. For optimization, we use the AdamW optimizer, which combines adaptive learning rates with weight decay to improve generalization. Our learning rate schedule follows Cosine Annealing with Warm Restarts, allowing for periodic resets of the learning rate to escape local minima. To prevent exploding gradients, we apply gradient clipping, limiting the maximum norm of gradients. Additionally, we utilize mixed precision training, which balances computational efficiency with numerical precision by using both float16 and float32 representations for different operations. For this work, we use top-1 and top-5 accuracy as our primary evaluation metrics. Top-1 accuracy measures the percentage of samples where the model's highest probability prediction matches the true label, while top-5 accuracy considers whether the true label is among the model's top 5 predictions.

7   Results and Discussion

We evaluated both our DA-CNN+Bi-GRU and EfficientNet-CNN-ViT models on multi-modal action recognition datasets containing synchronized RGB, IR, and Depth video streams. Table 3 presents our results compared to baseline methods.

Table 3. Performance comparison on multi-modal video classification

Model	Top-1 Accuracy
EfficientNet-B4 + Vision Transformer	87.8%
DA-CNN+Bi-GRU with ResNet	79.6%
DA-CNN+Bi-GRU without pre-trained weights	53.4%
Baseline model with TSM	86.43%

Our EfficientNet-B4 + Vision Transformer model outperforms both baseline methods and our initial DA-CNN+Bi-GRU approaches, demonstrating the effectiveness of our hybrid architecture in leveraging multi-modal data for action recognition. The improvement over the RGB-only EfficientNet baseline highlights the benefits of incorporating IR and Depth information.

The DA-CNN+Bi-GRU model with ResNet shows a significant improvement over the version without pre-trained weights, emphasizing the importance of transfer learning in this task. However, the EfficientNet-B4 + Vision Transformer model still outperforms this approach, showcasing the advantages of using more advanced architectures for feature extraction and temporal modeling.

The relatively low performance of the DA-CNN+Bi-GRU model without pre-trained weights (53.4%) highlights the challenge of training complex models from scratch on limited datasets. This result underscores the value of transfer learning and pre-trained weights in achieving competitive performance, particularly when dealing with multi-modal data and complex architectures.

The superior performance of our EfficientNet-B4 + Vision Transformer model (87.8%) can be attributed to several factors:

1. **Efficient feature extraction**: EfficientNet-B4 provides a strong foundation for extracting relevant features from each modality, benefiting from its optimized architecture and pre-trained weights.
2. **Multi-modal fusion**: The custom CNN layers effectively combine and refine features from RGB, IR, and Depth streams, allowing the model to leverage complementary information from each modality.
3. **Temporal modeling**: The Vision Transformer component excels at capturing long-range temporal dependencies, which is crucial for understanding complex actions that unfold over time.
4. **Transfer learning**: By utilizing pre-trained weights and fine-tuning strategies, our model effectively adapts to the specific challenges of multi-modal action recognition.

These results demonstrate the effectiveness of our hybrid approach in addressing the challenges of multi-modal action recognition. The significant performance gain over both our initial DA-CNN+Bi-GRU models and the RGB-only baseline highlights the benefits of combining advanced architectures with multi-modal data fusion (Fig. 4).

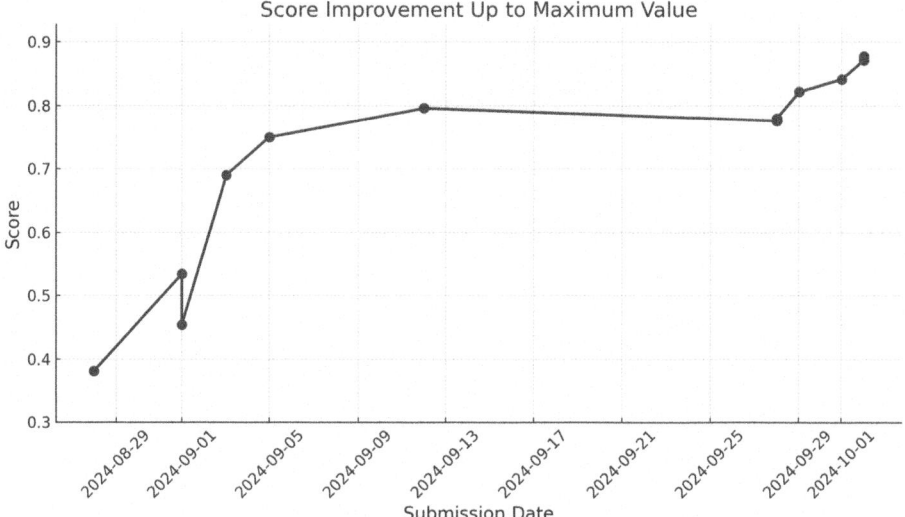

Fig. 4. Model performance over time

8   Conclusion

We have presented the evolution of our multi-modal action recognition research from the DA-CNN+Bi-GRU model to a more advanced EfficientNet-CNN-ViT hybrid architecture, which significantly improved the performance. The DA-CNN+Bi-GRU model, enhanced with ResNet and pre-trained weights, laid a strong foundation. However, the hybrid model-combining EfficientNet for feature extraction, CNN layers for refinement, and Vision Transformers for capturing long-range temporal dependencies-demonstrated superior handling of spatial and temporal features. This approach excels in processing RGB, IR, and Depth modalities, achieving state-of-the-art results on benchmark datasets and making it suitable for applications like autonomous driving, surveillance, and human-computer interaction.

References

1. Simonyan, K., Zisserman, A.: Two-stream convolutional networks for action recognition in videos. In: Advances in Neural Information Processing Systems, pp. 568–576. MIT Press (2014)
2. Wang, X., Girshick, R., Gupta, A., He, K.: Non-local neural networks. In: Proceedings of the IEEE Conference on Computer Vision and Pattern Recognition, pp. 7794–7803 (2018)
3. Carreira, J., Zisserman, A.: Quo vadis, action recognition? A new model and the kinetics dataset. In: Proceedings of the IEEE Conference on Computer Vision and Pattern Recognition, pp. 6299–6308 (2017)

4. Lin, J., Gan, C., Han, S.: TSM: temporal shift module for efficient video understanding. In: Proceedings of the IEEE/CVF International Conference on Computer Vision, pp. 7083–7093 (2019)
5. Feichtenhofer, C., Fan, H., Malik, J., He, K.: Slowfast networks for video recognition. In: Proceedings of the IEEE/CVF International Conference on Computer Vision, pp. 6202–6211 (2019)
6. Vaswani, A., et al.: Attention is all you need. In: Advances in Neural Information Processing Systems, pp. 5998–6008 (2017)
7. Ullah, A., Munir, K.: A computationally efficient framework for human activity recognition using dual attentional CNN and bi-directional GRU. IEEE Access 11, 45781–45793 (2023)
8. Pillai, R.R., et al.: Nuclei segmentation in histopathology images using UNet with EfficientNetV2. In: Advances in Communication and Computational Technology, pp. 667–677 (2023)
9. Sreelekshmi, D., et al.: SwinCNN: a hybrid model integrating swin transformer and CNN for breast cancer grade classification. In: 2023 IEEE Recent Advances in Intelligent Computational Systems, pp. 1–6 (2023)
10. Venugopal, K., et al.: A novel ensemble deep learning model for breast histopathology image classification. In: Intelligent Systems and Sustainable Development, pp. 593–603 (2023)
11. Shastri, A.A., et al.: A novel decision support system for breast cancer diagnosis using ensemble classification. Int. J. Sci. Res. Comput. Sci. Eng. Inf. Technol. 5(2), 509–517 (2019)

W16

Deep Learning-Based Building Footprint Extraction from UAV Acquired Fused Spectral and Elevation Information

Mohit Limba and Vaibhav Kumar$^{(\boxtimes)}$ (iD)

GeoAI4Cities Lab, Data Science and Engineering IISER Bhopal, Bhopal, India
vaibhav@iiserb.ac.in

Abstract. Unmanned Aerial Vehicle (UAV) images are increasingly being used for building footprint extraction due to their high spatial resolution, cost-effectiveness, flexibility, and accessibility. However, extracting building footprints from UAV images in unplanned dense regions of cities of developing nations such as India, is challenging. This study proposes Deep Learning (DL) approach to building footprint extraction by integrates UAV images with elevation data. The proposed approach involves development of five state-of-the art Deep Learning (DL) models on manually annotated RGBE (RGB + Elevation) imagery. We demonstrate the hypothesis that usage of elevation can be very effective in over-coming misclassifications primarily due to similar spectral information. The app-roach was evaluated on a dataset of UAV images acquired from a region of Bhopal city, India. The results show exceptional performance of all the models in seg-menting the building footprints. We also found that the use of elevation was very significant in training and helped boost the model performances by ~6%. The proposed approach has potential applications in a variety of real-world scenarios, such as urban planning, disaster management, and environmental monitoring.

Keywords: UAV · Deep Learning · DSM · Building Footprint Extraction

1 Introduction

Building footprints plays a vital role in various applications and domains of urban plan-ning, disaster management, environmental studies, real estate, traffic manage-ment, 3D city modeling and geospatial analysis. The precise and accurate geodatabase of buildings serves as an important and fundamental input in many decision-making systems, sus-tainable urban planning and development. The accuracy, availability and accessibility of building footprints aid city planners and policymakers in making im-portant decisions in disaster management, environment management and property management. Building footprint provides a comprehensive view of building distribu-tion, density and spatial arrangement [1, 2].

The utilization of UAV data has increased in recent years for building footprint extrac-tion, primarily owing to its capacity to deliver high-resolution aerial images. UAVs present a flexible and cost-effective alternative to conventional methods like satellite

S. Palaiahnakote et al. (Eds.): ICPR 2024 Workshops, LNCS 15617, pp. 353–364, 2025.
https://doi.org/10.1007/978-3-031-88217-3_27

imagery and manned aircraft, rendering them particularly well-suited for building footprint extraction [3]. In recent years, numerous studies have successfully extracted buildings from UAV images using Deep Learning (DL) models [4–10]. DL models can learn the features of buildings from training datasets and then use those features to predict buildings in unseen regions. This can help to automate the footprint extraction process and improve accuracy.

Many prior studies also used satellite information for automatizing building footprint extraction [11–14] for cities of developing nation like India. Unfortunately, the utilization of UAV data for this purpose remains underexplored in these regions. Primarily due to the lack of labeled training data. Models trained on images from more developed urban centers often struggle to generalize when applied to images obtained from cities in India. This challenge is particularly pronounced within densely populated informal settlements. The high density of buildings in these regions complicates the task of distinguishing between adjacent structures and accurately delineating their footprints. Factors such as occlusions from trees, similar spectral signatures of objects, presence of power lines, and other structures, as well as variations in elevation levels, further contribute to the complexity of building footprint extraction. These challenges can result in misclassification of buildings.

Incorporating elevation data, such as n-DSM (normalized Digital Surface Model), has shown promise in overcoming the challenges, leading to improved results [15, 16]. Researchers have explored methods that leverage elevation data alongside RGB data. Some of the studies are done in two steps rather than as an automatized learning-based tasks. For instance, Bittner et al. [17] concatenated the results from U-Net models trained on RGB images and n-DSM separately, resulting in enhanced outcomes. Another study [18] conducted in India utilized UAV RGB images for segmentation and then employed the Normalized Difference Vegetation Index (NDVI) and n-DSM data to refine features based on NDVI values and feature height. The exploration of combining UAV RGB data with elevation data as an additional channel in training Deep Learning (DL) models remains largely uncharted territory, particularly in developing countries like India.

Our proposed approach aims to tackle the challenges by integrating manually labeled UAV images with high-resolution elevation data obtained from Digital Surface Models (DSMs). We also leverage RGB images to leverage the spectral details of various objects materials, which enhances the segmentation accuracy. The paper makes the following significant contributions:

- Development of a manually labeled UAV data geodatabase that serves as the training dataset for the DL models. This geodatabase is not available in the literature.
- Trining of five DL models (BRNet, MC-FCN, SegNet, ResUNet, VGG16UNet) for benchmarking the segmentation of buildings from very high-resolution data acquired from UAVs in the Bhopal region of India. The models are trained on RGB and RGB with elevation (DSM) fused data.
- Exhaustive analysis of importance of DSM data in extraction of footprints in various built-forms.
- By applying the models to the Bhopal, region, we demonstrate the practical applicability and effectiveness of automating the approach of developing building footprints geodatabase for cities in developing nations like India.

2 Methodology

The methodology of this study involves a multi-step deep learning approach which utilizes both UAV data and elevation information. Firstly, the raw data of the study area was collected by UAV. The raw data was then processed to generate orthorectified RGB image, DSM, DTM. After generating this a preprocessing step was carried out to get normalized Digital Surface Model (n-DSM) and RGBE images. Following this, RGBE images were then manually annotated to get ground truth. Next, five state-of-the-art convolutional neural network (CNN) architectures were trained and evaluated on both RGB and RGBE images. Finally, post-processing steps including georeferencing and polygonise were implemented to generate a building footprint map.

2.1 Data Collection and Preprocessing

The study area used for this research is in the Gehun Kheda region of Bhopal city, India (see Fig. 1). This region is situated in the northern part of Bhopal city and is known for its mixed land use pattern, i.e., residential, commercial, and slum areas. Geographically, this area is located between 23° 9′ 35.0064″ N to 23° 11′ 32.0604″ N latitude and 77° 24′ 23.022″ E to 77° 26′ 6.5904″ E longitude. The study area covers approximately 6.63 km^2 area, includes various building structures (slums, high-rise buildings and densely populated buildings) and has been undergoing urbanization in recent years.

The data was collected using an Unmanned Aerial Vehicle (UAV) equipped with a high-resolution camera in the year 2021. The camera of UAV had a resolution of 1280 × 960, a focal length of 5.5 mm, and a pixel size of 3.75 × 3.75 μm. The UAV was flown at an altitude of 105 m, capturing a total of 88,155 images covering the complete study area. The captured images had R, G, B and NIR band. The ground resolution of each image was 7.24 cm/pix. To ensure accurate georeferencing of the captured UAV images, 20 Ground Control Points (GCPs) were selected. The X, Y, and Z errors of the GCPs were measured as 0.730763, 0.69848, and 0.131065, respectively. The GCPs were used to align and georeferenced the UAV images for further processing.

Photogrammetry techniques were then used to generate a dense point cloud which was then used to generate Digital Surface Model (DSM) of 7 cm. A normalized Digital Surface Model (nDSM) was generated by removing topographic variation. Shuttle Radar Topography Mission (STRM) DEM with a resolution of 30 cm was used to generate nDSM. DSM was also used to generate an orthomosaic image of the study area (See Fig. 1) with spatial resolution of 3 cm. After resampling the nDSM at 3 cm resolution it was fused with RGB channels resulting in a 4-channel RGBE image.

2.2 Manual Annotation of RGBE Images

The prepared RGBE image was manually annotated to get the accurate ground truth data. To manage the annotation process efficiently, 10 patches of size 2048 × 2048 were extracted from different regions which includes residential, slum and mixture of residential and slum within the study area. Figure 2 show some examples of images and their annotated ground truth. These patches were then manually annotated using

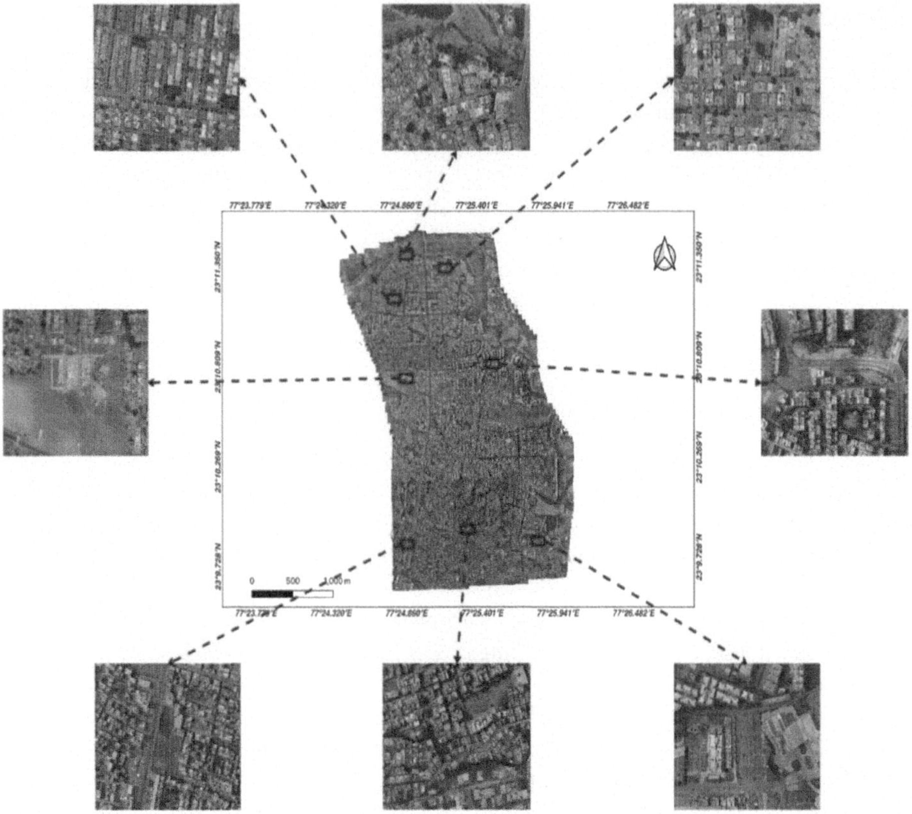

Fig. 1. Orthomap of the study area showing various landuse combinations

the OpenCV Computer Vision Annotation Tool (CVAT) and pixels were classified into two classes: building and non-building. Building class pixels were assigned a value of 1, while non-building class pixels were assigned a value of 0. The awning of balconies, windows and doors were also annotated as a building (Fig. 3).

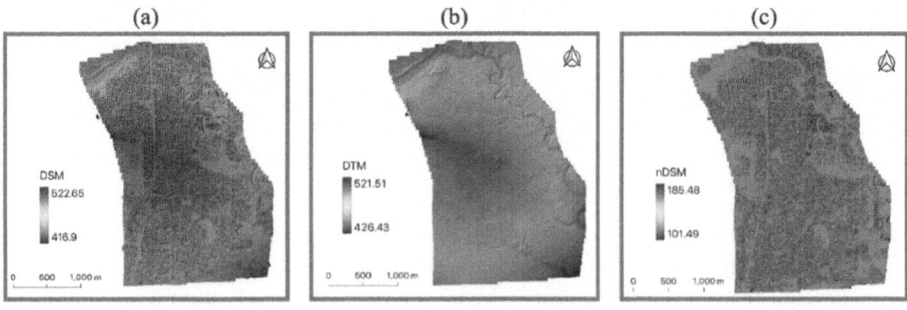

Fig. 2. A a) DSM, b) DEM and c) nDSM of the study area

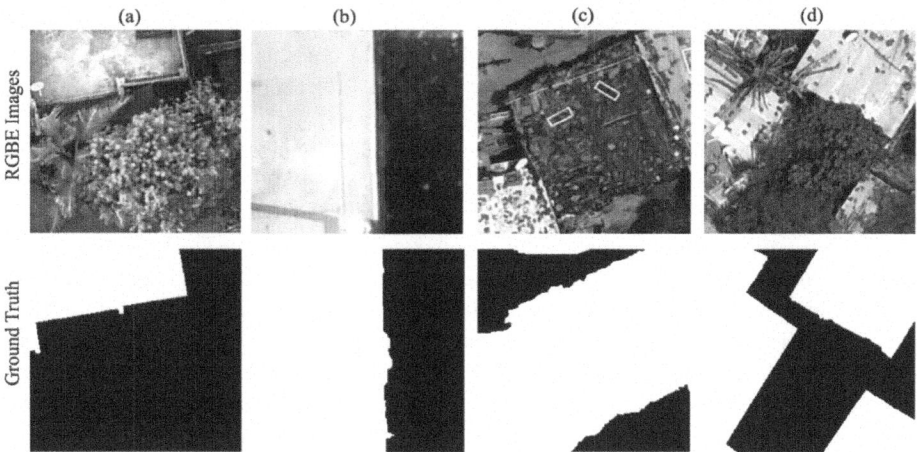

Fig. 3. RGBE images and their corresponding ground truth.

2.3 Training of Models

For the task of segmentation, manually annotated data were used to develop BR-net [19], SegNet [20], ResUNet [21], MC-FCN [22], and VGG16 [23] based models. BRNet, initially introduced by Wu et al. in 2018 [19], is a convolutional neural network model that utilises UNet styled architecture as a shaed backend with a multitask prediction approach, focusing on image segmentation and outline extraction. This model effectively uses both local and global information present in the images. This architectural design of BRNet was chosen due to its ability to effectively leverage image features at multiple scales, enabling accurate building footprint extraction in our study. SegNet, was introduced by Badrinarayanan, Kendall, and Cipolla in 2017 [20], is a notable neural network architecture for image segmentation. Its deep symmetrical encoder and decoder-based architecture makes it a valuable choice for image segmentation tasks, as it effectively captures and reconstructs important features within the data.

ResUNet, introduced by Xu et al. in 2018 [21], presents a notable model architecture featuring four encoder-decoder layers which draws inspiration from the ResNet architecture, however, ResUNet is composed of an upsampling operation coupled with a crucial residual block connection between the final layer of the encoder and the initial layer of the decoder. The ResUNet architecture's blend of ResNet's deep feature learning capabilities and UNet's effective image segmentation makes it suitable choice for our study. Further, MC-FCN, a convolutional neural network model, that was originally introduced by Wu et al. in 2018 [22] was also developed. MC-FCN's architectural arrangement has demonstrated its capacity to effectively capture and represent features in images, making it a good choice for segmentation tasks. Finally, a very widely used VGG16 Unet model [23], was adapted. Its architectural configuration encompasses four encoder-decoder. The model has been used in various studies related to segmentation of UAV images [24, 25]. It's noteworthy that for all the models employed in this study, adjustments were made to accommodate four channeled RGBE images input images, while keeping the remaining layers consistent with the original configurations. This adaptation ensures compatibility with our dataset and objectives for accurate image analysis and segmentation.

These image and label patches were systematically organized into tiles, each measuring 256 x 256 pixels. A deliberate strategy of employing 50% horizontal overlap and 50% vertical overlap was implemented to reduce prediction bias. This generated a total of 1575 pairs of RGBE images and their corresponding labeled masks. To ensure robust model training, approx. 90% of this dataset was allocated for training purposes, with the remaining 10% reserved for validation purposes. A separate test dataset containing 450 RGBE image-mask pairs was employed. Several data augmentation techniques were employed, including random rotations and translations. These augmentations were introduced to enhance the model's robustness and its ability to generalize to diverse scenarios. It must be noted that none of the models utilized pretrained weights; instead, all five models underwent training from scratch.

The training was conducted on a computer equipped with a 40 GB NVIDIA A100-PCI GPU and 256 GB of RAM. The training phase was executed using the Adam optimizer with a batch size of 8 and a learning rate set at 1e-4 for all the models. To facilitate convergence and model refinement, each model underwent training for 100 epochs. Throughout the training process, vigilant monitoring of both loss and accuracy metrics was conducted for both the training and validation datasets. The loss function employed for training was the Binary Cross Entropy (BCE) loss, which is well-suited for binary classification tasks like building footprint extraction.

3   Results and Discussion

The models when implemented generated exceptionally good results. The results were significantly good in dense regions, primarily due to the usage of elevation information. A comprehensive quantitative analysis was carried out to assess the performance of the models. We evaluated the outcomes using a range of metrics including Overall Accuracy (OAcc), Precision, Recall, F1-Score (F1Sc), Kappa (kapp), and Intersection over Union (IOU). Table 1 presents the outcomes for each model. Among these models, BRNet emerged as the top performer, achieving the highest Overall Accuracy (OAcc) at 0.948, followed closely by ResUNet with an OAcc of 0.933. MC-FCN exhibited an OAcc of 0.932, SegNet scored 0.912, and VGG16 recorded the lowest OAcc of 0.900. BRNet also exhibited the highest Precision at 0.961, signifying its low rate of false positive predictions. ResUNet, MC-FCN, and SegNet followed with Precision scores of 0.906, 0.897, and 0.863, respectively. VGG16Unet, on the other hand, displayed the lowest Precision at 0.839, indicative of higher false positive predictions.

However, the Recall: 0.953 of MC-FCN was better than other models, closely followed by VGG16Unet, ResUNet, and SegNet with Recall scores of 0.951, 0.948, and 0.945, respectively. The IOU outcomes, which is a better metric for evaluating semantic segmentation BRNet to be most accurate predictions with the highest IOU at 0.887. ResUNet achieved the second-highest IOU of 0.861, followed by MC-FCN with an IOU of 0.853, SegNet at 0.824, and VGG16 with the lowest IOU of 0.806. The results affirm

BRNet as the standout performer, excelling across various metrics including accuracy, precision, F1-score, Kappa, and IOU. ResUNet and MC-FCN also demonstrated strong performance, rendering them suitable for real-world building footprint extraction tasks. Conversely, VGG16Unet exhibited inferior performance, characterized by elevated false positive predictions and decreased true positive predictions. To further investigate the performance of the model we analyzed the outcome of the model in various built-up compositions.

Table 1. Quantitative evaluation results of five models BRNet, MCFCN, SegNet, ResUNet, and VGG16. The **bold** text represents the best outcome.

Model	OAcc	Precision	Recall	F1-Score	Kappa	IOU
BRNet	**0.948**	**0.961**	0.920	**0.940**	**0.890**	**0.887**
MC-FCN	0.932	0.897	**0.953**	0.924	0.862	0.853
SegNet	0.912	0.863	0.948	0.903	0.822	0.824
ResUNet	0.933	0.906	0.945	0.925	0.865	0.861
VGG16Unet	0.900	0.839	0.951	0.892	0.799	0.806

Figure 4 presents the visual representations of predicted building footprints by various models in various regions. Area3 and Area4 have sparse built-ups being sparse (Fig. 4-Area1 and Area3) were classified very accurately by every model, BRNet demonstrated exceptional performance particularly in generating sharp and accurate building boundaries. The other models in some instances misclassified objects such as cars, trees, and those sharing similar spectral signatures as buildings. This was true in almost all areas including slums and mix of slum and unplanned built-up (see Fig. 4-Area3 and Area4). Given the complexity of the built-ups in compact unplanned areas the outcomes demonstrate the capability of using the elevation-based approach in detecting building footprints with very high accuracy.

3.1 Impact of Elevation in Building Footprint Extraction

To assess the impact of incorporating elevation data as an additional channel into RGB imagery, we conducted a comparative analysis between the performance of the best performing BRNet model trained on RGB and RGBE datasets. The BRNet model was subsequently trained on the RGB dataset, employing identical parameters and hyper-parameters as those used for training on the RGBE dataset. Figure 4 shows the outcomes of the model prediction in various built-up cases. The discernible contrast in results between RGB (Fig. 5b) and RGBE outcomes (Fig. 5c) underscores the substantial impact of elevation data on building footprint extraction. By including the elevation channel, the height information as the primary feature reduced the misclassification on similar spectral signature due to height differences. Moreover, RGB images exhibited limitations near the boundaries of buildings, primarily attributable to the presence of awnings. These constraints led to inaccuracies in the results derived from RGB images.

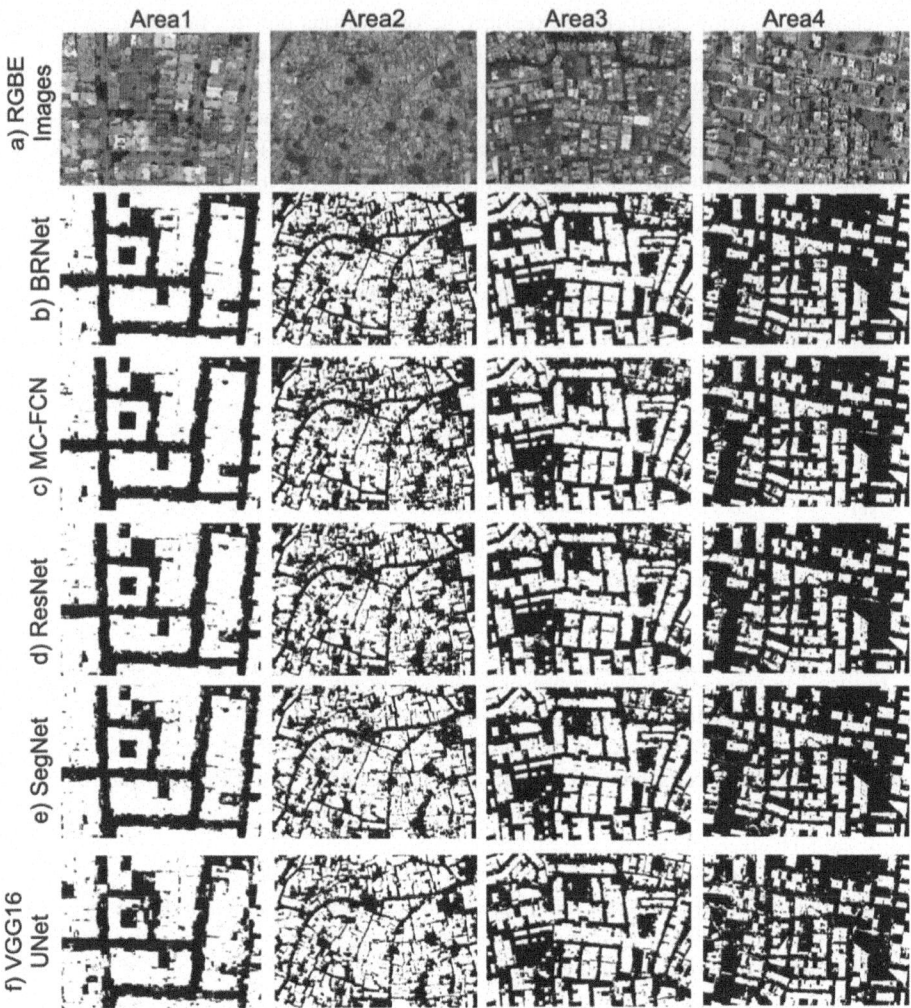

Fig. 4. Predicted building footprints by all five models for different areas of the study region.

The overall accuracy of RGBE images surpassed that of RGB images by a considerable 7%, with all other metrics displaying significant discrepancies in scores. Table 2 details the metric outcomes of the models on both the channels.

Table 2 encapsulates the performance disparity between the BRNet model trained on RGB and RGBE datasets, revealing substantial differences across all measured metrics. RGBE consistently outperforms RGB in all assessed metrics, with the most significant discrepancy observed in IOU metrics. This phenomenon can be attributed to the fact that RGB relies solely on spectral information, whereas RGBE benefits from the inclusion of elevation data. These results underscore the substantial improvement in building footprint extraction accuracy achieved through the integration of elevation data as an additional channel.

(a) Input Image   (b) BRNet RGB   (c) BRNet RGBE

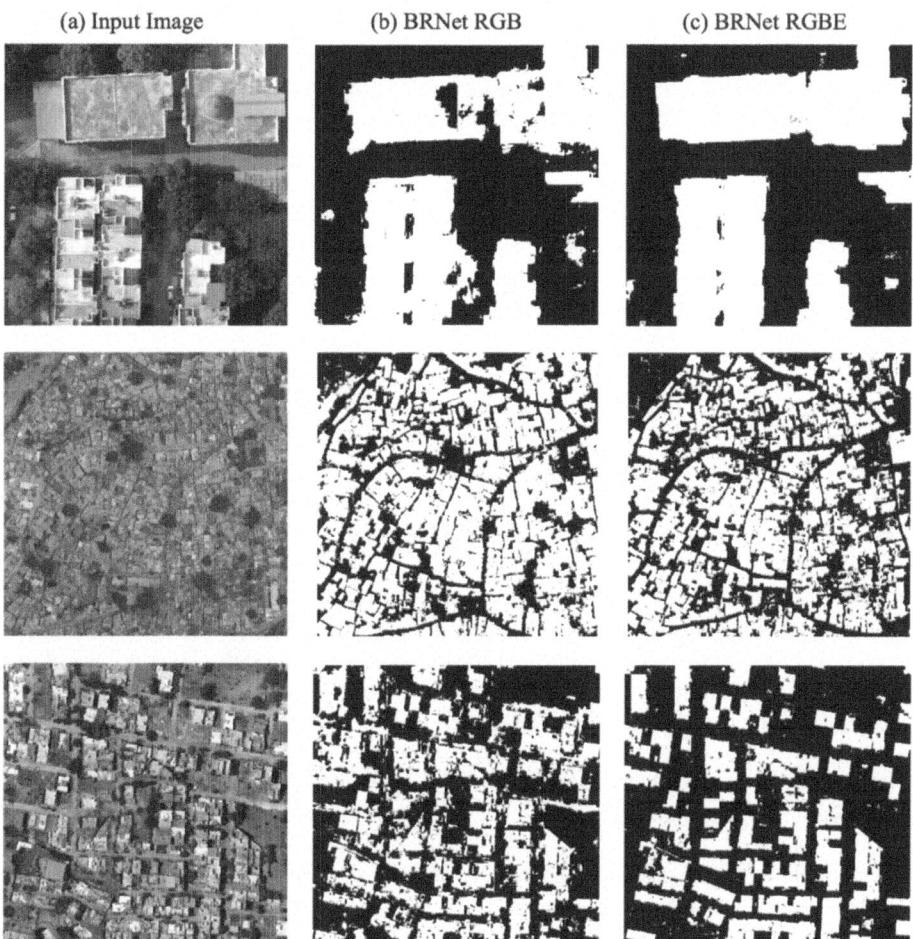

Fig. 5. Predicted building footprints for various (a) land combinations, by BRNet on (b) RGB (c) RGBE data

Table 2. Quantitative result of BRNet Model when trained on RGB and RGBE

Input Data	OAcc	Precision	Recall	F1-Score	Kappa	IOU
RGB	0.897	0.868	0.902	0.885	0.792	0.793
RGBE	0.948	0.961	0.920	0.940	0.890	0.887

4   Conclusion

Building footprint extraction from UAV images is a critical challenge, especially in densely populated and unplanned regions of developing nations. This study proposes an innovative approach by leveraging the power of deep learning techniques along with the integration of elevation data with UAV imagery. Five state-of-the-art deep learning models (BRNet, SegNet, MCFCN, ResUNet, VGG16Unet) were trained on manually annotated RGBE imagery. BRNet emerged as the standout performer, consistently achieving the highest scores across multiple metrics, including Overall Accuracy, Precision, Recall, F1-Score, Kappa, and Intersection over Union. This shows the model's robustness and its ability to generate exceptionally accurate building footprints, particularly in dense regions. BRNet's remarkable performance can be attributed to its utilization of elevation data, which enables it to accurately delineate building boundaries, even in complex and compact urban environments. ResUNet and MC-FCN also demonstrated strong performance, indicating their suitability for real-world building footprint extraction tasks.

The results show that incorporating elevation data as an addition channel to RGB data significantly improves the accuracy of building footprint extraction. The elevation data reduces the misclassification caused due to similar spectral signature, especially in areas with varying building heights. It also addresses limitations near building boundaries, where awnings and other factors can lead to inaccuracies in RGB-based predictions. A boost in model performance of approximately 6% is observed, due to the utilization of elevation data.

This research lays the foundation for using multi-spectral data (NIR, infrared) and high-resolution elevation data (LiDAR data) along with RGB data for further enhancing the accuracy and robustness of building footprint extraction models. The findings of this research can have significant implications for sustainable development, environmental impact assessment, and disaster management.

Funding Details. The work is supported by National Geospatial Program, DST, India, and M.P. State Electronics Development Corporation Ltd, Goverment of Madhya Pradesh.

Data Availability. The data that support the findings of this study are available from the corresponding author, upon reasonable request.

References

1. Touzani, S., Granderson, J.: Open data and deep semantic segmentation for automated extraction of building footprints. Remote Sens. **13**(13), 2578 (2021)
2. Li, W., He, C., Fang, J., Zheng, J., Fu, H., Yu, L.: Semantic segmentation-based building footprint extraction using very high-resolution satellite images and multi-source GIS data. Remote Sens. **11**(4), 403 (2019)
3. Crommelinck, S., Bennett, R., Gerke, M., Nex, F., Yang, M., Vosselman, G.: Review of automatic feature extraction from high-resolution optical sensor data for UAV-based cadastral mapping. Remote Sens. **8**(8), 689 (2016). https://doi.org/10.3390/rs8080689
4. Borba, P., de Carvalho Diniz, F., da Silva, N.C., de Souza Bias, E.: Building footprint extraction using deep learning semantic segmentation techniques: experiments and results. In: 2021 IEEE International Geoscience and Remote Sensing Symposium IGARSS, Brussels, Belgium, pp. 4708–4711 (2021). https://doi.org/10.1109/IGARSS47720.2021.9553855
5. Kang, Z., Kamran, M., Sohn, G.: Boundary regularized building footprint extraction from satellite images using deep neural network (2020)

6. Bischke, B., Helber, P., Folz, J., Borth, D., Dengel, A.: Multi-task learning for segmentation of building footprints with deep neural networks. In: 2019 IEEE International Conference on Image Processing (ICIP), Taipei, Taiwan, pp. 1480–1484 (2019). https://doi.org/10.1109/ICIP.2019.8803050

7. Chen, L.-C., Papandreou, G., Kokkinos, I., Murphy, K., Yuille, A.L.: DeepLab: semantic image segmentation with deep convolutional nets, atrous convolution, and fully connected CRFs. IEEE Trans. Pattern Anal. Mach. Intell. **40**(4), 834–848 (2018). https://doi.org/10.1109/TPAMI.2017.2699184

8. Huang, Z., Cheng, G., Wang, H., Li, H., Shi, L., Pan, C.: Building extraction from multi-source remote sensing images via deep deconvolution neural networks. In: 2016 IEEE International Geoscience and Remote Sensing Symposium (IGARSS), Beijing, China, pp. 1835–1838 (2016). https://doi.org/10.1109/IGARSS.2016.7729471

9. Liu, W., et al.: Building footprint extraction from unmanned aerial vehicle images via PRU-Net: application to change detection. IEEE J. Sel. Topics Appl. Earth Observat. Remote Sens. **14**, 2236–2248 (2021)

10. Li, Z., Xin, Q., Sun, Y., Cao, M.: A deep learning-based framework for automated extraction of building footprint polygons from very high-resolution aerial imagery. Remote Sens. **13**(18), 3630 (2021). https://doi.org/10.3390/rs13183630

11. Gopala Krishna, V.S.S.N., Pendyala, H.K., Kalluri, V.C., Rao,: An efficient multi-stage object-based classification to extract urban building footprints from HR satellite images. Traitement du Signal **38**(1), 191–196 (2021). https://doi.org/10.18280/ts.380120

12. Rastogi, K., Bodani, P., Sharma, S.A.: Automatic building footprint extraction from very high-resolution imagery using deep learning techniques. Geocarto Int. **37**(5), 1501–1513 (2022). https://doi.org/10.1080/10106049.2020.1778100

13. Prathiba, A.P., Rastogi, K., Jain, G.V., Govind Kumar, V.V.: Building footprint extraction from very-high-resolution satellite image using object-based image analysis (OBIA) technique. In: Ghosh, J.K., da Silva, I. (eds.) Applications of Geomatics in Civil Engineering: Select Proceedings of ICGCE 2018, pp. 517–529. Springer, Singapore (2020). https://doi.org/10.1007/978-981-13-7067-0_41

14. Tejeswari, B., Sharma, S.K., Kumar, M., Gupta, K.: Building footprint extraction from space-borne imagery using deep neural networks. Int. Arch. Photogramm. Remote. Sens. Spat. Inf. Sci. **43**, 641–647 (2022)

15. Hosseinpour, H., Samadzadegan, F., Javan, F.D.: CMGFNet: a deep cross-modal gated fusion network for building extraction from very high-resolution remote sensing images. ISPRS J. Photogramm. Remote. Sens. **184**, 96–115 (2022)

16. Bittner, K., Cui, S., Reinartz, P.: Building extraction from remote sensing data using fully convolutional networks. Int. Arch. Photogramm. Remote Sens. Spat. Inf. Sci. **42**, 481–486 (2017)

17. Bittner, K., Adam, F., Cui, S., Korner, M., Reinartz, P.: Building footprint extraction from VHR remote sensing images combined with normalized DSMs using fused fully convolutional networks. IEEE J. Selected Topics Appl. Earth Observat. Remote Sens. **11**(8), 2615–2629 (2018). https://doi.org/10.1109/JSTARS.2018.2849363

18. Shukla, A., Jain, K.: Automatic extraction of urban land information from unmanned aerial vehicle (UAV) data. Earth Sci. Inf. **13**(4), 1225–1236 (2020). https://doi.org/10.1007/s12145-020-00498-x

19. Wu, G., et al.: A boundary regulated network for accurate roof segmentation and outline extraction. Remote Sens. **10**(8), 1195 (2018)

20. Badrinarayanan, V., Kendall, A., Cipolla, R.: SegNet: a deep convolutional encoder-decoder architecture for image segmentation. IEEE Trans. Pattern Anal. Mach. Intell. **39**(12), 2481–2495 (2017). https://doi.org/10.1109/TPAMI.2016.2644615

21. Xu, Y., et al.: Building extraction in very high-resolution remote sensing imagery using deep learning and guided filters. Remote Sens. **10**(1) (2018). issn: 2072–4292. https://doi.org/10. 3390/rs10010144. https://www.mdpi.com/2072-4292/10/1/144

22. Wu, G., et al.: Automatic building segmentation of aerial imagery using multi-constraint fully convolutional networks. Remote Sens. **10**(3) (2018). issn: 2072–4292. https://doi.org/ 10.3390/rs10030407. https://www.mdpi.com/2072-4292/10/3/407

23. Shi, Y., Chen, X., Zhang, T.: Cloud-based deep learning on AWS open data registry: automatic building and road extraction from satellite and LiDAR. In: ACM SIGSPATIAL 2020 International Workshop on Geospatial Data Access and Processing APIs (2020)

24. Jung, H., Choi, H.-S., Kang, M.: Boundary enhancement semantic segmentation for building extraction from remote sensed image. IEEE Trans. Geosci. Remote Sens. **60**, 1–12 (2021)

25. Shao, Z., Tang, P., Wang, Z., Saleem, N., Yam, S., Sommai, C.: BRRNet: a fully convolutional neural network for automatic building extraction from high-resolution remote sensing images. Remote Sens. **12**(6), 1050 (2020). https://doi.org/10.3390/rs12061050

Generation of Dense Urban Features Using Conditional GANs

Anurag Nihal and Vaibhav Kumar[✉]

Department of Data Science and Engineering, Indian Institute of Science Education
and Research, Bhopal, India
{anurag19,vaibhav}@iiserb.ac.in

Abstract. This paper discusses the use of conditional Generative
Adversarial Networks (GANs) to generate dense urban features in satellite images and evaluate their effectiveness in semantic segmentation
tasks. High-resolution true-color satellite imagery of Mumbai, obtained
from Pleiades-1A at a 0.5 m resolution, is utilized for the study. The
proposed Multiple Discriminator pix2pix (MD-pix2pix) model, which
employs multiple discriminators and a modified training procedure, is
introduced to generate realistic satellite images. The performance of the
MD-pix2pix model is compared to the traditional pix2pix model using a
mix dataset of real and generated satellite images. The synthesized satellite images are assessed for their effectiveness in semantic segmentation
tasks using various CNN models, including VGG16-UNet, MobileNetV2-
UNet, and DeepLabV3+. The study aims to overcome the limitations of
existing datasets that do not include informal settlements, such as slum
areas, which are common in many cities. The results indicate that the
MD-pix2pix model produces more realistic satellite images with greater
variability in vegetation type, slum arrangements, and built-ups than the
traditional pix2pix model. The synthetically generated satellite images
are also effective in semantic segmentation tasks, with better segmentation accuracy achieved using the MD-pix2pix generated images for
computationally less expensive architectures such as MobileNetV2-UNet.
This study highlights the potential of GANs to generate realistic satellite
images for urban feature mapping and monitoring applications.

Keywords: Generative Adversarial Networks · Semantic
segmentation · Satellite images · Urban semantics

1 Introduction

Technological advancements in the last few decades have led to increased satellite
launches and the availability of satellite image datasets because of technological
cost reductions [1]. Consequently, satellite images have attracted tremendous
interest due to their various applications, including land use and land cover
(LULC) studies, forest and crop monitoring, urban planning (e.g., growth modeling, change detection, etc.), to mention a few [1]. However, for the above-
mentioned studies, semantic label maps are required for accurate and precise

S. Palaiahnakote et al. (Eds.): ICPR 2024 Workshops, LNCS 15617, pp. 365–379, 2025.
https://doi.org/10.1007/978-3-031-88217-3_28

predictions [29]. Deep neural networks have progressed to obtain semantic label maps for corresponding satellite images with higher performance [24]. Deep neural networks usually require large annotated datasets to achieve higher accuracy, where annotated datasets consist of raw data and corresponding labels (also termed as ground truths) [10]. However, generating labeled data is an exhaustive and resource intensive exercise.

Data augmentation techniques can increase the size and quality of smaller annotated datasets for training deep neural networks [26]. Enhancing the training dataset in size using basic image manipulation techniques of affine transformations (translation, rotation, scaling, sheer) and cropping have been used to increase the size of the dataset by multiples of thousands [15]. However, these manipulations are meaningful only when the transformed data follows the distribution close to actual data distribution [30]. The transformations such as translation and rotation suffer from the padding effect where the part of the image is lost. These drawbacks are overcome by the generative data modeling techniques [30].

Generative modeling offers to create synthetic examples from a training dataset to exhibit similar characteristics by approximating the distributions of the training dataset [26]. Synthetically generated data has been used in the training process of deep convolution neural networks to achieve better performance in the case of limited data [27]. Moreover, data augmentation using synthetic data can improve the ability of deep learning frameworks to perform well on unseen and unobserved inputs [4]. In the domain of remote sensing, synthetic data augmentation has been utilized in semantic segmentation [3], remote sensing image classification [30], data translation [2], and others. [11] introduced the generative adversarial network (GAN) that learns to produce synthetic examples with the matching characteristics of the data distribution on which they are trained . Various studies [14,22] demonstrate the use of GANs-generated data in the training process of deep learning models to improve their performance in case of insufficient training data. GANs have been utilized in the fields of remote sensing not only to generate missing data [21,25], but also to translate data among various domains [2,9]. However, in applications that require control over the data translation, conditional GANs by [18] is the suitable framework to allow the generation of data conditioned by auxiliary information such as text, tags, class labels, images, etc.

Conditional GANs can be used to augment smaller annotated dataset of raw satellite images and corresponding semantic labels by generating many synthetic satellite images with variations from the corresponding labels maps, i.e., for n semantic label maps, we aim to generate m synthetic satellite images with variations that can be used for scarce training data situations, where $m \geq n$. This method can overcome the problem of smaller annotated dataset by providing multiple variations of raw satellite images for the same ground truth for training deep neural networks. We test the multiple variations of generated satellite images mixed with real satellite images to evaluate the performance on segmentation task.

2 Background

2.1 Generative Adversarial Networks

GANs consist of two adversarial trained neural networks, namely, the generator G that attempts to generate images that can fool the discriminator D. The discriminator D tries to discriminate correctly between the generated and real images. The adversarial learning between the generator and discriminator promotes the generator G to learn the distribution close to real data distribution such that discriminator D can hardly differentiate between real and fake image. The objective function for the GAN with the generator G and the discriminator D is given by:

$$G^* = \arg \min_G \max_D \mathbb{E}_{x \sim p_{data(x)}} \left[\log D(x) \right] + \mathbb{E}_{z \sim p(z)} \left[\log(1 - D(G(z))) \right] \quad (1)$$

where $\mathbb{E}$ and log are the expectation and logarithmic operators respectively, and z is the random noise vector that follows prior known noise distribution $p(z)$.

2.2 Conditional Generative Adversarial Networks and pix2pix

Conditional GANs are the extension of GANs that considers auxiliary information on which both the discriminator D and the generator G are conditioned. In the generator G, the prior input noise $p(z)$, and y are combined in joint hidden representation whereas in the discriminator, x and y are presented as inputs and to a discriminative function. The modified objective function for conditional GAN is given by:

$$G^* = \arg \min_G \max_D \mathbb{E}_{x \sim p_{data(x)}} [\log D(x|y)] + \mathbb{E}_{z \sim p(z)} [\log(1 - D(G(z|y)))] \quad (2)$$

where $\mathbb{E}$ and log are the expectation and logarithmic operators respectively, and z is the random noise vector that follows prior known noise distribution $p(z)$. This provides the control to condition the networks on the auxiliary information in contrast to GAN in Eq. 1 where the user has no control over the network [18].

Building upon the conditional GAN, pix2pix offers as a general-purpose conditional GAN framework for image-to-image translation where the task is to translate the image data in the target domain from the native domain while preserving the pixel information. The overall pix2pix architecture is similar to conditional GAN with a generator G and discriminator D conditioned on the semantic label maps. The generator G used in pix2pix is a U-Net architecture with skip connections to circumvent the bottleneck of low-level information. While the discriminator is known as PatchGAN classifier, a patch-based fully convolutional network that tries to classify if each $N \times N$ patch in an image is real or fake. To reduce the blurriness in the generated image, [12] proposed to use L1 loss in addition to the conditional objective loss. Consequently, the objective function 2 modifies to Eq. 3 where λ represents the coefficient of the L1 loss. In our study, the objective function inputs x represents the semantic label map, and y represents the original satellite image.

$$G^* = \arg\min_G \max_D \mathbb{E}_{x,y} \left[\log D(x,y)\right] + \mathbb{E}_{x,z} \left[\log(1 - D(z, G(x,z)))\right] + \lambda L_1(G) \quad (3)$$

$$L_1(G) \ = \mathbb{E}_{x,y,z} \ ||y - G(x,z)||_1 \qquad (4)$$

3   Study Area and Data

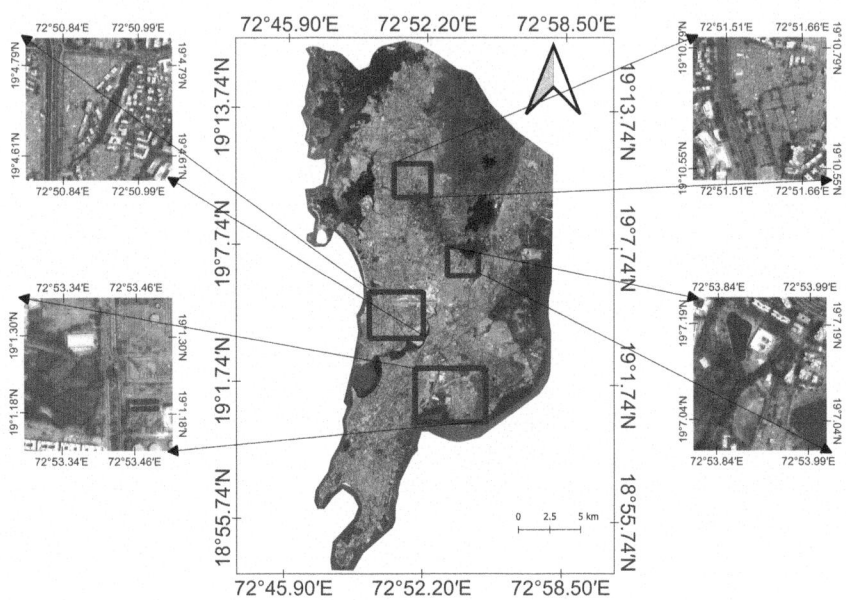

Fig. 1. Satellite image of Greater Mumbai. Best viewed in digital format.

GANs have been experimented with various datasets such as the INRIA Aerial Labeling dataset [16] in [17], UC-Merced Land-Use dataset [31] in [17] and others. However, these datasets contain planned infrastructural features and do not contain features of informal settlements such as slum areas. Hence, to have models that can generate congested and contrasting features and properly planned infrastructures is more desirable. We choose Mumbai as our test-bed for the experiments because of its contrasting infrastructural features and performed the experiments on the dataset proposed in [7]. In our study, high-resolution true-color satellite imagery of Pleiades-1A is utilized. Pleiades, a product of Airbus, offers image dataset at a 0.5 m resolution at various spectral combinations. The obtained images have pan-sharpened R, G, B bands dated 15th March 2017, that covers an area of approximately 541.66 square kilometers of Greater Mumbai (see Fig. 1).

4   Methodology

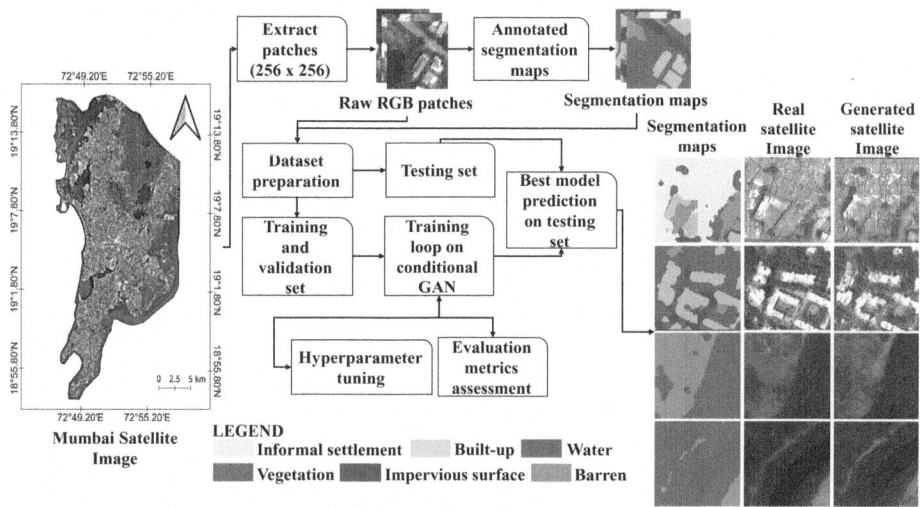

Fig. 2. Graphical representation of methodology. Best viewed in digital format.

The overall methodology involves preparation of dataset that consists of satellite images and corresponding semantic segmentation maps, data preprocessing, training and validation cycle of models and prediction on the testing set by the best model(s). The objectives of our work are implemented in two major phases (a) generation of dense urban features in satellite images from semantic segmentation maps (see Fig. 2) and (b) verification of the usage of the generated satellite images for task of semantic segmentation for better performance (see Fig. 3). In first phase, performance of pix2pix and our proposed MD-pix2pix models are studied for their ability to generate perceptually valid and realistic satellite images. Thereafter, a mix datasets of generated satellite images and real satellite images along with their corresponding semantic segmentation maps is prepared for training and validation cycles. Lastly, in the second phase, performance of various CNN models is studied for segmentation accuracy.

4.1   Training Data Preparation and Preprocessing

The patches of size 256×256 are extracted from the image tiles and paired with corresponding semantic patches. The semantic ground truth patches are obtained from work done by [7]. The patches are extracted with a stride of 256 to have zero vertical and horizontal overlapping within the images from the 110 tiles of 600×600 dimension. The number of manually labeled patches is further increased by finetuning the predictions of the VGG16-UNet model used in [6], resulting in a total of 22,397 annotated patches. These corresponding paired patches are then subjected to affine transformations, horizontal and vertical flipping along with random cropping. The dataset is split into training, validation and testing sets with the ratios of 70 : 10 : 20 split containing 15677, 2239 and 4481 tiles respectively for corresponding training and evaluation.

4.2 Proposed Multiple Discriminator Pix2Pix (MD-Pix2Pix)

The addition of multiple discriminators has also been effective in GANs where the adversarial learning is based on the multiple feed-backs [28]. Several studies have demonstrated the advantages of multiple discriminators for various applications such as obtaining high-quality generated samples in small numbers of iterations [8], specific reward system for dual discriminators [20], random low dimensional projections for meaningful gradient feedback to generators [19]. In our study, we modify pix2pix by using multiple discriminators and a modified training procedure. The architectures of discriminators are the same as PatchGAN used in pix2pix. The generator utilizes U-Net architecture with skip connections. We experiment with three random multiple discriminators. During training, at each step, any two discriminators are selected to update their parameters while averaging over the discriminator loss from all three discriminators. The generator is updated using the random discriminator's fake loss. This procedure attempts to accommodate the imbalance of sparse urban features to be accepted more often as real-like images than in case of pix2pix for our study. The random discriminator's fake loss update also provides the chance to provide meaningful feedback for the sparsely available urban features. Consequently, we obtain more variations in terms of vegetation type, slum arrangement, realistic color variations, built-ups, etc. The objective function for the proposed MD-pix2pix conditional GAN with the generator G and the discriminators D_1, D_2, D_3 can be modified from the objective function of pix2pix in Eq. 3 and Eq. 4 as,

$$G^* = \arg \min_G \max_D \mathbb{E}_{x,y}[\log D_{avg}(x,y)] + \mathbb{E}_{x,z}[\log(1 - D_m(z, G(x,z)))] + \lambda L_1(G)$$
(5)

$$L_1(G) = \mathbb{E}_{x,y,z} \|y - G(x,z)\|_1$$
(6)

where $D_{avg} = \frac{D_1 + D_2 + D_3}{3}$ and D_m is the random discriminator from the set of D_1, D_2, D_3 discriminators.

4.3 Implementation Details

The pix2pix and proposed MD-pix2pix models were trained for 200 epochs with batch size 4. The learning rate for both models was chosen to be 0.002 with Adam optimizer using momentum parameters of (0.5, 0.999). The coefficient λ for L1 was set to be 100. The optimization of the networks of the pix2pix model was achieved by alternating between one gradient step on discriminator D and then, one step on G [12]. The optimization of networks of the proposed MD-pix2pix was achieved by alternating one gradient step on any two discriminators from the set of three, then one gradient step on generator G. NVIDIA A100-PCIE of Ampere architecture with GPU memory of 40GB was used for training and evaluation of the models.

4.4   Segmentation Using Real and Generated Satellite Images

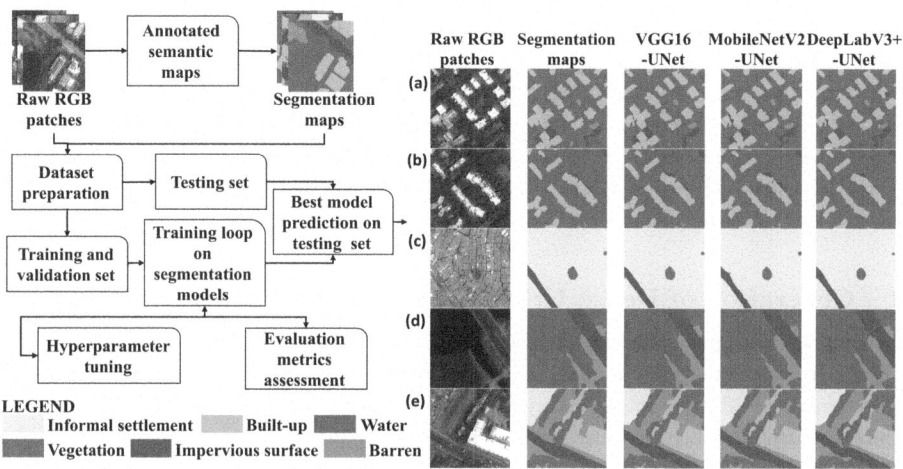

Fig. 3. Graphical representation for methodology of segmentation task using mixture of generated and real satellite images. Best viewed in digital format.

To evaluate the effectiveness of the synthetically generated satellite images, the segmentation task is performed using VGG16-UNet [23], MobileNetV2-UNet [13], and DeepLabV3+ [5] models on both MD-pix2pix and pix2pix generated satellite images. The selection of models is done on the basis of previously available benchmarks on the original dataset [7] used in [6]. The dataset for validating the use of generated satellite images in the segmentation task is made using 9378 pairs of satellite images and corresponding semantic segmentation. The training and validation set included a mix of real (25%) and generated (75%) samples of satellite images and their corresponding ground truth maps. In total, the training set consisted of 6717 pairs of satellite and segmentation map images, and the validation set contained 1050 pairs. The testing set comprised 1611 real satellite images and their corresponding ground truth maps. The experiment was performed twice for the generated outputs of pix2pix and MD-pix2pix where the models were trained for 40 epochs and evaluated on testing set to obtain evaluation metrics (see Fig. 3).

5   Results and Discussion

In this section, we present and thoroughly analyse the results of two crucial phases of our research, namely, the generation of dense urban features using conditional GANs, and the verification of the usefulness of the generated satellite images for the segmentation task. Firstly, we delve into the performance of two state-of-the-art conditional GAN models, namely, pix2pix and MD-pix2pix, for generating highly realistic and visually convincing satellite images. We provide a comprehensive comparison of the results obtained from these two models to identify the better-performing one.

Furthermore, we compare the generated dataset of satellite images from both pix2pix and MD-pix2pix for the segmentation task and evaluate their performance against the benchmark set by [6] for real satellite images. By doing so, we aim to determine the quality of the generated dataset and establish its reliability for use in various applications.

5.1   Generation of Dense Urban Features

Results of the Implementation of Pix2Pix. The outputs of the state-of-the-art pixp2pix is presented in Fig. 4. In Fig. 4 (a), the semantic map has informal settlements (or slums) as the major class along with barren land, built-up and vegetation in minor representation. The generation of informal settlements for the pix2pix is a difficult task because it generates perceptually incorrect settlement structures with random shapes. However, it fails to generate suitable impervious surfaces such as road, footpaths, etc. In Fig. 4 (b), the semantic map represents an urban locality with built-ups and vegetation. Compared to real satellite images, the pix2pix model can generate dense urban locality with the difference in color tone and increase in vegetation and different structure of built-ups while maintaining the overall shape of built-ups. The barren land pixels are also suitably generated to represent the same type of soil color. In Fig. 4 (c), the semantic map represents the barren land vegetation where the pix2pix model is able to generate appropriate satellite image with differences in colour tone and texture of the barren land. The vegetation pixels generated seem to represent dense vegetation where according to semantic map, water body is also blended accordingly. In Fig. 4 (d), the semantic map represents the water and vegetation pixels, where the pix2pix generates dense vegetation and water with different color tone as compared to the real satellite image.

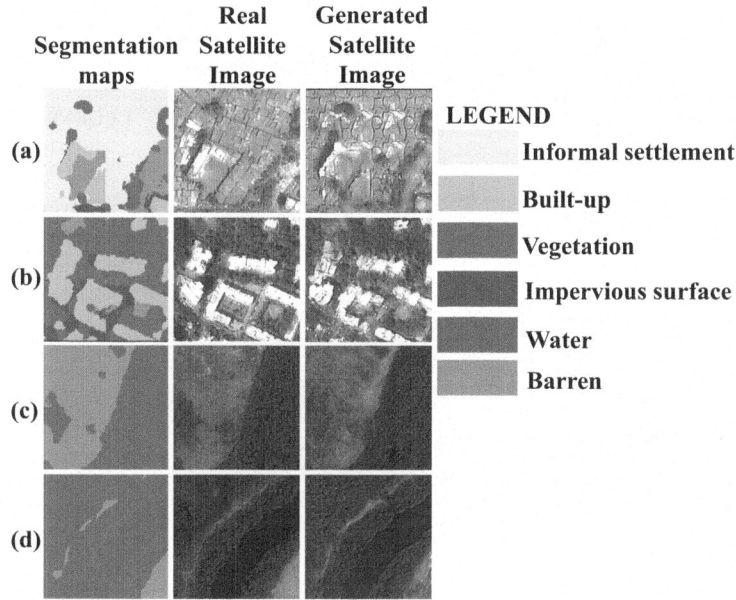

Fig. 4. Results from pix2pix model. Best viewed in digital format.

Results of the Implementation of MD-Pix2Pix. Fig. 5 represents the outputs of our proposed MD-pix2pix with possible variations of generated satellite images. Figure 5 (a) represents the informal settlements and barren land pixels in the majority where our MD- pix2pix is able to generate perceptually valid structures of slums with differences in color tone. The barren land pixels are also generated with different textures and color tone. It can also be observed that the minor class pixels of built-ups in semantic map, however, are not generated for small areas of built- ups in the second output of possible variations of generated satellite images. In Fig. 5 (b), all three output images have different number of built-ups generated for the same area of built-up pixels. In Fig. 5 (c), our model is able to generate suitable satellite images with differences in color tone and texture of the barren land. The vegetation area in the variations of generated images have different textures of vegetation. In Fig. 5 (d), all the generated satellite images have different textures and color tones of barren land. However, the vegetation has only differences in textures and internal shape composition of vegetation representing different types of vegetation.

We compare our work with the output of the state-of-the-art pix2pix from Fig. 4 and Fig. 5. For the sparse image inputs such as slums, the pix2pix faces difficulty in generating a suitable satellite image where artifacts are common to appear. The failure cases on sparse image inputs are reported in [12]. For image inputs containing major classes of vegetation, barren land and water body, both the models have significant generalizing power to generate images with adequate context and perceptually rationale images. However, our MD-pix2pix model

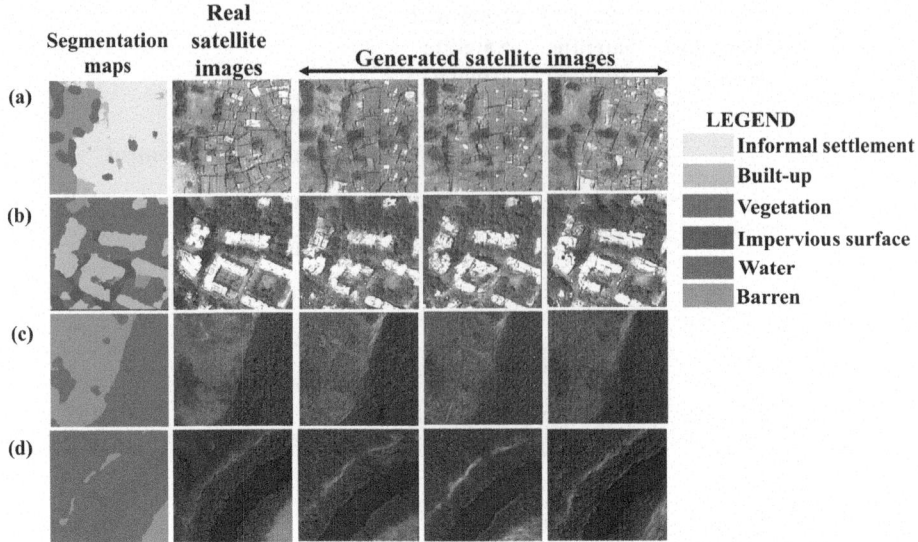

Fig. 5. Results from MD-pix2pix model. Best viewed in digital format.

generates better results for slums where there are suitable variations in terms of overall structure of the slum region and distinction of house structures. MD-pix2pix attempts to generate multiple scenarios of resultant generated images as the input image is subjected to image augmentation techniques such as random flipping and affine transformations. Comparing the results of Fig. 4 (b) and Fig. 5 (b), one can observe the variations in the architecture of the built-ups and the vegetation nearby. Though both pix2pix and MD-pix2pix tend to generate white-colored built-ups majorly, since the dataset utilized that contains the white-colored built-ups (skyscrapers, buildings, etc.) mostly. Our MD-pix2pix model yields recognizable output especially for built-ups, slums and vegetation in dense regions.

5.2   Segmentation Using Real and Generated Satellite Images

Noting from Table 1, VGG16-UNet is the best model for the pix2pix generated dataset. Observing Table 2, the experimental results show that MobileNetV2-UNet outperforms VGG16-UNet and DeepLabV3+ in overall and class-wise evaluation for segmentation using the MD-pix2pix generated dataset. Notably, for the MD-pix2pix generated dataset, MobileNetV2-UNet achieved ideal performance in built-up, vegetation, and water while improving the overall class metrics for most of the classes. This improvement in performance was not possible to obtain for the pix2pix generated dataset. Consistent with previous research, the segmentation of the water body showed higher metrics than other classes due to its distinct spectral signatures [6].

Table 1. Segmentation results using real and pix2pix generated satellite images. O. Acc represents overall accuracy and O. IoU represents the overall IoU.

Model	Class	Accuracy	IoU	O. Acc	O. IoU
VGG16-UNet	Informal Settlements	98.3	97.17	97.84	91.82
	Built-ups	94.8	90.75		
	Impervious Surfaces	95.02	91.19		
	Vegetation	97.94	95.14		
	Barren	98.52	96.86		
	Water	99.73	99.65		
MobileNetV2-UNet	Informal Settlements	98.86	93.2	96.04	76.62
	Built-ups	87.47	84.45		
	Impervious Surfaces	97.72	85.97		
	Vegetation	90.18	89.34		
	Barren	97.47	94.46		
	Water	98.77	98.73		
DeepLabV3+	Informal Settlements	98.09	96.63	97.11	93.20
	Built-ups	94.15	87.91		
	Impervious Surfaces	92.33	88.39		
	Vegetation	97.34	93.44		
	Barren	97.98	9578		
	Water	99.7	99.55		

We obtain better performance on semantic segmentation task on satellite images using the mixture real and generated satellite images on both, the pix2pix and the proposed MD-pix2pix which uses multiple discriminators with the tweaked training procedure. The evaluation metrics in Table 2 demonstrate the effectiveness of the proposed model in accurately generating the realistic images that can be used for accurate segmentation task. The overall performance displayed in Table 2 is higher than the overall performance achieved by all three segmentation models utilized in [6] using the Greater Mumbai region dataset [7]. This verifies the use of synthetically generated data to improve the ability of deep learning models to perform well on unobserved and unseen data, resulting in better performance.

Table 2. Segmentation results using real and MD-pix2pix generated satellite images. O. Acc represents overall accuracy and O. IoU represents the overall IoU.

Model	Class	Accuracy	IoU	O. Acc	O. IoU
VGG16-UNet	Informal Settlements	96.92	94.73	96.46	90.03
	Built-ups	92.84	88.32		
	Impervious Surfaces	94.14	89		
	Vegetation	97.19	93.99		
	Barren	95.78	90.89		
	Water	99.4	98.96		
MobileNetV2-UNet	Informal Settlements	97.56	95.07	96.74	91.16
	Built-ups	93.42	89.01		
	Impervious Surfaces	95.16	89.91		
	Vegetation	96.76	94.54		
	Barren	96.47	92.32		
	Water	99.54	99.03		
DeepLabV3+	Informal Settlements	96.74	93.74	95.72	88.48
	Built-Ups	92.85	86.74		
	Impervious Surfaces	93.17	86.93		
	Vegetation	96.49	92.87		
	Barren	94.38	89.77		
	Water	99.13	98.42		

6   Conclusion

In this study, we implement multiple discriminators in the pix2pix model to generate satellite images with dense urban features and assess their performance in semantic segmentation tasks. To achieve this, we utilize high-resolution true-color satellite imagery of Mumbai, which presents a challenging and contrasting infrastructure. Our proposed MD-pix2pix model is capable of producing satellite images that are visually accurate and realistic. The multiple discriminators offer meaningful feedback for sparse urban features, resulting in greater variability in vegetation types, slum arrangements, realistic color shades, and built-ups. Furthermore, we evaluate the effectiveness of synthetically generated satellite images in segmentation tasks using various CNN models. Our findings suggest that incorporating both real and generated images can enhance the accuracy of the segmentation process.

The potential impact of this work spans across several fields, including but not limited to urban planning, disaster response, and environmental monitoring. Synthetic satellite images can be employed to create high-resolution images of urban areas with diverse features, aiding in urban planning and disaster response planning. The images generated can also be used for environmental monitoring and tracking changes over time. The MD-pix2pix model proposed in this study has applications in other fields that require the production of high-quality images with dense features, such as street view imaging, robotics, and virtual reality. Although the methodology presented in this study is promising, further improvements can be made by exploring alternative datasets and employing different GAN architectures to produce more varied features. All in all, this study offers a promising approach to generating high-quality satellite images that can be applied in various fields.

Acknowledgements. This project is supported by the IIT Tirupati Navavishkar I-Hub Foundation (IITTNiF) through the CHANAKYA Graduate Internship program (IITTNiF/CHANAKYA/UGF/2022/11/15/10).

References

1. Abady, L., Cannas, E.D., Bestagini, P., Tondi, B., Tubaro, S., Barni, M., et al.: An overview on the generation and detection of synthetic and manipulated satellite images. APSIPA Trans. Sig. Inf. Process. **11**(1), 1–56 (2022)
2. Bermudez, J.D., Happ, P.N., Feitosa, R.Q., Oliveira, D.A.B.: Synthesis of multispectral optical images from SAR/optical multitemporal data using conditional generative adversarial networks. IEEE Geosci. Remote Sens. Lett. **16**(8), 1220–1224 (2019). https://doi.org/10.1109/lgrs.2019.2894734
3. Bittner, D., Ferreira, J.F., Andrada, M.E., Bird, J.J., Portugal, D.: Generating synthetic multispectral images for semantic segmentation in forestry applications. In: ICRA 2022 Workshop in Innovation in Forestry Robotics: Research and Industry Adoption (2022). https://openreview.net/forum?id=rtLgB7n14M9
4. Bowles, C., et al.: GAN augmentation: augmenting training data using generative adversarial networks. arXiv preprint arXiv:1810.10863 (2018)
5. Chen, L.C., Zhu, Y., Papandreou, G., Schroff, F., Adam, H.: Encoder-decoder with atrous separable convolution for semantic image segmentation. In: Proceedings of the European Conference on Computer Vision (ECCV), pp. 801–818 (2018)
6. Dabra, A., Kumar, V.: Evaluating green cover and open spaces in informal settlements of Mumbai using deep learning. Neural Comput. Appl. (2023). https://doi.org/10.1007/s00521-023-08320-7
7. Dabra, A., Kumar, V.: Manually annotated high resolution satellite image dataset of Mumbai for semantic segmentation (2023). https://doi.org/10.17632/XJ2V49ZT26.1
8. Durugkar, I., Gemp, I., Mahadevan, S.: Generative multi-adversarial networks. arXiv preprint arXiv:1611.01673 (2016)
9. Enomoto, K., et al.: Filmy cloud removal on satellite imagery with multispectral conditional generative adversarial nets. arXiv preprint arXiv:1710.04835 (2017)
10. Gong, S., Ball, J., Surawski, N.: Urban land-use land-cover extraction for catchment modelling using deep learning techniques. J. Hydroinf. **24**(2), 388–405 (2022). https://doi.org/10.2166/hydro.2022.124
11. Goodfellow, I., et al.: Generative adversarial nets. Adv. Neural Inf. Process. Syst. **27** (2014)
12. Isola, P., Zhu, J.Y., Zhou, T., Efros, A.A.: Image-to-image translation with conditional adversarial networks. In: Proceedings of the IEEE Conference on Computer Vision and Pattern Recognition, pp. 1125–1134 (2017)

13. Kanadath, A., Jothi, J.A.A., Urolagin, S.: Histopathology image segmentation using MobilenetV2 based U-Net model. In: 2021 International Conference on Intelligent Technologies (CONIT), pp. 1–8 (2021). https://doi.org/10.1109/CONIT51480.2021.9498341

14. Kim, J.H., Hwang, Y.: GAN-based synthetic data augmentation for infrared small target detection. IEEE Trans. Geosci. Remote Sens. **60**, 1–12 (2022). https://doi.org/10.1109/tgrs.2022.3179891

15. Krizhevsky, A., Sutskever, I., Hinton, G.E.: ImageNet classification with deep convolutional neural networks. In: Pereira, F., Burges, C., Bottou, L., Weinberger, K. (eds.) Advances in Neural Information Processing Systems, vol. 25. Curran Associates, Inc. (2012)

16. Maggiori, E., Tarabalka, Y., Charpiat, G., Alliez, P.: Can semantic labeling methods generalize to any city? The Inria aerial image labeling benchmark. In: IEEE International Geoscience and Remote Sensing Symposium (IGARSS). IEEE (2017)

17. Marín, J., Escalera, S.: SSSGAN: satellite style and structure generative adversarial networks. Remote Sens. **13**(19), 3984 (2021). https://doi.org/10.3390/rs13193984

18. Mirza, M., Osindero, S.: Conditional generative adversarial nets. arXiv preprint arXiv:1411.1784 (2014)

19. Neyshabur, B., Bhojanapalli, S., Chakrabarti, A.: Stabilizing GAN training with multiple random projections. arXiv preprint arXiv:1705.07831 (2017)

20. Nguyen, T., Le, T., Vu, H., Phung, D.: Dual discriminator generative adversarial nets. In: Guyon, I., et al. (eds.) Advances in Neural Information Processing Systems, vol. 30. Curran Associates, Inc. (2017). https://proceedings.neurips.cc/paper/2017/file/e60e81c4cbe5171cd654662d9887aec2-Paper.pdf

21. Panchal, P., Raman, V.C., Baraskar, T., Sinha, S., Purohit, S., Modi, J.: Reconstruction of missing data in satellite imagery using SN-GANs. In: Zhang, Y.-D., Senjyu, T., So-In, C., Joshi, A. (eds.) Smart Trends in Computing and Communications. LNNS, vol. 286, pp. 629–638. Springer, Singapore (2022). https://doi.org/10.1007/978-981-16-4016-2_60

22. Park, M., Tran, D.Q., Jung, D., Park, S.: Wildfire-detection method using DenseNet and CycleGAN data augmentation-based remote camera imagery. Remote Sens. **12**(22), 3715 (2020). https://doi.org/10.3390/rs12223715

23. Pravitasari, A., et al.: UNET-VGG16 with transfer learning for MRI-based brain tumor segmentation. TELKOMNIKA Telecommun. Comput. Electron. Control **18**, 1310 (2020). https://doi.org/10.12928/telkomnika.v18i3.14753

24. Rousset, G., Despinoy, M., Schindler, K., Mangeas, M.: Assessment of deep learning techniques for land use land cover classification in Southern New Caledonia. Remote Sens. **13**(12) (2021).https://doi.org/10.3390/rs13122257

25. Shao, M., Wang, C., Zuo, W., Meng, D.: Efficient pyramidal GAN for versatile missing data reconstruction in remote sensing images. IEEE Trans. Geosci. Remote Sens. **60**, 1–14 (2022). https://doi.org/10.1109/tgrs.2022.3188913

26. Shorten, C., Khoshgoftaar, T.M.: A survey on image data augmentation for deep learning. J. Big Data **6**(1) (2019). https://doi.org/10.1186/s40537-019-0197-0

27. Talukdar, J., Biswas, A., Gupta, S.: Data augmentation on synthetic images for transfer learning using deep CNNs. In: 2018 5th International Conference on Signal Processing and Integrated Networks (SPIN), pp. 215–219 (2018). https://doi.org/10.1109/SPIN.2018.8474209

28. Tran, N., Tran, V., Nguyen, N., Nguyen, T., Cheung, N.: Towards good practices for data augmentation in GAN training. arXiv preprint arXiv:2006.05338 (2020)

29. Wang, J., Bretz, M., Dewan, M.A.A., Delavar, M.A.: Machine learning in modelling land-use and land cover-change (LULCC): current status, challenges and prospects. Sci. Total Environ. **822**, 153559 (2022). https://doi.org/10.1016/j.scitotenv.2022.153559

30. Yang, S., Xiao, W., Zhang, M., Guo, S., Zhao, J., Shen, F.: Image data augmentation for deep learning: a survey. arXiv preprint arXiv:2204.08610 (2022)

31. Yang, Y., Newsam, S.: Bag-of-visual-words and spatial extensions for land-use classification. In: Proceedings of the 18th SIGSPATIAL International Conference on Advances in Geographic Information Systems, pp. 270–279. GIS '10, Association for Computing Machinery, New York, NY, USA (2010). https://doi.org/10.1145/1869790.1869829

Segment Using Just One Example

Pratik Vora and Sudipan Saha[✉]

Yardi School of Artificial Intelligence, IIT Delhi, New Delhi, India
{aib222687,sudipan.saha}@scai.iitd.ac.in

Abstract. Semantic segmentation is an important topic in computer vision with many relevant application in Earth observation. While supervised methods exist, the constraints of limited annotated data has encouraged development of unsupervised approaches. However, existing unsupervised methods resemble clustering and cannot be directly mapped to explicit target classes. In this paper, we deal with single shot semantic segmentation, where one example for the target class is provided, which is used to segment the target class from query/test images. Our approach exploits recently popular Segment Anything (SAM), a promptable foundation model. We specifically design several techniques to automatically generate prompts from the only example/key image in such a way that the segmentation is successfully achieved on a stitch or concatenation of the example/key and query/test images. Proposed technique does not involve any training phase and just requires one example image to grasp the concept. Furthermore, no text-based prompt is required for the proposed method. We evaluated the proposed techniques on building as target class.

Keywords: Semantic segmentation · One shot · Segment Anything

1 Introduction

Semantic segmentation is an important task in both computer vision [12] and Earth observation [1]. While there have been several works on supervised semantic segmentation [8,16], many Earth observation tasks work under constraints of limited data [15] and thus unsupervised semantic segmentation [25,26] is also a topic of interest for the Earth observation researchers. However, unsupervised semantic segmentation methods [7,26] are in essence clustering and their obtained segmentation outputs do not explicitly map to target class. Somewhat relaxing the conditions of unsupervised semantic segmentation, an example of nearly unsupervised semantic segmentation that also provides a mapping with desired target class(es) is the case when there is one training image available. As an example, imagine that we are interested to find buildings of a specific roof type. We are provided with an image that contains such roof type and its corresponding binary mask showing the pixels belonging to this roof type in one cluster and all other pixels in the other cluster. Then using this image as example or key image, we can retrieve from any query image the pixels belonging to the

S. Palaiahnakote et al. (Eds.): ICPR 2024 Workshops, LNCS 15617, pp. 380–394, 2025.
https://doi.org/10.1007/978-3-031-88217-3_29

same roof type. Such an one-shot scenario can be useful in many applications, including in disaster management where rapid identification of specific targets can be important for planning and resource allocation. To better illustrate this situation, consider an unmanned aerial vehicle (UAV) deployed in a disaster management operation. The UAV is provided with one example image for each target category it needs to find. Ideally, the UAV should be able to use this single example to identify targets without requiring any additional training.

An interesting recent development in computer vision is the development of the foundation models. Foundation models show strong generalization capability and have already found applications in semantic segmentation. While many foundation models can relate images and texts, in this work our interest is entirely on images. In more details, in the above-mentioned discussion, we only consider the case where we have example/key image and we are not interested in the cases where the example/key is instead expressed as text. Segment Anything (SAM) [17] is a vision foundation model that has shown strong capabilities for image segmentation. Taking prompts such as points, SAM can produce segmentation corresponding to the desired objects or classes. However, choosing the prompts in an autonomous manner to enhance the detection of the desired object is not a trivial process. In this work, we capitalize on the promptable segmentation capabilities of SAM to solve the above-mentioned problem of segmenting an object of interest using just one example and without any training. As such, our work is also related to target detection [22] as we focus on one target class, however instead of producing bounding boxes, we produce segmentation masks corresponding to the target class. Such segmentation masks can be easily converted into bounding boxes, if required for a specific application.

We emphasize that our problem statement and proposed solution are tailored for scenarios where we lack prior knowledge of our targets during deployment. The flexibility of our proposed method allows us to launch specific operations with just one example image. If we already knew in advance the specific targets of interest, it would be possible to collect a dataset and train a model for that particular category. However, our approach is designed for situations where such prior information is unavailable, enabling rapid identification using minimal data. Moreover, we do not need any text-based prompts. Although text-based prompts have gained popularity recently, our focus is on scenarios where the concept is provided to a model using only a single example image, without any textual description. In many practical applications, describing the target textually might be challenging, and it could be more intuitive to simply identify the target in an image.

Furthermore, our work does not rely on a training phase, making it a significant step towards reducing computational requirements and improving data efficiency. By eliminating the need for a training phase, our method not only speeds up the deployment process but also reduces the computational burden, making it suitable for real-time applications in dynamic environments. To further clarify our contribution, while the SAM demonstrates excellent capability in segmenting images, its ability to identify specific targets relies on the use of

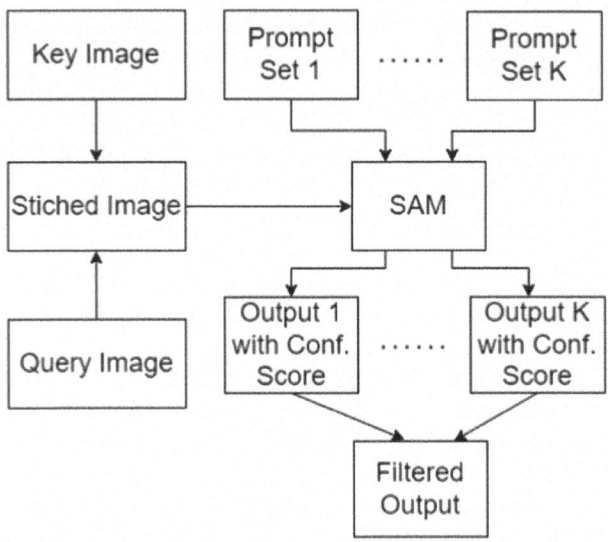

Fig. 1. Outline of the proposed method: given a key/example image for which the segmentation mask is known and a query image, proposed method concatenates them and feeds them to the SAM model as if they are single image. Furthermore, image-based prompts are fed to SAM that enables us to obtain the segmentation mask from the stitched image, i.e., also from the query image.

prompts-whether visual or textual. In the context of automated analysis, manually providing these prompts is not feasible. Therefore, there is a need for an automated mechanism to generate the appropriate prompts for SAM. Our work addresses this gap by introducing a method that requires only a single example/key image. Using this example, we automatically generate prompts that can then be applied to segment and identify specific targets in any other image. Furthermore, since our method requires only a single example image, it is reasonable to assume that this example image can be of high quality. Ensuring accurate and precise annotation in just one image is significantly more manageable compared to the complexity of maintaining consistent and correct annotations across a large-scale dataset.

The key contributions of this work are as follows:

1. We present an interesting and useful problem statement where only one example image of a specific category is provided, which is to be used for semantic segmentation on any query image without any training.
2. To solve the above-mentioned problem statement, we propose a solution exploiting recently popular foundation model SAM. Furthermore, we construct several novel automatic prompt engineering techniques employing SAM.
3. We evaluate the proposed method in the context of Earth observation, specifically in context of building segmentation. However, we emphasize that this

class is chosen merely for the challenges associated in delineating it, e.g., intra-class variability and different sizes. Otherwise, the practical utility of the proposed problem statement lies in its ability to handle unforeseen classes that may arise in various applications, particularly in disaster management scenarios where it is impossible to anticipate all potential targets in advance.

We organize the rest of the paper as follows. A few related works, such as semantic segmentation and foundation models, are briefly discussed in Sect. 2. Following this, Sect. 3 discusses the proposed method for target-specific semantic segmentation with single example image. Results are discussed in Sect. 4. Finally, the chapter is concluded in Sect. 5.

2   Related Works

2.1   Supervised Semantic Segmentation

Widely used segmentation architectures in deep learning include fully convolutional networks (FCNs) [18], U-Net [23], SegNet [3], and as DeepLab [6]. In the domain of Earth observation images, several supervised segmentation algorithms have been introduced leveraging these architectures [19,20,28,29]. Recently, Transformers have become popular in both computer vision and Earth observation semantic segmentation [4,13,27,30]. However, these supervised methodologies require substantial volumes of training data for supervised learning.

2.2   Semantic Segmentation with Limited Labels

Several works in the literature attempt to train semantic segmentation models with partial or no label, however generally with lower performance than supervised models. The work in [14] proposes a method to train semantic segmentation models with sparse annotations. An unsupervised semantic segmentation model is proposed in [26] exploiting contrastive learning. A Siamese network based method for one shot semantic segmentation in computer vision is proposed in [32].

2.3   Foundation Models

The vision foundation models represent an important advancement in computer vision, reshaping how we analyze visual data [2]. These models, which primarily rely on self-supervised learning on vast datasets, demonstrate robust generalization capabilities across a wide range of applications. Vision Transformers [9] are commonly utilized in these models for their effectiveness in capturing long-range dependencies within images [31]. Among other foundation models, SAM [17] is designed for promptable semantic segmentation and thus directly related to and used in our work. There are already some works using SAM for Earth observation tasks [5,11], however generally used in supervised context unlike our work.

The work in [5] trains category-specific prompt generator that enables generation of prompts to be fed to SAM. The work in [11] uses SAM for identifying green spaces, however by using dataset augmentation and fine tuning. Contrary to the existing works, our method is unsupervised and just uses a single example, which is not used for training. Furthermore, our method does not use any category-specific training unlike [11].

3   Proposed Method

3.1   Problem

Let us assume that we have an example/key image-label pair X_{key}, Y_{key}. The label image Y_{key} is a binary image that consists of two classes: all pixels belonging to a target category and all other pixels that do not belong to this category. As such this, example/key image can also be called training image, however we do not prefer to call so as there is no training step involved in our proposed method. Using this single example, we want to segment any query/test image X_{test}. We assume that the key and test images have same dimension, though this assumption can be easily relaxed. Moreover, this assumption does not limit the applicability of the proposed method to large-scale Earth observation scenes. Even in the case of such large scenes, the scene can be easily divided into smaller tiles of the required dimensions. Each tile can then be individually analyzed using our approach. Once the analysis is complete, the resulting segmented tiles can be stitched back together to create the segmentation output of the original large-scale scene.

To address the above-mentioned problem, we use SAM (Sect. 3.2), to which we feed a stitched image comprising of key and query images (Sect. 3.3) and prompts designed in one of several ways (Sect. 3.4). By repeating this process K times, we form an ensemble (Sect. 3.5) and further aggregate the ensembles (Sect. 3.6) and apply post-processing (Sect. 3.7). The outline of the proposed idea is demonstrated in Fig. 1.

3.2   SAM

Our method uses SAM which comprises of the following components:

- **Image Encoder**: Given an input image, the image encoder produces its embedding that captures the visual content of the image.
- **Prompt Encoder**: The prompt encoder encodes the prompt input to the model. There can be several types of prompts, however in this work we only consider point and mask prompts.
- **Mask Decoder**: The mask decoder takes the representations generated by the encoders and produces the segmentation mask.

SAM generally ingests a single image and the prompts. We must emphasize that the prompts can be both positive and negative, corresponding to the category of interest and to the other categories, respectively. SAM produces the desired segmentation mask and a confidence score. The pipeline of SAM is shown in Fig. 2.

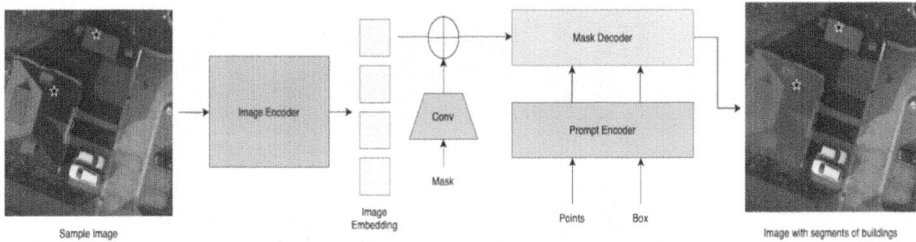

Fig. 2. SAM pipeline (green: positive prompt, red: negative prompt). The image encoder obtains representation of the image whereas prompt encoder obtains the representation of the prompt inputs. Using this information, the decoder obtains the segmented image. (Color figure online)

3.3   Image Concatenation

Since we are working with two images: X_{key} and X_{test}, we stitch them together, i.e., merely concatenate them side by side to produce a new image X_{cat} which we then feed to SAM. Recall that the segmentation mask for the X_{key} is known. Thus, if we assume Y_{cat} is the segmentation mask for X_{cat}, then we already know half of Y_{cat} (which is same as Y_{key}) and our task is to estimate the other half (Y_{test}).

3.4   Designing Prompts for SAM

We postulate that the above-mentioned task can be handled by cleverly choosing the prompts from the known half of Y_{cat} and exploiting SAM to produce the segmentation mask for the unknown half. Towards this, we design four different prompt techniques that are all image-based and requires no textual input. The first technique incorporates point-based prompts from the key image only. The following two techniques also cleverly incorporates the point-based prompts from the query image. The fourth technique additionally uses mask prompt from the key image.

Key-Only Prompts. As discussed above, one-half of Y_{cat} (i.e., Y_{key}) is known to us and we can simply choose positive and negative point prompts from Y_{key}, by randomly sampling a few points that that belong to the category of interest (positive prompts) and choosing some other points that do not belong to the category of interest (negative prompts). This is the most natural choice and positive and negative prompts are all correct. However, one issue with such choice of prompt is that all positive (and also negative) prompts are chosen from one half of the stitched input. This prompt technique is demonstrated in Fig. 3a. Though intuitive, in such an input scenario, SAM may get spatially biased and obtain an impression that the category of interest is likely to be present in only in this half of the stitched input. We will later see in the Sect. 4 that this is indeed a critical issue.

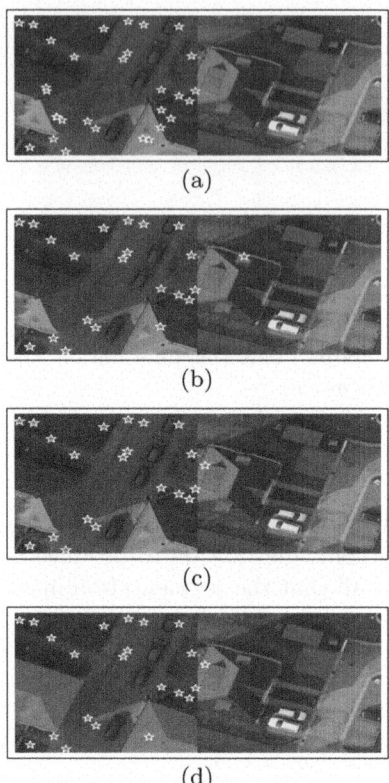

Fig. 3. Proposed prompt techniques: (a) key only prompts, (b) key prompts and positive prompts from query/test, (c) negative prompts from key and positive prompts from query/test and (d) masked key prompts and positive prompts from query/test. Left image is the key image and right image is the query/test image. Positive prompts are shown in green and the negative prompts are shown in red. (Color figure online)

Key Prompts and Additional Positive Prompt from Query/Test. As discussed above, the key limitation of the key-only prompt engineering is that SAM may get a spatial bias towards only the key image. To mitigate this issue, we need to somehow pursue SAM to also start considering the test image. This can be done by keeping the prompt engineering similar to above and additionally choosing positive point prompt from the test image. However, we do not know the segmentation mask of the test image and hence the question remains that how do we choose positive prompts from the test image. As there is no way to ensure this, we will simply choose some point randomly sampled from query/test scene as positive prompt. Note that now this positive prompt may or may not be correct. In other words, some points chosen as positive prompt from the query/test image may turn out to be actually not belonging to the category of interest and hence actually a negative point erroneously fed as positive prompt.

This might discourage us to design such prompt engineering, however we will see in Sect. 3.5 that this challenge can be tackled in a systematic manner. This prompt technique is shown in Fig. 3b.

Negative Prompts from Key and Positive Prompt from Test. In this approach, we go a step further and we choose positive prompt from the query/test (like above) and only negative prompts from the key, i.e., we do not choose any positive prompts from key. Since our negative prompts are sampled from key, they are all correct. Since our positive prompt is sampled from query/test for which we do not know the segmentation mask yet, it can be incorrect. However, this issue can be handled in a systematic manner, as described in Sect. 3.5. This prompt technique is shown in Fig. 3c.

Masked Key Prompts and Positive Prompt from Query/Test. In this approach we accompanied the prompt from the second approach with an input mask of the key. Let's say that we are interested in finding segment for buildings, so we will have the ground truth mask of all the buildings for the key image. This key mask will be a binary matrix of size equal to that of key image and will have value 1 where there is a building in the key image and 0 everywhere else. For the query image, we do not have any ground truth mask and so we will take a zero matrix of size equal to the query image. These two masks were stitched together to form a combined mask prompt. An example of this prompt technique is shown in Fig. 3d.

3.5   Using Ensemble and Confidence Score

As discussed above, all the three prompt engineering techniques have some merits and demerits. The first one selects all correct positive and negative prompts, however has a spatial bias towards the key image. The other two reduces the spatial bias, however may choose incorrect positive prompts. Thus, feeding X_{cat} and the chosen prompts using any of the above techniques to SAM does not guarantee generation of desired Y_{cat}. Here we adopt an ensemble technique. Sampling some positive and negative points and feeding the inputs once to SAM can be considered as one run of SAM. Similarly, we can sample another set of positive and negative points and feed to SAM again. By repeating this process K times, we can obtain $Y_{cat}^1, ..., Y_{cat}^K$. In addition to the segmentation output, SAM also provides a confidence score. Recall the discussion that in our second (and third) prompt engineering techniques, we are not certain about correctness of the positive prompts, which might lead to incorrect segmentation result. However, since our negative prompts are certainly correct, if randomly chosen positive prompts disagrees in concept with them, then the produced segmentation mask generally has a low confidence score. Thus, running the model K times, with different randomly sampled prompts, we may expect that some of these K runs will have relatively correctly chosen prompts, which will be aggregated in the next step to obtain the test image segmentation mask: Y_{test}.

3.6   Aggregation

After receiving the results for K number of prompts, we need to devise a strategy to aggregate them to form a single result. For this, we propose two different strategies: best selection and Confidence Weighted Majority Voting (CWMV).

Best Selection. In this approach, we simply choose the segmentation result with highest confidence score. This method operates on the assumption that the output with the highest confidence score is superior to all other possible outputs. Essentially, the confidence score represents a measure of reliability in the result. By selecting the outcome with the highest score, the method assumes that this particular outcome is the most accurate or optimal among all the available results.

CWMV. This strategy involves using confidence weighted average of all the results. This does not carry the assumption of the previous strategy that the output with highest confidence score is superior to all other possible outputs. CWMV [21] is an ensemble learning technique used in machine learning to improve the accuracy of predictions by leveraging the confidence levels of individual classifiers.

For a class C, let $\{Y_{test}^i\}_{i=1}^K$ be the predicted segments for the K different prompts and $\{c_{test}^i\}_{i=1}^K$ be their confidence scores. The weighted segment $\tilde{Y}$ is calculated as:

$$\tilde{Y} = \sum_{i=1}^K c_{test}^i * Y_{test}^i \tag{1}$$

Now, we will have $\tilde{Y}$ where every value $\tilde{Y}_{ij}$ will be the aggregated score over all the prompts for (i,j) pixel in the image. We calculate a threshold τ as:

$$\tau = \frac{\sum_{i=1}^K c_{test}^i}{m} \tag{2}$$

Here, value of m can be set as per this criterion: if we want to eliminate x% of the pixels with least confidence, then we can set m to 100/x. Thus, to remove 25%, we can set m to 4. Lower the value of m, higher will be τ (the threshold) and hence more number of pixels identified as our object of interest will be removed. For every pixel (i, j) of the weighted segment $\tilde{Y}$, the segment assignment $\tilde{S}_{ij}$ is performed as:

$$\tilde{S}_{ij} = \begin{cases} 1, & \text{if } \tilde{Y}_{ij} \geq \tau \\ 0, & \text{otherwise} \end{cases} \tag{3}$$

This segment assignment is the final aggregated result of all the K prompts. Unlike the best selection strategy, it does not suffer from the assumption that the highest confident result covers all the area from the ground truth.

3.7 Post-processing

To further refine the obtained segmentation mask, we use a traditional computer vision morphology technique to enhance our results. By now, we have the aggregated result from the previous stage which were found to be composed of spatially close but potentially disjoint blobs. For this we use morphological closing [10]. It helps us to connect disjoint blobs that are close to each other. We applied the process iteratively with progressively smaller structural elements to close blobs incrementally, targeting smaller remaining blobs with each step while avoiding closure of larger ones without constraint of a specific size.

4 Results

We carried out experiments targeting buildings as target class. This class is selected due to the difficulty of detecting them in complex urban environments and their differing sizes. 3457 test scenes/images are sampled from the ISPRS Potsdam dataset [24]. We stress that the real-world value of our approach is in its ability to manage unexpected classes that could emerge across different applications. Even though building class is chosen for evaluation, our approach is learning the concept of building from just one example image here. Thus, evaluating its performance on building in this case is equivalent to learning other challenging classes in practical deployment phase.

We used Intersection over Union (IoU) as our metric to evaluate the performance of our model. For an image with size $(m \times n)$, let its ground truth matrix be G and its predicted segmentation be denoted by P. For a class c, the IoU score is calculated as shown in Eq. 4.

$$\text{IoU}(G, P) = \sum_{i=1}^{m} \sum_{j=1}^{n} \frac{1\{G_{ij} = c \text{ and } P_{ij} = c\}}{1\{G_{ij} = c \text{ or } P_{ij} = c\}}$$

$$\text{where, } 1\{\text{condition}\} = \begin{cases} 1, & \text{if condition is true} \\ 0, & \text{otherwise} \end{cases}$$

(4)

A result for the building class is visualized in Fig. 4. In the stitched image, left half represents the key image and the right half represents the test/query image. Essentially, we are interested to obtain good segmentation result on the right half only, as the result for the key image (left half) is known to us. However, the key-only prompt technique produces a spatially biased result that almost excludes the right half, as shown in Fig. 4a. This shows that even though the key only prompt technique is most intuitive, the result produced by it is not useful for our task. On the other hand, by introducing positive prompts from the query, building detection accuracy on the query image improves significantly (Fig. 4b). As discussed in Sect. 3.5, the proposed method obtains segmentation masks K times with different prompts and then obtains the final result by aggregating them. A comparison of two different segmentation masks with different scores are shown in Fig. 5. This illustrates the relationship between better score and better segmentation performance on the test scene. The other proposed prompt technique (negative prompts from key and positive prompts from the test) performs similarly to the second prompt technique (Fig. 4c). However, for the proposed fourth prompt technique, the results degraded due to the imbalance between the key and query prompts (Fig. 4d). The fourth technique adds an input mask prompt to the second technique which one may expect intuitively to work better. But due to overindulgence of key prompts, i.e. introduction of key input mask with already present positive and negative key points created a spatial imbalance between key and query prompts leading to poorer results. The quantitative result is shown in Table 1. While results are provided using $K = 10$, increasing its value does not significantly change result.

We must note that with three advanced prompt engineering techniques, the performance on the key image (left part of the stitched image) actually degrades. However, this is not a concern to us, since the segmentation mask of the key image is known to us and we are not trying to find it here.

We can also see the effect of CWMV strategy of aggregation. In Fig. 5a, we can see the result of a prompt with highest confidence score. Even with highest confidence, it still misses out on providing segment of the second smaller building next to it. That building is identified in a lower confident result, which can be seen in Fig. 5b, albeit with some false positives. The selection of the best result would have deprived us of detection of the smaller building, which is where CWMV strategy comes into the picture. CWMV aggregates the results of all the prompts and eliminates the pixels identified as building with low aggregated confidence score. The result of this can be seen in Fig. 4b, where we can observe that both the buildings are well segmented and the false positives from Fig. 5b, are also eliminated. This strategy clearly helped us aggregate the prompt results in a more efficient manner.

In order to compare our method with a supervised method, we took a UNet based model with the backbone of ResNet-34 and pretrained on the ImageNet dataset. The model was fine-tuned on one labelled example; the same example that was used by our method as the key image. The fine-tuned model was then tested on the unseen test set which gave an IoU score of 0.3214. Thus, our SAM-based method proved to work better than a pretrained UNet.

We observe the the results of our post processing using morphology in Fig. 6. The results of this can be clearly seen by comparing Figs. 6a and 6c (where the results from CWMV had blobs unidentified due to its pixelwise thresholding) with Figs. 6b and 6d (after passing through closing morphology). The morphology helped us provide more complete segments as results and increased the efficiency of our overall methodology.

(a)

(b)

(c)

(d)

Fig. 4. Building detection on the stitched image (left: key image, right: query/test image) using four different proposed prompts shown in sub-figures (a), (b), (c) and (d)

(a)   (b)

Fig. 5. Building segmentation masks for two different confidence scores: (a) High - 0.8, (b) Low - 0.4.

Table 1. Quantitative performance of proposed prompt engineering techniques for the building class, shown as Intersection over Union (IoU).

Methods	Best Selection		CWMV	
	Raw	Processed	Raw	Processed
Prompt 1	0.0008	0.0015	0.0011	0.0019
Prompt 2	0.5662	0.6368	**0.6485**	**0.6930**
Prompt 3	0.2890	0.3323	0.2996	0.3954
Prompt 4	0.3918	0.4690	0.4372	0.4796

(a)   (b)

(c)   (d)

Fig. 6. Effect of the closing morphology. Figures (a) and (c) show the results after applying the CWMV aggregation strategy. Figures (b) and (d) show the result after passing them through the closing morphology as the blobs left behind by CWMV are filled up.

5   Conclusions

Foundation models are advancing significantly in computer vision due to their strong generalization capabilities. This paper demonstrated the generalizability of SAM, a foundation model for semantic segmentation, when applied to remote sensing images. We highlighted its application in segmenting the challenging building class. Since research in this area is still in its early stages, this paper represents a step towards understanding how to leverage robust foundation models in Earth observation. Future work will further explore segmentation for more challenging classes and explore segmentation for low-resolution Earth observation images, which may present greater challenges due to their substantial differences from typical computer vision images.

Acknowledgements. This work is partly funded by the project titled "Spatial and temporal monitoring of Indian urban dynamics from satellite images using deep learning" (SRG/2023/000669) funded by Science and Engineering Research Board (SERB), India.

References

1. Audebert, N., Le Saux, B., Lefèvre, S.: Semantic segmentation of earth observation data using multimodal and multi-scale deep networks. In: Asian Conference on Computer Vision, pp. 180–196. Springer (2016)
2. Awais, M., et al.: Foundational models defining a new era in vision: a survey and outlook. arXiv preprint arXiv:2307.13721 (2023)
3. Badrinarayanan, V., Kendall, A., Cipolla, R.: SegNet: a deep convolutional encoder-decoder architecture for image segmentation. IEEE Trans. Pattern Anal. Mach. Intell. **39**(12), 2481–2495 (2017)
4. Chen, J., et al.: TransUNet: transformers make strong encoders for medical image segmentation. arXiv preprint arXiv:2102.04306 (2021)

5. Chen, K., et al.: RSPrompter: learning to prompt for remote sensing instance segmentation based on visual foundation model. IEEE Trans. Geosci. Remote Sens. (2024)

6. Chen, L.C., Papandreou, G., Schroff, F., Adam, H.: Rethinking atrous convolution for semantic image segmentation. arXiv preprint arXiv:1706.05587 (2017)

7. Cho, J.H., Mall, U., Bala, K., Hariharan, B.: PiCIE: unsupervised semantic segmentation using invariance and equivariance in clustering. In: Proceedings of the IEEE/CVF Conference on Computer Vision and Pattern Recognition, pp. 16794–16804 (2021)

8. Diakogiannis, F.I., Waldner, F., Caccetta, P., Wu, C.: ResUNet-a: a deep learning framework for semantic segmentation of remotely sensed data. ISPRS J. Photogramm. Remote. Sens. **162**, 94–114 (2020)

9. Dosovitskiy, A., et al.: An image is worth 16x16 words: transformers for image recognition at scale. arXiv preprint arXiv:2010.11929 (2020)

10. Gonzalez, R., Woods, R.: Digital Image Processing. Addison-Wesley (1992). https://books.google.co.in/books?id=CfQeAQAAIAAJ

11. Gui, B., Bhardwaj, A., Sam, L.: Evaluating the efficacy of segment anything model for delineating agriculture and urban green spaces in multiresolution aerial and spaceborne remote sensing images. Remote Sens. **16**(2), 414 (2024)

12. Hao, S., Zhou, Y., Guo, Y.: A brief survey on semantic segmentation with deep learning. Neurocomputing **406**, 302–321 (2020)

13. He, X., Zhou, Y., Zhao, J., Zhang, D., Yao, R., Xue, Y.: Swin transformer embedding UNet for remote sensing image semantic segmentation. IEEE Trans. Geosci. Remote Sens. **60**, 1–15 (2022)

14. Hua, Y., Marcos, D., Mou, L., Zhu, X.X., Tuia, D.: Semantic segmentation of remote sensing images with sparse annotations. arXiv preprint arXiv:2101.03492 (2021)

15. Huang, B., Zhi, L., Yang, C., Sun, F., Song, Y.: Single satellite optical imagery dehazing using SAR image prior based on conditional generative adversarial networks. In: Proceedings of the IEEE/CVF Winter Conference on Applications of Computer Vision, pp. 1806–1813 (2020)

16. Kemker, R., Salvaggio, C., Kanan, C.: Algorithms for semantic segmentation of multispectral remote sensing imagery using deep learning. ISPRS J. Photogramm. Remote. Sens. **145**, 60–77 (2018)

17. Kirillov, A., et al.: Segment anything. In: Proceedings of the IEEE/CVF International Conference on Computer Vision, pp. 4015–4026 (2023)

18. Long, J., Shelhamer, E., Darrell, T.: Fully convolutional networks for semantic segmentation. In: Proceedings of the IEEE Conference on Computer Vision and Pattern Recognition, pp. 3431–3440 (2015)

19. Ma, B., Chang, C.Y.: Semantic segmentation of high-resolution remote sensing images using multiscale skip connection network. IEEE Sens. J. (2021)

20. Maggiori, E., Tarabalka, Y., Charpiat, G., Alliez, P.: High-resolution aerial image labeling with convolutional neural networks. IEEE Trans. Geosci. Remote Sens. **55**(12), 7092–7103 (2017)

21. Meyen, S., Sigg, D.M., Luxburg, U.V., Franz, V.H.: Group decisions based on confidence weighted majority voting. Cogn. Res. Principles Implications **6**, 1–13 (2021)

22. Qi, L., et al.: Ship target detection algorithm based on improved faster r-CNN. Electronics **8**(9), 959 (2019)

23. Ronneberger, O., Fischer, P., Brox, T.: U-Net: convolutional networks for biomedical image segmentation. In: International Conference on Medical Image Computing and Computer-Assisted Intervention, pp. 234–241. Springer (2015)
24. Rottensteiner, F., et al.: The ISPRS benchmark on urban object classification and 3D building reconstruction. ISPRS Ann. Photogramm. Remote Sens. Spatial Inf. Sci. I-3 **1**(1), 293–298 (2012)
25. Saha, S., Mou, L., Qiu, C., Zhu, X.X., Bovolo, F., Bruzzone, L.: Unsupervised deep joint segmentation of multitemporal high-resolution images. IEEE Trans. Geosci. Remote Sens. **58**(12), 8780–8792 (2020)
26. Saha, S., Shahzad, M., Mou, L., Song, Q., Zhu, X.X.: Unsupervised single-scene semantic segmentation for earth observation. IEEE Trans. Geosci. Remote Sens. **60**, 1–11 (2022)
27. Strudel, R., Garcia, R., Laptev, I., Schmid, C.: Segmenter: transformer for semantic segmentation. In: Proceedings of the IEEE/CVF International Conference on Computer Vision, pp. 7262–7272 (2021)
28. Su, Y., Cheng, J., Wang, W., Bai, H., Liu, H.: Semantic segmentation for high-resolution remote sensing images via dynamic graph context reasoning. IEEE Geosci. Remote Sens. Lett. (2022)
29. Volpi, M., Tuia, D.: Dense semantic labeling of sub-decimeter resolution images with convolutional neural networks. IEEE TGRS **55**, 881–893 (2017)
30. Wang, R., Cai, M., Xia, Z., Zhou, Z.: Remote sensing image road segmentation method integrating CNN-transformer and UNet. IEEE Access **11**, 144446–144455 (2023)
31. Wang, W., et al.: InternImage: exploring large-scale vision foundation models with deformable convolutions. In: Proceedings of the IEEE/CVF Conference on Computer Vision and Pattern Recognition, pp. 14408–14419 (2023)
32. Zhao, G., Zhao, H.: One-shot image segmentation with U-Net. J. Phys. Conf. Ser. **1848**, 012113 (2021)

Evaluating Sugarcane Yield Variability with UAV-Derived Cane Height Under Different Water and Nitrogen Conditions

Rajiv Ranjan$^{(\boxtimes)}$(ID), Tejasvi Birdh, Nandan Mandal, Dinesh Kumar, and Shashank Tamaskar

Plaksha University, Punjab, India
{rajiv.ranjan,tejasvi.birdh,nandan.mandal, dinesh.kumar1,shashank.tamaskar}@plaksha.edu.in

Abstract. This study investigates the relationship between sugarcane yield and cane height derived under different water and nitrogen conditions from pre-harvest Digital Surface Model (DSM) obtained via Unmanned Aerial Vehicle (UAV) flights over a sugarcane test farm. The farm was divided into 62 blocks based on three water levels (low, medium, and high) and three nitrogen levels (low, medium, and high), with repeated treatments. In pixel distribution of DSM for each block, it provided bimodal distribution representing two peaks, ground level (gaps within canopies) and top of the canopies respectively. Using bimodal distribution, mean cane height was extracted for each block by applying a trimmed mean to the pixel distribution, focusing on the top canopy points. Similarly, the extracted mean elevation of the base was derived from the bottom points, representing ground level. The Derived Cane Height Model (DCHM) was generated by taking the difference between the mean canopy height and mean base elevation for each block. Yield measurements (tons/acre) were recorded post-harvest for each block. By aggregating the data into nine treatment zones (e.g., high water-low nitrogen, low water-high nitrogen), the DCHM and median yield were calculated for each zone. The regression analysis between the DCHM and corresponding yields for the different treatment zones yielded an R^2 of 0.95. This study demonstrates the significant impact of water and nitrogen treatments on sugarcane height and yield, utilizing one-time UAV-derived DSM data.

Keywords: Sugarcane · Remote Sensing · UAV · DSM(Digital Surface Model) · CHM(Cane Height Model)

1 Introduction

Precision agriculture has revolutionized farming practices by integrating advanced technologies to enhance crop management and productivity. Among these technologies, the use of Unmanned Aerial Vehicles (UAVs) has gained significant attention due to their ability to capture high-resolution aerial imagery,

S. Palaiahnakote et al. (Eds.): ICPR 2024 Workshops, LNCS 15617, pp. 395–407, 2025.
https://doi.org/10.1007/978-3-031-88217-3_30

providing valuable data for crop monitoring and yield estimation. Sugarcane, a critical crop for many economies, serves as a primary source of sugar and bio-fuel. Accurate yield estimation is essential for effective resource management and optimizing production. Traditional methods of yield estimation such as crop cutting experiments are often labor-intensive and time-consuming. UAV technology offers a more efficient and precise alternative, enabling farmers to monitor crop growth and predict yields with greater accuracy.

Digital Surface Models (DSMs), representing the Earth's surface including vegetation, are crucial in this context. They are used to measure crop heights, a critical parameter for assessing crop health and estimating yield [24]. One significant area of research is the use of UAVs for creating DSMs to generate canopy height models (CHM) [2] and monitor crop growth. For instance, Li et al. [12] and Harkel et al. [9] demonstrated the application of UAV-derived heights in estimating the Above Ground Biomass (AGB) of maize and other crops, showing a good correlation between UAV-derived heights and actual biomass measurements. Similarly, Wang et al. utilized UAVs to generate DSMs for wheat [22], achieving accurate crop height measurements that correlated well with ground truth data. Similarly, many analyses have been done using UAV-derived height of crops like sorghum [23], corn [8], barley [1], maize [25], wheat [6], cotton [14], and sugarcane [5].

In the context of sugarcane, studies have shown promising results using remote sensing technologies for sugarcane canopy detection. Various studies have highlighted the advantages of satellite and UAV-based remote sensing over traditional methods, emphasizing its efficiency, accuracy, and cost-effectiveness. Shendryk et al. [18] employed satellite imagery to estimate field level sugarcane yield, while vargas et al. explored the use of LiDAR data for similar purposes [21]. Ranjan et al. [15] presented the study to predict the field level sucrose content (pol value) in sugarcane and optimal harvest date using time series satellite data. Maes et al. presented the effectiveness of UAVs in monitoring growth stages, assessing plant health, and estimating biomass and yield [13]. Chea et al. used high-resolution UAV images and DSMs to detect the sugarcane canopy in a field [3]. In sugarcane farming, UAVs have proven to be highly beneficial. They are used to monitor growth, assess plant health, and estimate biomass and yield [4,19]. These studies underscored the potential of remote sensing in providing timely and accurate yield estimates, although UAV-based approaches were not extensively covered. Building upon these foundational studies, our research employs UAV-derived DSMs to directly estimate sugarcane yield. In this work, the integration of UAVs in precision agriculture has been extensively researched, primarily due to their capability to capture high-resolution imagery for crop monitoring and yield estimation. By capturing DSM images at key growth stages and analyzing height variations is very efficient for the study, this study offers a novel approach that enhances the precision and reliability of yield predictions in sugarcane farming. We employed a Phantom 4 UAV to capture DSM images of a sugarcane farm just before harvesting. This DSM represented the crop at its optimal height. By analysing the DSM data with statistical method like pixel distribution, we obtained a detailed unimodel or bimodal distribution representing denser canopy cover and sparser canopy cover respectively. The primary objectives were to assess the impact of water and nitrogen levels on the cane's height and eventually on its yield. The reason for assessing water and nitrogen stress in sugarcane is that, these factors are the primary contributors to yield gaps in sugarcane production before crop management practices [7]. A yield gap is the difference between the potential yield of a crop, achieved under optimal conditions with maximum resource use and management, and the actual yield obtained by farmers under real-world conditions. The study area was divided into 62 small blocks, each subjected to different levels of water and nitrogen (fertilizer) treatment, and recorded yield values in tons per acre. We computed the trimmed mean cane height for each block by applying block-specific masks to the DSM image. A regression analysis was then performed to investigate the relationship between surrogate sugarcane derived height and yield, revealing a strong correlation with an R^2 value of 0.95. This paper aims to demonstrate the effectiveness of UAV-derived DSMs in estimating sugarcane yield and to highlight the potential of this technology for enhancing precision agriculture practices.

2 Experimental Setup

2.1 Study Area and Data Collection

Uttar Pradesh (India) is the main cane growing state in the country, allocating about 2.2 million ha area (43.7%) for cane cultivation [17]. We established a 3-acre test farm (Fig. 1) in Lakhimpur Khiri District (28°27′14.2″N 80°55′42.0″E), Uttar Pradesh, India, situated in the upper Gangetic plains agro-climatic zone with rains in a subtropical region. UAV data and ground truth were collected at regular intervals (monthly) throughout the crop cycle from February 2023 to February 2024. However, for this study, only the digital surface model (DSM) for 24th February 2024 was considered, just before the harvesting of the crop on 25th February 2024.

2.2 Farm Layout

The test farm is divided into three zones based on water application levels designated as LW (Low Water), MW (Medium Water), and HW (High Water) represented by different shades of blue. Within each water zone, there are blocks designated for low, medium, and high nitrogen levels represented as LN, MN, and HN respectively, indicated by different shades of green. For nitrogen stress estimation, LN, MN, and HN blocks received 0.25 kg, 0.5 kg, and 1 kg of fertilizer respectively for HW blocks, and 0.2 kg, 0.4 kg, and 0.8 kg for LW and MW blocks. The water levels applied were 50%, 100%, and 150% of the typical application for the LW, MW, and HW water blocks respectively. These amounts were determined based on the recommendations of an agronomist. Monthly drone flights were conducted over the test farm to collect aerial images for analysis.

Fig. 1. Test farm inside the red boundary at Lakhimpur Khiri, Uttar Pradesh, India (Color figure online)

Fig. 2. Farm layout

Eventually, 62 small blocks curated as shown in Fig. 2. An appropriate naming convention was used to identify each block. However, a combination of water and nitrogen blocks provides 9 treatment zones based on the treatment level of water and nitrogen explained in Table 1.

Table 1. Water and Nitrogen Levels Applied to Sugarcane Test Farm with Naming Conventions

Water Zone	Water Level	Nitrogen Zone	Fertilizer Applied	Abbreviation
LW (Low Water)	50%	LN (Low Nitrogen)	0.2 kg	LW_LN
		MN (Medium Nitrogen)	0.4 kg	LW_MN
		HN (High Nitrogen)	0.8 kg	LW_HN
MW (Medium Water)	100%	LN (Low Nitrogen)	0.2 kg	MW_LN
		MN (Medium Nitrogen)	0.4 kg	MW_MN
		HN (High Nitrogen)	0.8 kg	MW_HN
HW (High Water)	150%	LN (Low Nitrogen)	0.25 kg	HW_LN
		MN (Medium Nitrogen)	0.5 kg	HW_MN
		HN (High Nitrogen)	1 kg	HW_HN

2.3 Drone Flight

A single DSM image captured on 376 days after planting through a DJI Phantom 4 mounted P4 multispectral camera [16] was utilized. DJI GS Pro [10] was used for drone flight mission planning as shown in Fig. 3. This UAV was flown at two altitudes of 37.8 m and 75.6 m generating a spatial resolution (GSD - Ground sample distance) of 2 cm/px. and 4 cm/px. respectively. Front and side overlapping were kept at 80% and 75% respectively.

Fig. 3. UAV flight mission planning using DJI GS Pro

2.4   Data Preprocessing

Individual patches captured by a drone are stitched together to create a compre-hensive orthomosaic DSM image. This process is essential for accurately mapping and analyzing the farm's terrain and vegetation. We utilized Pix4Dfields soft-ware, a powerful tool specifically designed for agricultural applications, to achieve this [11]. It aligned and merged the drone-captured images, ensuring high preci-sion and consistency. The resultant orthomosaic DSM image as shown in Fig. 4 provides an accurate representation of the farm's surface, which is critical for subsequent analysis, including crop height measurement, yield estimation, and stress detection. This high-resolution image enables us to make informed deci-sions based on detailed visual and topographical data, ultimately enhancing the efficiency and effectiveness of our agricultural practices.

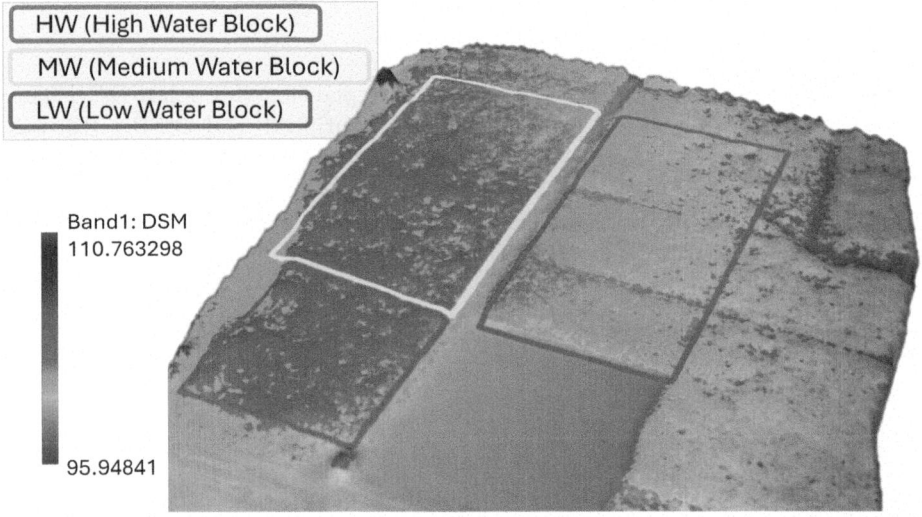

Fig. 4. DSM (Digital Surface Model) of the test farm

3   Methodology

We utilized a UAV-derived Digital Surface Model (DSM) of a farm, where sug-arcane was cultivated. The DSM was captured shortly before the harvest period from multiple altitudes, with the analysis focused on imagery obtained at a 37.8 meter height. The farm was segmented as discussed in Sect. 2.2 for detailed analysis, each of which was subjected to varying water and nitrogen treatments. Upon examining the histograms for each of the 62 plots, a bimodal distribution was observed in most cases. The initial peak on the x-axis indicated the presence of ground pixels within the DSM. This was corroborated by observations that plots situated at the field's periphery, which contained more ground and less crop coverage, exhibited a pronounced initial peak. Conversely, plots located centrally within the crop-planted area showed a diminished first peak, corresponding to gaps in the field as confirmed by ortho-imagery. In rare instances where the first peak was absent, the plots contained very dense sugarcane stands. To quantify the sugarcane height, we considered two distinct scenarios:

3.1   Case: 1

To analyze the bimodal distribution observed in the histograms of the majority of the blocks, we employed a Gaussian Mixture Model (GMM) [20] to separate the data into two distinct Gaussian curves as shown in Figs. 5,6 and 7. These two curves correspond to different components of the histogram, with one representing the crop height (right curve) and the other representing the ground level (left curve). The GMM fitting allowed us to isolate and model each curve independently. Once the curves were separated, we computed the trimmed mean for each component to obtain more robust estimates that are less sensitive to outliers. For the curve representing the crop height (right curve), we selected the data points corresponding to the highest 30% of frequency values, ensuring that the trimmed mean calculation focused on the most significant portion of the crop height distribution. Similarly, for the curve representing the ground level (left curve), we selected the highest 10% of frequency values to compute the trimmed mean, capturing the most prominent ground-level data. The difference between these two trimmed means provided a reliable estimate of the surrogate sugarcane height, as it effectively accounted for the height difference between the crop and the ground, minimizing the influence of noise and outliers.

3.2   Case: 2

In instances where a bimodal distribution was not observed, the histograms exhibited a single peak or unimodal distribution as shown in Fig. 8. This scenario typically occurred in plots with dense canopy cover, making it difficult to detect ground-level pixels and rendering the application of a GMM ineffective. To estimate the plant height in these cases, we adopted an alternative approach. We first computed the trimmed mean of the top 30% of frequency values from the histogram, representing the canopy height. Then, we identified the lowest pixel value within the plot, which corresponds to the ground level. The difference between the trimmed mean and this minimum pixel value provided an accurate estimate of the sugarcane height in plots with high canopy coverage.

4   Results and Discussion

In our study, the categorized 62 sugarcane blocks into 9 distinct groups based on the amount of water and nitrogen applied were analysed. This categorization, detailed in Table 1, facilitated a more granular analysis of how different levels of these inputs affect sugarcane yield. Specifically, we grouped the plots by three

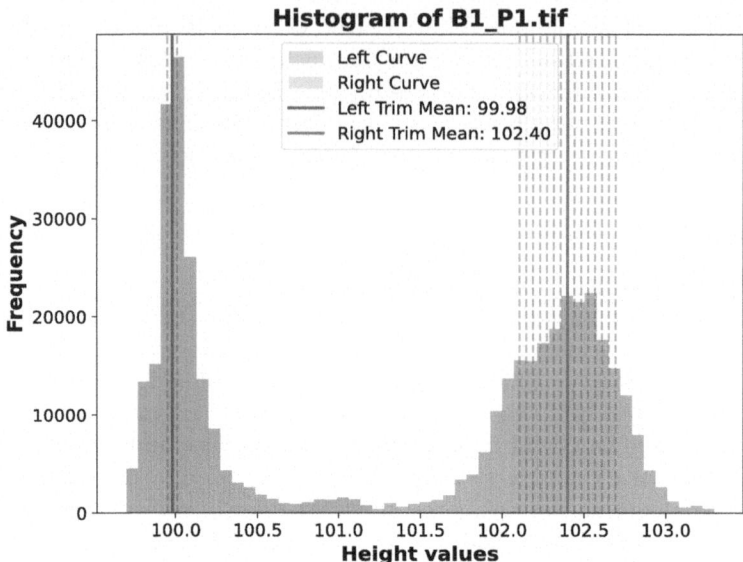

Fig. 5. Case 1a - Histogram of Block (B1_P1) showing a bimodal distribution

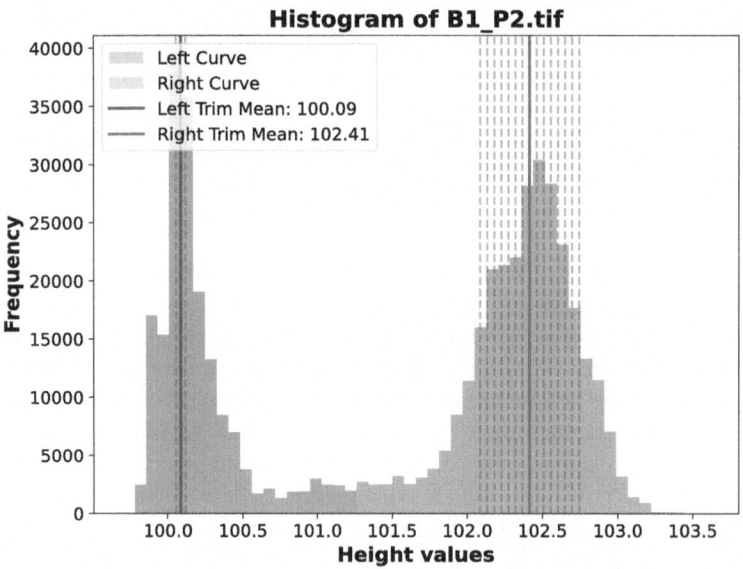

Fig. 6. Case 1b - Histogram of Block (B1_P2) showing a bimodal distribution

water levels (low, medium, high) and three nitrogen levels (low, medium, high), resulting in a comprehensive classification system that allowed for a robust examination of the effects of varying input levels. For each group, we calculated the

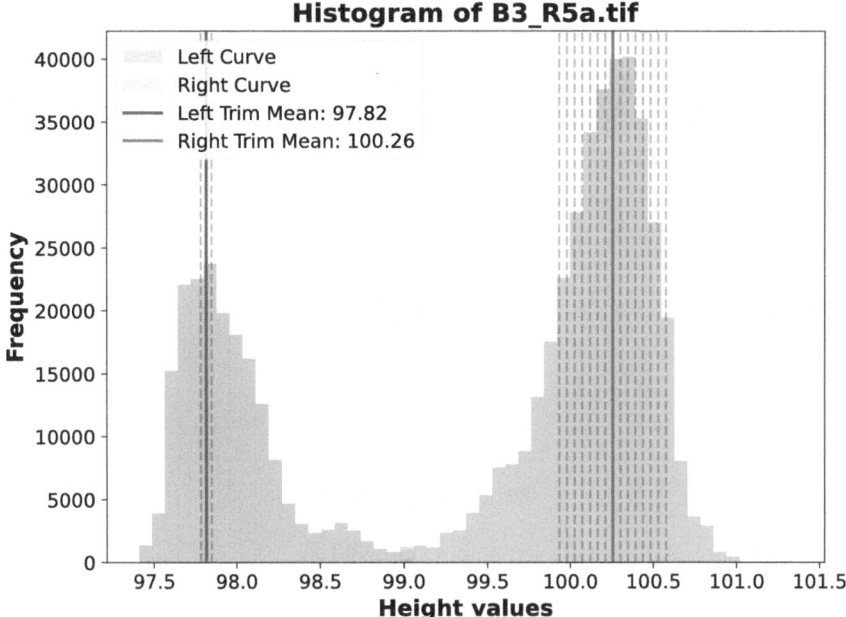

Fig. 7. Case 1c - Histogram of Block (B3_R5a) showing a bimodal distribution

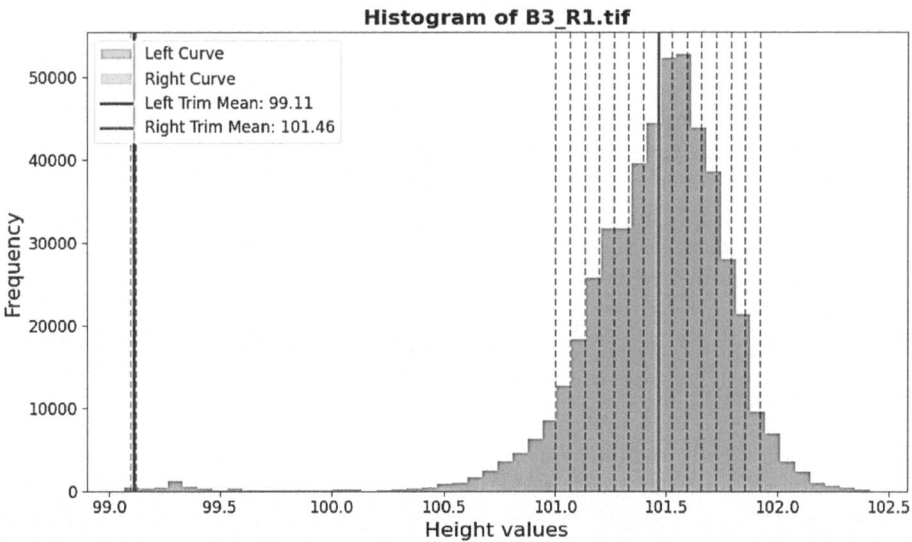

Fig. 8. Case 2 - Histogram of Block (B3_R1) showing a unimodal distribution

median cane height and yield, and subsequently conducted a regression analysis to explore the relationship between median crop height and yield across the nine

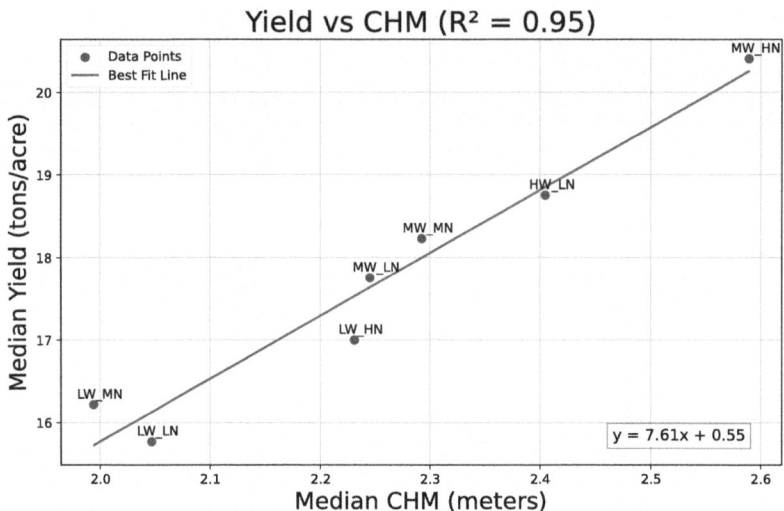

Fig. 9. Regression analysis between sugarcane yield and derived median crop height for each nine class

groups. The regression analysis revealed a strong linear relationship between these two variables, as shown in Fig. 9. The high R^2 value of 0.95 indicates that 95% of the variability in yield can be explained by the variability in crop height. The regression model, with the best-fit line equation $y = 7.61x + 0.56$, demonstrates a significant direct correlation between crop height and yield. This implies that as crop height increases, the yield also increases proportionally. The model's high explanatory power underscores the potential of using crop height as a reliable predictor of yield. This finding highlights the importance of optimizing water and nitrogen levels to enhance sugarcane growth and productivity. By understanding and leveraging the relationship between crop height and yield, we can make more informed decisions regarding resource management to improve overall sugarcane production efficiency.

5   Conclusion

This study effectively demonstrated the strong relationship between sugarcane height and yield at the block level, influenced by varying water and nitrogen treatments. By utilizing UAV-derived Digital Surface Models (DSM) and advanced analytical techniques such as Gaussian Mixture Models (GMM) and regression analysis, we observed a high correlation ($R^2 = 0.95$) between mean crop height and yield across the different treatment zones. The findings highlight the importance of precise water and nitrogen management in optimizing sugarcane yield, emphasizing that derived sugarcane height can serve as a reliable indicator of yield performance. Using a GMM model to extract surrogate cane height from a single DSM is more effective than the traditional CHM method.

Unlike CHM, our approach eliminates the need to capture two separate DSM images-one for the bare ground and another for the canopy cover-to obtain the CHM. Additionally, double DSM capture requires image coregistration, which is not necessary in our method. This research underscores the value of integrating UAV technology with data-driven approaches to enhance the precision and effectiveness of agricultural practices, providing valuable insights for better resource management and decision-making in sugarcane farming.

6   Future Work

Future work should focus on expanding the methodologies developed in this study to other regions, validating their generalizability across different agricultural contexts. Additionally, conducting longitudinal studies throughout the growing season would allow for a deeper understanding of how the relationship between crop height and yield evolves over time. Exploring more advanced machine learning models, such as deep learning, could also improve the precision of crop height estimation and yield prediction. Finally, developing user-friendly decision support systems to translate UAV data into actionable insights for farmers would increase the practical utility of this technology, aiding in more informed decision-making for irrigation, fertilization, and harvesting.

Acknowledgements. We would like to extend our heartfelt gratitude to CNH Industrial for their invaluable support in supplying the crucial resources and expertise that have significantly contributed to this work. Their dedication to driving innovation and promoting sustainable agricultural practices has been a key factor in the project's advancement. We are equally grateful to Mr. Vikram Bhalla for his generous provision of resources, farm land as well as his hospitality. His unwavering support have played a vital role in the progress of this work, for which we are deeply appreciative.

References

1. Bendig, J., Bolten, A., Bennertz, S., Broscheit, J., Eichfuss, S., Bareth, G.: Estimating biomass of barley using crop surface models (CSMS) derived from UAV-based RGB imaging. Remote Sens. **6**(11), 10395–10412 (2014). https://doi.org/10.3390/rs61110395
2. Chang, A., Jung, J., Maeda, M.M., Landivar, J.: Crop height monitoring with digital imagery from unmanned aerial system (UAS). Comput. Electron. Agric. **141**, 232–237 (2017). https://doi.org/10.1016/j.compag.2017.07.008
3. Chea, C., Saengprachatanarug, K., Posom, J., Wongphati, M., Taira, E.: Sugarcane canopy detection using high spatial resolution UAS images and digital surface model. Eng. Appl. Sci. Res. **46**(4) (2019)
4. Chiranjeeb, K., Shandilya, R., Rath, K.C.: Application of drones and sensors in advanced farming: the future smart farming technology. In: Artificial Intelligence and Smart Agriculture Applications, pp. 1–30. Auerbach Publications (2022)
5. De Souza, C., Lamparelli, R., Rocha, J.V., Magalhães, P.: Height estimation of sugarcane using an unmanned aerial system (UAS) based on structure from motion (SFM) point clouds. Int. J. Remote Sens. **38**(8–10), 2218–2230 (2017)

6. Demir, N., Sönmez, N.K., Akar, T., Ünal, S.: Automated measurement of plant height of wheat genotypes using a DSM derived from UAV imagery. Proceedings **2**(7) (2018). https://doi.org/10.3390/ecrs-2-05163

7. Dias, H.B., Sentelhas, P.C.: Sugarcane yield gap analysis in Brazil - a multi-model approach for determining magnitudes and causes. Sci. Total Environ. **637–638**, 1127–1136 (2018). https://doi.org/10.1016/j.scitotenv.2018.05.017

8. Furukawa, F., Maruyama, K., Saito, Y.K., Kaneko, M.: Corn height estimation using UAV for yield prediction and crop monitoring. In: Unmanned Aerial Vehicle: Applications in Agriculture and Environment, pp. 51–69 (2020)

9. ten Harkel, J., Bartholomeus, H., Kooistra, L.: Biomass and crop height estimation of different crops using UAV-based lidar. Remote Sens. **12**(1), 17 (2019)

10. Hasheminasab, S.M., Zhou, T., Habib, A.: GNSS/INS-assisted structure from motion strategies for UAV-based imagery over mechanized agricultural fields. Remote Sens. **12**(3) (2020). https://doi.org/10.3390/rs12030351

11. Ioja, I., Nedeff, V., Agop, M., Nedeff, F.M., Tomozei, C.: Software uses in precision agriculture based on drone image processing - a review. In: 2024 9th International Conference on Energy Efficiency and Agricultural Engineering (EEAE), pp. 1–6 (2024). https://doi.org/10.1109/EEAE60309.2024.10600556

12. Li, W., Niu, Z., Chen, H., Li, D., Wu, M., Zhao, W.: Remote estimation of canopy height and aboveground biomass of maize using high-resolution stereo images from a low-cost unmanned aerial vehicle system. Ecol. Ind. **67**, 637–648 (2016)

13. Maes, W.H., Steppe, K.: Perspectives for remote sensing with unmanned aerial vehicles in precision agriculture. Trends Plant Sci. **24**(2), 152–164 (2019). https://doi.org/10.1016/j.tplants.2018.11.007

14. Psiroukis, V., Papadopoulos, G., Kasimati, A., Tsoulias, N., Fountas, S.: Cotton growth modelling using UAS-derived DSM and RGB imagery. Remote Sens. **15**(5) (2023). https://doi.org/10.3390/rs15051214

15. Ranjan, R., Tamaskar, S.: Prediction of sugarcane sucrose content and optimal harvest date using multi-spectral time series image processing of satellite data. In: IGARSS 2024 - 2024 IEEE International Geoscience and Remote Sensing Symposium, pp. 4239–4244 (2024). https://doi.org/10.1109/IGARSS53475.2024.10640589

16. Sadenova, M.A., Beisekenov, N.A., Anuarbekov, T.B., Kapasov, A.K., Kulenova, N.A.: Study of unmanned aerial vehicle sensors for practical remote application of earth sensing in agriculture. Chem. Eng. Trans. **98**, 243–248 (2023). https://doi.org/10.3303/CET2398041

17. Sharma, A., Pathak, A.: Sugarcane production and productivity. Indian Farming **67**(02), 64–68 (2017)

18. Shendryk, Y., Davy, R., Thorburn, P.: Integrating satellite imagery and environmental data to predict field-level cane and sugar yields in Australia using machine learning. Field Crop Res. **260**, 107984 (2021)

19. Shikhar, S., et al.: Evaluation of computer vision pipeline for farm-level analytics: a case study in sugarcane. In: Proceedings of the 7th ACM SIGCAS/SIGCHI Conference on Computing and Sustainable Societies, pp. 238–247 (2024)

20. Skakun, S., et al.: Early season large-area winter crop mapping using MODIS NDVI data, growing degree days information and a Gaussian mixture model. Remote Sens. Environ. **195**, 244–258 (2017). https://doi.org/10.1016/j.rse.2017.04.026

21. Vargas, C.M., Heenkenda, M.K., Romero, K.F.: Estimating the aboveground fresh weight of sugarcane using multispectral images and light detection and ranging (LIDAR). Land **13**(5), 611 (2024)

22. Wang, D., Li, R., Zhu, B., Liu, T., Sun, C., Guo, W.: Estimation of wheat plant height and biomass by combining UAV imagery and elevation data. Agriculture **13**(1), 9 (2022)
23. Watanabe, K., et al.: High-throughput phenotyping of sorghum plant height using an unmanned aerial vehicle and its application to genomic prediction modeling. Front. Plant Sci. **8** (2017). https://doi.org/10.3389/fpls.2017.00421
24. Wu, M., et al.: Evaluation of orthomosics and digital surface models derived from aerial imagery for crop type mapping. Remote Sens. **9**(3) (2017)
25. Zhou, L., Gu, X., Cheng, S., Yang, G., Shu, M., Sun, Q.: Analysis of plant height changes of lodged maize using UAV-LIDAR data. Agriculture **10**(5) (2020). https://doi.org/10.3390/agriculture10050146

Unsupervised Deep Learning for Flood Segmentation in UAV Imagery

Georgios Simantiris[1]([✉])[iD] and Costas Panagiotakis[1,2][iD]

[1] Department of Management Science and Technology, Hellenic Mediterranean University, 72100 Agios Nikolaos, Greece
ddk230@edu.hmu.gr, cpanag@hmu.gr
[2] Institute of Computer Science, FORTH, Heraklion, Greece

Abstract. We present a novel unsupervised Deep Learning method for flood segmentation in Unmanned Aerial Vehicle imagery. This method utilizes automatically generated labels as masks for the training process, eliminating the need for actual ground truth data. On a public dataset consisting of 290 RGB images, we train two well-known Convolutional Neural Network architectures, typically used for semantic segmentation, to perform flood segmentation. The proposed method is tested and compared in a totally unknown public dataset consisting of 663 RGB images, yielding high-performance results, with 92.2% and 88.2% overall accuracy and F1-score, respectively.

Keywords: Unsupervised Image Segmentation · Deep Learning · Pseudo Labels · Flood Segmentation · Unmanned Aerial Vehicle (UAV)

1 Introduction

Natural disasters have historically imposed significant impacts on humanity and their intensity has been exacerbated by climate change. Increased frequency and severity of extreme weather events have caused substantial loss of life and property. These disasters also disrupt essential services such as water, electricity and transportation and pose serious health risks. The economic and psychological toll on affected populations is immense [17]. Technological advances, such as Deep Learning (DL) and Machine Learning (ML), offer promising tools for disaster detection, risk reduction, and efficient response management. These technologies, as reviewed in [1,14], have significant potential for future disaster response efforts.

In the context of natural disasters such as floods, DL methods are increasingly being employed for flood detection and segmentation to address the limitations of traditional flood mapping techniques [2]. However, they require large amounts of labeled data for training, which can be challenging to obtain, especially in disaster scenarios, and the labeling is also a time consuming process prone to human annotation errors.

S. Palaiahnakote et al. (Eds.): ICPR 2024 Workshops, LNCS 15617, pp. 408–423, 2025.
https://doi.org/10.1007/978-3-031-88217-3_31

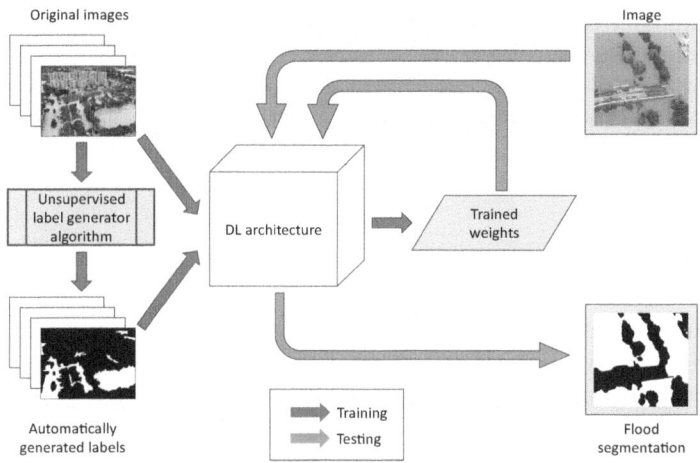

Fig. 1. Schematic overview of the proposed approach.

In this paper, we introduce an innovative unsupervised DL method for flood segmentation in Unmanned Aerial Vehicle (UAV) imagery that employs automatically generated labels as masks for training and validation sets, rendering the actual ground truth of these images unnecessary. We train two well-known Convolutional Neural Network (CNN) architectures, commonly used for semantic segmentation. Our results demonstrate that these CNN models can be effectively trained using this approach, achieving high prediction accuracies. We assessed the performance of our proposed method by applying the trained models to a larger test set of images not seen during training. The results are compared to those from the models trained with actual, human-annotated labels and the unsupervised approach used to generate the pseudo-labels. A schematic overview of our proposed approach is illustrated in Fig. 1.

The main contributions of our work can be summarized as listed below.

- To the best of our knowledge, this study presents the first fully unsupervised DL approach specifically designed for flood area segmentation in color images captured by UAVs.
- Our method leverages automatically generated labels via the UFS-HT-REM unsupervised pattern recognition algorithm [21], subtly adjusted to facilitate the training of DL architectures without relying on original ground truth labels.
- The proposed methodology results in an effective unsupervised algorithm for flood segmentation. Two semantic segmentation CNN models were successfully trained, yielding better performance results than the original UFS-HT-REM approach, and in one case outperformed also the training with the original ground truth labels, demonstrating the proposed method's applicability and potential.

The remainder of this paper is structured as follows: Sect. 2 provides a summary of related research. Our proposed unsupervised DL approach is described in Sect. 3. Section 4 outlines the experimental framework of this study, encompassing the datasets, the CNN architectures, and the training procedure. Section 5 presents the experimental results along with an in-depth discussion. Finally, conclusions and considerations for future work are discussed in Sect. 6.

2   Related Work

To overcome the limitations of traditional flood mapping techniques, DL methods are increasingly applied to remote sensing imagery. Convolutional layer-based models enhance the accuracy in capturing the spatial characteristics of flooding events, while fully connected layer-based models show potential when integrated with statistical methods. DL models are replacing remote sensing analysis, multi-criteria decision analysis, and numerical methods in flood mapping, where they are used to generate flood extent or flood inundation maps, susceptibility maps, and flood hazard maps to determine, categorize, and characterize flooding events [2].

CNNs have proven to be effective for flood detection using satellite imagery. They generate high-quality flood maps by analyzing temporal differences from various sensors, identifying changes between permanent and flooded water areas using synthetic aperture radar (SAR) and multispectral images [3,4]. However, these approaches require pre-disaster images as well. Bayesian CNNs have been recommended to quantify uncertainties in SAR-based water segmentation due to their ability to learn the mean and spread of parameter posteriors [7]. In addition, a CNN using the Deep Earth Learning, Tools, and Analysis (DELTA) framework has shown high precision and recall for water segmentation despite a diverse training dataset [20].

In [24], the effectiveness of CNNs in semantically segmenting water bodies was evaluated in high-resolution satellite and aerial images of various sensors for flood emergency response applications. Different CNN architectures, combined with encoder backbones, were used to delineate inundated areas under various environmental conditions and data availability scenarios. U-Nets and their variations have been extensively employed for water body segmentation and flood extent extraction. In [13], a modified U-Net was introduced, which, through careful parameter selection, the use of geomorphic elements, and training with pre-processed Sentinel-1 images for three-category classification, successfully distinguished flood pixels from permanent water and background.

In [8], an enhanced efficient neural network architecture (ENet) was selected to segment UAV video footage of flood disasters. This method employs atrous separable convolution as the encoder and depth-wise separable convolution as the decoder. Atrous convolutions have been also utilized to expedite search and rescue operations following natural disasters such as floods, high tides, and tsunamis. FASegNet, a novel CNN-based model that incorporates dilated convolutions, was specifically developed to segment flood and tsunami areas [19].

Transformers have also been applied effectively for semantic segmentation in remote sensing images. The Swin Transformer and a densely connected feature aggregation module as the backbone and the decoder respectively resulted in better capture contextual information [23]. Furthermore, the Bitemporal image Transformer (BiT) model excelled in a change detection approach, effectively capturing the changed regions [3].

A novel weak training data generation strategy and an end-to-end weakly supervised semantic segmentation (WSSS) method, called TFCSD, have effectively addressed urban flood mapping challenges [6]. By decoupling the acquisition of positive and negative samples, this weak label generation strategy significantly reduces data labeling efforts, facilitating rapid flood mapping in emergency situations. When such data are unavailable, the SAM-assisted interactive labeling method [10] can be used to achieve similar results. Unsupervised DL and the Normalized Difference Water Index (NDWI) was proposed in [12] for accurate water extraction from multispectral images. This framework utilized a simple and rapid binarization algorithm to segment potential water bodies from NDWI images, creating binarized images that serve as pseudo-samples and labels for DL training utilizing peer networks, thus transitioning from unlabeled learning to noisy label learning.

There have also been several unsupervised approaches to tackle the problem of flood segmentation, mainly employing k-means and region growing techniques. In [11], unsupervised object-based clustering has been applied to flood mapping in SAR images. The resulting clusters are classified based on centroids and refined using region growing. Furthermore, an automated method for mapping non-urban flood extents was developed through contextual filtering on multitemporal SAR imagery [16]. The approach utilized tile-based histogram thresholding, enhanced with post-processing filters such as multitemporal and contextual filters, resulting in high accuracy. In [22], an unsupervised graph-based segmentation method formulated within a Bayesian framework using probabilistic Markov random field (MRF) modeling is introduced.

Finally, in [21], the first fully unsupervised segmentation method (UFS-HT-REM) for fast and accurate flood area detection was proposed utilizing color images acquired from UAVs without the need of pre-disaster images. It progressively excludes non-flood image regions using binary masks derived from color and edge data. A probability map for the location of flooded areas is calculated with a weighted approach and a subsequent modified hysteresis thresholding yields the final segmentation. The results and computational efficiency of the proposed pattern recognition method show that it is suitable for onboard data execution and decision-making during UAV flights.

The advancement of DL methods in semantic segmentation has demonstrated their ability to enhance segmentation accuracy through adaptive mapping relationships based on contextual semantic information. However, DL approaches often necessitate extensive manual labeling of large datasets and can lack interpretability, highlighting areas for improvement. In contrast, traditional ML methods rely on manually crafted mappings. Recent systematic reviews spanning three decades of water body segmentation research examine the evolution and optimization of DL methods alongside traditional approaches at pixel and image levels [5].

3   Methodology

To train any DL model, a training and a validation set of images along with their corresponding ground truth images are essential. The accurate labeling of ground truth masks typically arises from human annotation, which is a time-consuming process and susceptible to errors. Generally, this task requires two or three experts to ensure a correct annotation. To bypass this step, we considered the UFS-HT-REM algorithm [21] as an automatic label generator.

UFS-HT-REM is a fully unsupervised approach for flood detection in color images captured by UAVs. Predicated on valid assumptions, masks are calculated where areas are classified as non-flood. The RGB vegetation index identifies visible vegetation which cannot be flooded, creating the first mask. The detected edges denote boundaries between flooded and non-flooded areas and borders of objects, generating the second mask. The remaining three masks are constructed out of the observation that in the CIELAB colorspace the value of each color component is usually higher in flooded areas. An automatically calculated thresholds for each component produce the corresponding binary mask with the non-flood areas. Combining these individual masks yields remaining zones representing potential flood areas (PFAs). Refined through fundamental morphological operations, these PFAs are utilized to estimate the dominant flood color using a probability map generated via a weighted approach. Pixels located further from the boundary of the non-flood class are assigned higher weights, as they exhibit a greater likelihood of being flooded. An adapted hysteresis thresholding technique is used to achieve the final flood segmentation through probabilistic region growing of an isocontour. While performance is high with only two tunable parameters, UFS-HT-REM does not surpass the performance of recent DL methods.

Utilizing the automatically generated labels from the UFS-HT-REM method instead of ground truth, we developed an unsupervised DL strategy. First, we refine the unsupervised algorithm by adjusting the user-defined parameters, namely T_L and T_H, which represent the low and high thresholds of the adapted hysteresis thresholding technique used for flood segmentation from the generated probability map. Pixels with probability greater than T_H have high confidence to belong to flood areas, and serve as seeds for a connectivity-based approach to track the flood. If neighboring pixels have a probability value higher than the low threshold T_L (weak flood pixels), they are ultimately considered part of the flood. We focus on the behavior of the method with different values in recall and precision. Recall measures the proportion of true positive instances correctly identified by the model from all actual positive instances in the dataset, while Precision measures the proportion of true positive predictions out of all positive predictions made by the model. We observed that increasing only T_L

was sufficient to affect these metrics, as detailed in Sect. 5. Second, the generated pseudo-labels are used to train two widely recognized CNNs for semantic segmentation, as illustrated in Fig. 1.

The original *U-Net*, as introduced in [18], features a depth of 5 and consists of an encoder path and a decoder path. The encoder path comprises convolutional blocks followed by max pooling, which increases the depth and receptive field while contracting the feature map size extracting complex contextual information. The decoder path mirrors the encoder with an equal number of convolutional blocks, transpose convolutions, and feature map concatenations from the corresponding encoder layers, thereby expanding and restoring the semantic information to the original input size. The convolutional block in both the encoder and decoder paths consists of two successive 2D convolutions, each followed by batch normalization and a ReLU activation. Batch normalization before the activation function allows for a higher learning rate and accelerates the network's training speed. All filter kernels are of size 3×3, starting with 64 kernels and doubling in each encoder layer, reaching 1024 at the bottleneck, and then halving again at each decoder layer. The final output is obtained with a 2D convolution with a kernel size of 1×1, resulting in two classes (flood and background). Overall, the model comprises approximately 31 million trainable parameters.

The second CNN used in this study is *the Fully Convolutional Network (FCN) model with a ResNet-50 backbone*, as described in [15]. FCNs efficiently learn to make dense predictions for per-pixel tasks such as semantic segmentation, while ResNet-50 facilitates training of very deep networks through skip connections, which mitigate the vanishing gradient problem. The concept of residual units in ResNet-50 allows deep layers to learn directly from shallow layers, easing network convergence. ResNet-50 includes an initial 7×7 convolutional layer followed by batch normalization, ReLU activation and max pooling, and four stages of residual blocks with 256, 512, 1024, and 2048 filters, respectively, each reducing and then restoring the spatial dimensions while increasing in depth. In the FCN, the fully connected layers of ResNet-50 are replaced with 1×1 convolutions to maintain spatial resolution. Skip connections from intermediate layers of the backbone to the corresponding upsampling layers enhance segmentation accuracy by combining detailed and contextual information, resulting in a final dense prediction map for segmentation. Overall, the model comprises approximately 33 million trainable parameters.

4 Experimental Setup

This Section describes the datasets and the training process for this study.

4.1 Datasets

We utilized two publicly available datasets for this study, both depicting flood-affected areas, along with corresponding ground truth images indicating water

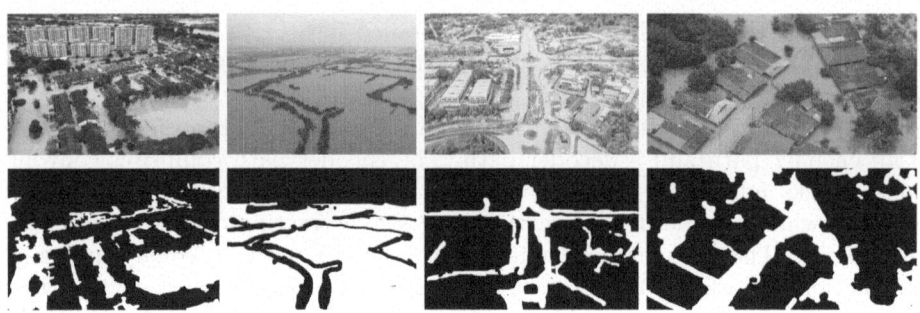

Fig. 2. Sample images from the Flood Area dataset (**top**) and their corresponding ground truths (**bottom**).

region segmentations. These images were captured by UAVs and helicopters. Both datasets feature a wide range of image variability, including urban, peri-urban, and rural areas, greenery, rivers, buildings, roads, mountains, and the sky. The images were acquired from various altitudes and angles.

The first dataset, "Flood Area" (FAD) [9], was used for training purposes and consists of 290 RGB images. Their corresponding masks were annotated by the dataset creators using Label Studio, an open-source data-labeling tool. Resolutions and dimensions vary. Representative images with their corresponding ground truths are shown in Fig. 2.

To evaluate the effectiveness of our approach, we employed the "Flood Semantic Segmentation Dataset" (FSSD) [25], which consists of 663 color images used exclusively as a test set. All images were resized and, if necessary, zero-padded to 512×512 pixels by the dataset creators, ensuring uniform dimensions, as shown in Fig. 3.

The datasets exhibit a similar balance in the distribution of flood and background pixels. In the Flood Area Dataset (FAD), flood pixels make up an average of 40.69% per image, while in the Flood Scene Segmentation Dataset (FSSD), this figure is 36.44%. The flood pixel percentage per image in FAD ranges from 4.25% to 87.87%, while in FSSD, it spans from 2.83% to 94.63%. It is important to note that in FSSD, many images include zero-padding to maintain uniform dimensions, with this padding contributing to the background pixel count.

4.2   CNN Training

Both CNNs were trained for 50 epochs with an initial learning rate of 1×10^{-5}. If no improvement was observed after 5 epochs, the learning rate was reduced by a factor of 0.1. Root Mean Squared Propagation (RMSProp) optimization was chosen, employing an adaptive learning rate strategy. RMSProp, a variant of gradient descent, offers advantages in reducing neural network training time and mitigating overfitting. RMSProp adjusts the learning rate individually for each parameter based on the magnitude of their gradients rather than using a uniform rate across all parameters. The loss function employed for training was

Fig. 3. Sample images from the Flood Semantic Segmentation dataset (**top**) and their corresponding ground truths (**bottom**).

cross-entropy, as it effectively handles class imbalance, provides a probabilistic interpretation, and ensures smooth gradient updates, facilitating robust and efficient training. Validation accuracy was assessed using the Dice score.

We used the 290 images from the FAD dataset randomly split into 90% for training and 10% for validation. Adaptations of the UFS-HT-REM method automatically generated the respective masks for the training process. All images were preprocessed to facilitate training by rescaling them to 800×600 and normalizing them to zero mean and unit variance. Given the relatively small number of training images, we employed simple augmentation techniques to enhance the training set and introduce variability to the network in each epoch. These augmentations, each with probability 0.5 of occurring, included vertical flipping, rotation within the range of $[-45, 45]$ degrees, and random uniform noise within the range of $[-0.2, 0.2]$. Training the models over 50 epochs could therefore result in approximately 13,000 different training images.

The DL models were built using PyTorch. Training was executed on an Intel I7 CPU processor at 2.3 GHz with 40 GB RAM and two NVidia Quadro RTX 4000 GPUs. The training time was about 1.4 h for each DL architecture. The inference is achieved in 0.8 and 0.5 milliseconds per image for the U-Net and the FCN_ResNet-50 model respectively. Detailed experimental results are presented and analyzed in the following section.

5   Experimental Evaluation

In this section, we present the experimental results of our proposed method[1]. We evaluated the original UFS-HT-REM method and refined variants of it to facilitate comparison with the results obtained from our unsupervised DL approach. Furthermore, we trained the same CNN models using actual ground truth

---

[1] Datasets and results will be publicly available at the following link (https://sites.google.com/site/costaspanagiotakis/research/flood-detection).

Table 1. The accuracy (ACC), intersection over union (IOU), precision (PR), recall (REC), F1-score (F_1), and average F1-score $(\overline{F_1})$ metrics for original UFS-HT-REM method [21] and its variants, tuned according to T_L, on the test dataset FSSD.

Method variant	T_L(%)	ACC (%)	IOU (%)	PR (%)	REC (%)	F_1(%)	$\overline{F_1}$(%)
UFS-HT-REM [21]	1	88.47	71.25	79.78	83.73	**81.71**	**79.41**
UFS-HT-REM var. A	2	88.58	**71.53**	79.01	**83.93**	81.39	79.36
UFS-HT-REM var. B	5	**88.69**	71.39	80.20	82.14	81.16	79.28
UFS-HT-REM var. C	10	88.55	70.68	81.46	79.68	80.56	78.78
UFS-HT-REM var. D	20	87.68	68.16	82.68	74.64	78.45	76.77
UFS-HT-REM var. E	30	86.36	64.73	**83.39**	69.41	75.76	74.05

labels for benchmarking. The evaluation metrics used include accuracy (ACC), intersection over union (IOU), precision (PR), recall (REC), and F1-score (F_1). Furthermore, we calculate the average F1-score $(\overline{F_1})$ across the entire dataset by averaging the F1-scores of each image. All metrics were conducted on the larger FSSD dataset comprising 663 images, which was exclusively used for testing.

Initially the suitability of automatically generated labels from the UFS-HT-REM method for training DL models was assessed. We aimed to determine whether fine-tuning this method could improve model training and metric scores. We observed that adjusting only the lower threshold T_L maintained performance within a consistent range but led to variations in precision and recall, as detailed in Table 1. As expected, the highest average F1-score 79.4% was achieved with the original method implemented and reported in [21], where T_L was configured to 1%. The highest precision 83.4% resulted from variant E, with $T_L = 30\%$. The highest recall was measured 83.9% in variant A, where $T_L = 2\%$. It has been observed that increasing T_L enhances the precision but decreases the recall of the method. This outcome is anticipated because a higher T_L excludes a larger number of pixels with weak probabilities classifying only the more certain pixels as flood.

We subsequently evaluated the performance of our unsupervised DL approach. We trained both CNNs with the FAD images and the pseudo-labels (PL) generated from UFS-HT-REM and its variants, and used the respective trained weights to segment the flood on the FSSD test dataset. All metrics are reported in Table 2 for the U-Net model and in Table 3 for the FCN_ResNet-50 model. Furthermore, in the last row of each Table, the performance on the test set is reported when the models are trained using the actual ground truth.

Firstly, it is important to note that the network demonstrates an ability to partially correct or disregard errors present in the initial pseudo-labels used as ground truth masks. Notably, the U-Net model increased the average F1-Score $(\overline{F_1})$ by 2.1%, primarily through an improvement in precision, rising from 81% in the initial pseudo-labels to 86.7% after training. These metrics, calculated on the training dataset (FAD), were derived from pseudo-labels generated using the

Table 2. U-Net accuracy (ACC), intersection over union (IOU), precision (PR), recall (REC), F1-score (F_1), and average F1-score ($\overline{F_1}$), when trained with pseudo-labels (PL) automatically generated with UFS-HT-REM method [21] and its variants, tuned according to T_L, and the actual ground truth images (last row), on the test dataset FSSD.

Trained with	T_L(%)	ACC (%)	IOU (%)	PR (%)	REC (%)	F_1(%)	$\overline{F_1}$(%)
UFS-HT-REM [21] PL	1	91.61	77.27	86.42	88.29	87.34	85.75
UFS-HT-REM var. A PL	2	92.06	78.04	87.61	87.90	87.76	86.41
UFS-HT-REM var. B PL	5	**92.17**	**78.50**	87.07	89.26	**88.15**	**86.73**
UFS-HT-REM var. C PL	10	92.16	78.07	87.95	87.83	87.89	86.31
UFS-HT-REM var. D PL	20	91.19	74.32	90.44	80.85	85.38	83.63
UFS-HT-REM var. E PL	30	91.67	75.50	**91.55**	81.73	86.36	84.49
Actual ground truth	-	91.20	77.02	83.78	**91.07**	87.27	85.69

Table 3. FCN_ResNet-50 accuracy (ACC), intersection over union (IOU), precision (PR), recall (REC), F1-score (F_1), and average F1-score ($\overline{F_1}$)), when trained with pseudo-labels (PL) automatically generated with UFS-HT-REM method [21] and its variants, tuned according to T_L, and the actual ground truth images (last row), on the test dataset FSSD.

Trained with	T_L(%)	ACC (%)	IOU (%)	PR (%)	REC (%)	F_1(%)	$\overline{F_1}$(%)
UFS-HT-REM [21] PL	1	90.85	**74.78**	83.67	87.78	85.68	84.17
UFS-HT-REM var. A PL	2	90.83	74.66	83.33	87.75	85.48	84.08
UFS-HT-REM var. B PL	5	**91.11**	74.36	87.02	84.08	85.52	83.89
UFS-HT-REM var. C PL	10	90.73	73.56	86.67	83.33	84.97	83.29
UFS-HT-REM var. D PL	20	90.34	71.95	87.59	80.15	83.71	81.90
UFS-HT-REM var. E PL	30	90.34	70.56	**90.90**	75.87	82.71	80.57
Actual ground truth	-	90.02	74.77	81.13	**90.97**	**85.77**	**84.21**

UFS-HT-REM variant B, with T_L set to 5%. This indicates that the network is robust to errors in the pseudo-labels.

From the resulting metrics in the test dataset (FSSD), we deduct that using the automatically generated PL in training, the performance is in the same range as training using the original ground truth. The U-Net model even performed better in $\overline{F_1}$ by 1.04%, F_1 (+0.88%), ACC (+0.97%) and IOU (+1.48%), when trained with variant B PL, where $T_L = 5\%$, as shown in Table 2. Also, PR was higher when trained with variant E ($T_L = 30\%$.) by 7.77%. It underperformed only in REC (−1.81%), compared to training with the actual ground truth labels. The FCN_ResNet-50 slightly underperforms in $\overline{F_1}$ by 0.13%, as does also in F_1 (−0.09%) and REC (−3.19%). But yields better ACC (+1.09%) and PR (+9.77%) when trained with PL generated by variant B ($T_L = 5\%$) and E ($T_L = 30\%$) respectively, compared to training with the original ground truth.

Overall, the proposed unsupervised DL approach outperforms the unsupervised UFS-HT-REM method and all its variants. As depicted in Fig. 4, any UFS-HT-REM variant generated with $T_L \in \{1\%, 2\%, 5\%, 10\%, 20\%, 30\%\}$ pseudo-labels, when used for training either the U-Net or FCN_ResNet-50 models, resulted in higher performance.

The robustness of our proposed U-Net approach is shown by the fact that any trained model scores better on the metrics than the respective UFS-HT-REM variant, and even the initial method, as implemented in [21]. The best performing U-Net, trained with pseudo-labels automatically generated with $T_L = 5\%$ improves the average F1-score ($\overline{F_1}$) by 7.5% of the corresponding UFS-HT-REM variant B, and by 7.3% compared to the result reported by the originally published, fine-tuned to the best performance method. As already mentioned, this trained U-Net also surpasses the model trained with the original ground truth data. Even the worst performing U-Net improves $\overline{F_1}$ by 4.2% compared to the result of UFS-HT-REM. Respectively, the FCN_ResNet-50 improved $\overline{F_1}$ by 4.7% compared to the initial method, while remaining in the same vicinity as when trained with the original ground truth data.

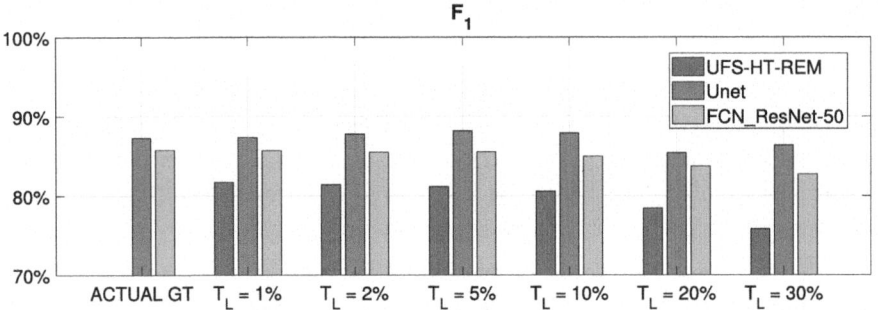

Fig. 4. The average F_1-score of UFS-HT-REM, U-Net and FCN_ResNet-50 under the actual ground truth and pseudo labels masks over the Flood Semantic Segmentation dataset.

Figure 5(a) and 5(b) show the histograms of the F1-score (F_1) values and the difference between the F1-scores for the best performing U-Net and the UFS-HT-REM method, respectively. As shown in Fig. 5(a), the unsupervised DL approach yields high performance results ($F_1 > 80\%$) in more images than the UFS-HT-REM method. Furthermore, according to Fig. 5(b), in 17.5% of the images in the test set, the results of U-Net are significantly better (with at least 15% higher F_1) compared to the results of the UFS-HT-REM method. Only in 3.6% of the 663 test images, U-Net resulted in significantly lower F_1 compared to the initial method.

Figure 6 presents the top segmentation results from the 20 40 60 80 percentiles according to the sorting of the F1-scores achieved by the U-Net predictions in descending order. The segmented flood is overlaid in blue over the image. The

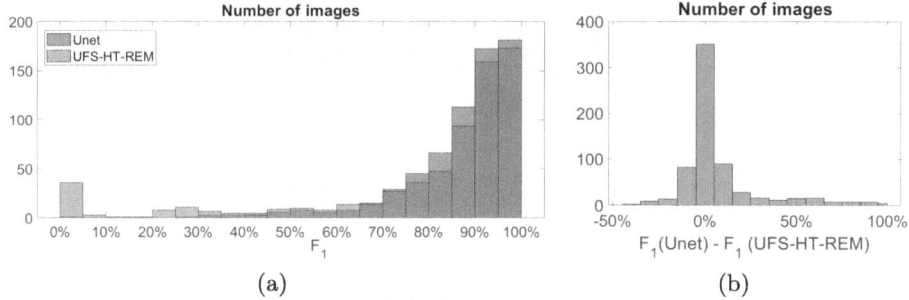

(a)   (b)

Fig. 5. (a)The histogram of the F_1-score values of U-Net and UFS-HT-REM. (b) The histogram of difference between the F_1-score of U-Net and UFS-HT-REM for pseudo labels masks with $T_L = 5\%$.

IMAGE

Fig. 6. Original images (a) to (d) and the respective top segmentations from the 20th, 40th, 60th and 80th percentile of the descending sorted F1-scores of the U-Net predictions (e) to (h). Flood segmentation is overlaid in blue color and each image's F1-score is also stated. (Color figure online)

best F1-score was 99.7%, while the average F1-scores in the 20th, 40th, 60th and 80th percentiles were 94.5%, 90.7%, 85% and 65.9%, respectively, verifying the improved effectiveness of the proposed approach.

Further segmentation results are presented in Fig. 7. Again, the flood is shown in blue, overlaid on the image. We show segmentations of the best performing U-Net trained with the automatically generated labels from UFS-HT-REM variant B (Table 2, row 3), and compare them with the corresponding UFS-HT-

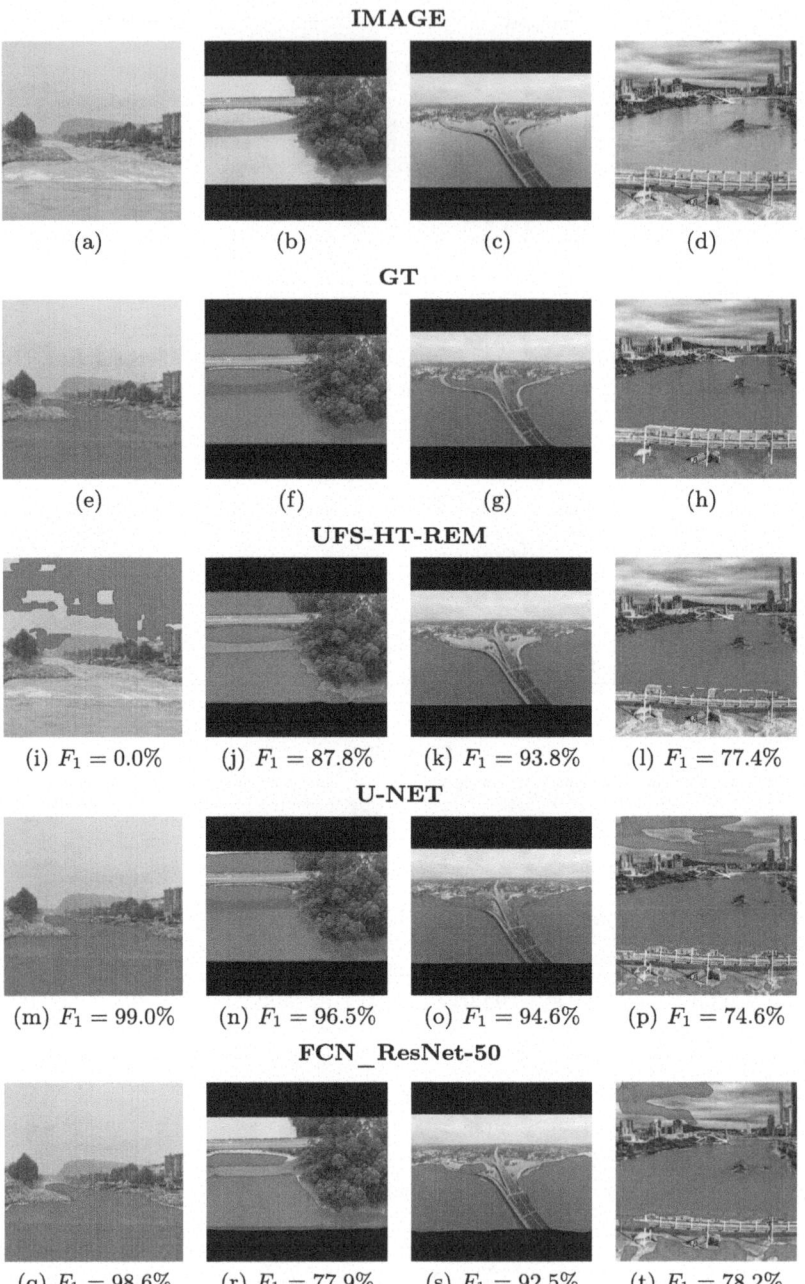

Fig. 7. Original images (a) to (d), respective ground truth (e) to (h), and segmentation results from UFS-HT-REM (i) to (l), U-Net (m) to (p), and FCN_ResNet-50 (q) to (t). The flood is overlaid in blue color and each segmentation's F1-score is also reported. We used the descending sorted differences between U-Net and UFS-HT-REM segmentations to showcase the top 0th, 25th, 50th and 75th percentile results for comparison. (Color figure online)

REM segmentations. The results exhibit improvements where the UFS-HT-REM method fails, and are depicted from the highest F1-score difference between the two methods (Fig. 7 first column) to the lowest (Fig. 7 last column). We have selected the images from the top 0, 25, 50 and 75 percentiles according to the sorted differences. There is considerable improvement in the U-Net segmentation results, with the average F1-score difference being +7.5%. Additionally, we also present the predictions from the FCN_ResNet-50, as well as the ground truth and the original image.

6   Conclusions

In this work, we have presented a novel unsupervised DL methodology for flood segmentation in UAV color images. We have utilized a pattern recognition method which automatically generates flood labels and tuned it so that training CNN models with these pseudo-labels has produced comparable or even higher performance metrics as when training with the actual ground truth. The models employed, namely U-Net and FCN_ResNet-50, are commonly used for segmentation purposes, and we did not focus on optimizing them. Our objective was rather to prove that pseudo-labels are effective in training DL models for flood semantic segmentation, thus making the ground truth obsolete. Our unsupervised DL approach also outperformed the initial unsupervised method for flood segmentation UFS-HT-REM. According to our experimental results, it is shown that DL models for flood segmentation do not necessarily need the ground truth to be trained.

The proposed approach offers lot of potential for future research with encouraging experimental results. We are currently working for an automated process to further discard unreliable pseudo-labels, where the UFS-HT-REM method lacks, i.e. sky areas falsely detected as flood, expecting better training and inference from the DL models. Also, we plan to extend this work by detecting flooded buildings and roads. Furthermore, we seek to evaluate the method's performance in identifying still water bodies in comparison to flood regions, and to determine the feasibility of distinguishing between these two types of areas. Finally, we intend to exploit the knowledge gained in order to construct specialized DL architectures and loss functions, directing the network's attention exclusively towards the flood.

Acknowledgements. This publication is financed by the Project "Strengthening and optimizing the operation of MODY services and academic and research units of the Hellenic Mediterranean University", funded by the Public Investment Program of the Greek Ministry of Education and Religious Affairs.

References

1. Algiriyage, N., Prasanna, R., Stock, K., Doyle, E.E., Johnston, D.: Multi-source multimodal data and deep learning for disaster response: a systematic review. SN Comput. Sci. **3**, 1–29 (2022)
2. Bentivoglio, R., Isufi, E., Jonkman, S.N., Taormina, R.: Deep learning methods for flood mapping: a review of existing applications and future research directions. Hydrol. Earth Syst. Sci. **26**(16), 4345–4378 (2022)
3. Dong, Z., et al.: Mapping inundation extents in Poyang lake area using Sentinel-1 data and transformer-based change detection method. J. Hydrol. **620**, 129455 (2023)
4. Drakonakis, G.I., Tsagkatakis, G., Fotiadou, K., Tsakalides, P.: OmbriaNet-supervised flood mapping via convolutional neural networks using multitemporal Sentinel-1 and Sentinel-2 data fusion. IEEE J. Sel. Top. Appl. Earth Obs. Remote Sens. **15**, 2341–2356 (2022)
5. Guo, Z., Wu, L., Huang, Y., Guo, Z., Zhao, J., Li, N.: Water-body segmentation for SAR images: past, current, and future. Remote Sens. **14**(7), 1752 (2022)
6. He, Y., Wang, J., Zhang, Y., Liao, C.: An efficient urban flood mapping framework towards disaster response driven by weakly supervised semantic segmentation with decoupled training samples. ISPRS J. Photogramm. Remote. Sens. **207**, 338–358 (2024)
7. Hertel, V., Chow, C., Wani, O., Wieland, M., Martinis, S.: Probabilistic SAR-based water segmentation with adapted Bayesian convolutional neural network. Remote Sens. Environ. **285**, 113388 (2023)
8. Inthizami, N.S., Ma'sum, M.A., Alhamidi, M.R., Gamal, A., Ardhianto, R., Jatmiko, W., et al.: Flood video segmentation on remotely sensed UAV using improved efficient neural network. ICT Express **8**(3), 347–351 (2022)
9. Karim, F., Sharma, K., Barman, N.R.: Flood area segmentation. https://www.kaggle.com/datasets/faizalkarim/flood-area-segmentation. Accessed Nov 2023
10. Kirillov, A., et al.: Segment anything (2023)
11. Landuyt, L., Verhoest, N.E., Van Coillie, F.M.: Flood mapping in vegetated areas using an unsupervised clustering approach on Sentinel-1 and-2 imagery. Remote Sens. **12**(21), 3611 (2020)
12. Li, J., et al.: Accurate water extraction using remote sensing imagery based on normalized difference water index and unsupervised deep learning. J. Hydrol. **612**, 128202 (2022)
13. Li, Z., Demir, I.: U-net-based semantic classification for flood extent extraction using SAR imagery and gee platform: a case study for 2019 Central US flooding. Sci. Total Environ. **869**, 161757 (2023)
14. Linardos, V., Drakaki, M., Tzionas, P., Karnavas, Y.L.: Machine learning in disaster management: recent developments in methods and applications. Mach. Learn. Knowl. Extr. **4**(2) (2022)
15. Long, J., Shelhamer, E., Darrell, T.: Fully convolutional networks for semantic segmentation. In: Proceedings of the IEEE Conference on Computer Vision and Pattern Recognition, pp. 3431–3440 (2015)
16. McCormack, T., Campanyà, J., Naughton, O.: A methodology for mapping annual flood extent using multi-temporal Sentinel-1 imagery. Remote Sens. Environ. **282**, 113273 (2022)
17. Ritchie, H., Rosado, P.: Natural disasters (2022). https://ourworldindata.org/natural-disasters

18. Ronneberger, O., Fischer, P., Brox, T.: U-Net: convolutional networks for biomedical image segmentation. In: Medical Image Computing and Computer-Assisted Intervention–MICCAI 2015: 18th International Conference, Munich, Germany, October 5-9, 2015, Proceedings, Part III 18, pp. 234–241. Springer (2015)
19. Şener, A., Doğan, G., Ergen, B.: A novel convolutional neural network model with hybrid attentional atrous convolution module for detecting the areas affected by the flood. Earth Sci. Inf. **17**(1), 193–209 (2024)
20. Shastry, A., Carter, E., Coltin, B., Sleeter, R., McMichael, S., Eggleston, J.: Mapping floods from remote sensing data and quantifying the effects of surface obstruction by clouds and vegetation. Remote Sens. Environ. **291**, 113556 (2023)
21. Simantiris, G., Panagiotakis, C.: Unsupervised color-based flood segmentation in UAV imagery. Remote Sens. **16**(12) (2024). https://doi.org/10.3390/rs16122126
22. Trombini, M., Solarna, D., Moser, G., Dellepiane, S.: A goal-driven unsupervised image segmentation method combining graph-based processing and Markov random fields. Pattern Recogn. **134**, 109082 (2023)
23. Wang, L., Li, R., Duan, C., Zhang, C., Meng, X., Fang, S.: A novel transformer based semantic segmentation scheme for fine-resolution remote sensing images. IEEE Geosci. Remote Sens. Lett. **19**, 1–5 (2022)
24. Wieland, M., Martinis, S., Kiefl, R., Gstaiger, V.: Semantic segmentation of water bodies in very high-resolution satellite and aerial images. Remote Sens. Environ. **287**, 113452 (2023)
25. Yang, L.: Flood semantic segmentation dataset. https://www.kaggle.com/datasets/lihuayang111265/flood-semantic-segmentation-dataset. Accessed April 2024

Self-Supervised Learning for Radio-Astronomy Source Classification: A Benchmark

Thomas Cecconello[1,2]($\boxtimes$), Simone Riggi[2], Ugo Becciani[2], Fabio Vitello[2], Andrew M. Hopkins[4], Giuseppe Vizzari[3], Concetto Spampinato[1], and Simone Palazzo[1]

[1] Pattern Recognition and Computer Vision (PeRCeiVe) Lab, Department of Electrical, Electronics and Computer Engineering, University of Catania, Catania, Italy
[2] INAF - Osservatorio Astrofisico di Catania, Catania, Italy
{thomas.cecconello,simone.riggi}@inaf.it
[3] University of Milano Bicocca, Milan, Italy
[4] School of Mathematical and Physical Sciences, Macquarie University, Sydney, Australia

Abstract. The upcoming Square Kilometer Array (SKA) telescope marks a significant step forward in radio astronomy, presenting new opportunities and challenges for data analysis. Traditional visual models pretrained on optical photography images may not perform optimally on radio interferometry images, which have distinct visual characteristics.

Self-Supervised Learning (SSL) offers a promising approach to address this issue, leveraging the abundant unlabeled data in radio astronomy to train neural networks that learn useful representations from radio images. This study explores the application of SSL to radio astronomy, comparing the performance of SSL-trained models with that of traditional models pretrained on natural images, evaluating the importance of data curation for SSL, and assessing the potential benefits of self-supervision to different domain-specific radio astronomy datasets.

Our results indicate that, SSL-trained models achieve significant improvements over the baseline in several downstream tasks, especially in the linear evaluation setting; when the entire backbone is fine-tuned, the benefits of SSL are less evident but still outperform pretraining. These findings suggest that SSL can play a valuable role in efficiently enhancing the analysis of radio astronomical data. The trained models and code is available at: https://github.com/dr4thmos/solo-learn-radio.

Keywords: Interferometry · Self-supervised learning · Benchmark

1 Introduction

Radio astronomy, a branch of astronomy that studies celestial objects through their radio emissions, has revolutionized our understanding of the universe.

S. Palaiahnakote et al. (Eds.): ICPR 2024 Workshops, LNCS 15617, pp. 424–439, 2025.
https://doi.org/10.1007/978-3-031-88217-3_32

Unlike traditional optical telescopes, radio telescopes are essentially highly sensitive antennas designed to detect faint radio signals from space. These sophisticated instruments can range from single dish antennas to vast arrays of interconnected antennas spread over large distances. By capturing and analyzing these radio waves, astronomers can observe phenomena invisible to optical telescopes, penetrating cosmic dust and gas to reveal hidden aspects of our universe. This field is now on the cusp of a data revolution, with next-generation telescope arrays like the Square Kilometre Array (SKA) [10] set to generate unprecedented volumes of high-resolution data.

The SKA, an international effort to build the world's largest radio telescope, promises unparalleled sensitivity and survey speed. Its precursors, such as MeerKAT [15] in South Africa and ASKAP [26] in Australia, are already producing vast amounts of high-quality data, foreshadowing the data deluge expected from SKA. This surge in data quantity and quality presents both opportunities and challenges for machine learning applications in astronomy.

Machine Learning (ML) techniques have become increasingly crucial in analyzing radio astronomical data. From source detection [30] to classification [31] and anomaly detection [22], ML algorithms are helping astronomers sift through terabytes of data efficiently. However, the unique characteristics of radio interferometry images pose challenges for traditional computer vision models, often pre-trained on optical images.

Self-supervised Learning (SSL) [21] has emerged as a powerful paradigm to address these challenges. By leveraging large amounts of unlabeled data, SSL enables models to learn meaningful representations without manual annotations. This is particularly valuable in radio astronomy, where labeled datasets are often limited but unlabeled data is abundant. Moreover, the labeling schemes in radio astronomical datasets can vary significantly depending on the specific study or survey objectives, making it challenging to create large, consistently labeled datasets. SSL offers a way to leverage the vast amounts of unlabeled data while potentially bridging the gaps between different labeling conventions.

While recent works have explored SSL in radio astronomy [20], they often focus on a single SSL method or a limited set of downstream tasks. This leaves a gap in our understanding of how different SSL techniques perform across various radio astronomy datasets and tasks.

Our study aims to provide a comprehensive benchmark of SSL methods applied to radio astronomical images, with the following objectives:

- Evaluate the performance of SSL-trained models compared to traditional models pretrained on natural images across various radio astronomy tasks.
- Assess the impact of data curation on SSL effectiveness in the radio astronomy domain.
- Investigate the transferability of self-supervised representations across different domain-specific radio astronomy datasets.
- Provide insights into the most effective SSL techniques for radio astronomical data analysis.

We conduct experiments using a range of state-of-the-art SSL methods, including SimCLR [7], BYOL [18], DINO [6], WMSE [13], SwAV [5] and All4One [14]. These methods are applied to both curated and uncurated radio astronomy datasets. Our evaluation encompasses multiple downstream tasks, focusing on source classification across diverse datasets such as Radio Galaxy Zoo (RGZ) [2], MiraBest [28], and VLASS [17]. Additionally, we present the Multi-Survey Radio Sources (MSRS) dataset, a curated collection from four existing radio surveys, labeled according to a new schema specifically developed for this study. This dataset provides a unique resource for evaluating self-supervised learning methods across different radio surveys and source morphologies.

Our results demonstrate the potential of SSL in radio astronomy, consistently outperforming ImageNet pre-trained baselines across all datasets, highlighting the value of domain-specific pre-training even by simply performing linear adaptation of SSL features. By providing this comprehensive benchmark of SSL methods in radio astronomy, we aim to contribute to the development of effective and efficient techniques for leveraging the vast amounts of unlabeled data in this domain. These insights may prove valuable not only for upcoming large-scale projects like SKA but also for informing similar approaches in other scientific fields characterized by abundant unlabeled data and domain-specific challenges.

2   Related Works

Computer vision techniques have become increasingly important in astronomy, finding applications across various wavelengths, including infrared, optical, and radio. Traditionally, machine learning approaches in astronomy have focused on unsupervised learning methods to extract representations from astronomical images, which are then visually explored using dimensionality reduction algorithms. These feature extraction techniques include autoencoders [4], self-organizing maps (SOM) [25], and SSL [24,32]. The extracted representations serve multiple purposes beyond visual inspection, including anomaly detection, classification, and instance segmentation.

In addressing these tasks, radio astronomy has followed a logical progression mirroring the broader evolution of computer vision techniques. Initially, astronomers primarily relied on supervised learning methods [31], favoring this approach due to its historical precedence and relative simplicity in implementation and interpretation. As the field advanced, researchers began to explore more sophisticated techniques, leading to the adoption of SSL in astronomy. However, a recent survey [20] notes that while SSL methods have gained traction, they have been applied primarily to non-radio images, such as optical data. This highlights a gap in the application of these techniques to radio astronomy, which presents unique challenges and opportunities.

In the specific domain of radio astronomy, recent work by Slijepcevic et al. [33] demonstrates the potential of SSL methods. They employed BYOL [18] on the Radio Galaxy Zoo Data Release 1 (RGZ-DR1) dataset [2] to pretrain a general model applicable to various downstream tasks. The model's performance was quantitatively evaluated using the MiraBest dataset [28], which provides physically meaningful morphological classifications. However, this evaluation was limited by the relatively small size of the MiraBest dataset (about 800 images) and its binary classification schema (FRI vs. FRII radio galaxies). Riggi et al. [29] addressed this limitation by constructing both curated and uncurated unlabeled datasets, reserving the labeled RGZ-DR1 data for the evaluation phase.

3   Materials and Methods

3.1   Overview

Deep radio sky observations are nowadays carried out with large arrays of radio telescopes, that collect sky visibility data across multiple frequency channels. These raw data undergo complex interferometric processing, including calibration and imaging, to produce either single-frequency radio continuum maps or multi-frequency spectral-line data cubes. Our study focuses on radio-continuum maps, which are single-channel grayscale images in FITS format. These images represent radio flux brightness in Jy/beam, with pixel values ranging from μJy/beam to several Jy/beam, including negative values often associated with imaging artifacts. The radio continuum maps generated by each survey presents different resolutions, but generally consist of very large images (e.g., for SMGPS [15], 7500×7500 pixels).

In this section, we present the methodology carried out for our systematic study of SSL approaches for radio-astronomy data analysis. We first introduce the dataset employed in this work for pretraining backbone models in a self-supervised fashion and describe data preprocessing modalities. We then introduce the variety of SSL techniques employed in this work, briefly presenting their characteristics and training objectives. Finally, we present the list of publicly-available datasets used in this work as downstream tasks, and the evaluation procedure for assessing the performance of SSL pretraining on those tasks.

3.2   Self-Supervision Datasets

Compared to traditional supervised learning, SSL approaches provide the important advantage of not requiring manual labeling of data samples, which is well-known as a time-consuming and error-prone task. However, while natural image datasets are inherently built ensuring that each data sample has meaningful and somewhat unique content, radio-astronomy data present significant challenges in this regard.

The easiest way to build a large *uncurated* radio dataset is to randomly extract (i.e., without any knowledge of the position of radio sources) cutout images from radio maps using a sliding window with fixed-size. This procedure can potentially sample a high variety of object morphologies, but, as the sky is dominated by compact point-like sources and by background, while the number of peculiar and extended objects is significantly smaller, the result is the unavoidable construction of an unbalanced dataset, where more interesting objects (e.g., diffused or extended sources) are relatively rare. As is known [1], SSL methods suffer when dealing with unbalanced data. Additionally, considering the multi-scale nature of objects in the sky, using a fixed size of the sliding window likely results in truncated or partially captured sources.

An alternative approach consists in building a *curated* dataset by extracting cutouts around known source celestial positions reported in existing radio source catalogues. In this case, it is possible to adaptively set the image cutout size to be large enough to fully include the catalogued source and part of its surrounding region (including the background or other nearby sources). As can be imagined, source catalogues need to be manually labeled, and inevitably include fewer objects than the totality that can be found in radio maps.

In our work, we assess the impact of data curation by using two different datasets for SSL training, indicated in the following as *Curated* and *Uncurated* dataset. These datasets are primarily collected from two radio surveys:

The SARAO MeerKAT Galactic Plane Survey (SMGPS) [15]: Covers a large portion of the 1st, 3rd and 4th Galactic quadrants ($l = 2°$-$61°$, $251°$-$358°$, $|b| < 1.5°$) in the L-band (886–1678 MHz), with 8" angular resolution and ~10–20 μJy/beam noise rms at 1.3 GHz.

The ASKAP EMU pilot survey [26]: Covers approximately 270 deg^2 of the Dark Energy Survey area, with 11"-18" angular resolution and ~30 μJy/beam noise rms at 944 MHz.

Uncurated Dataset. A set of 285,585 radio images of fixed size (256×256 pixels, equivalent to a ~6.4'×6.4' sky portion). As stated before, data are extracted from radio maps using a sliding windows, with a 50% overlap. Since an intrinsic limitation of that dataset is the fixed sliding window size, we choose it to be large enough to capture most of the extended sources in the maps. As the data are extracted from mosaicked maps, those images may contain missing values on the border (filled in with the minimum value from the corresponding cutout) and mosaicking artifacts (see Fig. 1).

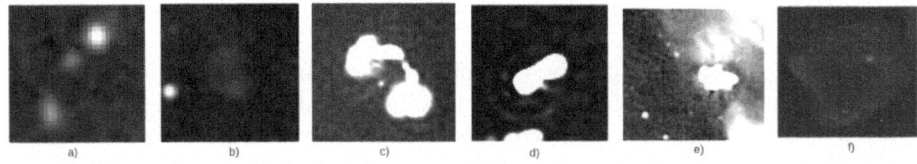

Fig. 1. Different visual characteristics of radio images. a) a multi-island radio source in low resolution; b) a faint diffuse source enhanced through a log scale transform; c) *mosaicking* artifact shown as a diagonal step line; d) *water ripple* artefact pattern around a bright source e) a large-scale diffuse emission region; f) a very large diffuse source with various nested compact sources along the line of sight.

Curated Dataset. A collection of 17,062 radio images, derived from the SMGPS integrated maps. These images are centered on objects cataloged in the SMGPS extended source catalogue [16]. Unlike fixed-size datasets, images have variable dimensions, each scaled to 2.5 times the bounding box of its central object. This adaptive sizing ensures comprehensive capture of source structures. The dataset encompasses a rich variety of radio source morphologies, including multi-component sources (e.g. radio galaxies), and diffuse structures.

Examples of images extracted from the Curated and Uncurated datasets are presented in Fig. 2.

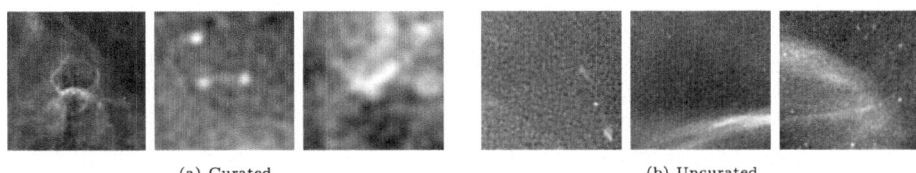

(a) Curated   (b) Uncurated

Fig. 2. Images extracted from Curated and Uncurated dataset. Curated samples correspond to well-fit crops of radio sources, while uncurated ones generally include more background and uncentered or partially-cropped objects.

3.3 Self-Supervision Methods

From the plethora of methods available from the state of the art, we select a subset of SSL techniques minimizing the overlap within training strategies, to provide readers with a comprehensive analysis. Given the limited research on applying SSL methods to radio-astronomy images and in order to favor a comparison with the literature, we believe it is prudent to build a solid baseline with well-established CNN models, leaving out vision transformers (as they require significantly amount of computational resources and since those can exhibit instability during training). Therefore, methods that principally rely on ViT [11] (e.g. MAE [19] or DinoV2 [27]) are not considered.

Additionally, we focus on methods based on view augmentation rather than on pretext tasks, since the latter may not make sense with some kinds of radio sources: for instance, some sources may be rotation-invariant, while the large amount of background in certain images (especially in the uncurated dataset) hinders the application of inpainting/jigsaw-based tasks.

In the following, we present an overview of the SSL methods employed in this study. As mentioned above, the methods under analysis all involve the generation of two augmented views, x' and x'', from the same starting image x, by means of random method-specific transformations. This approach is pivotal in learning robust feature representations, as it enables the model to understand and capture the intrinsic properties of the images across possible variants.

In **SimCLR** [7], the views are processed by a model producing representations z' and z''. The method relies on attracting representations of views generated by the same image, while repelling views generated by different images. To this aim, SimCLR uses a projection network and a loss defined as:

$$\mathcal{L}_{\text{SimCLR}} = -\log \frac{\exp(\text{sim}(h_i, h_j)/\tau)}{\sum_{k=1}^{2N} \mathbf{1}_{[k \neq i]} \exp(\text{sim}(h_i, h_k)/\tau)}$$

where h_i and h_j are the projections of z' and z'', sim is cosine similarity, and τ is a temperature parameter.

BYOL [18] tackles the problem from a slightly different perspective, without leveraging negative examples. It involves two networks, *online* and *target*, and a predictor on top of the online projector. Both networks are trained simultaneously in a teacher-student fashion, with the online target attempting to predict the target's representations; in turn, the target network does not receive parameter updates through gradient descent, but its parameters are obtained through an exponential moving average of the student's. BYOL's loss can be summarized as:

$$\mathcal{L}_{\text{BYOL}} = \|q_\theta(z_{\text{online}}) - z_{\text{target}}\|_2^2$$

where q_θ is the predictor network, and z_{online} and z_{target} are the representations obtained by the online and target networks, respectively.

DINO [6] addresses SSL using a similar teacher-student setting in a knowledge distillation framework, with the student network predicting the output of the teacher with a standard cross-entropy loss:

$$\mathcal{L}_{\text{DINO}} = H(\sigma(z_t/\tau_t), \sigma(z_s/\tau_s))$$

where z_t and z_s are the outputs of the teacher and student networks, respectively, σ denotes the softmax function, and τ_t and τ_s are temperature parameters.

WMSE [13] employs a single encoder network and positive samples only, preventing feature collapse by using a whitening operation that maps the representation space into a zero-mean and identity-covariance distribution. The loss could be represented as: uses the mutual information maximization in combination with whitening the representations.

$$\mathcal{L}_{\text{WMSE}} = \|W(z') - W(z'')\|_2^2$$

where $W(z)$ denotes the whitening transformation applied to representation z.

Clustering is traditionally one of the most suitable methods for unsupervised analysis. **SwAV** [5] adapts clustering to SSL by assigning pseudo-labels to different views of the same image. Given views x' and x'' of the same image, SwAV trains a model to compute features z' and z'', which are then mapped to soft assignments q' and q'' based on their similarity to a set of prototypes C. Then, the model is trained to predict the soft assignment of one view from the representation of the other view:

$$\mathcal{L}_{\text{SwAV}} = \ell(q', z'') + \ell(q'', z')$$

where (ℓ) is the cross-entropy.

Other approaches, such as NNCLR [12], propose to increase the diversity of positive pairs by pulling together a view of a sample with the nearest neighbor (NN) among the augmented views of another sample. **All4One** [14] builds upon this concept and extends it by efficiently including multiple neighbors through a self-attention mechanism and integrating a redundancy reduction loss inspired by Barlow Twins [35].

In our experiments, we use the implementations of the above methods provided by the *solo-learn* [9], ensuring that all experiments are implemented with a consistent standard, reducing variability and potential biases that might arise from different coding practices.

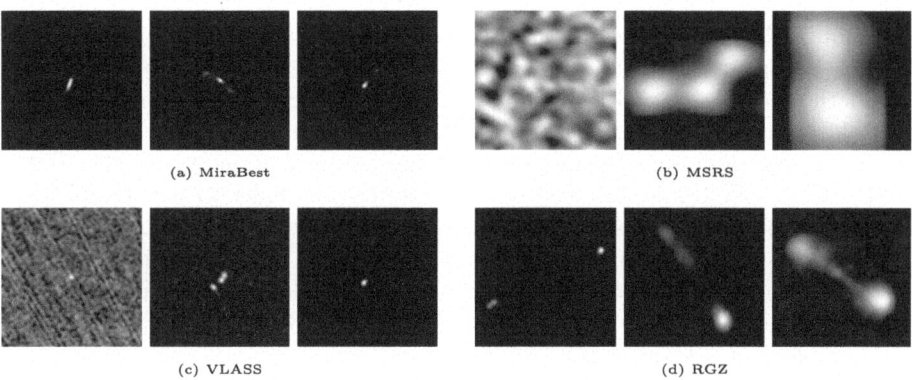

Fig. 3. Image samples for the downstream datasets employed in our study.

3.4   Downstream Datasets

To assess the effectiveness of self-supervised pretraining across the methods under analysis, we utilize publicly available radio-astronomy classification benchmarks as *downstream tasks*. We take into account datasets generated from various sky surveys, each encompassing distinct source types. Each dataset exhibits unique visual characteristics, as shown in Fig. 3. It should be noted that the original versions of the employed datasets feature a large class imbalance. Since this work addresses the quality of SSL representations, we resample each dataset so that all classes are balanced, either by undersampling more populated classes or by duplicating samples from less populated ones. The total number of samples included in each dataset after resampling is reported in the following.

Multi Survey Radio Sources (MSRS). This dataset is a collection of sources of different morphologies observed in various radio surveys (FIRST [3], EMU [26], SCORPIO [34], SMGPS [16]), covering galactic and extragalactic plane regions and showing different SNR ratios, angular resolutions, artifact patterns. Sources were labelled according to the following taxonomy: *1C-NP*: small single-island sources with N peaks, e.g., point-like (N = 1), double (N = 2), triple (N = 3); *Diffuse*: faint diffuse structures with roundish or irregular shape; *Extended*: single-component sources with extended morphology; *Extended-MI*: Multi-island extended sources, consisting in disjoint regions belonging to the same source. Besides being a multi-survey dataset, this is the only downstream dataset considered in this work that include samples of diffuse sources (the most challenging class) and images with pure background noise. Image cutouts are rectangular and equal to the original source size. The total number of samples in this dataset is 11,550.

Radio Galaxy Zoo (RGZ) [2] is retrieved from the crowd labeling campaign on Zooniverse[1]. This includes radio images from the VLA Faint Images of the Radio Sky at Twenty cm (FIRST) extragalactic survey (1.4 GHz, angular resolution ∼5") [3]. We use the data release 1, where angular size is also available for each source, therefore giving us the abilty to suitably crop the image around the source, extracting squared bounding boxes with side equal to 1.5 times the source size. The dataset classification schema includes 6 classes comprising different amount of components C and peaks P, namely: 1C-1P, 2C-1P, 2C-2P, 3C-1P, 3C-2P, 3C-3P. The resulting dataset includes 27,000 samples.

MiraBest [28] is a small dataset comprising FRI and FRII radio galaxies, as well as hybrid sources from extragalactic plane regions. For comparison with [33] we consider the sources tagged as "certain" and discarded hybrid source. Cutout size is fixed to 150×150 pixels. The dataset contains 397 FRI samples and 435 FRII samples, for a total of 832 (we do not perform resampling in this case).

VLASS is a survey [17] covering galactic and extragalactic plane regions. We use Quick Look epoch 1 version 3 and extract sources from the Table 2 of the catalogue[2], providing radio loud sources associated to their host spotted in the infrared band. The original source cutouts have a 500×500 size, probably to include the host galaxy in the infrared band, which however leads to the inclusion of a lot of background. For this reason, we reduce the cutout to 224×224: the background is still wide, but reasonable. The taxonomy of sources within the dataset includes: single-component sources; sources with two close components; sources with three close components; sources with two asymmetric radio components, many of which may be instances of a radio core blended with a lobe; sources that are notably brighter than their close neighboring components in the radio frequency. The total size of the resampled dataset is 14,500.

3.5 Downstream Evaluation

Following the literature on SSL, we compare the performance of the methods under analysis by carrying out a *linear evaluation* on the downstream tasks, i.e., by directly training a linear classifier mapping output features from the SSL backbone to the target classes. This procedure is intended to directly measure whether the representation learned by the model contains distinguishing features

---

[1] https://www.zooniverse.org/.
[2] https://cirada.ca/vlasscatalogueql0.

for the target classes. Additionally, given the relatively small size of the target datasets, we also perform *fine-tuning* of the SSL backbone on the downstream tasks, to investigate the effect of directly updating backbone features.

4   Experimental Results

4.1   Training and Evaluation Details

Following common practice in radio-astronomy, input images are normalized using the minimum and maximum values within a single cutout; we then resize them to 224×224. We employ both ResNet-18 and ResNet-50 as backbones for SSL. All methods are trained for using the LARS [8] optimizer, with a batch size of 512. Training on the Uncurated dataset is carried out for 100 epochs; on the Curated dataset, since it is significantly smaller, we train for 600 epochs. For all augmentation-based SSL methods, we apply the following set of transformations, with a certain probability p: horizontal/vertical flip ($p = 0.5$); Gaussian blur with σ between 0.1 and 2 ($p = 0.25$); contrast adjustment by a random value between 0.2 and 1.8 ($p = 0.5$); random crop with scale between 0.65 and 1 ($p = 1$). The selection of other hyperparameters is carried out independently for each SSL method, by manually varying key parameters and observing the average loss on the Curated and Uncurated datasets. In the following, we detail the final hyperparameters chosen for each method:

- **SimCLR**. Base learning rate: 1.2; output projection size: 512; temperature: 0.2.
- **BYOL**. Base learning rate: 1.2; projection size: 512; predictor hidden size: 1024.
- **DINO**. Base learning rate: 0.016; projection size: 256.
- **WMSE**. Base learning rate: 0.002; projection size: 128; whitening size: 256.
- **SWAV**. Base learning rate: 1.2; projection size: 128; number of prototypes: 300; temperature: 0.1.
- **All4One**. Base learning rate: 1.0; projection size: 512; predictor hidden size: 4096; temperature: 0.2.

When training on a downstream task with the fine-tuning strategy, we employ the AdamW [23] optimizer with a batch size of 256 and a learning rate of 0.0005, with a linear warmup followed by a cosine annealing schedule. For linear evaluation, we use a standard SGD optimizer, with the same batch size and initial learning rate. We employ a step scheduler, with learning rate decay steps of 0.1 factor at epochs 10 and 80. For both fine-tuning and linear evaluation, the total number of epochs is 100. During downstream training, we apply random vertical/horizontal flip ($p = 0.5$) and random crop with scale between 0.95 and 1 ($p = 1$).

Evaluation results on the downstream tasks are reported in terms of classification accuracy. Using the above final hyperparameters, we train each SSL method with each backbone on each pretraining dataset for three times with random initialization. The only exception is that, for the Uncurated dataset, we only use ResNet-18, for timing constraints. Then, we evaluate each trained model on all downstream tasks, using 3-fold cross-validation on each task. In practice, for a given combination of SSL method, backbone, pretraining dataset and downstream dataset, we have nine values of accuracy, for which we report the corresponding mean and standard deviation.

As an additional baseline for comparison, we also report the results obtained when pretraining BYOL on the ImageNet-100 (for ResNet-18) and ImageNet-1k (for ResNet-50) datasets. This provides useful information on the suitability of features extracted from natural images when applied to the analysis of radio-astronomy imaging data.

All experiments we carried out on a single NVIDIA A100-PCIE-40GB GPU.

Table 1. Linear evaluation: mean accuracies and standard deviations of each configuration. Best results in bold for each block.

Dataset	Backbone	Method	MiraBest	RGZ	MSRS	VLASS
Curated	ResNet-18	All4one	82.1 ± 0.5	$\mathbf{79.4 \pm 0.2}$	$\mathbf{78.2 \pm 3.9}$	$\mathbf{77.2 \pm 0.8}$
		BYOL	89.6 ± 0.4	77.6 ± 0.2	78.0 ± 4.2	76.2 ± 0.6
		DINO	64.2 ± 0.4	69.2 ± 0.6	73.8 ± 3.8	66.6 ± 0.8
		SimCLR	$\mathbf{91.0 \pm 0.5}$	69.5 ± 0.5	73.7 ± 4.1	71.9 ± 1.1
		SwAV	72.9 ± 0.4	74.6 ± 0.7	74.8 ± 2.9	69.6 ± 1.3
		WMSE	84.6 ± 0.0	70.6 ± 0.5	74.6 ± 4.6	70.6 ± 0.0
Curated	ResNet-50	All4one	88.5 ± 0.6	$\mathbf{78.8 \pm 0.2}$	77.1 ± 3.6	$\mathbf{77.0 \pm 0.4}$
		BYOL	$\mathbf{90.0 \pm 0.5}$	78.6 ± 0.5	76.5 ± 4.8	76.8 ± 0.4
		DINO	77.7 ± 1.1	70.2 ± 0.6	73.6 ± 3.5	67.7 ± 1.4
		SimCLR	85.8 ± 0.9	73.0 ± 0.1	71.7 ± 4.2	73.1 ± 0.9
		SwAV	82.3 ± 0.5	75.3 ± 0.2	74.4 ± 2.3	70.5 ± 0.5
		WMSE	81.2 ± 0.5	74.7 ± 0.3	75.7 ± 4.4	72.6 ± 0.4
Uncurated	ResNet-18	All4one	75.6 ± 0.8	68.4 ± 0.5	$\mathbf{74.2 \pm 3.8}$	$\mathbf{70.5 \pm 0.4}$
		BYOL	79.6 ± 0.4	$\mathbf{72.6 \pm 0.9}$	73.5 ± 3.0	69.6 ± 0.2
		DINO	83.6 ± 0.0	67.4 ± 1.0	71.4 ± 3.6	69.0 ± 0.8
		SimCLR	$\mathbf{84.8 \pm 0.7}$	68.2 ± 0.3	72.0 ± 3.4	68.1 ± 0.8
		SwAV	74.4 ± 0.8	65.2 ± 0.9	73.2 ± 3.1	62.5 ± 0.6
		WMSE	64.6 ± 0.4	60.2 ± 0.5	69.6 ± 3.5	60.5 ± 0.6
ImageNet-100	ResNet-18	BYOL	67.5 ± 0.9	63.6 ± 0.5	72.0 ± 4.2	62.8 ± 0.9
ImageNet-1k	ResNet-50	BYOL	73.5 ± 1.0	70.2 ± 0.8	76.0 ± 4.9	69.9 ± 0.3

4.2   Linear Evaluation

Results for linear evaluation are reported in Table 1. A high-level analysis across methods shows that All4one, BYOL and SimCLR generally achieve the best performance on the downstream tasks, while DINO, SwAV and WMSE seem to perform worse on average. In particular, All4one yields the highest accuracy on three downstream tasks out of four, excluding MiraBest. The superior trend of All4one is confirmed when varying across the backbone architectures, as well as on both the Curated and Uncurated pretraining datasets.

From a quantitative perspective, dataset curation positively impacts results, as all SSL methods benefit from the higher sample quality more than from a larger dimension of the dataset. Interestingly, even though MSRS partially over-laps with the Uncurated pretraining dataset (since both contain some of the same sky regions) the models pretrained on the Curated dataset perform better. This is likely because the Curated dataset includes entire, more complex structures, whereas the Uncurated dataset contains only portions of these structures. As a result, pretraining on the Curated dataset allows the models to learn more com-prehensive and transferable features. Backbone architecture has a more limited effect, with ResNet-18 generally yielding slightly better results than ResNet-50, which can be easily explained by the simplicity of the image patterns, not requiring a particularly high architectural complexity.

It is interesting to note that the SSL baseline using ImageNet variants almost always performs significantly worse than when using radio-astronomy data for pretraining. Only in the case of MSRS, which is characterized by larger and more structured object shapes, do the baselines yield closer (but still lower) accuracy, which might indicate that features learned from natural images may be overly complex (and thus less transferable) for the tasks at hand. However, it should also be noted that MSRS exhibits a significantly higher standard deviation, compared to the other downstream datasets. Hence, the similarity in terms of accuracy may also be due to an instability in the representations learned during self-supervision. Further investigations are therefore in order to clarify this aspect.

4.3 Fine-Tuning Evaluation

Fine-tuning results are reported in Table 2. As can be expected, results are higher than the linear evaluation setting, since the backbone models' features are explic-itly updated for each downstream task. Of course, this comes with a higher training cost, as gradients for the entire backbone must be computed at training time. In this setting, the differences between SSL methods observed for linear evaluation are basically flattened: there is no marked superiority of one approach over the others. Even the ImageNet-based baselines achieve results on par with models pretrained on the radio-astronomy datasets.

In this setting, we introduce, as an additional baseline for comparison, the results of the work by Slijepcevic et al. [33], where a ResNet-18 is pretrained on RGZ through BYOL, and then fine-tuned on MiraBest. To the best of our knowledge, this study is the most similar to ours from the literature, although it is significantly more limited in scope. Also in this case, the results are in line with the ones obtained in our study: however, due to the relative high performance that all approaches are able to achieve for MiraBest, we suggest that other downstream datasets might be more suitable for benchmarking in future works.

Table 2. Fine-tuning: mean accuracies and standard deviations of each configuration. Best results in bold for each block.

Dataset	Backbone	Method	MiraBest	RGZ	MSRS	VLASS
Curated	ResNet-18	All4one	96.2 ± 0.6	81.3 ± 0.5	76.7 ± 4.4	82.9 ± 0.3
		BYOL	96.5 ± 1.0	**81.6 ± 0.2**	76.5 ± 5.0	**83.5 ± 0.2**
		DINO	97.1 ± 0.6	80.0 ± 0.2	75.1 ± 4.1	82.1 ± 0.4
		SimCLR	94.2 ± 1.4	80.6 ± 0.3	76.0 ± 4.4	83.4 ± 0.6
		SwAV	94.2 ± 1.0	78.8 ± 0.4	76.8 ± 3.8	78.6 ± 1.3
		WMSE	**99.2 ± 0.4**	81.1 ± 0.6	**77.0 ± 4.1**	81.1 ± 1.0
Curated	ResNet-50	All4one	95.0 ± 1.4	82.1 ± 0.3	76.7 ± 4.6	84.4 ± 0.2
		BYOL	95.8 ± 1.8	**82.6 ± 0.4**	75.4 ± 4.1	84.9 ± 0.2
		DINO	**98.1 ± 0.9**	81.0 ± 0.4	74.8 ± 3.3	**85.1 ± 1.1**
		SimCLR	95.0 ± 1.4	82.1 ± 0.2	76.7 ± 3.6	84.2 ± 0.6
		SwAV	92.1 ± 0.7	80.9 ± 0.1	76.7 ± 3.9	81.7 ± 0.4
		WMSE	93.8 ± 1.2	81.5 ± 0.2	**76.8 ± 3.6**	83.8 ± 0.6
Uncurated	ResNet-18	All4one	**96.5 ± 0.5**	80.7 ± 0.4	75.2 ± 3.6	83.1 ± 0.4
		BYOL	94.8 ± 1.6	**81.0 ± 0.2**	**75.6 ± 4.5**	**83.7 ± 0.3**
		DINO	95.0 ± 0.7	79.3 ± 0.5	74.4 ± 4.5	81.1 ± 0.5
		SimCLR	95.6 ± 1.2	79.1 ± 0.1	75.0 ± 3.2	81.7 ± 1.0
		SwAV	94.6 ± 1.3	79.7 ± 0.3	75.3 ± 4.0	82.6 ± 0.4
		WMSE	93.5 ± 1.5	79.1 ± 0.2	74.8 ± 4.7	83.0 ± 0.9
ImageNet-100	ResNet-18	BYOL	96.2 ± 0.6	81.0 ± 0.2	75.4 ± 5.3	84.1 ± 0.6
ImageNet-1k	ResNet-50	BYOL	98.5 ± 0.8	81.4 ± 0.2	76.1 ± 6.1	83.9 ± 0.9
RGZ	ResNet-18	BYOL	98.1 ± 0.3	-	-	-

Despite the lack of significant differences in fine-tuning results, it is important to note that some tasks require data representations that are agnostic to specific classification schemas. For instance, visual data exploration tasks using dimensionality reduction techniques benefit from more general representations. In these scenarios, non-finetuned models can still provide valuable insights, offering representations that are useful for exploratory data analysis rather than specific classification tasks.

5   Conclusions

In this work, we investigated the potential of self-supervised learning (SSL) for enhancing the analysis of radio astronomical data, notably outperforming traditional models pretrained on natural images in several domain-specific downstream tasks. Our results indicate that SSL-trained models, particularly those using the All4one method, achieve notable improvements in accuracy during linear evaluation, suggesting that SSL can effectively leverage the unique characteristics of radio interferometry images. Advantages of SSL become less pronounced in the fine-tuning setting, though they still surpass the performance of models pretrained on natural images. Another key finding is the importance of data curation, which positively impacts SSL performance more significantly than the sheer size of the dataset.

Given that ResNet-50 did not outperform ResNet-18 (likely due to the simplicity of the image patterns) it might seem counterintuitive to explore more complex architectures like transformers. However, we propose that future work should investigate multimodal large language models and incorporate additional modalities such as infrared and optical bands. By integrating data from multiple spectral bands, these multimodal transformers could learn more meaningful and rich representations, potentially enhancing the analysis of radio astronomical data beyond what single-modality models can achieve.

Acknowledgements. This paper is supported by the Fondazione ICSC, Spoke 3 Astrophysics and Cosmos Observations. National Recovery and Resilience Plan (Piano Nazionale di Ripresa e Resilienza, PNRR) Project ID CN 00000013 "Italian Research Center for HighPerformance Computing, Big Data and Quantum Computing" funded by MUR Missione 4 Componente 2 Investimento 1.4: Potenziamento strutture di ricerca e creazione di "campioni nazionali di R&S (M4C2-19)" - Next Generation EU (NGEU). We also acknowledge partial funding from the INAF SCIARADA project.

We acknowledge the CINECA award under the ISCRA initiative, for the availability of high-performance computing resources and support. In particular, we sincerely thank Andrea Piltzer and Giuseppe Fiameni.

References

1. Assran, M., et al.: The hidden uniform cluster prior in self-supervised learning. arXiv preprint arXiv:2210.07277 (2022)
2. Banfield, J.K., et al.: Radio galaxy zoo: host galaxies and radio morphologies derived from visual inspection. Mon. Not. R. Astron. Soc. **453**(3), 2326–2340 (2015)
3. Becker, R.H., White, R.L., Helfand, D.J.: The first survey: faint images of the radio sky at twenty centimeters. Astrophys. J. **450**, 559 (1995)
4. Bordiu, C., Bufano, F., Cecconello, T., Sciacca, E., Riggi, S., Vizzari, G.: Patterns in the chaos: an unsupervised view of galactic supernova remnants. In: ML4Astro International Conference, pp. 61–65. Springer (2022)
5. Caron, M., Misra, I., Mairal, J., Goyal, P., Bojanowski, P., Joulin, A.: Unsupervised learning of visual features by contrasting cluster assignments. Adv. Neural. Inf. Process. Syst. **33**, 9912–9924 (2020)
6. Caron, M., et al.: Emerging properties in self-supervised vision transformers. In: Proceedings of the International Conference on Computer Vision (ICCV) (2021)
7. Chen, T., Kornblith, S., Norouzi, M., Hinton, G.: A simple framework for contrastive learning of visual representations. In: International Conference on Machine Learning, pp. 1597–1607. PMLR (2020)
8. Chowdhury, K., Sharma, A., Chandrasekar, A.D.: Evaluating deep learning in SystemML using layer-wise adaptive rate scaling (LARS) optimizer. arXiv preprint arXiv:2102.03018 (2021)

9. da Costa, V.G.T., Fini, E., Nabi, M., Sebe, N., Ricci, E.: solo-learn: a library of self-supervised methods for visual representation learning. J. Mach. Learn. Res. **23**(56), 1–6 (2022). http://jmlr.org/papers/v23/21-1155.html

10. Dewdney, P., et al.: SKA1 system baseline design v2. SKA Organisation, Design Report SKA-TEL-SKO-0000002, Rev, vol. 3 (2016)

11. Dosovitskiy, A., et al.: An image is worth 16x16 words: transformers for image recognition at scale. arXiv preprint arXiv:2010.11929 (2020)

12. Dwibedi, D., Aytar, Y., Tompson, J., Sermanet, P., Zisserman, A.: With a little help from my friends: nearest-neighbor contrastive learning of visual representations. In: Proceedings of the IEEE/CVF International Conference on Computer Vision, pp. 9588–9597 (2021)

13. Ermolov, A., Siarohin, A., Sangineto, E., Sebe, N.: Whitening for self-supervised representation learning. In: International Conference on Machine Learning, pp. 3015–3024. PMLR (2021)

14. Estepa, I.G., Sarasúa, I., Nagarajan, B., Radeva, P.: All4One: symbiotic neighbour contrastive learning via self-attention and redundancy reduction. In: Proceedings of the IEEE/CVF International Conference on Computer Vision (2023)

15. Goedhart, S., et al.: The SARAO MeerKAT 1.3 GHz galactic plane survey. arXiv preprint arXiv:2312.07275 (2023)

16. Goedhart, S., et al.: The SARAO MeerKAT 1.3 GHz galactic plane survey. Monthly Not. R. Astron. Soc. **531**(1), 649–681 (2024)

17. Gordon, Y.A., et al.: A quick look at the 3 GHz radio sky. II. Hunting for DRAGNs in the VLA sky survey. Astrophys. J. Suppl. Ser. **267**(2), 37 (2023)

18. Grill, J.B., et al.: Bootstrap your own latent-a new approach to self-supervised learning. Adv. Neural. Inf. Process. Syst. **33**, 21271–21284 (2020)

19. He, K., Chen, X., Xie, S., Li, Y., Dollár, P., Girshick, R.: Masked autoencoders are scalable vision learners. In: Proceedings of the IEEE/CVF Conference on Computer Vision and Pattern Recognition, pp. 16000–16009 (2022)

20. Huertas-Company, M., Sarmiento, R., Knapen, J.H.: A brief review of contrastive learning applied to astrophysics. RAS Tech. Instrum. **2**(1), 441–452 (2023)

21. Liu, X., et al.: Self-supervised learning: generative or contrastive. IEEE Trans. Knowl. Data Eng. **35**(1), 857–876 (2023). https://doi.org/10.1109/TKDE.2021.3090866

22. Lochner, M., Bassett, B.: Astronomaly: personalised active anomaly detection in astronomical data. Astron. Comput. **36**, 100481 (2021)

23. Loshchilov, I., Hutter, F.: Decoupled weight decay regularization. arXiv preprint arXiv:1711.05101 (2017)

24. Mohale, K., Lochner, M.: Enabling unsupervised discovery in astronomical images through self-supervised representations. Mon. Not. R. Astron. Soc. **530**(1), 1274–1295 (2024)

25. Mostert, R.I., et al.: Unveiling the rarest morphologies of the LOFAR two-metre sky survey radio source population with self-organised maps. Astron. Astrophys. **645**, A89 (2021)

26. Norris, R.P., et al.: EMU: evolutionary map of the universe. Publ. Astron. Soc. Austral. **28**(3), 215–248 (2011)

27. Oquab, M., et al.: DINOv2: learning robust visual features without supervision. arXiv preprint arXiv:2304.07193 (2023)

28. Porter, F.A.M., Scaife, A.M.M.: MiraBest: a data set of morphologically classified radio galaxies for machine learning. RAS Tech. Instrum. **2**(1), 293–306 (2023). https://doi.org/10.1093/rasti/rzad017

29. Riggi, S., et al.: Self-supervised contrastive learning of radio data for source detection, classification and peculiar object discovery. arXiv preprint arXiv:2404.18462 (2024)

30. Riggi, S., et al.: Astronomical source detection in radio continuum maps with deep neural networks. Astron. Comput. **42**, 100682 (2023)

31. Riggi, S., et al.: Classification of compact radio sources in the galactic plane with supervised machine learning. Publ. Astron. Soc. Austral. **41**, e029 (2024)

32. Sarmiento, R., Knapen, J.H., Sánchez, S.F., Sánchez, H.D., Drory, N., Falcón-Barroso, J., et al.: Capturing the physics of manga galaxies with self-supervised machine learning. Astrophys. J. **921**(2), 177 (2021)

33. Slijepcevic, I.V., et al.: Radio galaxy zoo: towards building the first multipurpose foundation model for radio astronomy with self-supervised learning. RAS Tech. Instrum. **3**(1), 19–32 (2023)

34. Umana, G., et al.: Scorpio: a deep survey of radio emission from the stellar lifecycle. Mon. Not. R. Astron. Soc. **454**(1), 902–912 (2015)

35. Zbontar, J., Jing, L., Misra, I., LeCun, Y., Deny, S.: Barlow twins: self-supervised learning via redundancy reduction. In: International Conference on Machine Learning, pp. 12310–12320. PMLR (2021)

Correction to: Advancing Multi-modal Visual Pattern Recognition: Object Detection

Arjun J. Nair, Swathi Jayakumar, Varalekshmy M. Mohan, Jyothisha J. Nair, Vishnu Thooprath Subran, and Hrishikesh Puthuvamana

Correction to:
Chapter 22 in: S. Palaiahnakote et al. (Eds.): *Pattern Recognition,* **LNCS 15617, https://doi.org/10.1007/978-3-031-88217-3_22**

In the originally published version of chapter 22, the author name had been rendered incorrectly as "Jyotisha J. Nair". This has been corrected as "Jyothisha J. Nair".

The updated version of this chapter can be found at
https://doi.org/10.1007/978-3-031-88217-3_22

Author Index

S. Palaiahnakote et al. (Eds.): ICPR 2024 Workshops, LNCS 15617, pp. 441–442, 2025.
https://doi.org/10.1007/978-3-031-88217-3

The manufacturer's authorised representative in the EU is Springer
Nature Customer Service Centre GmbH, Europaplatz 3, 69115 Heidelberg,
Germany. If you have any concerns regarding our products, please
contact ProductSafety@springernature.com

Printed and bound by CPI Group (UK) Ltd, Croydon, CR0 4YY
27/04/2026
02097845-0010